MEDIEVAL LITURGY:
An Introduction to the Sources

by
Cyrille Vogel

Revised and Translated by
William G. Storey
and
Niels Krogh Rasmussen, O.P.

with the assistance of
John K. Brooks-Leonard

The Pastoral Press
Washington, D.C.

The illustration on the front cover is taken from the Pontifical of John Vitéz *junior,* bishop of Veszprém in Hungary and dates from about 1490 A.D. It shows the handing over of the chalice and paten to a priest during his ordination (*traditio instrumentorum*) by the ordaining bishop. The manuscript is now at the Vatican Library (Codex Ottoboni Lat. 501, f. 15) and is reproduced through gracious authorization of Rev. L. Boyle, O.P., Prefect of the Vatican Library.

Medieval Liturgy: An Introduction to the Sources is the revised and updated translation of *Introduction aux sources de l'histoire du culte chrétien au moyen âge.*
© 1981 by Centro italiano di studi sull'alto medioevo, Spoleto.

ISBN: 0-912405-10-4

© The Pastoral Press, 1986

The Pastoral Press
225 Sheridan Street, NW
Washington, D.C. 20011
(202) 723-5800

The Pastoral Press is the Publications Division of the National Association of Pastoral Musicians, a membership organization of musicians and clergy dedicated to fostering the art of musical liturgy.

Printed in the United States of America

CONTENTS

LIST OF ABBREVIATIONS

ACC	Alcuin Club Collection
ACW	Ancient Christian Writers
AfL	Archiv für Liturgiewissenschaft
CC	Corpus Christianorum
CLLA	K. Gamber, *Codices liturgici latini antiquiores*, 2nd ed.
CSEL	Corpus scriptorum ecclesiasticorum latinorum
DACL	Dictionnaire d'archéologie chrétienne et de liturgie
DS	Dictionnaire de Spiritualité
DTC	Dictionnaire de théologie catholique
EL	Ephemerides liturgicae
ET	English translation
FC	Fathers of the Church
HBS	Henry Bradshaw Society
HS	Hispania sacra
JfL	Jahrbuch für Liturgiewissenschaft
JTS	Journal of Theological Studies
LMD	La Maison Dieu
LQF	Liturgiewissenschaftliche Quellen und Forschungen
MGH	Monumenta Germaniae historica
Mansi	J.D. Mansi, *Sacrorum conciliorum nova et amplissima collectio.*
NPNF	The Nicene and Post-Nicene Fathers
OCA	Orientalia Christiana Analecta
PG	Migne, Patrologiae cursus completus, Series graeca
PL	Migne, Patrologiae cursus completus, Series latina
RB	Revue bénédictine
RED	Rerum ecclesiasticarum documenta
RSR	Revue des sciences religieuses
SC	Sources chrétiennes
SE	Sacris erudiri
SeT	Studi e testi
TS	Theological Studies
TPL	Textus patristici et liturgici
TuA	Texte und Arbeiten
TuU	Texte und Untersuchungen
ZkT	Zeitschrift für katolische Theologie

PREFACE TO THE REVISED ENGLISH EDITION

Cyrille Vogel died unexpectedly at Strasbourg in November, 1982, at the age of 63. With his death the scholarly world lost one of the truly great historians of Christian worship in Antiquity and the Middle Ages. A native of Alsace, Vogel belonged to the clergy of Strasbourg and, as the concordat of Napoleon was still in vogue in Alsace-Lorraine, received a serious academic formation: first at the only French state School of Theology (the University of Strasbourg) and later at the Pontifical Institute of Christian Archaeology in Rome. In 1953 he began teaching in Strasbourg as successor to his mentor, Michel Andrieu, and was also a valued professor at the Institut Supérieur de Liturgie of the Institut Catholique of Paris.

Vogel's most learned works are the editions of the *Romano-Germanic Pontifical of the Tenth Century* (with R. Elze, 1963-1972) and his revised edition of Duchesne's *Liber Pontificalis (1971)*. Eleven other books and nearly 80 articles are found in his bibliography, reprinted as a testimonial to the author at the end of this edition. Among these works, however, one was written both for beginners in liturgical studies and for medievalists in general: the work at hand.

In his own preface Vogel stressed the difficulty so many medievalists seem to have in undertaking the study of the medieval liturgy, which they often consider an exclusively ecclesiastical discipline and one for which some particularly awesome rite of initiation is required. In order to make medieval forms of worship more accessible to both professional liturgists and to medievalists in general, he undertook the publication of the present work, first (parts one and two) in the renowned Italian periodical *Studi Medievali* and then in book form (incorporating part three) published by the *Centro Italiano di studi medievali* of Spoleto in 1966. The work was re-edited in 1975 and reprinted in 1981, with substantial additions of text and notes, but without incorporating the new material into the body of the book.

The present translators decided in 1982 that a translation of Vogel's work would provide in English-speaking countries the same handy access to the sources of medieval liturgy as Vogel had originally desired. When the author was approached he graciously acquiesced but requested that the 33 pages of additions of the 1975 edition be incorporated into the text. The translators have done this but they have also done more; recent scholarly material (post 1975) has been introduced; English translations have been added where appropriate; references have been checked, corrected, and simplified. One section of the book, on the Gregorian sacramentaries, was particularly difficult to revise in the light of the scholarship of the last 15 years. Rather than construct a patchwork of the often contradictory theories concerning the origins, affiliations, and developments of this important type of sacramentary, the entire section has been rewritten and simplified, providing the state of the question as it appears in 1985. Any further synthesis is still impossible to attain. The same is the case for the segment on the private mass. Minimal bibliographical indications have also been provided where the original version was completely silent as, for example, concerning liturgical poetry. The translators believe that the author would have approved of these revisions.

The translators wish to acknowledge the dedicated and competent collaboration of their successive graduate assistants; Edward Foley, Capuchin, and especially John Brooks-Leonard whose indefatigable checking of references, proof-reading, and linguistic suggestions have proven indispensable to this project. They also wish to express their appreciation to the Rev. Virgil Funk, publisher of the Pastoral Press, for his willingness to undertake the present edition and for his patience.

William G. Storey
Niels Krogh Rasmussen, O.P.

Graduate Programs in Liturgical Studies
Department of Theology
University of Notre Dame

AUTHOR'S PREFACE

The first two parts of the present work appeared in the form of articles in the *Studi Medievali*, 3rd series, tome III (1962), pp. 1-98 and in tome IV (1963), pp. 435-569; the third and final part was published by the *Centro Italiano di studi medievali* of Spoleto in 1966. Substantially, these two parts are notes stemming from a course in liturgical studies taught at the University of Strasbourg. With some hesitation, I have decided to publish them at the request of friends and colleagues.

With some hesitation, I say, because normally nothing is further from my mind than a production of a manual or textbook, especially in an area in which the sources themselves are still imperfectly catalogued and where, in important ways, agreement among specialists is still far from complete. Of its nature, therefore, any synthesis is both premature and of little interest to experts.

This is a very modest introduction to the sources of the medieval Latin liturgy and neither a full history of Christian worship nor even a full account of the sources of medieval worship. It is an introduction—and a limited one at that.

It will present only the Western liturgy and only liturgical documents properly speaking, i.e., the books that were actually used in and for the celebration of the liturgy: sacramentaries, *ordines*, pontificals and mass lectionaries. Consequently, it contains nothing about the hymns, tropes, sequences, lectionaries for the office, etc. The Christian East is excluded and so are certain forms of medieval literature which sometimes contribute to the history of worship, e.g., epics, mystery and miracle plays, stories, poetry, chronicles, etc. For the same reason, we felt obliged not to discuss—even briefly— medieval hagiography, even though the *vitae sanctorum* are a mine of valuable information on the liturgy. Despite the importance of medieval religious architecture and iconography for a knowledge of medieval worship, we have provided only a minimal bibliography on these subjects.

By the close of the Merovingian period and especially after the accomplishments of Pepin III the Short and Charlemagne, the history of Christian worship in the West is largely the story of how the Roman and papal forms of worship gradually eliminated, almost everywhere, the older, indigenous, non-Roman rites of Europe. We shall show how the documents that survive reflect that dynamic, thus explaining why we emphasize the Roman books so much.

The reason that I finally decided to publish this book—despite its many *lacunae*—is the lack of interest manifested by so many medievalists in the evidence of Christian worship and the embarrassment some of them apparently feel about trespassing into the supposedly special domain of the clergy. As one of the best historians of the liturgy has written: "One of the reasons so many historians . . . do not pursue liturgical studies is perhaps the difficulty they encounter in trying to discover the documents that describe the liturgical usages of the Middle Ages. The publication, therefore, of the texts which are needed is an urgent task for those who want to see the study of the medieval liturgy stop being the special preserve of the clergy. This intention has inspired the present work, with the conviction that a Carolingian mass *ordo* is as interesting a piece of historical evidence as the ritual of the Roman *Fratres Arvales*. The supposed benefits of the secularizing process of our time do not appeal to everyone; but surely no one could object to the 'secularization' of liturgical studies and its resultant progress towards a more thorough understanding of the medieval liturgy" [M. Andrieu, *Les Ordines romani du haut moyen âge* 2 (Louvain 1948) xv].

This book owes a great deal more than the footnotes show to the work of M. Andrieu (†1956), B. Botte (†1980), and to A. Chavasse of Strasbourg; I wish to thank them here for their unfailing assistance in putting their scholarly conclusions at my disposal. It is obvious that the present work would never have been possible without the studies and editions of L. Delisle (sacramentaries), H. Lietzmann (sacramentaries), L.C. Mohlberg (sacramentaries), E. Bourque (sacramentaries), V. Leroquais (sacramentaries, pontificals, psalters, books of hours), J. Deshusses and A. Dumas (sacramentaries), T. Klauser (mass lectionaries), K. Gamber (sacramentaries and other *codices liturgici*), P.E. Schramm (coronation *ordines*), R. Elze (imperial coronations), R.J. Hesbert (antiphonaries), P.M. Gy (rituals), J.B. Molin (rituals) and A.G. Martimort, and many others. I hope that I have been faithful to the results of their scholarly inquiries.

Special thanks are also due to my learned colleague and friend G. Vinay, the director of the *Studi Medievali*, who did more than read the proofs of this book with me; to the members of the Centro Italiano— especially its director Professor G. Antonelli—and to the Bottega d'Erasmo, who were so helpful in assisting this undertaking to a successful conclusion; and to Ms. Michelle Seyler who carefully perused the first edition and provided me with a list of spelling mistakes and typographical errors.

A word in conclusion: Since the first edition of this book in 1966, the implementation of the *Constitutio de sacra liturgia* (Dec 4, 1963) of the Second Vatican Council has proceeded apace. Among other liturgical reforms the Roman Catholic Church has now experienced its second linguistic revolution. The sharp break between the new liturgical *formulae* in the various vernacular languages and the older Latin *formulae* is as striking as the difference between the Carolingian arrangement of the mass readings and the new list of pericopes. Until about 1966, this book could introduce one into the complexities of a liturgy that was still current; henceforth it is a study of *antiquitates liturgicae.*

C. V.
Strasbourg, 1975/1981

I. GENERAL INTRODUCTION

The following pages contain neither a history of Christian worship in the West nor a detailed inventory of its literary sources; they are simply an introduction to the basic documents of the Latin liturgy.

This modest project aims at providing medievalists with an initial orientation to the written sources of the liturgies of the Western Church. This means that the professional liturgist will find in this informational work only those matters which are already well-known; it also means—inevitably—that the professional will also immediately discover certain *lacunae*. Because of the very nature of the project we have undertaken, we felt obliged to make a choice of a wide variety of materials. We hope that specialists in the various liturgical disciplines will not conclude that we have forgotten or deliberately overlooked certain areas of particular interest to them.

By their very nature, documents concerning Christian worship constitute a complex problem; not only are they hard to locate but they have never been adequately catalogued either chronologically or systematically. Scholarly opinion estimates that liturgical *codices* comprise some 10% of the surviving medieval MSS, which makes them more numerous than any other category.[1] Despite the paucity of catalogues and other obstacles, the scholarly efforts of the last several decades now permit us to discern, with a fair amount of confidence, the ebb and flow of liturgical books across the face of Europe and, therefore, that cycle of exchanges between Rome and the Christian countries of the West which underlies any grasp of the evolution of the Latin liturgy. Such an understanding will prevent us from making the false assumption that the Latin liturgy sprang up full-blown or that it originated in a single region or city (Rome) and then spread to other countries as they underwent the process of Christianization.

During the first stage of its dissemination—the VII and probably even the VI century—the Roman liturgy properly so-called, i.e., that form of worship worked out in and for the City of Rome, reached and began to spread throughout the Frankish territories north of the Alps. In the first instance, this was the result of private initiatives but soon its dissemination was supported and encouraged by the Frankish rulers themselves (Pepin III the Short and his successors), especially in Neustria (North Central Gaul) and, a bit later, in the

Rhineland. To varying degrees, depending on the rites in question, the Roman liturgy assimilated many older liturgical usages native to Gaul (often improperly called 'Gallican') and ended by producing a type of hybrid or mixed liturgy which may be termed Romano-Frankish. This is the liturgy we find preserved in the earliest surviving liturgical MSS, all of which were redacted in Frankish Gaul. This is also the liturgy which was explained and commented upon by such prominent figures as Walafrid Strabo (†849), Amalarius of Metz (†850/851) and Rabanus Maurus (†856) and which was definitively regulated—as regards the Eucharist—by St. Benedict of Aniane (†821) in the corrected *Hadrianum* and its famous *Supplement* (ca. 810-815). This is also the liturgy which—as regards its non-eucharistic components—was assembled and condensed in an imposing compilation in the *scriptorium* of St. Alban's abbey, Mainz, ca. 950: the *Romano-Germanic Pontifical of the X Century*.

In a second stage of its evolution, this mixed liturgy spread with surprising but understandable speed to all the churches of Northern Europe and, after the *Renovatio Imperii* (962), established itself without difficulty at Rome under the patronage of the Ottonian emperors. The somewhat distant but certainly authentic descendants of Benedict of Aniane's corrected and supplemented *Hadrianum* and the *Mainz Pontifical* installed themselves so thoroughly at Rome that, around a century later, canonists like Cardinal Deusdedit (†1097/ 1100) and Anselm of Lucca(†1073) were to cite excerpts from them as *ex ordine romano*, ignoring the fact that their quotations were from foreign books originating across the Alps. In 1145, the redactor of the *Ordo Officiorum Ecclesiae Lateranensis* reproduced entire passages from the *Mainz Pontifical*, clearly convinced that they came from an authentic Lateran ceremonial. With Pope Gregory VII (1073-1085), however, the influx of Northern Europe books began to slow down; his reign marked the end of an era during which, as the pope once remarked, *Teutonicis concessum est regimen Ecclesiae nostrae*.[2] Roman liturgists then tried, without much success, to revise copies of the *Mainz Pontifical*, producing what we call the *Roman Pontifical of the XII Century*. After further experiments, the *Pontifical of the Roman Curia of the XIII Century* appeared under Innocent III (1198-1216), still containing the distilled essence of the older Rhenish compilation.

At the beginning of the XIV century, this official compilation of the papal household, was carried from Rome to Avignon, but there it was soon replaced by the Pontifical assembled between 1291 and 1295 by William Durandus, bishop of Mende (S. France). In his collection Durandus included not only all the important elements of the

Romano-Germanic Pontifical but also the elaborations of the Roman liturgists of the XII and XIII centuries.

Subsequent attempts to adapt the *Pontifical of the Roman Curia* to that of the bishop of Mende failed because of the superiority of the latter's arrangements. At the end of the XV century, when Pope Innocent VIII charged Agostino Patrizzi Piccolomini and the celebrated master of ceremonies, John Burchard of Strasbourg, with the task of preparing the *editio princeps* of the *Roman Pontifical* (1485), they still used Durandus as their model, thereby making this collection of historic texts an official volume in the Latin liturgical library. In the same way, the XIII-century Missal of the papal chapel, the direct ancestor of the Tridentine Missal (1570-1970), was the authentic descendant of the *Hadrianum* and its *Supplement*.[3]

From this point on, the long, slow evolution of the Roman liturgical books drew to a close, more quickly in the case of the *Missale*, more slowly for the *Pontificale*.

The landmarks of this evolution, then, are these:
a) from Rome to *Francia* and Ottonian Germany;
b) from the Rhineland back to Rome;
c) from Rome to Avignon;
d) from Avignon back to Rome again;
e) and, finally, at the dawn of modern times, from Rome to the entire Latin Church, both in Europe and overseas.

The entire process was one of osmosis, amalgamation, and hybridization; liturgies were never simply substituted for one another; they influenced and modified one another, and even the dominant Roman liturgy issued from the process changed and enhanced. The study of the MS sources is particularly revealing in this regard: until the IX century, all Roman liturgical books are of Frankish execution and, conversely, all the books we term 'Gallican' are to some degree Romanized. As Theodor Klauser says so well: *Romana est sed etiam nostra.* "The liturgy which is performed by us today, is therefore, truly Roman, but it is at the same time also our own."[4]

*   *   *

Since the Council of Trent (1545-1563), the principal liturgical books of the Roman rite have been *seven* in number: *Missale, Breviarium, Graduale, Antiphonale, Martyrologium, Pontificale* and *Rituale*. There were, in addition, a variety of printed extracts from the offical books for special occasions (Holy Week) or to facilitate specific functions (baptism, confirmation, funerals) but these were never more than mere *excerpta* from the authorized books and had no special character of their own. That means that, from the Council of Trent until the II Vatican Council, the Roman rite had fewer than a dozen *libri liturgici*.

In the Middle Ages, the books one needed for the celebration of the liturgy were far more numerous and far more complex. If we employ the technical medieval terms for all these books, we can enumerate more than a hundred titles.[5] Even taking into account duplicate titles and synonyms, we can only reduce this figure by half, which means that we can still count at least fifty kinds of liturgical books.[6] Even for the XV century, twenty-seven varieties of liturgical books can be encountered among the *incunabula*[7]: *Sacramentarium*, *Lectionaria* (Epistle and Gospel books), *Antiphonarium missae* (as distinguished from the *Antiphonarium officii*) or *Graduale* or *Antiphonale* and with *Responsale*, *Troparium*, *Liber sequentialis*, *Psalterium*, *Passionarium*, *Hymnarium*, *Ordines*, *Pontificale*, *Benedictionale*, *Martyrologium*, *Liber manualis*, and others.[8]

Not only was there a profusion of separate books with a variety of confusing titles, but little uniformity existed even in any one category of book; each book derived from older types, styles and families of MSS, representing different liturgical usages.

Such diversity had two main causes:

1. Liturgical uniformity did not exist in the Middle Ages, not even within a single ecclesiastical province. Different worship habits— some of them quite remarkable—coexisted within the same family of liturgies and different liturgical families were often employed within the same country or region. As a result of such long periods of liturgical anarchy, we must make a real effort at imagining the kind of ritual chaos that existed in the Latin Church before the XIII century and even down to the invention of the printing press in the XV. Until the end of the Middle Ages, no amount of liturgical legislation could curb the prevailing situation.

2. The Middle Ages could not conceive of the situation which has prevailed in the Latin Church since the Council of Trent, i.e., *one* liturgical book for each *actio liturgica* (a *Missal* for the celebration of the Eucharist, a *Ritual* for the sacraments and blessings, a *Breviary* for the Office). Instead, the medieval Church had a book for each minister (one for the celebrant, bishop or presbyter, one for deacon, one for the lesser ministers and one for the choir) and often each

minister had a special book for each of his liturgical functions. But even here no system as such can be detected.

By definition, medieval liturgical books are MSS, but even today there are no fully satisfactory catalogues or collections of such MSS. Unfortunately, liturgical historians possess nothing comparable to the *Catalogi codicum hagiographicorum* of the Bollandists. Apart from those devoted to a particular region or a particularly important collection, the best descriptive catalogues, arranged according to type of liturgical book, are the following:[9]

L. Delisle, "Mémoire sur d'anciens sacramentaires," *Mémoires de l'Académie des Inscriptions et Belles-Lettres* 32(1886) 57-423; 1128 MSS of Sacramentaries before 1100.

W.H.J. Weale, *Bibliographia liturgica. Catalogus Missalium ritus latini* (London 1886); MSS and printed copies.

A. Ebner, *Quellen und Forschungen zur Geschichte und Kunst-Geschichte des Missale Romanum im Mittelalter. Iter italicum* (Freiburg/Br. 1896; reprint Graz 1961); 380 Sacramentaries and Missals.

M. Andrieu, *Les Ordines romani du haut moyen âge*, 1: *Les manuscrits*, Spicilegium sacrum Lovaniense 11 (Louvain 1931). This initial volume needs to be completed by the subsequent four vols., Spicilegium sacrum Lovaniense 23, 24, 28, 29 (Louvain 1948-61; repr. 1960-65) which include critical editions of 50 *ordines*. See also Andrieu's *Le Pontifical romain au moyen âge*, 1: *Le Pontifical romain du XII siècle*; 2: *Le Pontifical de la Curie romaine au XIII siècle*; 3: *Le Pontifical de Guillaume Durand*; 4: *Table alphabétiques*. SeT 86-88, 99 (Vatican City 1938-1940, 1941), wherein the several MSS are described.

T. Klauser, *Das römische Capitulare Evangeliorum*, 1: *Typen*. LQF 28 (Münster/Westphalia 1935). 1400 MSS from everywhere, see pp. 292-349 below.

E. Bourque, *Étude sur les sacramentaires romains*, pt. 1: *Les Textes primitifs* (Rome 1948); pt. 2: *Les Textes remaniés*, 2 vols. (Quebec 1952; Rome 1958).

K. Gamber, *Sakramentartypen: Versuch einer Gruppierung der Handschriften und Fragmente bis zur Jahrtausendwende.* TuA 49-50 (Beuron 1958). 219 MSS with an exhaustive bibliography; some of the classifications are dubious; see the review by B. Botte in *Revue d'histoire ecclésiastique* 55 (1960) 516-517. See also Gamber's *Codices liturgici latini antiquiores* (= CLLA), Spicilegii Friburgensis Subsidia 1. 2 vols. (2nd ed. Fribourg 1968; 1st ed. 1963).

A. Hughes, *Medieval Manuscripts for Mass and Office: A Guide to Their Organization and Terminology* (Toronto 1982).

R.W. Pfaff, *Medieval Latin Liturgy: A Select Bibliography* (Toronto 1982).

CIPOL: "Centre Interational de Publications Oecumeniques de Liturgies," publishes documents, manuscripts or books (especially those which are difficult to find) on microfiches. Directed by R. Buyse and P.M. Gy, CIPOL is attempting to prepare *the* liturgical *corpus*. The center relies on six task forces composed of liturgists from different regions (France, Italy, Spain, Germany, Scandanavia and Switzerland). To date there have appeared in the series "Liturgies orientales" 9 titles; under "Liturgies latines" 18 titles; under "Liturgies issues de la Réforme" 3 titles; and under "Subsidia" 2 titles. Address: CIPOL, 4 Avenue Vavin, 75006 Paris, France.

1. MANUALS AND COLLECTIONS.

General studies of the Roman liturgy exist in profusion but few are of much use to medievalists in quest of the sources. Most of them aim at explaining the Tridentine liturgy or that of the II Vatican Council, largely from a pastoral or theological point of view. They hardly ever provide the reader with careful, complete descriptions of how the rites were actually celebrated in any particular period.[10]

The following works are the best currently available:

L. Duchesne, *Les origines du culte chrétien: Étude sur la liturgie latine avant Charlemagne* (5th ed., Paris 1925); ET *Christian Worship: Its Origin and Evolution,* tr. L. McClure (London 1923). For a recent evaluation of this classic see V. Saxer, "Duchesne, historien du culte chrétien," *Monseigneur Duchesne et son temps,* Actes du Colloque organisé par l'École française de Rome (Rome 1975) 61-98.

T. Klauser, *Kleine abendländische Liturgiegeschichte* (Bonn 1965); ET *A Short History of the Western Liturgy,* tr. J. Halliburton (2nd ed. Oxford 1979).

E. Bishop, *Liturgica Historica* (Oxford 1918; repr. 1962). See the bibliography of liturgical works by Bishop compiled by N. Abercombie, *The Life and Work of Edmund Bishop* (London 1959).

A. Baumstark, *Liturgie comparée: Principes et méthodes pour l'étude historique des liturgies chrétiennes,* revised by B. Botte (3rd ed. Chevetogne 1953); ET *Comparative Liturgy* tr. F.L. Cross (Westminster, Maryland 1958).

C. Jones, G. Wainwright, and E. Yarnold (edd.), *The Study of Liturgy* (New York 1978).

A.-G. Martimort, *L'Église en prière: Introduction à la Liturgie,* new edition, 4 parts (Paris, 1983-1984);ET of the 1961 ed.,*The Church at Prayer,* 1: *Introduction to the Liturgy* (New York 1968), 2: *The Eucharist* (New York 1973), The rest never appeared in English. ET of the new edition, Collegeville, MN, 1985-.

H.B. Meyer *et al.* (edd.), *Gottesdienst der Kirche. Handbuch der Liturgiewissenschaft,* 8 parts (Regensburg, 1983 ff.; two parts published).

Marsili, S. *et al.* (edd.), *Anàmnesis: introduzione storico-teologica alla liturgia a cura dei professori del Pontificio Istituto Liturgico S. Anselmo di Roma,* (Rome 1978-; 5 vols., three published).

In addition to these works, one should consult the following manuals:

L. Hébert, *Leçons de liturgie à l'usage des séminaires,* 2 vols. (Paris 1920-21).

V. Thalhofer–L. Eizenhofer, *Handbuch der katholischen Liturgik,* 2 vols. (2nd ed. Freiburg/Br. 1912), new edition by Eizenhofer, 1932-33; new printing 1951.

C. Callewaert, *Liturgicae Institutiones,* 1: *De sacra liturgia universim* (5th ed. Bruges 1953) 2: *De breviarii romani liturgia* (2nd ed. Bruges 1939) 3: *De rebus cultus materialibus* (Bruges 1937).

P. Oppenheim, *Institutiones systematico-historicae in sacram liturgiam,* 11 vols. (Turin-Rome 1937-47).

A.I. Schuster, *Liber Sacramentorum: Note Storiche e liturgiche sul Messale Romano,* 10 vols. (3rd and 4th edd. Turin-Rome 1930-44); ET *The Sacramentary: Historical and Liturgical Notes on the Roman Missal,* 5 vols., tr. A. Levelis-Marke (New York 1930).

G. Dix, *The Shape of the Liturgy,* with additional notes by P.V. Marshall (New York 1982). Marshall offers a modern evaluation of Dix's classical work in his "Additional Notes." See also K.W. Stevenson, *Gregory Dix: 25 Years on,* Grove Liturgical Study 10 (Bramcote Notts 1977).

J.H. Strawley, *The Early History of the Liturgy* (2nd ed. Cambridge 1949).

L. Eizenhofer-J. Lechner, *Liturgik des römischen Ritus* (6th ed. Freiburg/Br. 1953); ET H.E. Winstone, *The Liturgy of the Roman Rite* (Freiburg-London-Edinburgh 1961).

M. Righetti, *Manuale di storia liturgica* 1: *Introduzione generale,* 2: *L'anno liturgico; Il Breviario,* 3: *L'Eucaristia,* 4: *I sacramenti e i sacramentali* (vols 1-2 in 2nd editions, Milan-Genoa 1950, 1955, 1956; vol 4. in first edition 1953).

B. Steuart, *The Development of Christian Worship* (London-New York 1953).

I.H. Dalmais, *Initiation à la liturgie* (Paris 1958); ET *Introduction to Liturgy* (Baltimore-London 1961).

A. Kirchgässner, *Die mächtigen Zeichen: Ursprünge, Formen und Gesetze des Kultus* (Freiburg/Br. 1959); FT *La Puissance des signes: Origines, formes et lois du culte,* tr. S.P. Marie, revised M.A. Barth (Tours 1962).

J.A. Jungmann, *La Liturgie de l'Église romaine* (Mulhouse 1957).

_____, *The Early Liturgy to the Time of Gregory the Great* (Notre Dame 1959).

_____, *Missarum Sollemnia: Eine genetische Erklärung der römischen Messe* (6th ed. Vienna 1966); ET from 2nd German edition of 1949: *The Mass of the Roman Rite,* 2 vols. tr. F.A. Brunner (New York 1951-1955); the abridged one-volume English translation (New York 1959) omits the references.

H.A.P. Schmidt, *Introductio in liturgiam occidentalem* (Rome 1960) esp. 742-746, has a more complete list of liturgical manuals than the survey offered here.

D. Busato, *La Liturgie: Magie, spectacle ou action divine* (Toulouse 1962).

A. Verheul, *Einführung in die Liturgie* (Vienna 1964); ET *Introduction to the Liturgy* (Collegeville, MN 1968).

F. Vandenbroucke, *Initiation liturgique* (Paris 1964); ET *Liturgical Initiation*, tr. K. Sullivan (Glen Rock, NJ 1965).

C. Vagaggini, *Il senso teologico della liturgia: saggio di liturgia teologica generale* (4th ed., Rome 1965); ET *Theological Dimensions of the Liturgy*, tr. L.J. Doyle-W.A. Jurgens (Collegeville, MN 1976).

K.F. Müller–W. Blankenburg, *Leiturgia: Handbuch des evangelischen Gottesdienstes*, 5 vols. (Kassell 1954-1970).

H.A.J. Wegman, *Christian Worship in East and West*, trans. G.W. Lathrop (New York 1985).

J.D. Crichton, *Christian Celebration* (London 1976; reprint Westminster, MD 1982).

E. Cattaneo, *Il culto cristiano in l'occidente* (Rome 1978). This is the 3rd edition: the 2nd ed. was published under the title: *Introduzione alla storia della liturgia occidentale* (1969).

H. Reifenberg, *Fundamentalliturgie: Grundelemente des christlichen Gottesdienstes*, 2 vols. (Klosterneuburg 1978).

The principal encyclopedias, dictionaries, periodicals and collections are listed here:[11]

ENCYCLOPEDIAS

Dictionnaire d'archéologie chrétienne et de liturgie
F. Cabrol–H. Leclercq–H. Marrou, edd. (Paris 1907–1953). 30 volumes composing a thesaurus of the most diverse information; care must be taken to separate the factual information from the commentary which often accompanies it.

Reallexikon für Antike und Christentum
T. Klauser, ed. (Stuttgart 1950-). Vol 1 begins with "Alpha und omega"; 13 vols. have appeared as of 1984 (up to "Gymnasium"). It has been supplemented by *Jahrbuch für Antike und Christentum* since 1958.

Clavis Patrum Latinorum
E. Dekkers, ed. (Steenbrugge 1951, 1961). The first edition appeared as *Sacris Erudiri* 3 (1951): the second edition is revised and enlarged (Steenbrugge 1961). A systematic classification of Christian Latin literature which includes liturgical works up to the mid-VIII century.

The New Catholic Encyclopedia 14 vols. and Index (New York 1967).

Enciclopedia Cattolica, P. Paschini *et al.* edd., 12 vols. (Vatican City 1949-1954).

Lexikon für Theologie and Kirche, 2nd ed., J. Höfer-K. Rahner, edd. 10 vols. and Index (Freiburg 1957-1967).

The Oxford Dictionary of the Christian Church
F.L. Cross–E.A. Livingstone, edd. (Oxford 1957; 2nd ed. 1974).

A New Dictionary of Liturgy and Worship
J.G. Davies, ed. (London–Philadelphia 1986).

PERIODICALS[12]

Archiv für Liturgiewissenschaft (Regensburg 1950–). This publication replaces the *Jahrbuch für Liturgiewissenschaft* 1-15 (Münster 1921-35 [1941]).
Ephemerides Liturgicae (Rome 1887–).
Liturgisches Jahrbuch (Trier 1951–).
Sacris Erudiri (Steenbrugge 1948–).
Jahrbuch für Liturgik und Hymnologie (Kassel 1955–).
La Maison-Dieu (Paris 1945–).
Vigiliae Christianae (Amsterdam 1947–).
Traditio (New York 1943–).
Worship (Collegeville, MN 1951–). This is a continuation of *Orate Fratres* (Collegeville 1926/7 to 1950/1, vols. 1–25); *Worship* begins with vol. 26.
Studia Liturgica (Rotterdam 1962–).

COLLECTIONS

Bibliotheca Ephemerides Liturgicae, Sectio historica (Rome 1932–).
Bibliotheca Ephemerides Liturgicae Subsidia (1975–).
Ecclesia Orans: Zur Einführung in den Geist der Liturgie (Freiburg/Br. 1918–).
Lex Orandi (Paris 1945-1971; 53 vols.).
Alcuin Club Collections (London 1899–).
Henry Bradshaw Society (London 1891–).
Surtees Society (London 1884–); this collection includes many liturgical texts from the Northumbrian region of Britain.
Liturgiegeschichtliche (since 1957 *Liturgiewissenschaftliche Quellen*) *und Forschungen* (Münster 1918–). Until 1928 there existed two collections a) *Liturgiegeschichtliche Quellen*, Heft 1-12, and b) *Liturgiegeschichtliche Forschungen*, Heft 1-10. After the merger in 1928, the latter were re-numbered vols. 13-22 and the collection continued until 1957 under the name *Liturgiegeschichtliche Quellen und Forschungen*, Heft 1-31. In 1957, the name was changed to *Liturgiewissenschaftliche Quellen und Forschungen* and fortunately continues the numbering from Heft 32– (= LQF in most citations).
Texte und Arbeiten: 1. Abteilung. *Beiträge zur Ergründung des älteren lateinischen christlichen Schrifttums und Gottesdienstes* (Beuron 1917–).

2. TYPES OF LITURGICAL DOCUMENTS

Liturgical literature includes three kinds of documents:
a. *The liturgical books properly so-called,* i.e., the books actually utilized in the course of Christian worship. They contain the prayer

formulae, the readings, the songs and the necessary directions (*ordines*) for the harmonious unfolding of actual celebrations in a given historical period. They are official Church books which the officiant and his ministers have in hand during a celebration of the Latin liturgy.

These are the primary books we shall consider in the following pages since they alone make up the essential and authentic sources of the Roman liturgy. At the same time, however, we must pay some attention to the interesting juridico-liturgical collections of the early Christian era.

b. *Works by Christians and non-Christians that treat of divine worship;* commentaries, expositions, explanations or descriptions of liturgies.

Works in this second category are important for two reasons:

i) Before the development of set liturgies, they permit us to view past liturgical events and see for ourselves the ongoing worship process of a certain period or geographical area. Given the paucity of authentic documents, on occasion such works are sometimes the only source of insight we have available.

ii) After the development of fixed rites, the importance of such documents fades, but they are sometimes still valuable because they contain the remnants of lost liturgies along with commentaries which make them indispensable sources of information.

The following are the principal such documents in their chronological order. Despite the fact that juridical sources contain important information on the arrangement of worship, conciliar collections, decretals, capitularies and episcopal regulations of the liturgy are not included here.[13]

I. THE EARLY CHRISTIAN ERA.

The most informative surviving ritual relic of the early Roman Church is the *Apostolic Tradition* of Bishop Hippolytus of Rome, composed around 215. It will be considered at length when we look at the liturgical documents proper.

Besides the incomparable *Apostolic Tradition* and the juridico-liturgical collections, the Fathers of the Church and other ecclesiastical writers often allude to the liturgy. Although valuable in itself, such information is usually fragmentary in nature—the mere shattered remnants of a once great construct—and therefore hard to understand and piece together.[14]

The most important texts of the Patristic era are the following:

Peregrinatio ad loca sancta Egeriae (381-384); CSEL 39, 37-101; CC 175, 32-106 and 175 =Indices; H. Pétré, *Ethérie: Journal de voyage* (Latin text, French Introduction and translation) SC 21 (Paris 1948) and P. Maraval, trans., SC 296 (Paris 1982); ET J. Wilkinson, *Egeria's Travels* (London 1971 and 2nd ed., Jerusalem 1981); also, G.E. Gingras, *Egeria: Diary of a Pilgrimage*, ACW 38 (New York 1970).

Augustine of Hippo (†430), *Ad Ianuarium*, PL 33, 199-223; "Letters 54 and 55 to Januarius," *St. Augustine: Letters*, vol.1 = FC 12, tr. W. Parsons (New York 1951) 252-293; *De symbolo ad catechumenos*, PL 40, 627-668; "De Symbolo," *St. Augustine: Treatises on Marriage and other Subjects*, R. Deferrari, ed., FC 27 (New York 1955) 285-307.

Fulgentius of Ruspe (†527), *Ad Monimum*, PL 65, 179-196; CC 91, 33-52.

Gregory the Great (†604), *Registrum epistolarum*, MGH, *Epistolarum* vols. 1-2.

John the Deacon (early VI century), *Ad Senarium comitem patrimonii*, PL 59, 399-408; SeT 59 (1933) 158-179.

Ambrose of Milan (†397), *De Mysteriis* and *De Sacramentis*, PL 16, 384-410, 410-462; CSEL 73, 13-116; B. Botte, *Des sacrements, Des mystères* (Latin/French) SC 25 bis (Paris 1961); ET T. Thompson, *St. Ambrose On the Sacraments and On the Mysteries* (London 1950); R.J. Deferrari, *Saint Ambrose: Theological and Dogmatic Works*, FC 44 (Washington, D.C. 1963) 3-28; 265-328.[15]

Pseudo-Maximus of Turin (†ca. 550), *De baptismo*, PL 57, 771-782.

Pseudo-Donysius the Areopagite (Syria, ca. 500), *De ecclesiastica hierarchia*, PG 3, 369-584; M. de Gandillac, *Oeuvres complètes du Pseudo-Denys l'Aréopagite* (Paris 1943); ET T.L. Campbell, *Dionysius the Pseudo-Areopagite: The Ecclesiastical Hierarchy* (Washington, D.C. 1981).

Roman Anonymous-Ambrosiaster (ca. 366-384), *Quaestiones veteris et novi testamenti*, PL 35, 2205-2298.

Marius Victorinus Afer (†after 362), *Adversus Arium*, PL 8, 1094-1095.

Germanus of Paris (†576), *Expositio brevis antiquae liturgiae gallicanae*, PL 72, 89-98; J. Quasten, *Opuscula et textus*: Series Liturgica 3 (Münster/Westf. 1934); K. Gamber, *Ordo antiquus gallicanus*, Textus Patristici et Liturgici 3 (Regensburg 1965); E.C. Ratcliff, ed., *Expositio Antiquae Liturgiae Gallicanae*, HBS 98 (London 1971). On the question of authorship, see A. van der Mensbrugge, "L'Expositio missae gallicanae est-elle de St. Germain de Paris?" *Messager de l'Exarchat du Patriarche russe en Europe occidentale* 8 (1959) 217-249 and "Pseudo-Germanus Reconsidered," *Studia Patristica* 5(1962) 172-184.

Isidore of Seville (†636), *De ecclesiasticis officiis libri duo*, PL 83, 737-826.

The decretals of some of the early popes should be added to this list; some of them are essential to any understanding of liturgical history. These are conveniently listed in chronological order in E. Dekkers, ed., *Clavis Patrum latinorum* (Steenbrugge 1961) section VII, 347-386

II. MEDIEVAL LITURGISTS[16]

For the celebrated letter of Charlemagne to his bishops on baptism, see P. Jaffé, *Bibliotheca Rerum Germanicarum* 6, 401-415; see also the basic document *Ad Odilbertum episcopum Mediolanensis* (805-814) of 809-812 and Odilbert's reply in MGH, *Capitularia regum Francorum* 1, 246-248 (also in MGH, *Epistolae selectae* 4, 529-31, 533-41; 5, 300 and 642).[17]

Alcuin (†804), *Ad Oduinum presbyterum*, PL 101, 611-614.
Leidrad of Lyons (†813), *Liber de sacramento baptismatis ad Carolum magnum*, PL 99, 853-872.
Angilbert of St. Riquier (790-814), *Institutio de diversitate officiorum*, F. Lot, ed., Hariulf (†1143), *Chronique de l'abbaye de Saint-Riquier* (625-1083) (Paris 1894) 296-306.
Magnus of Sens (†818), *Libellus de mysterio baptismatis iussu Caroli Magni editus*, PL 102, 981-984.
Theodulf of Orleans (†821), *De ordine baptismi*, PL 105, 223-240.
Maxentius of Aquileia (†833), *De significatu rituum baptismatis*, PL 106, 51-54.
Collectanea de antiquis ritibus baptismi, PL 106, 53-58.
Epistola de ritibus baptismi ad Carolum Magnum imperatorem, PL 98, 938-939.
Anonymous, Fragment *De baptismo*, PL 98, 939-940.
Jesse of Amiens (†836), *Epistola de baptismo*, PL 105, 781-796.
Hincmar of Rheims (†882), *Epistola ad presbyteros Remensis ecclesiae*, PL 126, 104-110.

In the Carolingian period, there arose a vast didactic literature for the clergy so that they could pass the examinations insisted upon by the reformers (since Carlomann, 742, under the influence of St. Boniface, the Apostle of Germany and reformer, of the Frankish Church. See MGH, *Capitularia regum Francorum* 1, 25). Such works were usually called *Expositiones missae, symboli, orationis dominicae*. There were also didactic collections of the old *Ordines Romani* turned into elementary manuals for the instruction of the clergy.[18]

This kind of clerical literature should be compared with the *Disputationes* and the *Ioca* of the same period. See the *Disputationes puerorum*, PL 101, 1099-1144, and the *Ioca episcopi ad sacerdotes* in A. Franz, *Die Messe im deutschen Mittelalter* (Freiburg/Br. 1902; repr Darmstadt 1963) 342.

The later Carolingian period also had many great liturgists:

Alcuin (†804), *Opera omnia*, PL 100 and 101.[19]
Amalarius of Metz (†ca 850), *Epistolae ad Petrum Nonantulanum, ad Carolum imperatorem de scrutinio et de baptismo, ad Carolum imperatorem de caeremoniis baptismi, ad Hilduinum abbatem de diebus ordinationis et Quattuor Temporum, Expositio missae, De canonis missae interpretatione, Liber officialis, De Ordine antiphonarii, Eclogae do ordine romano*: J. M. Hanssens, ed., *Amalarii episcopi*

opera liturgica omnia, 3 vols., SeT 138, 139, 140 (Vatican City 1948-1950); A. Cabaniss, *Amalar of Metz* (Amsterdam 1954).

Agobard of Lyons (†840), *Liber de correctione antiphonarii*, PL 104, 329-340; *Contra libros IV Amalarii*, PL 104, 339-350

Rabanus Maurus (†842), *De institutione clericorum libri III*, PL 107, 293-420; A. Knoepfler, ed., (Munich 1900). [20]

Walafrid Strabo (†849), *De exordiis et incrementis quarundam in observationibus ecclesiasticis rerum*, PL 114, 919-966; A Knoepfler, ed, (Munich 1890). *De sacris ordinibus, sacramentis divinis et vestimentis sacerdotalibus*, PL 112, 1165-1192.

Florus of Lyons (†ca 860), *Liber de divina psalmodia*, PL 104, 325-330; *De actione missae (i.e. de canone)* PL 119, 15-70. Florus is also published in part by Hanssens in his edition of Amalarius. See also P. Duc, *Étude sur l' "Expositio Missae" de Florus de Lyon suivie d'une édition critique du texte* (Belley 1937).

Remigius of Auxerre (†908), *Explicatio missae* in the *De divinis officiis* of Pseudo-Alcuin, cap. 40, PL 101, 1246-1271.

Pseudo-Bede (IX century), *De officiis libellus*, PL 94, 531-540.

Pseudo-Alcuin (before the *Ordo romanus antiquus = Ordo L*, thus, before 950), *De divinis officiis*, PL 101, 1174-1286. In regards to Pseudo-Alcuin and his significance for the history of worship, see M. Andrieu, "L'*Ordo romanus antiquus* et le *Liber de divinis officiis* du Pseudo-Alcuin," *Revue des Sciences Religieuses* 5 (1925) 642-650.

XI CENTURY:

Berno of Reichenau (†1048), *Libellus de quibusdam rebus ad missae officium pertinentibus*, PL 142, 1055-1080.

Humbert of Silva Candida (†ca. 1064), *Adversus Graecorum calumnias*, PL 143, 929-974.

Peter Damian (†1072), *De Dominus vobiscum*, PL 145, 231-252; *De horis canonicis*, PL 145, 221-232.[21]

Bonizo of Sutri (†1089), *Libellus de sacramentis*, PL 150, 857-866; W. Berschin, ed., *Bonizo von Sutri: Leben und Werk*, Beiträge zur Geschichte und Quellenkunde des Mittelalters 2 (Berlin-New York 1972).

John of Avranches (†1079), *De officiis ecclesiasticis*, PL 147, 27-116; R. Delamare, ed., *Le "De officiis ecclesiasticis" de Jean d'Avranches, archevêque de Rouen (1067-1079)*, Bibliothèque liturgique du Chanoine U. Chevalier 22 (Paris 1923).

Bernhold of Constance (†1100), *Micrologus de ecclesiasticis observationibus*, PL 151, 974-1022.[22]

Medieval music can barely be mentioned here. For a bibliography of Literature that deals with the liturgical music of the Middle Ages see A.

Hughes, *Medieval Music: The Sixth Liberal Art* (rev. ed. Toronto 1980) and the various articles in the *New Grove Dictionary of Music and Musicians*, 20 vols., S. Sadie, ed. (London 1980)[23]

XII CENTURY:

Sigebert of Gembloux (†after 1112), *De differentia Quattuor Temporum*, PL 160, 813–830.

Odo of Cambrai (†1113), *Expositio in canonem missae*, PL 160, 1053–70.

Ivo of Chartres (†ca 1117), *Sermones de ecclesiasticis sacramentis*, PL 162, 505-610.

Bruno of Segni (†1123) *De sacramentis ecclesiae, mysteriis atque ecclesiasticis ritibus*, PL 165, 1089-1110.

Alger of Liège (†1131), *De sacificio missae*, PL 180, 853–856.[24]

Rupert of Deutz (†1129/30), *Liber de divinis officiis*, PL 170, 9–332; H. Haacke, ed., CC, Continuatio Medievalis 7 (Turnhout 1967), cf. J. H. Van Engen, *Rupert of Deutz* (Berkeley 1983).

Hildebert of Tours (†1136), *Versus de mysterio missae*, PL 171 1177–1196.[25]

Drogo of Laon (†ca. 1135), *De divinis officiis*, PL 166, 1557–1564).

Stephen of Baugé (de Balgiaco) (†1136), *De sacramento altaris*, PL 172, 1273–1308.

Honorius of Autun (Augustodunensis) (†ca. 1145–1152), *Gemma animae*, PL 72, 541–738; *Sacramentarium seu de causis et significatu mystico rituum divini in ecclesia officii liber*, PL 172, 737–806; *Speculum Ecclesiae*, PL 172, 813–1108.

Hugh of St. Victor (†ca. 1141), *De sacramentis*, PL 176, 173–618,[26]ET R.J. Deferrari, *On the Sacraments of the Christian Faith*, Medieval Academy of America 58 (Cambridge, MA 1951).

Isaac of Poitiers (Stella) (†1169), *Epistola ad Iohannem Pictaviensis de officio missae*, PL 194, 1889-1896.

John Beleth (†1182), *Rationale divinorum officiorum*, PL 202, 9–167; *Summa de ecclesiasticis officiis*, H. Douteil, ed., CC Continuatio Medievalis 41–41ᴬ (Turnhout 1976).

Anon. *Liber Quare Symonis*, many MSS, no edition.

Anon. *Speculum de mysteriis Ecclesiae*, PL 177, 335-381 (Pseudo-Hugh of St. Victor).

Robert Paululus (late XII century), *De ceremoniis, sacramentis, officiis et observationibus ecclesasticis*, PL 177, 381-456 (Ps-Hugh of St. Victor).

XIII CENTURY

Sicardus of Cremona (†1215), *Mitrale seu de officiis ecclesiasticis summa*, PL 213, 13–436.

Lothar of Segni (Innocent III, †1216), *De missarum mysteriis*, PL 217, 763–916; D.F. Wright, *A Medieval Commentary on the Mass: "Particulae" 2-3 and 5-6 of the "De Missarum Mysteriis" (ca. 1195) of Cardinal Lothar of Segni (Pope Innocent III)*, Doctoral Dissertation, University of Notre Dame, 1977 (Ann Arbor, Michigan: University Microfilms); a translation of the Prologue and the section dealing with the Eucharistic Prayer (Part I, chapters 50-51; Part II, Part IV, and Part V, chapters 1-10) was submitted as a Master's Thesis by Michael O. Brown (University of Notre Dame 1982).

Praepositinus of Cremona (†ca. 1210), *Summa de officiis*, J. A. Corbett, ed. (Notre Dame 1969).

William of Auxerre (†1231), *Summa de officiis ecclesiasticis*, unpublished; cf. R.M. Martineau, "La *Summa de officiis eccles.* de Guillaume d'Auxerre," *Etudes d'histoire littéraire et doctrinale du XIII siècle* 2 (Ottowa 1932) 25-58.

Guy of Orchelles († ca. 1230), *Summa de officiis Ecclesiae*, V.L. Kennedy, ed., "The Summa de officiis Ecclesiae of Guy d'Orchelles," *Medieval Studies* 1 (1939) 23-62.

Alexander of Hales (†1245), *Summae Pars IV*, qu. 37: *De officio missae* (published by William of Melitona, †1260) J. A. Birretis-F. Gyrardengho, edd. (Pavia 1489).

Hugh of St. Cher (†1263), *Tractatus super missam* or *Speculum Ecclesiae*; G. Sölch, ed., *Hugonis a S. Charo tractatus super missam seu Speculum Ecclesiae* (Münster 1940) [see also G. Sölch, *Hugo von St. Cher O.P. und die Anfänge der Dominikanerliturgie* (Cologne 1938)]. cf. A. Franz, *Die Messe*, 274, n.2.

Albert the Great (†1280), *Liber de mysterio missae*; A. and A. Borgnet, edd., *Alberti Magni Opera Omnia* 38 (Paris 1890) 1-189; K. Illing, *Alberts des Grossen "Super Missam"* (Munich 1975).

Gilbert of Tournai († 1284), *Tractatus de officio episcopi et caeremoniis Ecclesiae*, Maxima Bibliotheca Patrum 25 (Lyons 1667) 401–420.

William Durandus (†1296), in addition to his famous *Pontificale*, composed a *Rationale divinorum officiorum* which is the liturgical synthesis *par excellence* of the Middle Ages. Innumerable MSS of the *Rationale* survive, especially in France, some almost contemporaneous with the author. It was the second printed work to appear (after the Psalter) at Mainz, in 1459. XV century: 43 editions; XVI century: 41 editions; XVII century: 9 editions. There is still no critical edition. One unsatisfactory modern edition (Naples 1859); French translation in 5 vols. by C. Barthélémy (Paris 1854); ET of Bk. I by J. M. Neale and B. Webb, *The Symbols of Churches and Church Ornaments* (London 1843) and of Bk. III by T. H. Passmore, *The Sacred Vestments* (London 1899). Cf. C.C. Ménard, *William Durand's Rationale divinorum officiorum. Preliminaries to a new Critical Edition*. Doctoral Dissertatin, the Gregorian University, Rome 1967; a critical edition is being prepared by P.M. Gy, *et al.*

XIV AND XV CENTURIES:

Guy of Mont Rocher (or Rother) (†1333), *Manipulus curatorum sacerdotum secundum ordinem septem sacramentorum perbreviter complectens;* cf. L. F. Hain, *Repertorium Bibliographicum* #8166 (Hain, vol. 1, p. 539; Hain-Copinger, pt. 1, p. 242; D. Reichling, *Appendices ad Hainii-Copingeri Repertorium Bibliographicum*, fasc. 2, p. 183).

Henry of Hesse (of Langenstein) (†1397), *Secreta sacerdotum quae sibi placent vel displicent in missa;* cf. Hain, ## 8375-8388 (Hain, vol 2, pp. 8-9; Reichling, fasc. 5, 136).

Ralph of Rivo, dean of Tongres (†1403), *Liber de officiis Ecclesiae; De canonum observantia liber; Tractatus de psalterio observando;* L. C. Mohlberg, ed., *Radulph von Rivo: Der letze Vertreter der altrömischen Liturgie,* 2 vols. (Louvain-Münster 1911-1915).

Vincent Gruner (†ca 1410), *Officii missae sacrique canonis expositio;* Hain-Copinger #2387, pt. 2, vol. 1, p. 237; Reichling, fasc. 2, p. 167).

Nicholas of Blonye (of Plove or Plone) (†ca. 1434), *Tractatus sacerdotalis de sacramentis deque divinis officiis et eorum administrationibus* (Strasbourg 1587).

Stephen Bodeker (†1459), *Tractatus (Brandenburgensis) de horis canonicis;* A. Schönfelder, ed. (Breslau 1902).

Denis the Carthusian (de Rickel) (†1471), "Expositio missae," *Opera* 1 (Cologne 1532) 211-228; *Hymnorum aliquot veterum Ecclesiae pia nec minus erudita narratio* (Paris 1542).

Gabriel Biel (†1495), *Literalis et mystica canonis missae expositio* (Reutlingen 1488); cf. Hain ## 3178-3179 (Hain, vol. 1, p. 435; Reichling, fasc. 1, p. 16); H. A. Oberman and W. J. Courtenay, edd., 5 vols. (Wiesbaden 1963-76).

Anonymous, *Quadruplex missalis expositio, litteralis, allegorica tropologica, anagogica* (Basle 1505); cf. Hain #6801 (Hain, vol. 1, pp. 339-340).

Josse Clichtove, *Elucidatorium ecclesiasticum* (Paris 1516).

Herrmann Torrentin, *Hymni et sequentiae cum diligenti difficilimorum vocabulorum interpretatione* (Cologne 1513).

John Adelphe, *Luculenta sequentiarum interpretatio* (Strasbourg 1513).

Albert of Ferrara, *Tractatus de horis canonicis:* cf. Hain ## 591-602 (Hain vol. 1, pp. 65-66).

Anonymous, *Tractatus misnensis de horis canonicis;* A. Schönfelder, ed. (Breslau 1902).

Other important texts of the XV century have been collected by F. Wasner "Fifteenth-Century Texts on the Ceremonial of the Papal *Legatus a latere*," *Traditio* 14 (1958) 295-358, 16 (1958) 405-416.

XVI CENTURY:

By the XVI century, the process of liturgical codification was over, although the documents liturgical scholars collected were to prove helpful for the study of medieval liturgy.[27]

George Cassander, († 1566), *Ordo Romanus de officio missae: Libelli aliquot pervetusti et authentici, etc.* (Cologne 1561), a collection of *ordines* from different periods; *Liturgica de ritu et ordine Dominica Caena celebranda* (Cologne 1558). Both of these appear in Cassander's complete works (Paris 1616).

Onofrio Panvinio († 1568), *Expositio missae* (Rome, Bibl. Vat. *codex lat.* 4973, unedited) includes extracts from the Fathers and old liturgies; *De urbis Romae stationibus* (Rome 1572); *De praecipuis Urbis Romae sanctioribus basilicis* (Rome 1570); *De baptismate paschali, de origine et ritu consecrandi Agnus Dei* (Rome 1560); *De ritu sepeliendi mortuos apud veteres christianos* (Cologne 1568).

Flacius Illyricus († 1575), *Missa latina quae olim ante Romanam circa 700 ann. in usu fuit* (!) (Strasbourg 1557), a document containing a X-XI century Roman liturgy saturated with sacerdotal *apologiae*; reprint PL 138, 1305-1336. A critical study is being prepared by Ms. Joanne Pierce, University of Notre Dame.

Melchior Hittorp († 1584), *De divinis catholicae Ecclesiae officiis ac ministeriis varia vetustorum aliquot Ecclesiae Patrum ac scriptorum libri* (Cologne 1568; reprint Bibliotheca Magna Patrum, tome X and in the Bibliotheca Maxima Patrum, tome XIII; Farnborough 1970). A collection of the work of different liturgists and of an *Ordo Romanus antiquus* which is, in fact, a witness to the *Romano-Germanic Pontifical of the X century* (which was then unknown).

Pamelius (Jaques de Joigny de Pamèle) († 1587), *Liturgia Latinorum*, 2 vols. (Cologne 1571; reprint Farnborough 1970). The same work appeared throughout the XVII century under different titles. T. I: a now worthless explanation of liturgical evolution; T. II: contains various liturgical documents, including *Hieronymi Comes sive Lectionarius: Antiphonarius ordinatus a S. Gregorio: Sacramentorum libri tres* (Gregory, Grimoald, Alcuin); and others. See DACL 13,966-974 for summary of the contents.

XVII AND XVIII CENTURIES:

Many scholarly works appeared during this period, remarkable both for the documents they assembled and for the learned commentaries which accompanied them. Many of these works are still indispensible today. In the following list, we give only those books that treat of the Latin liturgy; the year given is that of the first edition unless otherwise noted.

H. Ménard († 1644), *Divi Gregorii papae Liber Sacramentorum nunc demum correctior et locupletior editus ex missali MSS. S. Eligii bibliothecae Corbeiensis,* Paris, Bibliothèque Nationale *codex lat.* 12051; X century (Paris 1642; reprint PL 78, 25-263; Farnborough 1969). The title is erroneous; it is not a pure Gregorian but a mixed Gelasiano-Gregorian.

J. Gretser († 1625), *Opera,* 17 vols. (Regensburg 1734-1741). Fine treatises on many liturgical matters.

B. Ferrari († 1669). *De ritu sacrarum veteris Ecclesiae concionum* (Milan 1618); *De veterum acclamationibus et plausu* (Milan 1627).

C. Guyet († 1644), *Heortologia* (2nd ed., Lyons 1657).

J. Morin († 1659), *Commentarius historicus de disciplina in administratione sacramenti paenitentiae* (Paris 1651; reprint of the 1682 ed., Farnborough 1970); *Commentarius de sacris Ecclesiae ordinationibus* (Paris 1655; reprint of a 1695 ed., Farnborough 1970).

J.K. Suicerus († 1684), *Thesaurus ecclesiasticus,* 2 vols. (2nd ed. Amsterdam 1728).

L. d'Achery († 1685), *Spicilegium veterum aliquot scriptorum,* 13 vols. (Paris 1655-1677; 2nd ed. by De La Barre, 3 vols., Paris 1723).

J. J. Ciampini († 1698), *Vetera monumenta,* 2 vols. (Rome 1693-1699); *De sacris aedificiis a Constantino Magno exstructis* (Paris 1693).

L. Thomassin († 1695), *Vetus et nova Ecclesiae disciplina,* 3 vols. (Paris 1688; reprint Bar-Le-Duc 1864).

Other more ritual-rubrical commentators: B. Gavanti († 1638), C. Merati († 1744), M. Quarti († after 1650, J. Bona († 1674), and J. Catalani († 1764).

J. B. Thiers († 1703), *Traité des superstitions. 2: Des superstitions qui regardent les sacraments,* 4 vols. (Paris 1697-1704), new edition, Paris 1984. He also wrote several treatises on bells, porches, altars, choir lofts.

J. Mabillon († 1707), *De liturgia gallicana libri tres* (Paris 1685; reprint PL 72, 99-448).

J. Mabillon–M. Germain, *Museum italicum seu collectio veterum scriptorum ex bibliothecis italicis eruti* (Paris 1687-1689). Tome I: various documents including the Bobbio Missal under the title *Liber sacramentorum Ecclesiae gallicanae.* Tome II: *Liber ritualis sanctae romanae Ecclesiae* (reprint PL 78, 851-1408), a collection of *ordines,* the *Eclogae de ordine romano,* and other regulations.

C. de Vert († 1708), *Explication simple, littérale et historique des cérémonies de l'Église,* 2 vols. (Paris 1697-98; reprint of the 4-volume ed. of 1713-1720, Farnborough 1970).

J.M. Thomasius (Tommasi, † 1713), *Responsorialia et Antiphonaria Romanae Ecclesiae* (MS from later than IX century) (Rome 1686); *Antiqui libri missarum Romanae Ecclesiae* (Rome 1691), includes the *Comes* of Alcuin and a list of pericopes, etc.; *Psalterium cum canticis versibus prisco more distinctum* (Rome 1613); *Codices sacramentorum nongentis annis vetustiores* (Rome 1680), includes the Gelasian Sacramentary=*Vat. Reg.* 316, the *Missale Gallicanum*, the *Missale Francorum* and the *Missale Gallicanum Vetus*. A complete edition of Thomasius was edited by A. Vezzosi, *Opera Omnia*, 7 vols. (Rome 1717-1754). The fourth volume of this collection was reprinted: J.M. Thomasi, *Opera Omnia, Tomus Quartus in quo Responsorialia et Antiphonaria Romanae Ecclesiae* (Farnborough 1969).

J. Bingham († 1723), *Origines ecclesiasticae or the Antiquities of the Christian Church*, 8 vols. (London 1708-1722; reprint Oxford 1878). Latin translation by Grischovius, 10 vols. (Halle 1824).

P. Le Brun († 1729), *Explication littérale, historique et dogmatique des prières et des cérémonies de la messe*, 4 vols. (Paris 1716-1726; reprint Farnborough 1970).

B. Pez († 1735), *Thesaurus anecdotorum novissimus*, 6 vols. (Augsburg 1721-1728).

J. B. Sollier († 1740), *Martyrologium Usuardi* (Antwerp 1714; ed. J. Bouillart, Paris 1718).

E. Martène († 1739), *De antiquis Ecclesiae ritibus libri tres*, 1st ed., 3 vols. (Rouen 1700-1702) 2nd ed., 4 vols. (Antwerp 1736-1738; reprint Hildesheim 1967-69). The so-called Venice edition printed at Bassano (4 vols. 1788) was the most widespread edition: *De antiqua disciplina in celebrandis divinis officiis* and *De antiquis monachorum ritibus libri quinque*. Tome I: *De antiquis sacramentorum ritibus*: Tome II: *Benedictiones sacrae*: Tome III: *De variis ad ecclesiasticam disciplinam pertinentibus ritibus*: Tome IV: *Divina officia*=liturgy of the hours and the liturgical year. Cf. A. G. Martimort, *La Documentation liturgique de Dom Edmond Martène: Etude codicologique*, SeT 279 (Vatican 1978); Supplement *Ecclesia Orans* 3 (1986) 81-105.

E. Martène-U. Durand († 1773), *Thesaurus novus anecdotorum*, 5 vols. (2nd ed. Paris 1717); *Amplissima collectio veterum scriptorum et monumentorum*, 9 vols. (2nd ed. Paris 1724-1733).

L. A. Muratori († 1750), *Liturgia romana vetus*, 2 vols. (Venice 1748). An index for this collection of Roman and Gallican sacramentaries has been compiled by H. Wilson, *A Classified Index to the Leonine, Gelasian, and Gregorian Sacramentaries* (Cambridge 1892).

J. B. Gattico († 1754), *Acta selecta caeremonalia Sanctae Romanae Ecclesiae ex variis codicibus et diariis saec. XV, XVI, XVII*, Tome I (Rome 1753), Tome II (Rome: publication interrupted by order of the superiors); *De oratoriis domesticis et altari portatili* (Rome 1746; 2nd ed. J.A. Assemani, Rome 1770).

Donati († 1755), *Dei dittici degli antichi, profani e sacri, coll'appendice di alcuni necrologi e calendari finora non pubblicati* (Lucca 1753).

A. Gori († 1757), *Thesaurus veterum diptychorum consularium et ecclesiasticorum*, 3 vols (Florence 1759).

D. Giorgi († 1764), *Liturgia Romani pontificis in solemni celebratione missarum*, 3 vols. (Rome 1731-1744; repr. Farnborough 1970). Discusses sacred vessels, persons and liturgical books; *Martyrologium Adonis* (Rome 1745).

J. S. Assemani († 1768). *Kalendaria Ecclesiae universae*, 6 vols. (incomplete) (Rome 1755-57).

L. Selvaggio († 1772), *Antiquitatum christianarum institutiones* (Rome 1772-1774; 2nd ed., Mainz 1786).

J. A. Assemani († 1782), *Codex liturgicus Ecclesiae universae*, 13 vols. (incomplete) (Rome 1749-1766; reprint Paris-Leipzig 1902; Farnborough 1968-1969).

M. Gerbert († 1793), *Vetus liturgia alemannica, disquisitionibus praeviis, notis et observationibus illustrata*, 2 vols. (Saint-Blaise 1776; reprint Hildesheim 1967); *Monumenta veteris liturgiae alemannicae*, 2 vols. (Saint-Blaise 1777-1779; reprint Hildesheim 1967); *Principia theologique liturgicae quoad divinum officium, Dei cultum et sanctorum*, (Augsburg 1759); *De cantu et missa sacra a prima ecclesiae aetate usque ad praesens tempus* (Saint-Blaise 1744; reprint Graz 1968); *Scriptores ecclesiastici de musica sacra potissimum ex variis Italiae, Galliae et Germaniae codicibus MSS. collecti* (Saint-Blaise 1774; reprint Hildesheim 1963).

F. A. Zaccaria († 1795), *Bibliotheca ritualis* (Rome 1776-1781; reprint New York 1963), T. I: Sources; T. II: Catholic and Protestant material; T. III: Maldonnat's explanation of the Mass; various documents. *Onomasticon rituale*, 2 vols (Faenza 1787).

A. A. Pellicia († 1823), *De christianae ecclesiae primae, mediae et novissimae aetatis politia libri sex*, 3 vols. (Naples 1777; Cologne 1829-1838).

We must bring to an end this list of indispensable reference works. The literature of the XIX and XX centuries is immense and cannot be described here, even *per summa capita*.

For a more complete understanding of the concrete forms of medieval worship, however, we must refer the reader to the epics, dramas, mystery-plays, lyric poetry, fables, chronicles, etc. These other kinds of medieval literature literally teem with information on medieval worship. Although it is quite impossible to provide a working bibliography of such sources, by way of introduction we suggest the following classical repertories:

A. Molinier, *Les sources de l'histoire de France des origines aux guerres d'Italie*, - 1494 (Paris 1901-1906).

A. Potthast, *Bibliotheca historica medii aevi*, 2 vols. (Berlin 1896); new edition, *Repertorium fontium mediae aevi*; 1. *Series collectionum* (Rome 1962); 2. *Fontes, A-G* (Rome 1967-).

F. Dahlman and G. Waitz, *Quellenkunde der deutschen Geschichte* (9th ed. Leipzig 1931).

W. Wattenbach and R. Holtzmann, *Deutschlands Geschichtsquellen im Mittelalter: Deutsche Kaizerzeit* (Tübingen 1948): *Zeit der Sachsen und Salier* (Cologne 1967).

W. Wattenbach and F.-J. Schmale, *Deutschlands Geschichtsquellen im Mittelalter bis zur Mitte des 13 Jhs.* (Darmstadt 1976).

W. Wattenbach and W. Levinson, *Deutschlands Geschichtsquellen im Mittelalter: Vorzeit und Karolinger* (Weimar 1952-63).

H. Pirenne, *Bibliographie de l'histoire de Belgique* (Brussels 1931) and *Histoire de Belgique des origines à nos jours*, 4 vols. (Brussels 148-52).

L. J. Paetow, *A Guide to the Study of Medieval History* (Millwood, New York 1931, reprint New York 1980).

H. Barth, *Bibliographie der schweizer Geschichte enthaltend die selbständig erschienenen Druckwerke zur Geschichte der Schweiz bis 1912* (Basel 1914-15, reprint New York 1969).

B. Sanchez Alonso, *Fuentes de la historia española e hispano-americana*, (2nd rev. ed., Madrid 1927, Appendix 1946).

C. Gross, *The Sources and Literature of English History from the Earliest Times to about 1485* (Oxford 1975).

For a correlation between the history of the liturgy and the general history of the Church, see Weingarten—C.F. Arnold, *Zeittafeln und Ueberblicke zur Kirchengeschichte* (6th ed., Leipzig 1905).[28]

c. *Liturgical Monuments.*

One must add to the two literary sources just indicated (liturgical books properly so-called and the works of liturgists) the evidence provided by liturgical monuments: sacred buildings (basilicas, baptisteries, *consignatoria*), inscriptions, mosaics, paintings, sculptures, liturgical furniture and vestments. They often facilitate useful comparisons and sometimes—especially for the early Christian period—provide us with our only sources of information.

A meritorious synthesis of such sources was attempted by G. Ferretto, *Note storico-bibliografische di archeologia cristiana* (Rome 1942).

From the immense quantity of literature on this subject, we select only the following particularly valuable works:

In every instance it is helpful to consult the *Dictionnaire d'archéologie chrétienne et de liturgie*, edd. F. Cabrol-H. Leclercq-H. Marrou, 30 vols. (Paris 1907-1953)—even in spite of its sometimes astonishing *lacunae*.

Reallexikon für Antike und Christentum, T. Klauser, ed. (see above p. 8).

W. Smith-S. Cheetham, *Dictionary of Christian Antiquities*, 2 vols. (1875-1880). Dated but still useful.

E. Gause, *Der Einfluss des christlichen Kultus auf den Kirchenbau* (Jena, 1901). He wrongly denies the influence of liturgy on architecture.

P. Battifol, *Études de liturgie et d'archéologie chrétienne* (Paris 1919).

J. Braun, *Der christliche Altar*, 2 vols. (Munich 1924).

O. M. Dalton, *Early Christian Art. A Survey of the Monuments* (Oxford 1925).

H. W. Beyer, *Der syrische Kirchenbau* (Berlin 1925).

K. Liesenberg, *Der Einfluss der Liturgie auf die frückristliche Basilica* (Neustadt 1928).

T. Klauser, *Vom Heroon zur Märtyrerbasilika*. Kriegsvorträge of the University of Bonn 62 (Bonn 1942). Corrected by T. Klauser, *Christlicher Märtyrerkult heidnischer Heroenkult und spätjüdische Heiligenverehrung* (Cologne-Opladen 1961).

A. Grabar, *Martyrium. Recherches sur le culte des reliques et l'art chrétien antique. 1. Architecture; 2. Iconographie*, 3 vols. (Paris 1946). Important for early Christian worship.

J. Lassus, *Les sanctuaires chrétiens de Syrie* (Paris 1947).

W. Lowrie, *Art in the Early Church* (New York 1947). 500 illustrations.

A. M. Schneider, *Liturgie und Kirchenbau in Syrien*. Nachrichten der Akademie d. Wissen. in Gottingen. Phil.-hist. Kl. (1949) 45–68.

R. Krautheimer, *Corpus basilicarum christianorum Romae*. The Early Christian Basilicas of Rome, IV-IX Century. 5 vols. (Vatican City 1937-1980).

———, "The Beginnings of Early Christian Architecture," *Review of Religion* 3 (1939) 127–148.

———, "S. Pietro in Vincoli and the Tripartite Transept in the Early Christian Basilica," *Proceedings of the American Phil. Society* 84(1941) 353–429.

———, "The Carolingian Revivial of Early Christian Architecture," *Art Bulletin* 24(1942) 1–38.

———, "Il transetto nella basilica paleocristiana," *Actes du V congrès international d'archéologie chrétienne* (Aix-en-Provence 1954) 283–290.

———, *Early Christian and Byzantine Architecture* (2nd ed., Harmondsworth 1975).

———, "The Constantinian Basilica," *Dumbarton Oaks Papers* 21 (1967) 117–140.

———, *Studies in Early Christian, Medieval and Renaissance Art* (London-New York 1969); a collection of various articles.

J. B. Ward Perkins, "Constantine and the Origin of the Christian Basilica," *Papers of the British School at Rome* 22(1954) 69–90.

J. M. C. Toynbee-J.B. Ward Perkins, *The Shrine of St. Peter and the Vatican Excavations* (London–New York 1956). See especially chap. 7: "Constantine's Church."

J. W. Deichmann, *Versuch einer Darstellung der Grundrisstypen des Kirchenbaues in frühchristlicher und byzantinischer Zeit* (Würzburg 1957).

D. T. Rice, *The Beginnings of Christian Art* (London 1957).

F. van der Meer-C. Mohrmann *Atlas of the Early Christian World* (2nd ed.

London 1966). Helpful plates for the shape and decoration of churches and baptistries.

F. van der Meer, *Augustine the Bishop* (London 1961). See chap. 2. "The Town and the Country."

————, *Early Christian Art* (London 1968).

J. G. Davies, *The Origin and Development of Early Christian Church Architecture* (London 1952).

————, *The Architectural Setting of Baptism* (London 1962).

————, *The Secular Use of Church Buildings* (London 1968).

A. Khatchatrian, *Les baptistères paléochrétiens* (Paris 1962).

C. Heitz, *Recherches sur les rapports entre architecture et liturgie à l'époque carolingienne* (Paris 1963).

T. F. Mathews, "An Early Roman Chancel Arrangement and its Liturgical Uses," *Revista di archeologia cristiana* 38 (1962) 73–95.

————, *The Early Churches of Constantinople; Architecture and Liturgy* (University Park, PA–London 1971).

C. E. Pocknee, *The Christian Altar* (London–Westminster, MD 1963).

M. H. Shepherd, "Liturgical Expressions of the Constantinian Triumph," *Dumbarton Oaks Papers* 21 (1967) 59–78.

C. J. A. C. Peeters, *De liturgische dispositie van het vroechristelijk Kerkgebouw; plats en sammenhang van de 'Cathedra' de leesplats en het altar in de basiliek van de vierte tot de zevende eeuw* (Assen 1969).

J. Wilkinson, *Egeria's Travels* (2nd ed. Jerusalem 1983). "The Jerusalem Buildings."

C. Coüasnon, *The Church of the Holy Sepulchre in Jerusalem* (London 1974). See chap. 3: "Constantine's Basilica."

NOTES

1. V. Leroquais, *Les manuscrits liturgiques latins du haut moyen âge à la Renaissance*, Ecole pratique des Hautes Etudes. Sciences Religieuses (Paris 1931); T. Klauser, "Repertorium liturgicum und liturgischer Spezialkatalog," *Zentralblatt für Bibliothekwesen* 53 (1936) 2-16; G. Austin, "Liturgical Manuscripts in the United States and Canada," *Scriptorium* 28 (1974) 92-100.

2. Gregory VII, *Regula canonicorum*, ed. G. Morin, *Études, textes, découvertes*, Anecdota Maredsolana, series 2, vol. 1 (Tamines, Belgium-Paris 1913) 460.

3. For the printed editions of the Roman pontifical, see P. Batiffol, "La tradition du texte du Pontifical romain: Les éditions imprimées," *Bulletin d'ancienne littérature et d'archéologie chrétiennes* 2 (1912) 134-140. For the printed editions of the Roman Missal, see W.H.J. Weale and H. Bohatta,

Bibliotheca Liturgica: Catalogus Missalium ritus latini ab anno 1474 impressorum (London 1928). Chronological landmarks to keep in mind:

a) *Missale Romanum*: edited officially under Pius V (Bull, *Quo Primum*; July 14, 1570) with the title, *Missale romanum ex decreto sacrosancti concilii Tridentini restitutum, Pii V, P.M. iussu editum* (Rome 1570). From 1475 until the official 1570-edition, there were at least 211 printings of the Missal;

b) *Pontificale Romanum*: the *edito princeps* of the Pontifical came out under Innocent VIII in 1485 and was edited by John Burchard and A.P. Piccolomini. The edition made official for all the churches of the Latin Rite by Clement VIII (Bull, *Ex quo in Ecclesia Dei*; Feb. 2, 1596) agrees almost *ad litteram* with the edition of 1485;

c) *Caeremoniale Episcoporum*: Published in 1600 and made obligatory for all churches of the Latin Rite by Clement VIII, this book was based on the pontifical *Ordines* and on Paris de Grassis, Bishop of Pesaro (†1528), *De caeremoniis cardinalium et episcoporum libri duo* (Rome 1564);

d) The *Rituale Romanum*, in its official edition of Paul V (Bull, *Apostolicae Sedi*; June 17, 1614) was recommended rather than imposed on all Latin bishops;

e) The *Ordo missae secundum consuetudinem S.R.E.* or *Ordo servandus per sacerdotem in celebratione missae sine cantu et sine ministris* (Rome 1498) was also the work of J. Burchard of Strasbourg. For the other liturgical books, see the DACL at the appropriate entries; V. Thalhofer–L. Eizenhofer, *Handbuch der katholischen Liturgik* 1 (Freiburg/Br. 1912) 63-102 and the rev. ed. by Eizenhofer (1932) 57-111; F. Cabrol, *Les livres de la liturgie latine* (Paris 1930), ET *The Books of the Latin Liturgy* (London-St. Louis 1932); A.G. Martimort, *L'Église en prière* (Paris 1961) 68-70 for a list of books in use until Vatican II and ET *The Church at Prayer* (Shannon-New York 1968) 71-73 for books in use until 1968; L.C. Sheppard, *The Liturgical Books*, The Twentieth Century Encyclopedia of Catholicism 109 (New York 1962).

4. T. Klauser, *A Short History of the Western Liturgy* (Oxford 1982) 84.

5. Cf. W. Maskell, *Monumenta ritualia ecclesiae Anglicanae* 1 (2nd ed. Oxford 1882) cxxx-cxxxii.

6. The same total is obtained from analysing the lists in C. Du Cange, *Glossarium ad scriptores mediae et infimae latinitatis*, 3 vols. (1st ed. Paris 1673) re-edited with additions by Carpentier, Henschel, and Favre, 10 vols. (Niort 1883-88, reprint Paris 1938) clii-clv.

7. H. Bohatta, *Liturgische Bibliographie des XV. Jhds. mit Ausnahme der Missale und Livres d'Heures* (Vienna 1911).

8. For the types of liturgical books used in the Middle Ages—some authors are more accurate than others—see F.A. Zaccaria, *Bibliotheca ritualis* 1. 1 (Rome 1776, reprint: Burt Franklin Bibliography and Reference Series 58, New York 1963); W. Maskell, *Monumenta* (see note 5 above) iii-ccxxxiii; P. Guéranger, *Institutions liturgiques*, 3 (2nd ed. Paris 1883); W. Brambach, *Psalterium: Bibliographischer Versuch über die liturgischen Bücher des christlichen Abendlandes* (Berlin 1887); H. Ehrensberger, *Bibliotheca liturgica manuscripta*

(Karlsruhe 1887); F. Cabrol, *Les livres de la liturgie latine* (Paris 1930), ET *The Books of the Latin Liturgy* (London-St. Louis 1932); V. Leroquais, in the introductions to his works on sacramentaries, missals, breviaries and books of hours listed in note 9 below; a fascicle in the *Typologie des Sources du Moyen Âge Occidental* is in preparation by M. Huglo and A. Houssiau. Rather simplified, but containing much useful information is H. B. Swete, *Church Services and Service-Books before the Reformation* (3rd ed. London 1914); D. Balboni, "La catalogazione dei libri liturgici," EL 75 (1961) 223-36.

9. The following are the listings grouped according to region, particular library, or category of *libri liturgici*:

N. Sacksteder, "A Provisional List of Inventories of Latin Liturgical Manuscripts and Incunabula of the Middle Ages," EL 99 (1985) 60-82;

M. Pellechet, *Notes sur les livres liturgiques du diocèse d'Autun* (Chalon et Mâcon, Paris-Autun 1883);

L. Marcel, *Les livres liturgiques du diocèse de Langres* (Paris-Langres 1892-1912);

H. Ehrensberger, *Bibliotheca liturgica manuscripta* (Karlsruhe Library) (Karlsruhe 1889) and *Libri liturgici Bibliothecae Vaticanae* (Freiburg/Br. 1897) (with an unpublished supplement by H. M. Bannister, at the Vatican);

P. Salmon, *Les manuscrits liturgiques latins de la Bibliothèque Vaticane*, SeT 251, 253, 260, 267, 270 (Vatican City 1968-72);

R. Grégoire, "Repertorium liturgicum Italicum," *Studi Medievali*, Serie 3 Anno 9, fasc. 1 (1968) 465-592;

W.H. Frere, *Bibliotheca musico-liturgica*, 2 vols. (Cambridge 1901-1932 reprint Hildesheim 1967); a description of the muscial and liturgical MSS of the Middle Ages preserved in the libraries of Great Britain and Ireland;

S.J.P. Van Dijk, *Latin Liturgical Manuscripts* (Oxford 1952);

T. Haapanen, *Verzeichnis der mittelalterlichen Hss-Fragmente in der Universitätsbibliothek zu Helsingfors*, 1: *Missalien* (Helsingfors 1922);

P. Lindberg, *Die schwedischen Missalien des Mittelalters* (Berlin 1924);

P. Radò, "Mittelalterliche liturgischen Hss. deutscher, italienischer und französischer Herkunft in den Bibliotheken Südosteuropas," *Miscellanea K. Mohlberg* 2, Bibliotheca Ephemerides Liturgicae 23 (Rome 1949) 349-392;

———, *Libri liturgici manuscripti bibliothecarum Hungariae* (Budapest 1973);

A. Strittmatter, "Liturgical Manuscripts Preserved in Hungarian Libraries," *Traditio* 19 (1963) 487-507;

J. Plummer, *Liturgical Manuscripts for the Mass and the Divine Office* (New York 1964).

V. Leroquais, *Les sacramentaires et les missels manuscrits des bibliothèques publiques de France*, 4 vols. (Paris 1924); *Les Livres d'Heures manuscrits de la Bibliothèque Nationale*, 3 vols. (Paris 1927); *Les bréviaires manuscrits des bibliothèques publiques de France*, 6 vols. (Paris 1934); *Les pontificaux manuscrits des bibliothèques publiques de France*, 4 vols. (Paris 1937); *Les psautiers manuscrits latins des bibliothèques publiques de France*, 3 vols. (Paris 1940-41); *Supplément aux Livres d'"Heures manuscrits de la Bibliothèque Nationale: Acquisitions récentes et donation Smith-Lesouëf* (Paris 1943);

P.M. Gy, "Collectaire, Rituel, Processional," *Revue des sciences philosophiques et théologiques* 44 (1960) 441-469;

M. M. Bernard, *Répertoire de manuscrits médiévaux contenant de notation musicales*, 1: *Bibliothèque de Sainte-Geneviève*, 2: *Bibliothèque Mazarine* 3: *Bibliothèques parisiennes: Arsenal, Nationale, Universitaire, Ecole des Beaux-Arts et fonds privés* (Paris 1965-1974);

P. Ladner, *Iter Helveticum*, 3 vols., Spicilegii Friburgensis Subsidia 15, 16, 17 (Fribourg 1976-); it is a catalog of MSS in Swiss collections;

A. Olivar, *Els manuscrits litúrgics de la Biblioteca de Montserrat*, Scripta et Documenta 18 (Montserrat 1969). V. Saxer has a review of this in *Studia Monastica* 11 (1969) 442-448;

V. Saxer, "Manuscrits liturgiques, calendriers et litanies des saints du XII au XVI siècle, conservés à la Biblothèque Capitulaire de Tarazona," *Hispania Sacra* 23 (1970) 335-402; 24 (1971) 367-423; 25 (1972) 131-183; and "Les calendriers liturgiques de Saint-Victor et le sanctoral médiéval de l'abbaye," *Provence historique* 16 (Marseille 1966) 453-519;

G. Austin, "Liturgical Manuscripts in the United States and Canada," *Scriptorium* 28 (1974) 92-100;

F. Duine, *Bréviaires et missels des églises bretonnes de France antérieurs au XVII siècle* (Rennes 1905);

J. Koch, *Handschriftlichen Missalien in Steiermark* (Graz 1916);

J. B. Ferreres, *Historia del Missal Romano* (Barcelona 1929);

J. Baudot, *Le Missel plénier*, 2 vols. (Paris 1912).

10. Regarding the difficulties which arise in the composition of an up-to-date liturgical manual, see B. Botte, "A propos des manuels de liturgie," *Questions liturgiques et paroissiales* 33 (1952) 117-124; A. Bugnini, "Manuali italiani di liturgia," EL 59 (1945) 334-344. A fine listing of manuals, treatises, and periodicals which relate to liturgical matters can be found in H.A.P. Schmidt, *Introductio in liturgiam occidentalem* (Rome 1960) 742-785.

11. A detailed listing of lexicons, periodicals, collections, collected essays, Festschriften, Mélanges, and *Acta* of congresses can be found in H.A.P. Schmidt, *Introductio in liturgiam occidentalem* (Rome 1960) 747-785; see also the highly useful R.W. Pfaff, *Medieval Latin Liturgy: A Select Bibliography* (Toronto 1982) 4-9.

12. A more detailed list of periodicals is found in Schmidt, *Introductio*, 749-752. See also, for a more general listing, the detailed descriptions of collections in the *Repertorium Fontium Historiae Medii Aevii, I: Series Collectionum* (Rome 1962), *Additamenta 1962-1972* (Rome 1972).

13. It is obviously impossible to provide a bibliography of juridical and canonical bibliographies here. The following works can be consulted: A. van Hove, *Prolegomena* (2nd ed. Malines-Rome 1945)=the first volume of

Commentarium Lovaniense in Codice Juris Canonici; A.M. Stickler, *Historia iuris canonici latini*, I: *Historia fontium* (Turin 1950).

14. Concerning the juridico-liturgical collections (Church Orders), see below and Table A. A good introduction to the works of the Fathers and ecclesiastical writings (critical editions, contents, and studies) in the fundamental work of B. Altaner, *Patrologie* (5th ed., Freiburg/Br. 1958), ET *Patrology*, tr. H.C. Graef (New York 1964). For Latin authors before Bede (†735), see E. Dekkers, *Clavis Patrum Latinorum* (Steeenbrugge 1961) 423-467. Collections of liturgical texts drawn from the Fathers and from ecclesiastical writers are in F.Cabrol–H.Leclercq, *Reliquiae liturgicae vetustissimae ex Ss. Patrum necnon ecclesiasticorum monumentis selectae*, Monumenta Ecclesiae Liturgica I, 2 vols. (Paris 1900-02 and 1913); B. Geyer–J. Zellinger, *Florilegium patristicum tam veteris quam medii aevi auctores complectens* (Bonn 1914-1938), 43 vols. and 1 supplement; R. Stapper-A. Rücker, *Opuscula et textus . . . Series liturgica*, 9 fascs. (Münster 1933-1940); see especially, J. Quasten, *Monumenta eucharistica et liturgica vetustissima*, Florilegium Patristicum VII, 7 fasc. (Bonn 1935-37), well-edited texts accompanied by commentary; and *Patrology*, 3 vols. (Utrecht-Antwerp 1950-1960); A. Hänggi–I. Pahl, *Prex Eucharistica*, Spicilegium Friburgense 12 (Fribourg 1968).

15. On the *De sacramentis* of Ambrose, see K. Gamber, *Die Autorschaft von "De Sacramentis": Zugleich ein Beitrag zur Liturgiegeschichte der Provinz Dacia mediterranea*, Studia Patristica et Liturgica 1(Regensburg 1967); A. Paredi, "La liturgia del 'De sacramentis'," *Miscellanea Carlo Figini* (Milan 1964) 59-72, J. Schmitz, *Gottesdienst im altchristlichen Mailand*, Theophaneia 25 (Bonn 1975).

16. For bibliographies and biographical notices concerning liturgists, see H. Hurter, *Nomenclator literarius theologiae catholicae*, 4 vols (Innsbruck 1903-1913) where liturgists appear under different headings: "Theologia practica" or "Historia ecclesiastica et disciplinae annexae". The best systematic lists are those established by V. Thalhofer–L. Eizenhofer, *Handbuch der katholischen Liturgik* (2nd ed., 2 vols. Freiburg/Br. 1912) 63-102 = *Quellen*; 103-194= *Geschichte*. In the later editions of the *Handbuch*, (1932, 1951) the lists are given on pp. 57-118 and 118-148. A synoptic view of the chronology of liturgists is given in J. Creusen *et al.*, *Tabulae Fontium Traditionis Christianae* (2nd ed., Louvain 1925). A good general study of the work of medieval liturgists can be found along with a bibliography in A. Franz, *Die Messe im deutschen Mittelalter* (Freiburg/Br. 1902; repr. Darmstadt 1963); and *Die kirchlichen Benediktionem im Mittellalter*, 2 vols. (Freiburg/Br. 1909; repr. Graz 1960); J. Sauer, *Symbolik des Kirchengebäudes und seiner Ausstattung in der Auffassung des Mittelalters*, (Freiburg/Br. 1902). For Medieval liturgy one should always consult C. Du Cange, *Glossarium ad scriptores mediae et infimae latinitatis* 3 vol. (Paris 1673; re-edited with additions by Carpentier, Henschel. and Favre, 10 vols., Niort 1883-1888; reprint Paris 1938). For medieval liturgists see also the appropriate articles in the DACL and the excellent notices in the *Lexikon für Theologie und Kirche* edited by M. Buchberger, J.

Höfer, and K. Rahner, 10 vols. (1957-65) index and 3 supplemental vols. (1966-1968); and the *Realencyklopädie für protestantische Theologie und Kirche* by A. Hauck (3rd ed., Leipzig 1896-1913).

17. On this question see F. Wiegand, "Erzbischof Odilbert von Mailand über die Taufe: Ein Beitrag zur Geschichte der Taufliturgie im Zeitalter Karls des Grossen," *Studien zur Geschichte der Theologie und der Kirche* 4/1 (Leipzig 1899, reprint Aalen 1972); A. Werminghoff, "Die Beschlüsse des Aachener Concils in Jahre 816," *Neues Archiv für ältere deutsche Geschichtskunde* 27 (1902) 605-675; J. M. Heer, *Ein karolingischer Missions-Katechismus* (Freiburg/ Br. 1911); A. Wilmart, *Un florilège carolingien sur le symbolisme des cérémonies du baptême*, SeT 59 (Vatican City 1933) 153-179; S. Keefe, "Carolingian Baptismal Expositions: A Handlist of tracts and Manuscripts," in U.R. Blumenthal (ed.), *Carolingian Essays* (Washington, D.C. 1983) 169-237; see also A. Stenzel, *Die Taufe: Eine genetische Erklärung der Taufliturgie*, Forschungen zur Geschichte der Theologie und des innerkirchlichens Lebens 7-8 (Innsbruck 1958).

18. On the *expositiones missae* see A. Wilmart, DACL 5, 1014-1127. For the didactic collections of *ordines*, see M. Andrieu, *Les ordines romani*, 1, Spic. sac. Lov. 11 (Louvain 1931) 476-485.

19. See the bibliography of the liturgical works of Alcuin in DACL 1, 1072-1098 and in G. Ellard, *Master Alcuin, Liturgist* (Chicago 1956). These works need to be balanced by the more recent studies on the Carolingian liturgists such as J. Deshusses, "Le Supplément au sacramentaire grégorien: Alcuin ou S. Benoît d'Aniane?" AfL 9 (1965) 48-71.

20. The *Additio de missa* is not by Rabanus Maurus; cf. A. Franz, *Die Messe*, 399.

21. The *Expositio missae* which is attributed to Peter Damian is actually a poor extract of Innocent III's *De missarum mysteriis* IV, 2.

22. A critical edition of the *Micrologus* of Bernhold was being prepared by V.L. Kennedy (†1974); the materials are at the Pontifical Institute of Medieval Studies at the Universtiy of Toronto. Cf. "For a New Edition of the Micrologus of Bernhold of Constance," *Mélanges en l'honneur de Mgr. M. Andrieu* (Strasbourg 1956) 229-241.

23. See also H. Leclercq and A. Gatard, "Chant romain et chant Grégorien du IX au XIX siècle," DACL 3, 256-336; O. Söhngen–O. Brodde–W. Blankenburg *et al.*, *Leiturgia* 4 (1960) 1-266, 343-928. A large collection of the most important MSS has been published in *Paléographique Musicale* by the Monks of Solesmes (Tournai-Paris 1889–); H. Hucke, "Towards a New Historical View of Gregorian Chant," *Journal of the American Musicological Society* 33 (1980) 437-467; P.F. Cutter, *Musical Sources of the Old-Roman Mass*, Musicological Studies and Documents 36 (Neuhausen-Stuttgart 1979).

24. The attribution of *De sacrificio missae* to Alger is not absolutely certain. Cf. A. Franz, *Die Messe*, 428; L. Brigné, *Alger de Liège* (Paris 1936— unpublished thesis).

25. An *Expositio missae* which was attributed to Hildebert of Tours is inauthentic; cf. Franz, *Die Messe*, 434.

26. The following writings attributed to Hugh of St. Victor are inauthentic:

Speculum de mysteriis Ecclesiae, PL 177, 335; *De Caeremoniis, sacramentis et officiis ecclesiasticis*, PL 177, 381, possibly written by Robert Paululus, who is not be be confused with Robert Pullus (†ca. 1184); *De canone mystici libaminis* PL 177, 455. The actual author is not John of Cornwallis but Richard of Wedinghausen (Cologne; late XII century).

27. The liturgies produced in the XVI century in the Churches of the Reformation do not fall under our consideration here. For an introduction and bibliography, see Rietschel–Graff, *Lehrbuch der Liturgik*, 2 vols. (Göttingen 1951) and K.F. Müller–W. Blankenburg, ed., *Leiturgia: Handbuch des evangelischen Gottesdienstes*, 5 vols. (Kassel 1954-1970); L. Fendt, *Die lutherische Gottesdienste des 16 Jhs.*. (Munich 1923); collections of documents in E. Sehling, *Die evangelischen Kirchenordnungen des 16 Jhs.* vols 1-5 (Leipzig 1902-13), vols. 6-15 (Tübingen 1955-77). For the other churches of the Reformation, see the bibliography in R. Paquier, *Traité de Liturgique* (Neuchatel–Paris 1954) 217-218; For the Eucharistic liturgies of the Reformation see I. Pahl, *Coena Domini 1: Die Abendmahlsliturgie der Reformations-kirchen im 16 und 17 Jhd.*, Spicilegium Friburgense 29 (Fribourg 1983) and *Coena Domini 2: Die Abendmahlsliturgie der Reformations-kirchen vom 18 bis zum frühen 20 Jhdt.* Spicilegium Friburgense (vol. yet to appear); in English, B. Thompson, ed., *Liturgies of the Western Church* (Cleveland–New York 1961; and later printings).

28. For the works of modern liturgists, see N.K. Rasmussen, "Some Bibliographies of Liturgists," AfL 11 (1969) 214-218 with supplements 15 (1973) 168-171; 19 (1978) 134-139; 25 (1983) 34-42; this last article contains a cumulative index.

II. THE PERIOD OF CREATIVE BEGINNINGS, ORAL AND WRITTEN: FROM THE BEGINNING TO POPE GREGORY THE GREAT (590–604).
THE DOCUMENTS THAT PRECEDE THE SACRAMENTARIES PROPER

The ancient Christian era was one in which churches freely created their own liturgical *formulae*. Naturally, nothing survives of the earliest attempts at such oral improvisation. With the beginning of the III century, however, we start to have written evidence of how a church actually prayed and soon we have the famous *libelli missarum*, written evidence of how celebrants formulated their key prayers. There even survives an extraordinary collection of such Roman formularies under the misleading title of the Leonine Sacramentary.

Even at the time of Gregory the Great (590-604), there was no *liber sacramentorum* except for local use. The first such extant text, orgnanized along the lines of the liturgical year, is the Old Gelasian Sacramentary (*Vaticanus Reginensis* 316) copied at Chelles, near Paris, ca. 750, when Gisela, the sister of Charlemagne, was abbess. Its Roman prototype had appeared in the course of the VII century.

A. THE FIRST FOUR CENTURIES.

During the first four centuries, both in the Eastern and Western churches, even though the basic shape of the liturgy tended to become fixed, there were no definitive, uniform *formulae* obligatory for each *actio liturgica* in either individual or regional churches.

The texts preserved in the *Apostolic Tradition* of Hippolytus of Rome (ca. 215) are *an* example of how prayers were formulated, but they are not *the* formularies of the Roman church at that time. Each bishop was free to make up his own prayers as best he could. Less able or less eloquent bishops could borrow texts from their more facile neighbors, but no one was obliged to do so; such moves were left entirely to personal initiative.[29]

The use of extemporaneous prayer did not exclude the redaction of prayers according to set themes or fixed outlines. Such creations could then serve as models, sketches or guides for less gifted celebrants.[30]

Those who improvised liturgical prayers worked with the following essential sources:

a) the Bible, the first and most basic of all liturgical books.[31] One must remember that the Muratorian Canon of the late II century was established to serve the needs of public worship just as the much later VI-century *Decretum Gelasianum de libris recipiendis et non recipiendis*[32] was drawn up for liturgical purposes;

b) the *Symbolum fidei* which originally served as the profession of faith at baptism, e.g., the so-called Apostles' Creed, the baptismal creed of the old Roman Church;[33]

c) various liturgical doxologies and acclamations.[34] A large number of important fragments of early *formulae* can already be discerned in the New Testament, the Acts of the Martyrs,[35] early Gnostic writings, Christian inscriptions,[36] the writings of the Fathers[37] and in some pseudo-apostolic literature relating to law and ritual: The *Didache* (Antioch, ca. 50-70), the *Apostolic Tradition* of Hippolytus (ca. 215), the Syrian *Didascalia Apostolorum* (ca. 230), the *Apostolic Constitutions* in eight books (ca. 380), the *Constitutiones per Hippolytum* or the *Epitome* of Book VIII of the *Apostolic Constitutions* (V century), the *Canons of Hippolytus* (ca. 500), the *Testamentum Domini* (ca. 450).[38] Anaphora fragments survive in the *Prayerbook of Bishop Serapion of Thmuis* (†ca. 360)[39] and in certain Egyptian papyri.[40]

Of all these crucial documents, only the *Apostolic Tradition* of Hippolytus concerns us and our investigation of the development of the Western liturgy.

The *Apostolic Tradition*—earlier on called the *Egyptian Church Order*—is an authentic work of Bishop Hippolytus of Rome (217-235), the theological adversary of Callistus I (217-222) and other contemporary Roman pontiffs. Composed in Greek for a Roman community, the *Apostolic Tradition* comes down to us only in Coptic, Arabic, Ethiopic and Latin versions.[41] Nevertheless, it holds an absolutely central position among the various Church Orders (III-V centuries).

Although it is an invaluable documentary witness to the liturgy of a Roman Church at the beginning of the III century, the *Apostolic Tradition* is not *the* typical and official liturgy of *the* Roman Church; rather, it is one example—in Greek—of the way some Roman Christians worshipped, even though it claims for itself normative and even 'apostolic' authority.

The following is its ground plan (ed. Botte, 1963):

Part I: The Clergy.

    1. Prologue
  2-4. Episcopal ordination and a eucharistic prayer.
  5-6. Offerings of oil, cheese and olives.
  7-8. Ordination of presbyters and deacons.
 9-13. Appointment of confessors, widows, readers, virgins and sub-deacons.
   14. Gifts of healing.

Part II: The Laity.

   15. Admission to the catechumenate.
   16. Forbidden crafts and professions.
17-19. The organized stages of the catechumenate.
   20. Immediate preparation for baptism.
   21. The sacraments of initiation (Baptism, Consignation, Communion).

Part III. Various Church Observances.

   22. Sunday Communion.
   23. Fasting.
   24. Gifts to the sick.
25-29. The *Agape* (distinct from the Eucharist).
       The *Lucernarium* (communal supper).
   30. The meal for widows.
   31. Offerings due the bishop.
   32. The blessing of fruits and flowers.
   33. The paschal fast.
   34. The role of the deacons.
   35. Proper times for prayer.
36-38. Home care and use of the Eucharist.
   39. Daily assemblies of presbyters and deacons.
   40. Administration of the cemeteries.

41. Times of prayer.
42. The sign of the cross.
43. Conclusion.

B. LITURGICAL RENEWAL AT THE END OF THE IV CENTURY.

Judging from the liturgical flotsam and jetsam of the period before 375, very little creative activity took place up to that date. In the late IV century, however, a substantial liturgical literature appeared and is linked to that still unsolved phenomenon, the diversification of rites in the Church (Western and Eastern families of liturgy) and to the remarkable fact that in the West (unlike the East) each Mass of the temporal and sanctoral cycles came to be fitted out with a proper set of texts—aside from the anaphora (canon missae) which in some churches remained unchanged.[42]

A number of hypotheses have been advanced to explain the differentiation of rites but none of them are completely satisfactory. One that must surely be abandoned is the hypothesis that attributes the cause to the progressive formation of the liturgical year.[43] Such a development took place in both East and West at approximately the same time without affecting the Eastern liturgies as it did those of the West.[44]

One thing is sure: the beginnings of this creative renewal are not to be discovered at Rome. The Roman Church, a latecomer to the Latin tongue (ca. 380), was more cosmopolitan than Western, more Oriental than Roman. Rather, it was in Roman North Africa, the cradle of Latin Christianity, that the first creative stirrings were to be felt.[45]

1. Roman Africa.

Because large numbers of new texts loaded with barbaric expressions, solecisms and doctrinal errors were appearing, composed by homines imperiti et loquaces,[46]various African synods tried to control and direct such creative activity without, however, suppressing it. The Synod of Hippo (393), canon 25, stipulated that, at the altar, all prayers must be addressed to the Father and that one must avoid using prayers compiled in other localities until they have been examined by some of the fratres instructiores.[47] The Synod of Carthage (397) took the same line when faced with prayers suspected of containing false doctrine.[48] Henceforth, liturgical prayers would require official approval of some sort, and in 407 another Synod of Carthage insisted that a collection (*collectae*) of *preces, praefationes, commendationes and impositiones manuum*, composed under the supervision of the hierarchy, should become obligatory.[49] It seems clear that at the end of the IV and the beginning of the V century, there were already African collections of *libelli missarum*.[50] If the information passed on to us only by Gennadius of Marseilles (†492/505) can be taken at face value (*composuit etiam sacramentorum egregium volumen*), the African Church even had a sacramentary composed by Voconius (†460), bishop of Castellum in Mauretania.[51]

Unfortunately, nothing survives of an African sacramentary or other collection of prayers, not even a single fragment of a eucharistic prayer.[52]

2. Gaul.

Because of the vicissitudes of history, the African Church was not able to leave us much, but down to the year 1000, at least, the Frankish Churches took up the slack, not only because of the preponderant role they played in elaborating the Roman rite, but also because of the exceptional wealth of their own liturgical productivity.[53]

Musaeus, a presbyter of Marseilles (†ca. 460), drew up a lectionary (*lectiones totius anni*), a responsorial (*responsoria psalmorum capitula*), a sacramentary (*sacramentorum egregium et non parvum volumen*) and probably a book of homilies (*homilias dicitur declamasse*).[54]

Around 450, St. Mamertus, the archbishop of Vienne, also composed a lectionary.[55]

Sidonius Apollinaris (†ca. 480), bishop of Clermont, composed some *contestatiunculae* (prayers or prefaces for the Mass)[56] and even, according to Gregory of Tours, an entire collection of such *formulae* for the Eucharist.[57]

One can no longer, however, attribute a sacramentary to Hilary of Poitiers (†366) on the supposed authority of Jerome (†420)[58] or Berno of Reichenau (†1048).[59]

Unfortunately, none of the above liturgical productions have survived.

3. Spain.

The liturgical renewal in Spain seems to have been influenced by North Africa.[60] Priscillian (†386) or Bishop Instantius was the author of a *benedictio super fideles*[61] and Peter of Lerida (V-VI century) composed *orationes et missae*.[62]

Most of the prayers in the *Liber mozarabicus sacramentorum* and the *Liber ordinum* seem to derive from the first half of the V century.[63]

VI and VII-century Spain was an age of liturgical revision rather than one of original composition: Leander of Seville (†599), John of Saragossa (†613) and Conant of Palencia (†639) all had a hand in revising the *Libellus orationum* and the *Antiphonary*.[64] Braulio of Saragossa (†651), Quiricus of Barcelona (VII century) and Salvius of Albelda contributed in various ways to the elaboration of Spanish worship.[65] On the other hand, Isidore of Seville (†636), despite his literary productivity, left no liturgical compositions.[66]

It was only after the demise of Isidore that the great task of revising and enlarging the old liturgy of Spain began;[67] it was the work of three great bishops of Toledo: Eugene II (†657) who revised the chant and amended the *Ordines*,[68] Ildefonse (†667) who composed masses,[69] and Julian (†690) who corrected the Sacramentary or *Libellus orationum* and published certain musical items.[70] It is difficult to discern the exact part each bishop played in the *Liber ordinum* as it has come down to us.[71] Perhaps the only surviving Spanish sacramentary, the *Liber mozarabicus sacramentorum* (Toledo, Biblio. capit., *codex* 35.3; late X century) is a distant copy of the work of Julian of Toledo.[72] The more precise attributions attempted by Elipandus, primate of Toledo (†after 800), must be accepted with great caution.[73]

4. *Italy* (outside Rome).

Paulinus of Nola (†431) composed a sacramentary and a hymn book, neither of which survives.[74] Before the VI century, Ravenna had a respectable collection of liturgical books but only its famous *Rotulus* has survived.[75] Bishop Maximian (546-553) has a *missalis per totius circulum anni* (i.e., a sacramentary) attributed to him but it was merely a recasting of an earlier prototype and neither has survived.[76] It would be wrong—and simply disastrous for the history of our sources—to identify this book with the 'Leonine Sacramentary' or with the Old Gelasian Sacramentary; that would make the liturgy of Ravenna the ultimate source of all the Roman sacramentaries.[77]

A rather late but fairly well-informed source, the *Liber notitiae sanctorum Mediolani* (1304-1311), attributes liturgical compositions for the Church of Milan to Bishops Simplicianus (†401) and Eusebius (449-462)[78] and perhaps some of them survive among the Ambrosian prefaces.[79] Ambrose himself composed only hymns and antiphons.[80] Aside from these, no Milanese compositions before the VIII century have been preserved[81]. Towards the end of the IV century, pieces like a *Laus cerei* are pointed out at Piacenza[82] but the only surviving *laus* of the paschal candle is that which St. Augustine probably composed for Milan[83] and the two *Laudes* of Ennodius of Pavia (✝531).[84]

In enumerating the donations of F. Valila to a country church near Tivoli, the *Charta Cornutiana* of 471 lists the following books: *Codices, Evangelia IV, Apostolorum, Psalterium* and *Comitem* (probably a sacramentary in this context).[85]

In the anonymous Arian fragments of the V century, we find two prefaces composed for some Danubian church.[86]

5. Rome.

After Hippolytus and his *Apostolic Tradition* (ca. 215), complete silence reigns at Rome in regard to liturgical activity until the notice on the work of Pope Gelasius I (492-496) in the section of the *Liber Pontificalis* drawn up under Pope Hormisdas (514-523). In this passage some Lateran cleric attributes to Gelasius the composition of *sacramentorum praefationes et orationes, cauto sermone*, a quotation that was to become the source of a grave misunderstanding.[87] That was an expression of opinion of someone in the papal entourage at the end of the VI century; it simply means that at the close of the early Christian era nobody at Rome could recall any papal liturgical activity before the end of the V century.

Ordo XIX, 36 provides us with a list of liturgical pieces from Damasus I to Martin I (649-655) but it is too late a testimony to be reliable.[88] *Ordo* XIX belongs to a collection that used to be attributed to John, Archcantor of St. Peter's, Rome (680), but which is actually a compilation made at St. Gall around 780-790.[89]

For historians of the sources, the results of our brief survey are purely negative; nothing survives of the Roman liturgy of the first five centuries. Undoubtedly there must have been considerable liturgical activity but we have no way of evaluating either its extent or its results.

C. LIBELLI MISSARUM.

The Sacramentary, a complex liturgical book that we have yet to define, did not appear at once in its developed form. It was preceded and prepared by the *libelli missarum* which were leaflets or small booklets containing the *formulae* of one or more masses (prayers, preface, introductory formula for the *Hanc igitur*); they did not include the fixed Canon of the mass (whose history poses special problems all its own)[90] or the readings and chants belonging to the other ministers.[91]

One must not confuse the *libellus missarum* with the *libellus officialis* (a small ritual),[92] the *libellus ordinis* (a ceremonial agenda)[93] or with the Mozarabic *libellus orationum* (collects for the Office).

There were two kinds of *libelli missarum*:

a) Before the appearance of sacramentaries, the *libellus missarum* consisted of a single page or booklet containing several presidential prayers composed for a particular festival celebrated in a given church. The *libelli* are the missing links between the period of freely composed prayers and their collection and arrangement into a *Liber sacramentorum* properly so called. Isolated examples of such *libelli* have not survived but an impressive collection of them is contained in a Verona MS, formerly, but misleadingly, called the Leonine Sacramentary.

b) Even after sacramentaries developed, there were still *libelli missarum* in use, i.e., additional booklets containing either popular votive masses or extracts, substitutes or abridgements of sacramentaries made for missionaries and other travelers.

Several of the latter survive:

1. The *Stowe Missal* (792-812) whose archetype dates back to the early VII century.[94]

2. The seven *Masses of Mone* (ca. 650) of purely Gallican composition, with no trace of Roman influence.[95]

Votive *libelli* are represented by the Glagolitic *Missal of Kiev* (IX century)[96] and the votive Masses of Alcuin.[97]

D. THE VERONA COLLECTION OF LIBELLI MISSARUM.

A most interesting series of *libelli missarum* survives in the Verona collection, a kind of pre-sacramentary incorrectly labeled the Leonine Sacramentary since the edition of F. Bianchini (1735).

This compilation of *libelli* exists only in a single MS of Verona's Biblioteca capitolare, *codex* 85 (*olim* 80) and was copied in the first quarter of the VII century (Delisle, Duchesne, Feltoe, Lowe). The *Veronensis* was not transcribed at Rome but probably at Verona itself; others have suggested Spain, Africa, Bobbio or Luxeuil.[98]

The *Veronensis* is a private collection of authentically Roman *libelli* preserved in the Lateran archives after they had been partially adapted from papal use for the presbyters of the Roman *tituli*.[99] Despite innumerable studies devoted to the *Veronensis*, it remains somewhat of a mystery and somehow alien to the traditions of Latin liturgical prayer.[100] It is reasonably certain, however, that it is not a liturgical book properly speaking, i.e., it was not assembled to serve actual celebrants at the altar. It appears too haphazardly put together and too incomplete for that, and it follows the unusual plan of distributing its formularies according to the months of the civil calendar rather than according to the pattern of the liturgical year. It also contains prayers that seem too aggressively personal to be suitable for public worship. One cannot even be sure that the compiler of these numerous *libelli* had a liturgical end in view; perhaps ascetical or even polemical purposes dictated his choice of materials.[101]

1. CHRONOLOGY OF THE VERONENSIS AS A COLLECTION.

In his edition of the Verona MS in 1735, Bianchini attributed this work to Pope Leo the Great and began the bad habit of calling this MS the Leonine Sacramentary, a title which is incorrect on two scores, for it is neither a sacramentary properly speaking nor the work of Leo I. Other XVIII-century liturgists viewed it as a collection put together in the time of Pope Gelasius I (492-496): Merati (†1744), Assemani (†1782), Gerbert (†1793).[102] Nevertheless, the traditional and highly misleading title continued to be used until the edition of Dom Mohlberg in 1956.[103]

It was only at the end of the last century that the *Veronensis* was subjected to rigorous scientific analysis. L. Duchesne (1889) located it between 537-538 and 590, i.e., between the raising of the Gothic siege of Rome by Witiges (March, 538) and the beginning of Gregory I's pontificate (590).[104] Probst (1892) situated it in the pontificate of Felix III (483-492);[105] Feltoe (1896) placed it after 500;[106] Rule (1908-1909) believed he could discern three successive recensions: the first under Leo I (440-461), the second under Hilary I (461-468), and the third under Simplicius (468-483);[107] Buchwald (1908) proposed the time of Gregory of Tours (538/39-594);[108] and Klauser put forth 550 as the date of composition.[109]

Three hypotheses currently preoccupy liturgical historians:

a) The Common Hypothesis (Bourque).

The *Veronensis* is not a true sacramentary intended for public worship but a private collection of Roman formularies. It was assembled as a collection between 558/560 (the date of its most recent section, the September *libellus*) and 590 (before the supposed reforms of Gregory the Great).

The September *libellus*—which is certainly papal—contains a formulary (XXIX, IV; no. 983-988, ed. Mohlberg) in which there is an allusion to an episcopal anniversary (no. 987) held in close proximity to Holy Week or, more precisely, Holy Thursday (no. 986).[110] Between the years 200 and 700, there were only three possible anniversaries that coincided with Holy Week: March 29, 538 and 549, the anniversary of Pope Vigilius, and April 16, the anniversary of Pelagius I in 558.[111] The 549 date is ruled out because Vigilius was then in Constantinople; the year 538 has to be set aside because the formulary XXIV, IV contains no allusion to the siege of Witiges, an inconceivable silence in view of its importance. The only date left is 558.

Formulary XXIX, VII (Mohlberg, nos. 1003-1007) of the same September *libellus* directs us to an episcopal anniversary celebrated in paschaltide.[112] Such a coincidence can only be verified during the papacy of Pelagius I (556-561) who was made a bishop on Easter Day (April 16) and whose anniversary fell during Eastertide in 560 (Easter, March 28), 557 (Easter, April 1), 558 (Easter, April 21) and 559 (Easter, April 13). Because of the double coincidence of 558, it seems to have every chance of being the year in which this formulary was composed.

If the year 558 is the best *terminus ante quem non* of this collection, the *terminus post quem non* is 590, the opening year of the pontificate of Gregory I. No trace whatsoever of Gregorian influence can be found in the Verona MS.

The numerous *Hanc igitur oblationem* formulas of the *Veronensis* always appear without the Gregorian addition: *diesque nostros in tua pace disponas atque ab aeterna damnatione nos eripi et in electorum tuorum iubeas grege numerari.*[113] The presence of 'Gregorian' saints in the *Veronensis* does not stand in opposition to what has just been said; their presence simply shows that some of the masses of the *Veronensis* issue from about the same period as those of the 'Gregorian' Sacramentary.

If the *Veronensis* was compiled between 558/560 and 590, only a few years intervened between the original and our surviving copy, which can be located paleographically between 600 and 625. It may even be that the so-called copy is actually the original. Whatever may be eventually determined on that score, the *Veronensis* is and always has been an *unicum* among liturgical documents. No other copy or even partial copy exists and none of the catalogues of ancient libraries mention a *codex* that can be compared with it.

Two sets of facts seem, however, to stand in the way of this conclusion:

a) The existence, both in Italy and North of the Alps, of numerous parallels to the Verona formularies, e.g., the anonymous Arian fragments in the palimpsest of Mai-Mercati (IV, V, or beginning of the VI century),[114] the Ravenna *Rotulus* (V-VI century, Ceriani; mid-V, Cabrol; VI-IX Duchesne; mid-VI, Cagin; VI, Pinell),[115] the Stuttgart fragment (VII-VIII century),[116] some items in the Phillipps Sacramentary (Berlin, codex 1667; IX century)[117] and the Milanese fragment (VI-VII century).[118]

b) The presence of formularies proper to the *Ver.*in the Gallican sacramentaries (*Missale gothicum, Missale Francorum, the Bobbio Missal*),formularies that are not to be found in either the Old Gelasian or in the type of Gregorian Sacramentary represented by the *Paduensis.*[119]

To explain the presence of such *Ver.* pieces, we do not have to suppose some primitive Roman nucleus from which these formularies were borrowed before the final establishment of the *Ver.* text.[120] Beside the fact that such a primitive nucleus is practically indiscernible in a compilation like this, whose internal arrangement is by mere juxtaposition of a number of *libelli* without internal logic, it can be shown that the so-called 'borrowings' are from the most recent sections of the *Ver.*

It might appear, then, that there were copies of the *Ver.* and that such copies were circulating in Gaul some time before 700 (the approximate date of the Gallican sacramentaries). Such, however, was not the case. The borrowings never extend to a whole series of texts characteristic of the *Ver.* but are, in every instance, single formularies. Moreover, a critical examination of these texts shows that the Gallican books do not derive directly from the *Ver.* but come through some other intermediary.[121] Perhaps such an intermediary was a pre-Gelasian or pre-Gregorian Sacramentary circulating in Gaul since the VII century (Chavasse) or perhaps certain *libelli missarum* which passed North of the Alps as individual fascicles and were used in complete independence of the Verona compilation.[122]

b) The Stuiber Hypothesis.

In view of the obvious fact that some sections of the *Ver.* have several formularies which are substantially identical, Stuiber concludes that there must have been a common source for all of them. That would have been a collection of Lateran formularies or sketches of formularies used by the popes and transformed by them as they re-used them from time to time. The presbyters of Rome and its environs, too, may well have utilized the same archives in order to equip themselves for their eucharistic celebrations.

As such papal formularies were re-used again and again, they were adapted to specific liturgical occasions by different officiants and not simply repeated as they were found. This was still an era when extempore prayer would not have been unusual. Nevertheless, the same prayer *formulae* were simply bound to reappear in similar worship contexts.

Working outside the *Urbs*, the compiler of the *Ver.* must have procured his *libelli* from the various Roman churches but without necessarily acquiring either the best or the oldest. In such a case, the *Ver.* must have been put together in three stages:

1. more or less complete sketches or outlines borrowed from the papal archives;

2. *libelli* filled out by Roman presbyters along earlier lines;

3. the compiling of these *libelli* into one book by someone living outside the City: the *Veronensis*.

The compilation was done in the time of Gregory the Great (590-604) but was not influenced by any of his liturgical reforms. Working on his own, the compiler felt no need to 'publish' his texts.[123]

c) The Chavasse Hypothesis.

Some seventy masses in all belong to the time of Pope Vigilius (537-555); most belong to the turbulent year 537-538 when Witiges, the Ostrogothic king, was besieging Rome, and appear in the month of September; others show up in July and October (413-670 *Orationes et praeces diurnae*; 1111-1137 *De siccitate temporis*; 955-1102 *In natale episcoporum*). Here and there Vigilius apparently re-used earlier compositions, particularly those of Pope Gelasius I (492-496).

The compiler of *Ver.* must have employed two earlier collections, both deriving from the reign of Vigilius. The disorder of the *Ver.* comes from the fact that he wanted to maintain the arrangements he found in his two basic sources and not from mere carelessness on his part. He must have accomplished his work in the years 545-555, the final years of Vigilius' pontificate.[124]

As we examine the mass of *formulae* gathered together by Vigilius and others on the occasion of the bitter siege of Rome by Witiges, it becomes possible to discern, by means of literary and historical analysis, a certain number of sets deriving from Pope Gelasius: nos. 75-78, 181-182, 413-442, 445-460, 515-520,, 527-532, 550-552, 620-625, 1015-1020, 1039-1044, 1051-1056, 1074-1085, 1091-1096. In spite of recent studies of the vocabulary and style of Leo the Great in his authentic homilies, we cannot attribute mass *formulae* to that pope with any certainty.[125]

The studies we have just summarized seem to agree on several key points:

a) The *Ver.* is not an official sacramentary but a private collection of *libelli missarum* deriving, in the first instance, from the Lateran archives; some of them were rearranged and adapted for use in the Roman *tituli*.

b) Most of the *libelli* were composed in the V-VI centuries.

c) The apparent disorder of the *Ver.* stems not so much from the carelessness or inexperience of the compiler as from his pre-occupation with keeping intact the various groupings of masses as he found them.

d) The compiler worked outside Rome.

e) The *libelli* of the *Ver.* take us back to the earliest prayer forms of the Roman liturgy: *preces* (consecratory formulae), *oratio fidelium* (intercessory prayer) and *orationes* (brief prayers after the chants, the readings and at the conclusion of morning and evening prayer).

f) The *Ver.* was assembled at a period when the desire to collect all the documents of the popes was manifesting itself in the Latin Church. The first half of the VI century saw the appearance of the *Gesta pontificum*, the *Liber pontificalis*, the *Decreta pontificum* of the *Dionysiana*, the *Liber diurnus* and, finally, the forms of prayer used by the popes in the *Veronensis*.[126]

2. CHRONOLOGY OF THE FORMULAE THEMSELVES.

Whatever the date of the *Veronensis* as a collection, each of the *formulae* it contains has, in turn, its own proper date and a certain number of them can, in fact, be dated.

Some eighty-five attempts have been made at dating various sections of the *Ver.* but we cannot summarize them all here.[127] No set seems earlier than 400 A.D. (possibly sections IX, XXI, XXXV, XXXVII, 1 and XLII are of this period: Bourque). Most sets are after 440 and continue to appear until 560; more than half of them are later than 500.[128]

3. CONTENTS OF THE VERONENSIS.

The *libelli missarum* are all arranged according to the months of the civil calendar, some months having far more sets than others. The MS has lost its opening section (24 leaves or 48 pages missing, i.e., January 1-April 14) and begins in the middle of April with group VIII, set VI.[129]

APRIL

Group VIII. *Item alia:* 43 sets (nos. 1-168).
Masses of martyrs and confessors with no names indicated except for the following: a) 5 paschal sets (nos. 36-41 and 88-97) one with the rubric *E.F.S.P.–[Pascalis] est facta supra*; b) the martyr Tiburtius (no. 2), Lawrence (no. 72) and Gregory the Martyr (no. 126); c) a mass against relapsing into paganism (no. 75-78); d) *Item alia in dedicatione:* dedication of a church to St. Peter (no. 130-137).

MAY

Group IX. *Praeces in Ascensa Domini:* 6 sets of prayers (169-186).
Group X. *Orationes pridie Pentecosten:* 1 set (187-190) and *Item alia* (191-199). *In Pentecosten ascendentibus a fonte:* 3 sets (200-214). Interpolations: *In ieiunio quarti mensis* and *Praesumptio et reparatio primi hominis.*
Group XI. *In dominicum Pentecosten:* 3 sets (215-225). Interpolations: *Contra inimicos catholicae professionis, Contra inpetitores* and the indication PRAECE. *S.F.=praeces supra factae.*
Group XII. *In ieunio mensis quarti* (226-231).

JUNE

Group XIII. *VIII Kalendas Iulias. Natale Sancti Iohannis Baptistae:* 5 sets, the 4th entitled *Ad fontem* (232-256).
Group XIV. *In Natale sanctorum Iohannis et Pauli:* 8 sets (257-279).
Group XV and XVI. *In Natale Apostolorum Petri et Pauli:* 28 sets (280-379): one of these is a mass of all the apostles (351-356) and one, *Item ad S. Paulum* (372-374), actually concerns both Peter and Paul. Interpolated in this group is a *Hanc igitur* of a *Coniunctio oblationis virginum sacratarum* (283), three mentions of *Post infirmitatem* (308, 314, 334) and *In ieiunio* (353) and the indications *F.E. = facta est, F.E. SP. = facta est supra, P.SP.F.E. = prex supra facta est, P.F.E.SP. = prex facta est supra.*

JULY

Group XVII. *VI Iduum Iuliarum. Natale sanctorum martyrum Felicis, Filippi in cymeterio Priscillae. Vitalis et Martialis et Alexandri in cymeterio Iordanorum et*

Silani in cymiterio Maximi via Salaria et Ianuarii in cymiterio Pretextati via Appia: 9 sets (380-412) without names in the prayers = the seven sons of St. Felicitas martyred in the reign of Antoninus Pius (ca. 150). One interpolation: *In ieiunio* (386).

Group XVIII. *Incipiunt orationes et praeces diurnae:* 45 sets (413-670). Interpolations: *7 orationes matutinas vel ad vesperum* (587-593) and a new title: *Incipiunt praeces diurnae cum sensibus necesariis* (between 603-604, without interrupting the numbering system), and the indications: *Item ad Vesperum* (between 590 and 591), *In ieiunio* (612) and several rubrics like those we have already mentioned.

AUGUST

Group XIX. *IIII Nonas Augustas. Natale Sancti Stefani in cymeterio Callisti via Appia:* 9 sets for Stephen the Protomartyr, the last being a mass of dedication for a basilica of St. Stephen (671-703).

Group XX. *VIII Idus Augustas. Natale Sancti Xysti in cymeterio Callisti et Felicissimi et Agapiti in cymeterio Pretextati via Appia:* 8 sets for Sixtus II and his subdeacons (704-732). *In natale Sanctorum Felicissimi et Agapiti:* 1 set (733-738).

Group XXI. *IV Idus Augustas. Natale Sancti Laurenti:* 14 sets for Lawrence, the deacon of Sixtus II (739-789), the first and twelfth set being for the vigil of the feast (739-742, 777-778) and the last set for the octave day: *Ad Octabas* (786-789).

Group XXII. *Idus Augustas. Natale Sanctorum Ypolyti et Pontiani:* 2 sets, one for St. Hippolytus (790-794) and one for St. Agapitus (*sic*) (795-799).

Group XXIII. *III Kalendas Septembres. Natale Sanctorum Adaucti et Felicis:* 6 sets (800-822) and one preface of the apostles (823).

SEPTEMBER

Group XXIV. *XVIII Kalendas Octobres. Natale Sanctorum Corneli et Cypriani:* 3 sets (824-834) with a preface of St. Euphemia inserted under the title *PCES. H. SCE. EUFYMIAE* = praeces hae or *habendae in natale sanctae Eufymiae* (826).

Group XXV. *XVI Kalendas Octobres. In natale Sancte Eufymiae:* 2 sets (835-843).

Group XXVI. *Pridie Kalendas Octobres. Natale Basilicae Angeli in [via]Salaria:* 5 sets for the dedication of the basilica of St. Michael the Archangel (844-859).

Group XXVII. *Admonitio Ieiunii Mensis Septimi et Orationes et Praeces:* 8 sets (860-904).—*Invitatio Plebis in Ieiunio mensis decimi* (905) followed by 6 mass sets (906-941), one with a definite paschal character.

Group XXVIII. *Consecratio episcoporum* (942-947). *Benedictio super diaconos* (948-951). *Consecratio presbyteri* (952-954).

Group XXVIIII. *In Natale Episcoporum:* 7 sets (955-1007). One mass of consecration (1008-1014) with a *Hanc igitur* entitled *Pro episcopis offerendum* followed by 15 masses without a title, of the same type as the *Orationes et Praeces Diurnae* of Group XVIII (1015-1102).

Group XXX. *Ad Virgines Sacras* (1103-1104).

Group XXXI. *Incipit Velatio Nuptialis* (1105-1110).

OCTOBER

Group XXXII. *De siccitate temporis* (1111-1137): Times of drought and other trials.

Group XXXIII. *Super Defunctos:* 5 sets (1138-1160) with the last two mentioning S. Lawrence (1151-1160).

Group XXXIIII. *Sancti Silvestri:* 2 prayers (1161-1162) and then one of Pope Simplicius (1163).

NOVEMBER

Group XXXV. *In Natale Sanctorum Quattuor Coronatorum:* 2 sets (1164-1170).

Group XXXVI. *In Natale Sancte Caeciliae:* 5 sets (1171-1187).

Group XXXVII. *VIIII Kalendas Decembres. Natale Sanctorum Clementis et Felicitatis:* 4 sets for St. Clement (1188-1198) and 3 sets for St. Felicity (1199-1213).

Group XXXVIII. *VIII Kalendas Decembres. Natale Sanctorum Chrysogoni et Gregori:* 1 set (1214-1218).

Group XXXIX. *Pridie Kalendas Decembres. Natale Sancti Andreae Apostoli:* 4 sets (1219-1238).

DECEMBER

Group XL. *VIII Kalendas Ianuarias. Natale Domini et Martyrum Pastoris, Basilei et Ioviani et Victorini et Eugeniae et Felicitatis et Anastasiae:* 9 sets, all for Christmas despite the title (1239-1272).

Group XLI. *In Natale Sancti Iohannis Evangelistae:* 2 sets (1273-1283).

Group XLII *In Natale Innocentum:* 2 sets (1284-1293).

Group XLIII *In Ieiunio Mensis Decimi:* 5 sets (1294-1327).

Then, finally, there are 3 prayers in 3 different hands (1328-1330) and *Incipit Benedictio Fontis* in another hand (1331).[130]

NOTES

29. Freedom to improvise liturgical prayers is clearly attested in the texts. The following are two key examples: 1) Hippolytus of Rome, *The Apostolic Tradition*, chap. 9, trans. G.J. Cuming (1976) 14: "The bishop shall give thanks according to what we said above. It is not all necessary for him to utter the

same words as we said above, as though reciting them from memory, when giving thanks to God; but let each pray according to his ability. If indeed anyone has the ability to pray at length and with a solemn prayer, it is good. But if anyone, when he prays, utters a brief prayer, do not prevent him. Only he must pray what is sound and orthodox." 2) Gregory of Tours, *The History of the Franks* 2, 21, tr. L. Thorpe (Baltimore, MD 1974) 134: "The saintly Sidonius [Apollinaris] was so eloquent that he would often speak extempore in public without hesitating in the slightest and express whatever he had to say with the greatest clarity. One day it happened that he went to the monastery church ... for he had been invited there for a festival. Some malicious person removed the book (*libellus missarum*) with which it was his habit to conduct the church service. Sidonius was so well versed in the ritual that he took them through the whole service of the festival without pausing a moment." See also A. Bouley, *From Freedom to Formula: The Evolution of the Eucharistic Prayer from Oral Improvisation to Written Texts*, Studies in Christian Antiquity 21 (Washington, D.C. 1981): R.G. Coquin, "Une réforme liturgique du concile de Nicée (325)?" *Compte-rendus de l'Académie des Inscriptions et Belles-Lettres* (1967) 178-192; R.P.C. Hanson, "The Liberty of the Bishop to Improvise Prayer in the Eucharist," *Vigiliae Christianae* 15 (1961) 173-176.

30. We must give up the idea that because of the *disciplina arcani* the texts of the liturgical *formulae* would have been wrapped in secrecy; cf. P. Batiffol, *Études d'histoire et de théologie positive* 1 (7th ed. 1926) 1-41. On the other hand, it seems that around 250, at the earliest, liturgical *formulae* had to conform to those of the mother church of the metropolitan see.

31. This was still the case for the Bible in the Constantinian period. Cf. Eusebius, *Vita Constantini*, Bk. 4, 34-37 (PG 20, 1182-1187), ET *The Life of the Blessed Emperor Constantine in 4 Books*, NPNF ser. 2, vol. 1, pp. 548-549.

32. Editions: H. Lietzmann, *Das Muratorische Fragment*, Kleine Texte 1 (Berlin 1933); E. von Dobschütz, *Das Decretum Gelasianum de libris recipiendis et non recipiendis*, TuU 38 (Leipzig 1912). A review in English of Dobschütz' work is D.J. Chapman, "On the *Decretum Gelasianum de libris recipiendis et non recipiendis*," RB 30 (1913) 187-208, 315-333.

33. See H.J. Carpenter, "*Symbolum* as a Title of the Creed," JTS 44 (1943) 1-11; J.H. Crehan, *Early Christian Baptism and the Creed* (Oxford 1950); J.N.D. Kelly, *Early Christian Creeds* (3rd ed. New York 1981); T. Camelot, "Les récentes recherches sur le Symbole des Apôtres et leur portée théologique," RSR 39 (1951) 323-337.

34. The *formulae* are listed in F. Cabrol-H. Leclercq, *Reliquiae liturgicae antiquissimae*, Monumenta Ecclesiae Liturgica 1/1-2 (Paris 1900-1913) and in E. Norden, *Agnostos Theos: Untersuchungen zur Formengeschichte religiöser Rede* (4th ed. Darmstadt 1956).

35. Consult the Acts of the Martyrs in R. Knopf-G. Krüger, *Ausgewählte Märtyrakten* (4th ed. Tubingen 1965) or H.A. Musurillo *The Acts of the Christian Martyrs* (Oxford 1972);—Listings are in the *Bibliotheca hagiographica latina* 2 vols. (1908-10, 1911) and the *Bibliotheca hagiographica graeca* 3 vols. (2nd ed. 1957), both are the work of the Bollandists at Brussels.

36. The liturgical texts in gnostic writings are collected in E. von der Goltz, *Das Gebet in der ältesten Christenheit* (Leipzig 1901).—The liturgical texts included in inscriptions can be found in G. Lefebvre, *Recueil des inscriptions grecques chrétiennes d'Egypte* (Cairo 1907), for Nubia; T. Schermann, *Aegyptische Sepulkralinschriften liturgischen Inhalts* (Paderborn 1912); J.P. Kirsch, *Die Acclamationen und Gebete der altchristlichen Grabinschriften* (Cologne 1897); E. Peterson, *Eis Theos* (Göttingen 1926).

37. These texts are conveniently gathered in F. Probst, *Die Liturgie der drei ersten Jahrunderten* (Münster/Westf. 1870); See also E. Dekkers, *Clavis Patrum Latinorum* (Steenbrugge 1961).

38. For a listing of the various Church Orders, see B. Altaner, *Patrology*, tr. H.C. Graef (New York 1961) 47-61; J. Quasten, *Patrology* (Utrecht-Antwerp 1966) on the *Apostolic Church Order* vol. 2, 119-120; *Apostolic Constitutions* vol. 2, 184; *Apostolic Tradition* vol. 2, 180-194; *Canons of Hippolytus* vol. 2, 186; *Didache* vol. 1, 29-39; *Didascalia Apostolorum* (Syriac, Arabic, Ethiopic) vol. 2, 147-152; *Epitome of the Apostolic Constitutions* vol. 2, 181, 184; *Testament of Our Lord* vol. 2, 185. See also B. Botte, "Les plus anciennes collections canoniques," *L'Orient Syrien* 5 (1960) 331-350; A. Faivre, "La documentation liturgico-canonique," RSR 54 (1980) 204-219, 273-297; see Table A.

39. *Euchologion* of Serapion of Thmuis (†after 362): P. Nock, ed., "Liturgical Notes: The Anaphora of Serapion," JTS 30 (1929-30) 381-390; J. Wordsworth, *Bishop Serapion's Prayerbook*, (2nd rev. ed. London 1923, reprint, Hamden, CT 1964); F.E. Brightman, "The Sacramentary of Serapion of Thmuis," JTS 1 (1900) 88-113, 247-277.

40. C. del Grande, *Liturgicae preces, hymni christianorum e papyris collecti* (Naples 1934).

41. In an introduction such as this, we cannot include all the arguments, *pro* and *con*, for the authorship of Hippolytus. Instead, we offer a basic bibliography of the controversy and its principal elements:

1. The starting point for all modern research regarding the Apostolic Tradition is E. Hauler, *Didiscaliae Apostolorum fragmenta Veronensia latina: Accedunt canonum qui dicuntur Apostolorum et Aegyptiorum reliquiae* (Leipzig 1900) 101-121, which is the *editio princeps* of the document in its Latin version. A new edition, E. Tidner, *Didascaliae Apostolorum, canonum ecclesiasticorum, Traditionis Apostolicae versiones latinae*, TuU 75 (Berlin 1963) 117-150.

2. Those who attribute the *Apostolic Tradition* to Hippolytus of Rome (the "Schwartz-Connolly-Botte thesis"=the majority opinion) include the following: E. Schwartz, "Über die pseudo-apostolischen Kirchenordnungen," *Schriften der wissenschaftliche Gesellschaft in Strassburg* 6(1910; re-edited in *Gesammelte Schriften* 5 (Berlin 1963));—R. H. Connolly, "The so-called Egyptian Church Order and Derived Documents," *Texts and Studies* 8 (Cambridge 1916) 135-149;—H. Elfers, *Die Kirchenordnung Hippolyts von Rom* (Paderborn 1938) and "Neue Untersuchungen über die Kirchenordnung Hippolyts von Rom," *Abhandlungen über Theologie und Kirche* =Festschrift K.

Adam (Düsseldorf 1952) 169-211;—B. Botte, *Hippolyte de Rome: La 'Tradition Apostolique' de S. Hippolyte: Essai de reconstitution*, LQF 39 (Münster/West. 1963; reprint SC 11 bis, Paris 1968) and "Le texte de la 'Tradition Apostolique'," *International Conference on Patristic Studies* (Oxford 1967).

3. Those who are against attributing *Ap. Trad.* to Hippolytus of Rome: P. Cagin, *L'Anaphore apostolique et ses témoins* (Paris 1919) expresses some reservations. The same can be said of A. von Harnack in his *Geschichte der altchristlichen Literatur 2: Die Chronologie* (Leipzig 1904) 484-514, reprint in *Zeitschrift für neutestamentliche Wissenschaft und die Kunde der älterer Kirche* 36 (1937) 238-250, and of T. Schermann, *Die allgemeine Kirchenordnung* 3 (Paderborn 1916) 44, 618. The most lively opposition to the Schwartz-Connolly-Botte thesis is raised by the following authors: R. Lorentz, *De egyptische Kerkordening en Hippolytus van Rome* (Haarlem 1929): P. Nautin, *Hippolyte et Josippe: Contribution à l'histoire de la littérature chrétienne du 3ᵉ siècle*, Etudes et Textes pour l'histoire du dogme de la Trinité 1 (Paris 1947), a review of which by M. Richard appears in *Mélanges de Science religieuse de Lille* 7 (1950) 237-268 and 8 (1951) 19-50; P. Nautin, "Notes sur le catalogue des oeuvres d'Hippolyte," *Recherches de science religieuse* 34 (1947) 99-107; H. Engberding, "Das angebliche Dokument römischer Liturgie aus dem Beginn des 3 Jhs. Neue Untersuchungen zu der Frage nach dem Verfasser der heute sog, 'Apostoliki Paradosis'," *Miscellanea liturgica . . . Mohlberg* 1 (Rome 1948) 47-71; A. Salles, "La 'Tradition Apostolique' est-elle un témoin de la liturgie romaine?" *Revue de l'histoire des religions* 148 (1955) 181-213; M. Richard, "Quelques fragments des Pères anténicéens et nicéens," *Symbolae Osloenses* 38 (1963) 76-83, which deals with chapter 36 in Botte's edition; M. Richard, "Hippolyte de Rome," *Dictionnaire de Spiritualité* 7/1 (1969) 543-547, regarding the treatise "On the Charisms"; the problems concerning the Apostolic Tradition are referred to in the article "Tradition Apostolique" yet to appear; J. Magne, "La prétendue Tradition Apostolique d'Hippolyte de Rome s'appelait-elle Les 'Statuts des saints Apôtres'?" *Ostkirchliche Studien* 14 (1965) 35-67, reviewed by B. Botte, *Bulletin de Théologie ancienne et médiévale* 9 (1965) no. 2089; J. Magne, *Tradition Apostolique sur les charismes et Diataxeis des Saints Apôtres: Identification des documents et analyse du rituel des ordinations*, Origines Chrétiennes 1 (Paris 1975) includes an exhaustive bibliography.

Among those who oppose the common thesis, J.M. Hanssens occupies a place apart. In the works cited below, which are essential for the liturgical analysis of the *Apostolic Tradition*, the author agrees with the authorship of Hippolytus, but rejects the *Roman origin* of the document, in which he sees an example of the Alexandrian liturgy: *La liturgie d'Hippolyte: Ses documents, son titulaire, ses origines et ses caractères*, OCA 155 (Rome 1959) and *La liturgie d'Hippolyte: Documents et Etudes* (Rome 1970).

English Translations of the *Ap. Trad.*:

B.S. Easton, *The Apostolic Tradition of Hippolytus* (Cambridge 1934); G. Dix, *The Treatise on the Apostolic Tradition of St. Hippolytus of Rome*, rev. H. Chadwick (London 1968); M. Cotone, "The Apostolic Tradition of Hippolytus of

Rome," *The American Benedictine Review* 19 (1968) 492-514; G.J. Cuming, *Hippoytus: A Text for Students*, Grove Liturgical Study 8 (Bramcote Notts 1976).

42. Thus one can speak of a liturgical revolution with regards to the literary proliferation of liturgical material; cf. F. Cabrol, "Messe dans la liturgie: La révolution liturgique du IV siècle," DTC 10, 1365-1366. On the Latin *Canon Missae*, see B. Botte, *Le Canon de la messe romaine: Édition critique, Textes et études*, Études liturgiques 2 (Louvain 1935) and B. Botte–C. Mohrmann, *L'Ordinaire de la messe: Texte critique, traduction, et études*, Études liturgiques 2 (Louvain 1953); L. Eizenhöfer, *Canon missae Romanae* 1: *Traditio textus*, RED, Series Minor, Subsidia Studiorum 1 (Rome 1954), 2: *Textus propinqui*, RED, Series Minor, Subsidia Studiorum 7 (Rome 1966); E. Bishop, "On the Early Texts of the Roman Canon," *Liturgica Historica* (Oxford 1918, 1962) 77-115.

43. Tentatively made by F. Probst, *Die ältesten römischen Sakramentarien und Ordines* (Münster/Westf. 1892) 23-24.

44. Excellent account in W.S. Porter, *The Gallican Rite* (London 1958).

45. The hypothesis for a Roman orgin of the creative revival has been advanced by E. Bourque, *Étude sur les sacramentaires romains* 1 (Rome 1948) 34-38. For the actual situation at Rome during the early Christian era see F. Heiler, *Altkirchliche Autonomie und päpstlicher Zentralismus* (Munich 1941); G. Kunze, *Die gottesdienstliche Schriftlesung* 1 (Göttingen 1947) 103; A.M. Schneider, "Die ältesten Denkmäler der römischen Kirche," *Festschrift zur Feier des 200-jahrigen Bestehens der Akademie der Wissenschaften in Göttingen* 2(Berlin-Göttingen 1951) 166-198. On the liturgical revival in Africa see V. Saxer, *Vie liturgique et quotidienne à Carthage vers le milieu du 3. siècle*, Studi di antichità cristiana 29 (Rome 1969); A. Coppo, "Vita cristiana e terminologia liturgica a Cartagine verso la metà del 3. secolo," EL 85 (1971) 70-86.

46. Augustine, *De baptismate* 6, 26; CSEL 51, 323; *De catechizandis rudibus* 1, 9, 13; PL 40, 320; cf. W. Roetzer, *Des hl. Augustins Schriften als liturgiegeschichtliche Quelle* (Münster/Westf. 1930); F. van der Meer, *Augustine the Bishop* tr. B. Battershaw–G.R. Lamb (London-New York 1961) 347-387, 453-467.

47. Canon 25 of the Council of Hippo (393) is in G.D. Mansi *Sacrorum conciliorum nova et amplissima collectio* (31 vols., Florence-Venice 1759-1798; reprint Paris 1899-1922) 3, 922 and the Council of Carthage (397) is in Mansi 3, 891. For the African synods, see C. Munier, *Concilia Africae A. 345–A. 525*, CC 149 (Turnhout 1974); S. Lancel, ed., *Gesta conlationis Carthaginensis Anno 411*, CC 149A (Turnhout 1974).

48. Council of Carthage (397), see Mansi 3, 891.

49. Canon 10 of the Council of Carthage (407), see Mansi 3, 1163; and the Council *incerti loci* (wrongly placed in the Hispana Collection of Canons at Mileve, 416) Canon 12, Mansi 4, 330. K. Gamber, "Das Eucharistiegebet in der frühen Nordafrikanischer Liturgie," *Liturgica* 3 (Montserrat 1966) 51-65.

50. The existence of *libelli missarum*, perhaps even of sacramentaries, is certain; see G. Morin, "Formules liturgiques orientales en occident aux IV-V siècles," RB 40 (1928) 134-137; "Une particularité de *Qui Pridie* en usage en Afrique au V/VI siècle," RB 41 (1929) 70-73.

51. Gennadius, *Liber de scriptoribus ecclesiasticis*, ch. 79, PL 58, 1103-1104; E.C. Richardson, ed, *Gennadius: Liber de viris inlustribus*, TuU 14 (Leipzig 1896) 88. It was apparently a *volumen sacramentorum* much like the *De sacramentis* of Ambrose.

52. At one time, a homilary (Verona, Biblioteca capitolare, *cod.* 51, *olim* 49) was thought to represent a fragment of the African liturgy. This has been identified instead as the work of Maximus the Arian: B. Capelle, "Un *homiliare* de l'évêque airen Maximin," RB 34 (1922) 81-108, and "Les homiliaires 'de lectionibus evangeliorum' de Maximin l'Arien," RB 40 (1928) 49-86; E. Dekkers, *Clavis Patrum Latinorum*, 159, agrees with Capelle. However, E. Bourque, *Étude sur les sacramentaires*, 1, p. 14 n. 3, considers this attribution to be dubious.

53. For the famous *Statuta Ecclesiae antiqua* (late V century) and the many Gallican synods, both of which contain valuable information on the liturgy, see the edition of C. Munier, *Concilia Galliae 314-506*, CC 148 (Turnhout 1963); cf. H. Beck, *The Pastoral Care of Souls in South East France during the Sixth Century*, Analecta Gregoriana 51 (Rome 1950.)

54. Gennadius, *Liber de scriptoribus ecclesiasticis*, ch. 80, PL 58, 1104; Richardson, ed., TuU 14, 88-89. Some fragments of the liturgical work of Musaeus might be contained in a MS of the Bibliothèque Nationale of Paris; cf. G. Morin, "Fragments inédits et jusqu'à présent uniques d'Antiphonaire Gallican," RB 22 (1905) 329-356. In any case it is not a *missale plenum* (which is composed of an antiphonal, a lectionary, and a sacramentary). The sacramentary is possibly preserved in the MS Wolfenbüttel *codex* 4160. Cf. A. Dold, *Das älteste Liturgiebuch der lateinischen Kirche*, TuA 26-28 (Beuron 1936); G. Morin, "Le plus ancien monument qui existe de la liturgie gallicane: le lectionnare palimpseste de Wolfenbüttel," EL 51 (1937) 3-12. See L.C. Mohlberg's review of Dold in EL 51 (1937) 353-360 for some particular remarks concerning the responsorial.

55. Sidonius Apollinaris, *Epistola* 4, 11, PL 58, 516. G. Morin believed that the lectionary of Würzburg was the work of Claudianus Mamertus: "Le plus ancien *Comes* ou lectionnaire de l'Église romaine," RB 27 (1910) 41-74; "La lettre-préface du Comes *ad Constantium* se rapporterait au lectionnaire de Claudien Mamert?" RB 30 (1913) 228-231.

56. Sidonius Apollinaris, "Epistola ad papam Megethium," *C. Sollius Modestus Apollinaris Sidonius: Epistolae*, Bk. 7, 3; P. Mohr, ed. (Leipzig 1895) 144; ET *The Letters of Sidonius* vol. 2, tr. O.M. Dalton (Oxford 1915) 102.

57. Gregory of Tours, *Historia Francorum* 2, 22; MGH, *Scriptores Rerum Merovingicarum*, 1, 84-85; ET *The History of the Franks*, tr. L. Thorpe (Baltimore, MD 1974) 134.

58. Jerome, *Liber de viris inlustribus*, ch. 100; E.C. Richardson, ed., TuU 14/ 1, 48, he calls it a *"Liber hymnorum et mysteriorum"*. It seems to have been a treatise on mysticism, probably identified by Gamurrini; see p. 18 of A.

Wilmart, "Le De Mysteriis de St. Hilaire au Mont-Cassin," RB 27 (1910) 12-21.

59. Berno of Reichenau, "De initio Adventus Domini secundum auctoritatem Hilarii episcopi," PL 142, 1086-87: the author calls it a liber officium. The passage in question is not the work of Berno; cf. P. Blanchard, "Notes sur les oeuvres attribuées à Bernon de Reichenau." RB 29 (1912) 98-107. In any case, this is not the work of Hilary; cf. G. Mercati, "An Uncial MS of S. Cyprian," JTS 7 (1906) 269-270, inspite of W.C. Bishop, "The 'Three Weeks of Advent' of the Liber Officium S. Hilarii," JTS 10 (1909) 127-128; G. Morin, "Le prétendu Liber Officium de St. Hilaire et l'Avent liturgique," RB 27 (1910) 500-513.

60. Cf. A. Allgeier, Das afrikanische Element im altspanischen Psalter, Spanische Forschungen der Görres-Gesellschaft 1/2 (1930) 196-228.

61. Priscillian, Benedictio super fideles, CSEL 18, 103-106; cf. G. Morin, "Pro Instantio contre l'attribution à Priscillien des opuscules du MS de Würzburg," RB 30 (1913) 153-173.

62. Isidore of Seville, De viris illustribus liber, PL 83, 1090.

63. M. Férotin, ed, Le Liber Mozarabicus Sacramentorum, Monumenta Ecclesiae Liturgica 6 (Paris 1912; reprint Farnborough 1969).

64. Isidore of Seville, De viris illustribus liber, PL 83, 1104; Ildefonse, Liber de viris illustribus, PL 96, 201-203. The Libellus orationum of the Mozarabic Rite is a collection of prayers for the Liturgy of the Hours but not the Mass; it is preserved in two MSS: Verona, Bibliotheca capitolare codex 84 (VIII century); ed., P. Bianchini, (Rome 1741) and J. Vives, ed., Oracional Visigótico, Monumenta Hispaniae Sacra 1 (Barcelona 1946); and London, British Library, Add. codices 30852 (IX century, Silos); ed. J.P. Gilson, The Mozarabic Psalter, HBS 30 (London 1905). Cf. DACL 9, 2384-2387. Both of these MSS are considered in the work of J.M. Pinell, ed., Liber orationum psalmographus: Colectas de salmos del antiguo rito hispanico, Monumenta Hispaniae Sacra 9 (Barcelona–Madrid 1972) a review of which appeared in EL 87 (1973) 284-300 by A.M. Triacca and in JTS n.s. 24 (1973) 601-602 by H. Ashworth.

65. Braulio, Vita S. Aemiliani, PL 80, 701. Quiricus is mentioned in a hymn for the feast of St. Eulalia (Feb. 12) in the Breviarium Gothicum, PL 86, 1099-1100. Cf. M. Antonio, Bibliotheca Hispana Vetus 1 (1617) 517.

66. The disciple and biographer of Isidore—so descriptive elsewhere—never mentions liturgical compositions of his master. One must question the attribution of the Benedictio lucernae for Holy Saturday to Isidore based on the witness of Elipandus in his Epistola ad Albinum, PL 96, 875. On the other hand, the council of Toledo (633) where Isidore presided, concerned itself mightily with liturgical matters in a traditional way: P. Séjourné, Le dernier des Pères de l'Église, S. Isidore de Séville (Paris 1929).

67. Cf. Eugenius Dracontiana, MGH, Auctores antiquissimi 14, 27.

68. Ildefonse, Liber de viris illustribus, PL 96, 204. We cannot, however, discern the work of Eugenius in the surviving Liber Ordinum, M. Férotin, ed., (Paris 1904; Farnborough 1969). The Liber Ordinum is the rituale used in Spain before 712.

69. Julian and Cixilian of Toledo, *Vitae S. Ildefonsi Episcopi Toletani*, PL 96, 41-50.

70. Felix of Toledo, *Vita seu Elogium S. Juliani*, PL 96, 448 and 450.

71. Cf. note 68 above.

72. M. Férotin, ed., Monumenta Ecclesiae Liturgica 6 (Paris 1912; reprint Farnborough 1969).

73. Elipandus, *Epistola ad Albinum* [Alcuin] (ca. 793) PL 101, 1324 and 1328-1329. Cf. G. Mercati, "More Spanish Symptoms," JTS 8 (1907) 423-430, reprint in E. Bishop, *Liturgica Historica* (London 1918, reprint 1962) 203-210; D. De Bruyne, "De l'origine de quelques textes liturgiques mozarabes," RB 30 (1913) 421-436.

74. Gennadius, *De scriptoribus ecclesiasticis liber.* 49, PL 58, 1087, ed. Richardson in TuU 14, 79: he refers to it as "Sacramentorum [opus] et hymnorum".

75. Agnellus of Pisa, *Liber Pontificalis Ecclesiae Ravennatis* 2, 6 = PL 106, 610; MGH, *Scriptores rerum langobardicarum et italicarum* (1878) 332. For information on the opisthographic *rotulus* see A. Ceriani, "Il rotolo opistographico," *Archivio storico lombardo* 11 (1884) 11-16. The liturgical section is dated between the V and VII centuries: (Cagin: mid-VI; Cabrol: mid-V); cf. review in RB 22 (1906) 489-500. A new edition is included in L.C. Mohlberg, *Sac. Ver.* (Rome 1956) 173-178 and 202-203; and most recently in S. Benz, *Der Rotulus von Ravenna*, LQF 45 (Münster 1967). It is now in Milan.

76. Agnellus, see note 75 above.

77. A. Chavasse, "L'oeuvre littéraire de Maximin de Ravenne (546-553)," EL 74 (1960) 115-120, which expresses this position against that of G. Lucchesi, *Nuove note agiografiche Ravennati* (Faenza 1943) for the *Veronensis*, and K. Gamber, *Sakramentartypen* (Beuron 1958) 54-55, for the Gelasian.

78. M. Magistretti–U. Monneret de Villard, *Liber Notitiae* (Milan 1917) 369, 420.

79. A. Paredi, *I prefazi ambrosiani. Contributo alla storia della liturgia latina,* Publicazioni Università cattolica del Sacra Cuore, Scientia Philosophica 25 (Milan 1937), see Reviews in EL 52 (1938) 197-98 and in *Theologische Revue* 37 (1938) 42-47.

80. In spite of the late testimony of Walafrid Strabo, *De ecclesiasticarum rerum exordiis et incrementis*, cc. 22, 25, PL 114, 943-951 and 952-957. Cf. A. Bernareggi, *Ambrosius* 1 (1925) 130-135, 2(1926) 8-11, 3(1927) 45-48. As for the liturgical work of Ambrose, see K. Gamber, *Die Autorschaft von 'De Sacramentis'. Zugleich ein Beitrag zur Liturgiegeschichte der Provinz Dacia mediterranea*, Studia Patristica et Liturgica 1 (Regensburg 1967); and A. Paredi, "La liturgia del 'De Sacramentis'," *Miscellanea Carlo Figini* (Milan 1964) 59-72; J. Schmitz, *Gottesdienst im altchristlichen Mailand*, Theophaneia 25 (Bonn 1975).

81. O. Heiming, "Aliturgische Fastenferien in Mailand," AfL 2 (1952) 44-60.

82. Jerome, *Epistola 18* (to Praesidius) (ca. 384), PL 30, 182-188; cf. G. Morin, "Un écrit méconnu de St. Jérome: la lettre à Praesidius sur le cierge

pascal," RB 8 (1891) 20-27 and "La lettre de St. Jérôme sur le cierge pascal," RB 9 (1892) 392; cf. Pfaff, *Medieval Latin Liturgy*, 50.

83. Augustine, *De Civitate Dei*, 15, 22; CSEL 48, 488; PL 41, 467; ET *The City of God*, tr. D. Zema-G. Walsh, FC 7 (New York 1950) 469.

84. Ennodius, *Opuscula 9 & 10*, CSEL 6, 415-422; A similar formula can be found in VII-century Spain; cf. G. Mercati, "Una benedizione ritmica ispano-visigotica del cereo," SeT 12 (1904) 40-43 and P. Ewald–G.G. Löwe, *Exempla scriptura visigoticae* (Heidelberg 1883) tables II and III.

85. *Charta Cornutiana*, ed. L. Duchesne, *Liber pontificalis* 1 (Paris 1886; reprint 1955) cxlvii and *Origines du culte chrétien* (1925) 115, n.1, ET *Christian Worship: Its Origin and Evolution* (London 1925) 110, n.2.

86. See A. Mai, *Monumenta vetera ad Arianorum doctrinam pertinentia*, PL 13, 611-612, reprint from *Scriptorum veterum nova collectio* 3 (1827); This was re-edited by G. Mercati, "Tratti de un anonimo Ariano del Sec. IV/V," SeT 7 (1902) 51-53; A. Hänggi–I. Pahl, *Prex Euchristica*, Spicilegium Friburgense 12 (Fribourg 1968) 422.

87. *Liber pontificalis* 1, 225. Note that the text of the *Liber pontificalis* does not say Gelasius composed a sacramentary, but, some *praefationes sacramentorum* ('prefaces' in the modern sense?). For later witnesses see E. Bourque, *Étude sur les sacramentaires* 1 (Rome 1948) 297-298 and A. Chavasse, *Le Sacramentaire gélasien* (Tournai-Paris 1958) xx-xxiv.

88. M. Andrieu, *Les Ordines Romani du haut moyen âge* 3 (Louvain 1951) 223-224.

89. The conclusions of C. Silva-Tarouca, "Giovanni 'Archicantor' di S. Pietro a Roma e l'*Ordo Romanus* da lui composto," *Atti della pontificia Accademia Romana di Archeologia*, 3, Memorie 1 (Rome 1923) 159-219, are to be completely rejected according to M. Andrieu, *Les Ordines* 3, 3-21.

90. On the canon of the mass see above, note 42.

91. For the *libelli missarum* see E. Bourque, *Étude* and F. Cabrol, *Les livres de la liturgie latine* (Paris 1939) 34-36, ET *The Books of the Latin Liturgy* (St. Louis-London 1923). Gregory of Tours, *Historia Francorum* 2, 22 (see above, note 29) wrote: *ablato sibi nequiter libello, per quem sacrosancta sollemnia agere consueverat* [*Sidonius*].; and *Liber de vita Patrum* c. 16, MGH *Scriptores rerum merovingicarum*, 1, 661, where he says: *nec possum libellum aspicere*.

92. The IV Council of Toledo (633), canon 26, obliged every parish priest to have one.

93. Cf. *Capitulare Ecclesiasticum* (818-819) ch. 28, MGH, *Capitularia* 1, 279: *Quatenus presbyteri missalem et lectionarium sive ceteros libellos sibi necessarios bene correctos habeant*.

94. G.F. Warner, ed., *The Stowe Missal*, 2 vols., HBS 31-32 (London 1906-1915); cf. T.F. O'Rahilly, "The History of the Stowe Missal," *Eriu* 10 (1926) 95-109.

95. L.C. Mohlberg, *et. al.*, edd., *Missale Gallicanum vetus*, RED, series maior 3 (Rome 1958) 77-91; the masses of Mone are also found in PL 138, 863-882; cf. H. Brewer, "Der zeitliche Ursprung und der Verfasser der Moneschen Messen," ZkT 43 (1919) 692-703 where Venantius Fortunatus (†610) is

believed to be the author (!); P. Radò, "Verfasser und Heimat der Mone-Messen," EL 43 (1928) 58-65. See the sources in L. Eizenhofer, "Arator in einer *Contestatio* der Mone-Messen und einer mailandischen Praefation," RB 63 (1953) 329-332.

96. L.C. Mohlberg, ed., *Atti della Pontificia Accademia romana di Archeologia,* 3, *Memorie* 2 (1928) 207-320; cf. K. Gamber, "Das glagolitische Sakramentar der Slavenapostel Cyril und Method und seine lateinische Vorlage," *Ostkirchliche Studien* 6 (1957) 165-173.

97. PL 101, 445-466 (deficient edition); see G. Ellard, "Alcuin and the Votive Masses," *Theological Studies* 1 (1940) 37-61; H. Barré-J. Deshusses, "A la recherche du Missel d'Alcuin," EL 82 (1968) 3-44; J. Deshusses, "Les messes d'Alcuin," AfL 14 (1972) 7-41, which includes an edition of the votive masses; J. Deshusses, *Le sacramentaire grégorien* 2 (Fribourg 1979) nos. 1, 3, 9, 10, 14, 16, 17, 18, 63, 94, 105, 109, 110, 112, 120, 128, 132, 185, 223, 262, 264, and probably, 269.

98. The Ballerini edition is included in *Opera S. Leonis* 2, PL 55, 21-156; C.L. Feltoe, ed. *Sacramentarium Leonianum* (Cambridge 1896); L.C. Mohlberg, et. al., edd., *Sacramentarium Veronense,* RED, series major 1 (Rome 1956), the latest and best edition. Credit must be given the editors for having finally broken with the traditional way of naming the liturgical books which prevents an objective view of their formation. See the facsimile by A. Dold–M. Wolfe (Beuron 1957) and F. Sauer (Graz 1960). A. Stuiber, *Libelli sacramentorum Romani: Untersuchung zur Entstehung des sogennanten Sacramentarium Leonianum,* Theophaneia 6 (Beuron 1950) does not think the compiler was a cleric from Verona; be that as it may, his model was certainly Roman. See also D.M. Hope, *The Leonine Sacramentary: A Reassessment of its Nature and Purpose,* (Oxford 1971) and the review of the same by A. G. Martimort, *Bulletin de Littérature ecclésiastique* 73 (1972) 267-268; and A. Chavasse, SE 27 (1984) 151-190.

99. There is an immense bibliography of works which deal with the 'Leonine'. We indicate here those studies which provide more extensive bibliographies: E. Bourque, *Étude* sur les sacramentaires 1, 65-77; K. Gamber, *Sakramentartypen,* 48-50; L.C. Mohlberg, *Sacramentarium Veronense,* lxiv-lxix. A complete index is given by P. Bruylants, *Concordance verbale du Sacramentaire Léonien* (Louvain 1948) which is the one-volume edition of the work which first appeared in *Archivum latinitatis Medii Aevi* 18 (1945) 51-376 and 19 (1948) 39-405. See also the concordance by P. Siffrin, *Konkordanztabellen zu den römischen Sakramentarien* 1 (Rome 1958), and the *corpus* of concordances for all the sacramentaries: J. Deshusses-B. Darragon, *Concordances et tableaux pour l'étude des grands sacramentaires,* 1: *Concordances des pièces;* 2: *Tableaux Synoptiques;* 3: *Concordance verbale,* 6 vols, Spicilegii Friburgensis Subsidia 9-14 (Fribourg 1982-83).

100. For example, a certain preface (Mohlberg no. 1250) is probably an adaptation of a Mozarabic preface for Sundays (Férotin no. 1420). It was transformed into a preface for Christmas by changing the final words. Some of these *formulae,* however, may have been discovered in their

modified form at Rome itself; on this point see E. Bishop, *Liturgica Historica*, 197; G. Manz, *Ausdrucksformen der lateinischen Liturgiesprache bis das XI Jh.*, TuA 2/1 (Beuron 1941) 7-8; L. Brou, "Un passage de St. Augustin dans une oraison du sacramentaire léonien," *Downside Review* 64 (1946) 39-42; C. Coebergh, "Sacramentaire léonien et liturgie mozarabe," *Miscellanea Mohlberg* 2 (Rome 1949) 295-304. The problem of the symbols and marginal notes is dealt with by Mohlberg, *Sac. Ver.*, xxx; but a better interpretation appears in M. Andrieu, "Le sigles du Sacramentaire Léonien," RB 42 (1930) 127-135. The problem of 'leonine *cursus*' (*planus, tardus, velox,* trispondaic) is treated in Mohlberg, *Sac. Ver.*, lii-liii.

101. Certain marginal notes seem to indicate that this is the case; e.g. XVIII-1 (Mohlberg, p. 56 n. 416 line 11): *culpas relaxare fratri, corripere etiam inquietos non omitti, sicut scribtum est.*

102. See Mohlberg, *Sac. Ver.*, lxix-lxxxi for the various chronologies suggested.

103. Although Mohlberg broke with the traditional title, he replaced it with the still more ambiguous *Sacramentarium Veronense.* It is, however, neither a sacramentary nor is it designed for the Church at Verona. At best, it is a loose collection of *libelli missarum* probably taken from the archives of the Lateran. We will refer to the document as the *Veronensis/Veronense.*

104. No Gregorian influences, such as his conclusion to the *Hanc igitur,* can be detected in the *Veronensis.* Duchesne locates it after the lifting of the siege because of an allusion he finds contained in a *secreta* for Eastertide (Mohlberg, no. 570): *qui nos ab infestis hostibus liberatos, pascale sacramentum secura tribuas mente suscipere;* the *secreta* in question actually appears in the month of July but really belongs to Eastertide; cf. Duchesne, *Christian Worship,* 135-148.

105. F. Probst, *Die ältesten römischen Sakramentarien und Ordines* (Münster/ Westf. 1892)

106. C.L. Feltoe, *Sacramentarium Leonianum* (Cambridge 1896).

107. M. Rule, "The Leonine Sacramentary: An Analytical Study," JTS 9 (1908) 515-556, 10 (1909) 54-99.

108. R. Buchwald, *Das sogennanten Sacramentarium Leonianum und sein Verhältniss zu den beiden andern römischen Sakramentarien,* Weidenauer Studien 2 (1908) 187-251 and off-print (Vienna 1908) 1-67.

109. T. Klauser, "Die konstantinischen Altäre der Lateranbasilika," *Römische Quartalschrift* 43 (1935) 179-186, and "Ein Kirchenkalendar aus der römischen Titelkirche der hl. vier Gekrönten," *Scientia Sacra ... Festschrift Schulte* (1935) 11-40.

110. *Veronensis* XXIX-IV (Mohlberg, no. 987): *ut et de nostrae gaudeamus provectionis augmento et de congruo pascalis sacramenti obsequio.* (Mohlberg, no. 986): *Aptius siquidem atque decentius his diebus episcopalis officii suscepta principia celebramus ... quibus et aeclesiae totius observantia devota concurrit et ipsius ... natalis colitur sacramenti.* The classic interpretation has been given in E. Bourque, *Étude sur les sacramentaires* 1, 81-169.

111. H. Lietzmann, "Zur Datierung des Sacramentarium Leonianum," JfL 2 (1922) 101-102 (against R. Stapper, *Grundriss der Liturgik,* 184); A. Cappelli,

Cronologia, Cronografia e Calendario Perpetuo (3rd ed. Milan 1969) 62, and H. Lietzmann–K. Aland, *Zeitrechnung* (Berlin 1956).

112. *Veronensis* XXIX-VII (Mohlberg, no. 1004): *preces quas et pro reverentia paschali supplices adhibemus et pro sollemnitate recolenda primordii sacerdotalis.*

113. See the different *formulae* of the *Hanc igitur* in *Sac. Ver.* : nos. 1154, 1158: *"Hanc igitur"*; nos. 1107, 1140, 1162: *"Hanc igitur oblationem"*; nos. 203, 904: *"Hanc igitur oblationem quam tibi offerimus"*: no. 958: *"Hanc igitur oblationem quam tibi offero ego"*; no. 1012: *"Hanc itaque oblationem quam tibi offerimus".*

114. See above, note 86.

115. See above, note 75; J. Pinell, *Las Oraciones del Salterio o "per annum" en el nuovo libro de la liturgia de las horas,* Bibliotheca "Ephemerides Liturgicae," Subsidia 2 (Rome 1974) 355. E.A. Lowe, *Codices latini antiquiores* 3 (1938) 371, dates it VIII century.

116. Landesbibliothek HB. VII, 10., published in Mohlberg, *Sac. Ver.,*180-181.

117. Prayers and prefaces of Berlin (Phillipps *codex* 1667) O. Heiming (ed.), *Liber Sacramentorum Augustodinensis,* CC 149B (Turnhout 1984). See P. de Puniet, "Le sacramentaire gélasien de la collection Phillipps: 1, Son propre national; 2, Son propre national et ses emprunts au léonien," EL 43 (1929) 91-109, 280-303; and "Le Gélasien de la collection du Phillips et ses messes pour le commun des saints," EL 46 (1932) 379-395. Also, P. Siffrin, "De sacramentarii bibliothecae Phillipps proprio nationali eiusque cum sacramentario leoniano relationibus," EL 44 (1930) 47-50; Mohlberg, *Sac. Ver.,* 182-199.

118. Milan Fragment (Milan, *Ambrosiana* O.210 sup, f. 46) G. Mercati, SeT 7 (Rome 1902) 47-56; Mohlberg, *Sac. Ver.,* 178-180. Closely linked to the *Veronensis* formulary is the Mone Fragment (Karlsruhe, *codex Augiensis* 253, f. 96; VI century); F.J. Mone, *Lateinische und griechische Messen aus dem zweiten bis sechsten Jahrhundert* (Frankfurt 1850) 12.38-39. 151 (nr. 7); A. Holder, *Handschriften der Landesbibliothek Karlsruhe,* 5: *Die Reichenauer Handschriften* Bd. 1 (1906) 569-570. All of these texts are cited in Mohlberg, *Sac. Ver.,* 200-201.

119. See the tables constructed by H.M. Bannister, *Notes and Indices of the Missale Gothicum,* HBS 54 (London 1919); E.A. Lowe, *The Bobbio Missal: Notes and Studies,* HBS 61 (London 1934). See P. Siffrin, *Konkordantztabellen zu den römischen Sakramentarien* 1: *Sacramentarium Veronense;* 2: *Liber Sacramentorum Romanae Aecclesiae (Gelasianum);* 3: *Missale Gothicum,* RED, series minor, 4-6 (Rome 1958-1961).

120. E. Bishop, *Liturgica Historica,* 197-198.

121. A. Chavasse, *Le Sacramentaire gélasien* (Tournai-Paris 1958) 687-690. For Chavasse, the intermediary is a sacramentary—not preserved in the MS-tradition—which was pre-Gelasian/pre-Gregorian and was in circulation North of the Alps. On the basis of textual criticism, Chavasse denies that the Gallican sacramentaries are derived directly from the *Veronensis* or some similar collection. The *Veronensis* itself was never used North of the Alps.

122. Remember the numerous pilgrimages, trips, and exchanges of every sort between Gaul and Rome. See L. Gougaud, "Sur les routes de Rome avec

les pèlerins insulaires," *Revue d'histoire ecclésiastique* 29 (1923) 253-271; P.W. Finsterwalder, "Wege und Ziele der irischen und angelsachsischen Mission im fränkischen Reich," *Zeitschrift für Kirchengeschichte* 47 (1928) 203-226; P. Zettinger, *Die Berichte über Rompilger aus dem Frankenreich,* Römische Quartalschrift Supplementheft 11 (Rome 1900).

123. A. Stuiber, *Libelli Sacramentorum Romani: Untersuchung zur Entstehung des sogennanten Sacramentarium Leonianum,* Theophaneia 6 (Bonn 1950).

124. A. Chavasse, "Messes du Pape Vigile (537-555) dans le sacramentaire léonien," EL 64 (1950) 161-213; 66 (1952) 145-219. The same position is maintained by B. Capelle, "Retouches gélasiennes dans le sacramentaire léonien." RB 61 (1951) 3-14. The collection appeared during the time of Vigilius or in the years of Pelagius I (556-561), or perhaps early in the pontificate of John III (561-574).

125. See B. Capelle, "Messes du Pape Gélase dans le sacramentaire léonien," RB 56 (1945-46) 12-41, and "Retouches gélasiennes..." RB 61 (1951) 3-14; C. Coebergh, "Le Pape Gélase I, auteur de plusieurs messes du soi-dissant sacramentaire léonien," SE 4 (1952) 46-102; G. Pomarès, *Gélase I. Lettre contre les Lupercales et dix-huit messes du sacramentaire léonien,* SC 65 (Paris 1959). For possible masses by Leo I, see C. Callewaert, "S. Léon I et les textes du Léonien," SE 1 (1948) 139-150; and especially, in spite of the title, A.P. Lang, *Leo der Grosse und die Texte des Altgelasianums,* (Kaldenkirchen 1957) which includes a bibliography of earlier works; the following are also by A.P. Lang, " Anklänge an liturgische Texte in Epiphanie-Sermonen Leos der Grossen," SE 10 (1958) 43-126; "Leo der Grosse und die liturgischen Texte des Oktavtages von Epiphanie," SE 11 (1960) 12-135; "Leo der Grosse und die liturgischen Gebetstexte des Epiphaniefestes," Supplement to SE 14 (1963) 1*-22*. Consult also, A. Chavasse, *Le Sacramentaire gélasien, passim,* and *S. Leonis Magni Tractatus,* CC 138 and 138A (Turnhout 1973); R. Dolle, *Léon le Grand: Sermons,* SC 22, 49, 74, 200 (Paris 1964-1973).

126. See T. Klauser, "Entwicklung der abendländischen Liturgie bis zum Jahr 1000,"JfL 13 (1933) 347-362 which includes a review of L.C. Mohlberg, "Nuove considerazione sul così detto 'Sacramentarium Leonianum'," EL 47 (1933) 3-12. L.C. Mohlberg, "Des sogennanten *Liber diurnus romanorum pontificum* und das sogennanten Sacramentarium Leonianum," *Theologische Revue* 38 (1938) 297-303.

127. The details are in Mohlberg, *Sac. Ver.,* lxix-lxxxv.

128. A complete bibliography of works relating to the chronology of the *Veronensis* can be found in Mohlberg, *Sac. Ver.,* lxv-lxix, and in G. Pomarès, *Gélase I. Lettre contre les Lupercales...,* SC 65 (Paris 1959). According to Mohlberg, EL 47 (1933) 3-12, the majority of the masses are from the time of pope Symmachus (498-514). Stuiber assigns the greater part of the masses to the years 440-450. According to E. Bourque, the redaction of the *libelli* took place between 400 and 560. The Masses from section IX, XXI, XXV, XXXVII, and the first part of XLII are from ca. 400; those later than the year 500 are sections XIII, XIV, XVII, XXV, XXXII-XXXIV, XXXVII part 2, and XXXIX. These attempts at dating are not for the collection as a whole, but for the individual *libelli*.

129. A mass or formulary of the *Veronensis* is cited by the number of the section (in Roman numerals), followed by its numerical order within that section (also a Roman numeral); for example, VII-VI=section VII, mass VI. Each mass is then composed of various prayers which have been numbered using arabic numerals in a continuous fashion from 1-1331. In order to simplify citations, we will cite the section in Roman numerals and the individual prayers in Arabic, following the numbering in Mohlberg, *Sac. Ver.*

130. Several comparisons have been made between the Sanctoral of the *Veronensis* and other sources: a) between the *Veronensis* and the *Depositio martyrum* from the Chronographer of 354, by L. A. Muratori, *Liturgia romana vetus*, PL 74, 877-880; F. Probst. *Die ältesten römischen Sakramentarien und Ordines* (Münster 1892) 40-45; b) between the *Veronensis* and the saints venerated at Ravenna by G. Lucchesi, *Nuove note agiografiche Ravennati* (Ravenna 1943) 79-85, 93-98; c) between the *Veronensis* and the festal calendar of Roman and non-Roman antiquity by H. Lietzmann, *Petrus und Paulus in Rom: Liturgische und archäologische Studien*, Arbeiten zur Kirchengeschichte 1 (Berlin 1927) 73-83; G. Zunze, "Die gottesdienstliche Zeit," *Leiturgia* 1 (Kassel 1954) 481-485; W.H. Frere, *Studies in Early Roman Liturgy*, 1: *The Calendar*, ACC 28 (London 1930) 2-35; J.P. Kirsch, *Der stadtrömische christliche Festkalender im Altertum*, LQF 7-8 (Münster 1924); A. Chavasse, "Messes du pape Vigile . . . " EL 64 (1950) 197. For the feasts of saints in the months of August and September, it should be noted that the stations for these months are all in the *Southern* part of the city of Rome, which was spared from the invasions of the Goths in 537-538, an important fact for the chronology first noted by R. Buchwald in *Weidenauer Studien* 2 (1908) 187-251 (see note 108 above).

III. THE ROMANO-FRANKISH AND ROMANO-GERMANIC PERIODS: FROM GREGORY THE GREAT (590-604) TO GREGORY VII (1073-1085). *THE SACRAMENTARIES.*

The period that extends from Gregory the Great to Gregory VII is characterized by the following facts regarding liturgy:

a) the systematization of the liturgy of the City of Rome and of the papal court (the *Roman* liturgy in the strict sense);

b) the spread of this liturgy into the Frankish kingdom through the initiatives of individual pilgrims and, after 754, with the support of the Carolingian kings;

c) the deliberate Romanization of the ancient liturgy of Northern Europe (Gallican) at the behest of Pepin III and Charlemagne;

d) the progressive creation of a 'mixed' or 'hybrid' set of new rites in the Carolingian Empire through the amalgamation of the Roman liturgy with the indigenous ones;

e) the inevitable liturgical diversification resulting from these Romanizing and Gallicanizing thrusts;

f) the return of the adapted Romano-Frankish or Romano-Germanic liturgy to Rome under the Ottos of Germany, especially after the *Renovatio Imperii* of 962;

g) the permanent adoption of this liturgy at Rome because of the worship vacuum and the general state of cultural and religious decadence that prevailed in the City at the time.

This long period which we have just outlined is one of major importance for the history of Christian worship. The Latin liturgy which came into being in this era (in the *Hadrianum* supplemented by Benedict of Aniane, ca. 810-815, and in the *Romano-Germanic Pontifical,* ca. 950) and which continued to be the liturgy of the West for centuries to come, was not a purely Roman one; as a result of its long and turbulent history, it is better characterized as Romano-Frankish or even as Romano-Germanic.[131]

In presenting the sources of this 'hybrid' liturgy, we shall confine ourselves to two principal kinds of documents which made their appearance during this era: the sacramentaries and the *ordines*. In the form in which they are preserved, they illustrate perfectly the mixed character of the emerging Latin liturgy: paleographically, they all point to their Frankish origins, but their content reveals a primitive Roman substructure amalgamated, to a greater or lesser degree, with many ceremonies and rites proper to the Gallican and Germanic churches.

A. THE PECULIAR CHARACTER OF LITURGICAL MANUSCRIPTS.

Liturgical MSS have a specific character all their own and must be distinguished from other types of literature. In fact, they have to be submitted to a triple analysis:

a) First of all, there has to be a search for the chronological and geographical coordinates of the MSS in question and a description of the rites they contain. Since, by definition, we are dealing with liturgical *codices* in the strict sense—i.e., books used for the celebration of the liturgy—this first analysis will reveal the forms of worship that were used in a given church at a given time. No one, it seems, would continue copying books for the actual conduct of worship unless they intended to use them for exactly that purpose.[132] This means that if we discover the Old Gelasian was still being copied near Paris ca. 750, it must have been in use there at that time.

Even the presence of archaic elements in such MSS does not contradict the point we have just made. Liturgical uniformity was unknown in the Middle Ages and different ritual expressions from different eras coexisted in the liturgical books; celebrants could pick and choose among the various options available to them. Any adaptation to a new stage of liturgical evolution took place as fresh books were transcribed for actual liturgical use.

b) Secondly, we have to look for the *type* of liturgy presented in a particular *codex*. Our first analysis did not reveal the liturgical family to which the MS belonged nor the date of its archetype.

The problem is that in the Middle Ages 'pure' liturgical MSS as such did not exist. They were all the result of ritual cross-fertilization to some degree or other, e.g., the so-called Gallican sacramentaries were all Romanized to a greater or lesser extent and the surviving

Roman sacramentaries are only accessible in their Frankish transcriptions and adaptations. The rites themselves are the product of a long evolutionary process and if we want to uncover their specific character we have to sort out what belongs to their primitive Roman substratum from what has been added in Gaul or Germany at various stages of their development.

Looking for the *original* of such documents is largely futile and the very term "original" has little or no meaning here. Most liturgical texts are anonymous and come from a variety of contributors and, even when we know the author of a given book, its authenticity does not depend on that fact.[133]

When used in regard to liturgical texts, the words "authentic", "interpolated", or "modified" do not have the same meaning as they do when they are employed in regard to other forms of literature. A literary work is authentic when it comes directly from the hand of the author and from him alone. In the case of liturgical texts, what is authentic is what was actually used for divine worship. No matter how much such a text has been interpolated, enlarged or pruned, it is completely authentic if once utilized in an actual liturgy.[134]

c) Thirdly, we can try to restore the common ancestor lying behind our MSS and not just the archetype of a particular family. For example, a variety of attempts have been made at restoring the ancestor supposedly discernible in the various layers of a sacramentary even when, from a paleographical point of view, it is no longer available. This involves far more than relating MSS to one another; it is an actual attempt to reconstruct the primitive text not preserved in the MSS themselves.[135]

Such attempts at peering behind the MSS in order to get the 'original' or to examine an earlier stage of a given tradition is perfectly legitimate, but it is of little assistance to medievalists. Not only are such efforts too hypothetical but their positive results are too slight to be of much help. It seems preferable to follow the sage advice of Louis Duchesne in regard to such matters: "I prefer solid ground: I would rather go less far and walk securely *--non plus sapere quam oportet sapere, sed sapere ad sobrietatem.*"[136]

The coexistence of liturgical books of various types is a fact of capital importance for the history of the liturgy. The introduction of newer and more developed books did not, of itself, set aside earlier or less evolved texts. Even at Rome the Old Gelasian continued to be used side by side with the Gregorian Sacramentary. In Frankish Gaul this was even more the case since Roman innovations appeared only sporadically —before the Carolingians— as the result of private initiatives. Even the Romanizing process promoted by the Carolingians had no immediate impact on such a situation. Rather than eliminating the older liturgical books, it contributed to the multiplication of books both new and old. Further liturgical evolution came as a result of mutual interaction between the various strands of the tradition as books continued to be copied. In Gaul between 700 and 850, there existed simultaneously Old Gelasians like *Vaticanus Reginensis* 316, the Frankish Gelasians of the late VIII century like the Sacramentary of Gellone and the Sacramentary of Anglouléme, and the various Gregorians like the *Paduensis*, the Sacramentary of Trent, and the *Hadrianum*, with or without supplements. And what was true of the sacramentaries was equally true of the *Ordines*.[137]

B. THE SACRAMENTARY[138]

A Sacramentary is a presider's book containing all the texts he personally needs for the celebration of the Eucharist, the administration of the sacraments, the presiding of the Hours of Prayer, and for a variety of other liturgical events (the consecration of virgins, weddings, funerals, dedication of churches, etc.). By right it does not contain what the other ministers need for the performance of their specific liturgical functions, i.e., a Sacramentary has neither readings nor chants, because these are reserved to lectors, subdeacons, deacons or the *schola cantorum*. Nor does a Sacramentary normally have any but the sketchiest directions for carrying out the liturgy; these, are contained in special books called *Ordines*.[139]

A Sacramentary, in other words, did not resemble any of the late medieval or Tridentine books; it contained both more and less than the Missal, Pontifical, and Ritual of later centuries.

The technical Latin terms for Sacramentary are *Liber* or *Volumen sacramentorum*,[140] *Sacramentorium*[141] or *Sacramentarium*,[142] *Liber missalis* or *Missalis*.[143]

C. THE OLD GELASIAN SACRAMENTARY

The Sacramentary that we term 'Old Gelasian' is preserved in a MS of the Vatican Library, *Codex Vaticanus Reginensis latinus* 316, folios 3-245; its missing conclusion is found at Paris, *Bibliothèque* Nationale, *codex latinus* 7193, folios 41–56. It is clear that the indicated leaves of the latter MS used to belong to the *Reginensis* but had already been separated from it by 1651.[144]

The full title for the Sacramentary proper (folios 3-245) is: *In nomine Domini Iesu Christi Salvatoris. Incipit liber sacramentorum romanae aecclesiae ordinis anni circuli.* It concludes: *Explicit liber sacramentorum. Deo gratias.*[145] The Paris supplement contains a long exorcism, a penitential and a *Breviarium apostolorum*; it was probably added to the Roman materials when it was transcribed in Gaul.

The *Reg.* 316 was copied ca. 750—not at the end of the VII or the beginning of the VIII century (Delisle, Wilson, Bishop, Cabrol)[146]— near Paris, in the nunnery of Chelles[147]—not at St. Denis (Duchesne) or Corbie (Lowe, Wilmart). It is a Frankish recension of a Roman book and is the only one of its kind (an *unicum*). Other fragments that are sometimes connnected with it belong, in fact, to the family of Frankish Gelasian Sacramentaries of the late VIII century, except for the liturgical *Index of St. Thierry* (Rheims, *Bibliothèque municipale, codex 8,* fol. 1-2) which contains part of a *capitulatio* (table of contents) belonging to a *Gelasianum* analogous to the *Reginensis.*[148]

1. Contents.

Reg. 316 possesses two characteristics distinguishing it from the Gregorian Sacramentaries.

a) It is divided into three separate books with the Temporal and the Sanctoral kept distinct;

b) In every mass-set there are two very similar prayers appearing before the *secreta.* The first cannot be a stational collect since stations do not exist in this kind of sacramentary; perhaps they are alternative prayers left to the celebrant's choice or perhaps the first is an *oratio* proper and the second an *oratio super sindonem* as in the Ambrosian rite.[149]

LIBER PRIMUS: The Temporal Cycle with additional ceremonies.

1-14. Vigil of Christmas, Christmas, St. Stephen, St. John, Holy Innocents, Epiphany, Septuagesima, Sexagesima.

15-16. *Ordo* of public penance.

17-18. Quinquagesima, first week of Lent, Ember Days.

19-24. Ordinations of presbyters and deacons.

28-36. Second, third, fourth, fifth weeks of Lent with their baptismal scrutinies and the other ceremonies of the catechumenate.

37-38. Palm Sunday and Holy Week until Holy Thursday.

38-39. *Ordo* for the reconciliation of penitents.

40. *Ordo* for the blessing of chrism, *Coena Domini.*

41-45. Good Friday, Holy Saturday and the Paschal Vigil: the *ordo* of baptismal initiation.

46-87. Easter and Easter week; Ascension; Pentecost and several prayers for sick catechumens, for the reconciliation of heretics, etc.

[Pontifical additions:]

88-94. Dedication of churches and baptisteries.

95-99. Ordinations of doorkeepers, lectors, exorcists and subdeacons with extracts from the *Statuta Ecclesiae antiqua* (Gaul, late V century) relative to the Frankish clerical *cursus*.

100-102. The consecration of bishops.

103-107. The consecration of virgins.

LIBER SECUNDUS: *Orationes et praeces de nataliciis sanctorum.*

1-85. The Sanctoral Cycle (66 feasts), a *commune sanctorum*[150], five mass-sets for Advent and the Ember Days of September and December.

LIBER TERTIUS: *Orationes et praeces cum canone per dominicis diebus.*

1-23. Sixteen mass-sets for the ordinary Sundays throughout the year with the *Canon actionis* that prevailed throughout the Middle Ages, six *missae cotidianae.*

24-77. Masses for various occasions: for travelers, in time of trial, for seasonable weather, for monasteries, for weddings (*actio nuptialis*), in time of war, for rulers and judges, for the sick and dying, for the blessing of homes.

78-90. Miscellaneous prayers and blessings, morning and evening prayers; grace at meals.

91-96. *De cura mortuorum*: funeral and memorial masses.

97. Penance

The Gelasian Sacramentary (*Vat. Reg.* 316) is a 'mixed' book in two senses:

a) the primitive substratum is purely Roman but various Frankish liturgical elements have been added to it in the course of transcription;

b) the early Roman substratum itself is not entirely homogeneous but is the result of an intermingling of a variety of Roman *libelli* belonging to different periods and representing both papal and presbyteral usages. These *libelli* are distributed more or less successfully into three books according to the liturgical year, beginning with the Vigil of Christmas (Dec 24).

Liturgical historians have yet to reach agreement as to the nature and extent of the Frankish additions in *Reg.* 316. The Frankish origin of the following rites is, however, certain:

The minor orders, agreeable to the *Statuta Ecclesiae antiqua*;

The consecration of virgins;

The dedication of churches;

The blessing of holy water;

Funerals;

Public penance[151];

Some ceremonies of Holy Thursday and Holy Saturday;

A variety of *Benedictiones* and *orationes*, e.g., for travelers, for barren women;

The masses of Advent;

The great litanies of April 25 and a few additions to the Sanctoral Cycle.

These Gallican additions should not be regarded as blocks of material mechanically juxtaposed to the older Roman elements but as fresh additions or combinations which were gradually amalgamated, to varying degrees, with the older Roman structures.[152]

2. Origin.

The distant ancestor of our Frankish copy is undoubtedly a Roman Sacramentary, i.e., a Sacramentary used in the diocese of Rome. Agreement on this point is unanimous, except for A. Baumstark and his followers, and, more recently, K. Gamber and H. Schmidt.

According to Baumstark, the Old Gelasian Sacramentary is a work drawn up after the death of Gregory the Great (†604), probably in Frankish Gaul, using older Roman materials. *Reg.* 316, written towards the end of the VII century, is the only surviving example of it.[153] H. Hohlwein and H. Schmidt both adopted this thesis of Baumstark[154], but after the masterful work of M. Andrieu on the Lenten Thursdays (whose masses instituted by Gregory II, 715–731, were borrowed from an Old Gelasian like *Reg.* 316)[155] and that of A. Chavasse[156] on the Old Gelasian itself, such a thesis must be simply abandoned.

K. Gamber's hypothesis that the Old Gelasian was the work of Maximian of Ravenna (546–553) and subsequently passed into Gaul *via* Aquileia, has no MS evidence to support it. No Sacramentary of Maximian survives and none of the literary sources permit us to conclude that he composed a Sacramentary resembling the Old Gelasian.[157]

Using an older study of J. S. Sinclair, G. Dix thought that the Gelasian must not have come directly from Rome but from some city of Southern Italy (Capua perhaps?).[158] Although this an ingenious theory accounting for the presence of some Capuan saints in the Sanctoral, it cannot be seriously corroborated. The presence of Italian, non-Roman elements admits of other explanations.[159]

3. Date.

When the model for *Vat. Reg.* 316 was composed at Rome is still under discussion. It can no longer be attributed to Pope Gelasius (492–496) because that theory rests upon a faulty interpretation of a passage in the *Liber pontificalis*[160] and from an expression in the *Vita Gregorii* by the Roman deacon John which is too late to be helpful.[161]

An impressive array of liturgists (S. Bäumer, E. Bishop, F. Cabrol, and with some nuances, M. Andrieu) hold to the Gelasian origin of *some* parts of *Reg.* 316 or, at least, insist that—apart from certain post-Gelasian additions and Frankish interpolations—it is an old, VI-century Sacramentary of the Roman Church.[162]

Despite their authority, however, it does not appear possible to push the composition of the *Gelasianum* back into the VI century; it is too risky to base such conjecture simply on internal evidence and the progressive elimination of 'later' elements. There may well be some masses of Pope Gelasius in the so-called Gelasian Sacramentary, but they got there from the Lateran archives,[163] just as similar *libelli missarum* got into the *Veronensis* from the same source. The complex composition which we call the Old Gelasian is very largely made up of *libelli* used at Rome in the VII century.[164]

At the end of the most careful analyses, A. Chavasse came to some fresh conclusions, that *two* somewhat different kinds of Roman liturgy came together in the Old Gelasian:

a) the first was a presbyteral type of liturgy represented by a pre-Gelasian, pre-Gregorian Roman document which has not survived but which must have been a book rich in ancient *formulae;*
b) the second was another type of presbyteral book with a large number of Gregorian *formulae* drawn from the church of St. Peter-in-Chains and its neighborhood. The Old Gelasian belongs to the VII century and not to the VI as is commonly supposed.[165] Despite such influence, the liturgy of the Old Gelasian remains primarily 'Gelasian', i.e., of an older type than that represented in the Gregorian Sacramentaries (whether the *Paduensis* or the *Hadrianum* or the *Tridentinum*).

We shall not present in detail all the facts on which Chavasse's thesis is built since only the most specialized medievalist could make any use of them. His hypothetical pre-Gelasian and pre-Gregorian Sacramentary is not available to us and cannot be reconstructed in any precise fashion. Given this fact, it seems more useful simply to examine carefully the representative example that does survive (*Reg.* 316), without underestimating at all any serious attempt at discovering the pre-history of our only surviving source.

The *Vat. Reg.* 316 does not yet contain the masses for the Thursdays of Lent instituted by Gregory II (715-731).[166] On the other hand, it already has a *Capitulum S. Gregorii papae* (†604)[167], the *Canon actionis* contains the Gregorian embolism of the *Hanc igitur: Diesque nostros in tua pace disponas atque ab aeterna damnatione nos eripe et in electorum tuorum iubeas grege numerari*[168] and the *Pater noster* is situated immediately after the Canon[169]—exactly where St. Gregory I put it. The Sanctoral Cycle has both feasts of the Cross, although the *Exaltatio Crucis* (Sept 14) was introduced at Rome after the death of Gregory the Great, probably after the recovery of the True Cross from the Persians by the Emperor Heraclius in 628.[170] The Sanctoral also contains the four feasts of the Blessed Virgin (*Purificatio*, Feb. 2; *Annunciatio*, March 25; *Assumptio*, Aug 15; *Nativitas*, Sept 8) unknown at Rome in the time of Gregory but which were being celebrated during the reign of the Syrian pope, Sergius I (687-701).[171]

With such evidence before us, we have to conclude that the Roman ancestor of *Reg.* 316 must have been composed between 628 and 715, i.e., between the oldest possible date of the most recent feast and the beginning of Gregory II's pontificate.

4. Areas of Influence.

However old the Gelasian may be as a collection and whatever its original date of redaction, it is clear that it was used at Rome during much of the VII and the first part of the VIII century. In the reign of Gregory II (715-731), it still served side by side with a Gregorian-type Sacramentary and when Gregory decided to compose masses for the Lenten Thursdays (aliturgical until his time), he borrowed a few selections from a Gregorian book but took the greater number from a Gelasian.[172] That means it must still have been considered an authorized text. Again in the VIII century, the Old Gelasian was employed for the Saturday before Palm Sunday; as contained in the *Hadrianum*, the mass for this Saturday is that of the Monday of the fourth week of Lent as it appears in the Gelasian.

The Old Gelasian Sacramentary was not confined to Rome itself. It was carried into Gaul and widely used there, at least until around 750 when *Reg.* 316 was copied. Its Roman prototype must have left Rome before Gregory II because it did not yet contain masses for the Thursdays of Lent.[173] On the other hand, it is heavily connected to several Gallican Sacramentaries, especially the *Missale Gothicum (Vat. Reg. lat.* 317), ca. 690–700 A. D.), the *Missale Gallicanum vetus (Codex Vat. Pal.* 493, after 750) and the *Missale Bobbiense* (Paris, Biblio. Nat. *latin* 13246, after 700). Several liturgical items found in these books could only have come from an Old Gelasian. We have to draw the conclusion that the model for *Reg.* 316 must have arrived in Gaul by the late VII century, given the dates of redaction of the Gallican service books.[174]

We have no idea who first brought the Gelasian Sacramentary to Gaul. It was probably pious pilgrims who had come to admire the Roman rite as they saw it celebrated in the City itself; it might have been Benedictine (?) monks in view of the monastic *formulae* included in the book as it stands. In any case, it circulated widely in the Kingdom of the Franks, even before the reforms undertaken by Pepin III (751–768), and was one of the principle agents of Romanization there long before any royal initiatives on that score. Whichever hypothesis we accept, it remains clear that the archetype of *Reg.* 316 circulated in Gaul early on in the VIII century or that, at the very least, isolated Roman *formulae* of the Old Gelasian type were well known in Gaul in that period.

The *Reg.* 316 is a remarkable witness to the Romano-Frankish rite that was being worked out North of the Alps and particularly in the Kingdom of Neustria. As more and more copies were made outside Rome, they became replete with additions and interpolations from non-Roman practices until about the middle of the VIII century, the date of the sole surviving MS of this particular tradition.

When we eliminate the Gallican additions, *Reg.* 316 provides us with first-rate information on how presbyteral worship was conducted at Rome in the VII and VIII centuries. This particular form of worship coexisted with a Gregorian type liturgy in the same city. Insofar as it is a Romano-Frankish book, *Reg.* 316 preserves for us a type of liturgy that was celebrated in the churches that adopted it up to around the mid-VIII century; as at Rome, this liturgy coexisted in Gaul with other liturgical usages.

D. THE FRANKISH GELASIAN OR VIII-CENTURY GELASIAN SACRAMENTARY.—THE SACRAMENTARY OF FLAVIGNY AND ITS DESCENDANTS.

A dozen or more MSS still survive which preserve the text of a whole new class of sacramentaries belonging directly to neither the

Gelasian nor the Gregorian family of rites. The common characteristics of the MSS in question postulate the existence of a single archetype—the Sacramentary of Flavigny, now lost—of what is generally called the Frankish Gelasian or VIII-Century Gelasian Sacramentary. Edmund Bishop even termed it the Sacramentary of Pepin the Short.[175]

1. Surviving MSS.

a) *In Gaul*:

The Sacramentary of Gellone. Paris, Bibliothèque Nationale, MS *latin* 12048; 790–800 A.D. It was probably copied at Holy Cross Abbey (Meaux), possibly for Cambrai Cathedral during the episcopate of Bishop Hildoard (790–816), but was donated to the Abbey of Gellone, ca. 807. It is the only surviving example of the primitive recension of the Sacramentary of Flavigny. (edd.), A. Dumas-J. Deshusses, *Liber Sacraramentorum Gellonensis*, CC 159–159A (Turnhout 1981). CLLA no. 855, p. 392.

The Sacramentary of Angoulême. Paris, Bibliothèque. Nationale, MS *latin* 816; ca. 800, at Angoulême. Diplomatic edition by P. Cagin, *Le Sacramentaire gélasien d'Angoulême 1919*). CLLA no. 860 (Angoulême 1919) pp. 393-394, New edition in preparation for CC159C by P. Saint Roch.

The Phillipps Sacramentary. Berlin, Deutsche Staatsbibliothek, MS *lat.* 105 (*olim* Phillipps 1667); ca. 800, Eastern France, near Trier. O. Heiming (ed.), *Liber sacramentorum Augustodinensis*, CC159B (Turnhout 1984). CLLA no. 853, pp. 390-391.

The Sacramentary of Rheims or *of Godelgaudus* (now lost). Rheims, Bibliothèque de l'Abbaye de S. Rémi, ca. 800. Partial copy by J. de Voisin († 1685), Paris, Biblio. Nat., MS *lat.* 9493, fol. 43-71; ed. by U. Chevalier, *Sacramentaire et Martyrologe de l'Abbaye de Saint-Rémy*. Bibliothèque liturgique 7 (Paris 1900) 305-357. CLLA no. 862, pp. 394-395.

The Sacramentary of St. Amand=*The Colbertine Fragments.* Paris, Biblio. Nat., MS *lat.* 2296 (*olim* Colbert 1348, later Biblio. royale 4230.2); ca. 800, at St. Amand, by, in part, the same scribe as the Sacramentary of Arno (see below). Edd. by C. Coebergh-P. de Puniet *Liber Sacramentorum Romanae Ecclesiae Ordine Excarpsus*, CC, *Cont. Med.* 47 (Turnhout 1977) and by S. Rehle, *Sacramentarium Gelasianum Mixtum von Saint Amand*, TPL 10 (Regensburg 1973). CLLA no. 805, p. 374.

b) *In 'Alemannia'*:

The Sacramentary of St. Gall 348. St. Gall, Stiftsbibliothek, *codex* 348; ca. 790-800 or, better, 813-814 or 817; Northern Italy, Chur, then St. Gall. Edited by L. C. Mohlberg, *Das fränkische Sacramentarium Gelasianum in alamanischer Ueberlieferung*, LQ 1-2 (Münster/Westf. 1918; 2nd ed. 1939; reprint 1967). CLLA no. 830, pp. 381-382.

The Triplex Sacramentary of Zürich. Zürich, Zentralbibliothek, *codex* C.43; ca. 1020-1030; St. Gall; this is a corrected copy of the *Sangallensis* 348. The *Triplex* is not a true liturgical book but one assembled for didactic or scientific purposes. Edited by M. Gerbert, *Monumenta veteris liturgiae alemannicae* 1 (St. Blaise 1777; reprint Hildesheim 1967) 1-240 (a very poor edition); O. Heiming, ed., *Corpus Ambrosiano Liturgicum, 1: Das Sacramentarium Triplex*, Teil 1: *Text* LQF 49 (Münster/Westf. 1968). The *Triplex* also belongs among the Ambrosian Sacramentaries mentioned below. CLLA no. 535, p. 270.

The St. Gall Sacramentary Fragment 350. St. Gall, Stiftsbibliothek, MS. lat. 350; ca 800; Chur and then St. Gall. Edited by G. Manz, *Ein St.-Gallener Sakramentar-fragment*, LQF 31 (Münster/Westf. 1939). CLLA no. 831, p. 382.

The St. Gall Sacramentary Fragment 349. St. Gall, Stiftsbibliothek, MS *lat.* 349, pp. 5-56; late VIII or early IX century; St. Gall. Unedited. Cf L. C. Mohlberg, EL 42 (1928) 65-73; P. Siffrin, EL 45 (1931) 332-335. CLLA no. 1501, p. 549.

The Sacramentary of Rheinau 30. Zürich, Zentralbibliothek, MS *Rh.* 30; ca. 800; Northern France or Switzerland, then used at the Abbey of Rheinau in the IX century. Edited by A. Hänggi-A. Schönherr, *Sacramentarium Rhenaugiense, Handschrift Rh. 30 der Zentralbibliothek* Zürich, Spicilegium Friburgense 15 (Fribourg 1971). See the review by A. G. Martimort, *Bulletin de littérature ecclésiastique* (1972) 268-269.[176] CLLA no. 802, pp. 371-372.

c) *Italy:*

Sacramentary or Missal of Monza. Monza, Biblioteca capitolare, *codex* F 1-101: IX-X century; Bergamo then Monza. Edited by A. Dold-K. Gamber, *Das Sakramentar von Monza*, TuA 3 (Beuron 1957). CLLA no. 801, pp. 370-371, see Chavasse, "Le Sacramentaire de Monza," *Ecclesia Orans* 2(1985) 3-29.

The Sacramentary of Arno. Munich, Bayerische Staatsbibliothek, *Clm* 29164 I/la and various fragments in North America libraries (CLLA no. 806 pp. 374-375); from the scriptorium of Bishop Arno of Salzburg (785-821); this is a sister MS to the Colbertine Fragments which were written at St. Amand where Arno had been abbot for three years before becoming bishop of Salzburg in 785; they are written in part by the same scribe and correspond to each other in general layout. Edited by S. Rehle-K. Gamber, *Sacramentarium Arnonis. Die Fragmente des Salzburger Exemplars*, TPL 8 and 10 (Regensburg 1970 and 1973). Appendix: *Fragmenta Sacramentarii Arnonis nuper reperta.*

The Angelica Palimpsest. Rome, Biblioteca Angelica, *codex* F. A. 1408 (*olim* T.7.

22). Before 800; Northern Italy, perhaps Nonantola, used at Salerno. Edited by L. C. Mohlberg, "Un sacramentario palinsesto del secolo VIII dell'Italia centrale'" *Atti Pont. Acad. Rom. Archeol., Rendiconti* 3 (Rome 1925) 391-450. CLLA no. 833, pp. 383-384.

The Budapest Fragment. Budapest, Nationalmuseum, *codex lat. med. aevi* 441; before 800; N. Italy (Verona?). Edited by P. Lehman, "Mitteilungen aus Handschriften V," Sitzungsberichte der Bayerischen Akademie der Wissenschaften. Philos.-historische Abteilung, 1938, hft 4, 7-19. L. C. Mohlberg, "Note su alcuni sacramentari," *Atti Pont. Acad. Rom. Archeol., Rendiconti* 16 (Rome 1940) 131-170. CLLA no. 832, p. 383.

d) *Belgium, Germany and England:*

No complete Sacramentary is preserved in any of these three countries, but a few surviving fragments show that the Frankish Gelasian was known there.[177]

2. *Origin of the Frankish Gelasian Sacramentary.*

All the surviving MSS possess a series of common traits:

a) They have a "certain Benedictine flavor about them"[178] which points to a Benedictine abbey as their original place of redaction. They provide a mass in honor of St. Benedict the Abbot on July 11 and the *Sacramentary of Gellone* even adds a second formula which qualifies Benedict as *venerabilis pater, gregis pastor* and *decus monachorum;*[179] his name also appears in the *communicantes* of the *Canon missae,* where it concludes the list of the Latin Fathers. Moreover, in the MSS which provide a 'Book II' of supplementary materials, considerable attention is paid to rites useful only to monks and nuns.[180]

b) In addition to St. Benedict's July-feast (which may stem from the famous translation of his relics to Fleury-sur-Loire),[181] the Frankish Gelasian has another characteristically Frankish feast, that of St. Praeiectus the Marytr on Jan 25 (in competition with another festival of Frankish origin, the *Conversio Sancti Pauli Apostoli*)[182] The feast of Praeiectus (Preiectus, Proiectus, Priest, Prist, Projet, Prejet, Prix), bishop of Clermont, who died on Jan 25, 674/676 and who is invoked as *patronus semper fidelis,* is the only *natale* in the book of a native Gallican martyr. His successor, St. Avitus, built a basilica on the site of his martyrdom at Volvic (Puy-de-Dôme).[183] In 742 Pepin III founded an abbey at Flavigny-sur-Ozerain (Cote d'Or) in honor of St. Prix and of St. Peter the Apostle and the relics of the saint were transferred there after Volvic was destroyed in Pepin's 761 campaign in Aquitaine.[184] The Frankish Gelasians also have a mass in honor of St. Chrysogonus (Nov 24) which was probably composed when his basilica in the Trastevere district (Rome) was restored by Gregory III (731-741).[185] It is perhaps not too farfetched to think that this mass was introduced at the request of King Pepin himself who was devoted to this Roman saint as his *protector*.[186]

c) Large numbers of specifically Gallican practices appear in the Frankish Gelasians: Rogation Days, mixed Romano-Frankish rites for ordinations and the consecration of churches, episcopal blessings before communion. The *Canon actionis* adds Hilary, Martin, Gregory, Jerome and Benedict to the normal Roman list; such additions are frequent in Gaul and N. Italy, but rare elsewhere.

d) Finally, all the surviving MSS are of continental origin and the *Gellonensis*, the finest and earliest surviving example of the earliest recension, was copied in N. Gaul, probably at Meaux, for the cathedral of Our Lady of Cambrai during the episcopate of Hildoard (790-816), ca. 790-800.[187]

With such evidence before us, we can conclude that the archetype of the Frankish Gelasians was compiled in a Benedictine monastery that was closely connected with the veneration of St. Prix the Martyr, i.e. Volvic in Auvergne or, more probably, Flavigny in Burgundy.[188]

3. Contents and Structure.

The Frankish Gelasian is a careful fusion of the two kinds of Roman Sacramentaries which had penetrated Gaul by the mid-VIII century: the papal Sacramentary adapted to presbyteral use at St. Peter's on the Vatican (cf. *Paduensis* D. 47) and the presbyteral Sacramentary of the Roman *tituli* commonly called the *Gelasianum* (cf. *Vat. Reg.* 316).[189] The team of compilers also employed other materials drawn from the older Gallican books for the many additional ceremonies that were dear to Frankish hearts, and from a monastic customary for a variety of items in the so-called Pontifical section of the book; the Old Gelasian had merely included a Consecration of Virgins and a Blessing of Widows whereas the *Gellonensis*, for example, had an impressive number of entries suitable to monastic use, e.g., *Oratio ad abbate faciendum, Oratio quandum abbas vel abbatissa ordinatur in monasterio, Oratio pro renuntiantibus seculi et cenobio intrantibus*.[190]

Despite the generous use of Gelasian materials, the general groundplan of the new sacramentary is like that of a Gregorian Sacramentary (type II), i.e., the masses of the Temporal and Sanctoral cycles all appear in a single, unified series (according to a liturgical year in which Easter fell on April 3). On the other hand, the arrangement of the mass formularies is that of the Gelasian; there are normally six items for each mass: 2 collects, *secreta*, *praefatio*, *postcommunio* and a final prayer. The Gelasian also contributes far more formularies than does the Gregorian, the compilers obviously having a real predilection for the Old Gelasian materials. Moreover, all the MSS of both the first and second recension (except St. Gall 348) have a *Liber secundus* containing the kind of extra matter characteristic of the Old Gelasian as represented by *Vat. Reg.* 316 in the last part of Book I and in Book III (e.g., blessings, votive masses, dedication of churches, ordinations and funerals). A sharp division is discernible between the Sacramentary proper, which normally concludes with six *missae cotidianae* and the *Canon missae*, and the second half of the manuscript. Rheinau 30, the Colbertine Fragments and Brussels 10127-44 actually begin the section after the Canon with the title: *Incipit liber secundus de extrema parte*. Rheinau 30 has a very diminished Book II as compared with, say, Gellone and Angoulême, but only St. Gall 348 has none at all. However, since St. Gall 350 (which comes from the same scriptorium) does contain significant remains of a Book II, it may be that Book II of St. Gall 348 was bound in a second volume.

From the above considerations, it is clear what the monastic compilers of the Sacramentary of Flavigny were about. They wanted an authentic and eminently usable sacramentary which would incorporate as much as was feasible of the old Roman books still circulating in the Frankish kingdom and whatever else was needed by bishops and abbots for their peculiar ministries. Whether or not the Frankish Gelasian Sacramentary was officially inspired by the Frankish court, it certainly corresponded to the felt needs of Frankish churches and monasteries and was a genuine and well-ordered amalgam of traditional materials.[191]

4. Date of the Archetype.

The *terminus ante quem non* might seem to be the year of St. Prix's martyrdom in 676, but actually that date is far too early to be helpful. Since the Frankish Gelasian contains masses for the Thursdays of Lent—which were aliturgical until Gregory II (715-731)—an examination of these texts results in some important conclusions:

a) The compilers of our Gelasian did not possess a Gregorian Sacramentary with these *formulae* in it since the masses for these days differ from both those in the *Paduense* and in the *Hadrianum*. There would have been no need to search for fresh *formulae* if the compiler had had the masses of Gregory II before his eyes. What he did do to compose the masses he needed was borrow individual prayers from the masses bordering on the Lenten Thursdays in some Old Gelasian Sacramentary. It was a scissors-and-paste job to make up for the fact that the Gregorian he was using must have left Rome before the reign of Gregory II.

b) Since the compiler felt obliged to compose masses for the Thursdays of Lent, he must have known from some other source (antiphonary, lectionary, which had left Rome after Gregory II's reform) that, despite his old Gregorian Sacramentary, the Thursdays of Lent were no longer aliturgical. That means that the Frankish Gelasian must have been compiled in Gaul after the pontificate of Gregory II.

It is very likely that the Frankish Gelasian was assembled late in the reign of Pepin III (751-768), not too long after the momentous residence of Pope Stephen II in *Francia* (754-755), a time of great importance for every facet of church life.[192] It would be difficult to claim a date later than 770 since the surviving MSS—even the *Gellonensis*, the earliest and best example of the archetype—all show some signs of liturgical evolution beyond the archetype and appear in the last decade of the VIII century.

The rapid and widespread dissemination of the new book suggested to earlier scholars that it was more than a private project. Fascinated by the reforms instigated by St. Boniface, *missus sancti Petri*, and fostered by Carlomann and Pepin III,[193] some have tried to fasten its authorship on one or another outstanding Carolingian churchman such as Remedius of Rouen, the brother of Pepin III, or the famous Bishop Chrodegang of Metz.[194] Although both ecclesiastics were enamoured of things Roman, there is no concrete evidence to connect them with the Sacramentary of Flavigny. We must content ourselves with the claims of the editors of the *Gellonensis* that it was assembled by a team of Benedictine monks, ca 760-770, and underwent an early second redaction reflected in most of the surviving MSS.[195]

5. *Contents of the Sacramentary of Gellone* (ed. A. Dumas).

Title: IN NOMINE DOMINI NOSTRI IESU CHRISTI. INCIPIT LIBER SACRAMENTORUM.[196]

Book I: The Sacramentary Proper.

1-15. Vigil, masses and prayers of Christmas, Stephen, John, Holy Innocents, I Sun. after Christmas, Silvester, Octave of Christmas (2 mass-sets),[197] *Missa prohibendo ab idolis*,[198] II Sun. after Christmas.

16-34. Vigil, feast and prayers of Theophany, I Sun. after Theophany, Octave of Theoph., Felix, II Sun. after Theoph., Marcellus (2 sets), Prisca, Mary and Martha, Fabian, Sebastian, Agnes, Vincent, III Sun. After Theoph., Emerentianus and Macarius, Preiectus,[199] Agnes *de nativitate*, [IV Sun. after Theoph.][200]

35-45. Simeon,[201] Agatha, V Sun. after Theoph., Soteris, Zoticus, Irenaeus and Hyacinth, VI Sun. after Theoph., Valentine, Vitalis, Felicula and Zeno, Iuliana, Chair of Peter, Perpetua and Felicity, Gregory the Great.

46-54. Septuagesima, Sexagesima, Quinquagesima; *Ordo* of Public Penance; Announcement of the four Ember Seasons; *Caput de ieiuniis* (Ash Wed.), Thurs., Fri., Sat.

55-63. I Week of Lent (Ember days: Wed., Fri., and Sat.).

64-71. II Week of Lent.

72-79. III Week of Lent and the first scrutiny.[202]

80-87. IV Week of Lent and the second scrutiny.

88-97. V Week of Lent and further scrutinies and rites of the catechumenate.

98-108. [Holy Week] Palm Sun., Mon., Tues., Wed., Thurs: Reconciliation of Penitents, Chrism mass, evening mass; Good Fri., Holy Sat: *Redditio symboli.*

109-123. Easter Vigil: *Ordo baptismi*, Mass of the Holy Night; Easter Sun. and its octave (*alba*),[203] Morning and Evening Prayers for Paschaltide, *Pascha annotina*, mass *in parochiis.*

124-138. Annunciation of Mary and the Passion of Jesus,[204] I Sun. after the octave of Easter, Leo the Great, Euphemia, Tiburtius, Valerianus and Maximus, II Sun. after Easter, George, *Litania maior* and Rogations, Vitalis, III Sun. after Easter.

139-148. Philip and James, Juvenal, Alexander, Eventius and Theodolus, Finding of the Cross, IV Sun. after Easter, John *ante portam latinam*, Gordian, Nereus and Achilleus, Pancras, Dedication of the church of Mary *ad martyres.*

149-162. Vigil and feast of Ascension, Sun. after Ascension, Urban, Vigil, feast and octave of Pentecost, I Sun. after Pentecost.

163-187. Nicomedes, Marcellinus and Peter, II Sun. after Pent., Primus and Felicianus, Basilides *et al.*, III Sun. after Pent., Announcement of the Ember Days of the IV, VII and X months, Ember Days of the IV month, IV Sun. after Pent., Vitus, Mark and Marcellianus, Gervase, Protase and Nazarius, V Sun. after Pent., Vigil and feast of John the Baptist, Vigil and feast of John and Paul, VI Sun. after Pent., Vigil and feast of Peter and Paul.

188-201. Processus and Martinian, VII Sun. after Pent., Octave of Peter and Paul, Seven Brothers, VIII Sun. after Pent., Benedict (2 sets), IX Sun. after Pent., James, X Sun. after Pent., Simplicius, Faustinus and Beatrice, Felix, Abdon and Sennen, XI Sun. after Pent.

202-232. Peter *ad vincula* and the Holy Machabees, Stephen, Xystus, Felicissimus and Agapitus, Donatus,[205] Cyriacus, Vigil and feast of Lawrence, Tiburtius, Hippolytus, XII Sun. after Pent., Eusebius, Vigil and feast of Assumption, Octave of Lawrence, Agapitus, Magnus, Timothy, XIII Sun. after Pent., Bartholomew, Rufus, Augustine, Hermes, XIV Sun. after Pent., Sabinus, Passion of John the Baptist, Felix and Adauctus, Priscus, XV Sun. after Pent.

233-253. Nativity of Mary and Hadrian, Gorgonius, Protus and Hyacinth, XVI Sun. after Pent., Exaltation of the Cross, Cornelius and Cyprian, Nicomedes, Euphemia, Lucy and Geminian, XVII Sun. after Pent., Vigil and feast of Matthew, Ember Days of the VII month, XVIII Sun. after Pent., Cosmas and Damian, Dedication of the basilica of Michael the Archangel, Jerome, XIX Sun. after Pent.

254-263. Mark, Marcellus and Apuleius, XX Sun. after Pent., Callistus, XXI Sun. after Pent., Luke, XXII Sun. after Pent., Vigil and feast of Simon and Jude, XXIII Sun. after Pent.

264-276. Caesarius, XXIV Sun. after Pent., Four Crowned Martyrs, Theodore, Mennas, Martin, XXV Sun. after Pent., XXVI Sun. after Pent., Vigil and feast of Cecelia, Clement, Felicity, Chrysogonus.

277-295. Advent: V Sun. before Christmas and XXVII after Pent., Saturninus, Chrysanthus, Maurus and Daria, Vigil and feast of Andrew, XXIX Sun after Pent. and IV before Christmas, Daily masses for Advent, Octave of Andrew, Damasus, III Sun. before Xmas and XXX Sun. after Pent., Lucy, II Sun. before Xmas and XXXI after Pent., Ember Days of the X month, XXXII Sun. after Pent. (Last Sun. before Xmas), Thomas.

296-312. *Commune sanctorum.*

313-319. Votive masses.

320-326. Six *missae cotidianae* with the Roman Canon.

327-329. Blessings over the people.

Book II: [*INCIPIT LIBER SECUNDUS DE EXTREMA PARTE*].[206]

330. Episcopal Blessings throughout the Year.[207]

331-343. Prayers for the Liturgy of the Hours and at Meals.

344. *Ordo Baptisterii.*

345-512. A 'Pontifical':

1) Clinical baptism, reconciliation and exorcisms.

2) Dedication of churches and their furniture.

3) Minor and major ordinations and their anniversaries; Blessings of abbots and abbesses and other monastic exercises; Consecration of virgins; mass for kings; Weddings etc.

4) Miscellaneous prayers and masses.

5) Prayers and masses for the sick and dying.

6) Holy Water and Ordeals.

Breviarium Apostolorum: Their names, the places they preached the Gospel, circumstances of their deaths.

Martyrologium per circulum anni.

E. THE GREGORIAN SACRAMENTARIES.

In addition to the Gelasian sacramentaries (old and new) so prevalent in Gaul and Germany in the VIII and IX centuries, another type of Roman mass book, termed Gregorian, circulated widely North of the Alps and came to exercise a definitive influence.[208] In the course of the VII century, the Lateran *episcopium/patriarchium* developed its own distinctive collection of *libelli* and produced a sacramentary to be used by the pope both at the Lateran basilica (*ecclesia sanctissimi Salvatoris: omnium urbis et orbis ecclesiarum mater et caput*) and throughout the City as he celebrated his annual round of stational liturgies.[209] Although this distinctive book can no longer be attributed to Gregory the Great (590-604),[210] it was probably redacted under Pope Honorius I (625-638) and was gradually augmented as new stational liturgies and fresh feasts emerged in the course of the VII and VIII centuries.[211]

At dates difficult to pin down exactly, various copies of this book in different stages of development spread northward in Italy and were carried across the Alps; these stages are reflected in a variety of famous IX-century MSS. At first glance representative MSS of this class of sacramentaries can be distinguished from the Gelasians by two facts:

a) they are not divided into three books as the Old Gelasian was. Sometimes the masses of the temporal and sanctoral cycles are merged into a single, continuous series of Sundays and festivals (*Casinensis* 271[212] and Padua D. 47), sometimes the *orationes* or full mass-sets for the Sundays after Epiphany, Easter and Pentecost and other materials are assembled into appendices of various kinds (*Hadrianum*, Supplement of Benedict of Aniane, Sacramentary of Trent). *Cas.* 271 and *Pad.* D. 47 resemble most the layout of the Frankish Gelasians which combined into a single book an unbroken series of masses extending from Christmas until the last Sunday of Advent and set the rest of its materials in a 'Book II'. This arrangement should come as no surprise since the Sacramentary of Flavigny had adopted a type-II Gregorian like *Pad.* D. 47 as its groundplan;

b) the Gregorians normally have only three prayers for each mass: *oratio, super oblata, ad completa* or *ad complendum*, whereas the Gelasian books normally have several *orationes*, including a blessing *super populum* at the end. Moreover, the Gelasian books use the terms *oratio, secreta* and *post communionem* as well as *cotestata* or *contestatio* for the *praefatio* of the Gregorian MSS.

Of the 35 or so major Gregorian sacramentaries of the IX century, four demand our attention because of their special importance and distinguishing characteristics. With their assistance we shall be able to understand both the structure and evolution of the papal sacramentary and how it became fused with the Roman presbyteral book, in the course of the IX century, to produce the Roman-Germanic Missal known to the later Middle Ages.

1. The *Hadrianum*, the papal book that Pope Hadrian I sent to Charlemagne towards the end of the VIII century (= Gregorian, type I);

2. The *Hadrianum* as it was corrected and expanded by St. Benedict of Aniane in the early IX century (*Hadrianum* + Supplement);

3. The Sacramentary of Padua (*Paduensis*), a representative of the papal sacramentary as it had been adapted to presbyteral use at St. Peter's basilica on the Vatican, ca. 670-680 (= Gregorian, type II);

4. The Sacramentary of Trent (*Tridentinum*), whose core was a type-I Gregorian of the period just before the reign of Sergius I (687-701).

Padua and Trent permit us to recapture the Lateran sacramentary in its VII-century state; the *Hadrianum* in its fully developed VIII-century form.

1. The Hadrianum.

Whatever the exact role of Pepin III and his liturgical advisers may have been in unifying and romanizing the VIII-century Frankish liturgy, his mighty son and successor, Charlemagne (768-814), certainly fostered and promoted the Roman liturgy in his empire.[213] It was he who extracted a Gregorian Sacramentary from the then-reigning pontiff, set it in his archives and rendered it, in some sense, normative for his dominions.

As Paul Warnefrid (Paul the Deacon, Paul the Grammarian) departed from Aachen to return to Monte Cassino, King Charles commissioned him to ask Pope Hadrian I (772-795) for a pure (*inmixtum*) Gregorian sacramentary, i.e., the papal sacramentary as it had issued (suppposedly) from the very pen of St. Gregory I himself, free from all post- or extra-Gregorian additions.[214] The desire for Roman authenticity, so marked in St. Boniface and his Anglo-Saxon assistants and in the monks who had produced the Sacramentary of Flavigny, now took the form of an official, royal request for an authentic model, *the* Gregorian—which could be used without argument as the basis for all future reforms. Paul carried out his mission but the pope delayed satisfying Charlemagne's request until 784/785; possibly he had no convenient copy of such a 'pure' sacramentary at his disposal or perhaps because the very purpose of the Frankish liturgists escaped him. As can be seen in the accompanying papal letter, Abbot John of Ravenna delivered the long-awaited *Gregorian* to the Frankish sovereign:

De sacramentario vero a sancto disposito praedecessore nostro deifluo Gregorio papa: Inmixtum vobis emitteremus iampridem Paulus Grammaticus a nobis eum [lege: id] pro vobis petente secundum sanctae nostrae ecclesiae tradicionem, per sanctum Ioannem monachum atque abbatem civitatis Ravennantium Vestrae regali emisimus Excellentiae.[215]

This rather complex and faulty Latin sentence may be translated as follows: "As for the sacramentary arranged by our predecessor Pope Gregory [We remark the following]: some time ago Paul the Grammarian asked Us to send You a copy that would be free from all additions (*inmixtum*) and in accordance with the use of Our holy church [the Lateran]; we now dispatch it to Your Highness by means of John the Monk, abbot of Ravenna."[216]

Obviously the *Hadrianum* arrived at the Frankish court in the second half of Hadrian's pontificate (772-795). Paul the Deacon did not leave Aachen until at least 783 and was back in Benevento or Monte Cassino by 787.[217] Since the adverb *iampridem* of Hadrian's letter implies some delay between Paul's request and the dispatching of the *Hadrianum*, the years 784-791 seem to suit the evidence best.[218] Clearly the *Hadrianum* had arrived by the last decade of the century since the *Sacramentary of Gellone* (ca. 790-800) drew some dozen prayers from it.[219]

When it was received at Aachen, the *Hadrianum* was deposited in the palace library as a kind of *editio typica* from which subsequent copies were to be made. We know this because of the notice which appears at the head of all the MSS deriving from this original: *ex authentico libro bibliothecae cubiculi scriptum*, "copied from the authentic exemplar deposited in the palace library." A similar notice appeared in all the MSS of the Dionysio-Hadriana collection of canons forwarded to Charlemagne by Pope Hadrian in 774: *Iste codex est scriptus de illo authentico quem domnus Hadrianus apostolicus dedit gloriosissimo regi Francorum ... quando fuit Romae.*[220]

Unfortunately the liturgical *codex* sent by Hadrian I has not survived, but we do possess a copy made from the original (the

Sacramentary of Hildoard) and two other valuable IX-century copies which permit us to reconstruct the lost original in a satisfactory manner:[221]

a) The *Sacramentary of Hildoard of Cambrai* (Cambrai, Bibliothèque municipale, *codex 164 [olim* 159], folios 35ᵛ-203; Cambrai, 811-812). This is the only surviving, complete, uncorrected copy of the *Hadrianum*; it was made at the command of Bishop Hildoard, the same prelate who probably commissioned the *Sacramentary of Gellone* (790-800) and the *Lectionary of Alcuin* (✝804). Critical edition by J. Deshusses, *Le sacramentaire grégorien*, Spicilegium Friburgense 16 (Fribourg 1971) 85-348.

   b) Although Cambrai 164 is the only pure and complete transcription of the *Hadrianum*, two other MS-sacramentaries, both of Verona in the first half of the IX century, are careful, uncorrected— but unfortunately mutilated—copies that serve as excellent controls for the text presented in the Sacramentary of Hildoard: Verona, Biblioteca capitolare, MSS LXXXVI (mid-century) and XCI (first third), [CLLA 725 and 726]. Although uncorrected and without the Supplement of Benedict of Aniane, they are not without the *missae necessariae*. After the sacramentary proper, each MS has Sunday and votive masses drawn directly from the Frankish Gelasians and MS LXXXVI has, in addition, some of the famous votive masses of Alcuin.

The Sacramentary of Hildoard bears the title:

IN NOMINE DOMINI.
HIC SACRAMENTORUM DE CIRCULO ANNI EXPOSITO
A SANCTO GREGORIO PAPA ROMANO EDITUM
EX AUTHENTICO LIBRO BIBLIOTHECAE CUBICULI SCRIPTUM.

Clearly this is not the title of the *Hadrianum* itself (if it had one) but one added to the copies *ex authentico* to signal their very authenticity. On the basis of Pope Hadrian's letter to Charlemagne, it deems the authorship of Gregory I unquestionable and refers to him as the "Pope of Rome"—a title no Roman would employ.

   From the point of view of those in long possession of sacramentaries with all the necessary Sunday *formulae* in place, the new mass book must have been a grievous disappointment. For liturgists accustomed to the Frankish Gelasians it was a most peculiar and frustrating kind of sacramentary with the gravest kind of *lacunae*.

More than half the Sundays—those after Epiphany, Easter and Pentecost—appeared to be missing and there were no funeral services, no reconciliation of penitents, no votive masses and very few *benedictiones*. On the other hand, sections 201-226 contained a wealth of prayers for various circumstances. As a matter of fact, section 202 actually housed a multitude of collects (*orationes cottidianae*) designed to be used on the so-called missing Sundays and on other occasions. Apparently the hints given in sections 15 and 16 (*Oratio in alia dominica*) for the two Sundays after Christmas did nothing to persuade Carolingian liturgists to use section 202 *ad libitum*. Since they were accustomed already to a profusion of completely fitted out mass books, they were only confused and dismayed by the empty spaces of the *Hadrianum*.[222]

Contents:
Part I:
1. The *ordo missae* with the Roman Canon.
2-4. Ordinations: bishops, presbyters, deacons.[223]
Part II:
5-16. IN NOMINE DOMINI [original title before the addition of 1-2]. Vigil and masses of Christmas, Stephen, John, Holy Innocents, Sylvester, Octave of Christmas, 2 Sundays after Christmas [collects only].
17-26. Epiphany, Felix, Marcellus, Prisca, Fabian and Sebastian, Agnes, Vincent [No Sundays after Epiphany].
27-31. *Ypopanti*, Agatha, Valentine, Gregory, Annunciation.
32-37. Septuagesima, Sexagesima, Quinquagesima, Ash Wed., Thurs., Fri. and Sat.
38-44. I Lent, Mon., Tues., Ember Wed., Thurs., Ember Fri. and Sat.
45-65. II, III, and IV weeks of Lent.
66-72. V Lent=Passion Sun. and weekdays.
73-83. Holy Week: Palm Sun., Mon., Tues., Wed., Holy Thurs., and the Blessing of Oils, Good Fri., Holy Sat. (final stages of the catechumenate).
84-97. Vigil of Easter, Baptismal Rites, Vigil Mass; Easter Sun. and Octave, Low Sun. (*post Albas*), Paschal Prayers [No Sundays after Easter].
98-101 [April]. Tiburtius and Valerian, George, Great Litany, Vitalis.
102-107 [May]. Philip and James, Alexander *et al.*, John *ante portam latinam*, Gordian and Epimachus, Pancras, Mary *ad Martyres*.
108-118. Ascension, Urban, Vigil of Pentecost, Pentecost Sun. and Octave with Ember Wed., Fri. and Sat., I Sun after Pentecost [but no others].
119-131 [June]. Nicomedes, Marcellinus and Peter, Mark and Marcellinus, Protase and Gervase, Vigil and feast of John the baptist, John and Paul, Leo I, vigil and feast of Ss. Peter and Paul, Octave of the Apostles.
132-135 [July]. Processus and Martinian, Seven Brothers, Felix *et al.*, Abdon and Sennen.

136-154 [August]. Peter *ad Vincula*, Stephen, Xystus, Felicissimus and Agapitus, Cyriacus, Vigil and feast of Lawrence, Tiburtius, Hippolytus, Eusebius, Vigil and feast of the Assumption, Agapitus, Timothy, Hermes, Sabina, Felix and Adauctus.

155-169 [Sept]. Nativity of Mary, Protus and Hyacinth, Cornelius and Cyprian, Exaltation of the Cross, Nicomedes, Euphemia, Lucy and Geminian, Ember Days of Sept: Sun., Wed., Fri. and Sat., Sun. after the Ember Days; Cosmas and Damian, Dedication of St. Michael.

170-171 [Oct]. Mark, Callistus.

172-184 [Nov]. Caesarius, Four Crowned Martyrs, Theodore, Mennas, Martin, Cecilia, Clement, Felicity, Chrysogonus, Saturninus, Vigil and feast of St. Andrew.

185-193 [Dec]. I Sun of Advent, II Sun., Lucy, III Sun, December Ember Days: Wed., Fri. and Sat., and the Sun. after the Ember Days.

Part III:

194-200. Dedication of churches, ordination masses of popes and presbyters, wedding mass.

201-204. Miscellaneous prayers for sins, for ordinary Sundays (*cottidianae*) and for morning and evening prayer.

205-225. [Additions]: Clinical Baptism, Holy Water, miscellaneous prayers.

226. Ordination of a pope.

Explicit: Hildoardus Praesul Anno XXII Sui Onus Episcopatum Hunc Libellum Fieri Promulgavit.

An analysis of its contents clearly reveals that the *Hadrianum* is a mass book compiled for the exclusive use of the *domnus apostolicus* when he celebrated *de iure* at the Lateran and in the stational churches of the City. The preparation of a special sacramentary for the pope was a normal enough thing to do since, in his liturgical peregrinations, he was accompanied by the clerics of the *patriarchium* who carried with them, from the *secretarium* and *vestiarium* of the Lateran, the sacred vessels, utensils and books needed in the celebration of the papal liturgy.[224]

The *Hadrianum* is an VIII-century example of this mass book and is easy to distinguish from the fuller presbyteral sacramentaries used both in the Roman *tituli* and in Frankish Gaul. The famous Sacramentary of Padua preserves for us one of the larger presbyteral sacramentaries adapted from the primitive Gregorian and expanded for the use of St. Peter's basilica (= Type II Gregorian). The Old Gelasian Sacramentary (*Vat. Reg.* 316) preserves for us, in large measure, the more normal mass book used in the *tituli*. Both these books contained all that the clergy needed for the regular and normal conduct of eucharistic worship.

In sending King Charles the papal mass book, Pope Hadrian sent him neither a 'pure' sacramentary in the sense requested nor one that was 'complete'. Such a book was bound to confuse the liturgical experts of *Francia*. Perhaps the pope had misunderstood the seriousness and extent of the king's request; he sent him a gift when he wanted a document. In any case, whatever the accidents of history, the *Hadrianum* was destined to have un unforgettable future.

It is mere speculation to attempt to say if the *Hadrianum* corresponded exactly with the current papal sacramentary. Certainly it is a later redaction than those appearing in the Sacramentary of Padua and the Sacramentary of Trent, but whether it is a transcript of the late VIII-century book or of a somewhat earlier version is impossible to say. It has the fresh mass *formulae* for the Marian feasts introduced by Sergius I (†701), the masses for the Thursdays of Lent and the Saturday before Palm Sunday established by Gregory II (715-731) and the mass of St. Urban (May 25) created by Gregory III (ca. 735). It is therefore a redaction done at least as late as the latter pontificate of Gregory III. With the evidence on hand we may conclude that the *Hadrianum* may have been slightly out-of-date as well as 'incomplete'. In any case, it cannot have been, in any sense, a fresh recension of the papal sacramentary done by Pope Hadrian.[225]

To the somewhat undiscerning eyes of the Carolingian liturgists, the *Hadrianum* was not only incomplete when compared with the elegant 'Roman' sacramentaries already in use but it was also marred by other deficiencies. Its latinity was not as exquisite as theirs and it contained masses that could not have been in the 'original', i.e., in the very sacramentary of Pope Gregory I. Since they apparently had another and earlier recension of the papal mass book before their eyes—representing the state of the text as it had existed around 685—they felt they were in a position to handle the *Handrianum* critically as well as respectfully.[226]

2. *The Supplement to the Hadrianum.*

Since the labors of Bishop, Lietzmann and Bourque, scholars have agreed almost unanimously in attributing the authorship of the famous Supplement to Alcuin of Tours, the advisor to Charlemagne.[227] Recent studies have, however, thoroughly undermined this longstanding hypothesis. Alcuin did indeed compose a Missal for his Abbey of St. Martin of Tours but it is of an utterly different character from the *Hucusque*, both in regard to its main text and to its 'supplement'.[228]

From several important pieces of evidence presented by Jean Deshusses, it is now apparent that the Supplement was assembled in Septimania, ca. 810-815, during the reign of King Louis the Pious, by St. Benedict of Aniane (†821), the monastic founder and reformer *par excellence* of the Carolingian period. For his abbeys he produced a thoroughly up-to-date sacramentary which combined a corrected version of the *Hadrianum* with a copious, useful and even necessary series of appendices.[229]

The Supplement proper is preceded by an explanatory and justificatory prologue (*Hucusque*) which separates it from the text of the *Gregorianum*. The text of the Supplement itself is divided into two distinct parts, although the elements that compose them are drawn chiefly, but not exclusively, from the Frankish Gelasian Sacramentary.

Part I, the Supplement proper, composed mostly of Sunday and votive masses, was redacted between 810-815 to fill the *lacunae* of the *Hadrianum*.

Part II, the Appendix, is a series of additional materials originally drawn up in the late VIII century, to complement a Frankish Gelasian Sacramentary.

Contents of the Supplementum.

Part I: The Supplement Proper.

I-IV. Additions for the Vigils of Easter and Pentecost.
V-XLI. Masses for the Sundays after Christmas, Theophany, Easter and Pentecost.
XLII-XLVII. Six *missae cotidianae*.
XLVII-LV. *Commune Sanctorum*.
LVI-LVII. Tonsure of Clerics and Consecration of Virgins.
LVIII-LXIII. Consecration of altars, patens, chalices, fonts; anniversary of a basilica.
LXIII-XCVI. Votive Masses.
XCVII-XCVIII. Reconciliation of Penitents.
XCIX-CXII. Visitation of the sick and dying, funerals, requiem masses.
CXIII-CXLI. Miscellaneous blessings and prayers.
CXLII. Morning and Evening Prayers.
CXLIII-CXLV. Exorcisms.

Part II: The Appendix.

1. 221 Prefaces for Sundays, Festivals and every day of Lent.
2. 51 Episcopal Blessings for Sundays and Festivals.
3. Ordinations to the Minor Orders: Doorkeeper, Lector, Exorcist, Alcolyte and Subdeacon.

ENGLISH TRANSLATION OF THE PREFACE TO THE SUPPLEMENT: *Hucusque*

Up to this point the present sacramentary is obviously the work of the the blessed pope Gregory; the only exceptions are the feasts of the Nativity and the Assumption of the Blessed Virgin and the masses for the Thursdays of Lent; readers will find them marked with an *obelus* [to signify their dubious authorship]. We have been told that the pope does not celebrate stational liturgies on these Thursdays since he is worn out by his liturgical labors on the other days of the week and has to rest on these. Because he can escape the popular excitement at least one day a week, he can more readily distribute alms to the poor and devote himself to the external affairs [of the papacy]. Because of their love and veneration for St. Gregory, there is no doubt that his successors added the mass for his feast to the sacramentary he composed; it is also marked by an *obelus*. Although the aforegoing sacramentary is marred by a variety of scribal errors—not attributable to the author—we have tried to correct them as best we could in order to assist others in understanding the text. If the text is not corrupted once again by the carelessness of copyists, judicious readers will surely agree that we have restored the original readings.

Since there are other liturgical materials which Holy Church finds itself obliged to use but which the aforesaid Father omitted because he knew they had already been produced by other people, we have thought it worth our while to gather them like spring flowers, arrange them in a beautiful bouquet and—after carefully correcting and amending them and giving them appropriate titles—present them in this separate work so that diligent readers may find everything they need for the present. Note that almost everything included here has been drawn from other sacramentaries.

In order to distinguish [the sacramentary from the supplement], we have inserted this little preface between them so that it brings one book to a close and begins another. In this way, with one book before the preface and one after it, anyone can tell what Gregory composed and what was set forth by other Fathers.

Since it would be both impossible and unsuitable for us to ignore the wishes of those who want all kinds of first-rate religious observances, we hope that the present abundant collection will meet all their liturgical needs.

If what we have collected with such care and concern meets the approval of others, we hope that they will not be ungrateful for all our labors but join us in thanking the Giver of all good gifts. If, on the other hand, they judge what we have done is either superfluous or unnecessary, let them, at the very least, use the sacramentary of St. Gregory; they may not refuse to employ it without endangering their souls. Let them also be good enough to permit others to use our supplement for pious purposes.

We have made this collection of liturgical materials for the zealous and devout and not for ungrateful and disdainful critics. Those who find these prayers dear and familiar will be able to use them to pay their vows to the Lord and to offer Him divine worship in a pleasing and worthy manner. Readers may be assured that we have inserted nothing in this book except the careful compositions of authors of the highest reputation for virtue and learning. We have collected many items from many authors in order to serve the needs of all.

We ask those who like the prefaces which we have added to the end of this book to accept and sing them with love. On the other hand, we beg those who understand but do not like them and those who would like to use them but do not understand them to leave them alone.

We have also appended to this supplement the blessings which bishops are accustomed to confer on the people and the forms of ordination to the minor orders which are not contained in St. Gregory's sacramentary.

Those who use this book either for reading or for transcribing are asked to pray for me; I have tried hard to assemble and correct these materials to the advantage of all.

Please copy correctly so that the text will please the learned and not lead the uneducated astray. As St. Jerome said: "There is no point in correcting a book if copyists will not preserve accurately what has been corrected."

The prologue (*Hucusque*) and the subsequent *capitula* (*Incipiunt capitula praefati libelli:* no.1020)[230] set forth Benedict's intentions with admirable clarity:
1. He distinguishes the 'pure' Gregorian elements of the sacramentary from the later accretions, such as the Nativity and Assumption of the Blessed Virgin Mary, the Thursdays of Lent and the feast of St. Gregory himself. These *formulae* he has marked with an *obelus* in order to draw attention to their non-Gregorian origin. To be able to make such distinctions, he must have had before him an older text of the Gregorian which did not yet contain such late VII- and early VIII-century additions. This would have been a Mass-book like the core of the Sacramentary of Trent, representing the state of the papal sacramentary ca. 685.

2. He corrects the grammatical faults of the Gregorian text although, of course, he will not allow that they stem from the great Gregory himself. His corrected version superseded, for all practical purposes, the authentic text of the *Hadrianum*. Only Cambrai 164 and Verona 86 and 91 allow us to glimpse the kind of Latin used in the Roman liturgy before the Carolingian purists 'improved' upon it!

3. He fills in the notorious *lacunae* of the *Hadrianum*, explaining that Pope Gregory must have omitted, for example, the ordinary Sunday masses, because they were already to be found in earlier sacramentaries! Although Benedict betrays some kind of acquaintance with the Roman stational system, he does not grasp completely the connexion between it and the papal sacramentary and the 'use' of the Lateran.[231]

4. Besides the absolutely essential Sunday masses, Benedict adds to the *Hadrianum, alia quaedam quibus necessariae sancta utitur Ecclesia*. These include *missae cotidianae*, a rich variety of votive masses for all occasions, many occasional services such as weddings, funerals, dedications of churches, consecrations of sacred vessels, the reconciliation of penitents, the exorcism of the possessed, and so forth. In addition, there are a number of prayers and ceremonies essential to monastic communities, prayers and masses for the Kings of the Franks and an increased number of collects for morning and evening prayer.

Finally, in his Appendix, Benedict provides a profusion of prefaces drawn from the Gelasian books, episcopal benedictions throughout the year, and the full text and rubrics for the conferral of the minor orders according to normal Gallican usages.

Thanks to all these additions, Benedict of Aniane contributed mightily to the resulting hybrid Romano-Frankish liturgy destined to become the liturgy of the entire Latin patriarchate.

5. Benedict is completely candid about the fact that he derived most of his materials from previously existing liturgical books. However authoritative *Pater Gregorius* may be, his authors too are to be numbered among the *patres* with full right of citation as *probatissimi et eruditissimi viri*.

6. By way of suggestion only, Benedict also enriched the calendar with a few feasts dear to Gallican hearts: St. Prix (Jan 25), the Conversion of St. Paul the Apostle (Jan 25), the Chair of St. Peter (Feb 22), the Finding of the Cross (May 3), St. Benedict of Nursia (July 11), St. James the Apostle (July 25), the *Passio* or Martyrdom of St. John the Baptist (Aug 29), St. Matthew the Evangelist (Sept 21) and St. Luke the Evangelist (Oct 18). Unfortunately, neither the

prefaces nor blessings have been adjusted satisfactorily to the *Hadrianum*. They betray all too readily their purely adventitious character.

The MS-tradition has preserved Benedict of Aniane's Supplement in three ways:[232]

1) The *Hadrianum* + the Supplement (including the *Hucusque*) *in Two Distinct Sections.*
   In this instance the Supplement is maintained clearly distinct from the sacramentary proper and remains faithful to Benedict's recension. Representative examples:
   a) *Sacramentary of Marmoutier*: Autun, Bibliothèque municipale, *codex* 19 (*olim* Grand Séminaire, MS 19 bis); copied ca. 845 under Abbot Ragenaldus of Marmoutiers (*Martini monasterium*). It has been at Autun since the XI century (*Codex Augustodunensis*). This *codex* contains the full, corrected text of the *Hadrianum* and the best surviving copy of the Supplement. It also has a second supplement with all the mass *formulae* from the Frankish Gelasians for the feasts missing from the *Gregorianum* and, at the end, the famous masses of Alcuin for the vigil and feast of All Saints. CLLA no. 741, p. 351.
   b) *Sacramentary of Le Mans*: Le Mans, Bibliothèque municipale, *codex* 77; copied at St. Amand, shortly before the end of the IX century. It is one of the best MSS of the Supplement; there are two *lacunae:* no. 994-1009 and 1703-1805. CLLA no. 743, p. 352.
   c) *Sacramentary of Beauvais*: Paris, Bibliothèque Nationale, *codex lat.* 9429; copied in N. France in the second half of the IX century. An almost normal Supplement. CLLA no. 750, p. 354.
   d) *Sacramentary of Corbie*/Rodradus: Paris, Bibl. Nat., *codex lat.* 12050; copied at Corbie in 853 or a little later. It has Benedict's normal Supplement and a second supplement with the votive masses of Alcuin and some additional feasts and commons. CLLA no. 742, p. 351.
   e) *Sacramentary of Paris*: Rome, Bibliotheca Apostolica Vaticana, *codex Ottoboni lat.* 313; third quarter of the IX century for Notre Dame de Paris. This celebrated MS was long considered the best example of the *Hadrianum* & Supplement and was employed by H.A. Wilson as one of the basic MSS for *The Gregorian Sacramentary under Charles the Great* (London 1915). It now appears to be less reliable and Wilson's edition has been replaced by that of Jean Deshusses, *Le sacramentaire grégorien*, Spicilegium Friburgense 16 (Fribourg 1971) which uses Cambrai 164 for the *Hadrianum* and Autun 19 for the Supplement. CLLA no. 740, p. 350.

2) *The Hadrianum with an Irregular Supplement.*
   Benedict's Supplement still remains outside the main body of the Sacramentary proper but has undergone certain modifications.
   Representative examples:

a) Rome, Bibliotheca Apostolica Vaticana, *codex Reginensis* 337; copied at Lyons in the first half of the IX century. The *Greg.* is a quality example of Benedict's corrected text; the Supplement has been considerably re-arranged and re-edited, making the prefaces and episcopal blessings almost unrecognizable. *Reg.* 337 was used by H.A. Wilson as his base MS for the *Hadrianum.* CLLA no. 730, pp. 343-344.

b) *Sacramentary of Chelles*: New York, Pierpoint Morgan Library, *codex G* 57; copied at St. Amand, ca. 860, and given to Chelles by Charles the Bald. It has the corrected version of the *Greg.* with the *Hucusque* and Supplement but the latter is considerably re-arranged and constitutes the point of departure for the entire series of great sacramentaries copied at St. Amand, each of which reveals interesting and serious divergences from the classic Supplement. In Chelles the prefaces are removed from the Suppl. and inserted in the masses of the sacramentary proper; such is also the case for the first *formulae* of the Suppl. relating to the vigils of Easter and Pentecost. Moreover, the Suppl. is completed by the addition of Alcuin's popular votive masses and a few other texts. CLLA no. 760b, p. 356.

c) *Sacramentary of Mainz*: Mainz, Seminarbibliothek, *codex* 1; a deluxe MS copied towards the end of the IX century for St. Alban's Abbey, Mainz. The prefaces of the Suppl. are added to the masses of the sacramentary and the supplement is a creation of its own compiler. It has various new masses, e.g., of St. Alban, Sts. Sergius and Bacchus, All Saints; the episcopal benedictions of Aniane; prayers for a council; rites for the consecration of a church; Sunday masses from Aniane; a fresh series of requiem masses. CLLA no. 737, p. 346.

d) Florence, Biblioteca Medicea Laurenziana, *codex Aedili* 121; end of IX or even X century, probably in N. Italy. The *Greg.* is Aniane's corrected version but riddled with fresh errors. The prefaces of the Suppl. are incorporated into the sacramentary and into the Sunday masses. CLLA no. 755, pp. 354-355.

e) The Reichenau-St. Gall MSS. This is an easily recognizable group of MSS with three major representatives:

Sacramentary of Reichenau: Vienna, Öst. Nationalbibliothek, *codex lat.* 1815; copied at Reichenau ca. the mid-IX century. Several major items from Benedict's Suppl. were added to a very fine copy of the *Hadrianum.*

Sacramentary of Constance: Donaueschingen, Hofbibliothek, *codex* 191; a splendid MS copied in the third quarter of the IX century. Both its text and Supplement are very much like Vienna 1815, but the Sunday masses are added in a later hand. CLLA no. 738, p. 346.

Sacramentary of St. Gall: Oxford, Bodleian Library *MS Auct.* D.I. 20; copied at St. Gall in the second half of the IX century. Text of the *Hadrianum* much like the above two MSS. It was later adapted to the use of Mainz by adding the episcopal blessings, a calendar of St. Alban's Abbey and the *Exultet.* At the end of the sacramentary, there are copious extracts from the Supplement, especially the series of Sunday masses. CLLA no. 735, p. 345.

As can be seen from an inspection of the above list of MSS, there was nothing sacrosanct about the Supplement compiled by Benedict of Aniane. By actual count very few MSS preserved it intact. Editors seemed to understand well the permissive character of the *Huc-usque*.

3) *The Hadrianum and the Supplement Fused into a Single Book.*
In such cases Benedict's Supplement no longer appears as a kind of Book II; now its various sections are broken up and distributed into the sacramentary proper at the appropriate places. Sometimes the Supplement is incorporated wholesale, sometimes only portions of it appear in the body of the *Hadrianum* while others remain in a kind of appendix.[233]

Whatever form the *Hadrianum* with its numerous supplements may have taken, it did not at once supplant the Frankish Gelasians, Old Gelasians like *Vat. Reg.* 316, or even type-II Gregorians like the Sacramentary of Padua. Useful, valuable and especially sumptuous *codices* were not lightly or easily replaced despite the high authority of the 'Sacramentary of Charles the Great'. Nevertheless, its influence continued to be felt more and more and a progressive 'Hadrianization' can be discerned in the Frankish Gelasians of the IX century.[234]

Liturgical unification depended entirely upon a few famous *scriptoria* and their patrons and was never accomplished in a uniform manner. The full repercussion of the *Hadrianum* north of the Alps was to be a long time in coming and more or less archaic books would continue to be used (and even copied) because of the presence and prestige of older liturgical *codices*[235]. As can be seen from the MSS presented above, there was no religious authority capable, or even desirous, of imposing uniformity. A perfect example of how liturgical adaptation actually took place is the celebrated *scriptorium* of St. Amand Abbey, Flanders, and its successive editions of the *Hadrianum* which King Charles the Bald (840-877) used to reward prominent bishops and abbots of N. France.[236]

3. *The Sacramentary of Padua* (Padua, Biblioteca capitolare, *codex* D. 47).[237]

The *Paduensis* has two distinct parts:
a) Folios 11ʳ-100ʳ, which contain the sacramentary proper, were copied in a *scriptorium* of the Emperor Lothair (840-855) located either in N. France, Belgium or N. Italy[238]. Although it may have

originated in the Tyrol (Sept. 22: St. Maurice and his Companions), later marginal notes indicate that it was used in the diocese of Liège (Sts. Quentin and Foillan) and later migrated to Verona between 900 and 950, thanks to Bishop Iduin or Bishop Rathier, formerly of Liège. The primitive nucleus of the sacramentary seems to be contained in folios 11-100 and has the formularies for the saints intermingled with those of the Sundays.

b) Folios 1-10^v contain a variety of pontifical materials in a later hand and folios 136-162 present various IX-century additions and even complementary material added at Verona in the X century.[239]

CONTENTS OF THE SACRAMENTARY PROPER.

Part I: Sections I-CCIII (= *Hadrianum* 5-193)[240]

[No title]

1-10. Vigil and masses of Christmas, Stephen, John, Holy Innocents, Sylvester, Octave of Christmas, Sun. after Christmas.

11-24. Vigil and feast of Epiphany, I Sun. after Epiph., Felix, II Sun. after Epiph., Marcellus, Prisca, Fabian and Sebastian, Agnes, Vincent, III Sun. after Epiph., Agnes 2°, IV Sun. after Epiph.

25-28. *Ypapanthi* [with *collecta*][241], Agatha, V Sun. after Epiph., Valentine.

29-35. Septuagesima, Sexagesima, Quinquagesima, Ash Wed. and Fri. [no Thurs. or Sat. mass].

34-40. I week of Lent with Spring Ember Days.

41-61. II, III, and IV weeks of Lent [including *all* weekdays].[242]

62-67. V Week of Lent [no Sat. mass].[243]

68-73. [Holy Week]: Palm Sun., Mon.-Wed., *Caena Domini*, [no blessing of chrism], Good Fri. prayers.

74-84. Holy Sat.: Final exorcism and renunciation of Satan; Easter Vigil: 4 lessons [no blessing of font], Vigil Mass; Easter Sun. and Octave, Sun. *post albas*, Paschal prayers, *Pascha annotina*.

85-91. Annunciation and Passion [without *collecta*], I Sun. after the octave of Easter, Tiburtius, Valerian and Maximus, II Sun. after Easter, *Laetania maior*,[244] Vitalis, III Sun. after Easter.

92-99. Philip and James, Alexander, Eventius and Theodolus, Finding of the Cross*,[245] IV Sun. after Easter, John *ante portam latinam*, Gordian, Pancras, Mary *ad martyres* [Dedication: May 13, 609].[246]

100-110. Ascension, Sun. after Ascension, Urban, Vigil of Pentecost, Pentecost Sun. and Octave [no Thurs. Mass] with the Ember Days, Sun. of the Octave of Pent. (= Sun.).

111-129. Nicomedes, Marcellinus and Peter, II Sun. after Pent., III Sun. after Pent., Mark and Marcellinus, Protase and Gervase, IV Sun. after Pent., Vigil and feast of John the Baptist, John and Paul, V Sun. after Pent., Vigil and feast of Peter and Paul, Processus and Matinian, I week after Apostles, Octave of Apostles, Seven Brothers.

130-135. I Sun. after octave of the Apostles, II Sun., III Sun., Felix, Simplicius, Faustinus and Beatrice, Abdon and Sennen, IV Sun. after the Apostles.

136-157. Stephen, Xystus, Felicissimus and Agapitus, V Sun. after the Apostles, Cyriacus, Vigil and feast of Lawrence, Tiburtius, Hippolytus, I Sun. after Lawrence, Eusebius, Assumption [no vigil or *collecta*], Agapitus, II Sun. after Lawrence, Timothy, III Sun. after Lawrence, Hermes, Sabina, Passion of John the Baptist*, Felix and Adauctus, IV Sun. after Lawrence.

158-164. Nativity of Mary [without *collecta*], Protus and Hyacinth, V Sun. after Lawrence, Cornelius and Cyprian, *Ad crucem salutandam in Sancto Petro* (=one prayer), [247]Nicomedes, Euphemia, Maurice and Companions.*

165-172. Ember Days of Sept: Sun., Wed., Fri., Sat. and Sun;[248] Cosmas and Damian, Dedication of St. Michael, I Sun. after Michael.

173-178. Mark, II Sun. after Michael, Callistus, III, IV, V Sundays after Michael.

179-194. Caesarius[249], VI Sun. after Michael, Four Crowned Martyrs, Theodore, Mennas, Martin of Tours,[250] VII Sun., VIII Sun. after Michael, Cecelia, Clement, Felicity, Chrysogonus, IX Sun. after Michael, Saturninus, Vigil and feast of Andrew.

195-203. Advent: I Sun., II Sun., Lucy, III Sun. and Ember days, IV Sun., additional prayers for Advent.[251]

Part II: Sections CCIV–CCXIX.

204-210. *Commune sanctorum.*

211-217. Seven *missae cottidianae* [252]and the *Canon missae.*

218. Morning and Evening prayers for the Daily Office [*Had.* 203-204].

219. *Orationes pro peccatis* [*Had.* 201].

The Roman prototype of the *Paduensis* was executed at Rome for the use of St. Peter's basilica sometime between 650, more or less, and 680;[253] some interesting evidence even seems to point to 663, the year of the famous state visit to Rome of the Emperor Constans II. [254] It is referred to as a Gregorian sacramentary, type II, because it is now considered to be an adaptation of the Lateran sacramentary (= type I) of the mid-VII century for presbyteral use at the Vatican. It omits many of the pontifical items found in the *Hadrianum*—baptisms and ordinations—and adds other significant formularies to supply the growing pastoral needs of the famous Petrine shrine. It includes, for example, a *commune sanctorum*, a series of seven Sunday masses (with the Roman canon) and, *in loco proprio*, complete prayer texts for the 5 Sundays after Epiphany, the 5 after Easter, 5 after Pentecost, 6 after Peter and Paul (June 29), 5 after Lawrence (Aug 10), and 9 after Michael the Archangel (Sept 29). The *formulae* for these Sundays were 'borrowed' from the presbyteral sacramentary used in the Roman *tituli* (the Old Gelasian) and generally follow exactly the same order as they appear in *Reg.* 316. [255]

Various festivals help us date the Roman ancestor of the *Paduensis*. By around 680 the *Gregorianum* had acquired 77 feasts of the saints and such festivals are common to the *Pad., Had.* and Trent. Between 682 and 687 two more were added: the dedication feasts of St. George the Martyr *in Velabro* (Apr. 23, 683)[256] and of St. Peter-in-Chains (Aug. 1) and both appear in Trent and *Had.* but not in *Pad.* That means that the ancestor of the *Paduense* must have gone its separate way before 683 at the latest. In 688 Sergius I carried out a solemn translation of the remains of Pope Leo I (†461) and deposited them in a highly decorated shrine in the S. transept of St. Peter's basilica.[257] Since it is not recorded in the *Paduense* we have further proof of a prior separation. Significantly, too, the *Paduense* does not contain a vigil for the feast of the Assumption or the new mass of the Assumption composed by Sergius I (687-701). It does have the feast of the Presentation (*Ypapanthi,* Feb 2) with its preliminary *collecta*—whose text is identical in *Pad.*, Trent, and *Had.*— which had been introduced as early as Theodore (642-649). Reports from Rome must have forced the introduction into the Paduan tradition of two other late feasts—the Annunciation (March 25) and the Nativity of the Virgin (Sept 8), both instituted by Sergius I—but their texts are not those contained in the *Hadrianum.* This is also true of the Sacramentary of Trent which apparently acquired these feasts so late that it used for its texts the masses from the Frankish Gelasians. Moreover, even though both *Pad.* and Trent have the 'Marian' feasts of March 25, Aug 15 and Sept 8, they do not have any indication of the *collecta* at St. Hadrian-in-the-Forum and the procession to St. Mary Major which were arranged by Sergius I[258] and which appear in the *Hadrianum* (31, 148-149, 155-156). Finally, the singing of the *Agnus Dei* during the fraction after the *canon missae* is not yet indicated in the *Pad.*; it too was instituted by Sergius I.[259]

From these smatterings of evidence we can conclude that the prototype of our MS was completed before the reign of Leo II (682-683). Had it remained in Rome, it is inconceivable that it would not have been brought up to date by the addition of the new celebrations established during the last two decades of the VII century.[260]

Our suggested chronology is not affected by the fact that the *Paduense* has masses for the Thursdays of Lent. Although the Thursday celebrations were instituted by Gregory II (715-731), the *formulae* in the *Paduense* are not the same as those of the *Hadrianum* which undoubtedly contains the papal texts. Some Frankish scribe, knowing of the institution but not having the texts before him, worked up fresh *formulae* from older materials. His clumsiness and ignorance of actual conditions in the City are only too apparent.[261]

Something like a century and a half separates the Roman prototype of the *Paduense* from the Lotharingian *scriptorium* in which it was copied. It is impossible for us to ascertain either the time or the place of the intervening transcriptions during which non-Roman or more recent Roman additions of the VIII century could have penetrated the MS tradition. Nevertheless, in its peregrinations outside the City it absorbed the feast of the Martyrs of Agaunum, St. Maurice and his Companions (Sept 22; *Pad.* CLXIIII, 672-675), the *Inventio Sanctae Crucis* (May 3; *Pad.* XCIIII, 421-423) and the feast of the Passion of John the Baptist (Aug 29; *Pad.* CLV, 643-645).

As in the case of the Old Gelasian, we are completely ignorant of whatever Frankish pilgrim may have introduced the 'Sacramentary of St. Peter's' north of the Alps. He was perhaps an anonymous admirer of the Roman liturgy captivated by what he had experienced at St. Peter's basilica on the Vatican.[262]

Some scholars think they can penetrate behind the *Paduense* and its VIII-century intermediaries and attain the Roman *original* by analyzing the 'Sundays after Pentecost' and the feasts to which they are related, i.e.:

5 Sundays after Pentecost,
6 Sundays after Peter and Paul (June 29),
5 Sundays after Lawrence (Aug 10),
9 Sundays after Michael the Archangel (Sept 29).[263]

Such an arrangement of Sundays corresponds with, and only with, a year in which Easter falls on April 3 and Pentecost on May 22. Such a liturgical year ocurred several times in the course of the VI-VII century—under Symmachus in 511, Hormisdas in 516 and 522, Gregory I in 595; under Sabinian in 606, Deusdedit in 617, Agatho in 679 and under Sergius I in 690—but the first two dates should probably be eliminated as too early while those of Agatho and, especially, Sergius are too late. That leaves 595, 606 and 617 as the years when such a system of counting the Sundays after Pentecost may have been worked out. Although the type-I Gregorian was not assembled until the pontificate of Honorius I (625-638) and, consequently, the Sacramentary of St. Peter's only some time later, the *system* could have been incorporated into the latter mass book around the mid-century date we keep encountering.

The IX-century copyist did not have the Roman archetype before his eyes but transcribed the *Sacramentary of Padua* from one of the several intermediaries which had come into existence between his time and the latter half of the VII century. We must never forget that the *Paduense* is not a pure copy of the original but the form which the VII-century sacramentary came to have in the course of a century and a half after it left the City. If we want to restore the primitive shape of the Gregorian Sacramentary, we shall have to make the most careful comparison of the two surviving examples of Type I (*Tridentinum* and *Hadrianum*) and our prime example of Type II (*Paduense*).

Like *Vat. Reg.* 316, Padua D. 47 is an *unicum;* the only one of its kind. Nevertheless, there are a few surviving fragments of MSS of the same type:[264]

1. The fragments of the Palimpsest *Sacramentary of Salzburg:* Salzburg, Universitätsbibliothek (Studienbibliothek), *Codex* M. II. 296 (*olim codex* V I H 162); + Munich, Clm 15815[a] (*olim* 15815); + Vienna, Nationalbibliothek, *Codex Vindobonensis, Series nova* 4225. Edited by A. Dold–K. Gamber, *Das Sakramentar von Salzburg. Seinem Typus nach auf Grund der erhaltenen Fragmente rekonstruiert,* TuA 4 (Beuron 1960); first quarter of the IX century; Alpine regions of Austria-Bavaria. CLLA 883, p. 400.

2. The fragmentary *Sacramentary of Reichenau:* Karlsruhe, Landesbibliothek, *Fragment. Augien.* 23; early IX century; Abbey of Reichenau. CLLA 885. pp. 401-402.

3. The fragmentary Glagolitic *Sacramentary of Kiev:* Kiev Library of the Ukrainian Academy of Science (*olim.* Library of the Ecclesiastical Academy of Kiev), no. 42; Pannonia and later, Jerusalem. CLLA 895, pp. 405-406.

4. The fragments of the Palimpsest *Missal of Monte Cassino:* Monte Cassino, Abbey Library, *codex* 271 (*olim* 348); ed. A. Dold, *Vom Sakramentar, Comes und Capitulare zum Missale,* TuA 34 (Beuron 1943); ca. 700 (Wilmart and Deshusses), ca. 760-770 (Mohlberg), ca. 700 (Bischoff), N. Italy, probably Ravenna. CLLA 701, pp. 330-331.

These texts are also coroborated, of course, by the Sacramentary of Flavigny (ca. 760-770) in its many distinguished descendants, the Frankish Gelasians of the VIII century.

4. The Sacramentary of Trent (Salzburg).

Trent, Museo Nazionale (Castel del Buonconsiglio), no number (*olim Codex vindobonensis 700*). CLLA 724, pp. 340-341.[265]

This important sacramentary was executed for some monastery in the Tyrol, in the diocese of Sabiona (Sebana, Säben) which belonged to the ecclesiastical province of Salzburg. It may have been copied as early as 825-830 from an exemplar at Salzburg itself since, among its votive masses it contains one in honor of St. Rupert, the patron of Salzburg cathedral.[266] From 785-821 the bishop (archbishop after 798) of Salzburg was the famous Arno, sometime monk and abbot of St. Amand, the close friend and collaborator of both Abbot Alcuin of Tours and Abbot Benedict of Aniane. It is these latter two abbots who let us grasp how a pre-Hadrianic sacramentary (type-I Gregorian) could have been used at Salzburg as the base MS of a freshly composed mass book for this distinguished metropolitan see. Without Arno's connection with Alcuin and Benedict of Aniane, both the use of a papal sacramentary other than the *Hadrianum* and the presence of Benedict's corrected version of the *Hadrianum* in the Sacramentary of Trent are quite unintelligible.

CONTENTS OF THE SACRAMENTARY OF TRENT (Salzburg).

Title: INCIPIUNT CAPITULA. HOC SACRAMENTORIUM DE CIRCULO
    ANNI EXPOSIUM A SANCTO GREGORIO PAPA.   fol. 1[r]
    A table of contents of all the sections in Part I.
Title: IN NOMINE DOMINI.   fol. 8[r]
    HOC SACRAMENTORIUM DE CIRCULO ANNI EXPOSITUM,
    A SANCTO GREGORIO PAPA ROMANO EDITUM,
    EX AUTHENTICO LIBRO BIBLIOTHECAE CUBICULI SCRIPTUM.
    This is the title of the best copies of the *Hadrianum* although, as it turns out, Trent is not a copy of the *Had.* but of a VII-century MS.
    1. *Qualiter missa romana caelebratur.*   fol. 8[r]-20[r]
    In its initial supplement to the sacramentary proper, Trent maintains the *Ordo missae* (as in *Had.* 1) but incorporates into it the *Orationes cottidianae* (*Had.* 202) and a small number of secrets and postcommunions at the appropriate points. The ordination prayers for bishops, presbyters and deacons, however, (*Had.* 2-4) do not appear here but in the first supplement to the body of the sacamentary (cf. no. 4e below).
    2. Three blank pages intervene between the *Ordo missae* and the sacramentary proper. They signal the adventitious character of the *ordo* and indicate even better than the *Had.* that the primitive sacramentary began with the following title:
    3. Title: IN NOMINE DOMINI.   fol. 21[v]
    VIII KALENDAS IANUARII, ID EST DIE XXIIII MENSE
    DECEMBRIS IN VIGILIA DOMINI...DE ADVENTU.
The sacramentary continues without interruption to the top of fol. 141[r], i.e., from the Vigil of Christmas until the end of Advent (cf. *Had.* 5-193; *Pad.* 1-203), and also contains the material of the first supplement which follows.

4. *Supplement to the Sacramentary* (cf. *Had.* 194-226):
   a. *Commune sanctorum.*
   b. *Orationes pro peccatis (Had.* 201).
   c. *Orationes matutinales et vespertinales (Had.* 203-204).
   d. Miscellaneous prayers.
   e. Ordinations and anniversary masses (*Had.* 2-4 and 198-199).
5. *Second Supplement to the Sacramentary*:
Title: *INCIPIUNT CAPITULA SEQUENTI (sic) OPERIS.*   fol. 141ʳ, bottom
a. *Incipiunt missas Dominica prima post Theophaniam* ... The masses for the Sundays after Epiphany, Easter and Pentecost. As a whole they resemble the masses contained in the Supplement of Benedict of Aniane but they are drawn more directly from the Frankish Gelasians and do not have Benedict's corrections.
b. Two daily masses.
c. Masses *de communi* supplementing those contained in the *Commune sanctorum* of the first Supplement (4a, above).
d. Votive masses drawn both from the Frankish Gelasians. and from Alcuin's votive masses.
e. Ten requiem masses, 7 from Frankish Gelasian sources and at least one from Alcuin.
f. Seventy prefaces drawn mostly from the Frankish Gelasians. but also without the corrections and transformations of Benedict of Aniane.
g. A Martyrology. This is an abridged version of one contained in the *Sacramentary of Gellone* (ed. Dumas, 3038-3050).

A critical examination of the *Tridentinum* throws much fresh light on the nature and shape of the Gregorian sacramentary in the various stages of its development:
1) The base text of the sacramentary proper derives from a late VII-century Lateran sacramentary as it appeared shortly after 680 and before the liturgical innovations of Sergius I (687-701). If the Sacramentary of St. Peter's (cf. *Pad. D.* 47) was adapted from the papal mass book ca. 670-680, the ancestor of Salzburg-Trent must have left Rome shortly thereafter, ca. 685. It already has two new dedication feasts not represented in *Pad.*, George the Martyr (Apr. 23, 683) and St. Peter in Chains (Aug. 1) which were instituted by Leo II (682-683) but it does not yet contain the masses for Leo I (*Had.* 127) or Gregory I (*Had.* 30), the new feasts of the Annunciation (March 25) and the Nativity of Mary (Sept. 8), the fresh mass *formulae* composed for the older *Natale* or *Sollemnia S. Mariae* (Aug. 15) under the new title of *Pausatio, Dormitio* or *Adsumptio*, the processions from St. Hadrian-in-the-Forum to St. Mary Major on the above feasts, nor

the *Agnus Dei* chant at mass (cf. *Had*. 1, 20). Since all the latter items were instituted by Sergius I, our evidence reveals that Trent represents the state of the pre-Hadrianic sacramentary just before the pontificate of Sergius. A comparison/contrast of Trent and Padua permits us to see that core of common materials contained in the VII-century *Gregorian* just before the further evolution of its contents as they existed in the mass-book sent to Charlemagne by Hadrian I.

2) This VII-century core was much tampered with and improved upon in the IX century in the light of the Frankish Gelasians, the *Hadrianum* itself and the Supplement of Benedict of Aniane and the votive masses of Alcuin.[267] The redactor of Salzburg-Trent obviously knew and used the work of his abbot-friends but creatively shaped the materials he employed around the inner core of the pre-Hadrianic Gregorian he preferred even to the authorized *Hadrianum*.

Except for minor omissions of later liturgical developments and a certain amount of rehandling, the body of the sacramentary coincides largely, of course, with *Pad*. and *Had*.. Rather it is the first supplement to the sacramentary (cf. *Had*. 194-226) which has been considerably reworked and augmented. Trent, for example, removes section 202 of the original supplement, the *Orationes cottidianae*—a collection of collects to be used *ad libitum* on Ordinary Sundays throughout the year—and inserts it into the *Ordo missae* at the beginning of the MS.

The main innovations, however, are in the second supplement. It is clearly entitled: *In capitula sequenti (sic) operis* and opens with an organized series of Sunday masses: *Incipiunt missas Dominica prima post Theophaniam* and continues with mass-sets for the Sundays after Easter and Pentecost.

In other words, as regards the Ordinary Sundays, Trent maintains both the oldest and simplest ways of providing for them—a list of 59 undifferentiated collects to be used *ad libitum*—and inserts this list in its *Ordo missae* rather than in an appendix, *and* it presents a full complement of worked-out masses for the seasons of Epiphany, Easter and Pentecost. Unlike *Casinensis* 271 and *Padua* D. 47, however, Trent does not attempt to insert the mass *formulae* in the fixed sanctoral cycle but adds them in a supplement in the manner of Benedict of Aniane.

The second supplement also reveals the redactor's dependence on both the Frankish Gelasians and on the fresh compositions of his friend Alcuin of Tours.

3) When the *Tridentinum* was copied from its Salzburg model, it was also considerably corrected on the basis of Aniane's Gregorian, only some 15 years after it had appeared.

Where did Arno of Salzburg obtain his more primitive Gregorian and why did he think it so authoritative? The answer probably lies in the direction of Tours. Not only did Arno use Alcuin's votive masses in profusion but we have direct evidence that Alcuin also composed the special votive mass in honor of St. Rupert, the patron saint of Salzburg cathedral. Moreover, as the confusing but revealing sacramentaries of Tours (Paris, Bibliothèque Nationale, *nouv. acq. lat.* 1589 and Tours, Bibliothèque Municipale, *codex* 184) are submitted to closer and closer analysis, we see that Alcuin himself must have worked from a pre-Hadrianic MS before he obtained the *Hadrianum* and that it was this MS that was presumably copied and forwarded to his two influential friends, Arno of Salzburg and Benedict of Aniane.

As we saw in reading the *Hucusque*, Benedict was suspicious of several masses present in the *Hadrianum* and marked them with an *obelus* for his readers. How could he have done so without the assistance of some earlier witness to the authentic Gregorian (as he conceived it)?

The fact of the matter is that there probably were two authentic Gregorian MSS available to the three reformers in question. Somehow Alcuin of Tours had in his possession two papal sacramentaries representing two stages in the development of the Lateran liturgy. One was the *Hadrianum*, an up-to-date version of the VIII century, the other, a pre-Sergius I version of the same book. Where Alcuin could have obtained a copy of the latter is perhaps not so mysterious. All his life he remained in close contact with his homeland and particularly with York, his native city. Perhaps when he sent for his books in 797 there was among them an old-fashioned, i.e., a pre-Hadrianic sacramentary, from which he worked and drew his inspiration.[268]

When the Sacramentary of Trent is finally published and the two Sacramentaries of Tours disentangled, we should be able to decipher this story more perfectly. In the meantime we are able to draw the following conclusions:

1) Alcuin used both a pre-Hadrianic sacramentary and the *Hadrianum* to compose his famous Missal for the abbey of St. Martin of Tours and this Missal was later adopted/adapted for the cathedral of St. Maurice of Tours.[269] In performing this great task, Alcuin employed not only the recently arrived *Hadrianum* but the *Hadrianum* as it had been corrected and supplemented by Benedict of Aniane.

2) Alcuin probably sent both Arno of Salzburg and Benedict of Aniane copies of his 'English Sacramentary' and they worked—as the evidence shows—from this pre-Hadrianic sacramentary, from the

Hadrianum and from the current Frankish Gelasians, themselves so dependent on the Sacramentary of St. Peter's Basilica (type-II Gregorian). The result was a remarkable assimilation and fusion of Roman and papal materials in a variety of Carolingian books which were destined to transmit to the rest of the Middle Ages the heritage of this Romano-Germanic combination.

F. THE MIXED- OR GELASIANIZED-GREGORIANS OF THE X AND XI CENTURIES (Bourque).

In the X century there appeared a new class of sacramentaries which retained the major part of the *Hadrianum* supplemented by Benedict of Aniane and yet constituted a distinct type of 'fused' *Hadriana*.[270]

The somewhat equivocal term 'Gelazianized-Gregorians' or 'Gelasiano-Gregorians' will serve to characterize this family of MSS if we understand it in the following way:

a) the term 'Gregorian' designates the *Hadrianum* with Benedict's Supplement and not the type-II Gregorian typified by the *Paduensis*;

b) the adjectival 'Gelasiano' refers to the Frankish Gelasians of the late VIII century and not the Old Gelasian Sacramentary as typified by *Vat. Reg.* 316.

These Gelasiano-Gregorians must not be confused with the Frankish Gelasians (the descendants of the Sacramentary of Flavigny, ca. 760-770) which are also, in a sense, Gelasianized-Gregorians because the compilers used a type-II Gregorian like the *Paduense* and an Old Gelasian like *Vat. Reg.* 316 to create their new, enlarged and very 'Roman' mass book.[271] Nevertheless, these two kinds of sacramentaries are separated by a great divide.

These relationships may be diagrammed as follows:

The Frankish Gelasians of the VIII century	=	Gregorian type II + Old Gelasian
The Gelasiano-Gregorians of the X century	=	*Hadrianum* + Supplement + Frankish Gelasian materials

The latter books are large and crammed with liturgical materials of all kinds because of a kind of "compiling mania" (Bourque) which compelled the scribes to assemble as many documents as possible, even if there is no discernible logic or method involved. This mania appeared already in the IX and lasted until the XII century.[272]

The sub-groups within this family of MSS can be best distinguished by comparing them with the XIII-century Missal of the Roman Curia and with their ultimate *terminus*, the *Missale Romanum* of 1570.[273] These classifications are only provisional, however, and will be revised as the MSS become better analyzed and described.

1) Direct Types

There are MSS which conduct us directly from the *Hadrianum* + Supplement of the early IX century to the Missal of the Roman Curia of the XIII century. Representative types:

a) *Sacramentary of St. Vaast of Arras* in 2 volumes: Cambrai, Bibliothèque municipale, *codices* 162 and 163 (*olim* Cathedral 158), St. Vaast, second half of the IX century. There are many additions from the Frankish Gel. and the last part of the Sacramentary is re-arranged and combined with different parts of the Supplement and with the votive masses of Alcuin.[274]

b) The *Canterbury Missal*: Cambridge, Corpus Christi College, *codex* 260; X-XI century, St. Augustine's Abbey, Canterbury.[275]

c) The *Lateran Missal*: Rome, Archivio Lateranense, *codex* 65; XI-XII century; the Lateran.[276]

2. 'Exuberant' Types.

In accordance with the classification adopted, the following MSS are those containing *formulae* which do not appear in the *Missale Romanum*. These *codices* maintain the tradition of the 'fused' Gregorian but augment it with notable additions. Representative types:

a) *Sacramentarium Rossianum*: Rome, Cod. Vat. Ross. lat. 204; XI century, Abbey of Niederaltaich.[277]

b) *Sacramentary of Noyon*: Rheims, Bibliothèque municipale, *codex* 213; ca. 870-880.[278]

3. Eccentric Types.

This family of MSS has no direct connection with the *Missale Romanum* and left no direct descendants. Representative types:

a) *Sacramentary of Echternach*: Paris, Bibliothèque Nationale, *codex lat.* 9433; late IX century, Abbey of Echternach.[279]

b) *Sacramentary of Fulda*: Göttingen, Universitätsbibliothek, *codex theol.* 231; ca. 975, Abbey of Fulda.[280]

c) *Sacramentary of St. Eligius* (Eloi): Paris, Bibl. Nat., *codex lat.* 12051; second half of the IX century, St. Eloi of Corbie.[281]

In the second half of the X century, under the Ottos of Germany, the same thing happened to the sacramentary as happened to the Romano-Germanic Pontifical. The mixed Gregorians produced in France and Germany were carried to Rome and became *the* Roman mass book. This fact, which is so important for the history of Christian worship, can be deduced from the following pieces of evidence:

a) On April 22, 998, Gregory V (966-999) demanded that every year the *scriptorium* of Reichenau copy a *codex sacramentorum* for the use of the pope.[282] This obligation lasted for at least a century; Cardinal Deusdedit (1086-1087) discovered the papal decree inserted *in Missali Lateranensis palatii*.[283]

b) The *Vetus missale Lateranense* of Azevedo (XI-XII century), the Missal of the Papal Curia of the XIII century, and the Sacramentary of St. Peter's F. 15 (XII century) all belong to the family of Gelasiano-Gregorian sacramentaries.[284]

c) Burchard of Worms, *Decretum* (ca. 1012) III, 69; PL 140, 687-688, confirmed the false decretal on the proper prefaces, used only at Rome, by citing two that appear only in Gelasiano-Gregorian MSS.

As is well known, the new religious orders, especially the Franciscans, spread the Gelasiano-Gregorian—which had by then become the Missal of the Papal Chapel—across the whole face of Latin Christendom.[285]

The very proliferation of Gel.-Greg. *codices* must not let us forget the main evolution of the sacramentary; it was the *Hadrianum* supplemented by Benedict of Aniane which constituted the core of the Gelasiano-Gregorians and survived in the *Missale Romanum*. The Roman Missal was not, therefore, a direct prolongation of the Paduan-type book or of the Frankish Gelasian but of the *Hadrianum* as it was revised by Benedict of Aniane. The masses of the Thursdays of Lent and 45 out of 46 masses between Septuagesima and Wednesday of Holy Week come from the *Hadrianum* rather than from the Paduan or type-II Gregorian. Even beyond the Lenten Thursdays, the *Paduense* and the *Hadrianum* are by no means identical: they diverge in 26 instances. Ten Prayers of the *Paduense* are different from those in the *Hadrianum*. Eight of these prayers passed into the Frankish Gelasians but none of them survived in the Roman Missal.

Nine sanctoral feasts have different *formulae* in the *Hadrianum* than in the Frankish Gelasians: Octave of Christmas (Jan 1), Agnes (Jan 21), Gregory (Mar 12), Annunciation (Mar 25), George (Apr 23), Gervase and Protase (June 19), Exaltation of the Cross, *secreta* (Sept 14), Clement (Nov 23), Chrysogonus (Nov 24). None of the prayers from any of these nine feasts was received into the *Missale Romanum*; all were drawn from the *Hadrianum*.[286]

Even the many contributions which did survive form the Frankish Gelasians and played an important part in the Roman Missal, e.g., the Sundays after Epiphany, Easter, and Pentecost, did not enter it directly but came through the intermediary of the Supplement of St. Benedict of Aniane.

G. FROM THE SACRAMENTARY TO THE PLENARY MISSAL.

Although no date as such can mark a rigid divide, the era of the sacramentaries came to an end at the beginning of the XII century. Even by the end of the IX century, the *Liber sacramentorum* was giving way before the *Missalis plenarius*, a new kind of volume made up of four previous types of liturgical books: sacramentary, epistolary, evangelary and antiphonary.[287] By the second half of the IX century, the plenary missals were already beginning to be more numerous than the sacramentaries. In the first half of the XII century, the sacramentaries were a small minority, in the XIII they were exceptional and in the XIV, they were archaic leftovers.[288]

Why did the plenary missal come to replace the sacramentary? It was not only because celebrants found them easier to use, with all that was needed in one volume,[289] nor simply because of the multiplication of private masses.[290] It seems that the substitution is due more to the new obligation, at the end of the XI century, which demanded that the celebrant now recite to himself the sung parts of the mass even when they were duly executed by their proper ministers or by the choir.[291]

The plenary missal is therefore the result of a new way of regarding the mass. The eucharistic celebration ceases to be an *actio liturgica* in which the celebrant, ministers, singers and people collaborate and have distinctive and cooperative roles to play. As a result, the priest-celebrant, as the sole *actor* in this liturgical process, will be provided henceforth with a new kind of book.

From a technical point of view, the *Missalis plenarius* results from two operations which do not appear simultaneously or everywhere at once.

1) Reorganization of the Sacramentary for Practical Reasons.

Masses which had figured in the pontifical are put in the sacramentary; they are usually placed at the beginning of the second section of votive masses (*Missae votivae ad diversa*). The same is true for some other ceremonies and blessings: blessing of candles, ashes, palms.

The various *ordines* for Holy Week are inserted *in loco proprio* in the sacramentary (rites and rubrics).

On the other hand, the *benedictiones episcopales* and the prayers for the Liturgy of the Hours are removed and become distinct booklets: *Benedictionale, Collectarium, Orationale or Liber capitularis.*

Despite many previous attempts to fuse the *temporale* and *sanctorale*, (e.g., the *Paduense* and the Frankish Gelasians) the feasts of the saints are now carefully separated from the temporal cycle[292]—as had been the case in the *Hadrianum*. This was usually done in one of two ways: a separate *temporale* and *sanctorale* preceded by the *Canon missae* or a *temporale* separated by a *Canon missae* from the *sanctorale*.[293]

2) Addition of Other Books to the Sacramentary.

Four books were fused together to create the plenary missal: sacramentary, epistolary, evangelary and antiphonary of the mass; or if one prefers, three books: sacramentary, lectionary (epistles and gospels) and antiphonary. Such a process did not take place all at once, i.e., with all the readings and chants *in extenso* at their proper places. Sometimes, in older sacramentaries, the *initia* or even the texts themselves *in extenso* were added in the margins; these are plenary missals improperly so called. Sometimes the readings *or* the chants alone were put in their proper places; these are *augmented sacramentaries*. Sometimes a lectionary or an antiphonary were bound up with a sacramentary; this is a *factitious* plenary missal.[294] Despite all these variations, the fact is that in the *Missale Romanum* (1570-1970), there survived the papal, stational sacramentary of the VIII century (*Hadrianum*) and the Supplement of Aniane.

APPENDIX I

THE SACRAMENTARIES OF THE NON-ROMAN, WESTERN RITES

Given the confines of this study, it is impossible to provide adequate treatment of the non-Roman, Western rites which prevailed in the Latin West—outside Rome and its suburbicarian dioceses—before the introduction and general dissemination of the Roman rite.

The following is a list of basic studies helpful for an understanding of these ancient liturgies. Their origins, structures and manner of celebration are still poorly understood and pose serious problems for the liturgical historian.

A. *STUDIES* (in Chronological Order).

J. Mabillon, *De liturgia gallicana libri tres* (Paris 1685) 1-96, PL 72, 99-448.

J. M. Neale-G. H. Forbes, *The Ancient Liturgies of the Gallican Church* (Burntisland 1855-1857; reprint New York 1970).

L. Duchesne, *Origines du culte chrétien* (5th ed. Paris 1925) 89-109, 158-170, 200-240, 334-346, 382-395, 428-439; ET *Christian Worship: Its Origin and Evolution* (5th ed. London 1925) 86-105, 151-160, 189-227, 316-327, 363-375, 407-418.

R. Buchwald, *De liturgica gallicana* (Breslau 1890).

L. Duchesne, "Sur l'origine de la liturgie gallicane," *Revue d'histoire et de littérature religieuse* 5 (1900) 31-47, which is a review of P. Cagin, *Paléographic Musicale* 5 (Solesmes 1896).

G. Mercati, "Sull 'origine della liturgia gallicana," *Antiche reliquie liturgiche*, SeT 17 (Rome 1902) 72-75.

H. Lietzmann, *Kleine Liturgische Texte*. 2: *Ordo missae romanus et gallicanus* (Bonn 1923).

H. Leclercq, "Liturgie gallicane," DACL 6 (1924) 473-596.

J. B. Thibaut, *L'ancienne liturgie gallicane. Son origine et sa formation en Provence aux V et VI siècles* (Paris 1929).

F. Cabrol, "Les origines de la liturgie gallicane," *Revue d'histoire ecclésiastique* 25 (1930) 951-962.

T. Klauser, "Die liturgischen Austauschbeziehungen," *Historisches Jahrbuch* 53 (1933) 169-189.

J. Quasten, "Oriental Influences in the Gallican Liturgy," *Traditio* 1 (1943) 55-78.

M. Righetti, *Storia liturgica* 1 (Milan 1950, 1964) 123-129.

E. Griffe, "Aux origines de la liturgie gallicane," *Bulletin de littérature ecclésiastique* 52 (1951) 17-43.

A. Baumstark, *Comparative Liturgy* (London 1958) 209-212.

W.S. Porter, *The Gallican Rite*, Studies in Eucharistic Faith and Practice 4 (London 1958).

K. Gamber, *Ordo antiquus gallicanus. Der gallikanische Messritus des 6 Jahrhunderts*, TPL 3 (Regensburg 1965).

J.M. Pinell, "Anàmnesis y Epìclesis en el Antiguo Rito Galicano," *Didaskalia* 4 (1974) 3-130.

M. Curran, *The Antiphonary of Bangor* (Dublin 1984).

B. *DOCUMENTS* (The principal Sacramentaries only).

1) Gaul and Germany.

See E. Bourque, *Étude sur les sacramentaires romains*, 2/2 (Rome 1958) 389-404; K. Gamber, *Sakramentartypen* (Beuron 1958) 20-30; E. Dekkers, *Clavis Patrum Latinorum* (2nd ed. Steenbrugge 1961) 434-438; K. Gamber, *Codices liturgici latini antiquiores*, 2 vols. Spicilegium Friburgensis Subsidia, 1 (2nd ed. Fribourg 1968) nos. 201-229, pp. 156-169.

Germanus of Paris, *Expositio antiquae liturgiae gallicanae*, ed. E.C. Ratcliff, HBS 98 (London 1971); older editions in PL 72, 83-98, and J. Quasten, *Opuscula et textus. Series liturgica* 3 (Münster/Westf. 1934).

The seven masses published by F. J. Mone (Karlsruhe, *codex Augiensis* CCLIII, VII century); ed. L.C. Mohlberg, *Missale gallicanum vetus* (Rome 1958) 61-91; cf. P. Radò, "Verfasser und Heimat der Mone-Messen," EL 42 (1928) 58-65; PL 138, 863-882.

Missale Gothicum (Rome, *Vat. Reg.* 317; VII-VIII century); ed. H.M. Bannister, *Missale gothicum*, HBS 52 and 54   (London 1917-1919); L.C. Mohlberg, *Missale gothicum* (Rome 1961); PL 72, 225-318.

Missale Bobbiense (Paris, Biblio. Nat., *codex lat.* 13246; VIII century); ed. E.A. Lowe, *The Bobbio Missal*, HBS 53, 58, 61 (London 1917-1924); PL 72, 351-574 (*Sacramentarium Gallicanum*).

Missale Francorum (Rome, *Vat. Reg. lat* 257; VIII century); ed. L.C. Mohlberg, *Missale Francorum* (Rome 1957); PL 72, 317-340.

Missale Gallicanum vetus (Rome, *Vat. Pal.* lat. 493; VIII century); ed. L.C. Mohlberg, *et al.*, *Missale Gallicanum vetus* (Rome 1958).

2) Celtic Sacramentaries.

See E. Bourque, *Étude*, 2/2, 405-416; K. Gamber, *Sakramentartypen*, 30-34; E. Dekkers, *Clavis*, 438-439;

The Stowe Missal (Dublin, Library of the Royal Irish Academy, *codex* D. II.3; late VIII century); ed. G.F. Warner, *The Stowe Missal*, HBS 31-32 (London 1906-1915).
The *Libelli missarum* of St. Gall (Stiftsbibliothek, *codex* 1395; VIII/IX century); ed. F.E. Warren, *The Liturgy and Ritual of the Celtic Church* (Oxford 1881) 175-189.

3) Mozarabic Sacramentaries.

See E. Bourque, *Étude*, 2/2, 417-423; Gamber, *Sakramentartypen*, 15, 19; CLLA nos. 301 and 303, pp. 196-197; Dekkers, *Clavis*, 439; DACL 12 (1935) 390-491.

Liber Mozarabicus sacramentorum (Toledo, Capitular Library, *codex* 35.3; X century); ed. M. Férotin, Monumenta Ecclesiae liturgica 6 (Paris 1912).
Liber ordinum (Madrid Bibl. de la Real Accad. de la Historia, *codex*, 56; X century); ed. M. Férotin, Monumenta Ecclesiae liturgica 6 (Paris 1904) 227-448. See also J. Janini *Liber ordinum sacerdotal*, Studia silensia 7 (Silos 1981).

4) Ambrosian/Milanese Sacramentaries.

See Bourque, *Étude*, 2/2, 424-436; Gamber, *Sakramentartypen*, 34-36; 120-123; CLLA, nos. 501-535, pp. 262-270; Dekkers, *Clavis*, 432-433; M. Righetti, *Storia liturgica* 3 (Genoa 1949) 508-615; DACL 1 (1907) 1373-1442; A. Paredi, "Messali Ambrosiani antichi," *Ambrosius* 35 (1959) 1-25.

Sacramentarium Triplex (Zürich, Zentralbibl., *codex* C. 43; XI century); ed. M. Gerbert, *Monumenta veteris liturgiae alemannicae*, 1 (St. Blaise 1777) 1-241, and by O. Heiming, LQF 49 (Münster/Westf. 1968).
Sacramentarium Bergomense (Bergamo, S. Alexandri in Columna, *codex* 242; X—XI century); ed. P. Cagin, *Codex Sacramentarium Bergomensis saeculi X*, Supplementum sive Auctuarium Solesmense 1 (Solesmes 1900) and by A. Paredi, *Sac. Bergom., manoscritto del-secolo IX*, Monumenta Bergomensia 6 (Bergamo 1962); on the latter edition see F. Combaluzier, SE 13 (1962) 62-66 and his *Sacramentaires de Bergame et d'Ariberto. Index des formules*, Instrumenta patristica 5 (Steenbrugge 1962).

Sacramentary of Biasca (Milan, Biblioteca Ambrosiana, *codex* A. 24 *bis inf.*; IX-X century); incomplete edition by A.M. Ceriani, *Monumenta sacra et profana* 8 (Milan 1890); more recent edition by O. Heiming, *Das ambrosianische Sakramentar von Biasca*, LQF 51 (Münster/Westf. 1969).
Sacramentary of Ariberto (Milan, Bibl. capit. D.3.2.; XI century); ed. A. Paredi, *Il sacramentario di Ariberto*, Miscellanea A. Bernareggi (Bergamo 1958).

5) Other Italian Sacramentaries.

For the sacramentaries of Benevento, see Gamber, CLLA, nos. 430-459, pp. 238-258 and for the sacramentaries of Aquileia, CLLA nos. 880-898, pp. 397-407; see also Dekkers, *Clavis* 433-434.

NOTES

131. For the nature of these exchanges and their implications for the history of worship, see T. Klauser, "Die liturgischen Austauschbeziehungen zwischen der römischen und der fränkischdeutschen Kirche vom 8. bis zum 11. Jhd.," *Historisches Jahrbuch* 53 (1933) 169-189; M. Andrieu, "La liturgie romaine en pays franc et les *Ordines romani*," *Les Ordines romani* 2 (Louvain 1948) xvii-xlix; C. Vogel, "Les échanges liturgiques entre Rome et les pays francs jusqu'à l'époque de Charlemagne," *Le Chiese nei regni dell'Europa occidentale*, Settimane di studio Centro italiano sull'alto medioevo 7 (Spoleto 1960) 185-295.

132. There is a fundamental distinction between a liturgical book compiled for use at the altar in carrying out the sacred functions and a didactic collections of liturgical documents. Thus, the *Sacramentarium triplex* (Zürich, Zentralbibliothek *codex* C. 43) is not a liturgical book in the strict sense (cf. bibliography on *Sacramentarium triplex* in K. Gamber, *Sakramentartypen*, 122-123); the same should be said for the didactic collections of *Ordines romani* (cf. Andrieu, *Les Ordines romani* 1 (1931) 476-485). As for the problems and rules for critical editions, see the introductions in the works of M. Andrieu, *Les Ordines romani* (Louvain 1931-51; reprint 1960-65) and *Le Pontifical romain au moyen-âge*, 4 vols. (Rome 1938-1941); T. Klauser, "Repertorium liturgicum und liturgischer Spezialkatalog," *Zentralblatt für Bibliothekwesen* 53 (1936) 2-16, "Grundsätzliches für die Herausgabe alter Sakramentartexte," JfL 6 (1926) 205-206, and *Das römische Capitulare evangeliorum 1: Typen*, LQF 28 (1935) 9-13, 56-58, 100-102, 139-140 (under the heading "Editionsgrundsätze", regarding the Mass-lectionaires of different categories); L.C. Mohlberg, "Grundsätzliches für die Herausgabe alter Sakramentar-Texte," *Archivum latinitatis medii aevi, Bulletin du Cange* 2 (Brussels 1925) 117-133, *Norme per le pubblicazioni di opere scientifiche*, RED, series minor subsidia 2 (Rome 1956), *Ziele und Aufgaben der liturgiegeschichtlichen Forschung*, LQF 13 (Münster 1919), and *Nochmals Ziele und*

Aufgaben für das Studium des christlichen Kultus (Rome 1957), a printing of what had been two articles, the first of which appeared in *Miscel'anea Belvederi*, "Amici delle Catacombe" 23 (1954-55) 109-115; and the second in *Mélanges M. Andrieu* (Strasbourg 1956) 339-349.

133. Thus, it is not the fact of having been composed by William Durandus of Mende that made the Pontifical known under his name a liturgical document in the strict sense, but instead, the fact that the book was effectively received for the celebration of worship.

134. It follows that in a critical edition of liturgical documents all the variants, interpolations or modifications given by the different MSS should be carefully indicated and recorded.

135. Thus scholars try to get back beyond the surviving MSS of the *Gregorianum* in order to attain the supposed Sacramentary of Gregory I; see K. Gamber, *Sakramentartypen*, 82-85. In the same way., A. Chavasse has attempted to describe a pre-Gelasian/pre-Gregorian sacramentary, not preserved among the MSS, which possibly lay behind the Old Gelasian (A. Chavasse, *Le Sacramentaire gélasien* [Tournai 1958] 682-).

136. L. Duchesne, *Early History of the Christian Church* 1, tr. C. Jenkins (4th ed. New York 1909-1924) ix.

137. A special section will be devoted to the problems posed by the *Ordines, infra* pages 135 f.

138. In seeking more scientific precision, it would be desirable to dispense with the traditional and somewhat arbitrary titles under which many major liturgical documents are known (such as 'Leonine', 'Gelasian', 'Gregorian', etc.) and use instead the established numbers of the appropriate MS *codex* or *codices*. But in practice—especially in the case of the 'Gregorians'—it would be impossible to eliminate these titles altogether.

In order to simplify the citation of liturgical documents, several systems of abbreviations have been proposed. None of these has been so successful as to impose itself in a definitive and universal manner. We cannot give them here in detail. Most of the time—and this is a weakness—the abbreviations reflect the systematic classifications proper to each author; classifications which are less and less agreed upon today. The principal systems of abbreviations for the liturgical documents can be found in the following works:

L.C. Mohlberg, *Norme per le pubblicazioni di opere scientifiche* (Rome 1956) 10-11;

A. Chavasse, *Le Sacramentaire gélasien* (Tournai 1958) xxxv-xxxix;

K. Gamber, *Sakramentartypen* (Beuron 1958) xv-xxii—includes a leaflet joined to the publication;

———, *Codices liturgici latini antiquiores* (Fribourg 1968) 14-16;

P. Siffrin, *Konkordantztabellen* 1: *Sacramentarium Veronense* (Rome 1958) insert; 2: *Liber sacramentorum Romanae Ecclesiae* (Rome 1959) xiii-xvi; 3: *Missale Gothicum* (Rome 1961) insert.

J. Deshusses-B. Darragon, *Concordances et tableaux pour l'étude des grands sacramentaires*, Spicilegii Friburgensis subsidia 9-14 (Fribourg 1982-83).

139. It would be impossible to list all the works regarding the sacramentaries; such a bibliography would require an entire volume. An introduction to this literature can be found in L. Delisle, "Mémoires sur d'anciens sacramentaires," *Mémoires de l'Académie des Inscriptions et Belles-Lettres* 32 (Paris 1886) 57-423; F. Probst, *Die ältesten Sakramentarien und Ordines* (Munster/Westf. 1892); A. Ebner, *Quellen und Forschungen zur Geschichte und Kunstgeschichte des Missale Romanum, Iter Italicum* (Freiburg/Br. 1896); L. Duchesne, *Christian Worship: Its Origin and Evolution* (London 1925); E. Bourque, *Étude sur les sacramentaires romains*, 1: *Les textes primitifs* (Rome 1949), 2/1: *Les Gélasiens du VIII siècle* (Quebec 1952) and 2/2: *Les sacramentaire d'Hadrien. Le Supplement d'Alcuin (sic) et les Grégoriens mixtes* (Rome 1958); K. Gamber, *Sakramentartypen* (Beuron 1958)—an almost exhaustive bibliography of sacramentaries before 1000 A.D., with sources and studies; his classifications, however, are to be received with caution; his *Codices liturgici latini antiquiures*, 2 vols., 2nd ed. (Fribourg 1968) is much more reliable. V. Leroquais, *Les sacramentaires et les missels MSS des bibliothèques publiques de France*, 4 vols. (Paris 1924); A. Chavasse, *Le Sacramentaire gélasien* (Tournai 1958) 679-692; H. Schmidt, "De sacramentariis romanis," *Gregorianum* 34 (1953) 731-743. It would also be good to consult both the general overview presented in the various liturgical manuals as well as the introductions to the various critical editions. See A.G. Martimort, "Recherches récentes sur les sacramentaires," *Bulletin de littérature ecclésiastique* 63 (1962) 28-40, and J. Deshusses-B. Darragon, *Concordances et tableaux pur l'étude des grands sacramentaires*, Spicilegium Friburgensis Subsidia 9-14 (Fribourg 1982-83), and J. Deshusses, "The Sacramentaries: A Progress Report," *Liturgy* 18 (1984) 13-60.

140. Gennadius, *Liber de viris illustribus*, ch. 80; Richardson, (ed.) TuU 14, 88, The Old Gelasian Sacramentary and the Frankish Gelasians are also termed *Liber sacramentarum*.

141. Letter of Hadrian to Charlemagne, MGH, *Epistolae mer. et kar. aevi* 1 (1892) 626. The actual title of the *Hadrianum* reads: *In nomine Domini. Hic Sacramentorum de circulo anni exposito a sancto Gregorio papa romano editum ex authentico libro bibliothecae cubiculi scriptum.*

142. Possibly as early as Gennadius, *De vir. illustr.*, Richardson (ed.), TuU 14, 79, variant. The term is used by Alcuin, Agobard, Bernhold, *et al.* Thus by the end of the VIII century, the new term *sacramentarium* had become common, without, however, replacing *sacramentorium*.

143. Since the VIII century, by the same authors; cf. Alcuin, *Letter to Eanbald of York*, PL 100, 221-225; *Missalis libelli, libelli sacramentorii, sacramentaria maiora*; Alcuin's letter to Egbert of York, PL 89, 441; the *Capitulary* of 789; Amalarius, ed. Hanssens 3, 500-504; PL 105, 1158-59.

144. E.A. Lowe, "The Vatican MS of the Gelasian Sacramentary and its Supplement at Paris," JTS 27 (1925-26) 357-373—the supplement consists of an *Exorcismus contra energumenos*, a *Penitential*, and a *Breviarium Apostolorum* which were not part of the primitive sacramentary of which *Vat. Reg.* 316 is only a distant copy. Recent editions: H.A. Wilson (Oxford 1894); Mohlberg-Eizenhöfer-Siffrin, *Liber Sacramentorum Romanae aecclesiae ordinis anni circuli (Sacramentarium Gelasianum)*, RED, series maior 4 (Rome 1960). Bibliographies: E. Bourque, *Étude* 1 (Rome 1949) 173-298—includes studies up to 1940; H. Schmidt, "De sacramentariis romanis," *Gregorianum* 34 (1953) 731-733—works from 1939-1953; K. Gamber, *Sakramentartypen*, 56; A. Chavasse, *Le Sacramentaire gélasien (Vat. Reg. 316)* (Paris-Tournai 1958); Mohlberg-Eizenhöfer-Siffrin, *op. cit.*, xxix-xliv—bibliography up to 1960; *Sacramentarium Gelasianum: e codice Vaticano Reginensis latino 316 vertente anno sacro MCMLXXV iussu Pauli Pp. VI*, 2 vols. (Vatican City 1975)—a facsimile edition.

145. This *explicit* now appears after two final pieces which are not part of the sacramentary proper: a *Contestatio* (Gallican preface) and an *Incipit ad paenitentiam dandam* (rite of Penance). Nor do the *Orationes in natali presbyteri qualiter sibi missam debeat celebrare* (Wilson 254; Mohlberg 199-200), inserted on folio 195ᵛ by a hand of the IX century, belong to the primitive sacramentary: cf. A. Wilmart, "Pour une nouvelle édition du sacramentaire gélasien: une messe fourvoyée," RB 50 (1938) 324-328.

146. Cf. E.A. Lowe, *Codices latini antiquiores* 1 (Oxford 1934) no. 105, p. 31, and H. Lietzmann, *Das Sacramentarium Gregorianum* (Münster/Westf. 1921) xxvii. A. Wilmart, *Bibl. Apost. Vaticanae Codices Reginenses* 2 (Rome 1945) 203, opted for a date a little before 750.

147. B. Bischoff, *Die Kölner Nonnenhss. und das Scriptorium von Chelles: Karolinische und Ottonische Kunst* (Wiesbaden 1957) 408, and E.A. Lowe, *Codices lat. antiquiores* 6 (Oxford 1953) xxi-xxii.

148. The Liturgical *Index of St. Thierry*, ca. 780; ed. A. Wilmart, RB 30 (1913) 437-450; Mohlberg et al., *op. cit.* 267-275. Fragments improperly associated with *Vat. Reg.* 316: 1) Masses from the collection of Saint-Amand-en-Pevèle (Paris, Bibl. Nat. 1603) inserted on the empty spaces of various pages; late VIII century, Monastery of Elnone, diocese of Tournai according to A. Wilmart, "Les messes de la collection de St.-Amand," JfL 3 (1923) 67-77; 2) the Formularies of Caesarius of Arles (Munich, Bayerische Staatsbibl. 28118; IX century, Arles); G. Morin, "S. Caesarii Arlatensis episcopi, Regula Sanctarum Virginum: orationes super defunctae corpus, ... supra sepulchram quando sepelitur," *Florilegium Patristicum* fasc. 34 (Bonn 1933) 30-31; 3) The morning and evening orations of London (London British Library Add. 37518, folios 116-117; VIII century); A. Baumstark, "Ein altgelasianisches Sakramentarbruchstück insularer Herkunft," JfL 7 (1927) 130-136; 4) the Commentary of Pseudo-Rufinus (according to a lost MS of Isle-Barbe; PL 21, 849); G. Morin, "Une collecte romaine du sacramentaire gélasian citée par un écrivain provençal des environs de 494," RB 30 (1913) 226-228; A.

Wilmart, "Le commentaire sur les psaumes imprimé sous le nom de Rufin," RB 31 (1914-1919) 258-276.

149. Detailed concordances have been prepared by P. Siffrin, *Konkordanztabellen*, 2:, *Liber sacramentorum romanae Aecclesiae* (*Vat. Reg. lat.* 316, RED, series minor 5 (Rome 1959); see also J. Deshusses-B. Darragon, *Concordances et tableaux*, 6 vols. Spicilegii Friburgensis Subsidia 9-14 (Fribourg 1982-83).

150. Study of the Sanctoral in W.H. Frere, *Studies in Early Roman Liturgy* 1: *The Calendar*, ACC 28 (Oxford-London 1930) and A. Chavasse, *Le Sac. gél.*, *passim*.

151. For the Gallican additions and the criteria for determining them, see A. Chavasse, *Le Sac. gél.*, 5-61. On the rite of public penance see C. Vogel, *La discipline pénitentielle en Gaule* (Paris 1952) 182-194 and "Sin and Penance in the Latin Church," P. Delhaye, ed., *Pastoral Treatment of Sin* (New York 1968) 177-282, esp. 213-259; A. Chavasse, *Le Sac. gél.*, 140-153.

152. Cf. E. Bourque, *Étude* 1, 225-261 and A. Chavasse, *Le Sac. gél.*, 5-77.

153. A. Baumstark, "Untersuchungen," in L.C. Mohlberg, *Die älteste er reichbarre Gestalt des Liber sacramentroum anni circuli der römischen Kirche*, LQF 11-12 (Münster/Westf. 1927) 1*-120* and *Comparative Liturgy* (London 1958), 203. Baumstark's thesis is part of a theory that deals with the origin of the *Missale Romanum*; this will be discussed later.

154. H. Hohlwein, "Untersuchungen über die überlieferungsgeschichtliche Stellung des Sakramentarium Gregorianum," EL 42 (1928) 231-257— the author follows Baumstark's view of the origin of the VIII-century Frankish Gelasians; H. Schmidt, "De lectionibus variantibus in formulis identicis sacramentorum Leoniani, Gelasiani, Gregoriani," SE 4 (1952) 725-743 and "De sacramentariis romanis," *Gregorianum* 34 (1953) 725-743. At the end of his remarkable analyses, H. Schmidt proposed that a Roman collection of *libelli* made its way across the Alps and was joined together with native (Gallican) formularies in order to form the Old Gelasian. The fact, however, that characteristics of the *Sanctoral* and *Temporal* conform to other documents of the City, opposes Schmidt's hypothesis. See the critique by B. Capelle, "Le sacramentaire romain avant S. Grégoire," RB 64 (1954) 157-167.

155. M. Andrieu, "Les messes des jeudis de Carême et les anciens sacramentaires," RSR 9 (1929) 343-375; 451-455, and "Quelques remarques sur le classement des sacramentaires," JfL 11 (1931) 46-66. The same view is taken by B. Capelle, "Le sacramentaire romain avant s. Grégoire," RB 64 (1954) 157-167.

156. A. Chavasse, *Le Sac gél.*, x-xxix.

157. K. Gamber, *Sakramentartypen*, 54-60, and "Das kampanische Messbuch als Vorläufer des Gelasianum: Ist der hl. Paulinus von Nola der Verfasser?" SE 12 (1961) 5-111. The hypothesis is based on a text of Agnellus of Pisa (ca. 830), *Liber pontificalis ecclesiae Ravennatis* 2, 6=MGH, *Script. rer. lang.*, 332; PL 140, 610, disproved by A. Chavasse, "L'oeuvre littéraire de Maximien de Ravenne," EL 75 (1960) 115-120. Gamber's initial hypothesis influenced the classification of all the sacramentaries with which he dealt.

158. G. Dix, *The Shape of the Liturgy* (2nd ed. London 1945) 532, 565-566; J. S. Sinclair, "The Development of the Roman Rite during the Dark Ages," *Theology* 32 (1936) 142-155. Agreeing with Dix, W.H. Frere, *Studies* 1, ACC 28 (London 1930) 142. For the same reasons, B. Botte, "Le rituel d'ordination des *Statuta Ecclesiae antiqua*," *Recherches de Théologie ancienne et médiévale* 11 (1939) 241, and C. Coebergh, "Le sacramentaire gélasien ancien," AfL 7 (1961) 45-88, proposed that the Old Gelasian was composed in Italy, but outside of Rome.

159. A. Chavasse, *Le Sac. gél.*, 282-285, 340-344.

160. *Liber pontificalis: Vita Gelasii*, ed. Duchesne, 1, 225; *Fecit etiam et sacramentorum praefationes cauto sermone*. This passage says that Gelasius was the author of liturgical compositions: prefaces and orations—a fact that has been verified by literary and historical criticism—but not that he had composed a sacramentary.

161. John the Deacon (872-882), *Vita Gregorii* 2, 17; PL 75, 94: *Sed et gelasianum codicem de missarum solemniis multa subtrahens pauca convertens nonulla vero superadiciens pro exponendis evangelicis lectionibus in unius libri volumine coarctivit*. On the impossibility of attributing a sacramentary to Gelasius, see A. Chavasse, *Le Sac. gél.*, xx-xxiv.

162. S. Bäumer, "Über das sog. Sacramentarium Gelasianum," *Historisches Jahrbuch* 13 (1893) 241-301; E. Bishop, *Liturgica Historica*, 39-61; F. Cabrol, DACL 6 (1924) 747-777; M. Andrieu, "Les messes des jeudis de Carême," RSR 9 (1929) 347—note Andrieu's significant remark that a sacramentary of the same type as *Vat. Reg.* 316 was still in use at Rome during the time of Gregory II (715-731).

163. See B. Capelle, "Messes du pape Gélase dans le sacramentaire léonien," RB 56 (1945-46) 12-41; G. Pomarès, *Dix-huit messes du pape Gélase dans le sacramentaire léonien*, SC 65 (Paris 1959)—includes a bibliography of the subject.

164. This was proposed as early as L. Duchesne, *Christian Worship* (1925; but also in the earlier editions) 127-128. See especially E. Bourque, *Étude* 1, 187-269, who isolates different strata.

165. A. Chavasse, *Le Sac. gél.*, 679-692, and *passim*. Chavasse' thesis leads to a reclassification of the sacramentaries or, rather, to some new views concerning the history of their formation. The Gregorian of the *Paduensis*-type would not be the oldest form of the Gregorian, but a revision of a Gregorian of the *Hadrianum*-type composed at Rome between 650 and 682/683, with the assistance of the old Gelasian. The entire theory depends on the existence of an ancient Roman sacramentary, not preserved in the MS-tradition, that would have been pre-Gelasian and pre-Gregorian. Cf. B. Capelle, "Origine et vicissitudes du sacramentaire gélasien d'après un livre récent," *Revue d'Histoire ecclésiastique* 54 (1959) 877-878. The critique of Chavasse' hypothesis by C. Coebergh, "Le sacramentaire gélasien ancien," AfL 7 (1961) 46-88 must be taken into account as well.

166. *Liber pontificalis: Vita Gregorii II (715-731)*; ed. Duchesne, 1, 402: *Hic quadragesemali tempore ut quintas ferias missarum celebritas fieret in ecclesia, quod non agebatur, instituit*. For these Masses and the basic conclusions regarding

the classification of the principal Roman sacramentaries, see M. Andrieu, "Les messes des jeudis de Carême," RSR 9 (1929) 343-375—formularies from the *Hadrianum*, pp. 345-346; from *Paduensis* D. 47, p. 351; from the Frankish Gelasians, pp. 354-355. If the *Roman* ancestor had been composed *after* the pontificate of Gregory II, it would be difficult to account for the absence of these masses instituted by this pope.

167. *Old Gelasian Sacramentary*, 1, 21; Wilson 26; Mohlberg 26. It is actually an extract from a letter; cf. Gregorius I, *Registrum*, 9, 218; MGH *Epistolae* 2, 205-206.

168. *Liber pontificalis: Vita Gregorii I (590-604)*; ed. Duchesne, 1, 312: *Hic augmentavit in praedictionem canonis: Diesque nostros in tua pace dispone, et cetera.*

169. Gregorius I, *Registrum* 9, 12; PL 77, 956; MGH, *Registrum* 9, 26 in *Epistolarum Tomus* 2 (1899) 59: : *Orationem vero dominicam idcirco mox post precem*[=*canon missae*] *dicimus*, etc.

170. Cf. L. Duchesne, *Liber pontificalis* 1, 374. The two feasts of the Holy Cross—*Inventio* on May 3 and *Exaltatio* on Sept. 14—originally celebrated the same fact.

171. L. Duchesne, *Liber pontificalis* 1, 376 and 381. Gaul came to celebrate these feasts after Rome; there is no mention of them in the Auxerre-recension of the Martyrology of Jerome (ca. 592-605). The ironic remark of E. Bourque—*Étude* 1, 226, note 2—does not apply to the chronological conclusions drawn by Duchesne from his examiniation of the *Sanctorale* of the Gelasian. Duchesne used *Vat. Reg.* 316, not some hypothetical prototype which is supposed to have existed prior to the extant MSS.

172. The Mass formularies for the Thursdays of Lent instituted by Gregory II appear in the *Hadrianum*. An analysis of these prayers shows that the Roman clerk in charge of providing the orations, copied them from an Old Gelasian, except for two cases in which he repeated the first oration which the *Hadrianum* had assigned for the previous day. Ordinarily, the clerk chose the Gelasian formularies from either a Wednesday or Friday of the same week. This proves a) that the Thursdays of Lent still had no mass formularies in the copy of the Gelasian that this Lateran liturgist had at his disposal; otherwise, following the law of least resistance, he would simply have copied them. Thus, the Gelasian he had in front of him must have resembled our *Vat. Reg.* 316; b) that the Old Gelasian was still considered an authorised liturgical book. Cf. M. Andrieu, "Les messes . . . " RSR 9 (1929) 345-347.

173. Further on we shall explain how the masses for the Thursdays Lent were completed for the Frankish Gelasians of the late VIII century.

174. According to Chavasse (*Le Sac. gél.*) and his hypothesis on the history of the Roman sacramentaries, the Old Gelasian and the Gregorians of the *Paduensis*-type arrived in Gaul later than has heretofore been supposed. They must have arrived in Gaul toward the *end* of the VII or beginning of the VIII century. Early on in the VII century, a pre-Gelasian/pre-Gregorian sacramentary containing *formulae* proper to both the so-called Gelasian and

Gregorian sacramentaries must have appeared in Gaul. The Gallican books mentioned above must have gotten their Roman prayers from this hypothetical sacramentary. It must be said, however, that the difference between the conclusions of Chavasse regarding the places in which the Old Gelasian was used and the chronology of the sacramentaries that have actually been preserved, and the earlier theories are more apparent than real.

Whatever one may think about Chavasse' attempts to re-construct lost texts, his opinions leave intact the standard way of classifying the sacramentaries that do exist. It will be easier to see this by referring to the simplified table which has been reproduced with the permission of Chavasse, my colleague and my friend. Given the age of the MSS, there is no question about the Romanization of the Gallican Sacramentaries under the influence of a liturgy of the Old-Gelasian-type; something that must have occured at the very beginning of the VIII century. Chavasse thinks this Romanizing process does not stem from direct contact with an ancestor of *Vat. Reg.* 316 but from an intermediary sacramentary (pre-Gelasian/pre-Gregorian) which must have been circulating in Gaul at least as early as the beginning of the VII century. See Table C.

175. Lists of witnesses to the Frankish Gelasian can be found in Bourque, *Étude* 2/1, 3-223; Gamber, *Sakramentartypen*, 99-119 and *passim*; E. Dekkers, *Clavis*, 429-432. A critical edition of the Frankish Gelasian based on all of the surviving MSS still does not exist; the best representative of the family, the *Gellonensis*, has appeared in a critical edition: A. Dumas-J. Deshusses, *Liber Sacramentorum Gellonensis*, CC 159 and 159A (Turnhout 1981) which gives fuller and more accurate information than the earlier tables and introduction provided by P. de Puniet, "Le sacramentaire romain de Gellone," EL 48 to 52 (1934-1938) reprinted in one volume as *Bibliotheca Ephemerides Liturgicae* 4 (Rome 1938). See also K. Gamber, "Heimat und Ausbildung der Gelasiana saec. VIII (Junggelasiana)," SE 14 (1963) 99-123. New tables appear in A. Chavasse, *Le sacramentaire dans le groupe dit 'Gélasiens du VIII siècle.' Une compilation raisonnée, Étude des procédés de confection et Synoptiques nouveau modèle*, 2 vols. Instrumenta Patristica 14 A-B (Steenbrugge-the Hague 1984).

176. The Sacramentary of Reichenau *(Insula Augiensis)*; Karlsruhe, Landesbibl. *codex Augiensis* CXII; ca. 800, probably Reichenau. Cf. A. Dold-A. Baumstark, *Das Palimpsest-Sakramentar in Codex Augiensis*, TuA 1/12 (Beuron 1925) and the lists cited in note 175, above.

177. For a more complete list, see the works in note 175 above.

178. B. Moreton, *The Eighth-Century Gelasian Sacramentary* (Oxford 1976) 15.

179. Gellone 194, 1237-1240; cf. Deshusses, *Sac. grég.* 1, 698-699; 2, 299-300 and 302.

180. Gellone prefixes the selections drawn form the Old Gelasian with additional sections of more pronounced character (391-393) while Angoulême contents itself with the older materials (sections LXXIX-LXXXII): *Missa monachorum, missa in monasterio, oratio in monasterio, orationes mona-*

chorum. Rheinau, with its diminished Book II, does not contain the blessings of abbots and abbesses, the making of monks and nuns and the other monastic exercises, not even those contained in the Old Gelasian.

181. *Annales* of Lorsch, A.D. 703. The *translatio* is reported in a palimpsest of Munich from the end of the VIII century; cf. E. Munding, *Palimpsesttexte des Codex lat. monacensis 6333*, TuA 15-18 (Beuron 1932) 218. Note, however, that the Martyrology attached to the *Gellonensis* assigns Dec. 4 as the *translatio S. Benedicti abbatis.*

182. They also contain the feasts of Sts. Augustine and Jerome and the Apostles. The *cultus* of St. Augustine had been popular since the VI century (*Vita Caesarii Arelatensis* 2, 46) and the *cultus* of the Holy Apostles was in evidence ca. 750; cf. T. Klauser, *Das römische Capitulare Evangeliorum*, LQF 28 (1935) 131-132.

183. *Passio Preiecti*, MGH, *Scriptores rerum merovingicarum* 5 (1910) 212-248; cf. *Analecta Bollandiana* 13 (1894) 63; see also B. Moreton, "A Patronal Festival? ST. Praeiectus and the Eighth-Century Gelasian Sacramentary," JTS 27 (1976) 370-380.

184. See E. Bourque, *Étude* 2/1 (Quebec 1952) 225.

185. *Liber pontificalis, Vita Gregorii III (731-741)*, ed. Duchense 1, 419-420. Mass formula: Gellone 276, 1645-1649; Angoulême CCLXXXIX, 1511-1514; St. Gall *codex* 348 (ed. Mohlberg), 257, 1354-1357; this mass-set does not appear in Rheinau.

186. Paul I (757-767), Letter to Pepin III (761): *Per aliam quippe epistolam suam a Deo protecta Eximietas vestra, sicut certe suo bene cupienti patri direxit, quatenus titulum protectoris vestri, beati Christi martyris Chrysogoni, cum omnibus sibi pertinentibus dilectissimo atque fidelissimo nobis Marino presbitero concedere deberemus; de quo et praeceptum nobis dirigi petistis:* MGH, *Epistolarum* 3, 529. Cf. L.C. Mohlberg, "Elementi per precisare l'origine del sacramentario Gelasiano del secolo VIII," *Atti della Pontificia Accademia di Archelogia, Rendiconti* 7 (1932) 25-33.

187. A. Dumas-J. Deshusses, *Liber Sacramentorum Gellonensis*, CC 159 A =*Introductio* (Turnhout 1981) xviii-xxi.

188. E. Bourque, *Étude* 2/1 (Quebec 1952) 227, opted for Flavigny because of the special connections of this abbey with King Pepin III. The Frankish Gelasian spread throughout East *Francia*, in particular, and from there into Germany; cf. P. de Puniet, "Le sacramentaire gélasien de Phillipps," EL 43 (1929) 96.

189. The redactor used a Gregorian sacramentary that was more like the *Sacramentary of Padua* than the *Hadrianum.* Among other indications is the fact that for the Lenten period the *Paduense* is not identical with the *Hadrianum*; the masses for the Thursdays of Lent are, in fact, quite different. Eight out of ten prayers of the *Paduense* passed into the Frankish Gelasian Sacramentary and finished their career there; cf. M. Andrieu, "Les messes des jeudis de Carême," RSR 9 (1929) 352-370; E. Bourque, *Étude* 2/1 (Quebec 1952) 283-321. —For the two redactions of the Frankish Gelasian, which cannot be discussed here, see A. Chavasse, "Le sacramentaire gélasien du VIII siècle: Ses deux principales formes," EL 73 (1959) 249-298.

190. Ed. Dumas, 391-404, 440f.

191. Perhaps a critical edition based on all the surviving MSS of the Frankish Gelasian will eventually allow us to penetrate more surely into the principles underlying the construction of this sacramentary. The *status quaestionis* is presented in Bourque, *Étude* 2/1, 255-402, in A. Chavasse, *supra*, note 189 and in our Table D—Many important sections of the Frankish Gelasian survived by means of the Supplement to the *Hadrianum* compiled by St. Benedict of Aniane; he drew heavily upon this sacramentary and passed on its contributions to the remainder of the Middle Ages and to the *Missale Romanum* of the Tridentine reform (1570). It is also important to remember how much the Frankish Gelasian contributed to the Milanese liturgy and to the *Romano-Germanic Pontifical of the X Century*.

192. On the liturgical significance of Stephen II's sojourn in France, see T. Klauser, "Die liturgischen Austauschbeziehungen," *Historisches Jahrbuch* 53 (1933) 174.

193. For the liturgical initiatives of Pepin III (741-768), his motives and their results, see C. Vogel, "Les échanges liturgiques entre Rome et les pays francs jusqu'à l'époque de Charlemagne," *Le Chiese nei regni dell'Europa occidentale*, Settimane di studio sull' alto medioevo 7 (Spoleto 1960) 229-246.

194. Remedius went to Rome in 760 to examine the Roman liturgy and with Paul I's permission brought back to Rouen, Simeon, the *secundus* of the papal *schola cantorum*, to instruct his clergy in Roman chant; Paul I, *Epistola 41* to Pepin III: *In eis [litteris vestris] siquidem conperimus exaratum quod praesentes Deo amabilis Remedii germani vestri monachos Symeoni scole cantorum priori contradere deberemus ad instruendum eos in psalmodii modulationem quam ab eo apprehendere (=apprendere) tempore, quo illic in vestris regiminibus exstitit nequiverant; pro quo valde ipsum vestum asseritis germanum tristem in eo quod non eius perfecte instruisset monachos. Et quidem, beginissime rex, satisfacimus Christianitatem tuam, quod, nisi Georgius qui eidem scolae praefuit, de hac migrasset luce, nequaquam eundem Simeonem a vestri germani servitio abstolere niteremur. . . . Propter quod et praefatos vestri germani monachos saepe dicto contradidimus Simeoni eosque obtine collocantes sollerti industria eandem psalmodii modulationem instrui praecipimus et crebro in eadem, donec perfectae eruditi efficiantur . . . ecclesiasticae doctrinae cantilena disposuimus efficaci cura permanendum;* MGH, *Epositolae mer. et kar. aevi* i,=*Tomus Epistolarum* 3 (1892) 553-554; PL 89, 1187. —For the *schola cantorum* see M. Andrieu, "Les ordes mineurs dans l'ancien rit romain," RSR 5 (1925) 323-374; J. Quasten, *Musik und Gesang der heidnischen Antike und der christlichen Frühzeit*, LQF 25 (Munster/Westf. 1930), ET *Music and Worship in Pagan and Christian Antiquity*, tr. B. Ramsey, (Washington, D.C. 1983); E. Josi, "Schola cantorum, clerici, lectores," EL 44 (1930) 281-290. Chrodegang of Metz (742-766), another fervent admirer of the Roman liturgy, went to Rome in 753 and, according to Paul the Deacon, subsequently introduced the *cantilena romana* and the *Ordo romanae ecclesiae* at Metz; Paul, *Gesta episcorporum Mettensium*; MGH. *Tomus Scriptorum* 2, 268; PL 95, 720: *Cumque esset in omnibus locuples [Chrodegang], a Pippino rege omnique Francorum caetu singulariter electus, Romam directus est Stephanumque venerabilem papam, ut*

cunctorum vota anhelabant, ad Gallis evocavit. . . . *Ipsumque clerum abundanter lege divina romanaque imbutum cantilena morem atque ordinem Romanae ecclesiae servare praecepit, quod usque ad id tempus in Mettensi ecclesia factum minime fuit.* Paul the Deacon wrote his *Gesta* around 783 at the request of Angilramnus of Metz. See T. Klauser, "Eine Stationsliste der Metzer Kirche aus dem 8 Jhd. wahrscheinlich en Werk Chrodegangs," EL 44 (1930) 162-193; T. Klauser-R.S. Bour, "Un document du IX siècle," *Annuaire de la Société d'Histoire et d'Archéologie de Lorraine* 34 (1929); M. Andrieu, "Règlement d'Angilramne de Metz fixant les honoraires de quelques fonctions liturgiques," RSR 10 (1930) 349-369. Chrodegang also tried to conform to Roman usages in other matters: ordinations (*consecrare . . . sicut moris est Romanae ecclesiae in diebus sabbatorum quaternis temporibus anni*: Paul the Deacon, *Gesta*, PL 95, 722); vestments (*sicut habet ordo romanus; Regula canonicorum*, PL 89, 1102); cf. C. Vogel, "Les échanges liturgiques," 242-244.

195. A. Dumas–J. Deshusses, "Introductio," pp. xxiii-xxvi.

196. Other versions of the title: IN NOMINE SANCTAE TRINITATIS. INCIPIT LIBER SACRAMENTORUM ANNI CIRCULUM ROMANE EC-CLESIE (St. Gall 348); IN NOMINE DEI SUMMI. INCIPIT LIBER SAC-RAMENTORUM ROMANAE ECCLESIAE ORDINIS PER CIRCULUM ANNI (Phillipps); INCIPIT LIBER SACRAMENTORUM ROMANAE EC-CLESIAE ORDINE EXCARPSUS (St. Amand).

197. All the Frankish Gelasians have a proper mass for the Octave of Christmas (Jan. 1) taken directly from the Old Gelasian tradition (*Reg.* 316, IX, 48-53) but Gellone adds an *Alia Missa de Octabas Domini* (13, 82-87) composed of three prayers from the *Hadrianum* (14, 82-84) and three others taken from the *Hypapante*, Feb. 2 (sect. 27, nos. 123, 125, 127). Since the *Hadrianum* did not arrive in Gaul until between 784 and 791, this is good evidence that the Gellone was not copied until the last decade of the VIII century.

198. This formula is also drawn directly from the Old Gelasian (*Reg.* 316, X, 54-56) and reappears in almost all the Frankish Gelasians (Gellone 14, Angoulême XIII; *Sangall.* 348, 13). Rome probably got this usage from S. Italy where it was already recorded in the Epistolary of Capua of 546: After the mass of the Circumcission on Jan 1, it has *De eodem die, contra idola*; cf. Chavasse, *Le Sac. gél.*, 208.

199. *Eodem die*, other Frankish Gelasians add the *Conversio Sancti Pauli Apostoli* (Angoulême XXX, 181-185; *Sangall.* 348, 31, 169-172; Phillips). Since it was in closer proximity to the archetype of Flavigny, Gellone provides only the patronal feast of that abbey.

200. Omitted by a negligent scribe, this mass appears, naturally, in all other MSS.

201. In the Frankish Gelasians, this is always referred to as 'St. Simeon' with the *collecta* at St. Hadrian-in-the-Forum and the mass at St. Mary Major. In *Reg.* 316 it is termed *Purificatio Sanctae Mariae*, in the *Paduense, Hypapanthi,* spelled *Ypopanti* in the *Hadrianum* and in the *Liber Pontificalis* under Sergius I, *dies S. Simeonis quod Ypapanti Graeci appelant* (ed. Duchesne 1, 376). The title

Purificatio became more popular at Rome in the XI and XII centuries and came to oust the old Greek title permanently.

202. At this point the scribe forgets to include the *missa pro scrutinio* and replaces it with the *ordo* of the I Scrutiny. He muddles things further on the Sat.-Sun. of Week V. What is scattered across Lent in Gellone is bunched together in Holy Week in Angoulême and omitted entirely from *Sangall.* 348. Note that the entire *Ordo baptisterii* reappears in 'Book II' in sect. 344 of Gellone.

203. The Sun. of the Octave of Easter is entitled *Dominica I Octabas Paschae* but in Angoulême CXXV, *Sangall.* 348, 107 and Rheinau LXXVI, *Dominica post Albas.*

204. March 25: *Denuntiacio Sanctae Mariae et Passio Domini Nostri Iesu Christi* (Gellone 124, 849-860); *Adnuntiatio Sanctae Dei Genetricis et Passio eiusdem Domini (Paduense LXXXV, 385-389): In Adnuntiatione Sanctae Mariae Matris Domini Nostri Iesu Christi* (Angoulême CXXVIIII, 541-543); *Adnuntio Sanctae Mariae (Sangall.* 348, 111, 677-686). See *infra,* page 95.

205. Since at this point the scribe forgot to insert the XII Sun. after Pent. (after section 206), he mistakenly put the text of the XII Sun. in the place of the XIII Sun. but still called it the XII Sun. The XIV Sun. appears in the right place but is called the XIII. The missing text of the XIII Sun. turns up as an *alia missa XIII post Pent.* at 222. Subsequently, the Sunday mass-sets come in their regular order but numbered incorrectly until the V Sun. before Christmas or XXVII after Pent., *recte* XVIII. At the IV Sun. before Christmas the numbering is rectified and called the XXIX Sun. after Pent. That makes the last Sun. before Christmas the XXXII Sun. after Pentecost.

206. 'Book II' has this title in the Sacramentaries of St. Amand and Rheinau but despite a clear demarcation between the sacramentary proper and the supplementary material, Gellone and Angoulême do not. 'Book II' is completely missing in St. Gall 348, possibly because it was bound under separate cover.

207. Perhaps the editors of Gellone had forgotten how Pope Zachary (741-752) had raged against the solemn benedictions the Frankish bishops employed to bless their people after the *Pater noster* and before Holy Communion; cf. Zachary, *Epistola 13 ad Bonifatium* in PL 89, 951-952. By perpetuating them in the Frankish Gelasians, they also assured their continuance in the Supplement of Benedict of Aniane(q.v.) and in most of the Northern churches for the rest of the Middle Ages. See E.E. Moeller, *Corpus benedictionum episcopalium missae,* CC 162, 4 vols.(Turnhout 1971-1973) and J. Deshusses, "Le Bénédictionnaire gallican," EL 77 (1963) 169-187.

208. Standard reference tools on the Gregorian sacramentaries: E. Bourque, *Étude sur les sacramentaires romains* 1 (Rome 1948) 301-391 *(Paduensis);* 2/2 (Rome 1958) 13-72 *(Hadrianum* and Supplement); K. Gamber, *Sakramentartypen,* TuA 49-50 (Beuron 1958) 81-98, 135-144, *passim;* E. Dekkers, *Clavis Patrum Latinorum* (2nd ed. Steenbrugge 1961) 426-428 (the Supplement to the *Hadrianum* is not included); CLLA nos. 701-796, pp. 325-367. All of the above information must now be rectified, to a greater or lesser

degree, by the research of J. Deshusses; see his introduction to *Le Sacramentaire grégorien*, Spicilegium Friburgense 16 (Fribourg 1971) and his magisterial review of the *status quaestionis*, "Les sacramentaires. État actuel de la recherche," AfL 24 (1982) 19-46, ET "The Sacramentaries: A Progress Report," *Liturgy* 18 (Gethsemani, Kentucky 1984) 13-60. See also A. Chavasse, "L'organisation générale des sacramentaires dits Grégoriens," RSR 56 (1982) 179-200, 253-273; 57 (1983) 50-56.

209. For the Roman stational system and its pastoral purposes, see *Ordo romanus primus* 1-28, ed. M. Andrieu, *Les Ordines romani du haut moyen âge* 2, Spicilegium sacrum Lovaniense 23 (Louvain 1948) 67-76; G.G. Willis, "Roman Stational Liturgy," *Further Essays in Early Roman Liturgy*, ACC 50 (London 1968) 1-87 with complete bibliography; J.F. Baldovin, *The Urban Character of Christian Worship in Jerusalem, Rome, and Constantinople from the 4th to the 10th Centuries*, PhD Dissertation (Yale 1982) [presently available through University Microfilms, Ann Arbor Michigan; soon to be published]; A. Chavasse, "L'organisation stationale du carême romain avant le VIII siècle. Une organisation pastorale," RSR 56 (1982) 17-32.

210. H. Ashworth, "Did St. Gregory the Great Compose a Sacramentary?" *Studia Patristica* 2=TuU 63 (Berlin 1957) 3-16; "Did St. Augustine Bring the *Gregorianum* to England?" EL 72 (1958) 39-43; "Sacramentaries," *New Catholic Encyclopedia* 12 (1967) 792-800; "The Liturgical Prayers of St. Gregory the Great," *Traditio* 15 (1959) 107-161; B. Capelle, "La main de St. Grégoire dans le sacramentaire grégorien," RB 49 (1937) 13-28. On St. Gregory and the Chant, see S.J.P. Van Dijk, "Gregory the Great, Founder of the Urban *Schola Cantorum*," EL 77 (1963) 336-356. Article by P.M. Gy, to appear QL 1986.

211. Attempts at classifying and identifying the various witnesses to the Gregorian family have been particularly long, complex and confusing. J. Pamelius, *Liturgicon ecclesiae latinae* 2 (1st ed. Cologne 1571, reprint Farnborough 1970) 177-387, reproduced by P. Goussainville, *S. Gregorii Magni opera* (Paris 1675) and by A. Rocca, *Opera S. Gregorii Magni* 8 (Rome 1593), *Sacramentarium Gregorianum* (1595), published MSS under the name of Gregory that proved to be both late and contaminated. Dom Ménard, *Divi Gregorii papae I Liber Sacramentorum* (Paris 1642) reprinted in *Opera omnia* 10 (Venice 1773) 118-404 and in PL 78, 25-264, gave up on his original idea of publishing the Sacramentary of Rodradus (Paris, Bibl. Nat. *codex lat.* 12050; Amiens, 853) and edited instead the Sacramentary of St. Eligius (Paris, Bibl. Nat., *codex lat.* 12051; Corbie, last half of the IX century) as the work of St. Gregory; unfortunately, the latter *codex* was one of the most corrupt MSS of the Gregorian family and his work confused research on the *Gregorianum* for long years to come. Cardinal Tommasi did not live long enough to produce an edition he would have based on *Vat. Reg.* 337 and the *Codex Ottobonianus* 313. M. Gerbert, *Monumenta veteris liturgiae alemannicae* 1 (Saint Blaise 1777; reprint Hildesheim 1967) 1-240 also printed a late text included in the *Sacramentarium triplex* (Zürich, Zentralbibliothek C. 43). The edition of L. A. Muratori, *Liturgia romana vetus* 2 (1748) 1-361, was based on two excellent

MSS (*Vat. Reg.* 337 and *Ottobon.* 313) but was severely damanged by mistakes in layout; it has to be read in the following order: 1-6, 357-361, 7-138, 241-272; cf. E. Bishop, *Liturgica Historica* (Oxford 1918, 1962) 75. Firm ground was reached only with the research of L. Duchesne (1889), and E. Bishop (1915) and with the editions of H.A. Wilson (1915), H. Lietzmann (1921), L.C. Mohlberg (1927) and J. Deshusses (1971). The story of the vicissitudes of the Gregorian may be found in E. Bourque, *Étude* 2/2 (1958) 75-92.

212. This is a palimpsest sacramentary-lectionary copied in N. Italy ca. 700 and represents the first tentative, experimental introduction of mass-sets for the ordinary Sundays into the series of major Roman feasts, e.g., the 7 Sundays *post Angeli*. It also provides 2 readings for each Sunday of the *temporale* but not for the *sanctorale*. Its terms for the mass prayers are unusual: *oratio, secreta, ad. com.*; cf. CLLA 701, pp. 330-331; A. Chavasse, "Les fragments palimpsestes du *Casinensis* 271 (Sigle Z 6). A côté de l'*Hadrianum* et du *Paduense* un collateral, autrement remanié," AfL 25 (1983) 9-33.

213. For the intentions of Charlemagne himself and his recollections of his father's aims, see especially his *Capitulare Generale* (March 23, 789); MGH, *Capitularia regum francorum*=Tomus *Legum* I (1835) 68-69, the *Encyclica de litteris colendis* (ca. 786-800); MGH, *ibid.*, 52-53, and the *Caroli Magni Capitulare de imaginibus* (=*Libri Carolini*), ca. 791; MGH, *Concilia Tomi II Supplementum*=*Legum Sectio III* (1924). On the liturgical reform of Charlemagne, see F. Cabrol, DACL 3 (1914) 807-923 (major texts but inaccurate chronology); E. Bishop, "The Liturgical Reforms of Charlemagne, their Meaning and Value," *Downside Review* 38 (1919) 1-16; E. Bishop–A. Wilmart, "La réforme liturgique de Charlemagne," EL 45 (1931) 186-207; C. Vogel, "Les échanges liturgiques entre Rome et les pays francs jusqu'à l'époque de Charlemagne," *Le Chiese nei regni dell'Europa occidentale*, Settimane di studio sull'alto medioevo 7 (Spoleto 1960) 265-295. On Charlemagne and Alcuin, see R. Wahl, *Karl der Grosse* (Frankurt/Main 1954). Much of this information must now be rectified in the light of more recent research, especially that of J. Deshusses.

214. The meaning of the term *sacramentarium inmixtum* i.e. free from all post-Gregorian or extra-Gregorian additions, can be discerned by a careful reading of its context in the prologue to the Supplement added to the *Hadrianum: Hucusque praecedens sacramentorum libellus a beato papa Gregorio constat esse editus . . . . Licet a plerisque scriptorum vitio depravante, quia non ut ab auctore suo est editus haberetur. . . . Si vero superflua vel non necessaria sibi illa iudicaverit, utatur praefati patris opusculo quod minime respuere sine sui discrimine potest* (ed., J. Deshusses, *Sac. grég.* 1 [1971] 351-352).

215. Hadrian I, Letter to Charlemagne (Jaffé-Wattenbach, 2473); *Codex Carolinus, Epistola 89*; MGH, *Epistolae merov. et karol. aevi* 1 (1892) 626; *Epistolae selectae* 3, 626. Text and translation in accordance with the reconstruction of H. Lietzmann, *Das Sakramentarium Gregorianum*, LQ 3 (Münster/Westf. 1921) xv. Other translations with differences of detail by R. Strapper, *Karls des Grossen römisches Messbuch* (Leipzig 1908) 14; F. Probst,

Die Ältesten Sakramentarien und Ordines (Münster/Westf. 1892) 316, Note 1; L.C. Mohlberg, "Il messale glagolitico di Kiev (Sec. IX) ed il suo prototipo Romano del Sec. VI-VII," *Atti della Pontificia Accademia di Archeologia, Memorie* 2 (1928) 271.

216. *Secundum sanctae nostrae ecclesiae traditionem*: according to the use of Our holy church. In his 42 letters Pope Hadrian carefully distinguishes between the Roman Church as an ecclesial community, the church-building (basilica) of St. Peter's on the Vatican, and *ecclesia nostra*, i.e. the Lateran; e.g., Hadrian put the cross King Charles sent him as a gift in the Lateran treasury: *crucem quam nobis misistis, in sanctam nostram ecclesiam recondentes, vestra memoria in aeterna in ea remanebit*. To the pope's mind, Charlemagne was requesting a book containing exactly what went on at the Lateran, in the *basilica sanctissimi Salvatoris*; cf. A. Chavasse, "Les oraisons pour les dimanches ordinaires," RB 93 (1983) 178, note 1.

217. T. Klauser, "Die liturgischen Austauschbeziehungen," *Historisches Jahrbuch* 53 (1933) 179, note 31. See also L.C. Mohlberg, *Atti della Pontificia Accademia di Archeologia, Rendiconti* 16 (1940) 147-154.

218. Jaffé-Wattenbach 2473 suggest the years between 784 and 791; J. Deshusses agrees, *Sac. grég.* 1 (1971) 61.

219. An *alia missa* for the octave of Christmas (Jan 1), nos. 82-87, composed of two masses drawn from the *Hadrianum* (sections 14 and 27) and four other prayers (132, 200, 1433, 1434); cf. A. Chavasse, *Le Sac. gél.*, 556.

220. This notice is contained in 3 MSS of the *Dionysio-Hadriana* (ed. in Lietzmann, *Das Sacramentarium Greg.*, p. vi). The *cubiculum* in question is that of the king and not of the pope as Duchesne, De Puniet, Dold and others have thought. No Carolingian edict survives which imposes the use of the *Hadrianum* but the subsequent Gregorians derive from the *authenticum*, either in the corrected version of Benedict of Aniane or in the actual style of the original. "Though we have no extant copies of any royal edicts imposing the use of the Roman sacramentary in the Carolingian kingdom, one feels that such decrees must have existed." J. Deshusses, "The Sacramentaries: A Progress Report," *Liturgy* 18 (Gethsemani 1984) 48.

221. Editions of the *Hadrianum*: H. A. Wilson, *The Gregorian Sacramentary under Charles the Great*, HBS 49 (London 1915), a diplomatic edition reproducing the 3 MSS which Wilson considered the best: *Vat. Reg. 337*, Cambrai 164, and *Ottoboni 313*; H. Lietzmann, *Das Sacramentarium Gregorianum nach dem Aachener Urexemplar*, LQ F3 (Münster/Westf. 1921; reprint 1958), using Cambrai 164 and *Ottoboni 313* with assistance from *Vat. Reg. 337*; K. Gamber, *Sacramentarium Gregorianum*, TPL 4 and 6 (Regensburg 1966-1967), which attempts to restore the primitive text of the Gregorian by eliminating anything not in it towards the beginning of the VII century; J. Deshusses, *Le sacramentaire grégorien, ses principales formes d'après les plus anciens manuscrits*, 3 vols., Spicilegium Friburgense 16, 24, 28 (Fribourg 1971, 1979, 1982). See also E. Bishop, *Liturgica Historica*, chap. 15: "A Letter of Abbot Helisachar," (Oxford 1918, 1962) 333-348. Bibliography in *Sakramentartypen* and in CLLA; E. Bourque, *Étude* 2/2 (Rome 1958) 13-16; A. Chavasse, *Le Sacramentaire gélasien* (Paris-Tournai 1958), is the best over-all

study of the Romano-Frankish sacramentaries and the problems they raise. For the MSS see H. Lietzmann, "Handschriftliches zur Rekonstruktion des Sakramentarium Gregorianum," *Miscellanea Ehrle*, SeT 38 (Rome 1924) 13-26 and in JfL 5 (1925) 68-79; A. Dold, "Bedeutsame Reste dreier gregorianischer Sakramentare," EL 50 (1936) 359-365 (Clm 29164). R. Amiet, "Le prologue *Hucusque* et la table des *Capitula* du Supplément d'Alcuin au sacramentaire grégorien," *Scriptorium* 7 (1953) 177-209, "Les sacramentaires 88 et 137 du Chapitre de Cologne," *Scriptorium* 9 (1955) 76-84 and the introduction, pp. 34-47, of Deshusses' edition of the *Hadrianum* (Spicilegium Friburgense 16). For the *formulae* 205-226, see G. Manz, *Ausdrucksformen der lateinischen Liturgiesprache*, TuA 1/1 (Beuron 1941) 17-23.

222. A. Chavasse, "Les oraisons pour les dimanches ordinaires," RB 93 (1983) 31-70, 170-244.

223. "Towards 682-683, a little *Ordo missae romanae* (with the canon) and the formulaires for the ordination of bishops, presbyters and deacons were all added to the opening pages of the book (section 1-4); and at the end of the book there was a similar supplement with a few masses for special occasions, some blessing-formulas and analogous texts (sections 198-200, 205-226)." J. Deshusses, "The Sacramentaries," *Liturgy* 18 (1984) 39. But note Chavasse, "Les oraisons," RB 93 (1983) for additional and essential information about the *orationes cottidianae* (section 202), *supra*, note 222.

224. See Ordo I (*Ordo romanus primus*), nos.18-22, ed. M. Andrieu, *Les Ordines romani* 2 (Louvain 1948) 72-73: *Apostolum autem subdiaconus qui lecturus est sub cura habebit; evangelium archidaconus. Aquamanus, patena cotidiana, calicem, sciffos et pugilares et alios aurios et gemelliones argenteos . . . cantatorio et cetera vasa aurea et argentea, cereostata aurea et argentea de ecclesia Salvatoris . . .*

225. Cf. T. Klauser, "Die liturgischen Austauschbeziehungen," *Historisches Jahrbuch* 53 (1953) 181, note 42 as against E. Bishop, *Liturgica Historica*, 63, note 1 and A. Wilmart in E. Bishop, *Le génie du rit romain* (Paris 1920) 77, note 26.

226. J. Deshusses thinks that Alcuin of Tours probably circulated to his close friends Arno of Salzburg and Benedict of Aniane a Romano-English copy of a primitive version of the *Gregorianum*. That meant they were in a position to critique their current *Hadrianum* from the evidence of an earlier MS.; cf. *Sac. grég.*, pp. 71-72.

227. The Supplement to the *Hadrianum* was edited by H. A. Wilson in 1915 and by J. Deshusses in 1971 (*supra*, note 221). Deshusses' edition is based primarily on the Sacramentary of Marmoutier (Autun, Bibliothèque municipale, *codex* 19), but is compared with several other IX-century MSS. For a recent study of the MS of the Sacramentary of Marmoutier, see J. Decreaux, "Le sacramentaire de Marmoutier conservé à la Bibliothèque Municipale d'Autun," *Mémoires de la Société eduenne* 51 (Autun 1970) 237-292; a further study by this author will be published by the Pontifical Institute of Christian Archeology, Rome (1986). For the liturgical work of Alcuin, see L.C. Mohlberg, "L'oeuvre liturgique d'Alcuin," *Annuaire de l'Université de Louvain* 73 (1909) 418-428; F. Cabrol, "Les écrits liturgiques d'Alcuin," *Revue*

d'Histoire Ecclésiastique 19 (1923) 507-521; F. Ganshof, "La révision de la Bible par Alcuin," Bibliothèque d'Humanisme et de Renaissance. Travaux et documents 9 (Geneva 1947) 7-20; G. Ellard, Master Alcuin Liturgist (Chicago 1956); E. Bourque, Étude 2/2 (Rome 1958) 139-250. The standard arguments for attributing the Supplement to Alcuin are in E. Bishop, Liturgica Historica (Oxford 1918, 1962) 55; A. Wilmart, "Les messes de la collection de St. Amand," JfL 3 (1923) 67-77.

228. The Missal (ca. 800) can be recovered from 2 surviving MSS, the Sacramentary of the Cathedral of Tours (Bibl. Nat. nouv. acq. lat. 1589; early X century) and the Sacramentary-Antiphonary of St. Martin's Abbey (Tours, Bibliothèque municipale, codex 184; last quarter of the IX century). It unites, combines and modifies the Hadrianum and the Frankish Gelasian material quite drastically and criticizes and corrects them in the light of older MSS of the Gregorian Sacramentary of Romano-Frankish and Romano-English origin. It proves that, whatever the authority of the authenticum of Aachen, one, at least, of the outstanding Carolingian liturgists could use it very freely. Alcuin also composed fresh masses that were to have enormous influence on medieval piety; these 21 or 22 votive masses have been published by J. Deshusses, "Les messes d'Alcuin," AfL 14 (1972) 7-41 and even more critically in Sac. grég. 2, Spicilegium Friburgense 24 (1979), nos. 1,3,9,10, 14,16,17,18,63,94,105,109,110,112,120,128,132,185,223,263,264, and possibly, 269. See also H.Barré-J. Deshusses, "A la recherche du Missel d'Alcuin," EL 82 (1968) 3-44; cf. N.K. Rasmussen, "Une cartula missalis retrouvée," EL 83 (1969) 482-484. Alcuin's biographer depicts him as celebrating mass daily by means of his votive masses: Celebrabat omni die missarum solemnia, multa cum honestatis diligentia, habens singulis hebdomadae diebus missas deputatas proprias (Alcuini vita 26; PL 100, 104).

229. J. Deshusses, "Le Supplément au Sacramentaire grégorien: Alcuin ou S. Benoît d'Aniane?" AfL 9 (1965) 48-71 and "Le sacramentaire grégorien préhadrianique," RB 80 (1970) 213-237 and a review by A.G. Martimort, Bulletin de Littérature ecclésiastique 73 (1972) 273 who agrees that the Supplement must be attributed to Benedict of Aniane.

230. The prologue Hucusque and the Capitula were published by R. Amiet, "Le prologue Hucusque et la table des Capitula du Supplément d'Alcuin," Scriptorium 7 (1953) 177-209 and reproduced by G. Ellard, Master Alcuin Liturgist, 111-173. The text of the prologue appears in L.A. Muratori, Liturgia Romana vetus 2 (Venice 1748) 741 and in H.A. Wilson, The Gregorian Sacramentary, 145-146. In the present volume references to the prologue and Capitula are, naturally, to J. Deshusses, Sac. grég, vol. 1 (1971).

231. We refer the reader again to A. Chavasse, "Les oraisons pour les dimanches ordinaires," RB 93 (1983) 31-70; 177-244.

232. This is the classic distribution since A. Ebner, Quellen und Forschungen zur Geschichte und Kungstgeschichte des Missale Romanum in Mittelalter. Iter Italicum (Freiburg/Br. 1896; reprint Graz 1957) 232-391. For all the following MSS, refer to the repertoria listed in note 221. supra.

233. There are provisional lists of such MSS in Ebner, Bourque and Gamber, but satisfactory *repertoria* will only be compiled after all the MSS have been described in detail.

234. How the Frankish Gelasians of the IX century were gradually 'Gregorianized' and 'Hadrianized' was set forth in magisterial fashion by M. Andrieu, "Quelques remarques sur le classement des sacramentaires," JfL 11 (1931) 46-66.

235. After his trip to Rome in 831, Amalarius of Metz added a preface to the third edition of his *De ecclesiasticis officiis* in which he noted the different usages of Rome and *Francia* at the same period: cf. J.M. Hanssens, ed., *Amalarii episcopi opera liturgica omni*, SeT 138 (Vatican City 1948) 13-19; PL 105, 987-992.

236. J. Deshusses, "Chronologie des grands sacramentaires de Saint-Amand," RB 87 (1977) 230-237 and "Encore les sacramentaires de Saint-Amand," RB 89 (1979) 310-312. This sumptuous series of gift editions integrated the Supplement of Benedict of Aniane more and more into the body of the sacramentary proper and added additional material until an ultra-complete edition was achieved.

237. Bibliography on the *Paduensis* in K. Gamber, *Sakramentartypen*, 130-131 and CLLA 880, pp. 389-399 and in Bourque, *Etude* 1, 301-391. Critical edition by L.C. Mohlberg, *Die älteste erreichbare Gestalt des Liber Sacramentorum anni circuli der römischen Kirche mit Untersuchungen von A. Baumstark (codex Paduensis D. 47, folios 11-100),* LQF 11-12 (Münster/Westf. 1927; reprint 1967); a very convenient edition will also be found in J. Deshusses, *Sac grég.* 1, 609-684. Mohlberg's title may lead unwary readers astray; *Vat. Reg.* 316 actually contains the oldest MS of a Roman Sacramentary (aside from the *Veronensis* which is not a sacramentary properly speaking). What the *Paduensis* actually does, is help us attain an earlier stage of evolution of the papal sacramentary than that contained in the *Hadrianum*. In his *Untersuchungen* to the critical edition, Baumstark presented conclusions which were subsequently contradicted by Mohlberg's own work; see the latter's refutations in "Il Messale glagolitico di Kiev, "*Atti della Pontificia Accademia di Archeologia, Memorie* 2 (1928) 267-269 and in his "Note liturgiche per precisare l'origine del Sacramentario del secolo VIII," *Atti della Pont. Accad. Archeol, Rendiconti* 7 (1932) 28-31.

238. The paleographical evidence is confirmed by the fact that the Emperor Lothair is alone named at the end of the *Exultet*; that means the MS could only have been copied when he was sole ruler (840-855). Provenance has to be determined from the additions to the *sanctorale* and from the style of the illuminations.

239. Folios 1-10 and 100-136 contain non-eucharistic elements of considerable antiquity, some of which may even have belonged to the primitive redaction of this sacramentary; their disorderly arrangement and their Gallican interpolations seem to indicate that they could not, however, have belonged to the Roman *prototype* (ed., Mohlberg, xxv-xviii; *cf.* M. Andrieu, "Les messes de Jeudis," RSR 9 (1929) 454).

240. The *Ordo missae* and the prayers for the ordinations of bishops, presbyters and deacons had not yet been added to the prototype. Deshusses judges that such an addition was accomplished towards 682-683; "The Sacramentaries: A Progress Report" *Liturgy* 18 (1984) 39.

241. This ancient feast of the Meeting/Encounter of Jesus and the aged Simeon in the Temple has almost identical texts in *Pad*. 25, Trent, and *Had*. 27; all three have a prayer *ad collectam* indicating a preliminary procession before the mass of the feast. Sergius I (687-701) extended this custom of gathering at St. Hadrian-in-the-Forum and going in procession to St. Mary Major for mass to the other three 'Marian' festivals of March 25, Aug. 15 and Sept. 8. Cf. *Liber Pontificalis, Vita Sergii* (ed. Duchesne 1, 376): *Constituit Sergius ut diebus Adnuntiationis Domini, Dormitionis et Nativitatis sanctae dei genetricis semperque virginis Mariae ac sancti Symeonis, quod Ypapanti Graeci appellant, letania exeat sanctae Hadrianae et ad sanctam Mariam [ad praesepe] populus occurrat.*

242. Including the Thursdays of Lent which had been aliturgical until the pontificate of Gregory II (715-731): *Hic quadragesimali tempore ut quintas ferias missarum celebritas fieret in ecclesiam, quod non agebatur instituit: Liber Pontificalis, Vita Gregorii II* (ed. Duchesne 1, 401). It is possibly Gregory II who also instituted the feast of his sainted predecessor Gregory I which does not appear in *Pad*. or Trent, but is in the *Hadrianum* (cf. *Had*. 30).

243. Cf. *Had*. 72: *Sabbato ad S. Petrum quando helesmosyna datur* (with a mass-set).

244. The Greater Litany did not yet imply the Gallican devotion of the 3 Rogation days (*litaniae minores*), whereas the Frankish Gelasians already included them; cf. *Gellone* (ed. Dumas), 133-136.

245. The *Inventio crucis* (May 3), *Passio sancti Johannis Baptistae* (Aug. 29) and *Mauricius cum sociis suis* (Sept. 22) are 'Gallican' feasts which the Sacramentary of St. Peter's absorbed in its sojourn north of the Alps.

246. With the permission of the emperor, Boniface IV dedicated the Pantheon to Mary and all the Martyrs (May 13, 609); cf. *Liber pontificalis, Vita Bonifatii IV* (ed. Duchesne 1, 317).

247. The *Had*. (159) has a complete mass and calls it *Exaltatio sanctae Crucis*. The *Tridentinum* (ed. Deshusses, *Sac. grég*. 1, 368-370) has an *oratio* and *super oblata* taken from the votive mass *de s. Cruce* of Alcuin (=*Sac. grég*, 2, nos. 1835-1836, p. 44). Sergius I rediscovered a significant portion of the True Cross in St. Peter's sacristy and *ex die illo pro salute humani generis ab omni populo christiano, die Exaltationis sanctae Crucis [Sept. 14], in basilicam Salvatoris quae appellatur Constantiniana [the Lateran] osculatur et adoratur: Liber Pontificalis, Vita Sergii*; ed. Duchesne 1, 374). From the description in the *Liber pont*. this Cross must have closely resembled the famous Cross of Justin II still preserved at St. Peter's. This is the first documentary evidence for the feast of the Exaltation of the Cross.

248. Note that two Sundays frame the Sept. Ember days and that this stable group of five masses appeared between the V Sun. *post Laurenti* and the I Sun. *post Angeli*. As this older method of subdividing Sundays was

discarded in favor of a continuous series of Sundays *post Pentecosten*, the ancient Sunday mass-sets before and after the Ember days disappeared. Although they are still present in the *Hadrianum* (163 and 167), they are already absent from the Sunday list of Benedict of Aniane's Supplement; cf. A. Chavasse, "Les oraisons," RB 93 (1983) 185-186.

249. St. Caesarius, the martyr-deacon of Terracina in Campania, a constant feature of the Lateran sacramentary and its descendants (*Pad.*, 179, *Had.*, 172-173 and *Trid.* etc., and the Frankish Gelasians), was eventually to be replaced by the feast of All Saints so widely promoted by Alcuin of Tours and his friends. The *Festivitas omnium sanctorum* appears in the Sacramentary of Essen (Corbie, late IX century; CLLA 915) and by the late X century some direct descendants of the *Had.* + *Suppl.* tradition had both a vigil and feast of All Saints; cf. *The Missal of St. Augustine's Abbey, Canterbury*, ed. M. Rule (Cambridge 1896) 118-119.

250. Nov. 11: Martin of Tours (315?-397) was one of the first non-martyr bishops to be venerated in the Roman liturgy and the oldest existing church in England already bore his name when Augustine arrived in Canterbury in 597: *Erat autem prope ipsam civitatem ad orientem ecclesia in honorem sancti Martini antiquitus facta dum adhuc Romani Britanniam incolerent*; Bede, *Historia eccles.* 1, 26 (Cambridge 1971) 112. Bede may have been right about the age of the church but wrong about its dedication to St. Martin during the Roman occupation. Perhaps Bishop Liuthard of Senlis, chaplain to Queen Bertha, created the dedication when he accompanied her from Gaul to Canterbury; cf. M. Deanesly, *The Pre-Conquest Church in England* (London 1963) 48.

251. The *Veronense* reveals only the slightest traces of an Advent liturgy in its December Ember Days (section XLIII) but by the mid-VII century the Lateran sacramentary contains four Sunday masses and three Ember Day Masses with strong Advent themology. Their stress seems to be primarily on the incarnation and its liturgical celebration rather than on the second coming as in Gaul.

252. In the primitive Gregorian, [cf. *Had.* 202] there was a complete section of *orationes cottidianae* to be used by celebrants *ad libitum* to compose Sunday masses in ordinary time. When full lectionaries had already been developed for all the Sundays of the year, celebrants were still free to choose their *orationes* from this rather lengthy list (59 collects in the *Had.*); cf. A. Chavasse, "Les oraisons," 35-36. Here, in the *Pad.*, there are 7 complete mass-sets for ordinary Sundays, even though all the Sundays throughout the year have already been filled at their proper places in the sacramentary. In this instance, the seven full *missae cottidianae* have replaced the *orationes cottidianae* whereas in the *Tridentinum* these collects are inserted in the *Canon missae* after the words, *oratio dicitur una ex his.*

253. Chavasse, *Le Sac. gél.*, 526 and 567.

254. Deshusses considers it a "reasonable hypothesis" because the Good Friday prayer for the emperor is in the plural and may be connected with the famous events of 663; "The Sacramentaries," 42-43; cf. Chavasse, *Le Sac gél.*,

510-514 on the genesis of formulary LXII of *Vat. Reg.* 316, *Pro regibus*. For an official account of this unusual visit and of the emperor's two Sunday masses at St. Peter's, see *Liber Pontificalis, Vita Vitaliani*; ed. Duchesne 1, 343-344.

255. Cf. the VII-century entries of the *Liber pontificalis* and A. Chavasse, "L'organisation générale des sacramentaires dits Grégoriens. L'apport du sacramentaire conservé à Trente. Le Sanctoral de H. P. et O," RSR 56 (1982) 179-200, 253-273; 57(1983) 50-56, particularly his compiling of evidence from the *Liber pontificalis*, the sacramentaries and the early Roman lectionaries to establish the chronology of the VII-VIII century feasts.

256. *Liber pontificalis, Vita Leonis II*; ed. Duchesne 1, 360; cf. J.P. Kirsch, *Der altrömische Festkalendar im Altertum* (Freiburg/Br. 1924) 144-145.

257. *Liber pontificalis, Vita Sergii I*; ed. Duchesne 1, 375.

258. Cf. note 241 *supra* and Chavasse, *Le Sac. gél.*, 375-402.

259. *Hic [Sergius] statuit ut tempore confractionis dominici corporis 'Agnus Dei, qui tollis peccata mundi, miserere nobis' a clero et populo decantetur: Liber pontificalis, Vita Sergii I* (Duchesne 1, 376).

260. Our argument is strengthened by the fact that a sacramentary of the Paduan-type was already circulating in Gaul before the middle of the VIII century since the Benedictine compilers of the Sacramentary of Flavigny (ca. 760-770) used it to create their composite work; cf. M. Andrieu, "Les messes des jeudis," RSR 9 (1929) 352-360. Their type-II Gregorian did not yet contain the masses for the Thursdays of Lent, for if such had been the case, they would have copied its *formulae* as they stood instead of creating their own. J. Deshusses, "The Sacramentaries," 43, asserts however, that the Roman ancestor of the *Paduensis* already contained the Lenten Thursdays before leaving Rome.

261. For example, the Thursday *formulae* are all off by a week in comparison with the *Hadrianum*. Only the 4th and 5th Thursdays have the stational churches indicated and they are the wrong ones, being the churches for the 3rd and 4th Thursdays; such awkward errors are inconceivable if these *formulae* had been added already at Rome. How the Frankish compiler knew the Thursdays were no longer aliturgical is not apparent, but he could have learned it in a variety of ways, *via* pilgrims, lectionaries, letters, *etc.*

262. In his investigations of the Old Gelasian, A. Chavasse was led to conclude that *Pad*. D. 47 represented a revision of the papal sacramentary made at Rome between 650 and 682-683 with the help of an Old Gelasian sacramentary: cf. *Le Sac. gél.*, 684. By so doing, Chavasse corrected his older hypothesis which maintained that a Gregorian like *Pad*. D 47 had been composed in 3 stages: in 594 (for the portion before Easter), in 595 (Easter to Sept 29), and in 596 (Sept 29 to the vigil of Christmas); cf. Chavasse, "Temps de préparation à la Pâque d'après quelques manuscrits liturgiques romains," RSR 37 (1950) 125-145 and "Peut-on dater le sacramentaire grégorien?" EL 58 (1953) 108-111. Obviously Chavasse' hypotheses concern the *types* of sacramentaries and not the texts in which they survive; as a text the *Hadrianum* (Sacramentary of Hidoard *et al.*) is of the early IX century and *Pad*. D. 47 of the mid-IX century, but as a *type* the Paduan-kind of mass book

(Gregorian type II) is earlier than the fully developed *Hadrianum* (Gregorian, type I, late VIII century).

263. P. de Puniet, "Le sanctoral romain et les dimanches après la Pentecôte," *Vie et les arts liturgiques* 12 (1925-1926) 343-349; 385-392; L.C. Mohlberg, *Die älteste erreichbare Gestalt* (Pad. D. 47), xxxviii-xxxix.

264. See the bibliography in Gamber, *Sakramentartypen* and CLLA, *passim*; E. Dekkers, *Clavis Patrum Latinorum* (1961) 426-428, and E. Bourque, *Étude 1*, 301-309.

265. *The Sacramentary of Trent* will appear in 1986 in an edition by F. Dell'Oro and B. Baroffio. Literature: Bonelli, *Monumenta Ecclesiae Tridentinae* (Trent 1760-1765) 1,321; 2, 219; 3, 65 and 485; 4,399; cf. A.M. Triacca, EL 81 (1967) 447, note 3; Weinberger, *Abhandlungen für die Fortschritte der Klassischen Altertumswissenschaften* (1913) 103; G. Gerola, "Il Sacramentario della Chiesa di Trento," *Dedalo* 2, vol. 1 (Milan 1921); J. Deshusses, "Le sacramentaire grégorien de Trente," RB 78 (1968) 261-282; "Le sacramentaire grégorien pré-hadrianique," RB 80 (1970) 213-237, *Sac. grég.* 1, 71-72 and the *Additiones Codicis Tridentini* on pp. 708-715 of the same vol.; and "Sacramentaries," 55-56; A. Chavasse, "L'organisation générale des sacramentaires dits grégoriens," RSR 56 (1982) 179-200, 253-273; 57 (1983) 50-56. Other recent studies by Chavasse help us discern the on-going organization and development of *Pad.*, Trent and *Had.*: "Le Sermonnaire Vatican du VII siècle," SE 23 (1978/79) 225-289; "L'Epistolier romain du Codex de Wurtzbourg," RB 91 (1981) 280-331; "L'Evangéliaire romain de 645: un recueil," RB 92 (1982) 33-75.

266. Two of Alcuin's letters—to the monks of St. Vaast of Arras and to those of Fulda— (Letters 250 and 296, MGH *Epistolarum* 4, 454f and 404f) contain lists of his votive masses. The mass of St. Rupert in Trent—*Orationes ad Missam in Natale Sancti Hrodperti Confessoris* (Deshusses, *Sac. grég*, 2, no. 347, p. 303)—has the same structure and style as Alcuin's other votive masses and was surely composed especially for Arno of Salzburg. Again, the letters of Alcuin also reveal that, as early as 799, Alcuin and Arno were celebrating in their respective abbeys the still unusual feasts of all Saints; once again structure and style betray the hand of Alcuin (cf. Deshusses, *Sac. grég.*, 2, nos. 385 and 386, pp. 330-332).

267. Barré-Deshusses, "A la recherche du Missel d'Alcuin," EL 82 (1968) 3-44; J. Deshusses, "Les Messes d'Alcuin," AfL 14 (1972) 7-41 and *Sac. grég.* 1 (1979), nos. 1,3,9,10,14,16,17,18,63,94,105,109,110,112,120,128,132,185,223, 263,264.

268. In his 1970 article on the pre-Hadrianic Gregorian, Deshusses suggests, however, that both the *Hadrianum* and the pre-*Hadrianum* may have both been dispatched from Rome by Pope Hadrian and that therefore both merit the name *Hadrianum*. In any case, it seems sure now that sometime before the end of the IX century, the Carolingian reformers had at their disposal both an VIII-century and a VII-century (pre-Sergius I) papal sacramentary.

269. This is the famous composite sacramentary described in the Chron-

icle of St. Riquier: *Missalis gregorianus et gelasianus modernis temporibus ab Albino ordinatus (Chronicon Centulense* 3,3; ed. F. Lot, Paris 1894). Deshusses reminds us that Alcuin, for all his interest in the genuine Gregorian, was not at all opposed to the sacramentary formerly composed in one of the abbeys dependent on St. Martin of Tours, i.e. Flavigny.

270. Because of the proliferation of such *codices*—many of which are not yet properly catalogued—we still do not have a completely satisfying list of these MSS. Aside from the inventories of V. Leroquais which are only for MSS preserved in France, the most complete accounting is that of E. Bourque, *Étude sur les sacramentaires romains,* 2/2 (Rome 1958) 253-385. On how to classify such MSS, see P. Séjourné, *L'Ordinaire d'Utretcht (1919-1921)* 142 and E. Bishop-A. Wilmart, "La réforme liturgique de Charlemagne," EL 45 (1931) 205-207. A variety of names have been suggested for the present category of MSS: *Mixed Gregorians of the X Century or Gelazianized Gregorians* (A. Ebner, *Das Missale Romanum im Mittelalter* 389-394, 362-387), the *Gelasiano-Gregorian Missal of the X Century* (E. Bishop, EL 45 (1931) 207.)

271. Such confusion was created by M. Andrieu, JfL 11 (1931) 50-66, when he considered the *Fuldense* and the *Rossianum* as related to the Frankish Gelasians while they really belong among the Gelasiano-Gregorians described above. P. de Puniet provided a method for distinguishing them when he set up his concordances of the Frankish Gelasians of the VIII century: *Le sacramentaire romain de Gellone* (Rome 1938) 1-333; a simple comparison of his tables with the arrangement of the Gelasiano-Gregorians will suffice to tell the difference. For a critique of these kinds of tables, see A. Chavasse, *op. cit.,* note 175, i-iv.

272. Cf. E. Bourque, *Étude* 2/2, 492-499.

273. The official edition of the *Missale Romanum* published by Pius V (July 14, 1570) hardly differs at all from the *editio princeps* which appeared at Milan in 1474 [reprinted by R. Lippe, *Missale Romanum Mediolanensis anno 1474,* HBS 17 and 33 (London 1899 and 1907) with the variants of the 14 editions which preceded 1570]. Except for the addition of new feasts, the Milanese edition of 1474 reproduced the missal of the XIII century; cf. M. Andrieu, "Le missel de la chapelle papale à la fin du XIII siècle," *Miscellanea F. Ehrle* 2, SeT 38 (Rome 1924) 348-376. For more recent controversy on this point see, S.J.P. Van Dijk, "The Legend of the Missal of the Papal Chapel," SE 8 (1956) 76-142 and M. Andrieu, "Une controverse récente sur le Missel de la Chapelle papale," *Scriptorium* 11 (1955) 17-34. The type of classification used here was first proposed by E. Bourque, *Étude,* 2/2 444-472; see also A.P. Frutaz, " Due edizioni rare del 'Missale romanum' pubblicato a Milano nel 1482 e nel 1492," *Miscellanea G. Belvederi* (1954-1955) 55-107.

274. Nordenfalk, *Acta Archeologica* 2/3 (1931) 207-244; Bourque, *Étude* 2/2, pp. 255 and 447-448; CLLA 761, p. 356.

275. Ed. M. Rule, *The Missal of St. Augustine's Abbey,* Canterbury (Cambridge 1896); Bourque, *Étude* 2/2, pp. 271 and 447-452.

276. Ed. M. De Azevedo, *Vetus missale romanum monasticum Lateranense* (Rome 1752-1754); N. Antonelli, *Vetus missale monasticum* (Rome 1756);

Bourque Étude 2/2, 301 and 453-454; CLLA 1187ᵇ, p. 469.

277. Ed. J. Brinktrine, *Sacramentarium Rossianum*, Römische Quartalschrift Supplement-Heft 25 (Freiburg/Br. 1930); CLLA 985, 426-427.

278. Partial edition in PL 78, 25-264, 605-628; E. Martène, *De antiquis Ecclesiae ritibus* 1, 541-547 Martimort, *Martène* nos. 354 and 553.

279. Extracts in V. Leroquais, *Sacramentaires et missels manuscripts des Bibliothèques publics de France* 1 (1924) 122-125; CLLA 920, pp. 412-413.

280. Edd. G. Richter–A. Schönfelder, *Sacramentarium Fuldense saeculi X*, Quellen und Abhandlungen zur Geschichte der Abtei und der Diözese Fulda 9 (Fulda 1912; reprint HBS 101, London 1972-1977); CLLA 970, pp. 422-423.

281. Ed. H. Ménard, *Divi Gregorii I papae Liber Sacramentorum* (Paris 1641-1642, reprint Farnborough 1969)) 1,1-288; PL 78, 25-264 and vol. 2, 25-582 (*notae et observationes*). Dom Ménard published the Sacramentary of St. Eligius thinking it to be a pure Gregorian whereas it is one of the most hybrid examples of a Gelasiano-Gregorian; research on the Gregorian was severly hampered for many years to come as a result of his mistake. CLLA 901, pp. 409-410.

282. Cf. A. Brackmann, *Germania Pontificia* 3 (1923) 152: *Statuens ut monasterium debeat pensionis nomine in sui consecratione codicem sacrementorum I, Evangeliorum I, Equos albos II.*

283. Cf. T, Klauser, "Austauschbeziehungen," *Historisches Jahrbuch* 53 (1933) 185, and M. Andrieu, *Les ordines romani* 1, 515-516. The text of Deusdedit is in his collection ed. V. Wolf von Glanvell, *Die Kanonessamlung des Kardinals Deusdedit* (Paderborn 1905) 362.

284. Cf. L. Brou, "Étude historique su les oraisons des dimanches après la Pentecôte," SE (1949) 123-224, esp. 212-223.

285. Cf. M. Andrieu, "Le missel de la chapelle papale à la fin du XIII siècle," *Miscellanea F. Ehrle* 2, SeT 38 (Rome 1924) 348-376. The title of the missal was *Ordo missale secundum consuetudinem curiae romanae* (or *Ecclesiae romanae*) and survives in 2 MSS: Avignon, Bibliothèque municipale, *codex* 100, ca. 1276-1288 and Rome, *Vat. Ottoboni* 326, ca. 1288-1292. This is the immediate ancestor of the Tridentine Missal of 1570 and differs little from the *Vetus missale romanum monasticum Lateranense* published by E. de Azevedo, (Rome 1752). S.J.P. Van Dijk comes to different conclusions than those of Andrieu in his "The Lateran Missal," SE 6 (1954) 125-129; see also Van Dijk–J.H. Walker, *The Origins of the Modern Roman Liturgy* (London 1960), esp. chap. 2.

286. See the important articles of M. Andrieu, "Les messes des jeudis de Carême et les anciens sacramentaires," RSR 9 (1929) 360-364 which contradicts the points developed by A. Baumstark and his school: résumé in A. Baumstark, *Missale romanum. Seine Entwicklung, ihre wichtigsten Urkunden und Probleme* (Einhoven-Nijmegen 1929).

287. *Missalis plenarius* is not a new term; cf. The *False Decretal of Leo IV*, PL 115, 878; Rathier of Verona (974); PL 136, 559, etc.. For an understanding of this complex terminology, see S.J.P. Van Dijk–J.H. Walker, *The Origins of the*

Modern Roman Liturgy (London 1960) 57-66.

288. See the figures of V. Leroquais: For the years 1000-1050, 5 plenary missals and 14 sacramentaries; 1050-1100, 17 plenary missals and 7 sacramentaries; XII century, 41 sacramentaries, all from the beginning of the century, and 111 plenary missals; XIII century, the plenary missal is the rule; XIV century, only 4 sacramentaries. Ebner's figures for Italy agree with those of Leroquais for France. Plenary missals already existed in both France and Italy in the X century: Leroquais, *op. cit.*, no. 37; Milan, *codex* L. 77.

289. See A. Wilmart, "Les anciens missels de France," EL 46 (1932) 240.

290. J.A. Jungmann, *The Mass of the Roman Rite* 1 (New York 1951) 212-233.

291. L. Fischer, *Bernhardi cardinalis et Lateranensis ecclesiae prioris Ordo officiorum ecclesiae Lateranensis* (Munich 1916) 80-81—From that time on, the celebrant repeated the parts read or sung by the deacon, subdeacon, lectors and the schola; as this practice became more extensive it became, little by little, obligatory.

292. This had already occured in some 'fused' *Hadriana*: *the Sacramentary of Brescia* (Bologna, University Library, *codex* 2547; Brescia, end of the XI century) and in the *Sacramentary of Lorsch* (Rome, *Vat. Pal.* 495; Lorsch, X-XI century).

293. E. Bourque, *Étude* 2/2, 503-533.

294. There is still no good history of the plenary missal or of the Roman Missal. Baumstark's *Missale romanum* (1929) is marred by too many false or unverifiable hypotheses.

IV. THE ROMANO-FRANKISH/ ROMANO-GERMANIC PERIOD: FROM GREGORY THE GREAT (590-604) TO GREGORY VII (1073-1085).
THE ORDINES ROMANI.

Strictly speaking, an *ordo* is a description of a liturgical action (*actio liturgica*), a directory or guide for the celebrant and his ministers setting forth in detail the arrangement of the entire ritual procedure and how to carry it out.[1] As descriptive of the actual rite, the *ordines* are the indispensable complement to the Sacramentary. The *Liber sacramentorum* contains only the prayers and other formulas needed by the officiant in the course of the liturgy and is either completely without ceremonial indications or contains only a few, brief, general directions of little use to the average celebrant. Neither the celebrant nor his ministers would discover in the Sacramentary enough information for a given liturgical function, especially a complicated one. Unless they had been previously initiated into the ritual process by an experienced master of ceremonies, they would find it quite impossible, without an *ordo*, to perform the rite in question.[2] An *ordo* would prove even more indispensable to a church which acquired a new Sacramentary that supposed a different style of celebration than the one to which the local clergy were accustomed. From the VIII century on, such was often the case North of the Alps.

1. *Terminology*

In a more general sense, the term *ordo* means an arrangement, disposition, grouping, composition or plan and is equivalent to the term *regula* or *canon*.[3] For example, in the letter of Pope Innocent I (416): *Si instituta ecclesiastica . . . vellent servare Dei sacerdotes, nulla diversitas . . . in ipsis ordinibus et consecrationibus haberetur.*[4] As regards institutional arrangements in the Church, *ordo* stands in opposition to *plebs; ordo* stands for the clergy, *plebs* for the laity; Tertullian speaks in this way: *Nonne et laici sacerdotes sumus?...Differentiam inter ordinem et plebem constituit ecclesiae auctoritas, et honor, per ordinis consessum sanctificatus.*[5] With the same semantic background, *ordo* and *ordines* came to designate those in holy orders or the degrees themselves within the clerical *cursus honorum.*[6]

Confined to the liturgical domain, sometimes *ordo* means the eucharistic prayer; thus the Council of Braga (563): *Placuit ut eodem ordine missae celebrantur ab omnibus, quem Profuturus, quondam huius metropolitanae Ecclesiae episcopus, ab ipsa apostolicae Sedis auctoritate accepit scriptum.*[7]

In the strict sense used here—a description of rites—the word *ordo* came into use sometime after Gregory the Great (✝604), i.e., after the period of liturgical improvisation was over. It does not seem to have been much used before the VIII century. It appears in various places in the Old Gelasian Sacramentary (*Vat. Reg.* 316) copied in Gaul (Chelles, Northern France) around 750: e.g., I, XX (Wilson, p. 22; Mohlberg, p. 24): *Ordo qualiter ... presbyteri, diaconi vel subdiaconi eligendi sunt;* I, XXXVIII (Wilson, p. 64; Mohlberg, p. 56): *Ordo agentibus publicam paenitenciam.* In the collections of *ordines*, the term *ordo* appears a bit earlier if, indeed, that title was really an authentic part of the original document. Thus *Ordo* XI (composed at Rome, ca. 650 and in Gaul, ca. 750): *Incipit ordo scrutinii ad electos qualiter debeant baptizari* (in the Montpellier MS, Biblio. Fac. Médicine, *codex* 412; early IX century); *Ordo* I (composed at Rome ca. 687/701 at the earliest and present in Gaul, ca. 750): *Incipit ordo ecclesiastici ministerii romanae ecclesiae vel qualiter missa celebratur* (the same Montpellier MS as *Ordo* XI). With Amalarius of Metz, liturgists came to use *ordo* in the strict sense: Amalarius (✝ca. 850), *De ordine antiphonarii: Ut ex scriptis discimus quae continent per diversos libellos ordinem romanum* (PL 105, 1295; ed. Hanssens, III, 83).[8]

In the XII century, *ordines* were enlarged by the addition of extraliturgical elements (historical and political notices, etc.): thus *Ordo* 11 of Mabillon or *Liber politicus* (ca. 1143) and *Ordo* 12 of Mabillon or *Ordo* of the *Liber censuum* of Cencius (ca. 1188-1197).

In the XIII century, the term *ordo* tended to disappear in favor of *Ordinarium, Caeremoniale, Liber de caeremoniis, Liber Caeremoniarum;* thus *Ordo* 13 of Mabillon or *Caeremoniale Romanum* (under Gregory X, ca. 1274); *Ordo* 14 of Mabillon or *Ordinarium Sanctae Romanae Ecclesiae* or *Ordo* of Cardinal G. Gaetano Stefaneschi (ca. 1304-1328); Mabillon's *Ordo* 15 or *Liber de caeremoniis ecclesiae romanae* or the *Ceremonial* of Pierre Amiel (✝1398). A *Liber caeremoniarum S.R.E.* can be found in Gattico, *Acta selecta caeremon. S.R.E.,* 1 (Rome 1753) 9.

Normally, liturgical historians and medievalists are more interested in the *ordines* than they are in the Sacramentaries since the
former allow them to reconstruct the actual ways of worshipping of a
given period and geographical area, a task that would be quite
impossible using the Sacramentaries alone.

As liturgical documents, the *ordines* can be viewed in three ways:

a) They permit us to witness a liturgy as it was actually celebrated
when the *codex* was drawn up and for as long as it remained in use.
Since we are dealing with a liturgical document in the strict sense
(and not with a work of erudition or instruction) we ordinarily
maintain that a MS containing *ordines* would not have been recopied
if it were not destined for practical use. On the other hand, it must be
confessed that, because of the archaizing tendency of some *scriptoria*
and a kind of craze for collecting everything in sight, in some MSS
there can be found out-of-date *ordines* side by side with current ones.
It is comparatively easy to distinguish one from the other.

b) They encourage us to get back behind the example in hand and
attain the archetype or common ancestor of an *ordo* or family of
ordines. By so doing, we can both arrive at the time certain rites began
to appear and also discover the amount of time they endured in use,
i.e., from the composition of the archetype until the transcription of
the most recent copy.[9]

c) Since paleographically speaking, the *ordines* are all of Frankish
manufacture and are, for the most part, of mixed or hybrid character
(Romano-Frankish/Romano-German), we must carefully separate
out the primitive or original form of the *ordo* from the additions made
at the time of its transcription and discover—if possible—both the
date of the primitive recension and the date it arrived in Gaul or
Germany (in the case of a Roman *ordo*). The Roman recension of the
ordo bears witness to a style of worship in the City of the Popes or in
the suburbicarian dioceses of Rome at a given historical moment; the
Frankish recensions permit us to see the changes the Roman rites
underwent after they crossed the Alps. Since a multiplicity of rites
was then normal, a variety of ritual descriptions could coexist in
regard to the same *actio liturgica* at the same period and in the same
locality, even if they were of different cultural and cultic back-
grounds. Only exceptionally were books brought up to date through
the direct intervention of some central authority, such as the Frankish
monarchy and its Romanizing policies. Normally books were
updated only gradually as MSS were transcribed for use. Consequently, the updating process was almost entirely dependent upon
the local initiatives of bishops and abbots or even the civil authority

on occasion (e.g., the *missi* of Charlemagne were authorized to intervene in matters liturgical as well as political and military) and upon the presence of *scriptoria* equipped to prepare liturgical *codices*.[10]

As documents designed to facilitate public worship, the *ordines* are, by nature, texts reserved to the exclusive use of masters of ceremonies, officiants and their ministers. In this regard, they are like the *libri paenitentiales*.[11] On the other hand, they do not constitute some kind of secret literature and there is no point in invoking the *disciplina arcani* in their regard. They were *functional* documents—at least in the early Middle Ages—and remained such so long as the rites described in the *ordines* remained accessible to all.[12] Only later, when the majority of rites became unintelligible to the faithful and often even to the celebrants themselves, did masters of ceremonies try to prohibit their dissemination and even their redaction.[13] In this regard it is helpful to discover the protest raised by the master of ceremonies, Paris de Grassis, against the edition of the *Ceremonial* published at Venice in 1516 under the title *Rituum ecclesiasticorum sive sacrarum caeremoniarum sanctae romanae Ecclesiae libri tres* by Cristoforo Marcello, bishop of Corfu, in accordance with the compilation of the papal ceremonial ordered by Innocent VIII in 1485. In his letter to Pope Leo X (March 11, 1516)), Paris de Grassis expresses the fear that making public the often unintelligible rites of the Church might furnish an occasion for deriding Christian worship and for damaging the prestige of the bishops [*quos*] *non tamquam mortales homines, sed tanquam deos in terris existimant et credunt*.[14]

Before they were gathered together in collections, each *ordo*—which described a single *actio liturgica* or some part thereof—existed completely on its own. The various Roman *ordines* which traveled northward across the Alps arrived independently and were gathered together for the first time only in Gaul.[15] Just as, early on, there were *libelli missarum* for each separate eucharistic celebration, there were also *ordines* corresponding to each liturgical function.

The *ordines* vary in dimension from a single page or leaflet to the size of a real book. As for the prayers which accompany such ritual instructions, sometimes an *ordo* refers to the Sacramentary (*ut in sacramentario continetur*), sometimes it contains the *incipit* of the prayers or other *formulae*, sometimes it even provides the prayers *in extenso*. In the latter case, we have either the forerunner of the Pontifical (non-eucharistic *ordines* + the corresponding prayers) or the Missal (*ordo* of the Mass + the necessary prayers).

Although we are sure that the Roman *ordines* arrived independently in the Frankish kingdom, we also know that they were gathered into collections very early on and that that is why they could spread so readily throughout Northern Europe. The *ordines* have survived only as collections; there is not a single *ordo* with an independent MS tradition of its own.

The collections of *ordines* are either strictly liturgical (created for practical liturgical use) or didactic (combining commentaries and *ordines* for the instruction of the clergy) or juridico-liturgical (combining administrative and canonical texts with *ordines*). Only those that are strictly liturgical in nature will be considered here.[16]

Like the oldest Sacramentaries, the *ordines* are all of Frankish or Germanic execution. This is true even when we are dealing with authentically Roman *ordines* which come to us only in northern MSS; such is also the case when it is a question of mixed or hybrid *ordines* of Romano-Frankish or Romano-Germanic composition in which native or local usages are superimposed on a Roman foundation to a greater or lesser degree, depending on the rites in question.

Until the appearance of Pontificals around the middle of the X century, the *ordines* are of major importance for the history of the liturgy. Sometime around 950, a compilation now called the *Romano-Germanic Pontifical of the Tenth Century* superseded the older *ordines* by absorbing and combining them into a single book. This fresh and superior composition soon spread far and wide throughout Latin Christendom, including Rome and the suburbicarian dioceses.[17] After the year 1000, we have to examine this Pontifical and its descendants if we want to appreciate the ceremonial details of medieval worship.

2. Bibliography

Historians of the liturgy have always been interested in the *ordines* but they have not been able to put them to full and systematic use until recently because they lacked both critical editions and sound chronological indications. The scholarly work of Michel Andrieu (born at Millau in 1886; died at Strasbourg in 1956) marked a turning-point in the study of the *ordines* as well as of the Roman Pontificals which succeeded them. All the editions of the *ordines* which appeared before those of Andrieu are now out-of-date, including those of Mabillon and Duchesne, and so are most of the studies of the *ordines* published before his time.

We shall cite the most important editions and studies that appeared before Andrieu because they are so often referred to in scholarly publications. Later, we shall also provide a concordance for the editions of Mabillon, Duchesne and Andrieu.

a. EDITIONS.

1. Major Editions:

Melchior Hittorp, *De divinis catholicae ecclesiae officiis et mysteriis varii vetustorum aliquot Ecclesiae Patrum ac scriptorum ecclesiasticorum libri* (Cologne 1568; reprint Farnborough 1970). Hittorp was reprinted at Rome in 1591 by G. Ferrari =*Magna Bibliotheca veterum Patrum* (Paris 1610) tome X =*Maxima Bibliotheca veterum Patrum* (Lyons 1677) tome XIII. Migne did not reprint Hittorp in the *Patrologia Latina*.

J. Mabillon, *De liturgia gallicana libri tres* (Paris 1695) =PL 72, 99-448.

J. Mabillon–M. Germain, *Museum Italicum*, 2 vols. (Paris 1687-1689). Volume 2, the one that concerns us, was Mabillon's alone and has the title *Musei Italici t. II complectens antiquos libros rituales sanctae romanae Ecclesiae cum commentario praevio in Ordinem romanum* (PL 78, 851-1408). This is still an indispensable book because of the *ordines* it contains which were not published by Andrieu and because of the commentaries which accompany them.

E. Martène, *De antiquis Ecclesiae ritibus libri tres* (1st ed., 3 vols., Rouen 1700-1702; 2nd ed., 4 vols., Antwerp 1736-1738 =the best edition); the Venice-Bassano ed., 4 vols., 1788 =the most widespread edition; this edition must be used with the work of A.G. Martimort cited above, pp. 19

L. Duchesne, *Origines du culte chrétien* (Paris, 1889; 5th ed., Paris, 1925) "Les Ordines romains du MS de Saint Amand," pp. 475-504, ET *Christian Worship: Its Origin & Evolution*, tr. M. McClure, (3rd ed. London 1923) 455-484.

M. Andrieu, *Les Ordines romani du haut moyen âge*. Vol 1: The Manuscripts; vols. 2-5: The Texts (*Ordines* I-L) = *Spicilegium Sacrum Lovaniense* 11, 23, 24, 28, 29 (Louvain 1931-1961). Vol 6 (tables) is in the press.

2. Partial Editions:

The following are outstanding:

C. Lambot, *North Italian Services of the Eleventh Century* (Milan, Bibl. Ambros., T.27 Sup.), HBS 67 (London 1931). The importance of this collection of *ordines* will be seen in the chapter on Rituals.

P.E. Schramm, "Die *Ordines* der mittelalterlichen Kaiserkrönung" in *Archiv für Urkundenforschung* 11 (1930)285-390.

_____,"Die Krönung bei den Westfranken und Angelsachsen von 878 bis um 1000," *Zeitschrift für Rechtsgeschichte* 54, Kan. Abt. 23 (1934) 177-242.

_____, "Die Krönung in Deutschland bis zum Beginn des Salischen Hauses (1028)", *ibid.*, 45, Kan. Abt. 24(1935)184-332.

_____, "Ordines Studien II. Die Krönung bei den Westfranken und den Franzosen", *Archiv für Urkundenforschung* 15(1938)3-55.

_____, "Die Krönung in Katalanisch-Aragonesischen Königsreich," *Miscellanea d'Estudis literaris historica i linguistica* 3 (Barcelona 1936-1937) 577-598.

_____, *Geschichte des englischen Königtums im Lichte der Krönung,* (Weimar 1937; reprint Darmstadt 1970), ET J. Wickham Legg, *A History of the English Coronation* (Oxford 1937).

_____, "Ordines Studien III. Die Krönung in England," *Archiv für Urkundenforschung* 15(1938)305-391; with an index of the pertinent MSS.

_____, "Der 'Salische Kaiserordo' und Benzo von Alba," *Deutsches Archiv für Geschichte des Mittelalters* 1 (1937)389-407.

_____, "Nachträge zu den Ordines Studien II-III," *Archiv für Urkundenforschung* 16 (1939) 279-286.

_____, *Der König von Frankreich. Das Wesen der Monarchie vom 9 bis zum 16 Jhd.,* 2 vols. (Weimar 1939; 2nd ed. revised and enlarged, Weimar-Darmstadt, 1960); with complete bibliography.

_____, *Kaiser, Könige, und Päpste.* 4 vols. in 5 (Stuttgart 1968-1971). Several of the early monographs cited above are available in these collected papers. They reveal a change of heart on several key points. Percy Schramm's studies are essential for a grasp of both imperial coronations and for those of Germany, France, England and Spain. See also R. Schneider, *Königswahl und Königserhebung im Frühmittelalter* (Stuttgart 1972).

R. Elze, *Ordines coronationis imperialis,* Fontes iuris germanici antiqui 11 (Hanover 1960). This is the classic work on imperial coronations with a complete bibliography of earlier publications.

P. Fabre- L. Duchesne- G. Mollat, *Le Liber Censuum de L'Église romaine,* 3 vols. (Paris 1905-1952). Indispensable for the *Liber politicus* and the *Ordo* of Cencius.

C. Erdmann, *Forschungen zur politischen Ideenwelt des Frühmittelalters* [published posthumously by F. Baethgen] (Berlin 1951) 83-90.

C.A. Boumann, *Sacring and Crowning. The Development of the Latin Ritual for the Anointing of Kings and the Coronation of an Emperor before the Eleventh Century* (Groningen 1957).

More partial editions of the *ordines:*

G. Cassander, *Liturgica de ritu et ordine Dominicae caenae celebrandae ...ex variis*

_____, *Ordo romanus de officio missae. Libelli aliquot pervetusti et authentici...iam primum typis expressi* (Cologne 1561). These two works are contained in the *Opera omnia G. Cassandri* (Paris 1616) 2-28 (*Liturgica*), 87-145 (*Ordo romanus*).

J. Morin, *Commentarius historicus de disciplina in administratione sacramenti paenitentiae...in decem libros distinctus* (Paris 1651; reprint Farnborough 1971); the *ordines* for private penance are contained in the appendix.

_____, *Commentarius de sacris ordinationibus...in tres partes distinctus* (Paris 1655; Antwerp 1695; reprint Farnborough 1971).

Martène et Durand, *Thesaurus novus anecdotorum,* 13 vols. (Paris 1717-1733).

F. Bianchini, *Anastasii Bibliothecarii de vitis romanorum pontificum* 3 (Rome 1728).

D. Giorgi, *De liturgia romani pontificis in solemni celebratione missarum,* 3 vols. (Rome 1731-1744; reprint Farnborough 1970).

J.M. Tommasi (Thomasius), *Opera omnia*, ed. A.F. Vezzosi, 7 vols., (Rome 1747-1754).

L.A. Muratori, *Liturgia romana vetus*, 2 vols. (Venice 1748).

M. Gerbert, *Monumenta veteris liturgiae Alemannicae*, 2 vols. (Saint Blaise 1777-1779; reprint Hildesheim 1967). Still necessary for the Gallican Liturgies.

H. Lietzmann, *Kleine Texte für Vorlesungen und Übungen* [*Liturgische Texte*] (Bonn 1910-1911).

C. Silva-Tarouca, "Giovanni 'archicantor' di S. Pietro a Roma e l'Ordo Romanus da ui composto." *Atti Pont. Accad. Rom. Archeol.* Memorie 1/1 (Rome 1925) 160-219. Wrong dates and wrong author of the *Capitulare ecclesiastici ordinis*.

F.W.H. Wasserschleben, *Die Bussordnungen der abendländischen Kirche*, 2 vols. (Mainz-Düsseldorf 1883-1898; reprint Graz 1958). *Ordines* for tariff penance; false classification of the *libri paenitentiales*.

H.J. Schmitz, *Die Bussbücher und die Bussdisziplin der Kirche* (Mainz 1883; reprint Graz 1958).

C. Vogel, *Les 'libri paenitentiales'*, Typologie des Sources du Moyen Age occidental 27 (Turnhout 1978).

G.B. De Rossi, *Inscriptiones christianae Urbis Romae septimo saeculo antiquiores*, 2/1 (Rome 1888) 34-36=*Ordo* XXIII of Andrieu.

b. STUDIES.

All the works cited above under "Editions" have introductions and commentaries. Remember that editions of the *ordines* or commentaries on them that appeared before the work of Andrieu are largely of historical interest only.

H. Grisar, "Die Stationfeier und der erste römische Ordo," *Zeitschrift für kath. Theologie* 9 (1885) 385-422.

———, *Analecta Romana* 1 (Rome 1899); the only vol. to appear.

G.G. Willis, "Roman Stational Liturgy," in *Further Essays in Early Roman Liturgy*, ACC 50 (London 1968) 1-85.

F. Probst, *Die ältesten römischen Sacramentarien und Ordines* (Münster/Westf. 1892).

J. Kösters, *Studien zu Mabillons römischen Ordines* (Münster/Westf. 1905).

J.A. Jungmann, *Missarum solemnia*. Eine genetische Erklärung der römischen Messe, 2 vols. (Vienna, 1st ed. 1948; 5th ed. 1962), ET F.A. Brunner, *The Mass of the Roman Rite*, 2 vols. (New York 1951-1955, from the 2nd rev. [1949] German edition). New revision, abridged to one volume without notes, New York, 1959; not recommended.

S.J.P. van Dijk, "The Old Roman Rite," *Studia Patristica* 5, TuU 80 (Berlin 1962) 185-205.

_____, "The Urban and Papal Rites in the VII and VIII Century in Rome," SE 12 (1961)411-487.

_____and J.H. Walker, *The Origins of the Modern Roman Liturgy* (Westminister 1960).

_____, "The Medieval Easter Vespers of the Roman Clergy," SE 19 (1969-70) 261-363.

K. Hallinger, "Die römischen *Ordines* von Lorsch, Murbach, und St. Gallen," *Universitas, Festschrift für Bischof Dr. A. Stohr* 1, ed. L. Lenhardt (Mainz 1960) 466-477.

A.A. King, *Liturgy of the Roman Church* (London 1957).

_____, *Liturgies of the Primatial Sees* (London 1957).

_____, *Liturgies of the Past* (London 1959).

Obviously, all liturgical historians use the *ordines* and the Pontificals as well as the Sacramentaries in their research. If we were to begin to cite even the titles of the greatest among them, we would be attempting a kind of universal liturgical bibliography—which cannot be the aim of this introduction to the sources. Nevertheless, it seems useful to provide a list of general works which treat of the Latin liturgy, and especially of the *Ordines,* the Pontificals and the Rituals.

In addition to the titles referred to above on pages 6-9, one might consult the following:

J. Oehler, "Leiturgia," *Real Encyklopädie* 12, 2 (1871-1879).

C. Clemen, *Quellenbuch zur praktischen Theologie. 1: Quellen zur Lehre des Gottesdienstes* (Giessen 1910).

A. Baumstark, *Vom geschichtlichen Werden der Liturgie* (Freiburg/Br. 1923).

E. Raitz von Frentz, "Der Weg des Wortes Liturgie in der Geschichte," EL 55 (1941)874-880.

Strathmann-Meyer, "Leiturgia," (and derivatives) in G. Kittel, *Theological Dictionary of the New Testament* 4 (Grand Rapids, MI 1962) 215-231.

L. Beauduin, "La Liturgie: définition, hiérarchie, tradition," *Questions de liturgie paroiss.* 29(1948)123-144.

E. Bishop, *Liturgica Historica* (Oxford 1918/1962). For Bishop's bibliography, see N.J. Abercrombie, *The Life and Work of Edmund Bishop* (London 1959) 492-508.

E. Underhill, *Worship* (New York 1937).

J.A. Jungmann, *Die liturgische Feier. Grundsätzliches und Geschichtliches über Formgesetze der Liturgie* (Regensburg 1939), ET *Liturgical Worship* (Collegeville 1941).

U. Altmann, *Hilfsbuch zur Geschichte des christlichen Kultus,* 1-3 (Berlin 1941-1947).

G. Rietschel-P. Graff, *Lehrbuch der Liturgie* (2nd ed., 2 vols., Göttingen 1951).

A. Stenzel, "Cultus publicus," *Zeitschrift für kath. Theologie* 75 (1953)174-214.

B. Steuart, *The Development of Christian Worship* (London 1953).

J.A. Kay, *The Nature of Christian Worship* (New York 1954).

J. Beckmann, *Quellen zur Geschichte des christlichen Gottesdienstes* (Gütersloh 1956).

W.J. O'Shea, *The Worship of the Church. A Companion to Liturgical Studies* (Westminster, MD 1957).

J.H. Miller, "The Nature and Definition of the Liturgy," *Theological Studies* 18(1957)325-356 and *Fundamentals of The Liturgy* (Notre Dame 1960).

I.H. Dalmais, *Initiation à la liturgie.* Cahiers de la Pierre-Qui-Vire 12 (Paris 1958), ET *Introduction to the Liturgy* (Baltimore 1961).

L.C. Mohlberg, *Ziele und Aufgaben der liturgiesgeschichtlichen Forschung,* Liturgiegeschictliche Forschungen 1 =LQF 13(Münster/Westf. 1919).

————, *Nochmals Ziele und Aufgaben für das Studium der christliche Kultus* (Rome 1957): a rewrite and fusion of two articles on the same subject published in *Miscellanea Belvederi* 23 (1954) 109-115 and in *Mélanges Msgr. M. Andrieu* (Strasbourg 1956) 339-349.

On how to edit liturgical texts:

L.C. Mohlberg, *Norme per le pubblicazioni di opere scientifiche,* RED, series minor, Subsidia studiorum 2 (Rome 1956). See the list of *sigla* for Sacramentaries, pp. 10-11.

In his editions of the *Ordines* and Pontificals, M. Andrieu carefully indicated the rules he followed for the critical editions of his documents. His remarks are indispensable to any editor of liturgical texts. He was practically the first scholar to set forth the specific character of liturgical documents and to show that their special problems in regard to authenticity and origin are quite different from those of classic literary texts. In addition to the editorial principles he provides before each text he published, see *Le Pontifical au moyen âge* 1, SeT 86 (Vatican City 1938) 115-119; *Les Ordines romani* 2, Spic. Sac. Lov. 23 (Louvain 1948) vii-xiii.

A. COLLECTIONS OF ORDINES

Just as *libelli missarum* existed separately before the appearance of Sacramentaries, separate *ordines* existed on their own before being gathered together into collections.[18] Each *ordo* contained instructions and directions concerning the actual performance of a particular liturgical function. When they crossed the Alps, each of the Roman *ordines* did so as a separate booklet, quite independent of any other.[19]

Despite their origin, the older *ordines* survive only in collections of *ordines* and these can differ widely in both size and scope. It was in and through such collections that these directories of worship succeeded in infiltrating the northern churches and influencing their liturgical patterns.[20] Like the Sacramentaries, the oldest collections of *ordines,* even those of purely Roman origin and character, are all of Frankish or Germanic composition.

1. *The Roman Collection of Ordines or Collection A* (Andrieu).

This collection appeared in the IX century; the following are the principal MSS:

Montpellier, Bibl. Fac. de Médecine, *codex* 412 (early IX century; Tours)

Copenhagen, Royal Library, *codex* Gl. Kgl. S. 3443 (early X century; *Francia*)

London, British Library, *codex addit.* 15222 (early XI century; E. France; Besançon?)

Rome, *Vat. Palat. lat.* 487 (IX century; Corbie)

Rome, *Vat. Ottobon.* 312 (late XI century for the *ordines* section; Aquitaine)

Paris, Bibl. Nat., *codex lat.* 2399 (XI century, probably reproducing one of the IX century; Frankish monastic scriptorium)

Leningrad, Publichnaja Biblioteka im M.E. Saltykova-Shchedrina, *codex* Q. v. II, no. 5 (IX-X century; part of the old MS *Corbeiensis* 230; Corbie?)

a) The Elements Composing Collection A.

The various *ordines* which compose Collection A are a rather coherent whole permitting a liturgist to celebrate according to the Roman Rite. The following arrangement is that of Montpellier 412:

Ordo I—solemn papal Mass.

Ordo XI—baptismal *ordo.*

Ordo XXVII—*ordo* for Holy Week.

Ordo XLII—*ordo* for the deposition of relics in a new church.

Ordo XXXIV—ordinations in the Roman style from acolyte to bishop.

Ordo XIII A—a list of readings for the liturgical year (Night Office).

At the beginning of the Montpellier MS stands the *Capitulare ecclesiastici ordinis* (*Ordo XV*) which is not really part of Collection A; it must have been added to the collection when Montpellier 412, or one of its immediate predecessors, was being copied.

b) Date of Collection A as a Collection.

The *terminus post quem non* is the date of transcription of the oldest surviving MS (early IX century). The collection itself is, however, much older than that.

After comparing the text provided by the various MSS, we find that we cannot construct a geneological tree for the surviving witnesses to the original. Although all the MSS reproduce the same *ordines*, no trace of literary dependence can be discovered. That implies that the number of transcriptions separating the surviving MSS from their common ancestor must have been very numerous and that, consequently, the archetype must have existed a long time before the oldest copy we now have (ca. 800). We could hardly be wrong in saying that Collection A was already in existence ca. 750 or, more likely, as early as 700-750. At any rate, it is certainly earlier than the systematic policy of Romanization undertaken by Pepin the Short.

Collection A was put together by some private individual who admired the Roman liturgy and wanted to propagate it in those areas where the Gallican liturgy still flourished.

c) Place and Date.

As we shall prove later when we examine each *ordo* individually, all the documents making up Collection A are Roman in origin. Each *ordo* left Rome for Gaul independently, at the private initiative of some monk or pilgrim enamored of the liturgy experienced on the banks of the Tiber, and after they arrived in Gaul, they circulated, at first, as independent items. The *ordines* composing Collection A could not have been gathered together at Rome itself; this is obvious because *Ordo XXVII*, for example, although clearly Roman in origin, shows unmistakable signs of Frankish alterations.[21] Its presence in Collection A tells us that the compiling of such documents must have been accomplished in Gaul or Germany.

Moreover, the original location of the several *codices* which have survived indicate not only Gaul but a rather well marked area of Gaul delimited by Tours, Corbie and Besançon.

It must have been around 750, when Pepin's Romanization of worship had officially begun, that a Frankish monk conceived the idea of bringing together into one collection (our Collection A) the *ordines* that had been penetrating his part of the world since around 700.[22] Like the Roman Sacramentaries already in circulation, Collection A was to contribute to the spread of Roman usages in Gaul.[23]

d) Stages of the Romanizing Process

For a bibliography on this subject, see T. Klauser, *A Short History of the Western Liturgy*, M. Andrieu, *Les Ordines romani*, and the synthesis of C. Vogel, "Les échanges liturgiques entre Rome et les pays francs jusqu'à l'époque de Charlemagne," *Settimane di studio del Centro ital. di studi sull'alto medioevo* 7 (Spoleto 1960) 185-285.

The years of Pepin III's reign (751-768) mark a clear divide between the earlier and later period of Romanizing influence. Before him, the appearance of Roman usages in Gaul was the result of purely private initiatives by pilgrims, monks, clerics and bishops, without any coordination whatsoever. During his reign, the Frankish monarchy openly favored and tried officially to impose the Romanizing process, although success came only under his son, Charlemagne.

The best testimonies to this process are the liturgical books themselves (Sacramentaries, *ordines* and, ultimately, the *Romano-Germanic Pontifical of the Tenth Century* in which so many influences—Roman, Frankish, German—converge). All these liturgical books emerge from a mixed or hybrid background. The 'Roman' Sacramentaries are filled with Gallican interpolations and the 'Gallican' Sacramentaries are Romanized to various degrees; from a paleographical point of view, all the collections of *ordines* are of Frankish origin and the collections of Gallicanized *ordines* are by far the most numerous. In this introduction our main objective is precisely the study of these very documents.

1. *Before the Mid-Eighth Century.*

Information is meager on the penetration of the Roman liturgy into Gaul before Pepin III, although the fact itself is certain.

Since the conversion of Clovis (496), numerous Frankish pilgrims had visited Rome and its martyrs, particularly the illustrious shrines of the holy apostles Peter and Paul. On their return, they brought back with them *patrocinia* (relics), *brandea* or *encolpia* (linen or silk cloths which had touched relics) and *codices*; Pope Gregory I, Letter to Queen Brunhilda, A.D. 597 (Jaffé-Wattenbach, 1491); Gertrude, abbess of Nivelles (626-659) had people search for *volumina* in Rome (MGH, *Sriptores rerum merovingicarum* 2, 457); Godo brought St. Wandregisilis (Wandrille), abbot of Fontenelle, a *codicum sacrorum copiam non minimam*, between the years 657 and 672 (*Acta Sanctorum*

Jul. V, July 22, 276); St. Amandus, bishop of Maastricht, Flanders (ca. 647-684), after visiting Pope Martin I (649-653), brought back from Rome various *codices et tractatus* (*Acta Sanctorum* I, Febr. 6, 860); Gregory, abbot of Utrecht, did the same in the time of Boniface II (530-532) (MGH, *Scriptores* 15, 73); Benedict Biscop (†690), the founder of Wearmouth-Jarrow (Northumbria), made several visits to Rome, bringing back icons, relics, books, stonemasons, glaziers, and even the archcantor of St. Peter's church *quatenus in monasterio suo cursum canendi annuum, sicut ad sanctum Petrum Romae agebatur, edoceret . . . Non solum autem idem Iohannes ipsius monasterii fratres docebat, verum de omnibus pene eiusdem monasteriis ad audiendum eum, qui cantandi erant periti, confluebant.* (Bede, *Historia ecclesiastica gentis anglorum* IV, 18, ed. C. Plummer I, 240-241; cf. his *Vita beatorum abbatum* I, 4. 5, 11, ed. Plummer, I, 367, 369, 375).

On the other hand, the popes themselves did not try to promote the Roman liturgy outside the City and its suburbicarian dioceses. A few general affirmations (Pope Innocent I, Epistle 25 to Decentius of Gubbio, Feb. 15, 404; PL 20, 551-552, and to Victricius of Rouen, March 19, 416, PL 56, 519-527) were known in Gaul through the intermediary of collections of canons but there were few concrete commands (Vigilius to Profuturus of Braga, June 29, 538, PL 69, 15-19; John III to Edaldus of Vienne, ca. 560-573, (of dubious authenticity) Mansi, *Concilia*, 9, 760; Gregory II to Martinianus of Bavaria, May 15, 716, PL 89, 531-532; Zachary I to Boniface, Nov 4, 751, PL 89, 951-952).

Councils and synods of this early period did not address the question of liturgical uniformity, much less the possible Romanization of the liturgy; the only exceptions were some rather timid canons on provincial observances issued by the Synods of Vannes, ca. 465, canon 15 (CC 148, 155), Agde, 506, canon 30 (CC 148, 201), Epaone, 517, canon 27 (CC 148 A, 30), Vaison, 529, canon 3 (CC 148 A, 79) and Arles, 554, canon 1 (CC 148 A, 171).

Even St. Boniface, *missus sancti Petri*, apostle of Germany and reformer of the Frankish church, did not seem anxious to impose the Roman liturgy north of the Alps, despite his insistence on total *subjectio* to the Apostolic See (cf. Vogel, " Les échanges liturgiques," pp. 194-196).

The capitulary of Duke Carloman sanctioning the *Concilium Germanicum* of April 21, 742 (MGH, *Capitularia* 1, 25) prescribed that every priest must give an account to his bishop of his *ratio et ordo ministerii sui* but it did not insist that priests had to celebrate in the Roman manner (cf. Vogel, *op. cit.*, 195-196).

Until about 750 therefore, the penetration of the Roman liturgy into *Francia* appeared to be somewhat sporadic and haphazard and was the result of private initiatives only.

2. Pepin the Short (751-768) and his Successors.

It is very generally agreed that Pepin III (751-768) was the first ruler to bring about the Romanization of the liturgy. Charlemagne was merely to expand and consolidate the movement begun by his father.

Charlemagne, *Admonitio generalis* (March 23, 789), caput 80: *Ut cantum Romanum* [=solemn recitation of a text] ... *secundum quod* ... *genitor noster Pippinus rex decertavit ut fieret, quando Gallicanum tulit ob unanimitatem apostolicae sedis* (MGH, *Capitularia* 1, 61).

Charlemagne, *Epistola generalis* (786-800): *Accensi praeterea* ... *Pippini genitoris nostri exemplis, qui totas Galliarum ecclesias Romanae traditionis suo studio cantibus decoravit, nos,* etc. (MGH, *Capit.* 1, 80).

Charlemagne, *Capitulare de Imaginibus (Libri Carolini)* I, 6: *Quae* [the Frankish Church] *dum a primis fidei temporibus cum ea* [the Roman Church] *perstaret in sacra religionis unione et ab ea paulo distaret* ... *in officiorum celebratione,* ... *genitoris nostri* ... *Pippini regis cura et industria sive adventu in Gallias* ... *Stephani romanae urbis antistitis* [Stephen II], *est ei etiam in psallendi ordine copulata* (MGH, *Concilia* 2, Suppl. 21).

Walafrid Strabo (†849), *Liber de exordiis et incrementis,* caput 26: *Stephanus papa cum ad Pippinum patrem Karoli Magni imperatoris in Francia pro iustitia sancti Petri a Longobardis expetenda venisset, per suos clericos (cantilenae perfectiorem scientiam) petente eodem Pippino invexit indeque usus eius longe lateque convaluit* (MGH, *Capit.* 2, 508).

Charles the Bald (Charles III), *Epistola ad clerum Ravennatis: Nam et usque ad tempora abavi nostri Pippini Gallicanae et Hispanae ecclesiae aliter quam Romana vel Mediolanensis ecclesiae divina officia celebrabant* (**Mansi**, *Concilia* 18 B, 730).

In two of these documents (*Capit. de imaginibus* and Walafrid Strabo), the beginning of Pepin's reforms seem to have coincided with Pope Stephen II's residence in *Francia.* Stephen left Rome on Oct 14, 753, met Pepin at Ponthion at the beginning of 754, anointed him king at St. Denis on July 23, 754 (he had been anointed previously by St. Boniface in 751) and returned to Rome only in 755, having stayed in Gaul almost two years. Since the pope traveled with a whole retinue of Roman ecclesiastics, the Frankish clergy had a rather extensive opportunity for viewing celebrations of the liturgy in the Roman and papal style.

Why the liturgy was Romanized is still not completely clear.

a) Theoretically, the unification and reform of worship in the Frankish kingdom could have been accomplished by using the old Latin liturgy native to Gaul, i.e., the so-called Gallican liturgy, a typical Western, non-Roman liturgy (see *supra,* pp. 107-8 and *infra,* pp. 275-7).

As a matter of fact, however, if such an attempt had been made, it could hardly have been a success. By the latter part of the VIII century, only tattered remnants remained of the old Gallican service books; cf. Hilduin, abbot of St. Denis (ca. 835), Letter to Louis the Pious, nos. 5-6: *Antiquissimi et nimia pene vetustate consumpti missales libri, continentes missae ordinem more gallico, qui ab initio receptae fidei usu in hoc occidentali plaga est habitus, usque quo tenorem quo nunc utitur romanum susceperit* (MGH, *Epistolae aevi Karolini* 3, 330).

b) Well before the official efforts of Pepin III, the Romanization process had been initiated by Frankish clerics and fervent pilgrims to Rome who admired the liturgy they experienced there. See the studies of Zettinger, Kötting, Schneider, Zwölfer and Pfeil relating to the Frankish veneration for papal Rome and their pilgrimages to it in Vogel, "Les échanges liturgiques," pp. 234-235; see also J.M. Wallace-Hadrill, *Early Medieval History* (Oxford/New York 1975) 138-154.

c) Besides the real veneration felt by Pepin and Charlemagne for all things Roman, there were excellent political reasons in favor of Romanization. Liturgical unification would both foster unity within the kingdom and help consolidate the alliance between the Holy See and the Frankish monarchy, the protector of the *iustitia sancti Petri*; cf. A. Baumstark, *Vom geschichtliche Werden der Liturgie* (Freiburg/Br. 1923) 61-64.

d) Until 780, Iconoclasm may have contributed, at least indirectly, to the Romanizing process. The adoption of the Roman rite was an effective means of parrying whatever Byzantine liturgical influences may have been encouraging the survival of the Gallican rite; for documents on this subject see G. Haendler, *Epochen karolingischer Theologie. Eine Untersuchung über die karol. Gutachten zum byz. Bilderstreit* (Berlin 1958) 17-22, 30; Vogel, " Les échanges liturgiques," pp. 235-237.

On the liturgical reforms of Charlemagne—besides the liturgical books themselves which are surely the best witnesses to what was accomplished—see F. Cabrol, "Charlemagne et la liturgie," DACL 3, 807-823 (major texts, dates need correction); E. Bishop, "The Liturgical Reform of Charlemagne," *Downside Review* 38 (1919) 1-16; E. Bishop-A. Wilmart, "La réforme liturgique de Charlemagne," EL 45 (1931) 186-207. On Charlemagne and Alcuin, see R. Wahl, *Karl der Grosse* (Frankfurt/Main 1954) and G. Ellard, *Master Alcuin, Liturgist* (Chicago 1956). All the above must be corrected, of course, in the light of the Deshusses hypothesis, *supra*, pages 79-89.

2. The Gallicanized Collections of Ordines; Collection B (Andrieu).

Besides the Roman *ordines* forming Collection A, there were other *ordines* circulating in Gaul from the time of Pepin III. These were hybrid items resulting from a greater or lesser degree of adaptation of Roman *ordines* to Gallican usages. Such forms of adaptation proved necessary because Collection A was still too close to its origins, both topographically (too linked to certain Roman basilicas) and liturgically (the bishop of Rome was also the pope and the papal liturgy, as such, could not be used by the bishop of another city, much less by simple priests). It was also important not to offend unnecessarily the local usages and customs dear to Gallican hearts.

In this instance the same process occurred as in the case of the Sacramentaries; all the Roman Sacramentaries circulating in Gaul were Gallicanized to some degree and all the Gallican Sacramentaries were Romanized. Benedict of Aniane himself, in supplying the *Hadrianum* with its indispensible *Supplement*, employed many Gallican and even Visigothic usages.

Collection B is an example of the Gallicanization of the Roman *ordines*. The two best representatives of this process are the Verona MS, Bibl. capit., *codex* 92 (under Louis the Pious, 815-817; before 820) and the Cologne MS, Dombibliothek, *codex* 138 (early IX century).[24]

a) The Elements Composing Collection B.

Collection B includes a certain number of *ordines* already known through Collection A but, in this case, they have undergone a fair amount of Frankish processing; it even contains a few proper items of its own. The arrangement of Collection B in *Veronensis* 92 is as follows:

Ordo XIII B—list of readings for the Office throughout the year (an enlarged edition of XIII A).

Ordo I—solemn papal Mass with very small Gallican additions.[25]

Ordo XI—baptismal *ordo* reshaped to make it self-sufficient so that reference to the Sacramentary would not be necessary.

Ordo XXVIII—*ordo* for Holy Week, replacing *Ordo* XXVII in Collection A.

Ordo XLI—dedication of churches, proper to Collection B and the result of the Romanizing reform of Pepin and Charlemagne.

Ordo XLII—the deposition of relics in a new church, taken over from Collection A.

Ordo XXXVII A—Ember Days according to the Gallican arrangement. Ordinations in the Gallican manner, from psalmist to bishop.[26]

b) Place and Date of Collection B as Collection.

As an adaptation of Collection A to the needs of the Frankish Church, this new collection came into existence after the composition of the Frankish Gelasian Sacramentary (760-770). The *terminus post quem non* is provided by the date of *Veronensis* 92, executed at Verona itself, in the kingdom of Lothair, between the years 814 and 817 (while Louis was sole emperor) and 820 (the year Lothair married Hermingard of Alsace).[27] Collection B itself must have been assembled in the early years of Louis the Pious (814-818).

Collection B was not only better adapted to Frankish conditions than Collection A, it was deliberately designed for ordinary episcopal

use and may be regarded as one of the first examples of a true
Pontifical—a forerunner of the great Mainz Pontifical of the X
Century.

3. The Gallicanized collections: The Saint Amand Collection.

This collection of *ordines* is only preserved in a single MS, Paris,
Bibliothèque Nationale, *codex latinus* 974 (IX century), deriving from
the ancient abbey of St. Amand-les-Eaux (N. France) where the MS
was discovered in the XV century. It owes its name to its first editor,
Louis Duchesne.[28]

a) Elements Composing Collection of St.Amand.

Ordo IV—a second version of the solemn papal Mass; a recasting of
  Ordo I and its two supplements: *Ordo II (Roman) and Ordo* III
  (Frankish).
Ordo XXX B—Holy Week and Easter Week, using *Ordines* XI, XXVII,
  XII and XXX A.
Ordo XXI—the Greater Litanies of April 25.
Ordo XXXIX—the ordinations of deacons and presbyters.
Ordo XLIII—the deposition of relics, using *Ordines* XLI and XLII.
Ordo XX—the feast of the Purification, Feb. 2.

b) Origin and Date

The *Parisinus* 974 was copied in the IX century but is only a
mediocre and faulty transcription of an older original (the copyist
could not read the ligatures of the original). The vulgar Latin of this
original proves that it was earlier than the Carolingian Renaissance,
i.e. ca. 800, and yet it is later than Collection A (ca. 750 as a
collection), several items of which were used by the compiler of the
St. Amand Collection (*Ordines* I, XI, XXVII, XLII). We can conclude
that this collection was put together late in Pepin's reign or early in
Charlemagne's (ca. 770-790).

Although it did not spread very widely, the St. Amand Collection
is a valuable witness to how the liturgy was celebrated in Northern
Francia.

*4. The Gallicanized Collections: the Capitulare ecclesiastici ordinis
or the St. Gall Collection.*

The St. Gall MS, Stiftsbibliothek, *codex* 349 (late VIII century)[29]
preserves the most complete form of the *Capitulare* and often gives it
its name.

a) Composition.

Ordo XIV—the readings for the Night Office in St. Peter's basilica.

Ordo XVI—*Instruccio aecclesiastici ordinis*: monastic ceremonial for the liturgical year.

Ordo XV—*Capitulare ecclesiastici ordinis*: Roman ceremonial for the liturgical year.

Ordo XVIII—*De cursu divino*: the monastic Office.

Ordo XIX—*De convivio . . . monachorum*: ceremonial for monastic meals. Obviously, the *Capitulare* is a customary for monasteries.

b) Origin and Date.

Ordines XV, XVI, XVIII and XIX had the same author and formed one collection from the time they were first put together; these four alone constitute, properly speaking, the St. Gall Collection. *Ordo* XIV was prefixed to this block of material early on, but remains an extraneous element. The grouping of items was not done by the copyist of *Sangallensis* 349 but by the liturgist who originally redacted these *ordines*; there is evidence for this in MSS that are earlier than and independent of St. Gall 349, e.g., the *Parisinus* 3836 (early VIII Century) and the *Metensis* 134 (early VIII century). The four *ordines* of the *Capitulare* are little works of propaganda designed to facilitate the Romanization of worship in the homeland of the Gallican liturgy and to promote liturgical unity by the adoption of usages which came from Rome.

The anonymous author, a Frankish monk, who much admired the Roman liturgy but had little experience of the City and its liturgical peculiarities, worked in Austrasia or Burgundy, a little before 787. This can be ascertained from the fact that a) he used the Gallicanized form of *Ordo* I dating from ca. 750 and b) in *Ordo* XIX, 44-45, there is a clear allusion to the first six Ecumenical Councils held against the "oriental" heresies which attacked the Roman Church (the sixth closed at Constantinople, Sept 16, 681) and to a seventh heresy which will be that of the end of time. Such a prediction had to have been made before Sept 24, 787, the opening date of II Nicea.[30] The original redaction of our collection must, therefore, have taken place between 750 and 787, and more exactly, around 775-780, since copies were already numerous by the end of the century.

The birthplace of the *Capitulare* was some western region that venerated the memory of bishops Hilary, Martin, Germanus and Ambrose (*Ordo* XIX, 39), i.e., an area which included Northern Italy and Gaul, the homeland of the Gallican liturgy (Paris, Poitiers, Tours, Milan). The geographical spread of the MSS (Wissembourg, Tours, Angoulême) directs our attention to Burgundy and the old German borderlands, to Alsace and the Vosges Mountains, in Luxeuil's zone of influence. The anonymous author must, therefore, have been a Burgundian or Austrasian monk.

We must discard the old hypothesis that the *Capitulare* was the work of John, archcantor of St. Peter's, around 678-681.[31]

Two lesser collections of *ordines* have to be added to the four major ones listed above:

5. *A Collection of the Brussels MS*, Bibliothèque royale, *codex latinus* 10127-10144 (around Liège, late VIII century).[32]

This is a kind of manual for a country priest—a first stab at creating a Ritual—containing directions for the more ordinary worship situations. Only *Ordo* XIII appeared in the other collections.

Ordo XIII—*Ordo librorum catholicorum*: lessons for the Night Office.

Ordo XXVI—*ordo* for the Night Office (*Tenebrae*), Holy Thurs. to Easter.

Ordo III—the second Frankish complement to *Ordo* I.

Ordo XXIV—*ordo* for Holy Thurs. through Easter Sat.

Ordo XXX A—*ordo* for Holy Week.

6. *The Collection of the St. Gall MS*, Stiftsbibliothek, *codex latinus* 614 (second half of the IX century).[33]

This is an interesting collection because, for some *ordines*, the compiler used sources earlier than those in Collections A and B (e.g., for *Ordo* I), and because it contains certain documents that appear here for the first time (*Ordines* II, XXII, XII, XXXVI, VIII, IX).

The *Sangallensis* 614 came to play an important role in the literary history of *ordines*. It provided the majority of texts for *Sangallensis* 140 (St. Gall, Stiftsbibliothek, *codex latinus* 140; X century)[34] and *Sangallensis* 140 was used by the compilers of St. Alban's Abbey, Mainz, when they assembled the *Romano-Germanic Pontifical* in the mid-X century. Consequently, *Sangall.* 614 contributed to the survival of an important group of *ordines*.

Particulars concerning the didactic and juridico-liturgical collections will not be provided here, because they are not liturgical documents in the strict sense (i.e., meant for an actual celebrant).

Rather, they correspond to the church renewal and reform programs of Carlomann, Pepin III and Charlemagne.[35] They reflect both the prescriptions of the reforming councils and those of the central authority which directed the clergy to inform themselves on matters of religion and worship: *Capitulare* of Carlomann (742)[36], the *Admonitio generalis* of Charlemagne (March 23, 789)[37], the Synod of Frankfort (794)[38], the *Interrogationes examinationis* of Bavaria (803)[39] and the *Statuta synodalia* of Hincmar of Rheims (852).[40]

Although these collections are of great interest to those who want to study the formation of clergy and people in the Carolingian period, they do not fall within parameters of the present study.

B. INDIVIDUAL ORDINES BEFORE THE YEAR 1000.

We had to present the collections of *ordines* before undertaking a detailed analysis of each *ordo*. Although it is true that each *ordo* originally enjoyed an independent existence of its own as a booklet of ceremonial directions for the guidance of a practical liturgist performing a particular liturgical function, such *ordines* survived only in the established collections. It was also thanks to their existence in collections that they attained wider dissemination.

Since we shall use the editions published by Michel Andrieu, we shall also employ his nomenclature and numbering system (*Ordo* I-L).

ORDO I. INCIPIT ORDO ECCLESIASTICI MINISTERII ROMANAE ECCLESIAE VEL QUALITER MISSA CAELEBRATUR.[41]

Mabillon called this the *Ordo romanus primus*, not to be confused with Hittorp's *Ordo romanus antiquus* (=*Ordo* L of Andrieu).

This is the first surviving *ordo* of the solemn papal Mass. It not only describes in detail the papal ceremonial at Mass (nos. 24-126) but also the major structures of the Roman Church and its internal organization: the seven ecclesiastical precincts of the City, the *tituli*, the deaconries, the *episcopium* or *patriarchium Lateranense*, the stational liturgies, the precedence among the various dignitaries and a description of the papal cavalcade.[42] It is an extremely important document because it contains the first full description of eucharistic worship at Rome. In the Middle Ages, the solemn or high Mass, episcopal or parochial, was a direct descendant of this papal liturgy and even the so-called private Mass was merely a reduced version of it.

EXCURSUS: THE "PRIVATE" MASS[43] [Revised by translators]

The reduced version of the solemn mass was the result of a number of factors that appeared at different times and places but eventually became almost universal in the Western Church. Some of the more important factors were the following:

1. The attempt to replicate the liturgy of the Roman basilicas and shrines with their manifold eucharistic celebrations in the local church(es) of an episcopal city or monastery;[44]

2. the establishment of daily mass in cathedrals and monasteries and then several daily conventual and non-conventual masses including the *missa matutinalis*, *missa maior* and others, as well as the need to create more and more priest-monks;[45]

3. the view of the mass as an *opus bonum* to be offered frequently in intercession, or as an act of subjective piety;[46]

4. the *redemptiones paenitentiales*, which advised the saying of impressive numbers of masses (as commuted penances) which could only be accomplished if many monks and canons were henceforth ordained;[47]

5. increasing devotion to the Blessed Virgin and to the faithful departed with the growing custom of having at least one mass per day *de Beata* and *de requie* in communities;[48]

6. the endowment of more and more 'chantries' in cathedrals and monasteries (and much later even parishes) and the resulting need for more priests;[49]

7. the stipend system itself which encouraged even slovenly priests to celebrate daily for their mass-penny.[50]

Various approaches have been taken to explain these phenomena. Scholars such as Otto Nussbaum and Cyrille Vogel have stressed certain of these factors in order to explain the appearance of the so-called private mass.[51]

To begin, these scholars consider *missa privata* to be synonymous with *missa lecta* and *missa solitaria*, i.e. a mass wherein a single priest assumes the liturgical functions normally reserved to the other ministers (readings), choir (chants) and congregation (responses, etc.).[52] For Vogel in particular, this 'sacerdotalization' of the entire mass is due to a basic changeover in religious and liturgical psychology—radically different from that of the early church. The mass has become a good work, "which takes its place among the other ascetical exercises through which the religious sanctify themselves."[53] The mass is now celebrated out of personal devotion as a means of ensuring salvation.[54]

A different approach is taken by A. Häussling.[55] Basing his conclusions on much of the same historical data but seen from a different perspective, Häussling argues first of all that the use of the term "private" in the sense of "solitary" as used by Nussbaum, betrays a post-Tridentine understanding of the term. "Private" in the early Middle Ages did not refer to something done alone but more than likely something "privated" or deprived of the elaborate or special.

A *missa privata*[56] is one celebrated not with the entire community with all the ministers functioning as on Sundays and other 'liturgical' days, but on ordinary days (even daily) with a small group. *Privata* is opposed to *publica* as "secondary" or "subordinate" is opposed to "principal," "solemn," and "official". *Missae privatae* in this earlier sense included those celebrated at the Roman shrines/basilicas not on the Sundays or festivals when the entire community was scheduled to worship there, but whenever the need arose, e.g., when there were enough pilgrims present.[57]

These masses, then, were not in origin celebrated by a priest alone, but were nonetheless subordinate to the liturgies of the entire community such as those of the stational system for Sundays and feasts.

The smaller groups who gathered at the shrines on ordinary days celebrated the Eucharist not only to honor the saints and martyrs, but took the opportunity to intensify the intercessory aspect of the celebration: to give thanks or praise for recovery from sickness, to ask for safe childbirth, to pray for the departed, etc. and to do so more intently (and effectively) at the very place where the martyr-patron "lived" as a guarantee that God hears and answers the prayers of the individual and the community.[58]

Of course there were festivals of the martyr-patrons in the stational system as well, when the entire community celebrated at the shrine and where the pressing needs of the entire community or of special members of the community were likewise included as *vota* in the celebration of the Eucharist. These were among the first "votive masses" to be included in the earliest *libelli* and sacramentaries.[59]

As has already been shown, the spread of the Roman liturgy North of the Alps began very early and unsystematically-even before the VIII century. In order to use the Roman books, the Franks needed to modify their own cities and monasteries in order to carry out the prescriptions of the stational and non-stational liturgies in which they had participated while visiting Rome and/or found in the various books. This is not to say that stational liturgies are exclusively Roman in origin,[60] but there is ample evidence that in many places by the late VIII century, there was a conscious attempt to replicate the Roman liturgies as best they could in their own situations.[61]

It is undeniable that there is a difference in the theology of Church, Orders, and Eucharist between that of the early Church and that of the medieval Church. Häussling argues, however, that for the early Middle Ages when the frequency of the Eucharist increased dramatically, there is no complete break—there is a gradual change of emphasis until the intercessory aspect overshadows the building-up of the gathered community.[62]

Without such a change in Eucharistic understanding the actual practice of the early Middle Ages would be unthinkable—the piling up of masses and the "offering of the sacrifice for" so many reasons. And yet, the actual *formulae* and the ritual itself does not change so drastically that nothing from the Church of late Antiquity remains. In fact, the forms and *formulae* that developed during late antiquity and the early Middle Ages were left as a treasured inheritance in the Liturgy, guarded as the tradition of the Apostles from the City of the Apostles.

Still, although the possibility of a Eucharist celebrated by a priest at a side altar or chapel existed as early as the VI century[63] and was common in Frankish monasteries by the IX,[64] it is important to understand these celebrations as part of a whole—not individual "private" affairs occasioned by personal option or piety.[65] Indeed, what eventually became a thoroughly "private" mass in the post-Tridentine church, kept intact all the structural features of the solemn Mass, but with some additions:

Various prayers of preparation and devotion were added (at the beginning, at the offertory, before and after communion) perhaps influenced by ancient Gallican usages. Such prayers are very diverse and vary from MS to MS. These various, adapted ordinaries of the Mass were gradually reabsorbed by the Roman structure, fixed in the XIII-century Missal of the Roman Curia and passed into the *editio princeps* of the *Missale Romanum* of 1474.[66] The Roman rite of the mass was only imposed on the Western Church by the *Misssale pianum* (Pius V) in 1570.[67]

The *Hadrianum* forwarded to Charlemagne by the pope in the late VIII century contained a short *ordo* suitable for both solemn and private Mass:

QUALITER MISSA ROMANA CAELEBRATUR. Hoc est in primis *introitum* qualis fuerit statutis temporibus sive diebus festis seu cottidianis, deinde *kyriae eleison*. Item dicitur *gloria in excelsis deo*, si episcopus fuerit, tantummodo die dominico, sive diebus festis; a praesbyteris autem minime dicitur nisi solo in pascha. Quando vero laetania agitur, neque *gloria in excelsis deo* neque *alleluia* canitur. Postmodum dicitur *oratio*, deinde sequitur *apostolum*. Item *gradalem* seu *alleluia*. Postmodum legitur *evangelium*, deinde *offerturium* et *oblationem super oblatam.* qua completa dicit sacerdos excelsa voce: *Per omnia saecula saeculorum. Amen. Dominus vobiscum*, etc. Then follows the *Canon missae*: initial dialogue, *praefatio, sanctus, Te igitur, Pater noster* and its embolism *pax* and *Agnus dei*; the *Hadrianum* terminates here without any further indications.[68]

The best commentaries on the structure of the Roman Mass are B. Botte-C. Mohrmann, *L'Ordinaire de la messe. Texte critique, traduction et études.* Études liturgiques 2 (Louvain/Paris 1953); B. Botte, *Le canon de la messe romaine.* Textes et études liturgiques 2 (Louvain 1935); L. Eizenhöfer, *Canon missae romanae, RED, Series minor* 1: *Traditio textus* (Rome 1954) and 7: *Textus propinqui* (Rome 1966) and the classic work of J.A. Jungman, *Missarum sollemnia. Eine genetische Erklärung der römischen Messe,* 2 vols., 6th ed., Vienna, 1966; ET F.A. Brunner, *The Mass of the Roman Rite,* 2 vols. (New York 1951-1955, from the 2nd German ed., 1949)—On the term *missa,* see C.

Mohrmann, "Missa," *Vigiliae Christianae* 12(1958) 67-92 (best critical synthesis and bibliography); see also C. Callewaert, "Histoire positive du canon romain," SE 2(1949) 102-110 and A. Coppo, "Una nuova ipotesi sull'origine di *missa*," EL 71 (1951) 225-267. In the time of Gregory the Great, mass lasted 2-3 hours, Gregory I, *Registrum* 10, 14; MGH, *Epistolarum* 2, 248.[69]

Ordo I survives in two recensions: a long text and a short one which represents its oldest form (accessible only in *Sangallensis* 614). *Both* recensions are of Roman origin.[70]

1. Date of its Passage into Gaul.

Ordo I left Rome for Gaul sometime between 700 and 750:

a) As early as the beginning of the IX century, we find MSS testifying to its existence North of the Alps: Paris, Biblio. Nat., *codex latinus* 2399 (an XI century copy of the IX century model); St. Gall, Stiftsbibliothek *codex* 614 (second-half of IX century); Montpellier, Bibl. Fac. Méd., *codex* 412 (Collection A, early IX century); Verona, Biblio. capit., *codex* 92 (early IX century); and Cologne, Biblio. capit., *codex* 138 (early IX century); the last two MSS belong to Collection B.

b) Before the end of the VIII century, the compiler of *Ordo* IV (*Ordo S. Amandi*) used *Ordo* I with its second (Frankish) supplement, *Ordo* III, and therefore Collection A of which *Ordo* I was a part.

c) *Ordo* I certainly arrived before 787 (probably ca. 770-780) because it was used, with its Frankish alterations, by the Austrasian or Burgundian monk who authored the *Capitulare ecclesiastici ordinis* (cf. *Ordo* XVI).

d) Finally, *Ordo* I was the indispensable directory for the Frankish clergy using the Gregorian Sacramentary of the Paduan type (*Paduensis* D. 47) and such a Sacramentary had circulated in Gaul since the early VIII century.

2. Roman Date of Composition.

Our only help here is internal criteria. *Ordo* I refers to stational Masses celebrated in a *diaconia*, something that could hardly have occurred before Pope Gregory II (715-731).[71] The Lateran palace is called the *patriarchium*, a term that came into use only under Sergius I (687-701).[72] Our text presupposes a highly developed and hierarchically organized papal court with numerous personnel: *vicedominus, vesterarius, nomenclator, sacellarius, et al.*, all of whom appeared only towards the end of the the VII century.[73] Finally, even the shorter and older recension mentions the *Agnus dei* which was inserted in the eucharistic celebration by Sergius I (687-701).[74] In all probability, therefore, the Roman redaction of *Ordo* I took place after the pontificate of Sergius I, but not very long after it, since we find *Ordo* I in Gaul by 750.

ORDO II (no title). *Si autem contigerit summum pontificem . . .* [75]

This is the first *Roman* supplement to *Ordo* I, regulating the celebration of the Eucharist whenever a bishop or presbyter replaces the pope at a stational liturgy.

Its Roman origin is clear since certain of its peculiarities suit only the context of the papal City. The redactor may be the same person who composed nos. 24-126 of *Ordo* I.

The chronological problems are the same of those for *Ordo* I; *Ordo* IV already uses *Ordo* II.

ORDO III (no title). *In diebus festis, id est pascha, pentecosten . . .* [76]

This is the second supplement to *Ordo* I, this time a *Frankish* or, better, a Romano-Frankish one.

From a literary point of view, this document can be divided into six paragraphs that were put together at different periods and in no particular order.

They treat of (1) the concelebration by cardinal presbyters on Christmas, Easter, Pentecost and the feast of Sts. Peter and Paul (June 29), (2) a modified order of communion, (3) a simplified *commixtio* rite, (4) a description of the *fractio* in an ordinary episcopal Mass, (5) some new rubrics on vestments and (6) the case in which a presbyter replaces a deacon in an episcopal Mass.

Fragments 1-2 are Roman; fragments 3-6 are Frankish. *Ordo* III began to circulate North of the Alps between 750-780. The archetype of the Roman sections comes from the same period as *Ordo* I (ca. 700); sections 3-6 date from 750-780.

ORDO IV. IN NOMINE DOMINI NOSTRI IESU CHRISTI INCIPIT ORDO QUALITER IN SANCTA ATQUE APOSTOLICA ECCLE- SIA ROMANA MISSA CAELEBRATUR QUAM NOS CUM SUMMO STUDIO ATQUE CUM DILIGENTIA MAXIMA CURAV- IMUS, NON GRAMMATICO SERMONE, SED APERTE LOQUENDO VERITATEM INDICARE, ID EST QUALITER PONTIFEX PROCEDIT IN DIE SOLEMNI CUM HONORE MAGNO SICUT INVESTIGATUM EST A SANCTIS PATRIBUS.[77]

This is the second full *ordo* for a papal Mass; it is a hybrid or Romano-Frankish composition.

Ordo IV is not the result of direct observation nor is it a description of a current eucharistic rite in Gaul. Rather, it is a literary work dependent on *Ordo* I supplemented already by *Ordo* III. The compiler adds to the Roman elements of his main source several modifications indicating local Frankish usages and conditions: a regrouping of ministers dependent on the kind of orientation characteristic of Frankish churches, the transformation of the final doxology of the *canon missae* into a simple rite of displaying the consecrated elements to the people, the simplification of the *immixtio* rite, the suppression of the *fermentum* rite, the addition to *Ordo* III, of four new feasts.

Ordo IV is not a Roman document but a deliberate adaptation of *Ordo* I to Frankish conditions. The author was trying to establish the Roman rite in Gaul by means of a compromise with prevailing Frankish customs. It is a typical example of ritual hybridization ca. 780-790. Its chronology is that of the *Collection of St. Amand* of which it is a part (cf. p. 152 *supra*).

ORDO V. ORDO PROCESSIONIS AD ECCLESIAM SIVE AD MISSAM SECUNDUM ROMANOS.[78].

This is the third *ordo* for a papal Mass and another hybrid, Romano-Germanic *ordo* for solemn Mass.

From a paleographical point of view, *Ordo* V only appears in the MSS of the *Romano-Germanic Pontifical*. The compilers of St. Alban's Abbey, Mainz, inserted it into their voluminous composition and since it dates from 950-962, *Ordo* V itself must have been created earlier on. It uses *Ordo* I (ca. 750 in *Francia*), the *Liber officialis* of Amalarius of Metz (823)[79] and the *Eclogae de ordine romano*.[80] On the other hand, it is not sure that the *Expositio totius missae ex concordia divinarum scripturarum* or *Missa pro multis causis celebratur* . . . is one of the sources of *Ordo* V; the opposite is, indeed, quite possible.[81] Since both works come from about the same period, the literary problem is of little interest anyway.

The most suitable date for the redaction of *Ordo* V is 850-900, but closer to 900 than to 850.

This is a Romano-Germanic *ordo* for solemn Mass, redacted in the Rhineland, in an abbey or episcopal city. The changes and additions it contains make it diverge widely from *Ordo* I. Although it was long considered a purely Roman document, it is a directory for the German clergy taking account of local usages.[82]

ORDO VI. IN NOMINE DOMINI INCIPIT LIBER DE ROMANO ORDINE. QUALITER CELEBRANDUM SIT OFFICIUM MISSAE.[83]

Ordo VI is only known through the edition of G. Cassander[84] and the date of his original is hard to fix. It is later than Amalarius of Metz (†850) whom it uses and it mentions *diacones stationarii* (no. 3) which reminds us of the clergy of Metz.

This is a text of little documentary value; in abridging *Ordo* I, it understands it badly on occasion and adds nothing of interest to the text.

ORDO VII. QUALITER QUAEDAM ORATIONES ET CRUCES IN TE IGITUR AGENDAE SUNT.[85]

This is a directory telling celebrants where to make signs of the cross over the *oblata* during the *canon missae*.

It is a fragment of a Paduan-type sacramentary (although not identical with *Paduensis* D. 47), redacted either in the diocese of Metz or Besançon, after *Ordo* I arrived in Gaul (ca. 750) and before the transcription of *Sangallensis* 150 (late IX century) which contains the *canon missae* of the Sacramentary.

It exists in both a short and long version, the latter representing its primitive form stemming from the Carolingian period; the abridged version may be due to the compilers of the *Romano-Germanic Pontifical* (ca. 950) which contains the shorter text.

The author is a Frankish scribe favorable to the Romanization of the liturgy. *Ordo* VII must not be viewed as the treatise of Pope Zachary (741-752) which he mentioned in a letter to St. Boniface in 752.[86]

Ordo VII completes the series of ancient *ordines* for eucharistic worship. To obtain a more detailed view of the medieval Mass, we have to take into consideration the didactic kind of material contained in the *Expositiones missae*[87] and the other manuals composed for the instruction of the clergy.[88]

The following documents may also be of assistance:

1. *The Missa Illyrica.*
This is a document published by Mathias Flacius Illyricus (Flach or Flacich Francowitz, 1520–1575), *Missa latina quae olim ante Romanam ca. 700 A.D. in usu fuit,* (Argentinae=Strasbourg 1557) = E. Martène, *De antiquis Ecclesiae ritibus* I, 4, *Ordo* XII (ed. Antwerp 1736) pp. 490-518 = PL 138, 1305-1336.

This is neither a Gallican style Mass before the Romanization process of the VIII century nor a Romano-Frankish type characteristic of the Carolingian era[89], but a pontifical Mass for the Church of Minden (Westphalia), composed ca. 1030,[90] and crammed with subjective devotional prayers of the *apologiae* kind.[91]

2. *Parodies of the Mass.*

a) *Incipit officium lusorum, Carmina Burana*, ed. J.A. Schmeller (3rd ed., Breslau 1894) 248-250.

b) *Missa de potatoribus*, ed. T. Wright-J.O. Halliwell, *Reliquiae antiquae* 2 (London 1843) 208-210.

c) *Missa potatorum et lusorum* or *Missa in honorem Bachi*, ed. A. Franz, *Die Messe*, 755-758.

d) *Introitus patronorum Bohemiae* (polemics against the Hussites) ed. Franz, 758-761.

3. *Popular Superstitions.*

Belonging to this category are the *missa nautica* (at sea), *missa venatoria* (for good hunting), *missa sicca* (no offertory, Canon, or Communion), *missa bi-, tri-,* or *quadrifaciata* (several Mass formularies with only one canon and communion).[92]

Also belonging to this category of popular deformations of the Mass are the all-too popular votive Masses illustrating certain concrete forms of medieval devotion: *missa de XIV sanctis auxiliatoribus* (ca. 1348), *missa de XXIV senioribus* (XIV-XV centuries), *missa S. Sebastiani contra pestilentiam, missa S. Rochi contra pestem et languorem epidemiae, missa Recordare contra pestem* (after 1342/1352), *missa S. Liborii contra calculum* (gallstones, XIII century), *missa B. Iob contra morbum gallicum* (venereal disease, late Middle Ages), *missa Sigismundi pro febricitante* (VII century), *missa contra episcopos male agentes* (a cursing formula), *missa contra Hussitas, contra Turcos, missa pro furto,* Mass said on the occasion of ordeals, *missa adversus sagas, veneficas et maleficas omnes daemonum praestigias, missa pro iter acturis* (Mass of the Three Kings), *missa S. Ioseph contra infamiam malorum hominum, missae pro defuncto de cuius anima dubitatur vel desperatur* (for the damned). Note also the series of 3, 5, 7, 9, 13, 30, 41, 44, and 48 masses for the faithful departed or for other intentions.

ORDO VIII. DE VESTIMENTIS PONTIFICIS.[93]

Episcopal vestments: *camicia* (tunic), *cingulum* (cincture), *linea cum costis sirica* (alb), *anagologium* (amice), *dalmatica minor et maior* (dalmatics), *orarium* (stole), *planeta* (chasuble), *pallium* (a woolen band sewn with black crosses which hangs over the shoulders), *sestace* (maniple), *odhones, odones* or *udones* (white stockings), *campagi* (sandals); some of these vestments are of Frankish origin.[94]

Ordo VIII was drawn up in Gaul ca. 850-900, on the basis of *Ordo* I but with additions that sometimes correspond more with the author's fantasies than with actual usage.

ORDO IX (no title). *In primis etenim vestietur episcopus* . . . [95]

The first ritual description of an episcopal Mass proper.

Ordo IX describes an ordinary episcopal Mass when the celebrating bishop is not the pope. It derives from the papal Mass described in *Ordines* I and V which the redactor knew and simplified.

It originated in the Frankish kingdom, probably in its Germanic section (peculiarities in vocabulary).

It was put together before the end of the IX century (date of that part of *Sangallensis* 614, containing *Ordo* IX) but not much before this date since *Ordo* V, one of its sources, dates from the end of the IX century. Most likely *Ordo* IX was redacted ca. 880-900.

ORDO X. ORDO PROCESSIONIS SI QUANDO EPISCOPUS FESTIVIS DIEBUS MISSAM CELEBRARE VOLUERIT, ITA UT AB ANTIQUIS PATRIBUS OCCIDENTALIUM INSTITUTIONE EST CONSTITUTUM, HIC ADESSE CERNITUR SCRIPTUS.[96]

This is the second description of an episcopal Mass proper; this one was celebrated in a catherdral served by canons regular.

The sources of *Ordo* X are *Ordo* V and *Ordo* IX, but not *Ordo* I directly.

Ordo X was used by the compilers of the Mainz pontifical (ca. 950). Since *Ordines* V and IX used by *Ordo* X are of the late IX century, our document can be situated between 900 and 950.

The redactor was a Frank (Gallican peculiarities) and perhaps worked at Mainz itself.

ORDO XI. INCIPIT ORDO VEL DENUNTIATIO SCRUTINII AD ELECTOS QUOD TERTIA EBDOMADA IN QUADRAGESIMA, SECUNDA FERIA, INITIATUR.[97]

A directory for the liturgy of baptism.

Ordo XI provides a detailed description of the seven *scrutinia* of Lent, from Wed. of the third week of Lent until the morning of Holy Saturday (these *scrutinia* are vestiges of the ancient catechumenate;

their didactic elements have been largely eliminated but their ritual elements were retained), and of the full baptismal rite celebrated during the Paschal Vigil (including Confirmation and first Communion).[98]

Ordo XI is undoubtedly a Roman document, both because of its presence in Collection A and because of the local peculiarities it contains; it was used by the presbyters of the Roman *tituli* and basilicas with baptismal privileges and has affinities with the baptismal *ordo* of the Old Gelasian Sacramentary (*Vat. Reg.* 316).

This relationship between *Ordo* XI and the Gelasian Sacramentary can be viewed, in principle, in two ways:

a) *Ordo* XI is the source of the baptismal *ordo* in the Gelasian Sacramentary (Andrieu), or

b) *Ordo* XI derives from the Gelasian's baptismal *ordo* (Chavasse); the latter seems the more probable hypothesis.[99]

Ordo XI was redacted at Rome later than the creation of the baptismal *ordo* of *Vat. Reg.* 316 (ca. 650). *Ordo* XI may well have appeared around 650-700 and is therefore one of the oldest *ordines* to have survived.

A variety of baptismal rites are described in the Old Gelasian Sacramentary (*Vat. Reg.* 316):

1. a succinct Roman ritual for normal baptism, older than *Ordo* XI but already including several *scrutinia*:

I, XXIX: *Denuntiatio pro scrutinio quod tertia hebdomada in Quadragesima, secunda feria, initiarum* (Wilson, 45; Mohlberg, 42)

I, XXX: *Orationes super electos ad caticumenum faciendum* (Wilson, 46-47; Mohlberg, 42-43)

I, XXXI: *Benedictio salis dandum caticuminis* (Wilson, 47-48; Mohlberg 43)

I, XXXII: *Benedictio post datum sale* (Wilson, 47; Mohlberg, 44)

I, XXXIII: *Item exorcismi super electos* (Wilson, 48-49; Mohlberg, 44-46)

I, XXXIV: *Incipit expositio evangeliorum in aurium apertione ad electos* (Wilson, 50-52; Mohlberg, 46-48)

I, XXXV: *Incipit praefatio symboli ad electos* (Wilson, 53-56; Mohlberg, 48-51)

I, XXXVI: *Item praefatio orationis dominicae* (Wilson, 57-59; Mohlberg, 51-53)

I, XLII: *Sabbatorum die* (Holy Sat). *Sequitur ordo qualiter sabbato sancto ad vigiliam ingrediantur* (Wilson, 78-81; Mohlberg, 67-70)

I, XLIV: *Inde discendis cum laetania ad fonte. Benedictio fontis* (baptism and confirmation; Wilson, 84-87; Mohlberg, 72-74)[100]

2. The Old Gelasian also contains baptismal rites for other, extraordinary occasions: for the sick, for converted pagans (Vigil of Pentecost):

I, LXVI-LXX: *Egrotanti caticumino impositio manuum* (Wilson, 110-113; Mohlberg, 91-93)

I, LXXI: *Item ad catecuminum ex pagano faciendum* (Wilson, 113-114; Mohlberg, 93-94)

I, LXXII-LXXVI *Item ad succurrendum infirmum catechuminum* (Wilson, 114-117; Mohlberg, 94-97)[101]

3. In the *Supplement* to the *Hadrianum* there is also a baptismal rite: *Oratio ad caticumenum faciendum ... In sabbato sancto oratio ad catecizandum infantem* (Wilson, 159-163; Deshusses, 1064-1089, pp. 371-379). This is the first baptismal rite in which all the separate *scrutinia* of the older rites are reduced to *one*—and one not designed for the sick or dying. In substance, this *ordo* of the *Supplementum Anianense* is identical with the Tridentine *Ordo baptismi adultorum* and therefore with the reduced form of that rite, the *Ordo baptismi parvulorum*. Although the baptism of infants became the rule, the medieval Church never developed a proper rite of baptism for such occasions. Earlier on, it used *Ordo* XI and its variants even for children and, later, this order of the *Supplement* and another abbreviated *Ordo baptismi infirmum* for those in danger of death (clinical baptism).[102] A new *ordo* of baptism with the *scrutinia* reduced to one appeared in the *Romano-Germanic Pontifical* (ca. 950).[103]

From Northern Italy (Grado?) we have an *Ordo scrutiniorum* (baptismal rite) in the Milanese MS, Bibl. Ambrosiana, *codex* T. 27 Sup. (XI century) ed. C. Lambot, *Northern Italian Services of the Eleventh Century*, HBS 67 (London 1931).[104] The baptismal ordo sent by Pope Vigilius *e scrinio nostro* to Bishop Profuturus of Braga (June 29, 538) has not been preserved. (PL 69, 18).

ORDO XII. ORDO ANTIPHONARUM.[105]

An incomplete directory for the antiphons and responsories to be used at the Liturgy of the Hours.[106] It supposes the existence of a *Capitulare=Liber antiphonarum* or *Liber responsalis, Responsoriale* and only points out certain peculiarities and modifications.

The redactor was a Frankish monk well versed in Roman usages and perhaps a contemporary of Pope Hadrian I (772-795); (*Ordo* XII, 25: *Passiones sanctorum vel gesta ipsorum usque ad Adriani tempora)*, or of a slightly later period. *Ordo* XII is certainly earlier than 850, the date of its earliest witness, *Sangallensis* 614.

ORDO XIII A. INCIPIT ORDO LIBRORUM CATHOLICORUM QUI PONUNTUR IN ANNO CIRCULO IN ECCLESIA ROMANA.[107]

A list of the biblical books used during the Night Office (*Vigiliae*) throughout the liturgical year, beginning at Septuagesima with the Heptateuch (probably the first seven books of the Bible). This *ordo* is too concise to permit us to study the Night Office.

Aside from nos. 3-5, the Roman origin is clear; the redactor was probably a master of ceremonies of the Lateran Palace, the papal residence. Since this document belongs to Collection A, the original of XIII A must have been drawn up around 700-750.

ORDO XIII B. INCIPIT ORDO LIBRORUM CATHOLICORUM QUI IN ECCLESIA ROMANA PONUNTUR AD LEGENDUM.[108]

A new, enlarged and somewhat modified edition of *Ordo* XIII A in a recension containing the Gallican interpolation (*Ordo* XIII A, nos. 3-5).

Its Frankish origin is certain. *Ordo* XIII B belongs to the Gallicanized Collection B of the beginning of the IX century. *Ordo* XIII B may, therefore, come from the years 770-780.

ORDO XIII C. QUANDO ET QUO TEMPORE LIBRI VETERIS ET NOVI TESTAMENTI LEGENDI SUNT.[109]

A combination of *Ordines* XIII A and B, predominantly the former.

It is part of the *Decretum* of Burchard of Worms (*Decretum* III, 222; PL 140, 720-721) and is probably the work of Burchard himself (✝1025); around 1120 it was copied from the *Decretum* by the scribe of *Vindobonensis* 701 and thus preserved.

ORDO XIII D. INCIPIT ORDINATIM BREVIATUM QUALITER LIBRI CUM RESPONSORIIS SIBI CONVENIENTIBUS PER ANNI CIRCULUM AD LEGENDUM PONUNTUR.[10]

This recension of the *ordo* of readings combines the preceding ones; part I (nos. 1-21) follows the arrangement of *Ordines* XIII A and B; part II (nos. 22-34) is based on XIII A.

Ordo XIII D is of Germanic origin and was transcribed in the XII century, after the *Micrologus* of Bernhold of Constance, in *Sangallensis* 164. In all probability, it represents the usages of the XI century German churches.

ORDO XIV (no title). *Cantatur autem omni scriptura* . . . [111]

A list of readings for the Office in St. Peter's on the Vatican, giving the lessons as they were read in the monasteries serving the basilica.

Both recensions are of Frankish origin, the earlier one recording pure Roman use, the later a revised and rearranged use for Frankish churches.

Paleographical evidence shows that *Ordo* XIV forms the second part of the *Sententiae papae Leonis de apocrifae scripturae* of the MS *Vat. Pal. lat.* 277 (uncial, VIII century).[112] The original, drawn up most probably in the second half of the VII century, is already found in the collection of *ordines* of *Sangallensis* 349 (late VIII century).

ORDO XV. INCIPIT CAPITULARE ECCLESIASTICI ORDINIS QUALITER IN SANCTA ATQUE APOSTOLICA ROMANA ECCLESIA CELEBRATUR, IBIDEM A SAPIENTIBUS ET VENERABILIBUS PATRIBUS NOBIS TRADITUM FUIT.[113]

A directory designed for all ecclesiastics, secular and regular, containing a variety of liturgical prescriptions spanning the liturgical year, beginning with Advent (readings, ordinations, Masses, baptismal scrutinies, various celebrations of the temporal and sanctoral cycles, exhortations to follow Roman usages).

The document has two main recensions, both amalgamating Roman and Frankish elements. Its principal sources are *Ordines* I and XI and the baptismal rite of a Frankish Gelasian Sacramentary of the earliest kind, i.e., the *Gellonensis*.

For origin and date, refer to the Collection of the *Sangallensis* 349 (*Capitulare eccl. ordinis; supra*, pp. 152-154).

ORDO XVI. INCIPIT INSTRUCCIO AECCLESIASTICI ORDINIS QUALITER IN CAENUBIIS FIDELITER DOMINO SERVIENTES . . . MISSARUM SOLEMNIIS VEL NATALICIIS SANCTORUM SEU ET OFFICIIS DIVINIS ANNI CIRCULI DIE NOCTUQUE . . . DEBEANT CELEBRARE.[114]

A liturgical directory for Benedictine monks, adapting *Ordines* XIV and XV; It has two parts: a) the liturgy of the Hours (nos. 1-17) based on *Ordo* XIV, and b) the liturgical cycle (nos. 18-54) based on *Ordo* XV. It also uses the *Rule* of St. Benedict.

For origin and date, refer to *Sangallensis* 349 (*supra*, pp. 152-154).

ORDO XVII. INCIPIT BREVIARIUM ECCLESIASTICI ORDINIS QUALITER IN CAENOBIIS FIDELITER DOMINO SERVIENTES . . . DEBEANT CAELEBRARE . . .[115]

A compilation made up of elements borrowed from *Ordo* XV and *Ordo* XVI. Its most interesting part is a description of the Mass (nos. 17-63) in its simplified and Gallicanized form. The alterations of *Ordo* I it contains come by way of *Ordo* XV.

If *Vat.pal. lat.* 574 (late VIII century) is the archetype, the author was a Frankish monk working around 790; if this MS is only a copy, he may have worked some ten years earlier. In any case, because of its use of *Ordines* XV and XVI, it cannot be earlier than 780-790.

ORDO XVIII. ITEM DE CURSU DIVINO VEL NOCTURNO QUALITER ORAS CANONICAS NUNTIANTUR IN SANCTAE SEDIS ROMANE ECCLESIE SIVE IN MONASTERIIS CONSTITUTIS.[116]

A directory showing how the several parts of the Office are distributed throughout the day in a small Benedictine community; it seems based on older documents.

For date and author, see the *Sangallensis* 349 (*supra*, pp. 152-154).

ORDO XIX. INCIPIT DE CONVIVIO SIVE PRANDIO ATQUE CENIS MONACHORUM QUALITER IN MONASTERIA ROMANAE ECCLESIAE CONSTITUTIS EST CONSUETUDO.[117]

The most essential part of this document is a set of monastic customs regulating the meals of an important community according to principles deriving from an ancient Rule originating at Luxeuil. It contains curious details, such as numerous signs of the cross like those in the *Regula coenobialis* of St. Columbanus.

For date and author, see the *Sangallensis* 349 (*supra*, pp. 152-154).

ORDO XX. ORDO QUALITER IN PURIFICATIONE SANCTAE MARIAE AGENDUM EST.[118]

The disposition of the procession which went from S. Hadrian-in-the-Forum to St. Mary Major, according to the itinerary prescribed by Sergius I (687-701) on the four major feasts of the Blessed Virgin: Purification (Feb 2), Annunciation (March 25), Dormition (Aug 15), and her Nativity (Sept 8).[119]

This document derives in some fashion or other from the *Collection of St. Amand* and is the work of a Frankish monk at the time of Pepin III; he is probably the same person who redacted *Ordo* IV, around 780-790.

ORDO XXI (no title). *Quando letania maior debet fieri . . .* [120]

This is a Frankish arrangement of the Rogation procession of April 25 (replacing the ancient *Robigalia*) which, at Rome, went with several *stationes* from St. Lawrence in Lucina to St. Peter's basilica. It was a venerable Roman observance attested to already in the time of Gregory the Great (590-604).[121]

The Frankish editor omitted all Roman topographical indications, thus making it suitable for any bishop of any episcopal city.

This document is part of the *St. Amand Collection* and is probably by the same author as *Ordines* IV and XX (similar expressions). It was composed after the introduction of the Roman liturgy in *Francia* (the Rogations appear already in the Frankish Gelasian, ca. 760-770) and before the Carolingian Renaissance (for stylistic reasons). It can therefore be dated 770-790.

ORDO XXII (no title). *Feria quarta initium Quadragesimae . . .* [122]

The liturgy for Lent, composed in *Francia* (XXII, 4: the celebrant faces the East with his back to the congregation) with the help of Roman documents or from information acquired in Rome while on pilgrimage, in order to disseminate the Roman liturgy north of the Alps.

To understand the rather complex problems of the Lenten liturgy appearing in *Ordines* XXII and XXIII, see the studies of A. Chavasse.[123]

This document is earlier than 800 (Charlemagne is still called *rex;* XXII, 13: *flectere pro Carolo rege*) and later than Pope Hadrian (†795) (XXII, 13: *tempore Adriani*).[124]

ORDO XXIII (no title). *Feria quinta ad matutinum . . .* [125]

A short, precise directory for the last three days of Holy Week (Einsiedeln, Monastery Library, *codex* 326; IX century); whence its title, the *Ordo of Einsiedeln.*[126]

The original redactor, who seems to have been German (*lumen* or *facula* for *cereus; chorus* for *presbyterium*) must have assisted at the Sacred Triduum in Rome and composed his *ordo* as early as 700-750 since it still contains no blessing of the Paschal Candle.[127]

ORDO XXIV (no title). *Feria quarta quae est pridie in caena domini . . .* [128]

The liturgy of the last days of Holy Week, Wed. through Holy Sat. This document has no direct connection with Rome and could have served as a directory for any bishop. Overall, however, it has strong Roman characteristics and is a kind of transposition of the papal ceremonial or, more likely, of that of some suburbicarian church. It supposes the use of a Gelasian Sacramentary of some kind (Old Gelasian or Frankish Gelasian). Andrieu thinks the derivation was as follows: papal, suburbicarian, *Ordo* XXIV.[129]

ORDO XXV (no title). *Eodem die sabbato sancto* . . . [130]

The blessing of the Paschal Candle. This brief document is a Frankish complement to *Ordo* XXIV. A blessing of the Paschal Candle was already in use in Northern Italy in the IV century and in the suburbicarian churches of Rome since the V century.[131] The proclamation *Exultet iam angelica turba caelorum* is of Gallican origin *(Bobbio Missal, Missale Gothicum, Missale Gallicanum vetus,* the Frankish Gelasian Sacramentaries, the *Supplementum Anianense,* the Bari *rotulus).* These documents combine to show that the blessing of the Paschal Candle existed in the Gallican rite at an early date.[132]

The author of *Ordo* XXV was a monk of Wissembourg (Alsace), the compiler of the *Guelferbytanus* 4175; it was composed early in the IX century but after *Ordo* XXIV which it uses.

ORDO XXVI. DE OFFICIIS IN NOCTIBUS A CAENA DOMINI USQUE IN PASCHA.[133]

In spite of its title, this is a directory extending from *dominica in mediana* (V Sun. of Lent) to Holy Sat. Like *Ordo* XXV, it too complements *Ordo* XXIV.

Ordo XXVI derives from a Roman style liturgy (terminology, manufacture of the *Agnus dei* on Holy Sat.) drawn up for a suburbicarian church near Rome; it differs from standard papal practice by having the blessing of the New Fire and of the Paschal Candle.

This document probably comes from the years 750-775; it is earlier than *Ordo* XXV because *Ordo* XXV, 2=*Ordo* XXVI, 6.

Compare these *ordines* with an *Ordo feria quinta in Cena Domini, hora sexta, celebratur missa* studied by A. Chavasse[134] and A. Mundò.[135]

ORDO XXVII. DE OFFICIIS IN NOCTIBUS A CAENA DOMINI USQUE IN PASCHA.[136]

The liturgy of the last four days of Holy Week (nos. 1-66) and of the special Vespers of Easter Week (nos. 67-94). The two divisions are of different origin and existed as separate documents before being brought together here. The first section is an amalgamation of *Ordines* XXIV and XXVI and was compiled—rather clumsily—in *Francia*, perhaps by the compiler of Collection A, in the second half of the VIII century. The second section is a Roman *ordo* which circulated independently in Gaul before being united with the first section, during the composition of Collection A, ca. 750-800.

ORDO XXVIII. INCIPIT ORDO A DOMINICA MEDIANA USQUE IN OCTABAS PASCHAE.[137]

A complete liturgical directory from the V Sunday of Lent until the Sunday after Easter (*octabas paschae = dominica in albis*) with the help of *Ordines* XXIV, XXVI, XXVII, XI, XIII B, XXX A and a Frankish Gelasian Sacramentary like that of *Gellone.*

Ordo XXVIII was drawn up in *Francia* ca. 800, probably by the person who compiled Collection B.

ORDO XXVIII A (no title). *Deinde pontifex procedens de ecclesia . . .* [138]

The blessing of the font and the administration of Baptism during the Easter Vigil.

Its author is a Frankish monk who worked in *Francia* (Wissembourg) toward the beginning of the IX century. See the *Collection* of the Wissembourg monk.

ORDO XXIX (no title) *Igitur a dominica quam sedis apostolica . . .* [139]

A detailed directory for Holy Week; a monastic adaptation of an *ordo* originally composed for a cathedral church; its sources are *Ordines* XXVII (or XXIV and XXVI, *Ordo* XXVII being an amalgam of the former).

Ordo XXIX has an appendix (*Et interrogavimus nihilominus domnum apostolicum Adrianum . . .*) in the form of a question addressed to a Pope Hadrian, i.e., Hadrian II (867-872) or Hadrian III (884-885). The question and answer relate to the matters contained in *Ordo* XXIX (the liturgy of Holy Sat.).

The MSS containing this document: *Vat. Pal. lat*, 487 (IX century) and its copy, *Corbeiensis* 230 (=Leningrad, *codex* Q.V.II.5; cf. Andrieu,

Ordines I, 348), of around 900, put *Ordo* XXIX and its appendix in the years 870-890 (allusion to Hadrian II or III).

The author was a Frankish monk who had been a pilgrim to Rome and perhaps worked at Corbie itself.

ORDO XXX A (no title). *Feria V in cena domini. Media illa nocte* . . . [140]

The arrangement of the Night Office from Holy Thursday to the Saturday of Easter Week, composed for a community of monks or canons regular.

It orginated in Flanders or Lotharingia, the homeland of its only MS, Brussels, *Bibliothèque royale, codex lat.* 10127-10144. It was composed before 800 (date of the MS) and after 750 (connections with an Old Gelasian Sacramentary like *Vat. Reg.* 316 and not with the *Hadrianum*).

ORDO XXX B (no title). *Qualiter feria V caenae domini agendum sit.*[141]

The arrangement of the Office from the Thursday of Holy Week to the Saturday of Easter Week. It appears to be a compilation of *Ordines* XXX A, I, XXVII, and XII (in that order).

For origin and date, consult the *Collection of St. Amand, (supra,* p. 152).

ORDO XXXI (no title). *De dominica quae mediana nuncupatur* . . . [142]

The arrangement of the Office from the V Sunday of Lent until the end of the octave of Easter; it appears to be a recasting of *Ordo* XXVIII with some older material from *Ordines* XI, XXIV, XXVII and XXX.

In the only surviving MS (Paris, *Biblio. Nat., codex lat.* 9421) this document follows the first edition of Amalarius of Metz's *Liber officialis* (ca. 823). It originated in the North or North-East of *Francia occidentalis* before 900; it was already an anachronism in the X century.

ORDO XXXII (no title). *Item ordo. In caena domini reservant* . . . [143]

The liturgy of the last three days of Holy Week.

This *ordo* uses the earlier *ordines* on the same subject although we cannot establish which one it prefers. Its contact with a Gelasian Sacramentary shows that the Gregorian had not yet completely replaced it.

Ordo XXXII was probably composed around the end of the IX century, at the abbey of Corbie.

ORDO XXXIII (no title). *Alia ordo. In caena domini ad primam* . . . [144]

A succinct ceremonial description of the last three days of Holy Week with emphasis on the Liturgy of the Hours.

It originated in *Francia* but its exact locale still depends on the as yet unidentified chapel *ad Sanctum Gregorium* (XXXIII, 2).

Its only surviving MS, *Parisinus* 1248 (end of the X century?), comes from St. Martial of Limoges.

ORDO XXXIV. QUOMODO IN SANCTA ROMANA ECCLESIA ACOLITUS ORDINATUR.[145]

The Roman rites of ordination: acolyte (no doorkeepers or exorcists because these orders had fallen out of use by this time; omission of lectors also, although this order was still in use), subdeacon, deacon, presbyter and bishop.[146] The candidates are expected to be tonsured clerics although there is no mention of a ceremony of admission to the clerical state. Clerics do not have to pass through each stage of the *cursus* in order to reach a higher rank.

The Roman origin of *Ordo* XXXIV is clear: the *domnus apostolicus* is regarded as the consecrating prelate, and those to be ordained bishop swear to their innocence of the four, capital, sexual crimes before the *confessio* of St. Peter. Pope Hadrian I cited this document to illustrate his own practice (see *below, Ordo* XXXV B).

Ordo XXXIV belongs to Collection A which was circulating in Gaul—as a collection—from around 750. It was written at Rome, but the author understood Frankish terminology and may have picked it up while staying in Gaul with Pope Stephen II (753-754). Nevertheless, this *ordo* was not assembled for the special use of the Frankish churches; certain of its prescriptions were quite inapplicable there. It had small success north of the Alps and was much criticized.

The author appears to have been a Lateran cleric who, shortly before 750, put in writing the practices of his time while taking into account older usages. *Ordo* XXXIV contains the Roman rites of ordination as they were performed in the *early* Middle Ages; they do not represent the original Roman practices of the patristic period (before the VI century).

*   *   *

The original Roman rites of ordination are contained in Hippolytus of Rome, *The Apostolic Tradition* (ca. 215),[147] but there is no ceremonial description of such rites until *Ordo XXXIV*. *Prayers* of ordination used in late antiquity can be found in the *Verona Sacramentary* and in the *Hadrianum* but not ceremonial indications.[148]

In Gaul, a different way of conferring orders was in use. The basic ritual documents are the following:

1. The *Statuta Ecclesiae antiqua* (by a presbyter of S. Gaul, ca. 476-485) under the sub-title *Recapitulatio ordinationis officialium ecclesiae*. There is a short, descriptive canon for each order, introduced by a stereotyped formula: *Episcopus, presbyter, diaconus, subdiaconus, acolythus, exorcista, lector, ostiarius cum ordinatur. . . .* The final grade mentioned, the *psalmista, id est, cantor,* is not introduced by the words *cum ordinatur.*[149]

The *Statuta* preserve certain early Roman practices adapted to Gallican usage.

2. The Romano-Gallican rite compiled in Gaul (late VII or early VIII century) and added to the *Old Gelasian Sacramentary (Vat. Reg.* 316) when it was reproduced in *Francia.*[150]

As it stands now, the ordinations to the various ministries are scattered through Book I in three different locations whereas all the ordination rites are grouped together in the Old Gelasian *Index* of Saint Thierry I, 90-97 (Mohlberg, 268-269) and in the *Missale Francorum* I-IX, along with fresh additions such as the *Benedictio super virgines* and the *Orationes et preces pro regibus* (ed. Mohlberg 1-13)=prayers only, no rubrics.

a) The *Old Gelasian Sacramentary (Vat. Reg.* 316) I, XX-XXIV (Wilson, 24-29; Mohlberg, 20-24): *Ordo qualiter in romana sedis apostolicae ecclesia praesbiteri, diaconi vel subdiaconi eligendi sunt.*

b) *Old Gel. Sac.* I, XCV-XCVI: *Incipit ordo de sacris ordinibus benedicendis* (Wilson, 144-145; Mohlberg, 115-117): *Item benedicciones super eos qui sacris ordinibus benedicendi sunt (ostiarius, lector, exorcista, subdiaconus)* (Wilson, 147-148; Mohlberg, 117-119).

c) *Old Gel. Sac.* I, XCIX: *Orationes de episcopis ordinandis* (prayers only) (Wilson, 151-152; Mohlberg, 120-122).

3. The Frankish Gelasian (or VIII-Century Gelasian) Sacramentaries.[151]

a) The *Sacramentary of Gellone* (ed. A. Dumas, pp. 381-396): *Incipit ordo de sacris ordinibus benedicendum (ostiarius, lector, exorcista, acolitus).—Ordo qualiter in romana sedis apostolicae ecclesiae presbyteri, diaconi vel subdiaconi elegendi sunt.—*[Ordo episcopi] *Exortacio ad populum cum episcopi ordinantur.*

b) The *Sacramentary of Angoulême* (ed. P. Cagin, fol. 146-152): *Incipit ordo de sacris ordinibus . . . Ordo qualiter . . .* and *Exortatio . . .*

4. The Gallican rites contained in Collection B (2nd half of the IX century); e.g., Cologne, Biblio. capit., *codex* 138, fol. 34-35: *Ordo de sacris ordinibus ad benedicendum. Item qualiter in romana sedis apostolicae presbyteri, diaconi vel*

subdicaoni eligendi sunt. Ordinatio episcopi and in Verona MS, Biblio. capit., *codex* 92, fol 57-60 (=*item*).[152]

These Romano-Gallican ordination rites became part of the first attempts at creating the Carolingian Pontificals and those of the subsequent period.

With fresh additions, these rites appeared again in the *Romano-Germanic Pontifical of the Tenth Century* (ca. 950) and were introduced at Rome by the Ottos of Germany.[153]

ORDO XXXV. ORDO QUOMODO IN SANCTA ROMANA ECCLESIA LECTOR ORDINATUR.[154]

Despite its restrictive title, this is a Romano-Gallican *ordo* for the ordination of lectors, (1-16), acolytes and subdeacons (7-14), deacons and presbyters (15-37) and bishops (38-74).

Ordo XXXV is an interpolated recasting of *Ordo* XXXIV. It belongs to the years 900-950, i.e., to the period intervening between *Ordo* XXXIV and the corresponding rites of the RGP. It must have been drawn up at Rome around 925, at the latest, because the compilers of the RGP used it ca. 950, and towards 900, at the earliest, because of certain peculiarities that were received at Rome only around that time (the Frankish anointing of the hands of those ordained to the presbyterate was still not used at Rome in 864; see the letter of Pope Nicholas I to Ralph of Bruges in *MGH, Epistolae karolini aevi* 4, 634-635).

ORDO XXXV A (no title). *Progreditur domnus apostolicus* . . . [155]

A rite for episcopal ordination elaborated ca. 970 by a Roman master of ceremonies with the help of the RGP which Otto I (951-973) had brought to Rome; although he used the Mainz Pontifical, he did not follow it faithfuly. *Ordo* XXXV A is a witness to the liturgical decadence that prevailed at Rome before all sections of the RGP were imposed on the City.

ORDO XXXV B. ORDO AD VOCANDUM ET EXAMINANDUM SEU CONSECRANDUM ELECTUM EPISCOPUM.[156]

A rite for episcopal consecration containing two distinct sections: a preliminary synaxis on Saturday (nos. 1-8) which is a recasting of the corresponding parts of *Ordines* XXXIV and XXXV, and a Sunday morning ceremony (nos. 9-52) which is a recasting of the corresponding section of the RGP.

Ordo XXXV B is a part of *Alexandrinus* 173, copied near Rome a little after 1000; except for this *ordo*, the MS is a literal copy of extracts from the RGP. *Ordo* XXXV B appears to be the rite of episcopal ordination adapted to the use of the suburbicarian dioceses of Rome.

In his letter to Charlemagne (790-791), Pope Hadrian cites the first part of *Ordo* XXXV B (*Ordo* XXXV A, 52 = *Ordo* XXXIV, 28).[157]

Ordo XXXV B, as a whole, was assembled around 975-1000 and the *Alexandrinus* 173 belongs to the first years of the XI century. The first part, the section cited by Hadrian, was used just about as it stood. The *decretum* announcing the ordination is addressed to a pope whose initial is A (*Ordo* XXXV B, 3: *Beatissimo papae A . . .*); given the other chronological indications, this can only be Anastasius III (911-913) or Agapetus II (946-955). Like the first part of our document, this section was drawn from an earlier source.

ORDO XXXVI. DE GRADIBUS ROMANAE ECCLESIAE.[158]

Ordination rites of deacons, presbyters and bishops, with only the briefest mentions of the minor orders. This *ordo* retraces the general outline of the ceremonies missing from *Ordo* XXXIV; it has, e.g., the rite for the ordination of a pope, which does not appear in XXXIV.[159]

Apparently a Roman document, it is actually a Romano-Frankish rite of ordination making a bit more explicit the prescriptions of the *Statuta Ecclesiae antiqua* which, since the late VI century, had been normative for the Frankish church.

Ordo XXXVI is the product of a Frankish liturgist working rather unevenly from either Roman texts or from personal memories of a visit to Rome. The author does not seem to have aimed so much at spreading the Roman liturgy north of the Alps as at providing information on Roman usages.

The oldest witness to *Ordo* XXXVI is the St. Gall MS, Stiftsbibliothek, *codex* 614 (ca. 850-900, hard to locate after 900). It declares that a bishop cannot become pope (no. 40: *Summus namque pontifex . . . episcopus esse non poterit*): such a judgment coincides with that of the synod of 897, a synod which condemned Pope Formosus after his death for—among other things—having been transferred from the bishopric of Porto to the see of Rome. No 54 acclaims a *Domnus Leo papa*, who can be no other than Leo IV (847-855), but the problem of bishops seeking the papacy had not yet surfaced at the time of his pontificate. It is more prudent, therefore, to date *Ordo* XXXVI around 897, especially because *Sangallensis* 614 may well be the original of our *ordo* and was produced in the St. Gall scriptorium itself.

ORDO XXXVII A. ORDO QUATTUOR TEMPORUM IEIUNII PRIMI, QUARTI, SEPTIMI ET DECIMI MENSIS.[160]

A directory for the Ember Days. These were the seasonal fast days (Wed., Fri. and Sat.) of March (the first month according to ecclesiastical reckoning), June (fourth month), September (seventh month) and December (tenth month). At Rome and elsewhere since the V century, these four fasts had replaced the earlier fasting periods of the fourth, seventh and tenth months.[161] Because of this change, two March fasts might henceforth coincide: the *ieiunium primi mensis* and the fast of the first week of Lent when this week fell in March. The *Old Gelasian Sacramentary* (*Vat. Reg.* 316) still registered two distinct fasts for the first month, whereas the *Gregorian Sacramentary* (both the *Paduense* and the *Hadrianum*) presented them as a single fast of the first week of Lent (as in the Tridentine Missal). The Ember Days have been abolished in the Missal of the II Vatican Council.

The Gallican and Roman dates for the Ember Days were quite different.

Gallican Dates (kept north of the Alps, IX-XI centuries):[162]

    I fast—I week of March
    II fast—II week of June
    III fast—III week of September
    IV fast—December, before Christmas
    Roman Dates (differing for March and June):[163]
    I fast—I week of Lent
    II fast—June, in the octave of Pentecost

The Frankish origin of *Ordo* XXXVII A is clear since its Ember Days do not coincide with those of Rome. The oldest witness to this document is Verona, Biblioteca capitulare, *codex* 92 (814-817). The *ordo* itself was put together a bit earlier, ca. 800 (it uses *Ordo* XXXVIII, belonging to Collection B) and probably before 813 because of the canon of the Synod of Mainz held that year.[164]

ORDO XXXVII B. DE QUATTUOR TEMPORIBUS IEIUNII PRIMI, QUARTI, SEPTIMI ET DECIMI MENSIS.[165]

A directory for the Ember Days. This document has two recensions: an older one which is an abridged edition of XXXVII A and a more recent one which is a revision of the former made by the compiler of the RGP.

The older recension can be located around 825, the date of its oldest witness, Cologne, Biblio. capit., *codex* 138, which may be the original itself. The more recent is that of the Mainz Pontifical where it appears in two locations (independently and within the framework of *Ordo* L) and can, therefore, be dated around 950.

ORDO XXXVIII. ITEM DE QUATTUOR TEMPORIBUS IEIUNIORUM QUANDO FIUNT XII LECTIONES.[166]

This document is preserved only in the MSS of the RGP and is perhaps due to the compiler of *Ordo* L, a foundational piece in the Mainz Pontifical.[167]

ORDO XXXIX. ORDO QUALITER IN SANCTA ATQUE APOSTOLICA SEDE, ID EST BEATI PETRI ECCLESIA, CERTIS TEMPORIBUS, ORDINATIO FIT QUOD AB ORTHODOXIS PATRIBUS INSTITUTUM EST, ID EST MENSE PRIMO, IIII, VII, X, HOC EST IN XII LECTIONES.[168]

A brief directory for the ordinations of deacons and presbyters on the Ember Saturdays. In fact, however, the meetings and scrutinies for these ordinations began on Monday of each Ember Week. This *ordo*, like *Ordo* XXXVI, is a compliment to *Ordo* XXXIV.[169]

This document belongs to the *St. Amand Collection*,[170] which means that it is a Frankish composition of the late VIII century adapting Roman customs to Frankish purposes. The Roman documents were, of course, completely free from all Gallican interpolations.

ORDO XL A. DE ORDINATIONE ROMANI PONTIFICIS.[171]

A brief description of the ordination of a pope by the bishop of Ostia, assisted by the bishops of Albano and Porto as co-consecrators.[172]

This *ordo* was drawn up at Rome and originally stood by itself, but in the VII century it was incorporated into the *Liber diurnus*, the official book of *formulae* used by the papal chancery,[173] and reflects VI-century Roman usages, both institutional and liturgical.

ORDO XL B. ORDO QUALITER ORDINETUR ROMANUS PONTIFEX.[174]

A new and enlarged edition of *Ordo* XL A, belonging to the original strata of the RGP. The *incipits* of the prayers corresponded to those used for the ordination of a bishop in the *Gregorian Sacramentary*, with the special phraseology provided by the *Hadrianum* for the consecration of a pope (Desshuses, no. 1018).

The elements making up this *ordo* seem as old and as Roman as those of *Ordo* XL A, but we cannot locate MSS of it earlier than those of the RGP. *Ordo* XL B is a new recension of a Roman original produced in the scriptorium of St. Alban's Abbey, Mainz.

ORDO XLI. DENUNTIATIO CUM RELIQUIAE SANCTORUM MARTYRUM PONENDAE SUNT. ORDO QUOMODO ECCLESIA DEBEAT DEDICARI.[175]

The initial *denuntiatio* does not belong here and has been borrowed from the Old Gelasian Sacramentary.[176] The second half of the title corresponds to the contents of this *ordo*.

The dedication of churches:[177] initial entry procession, great litany, prostration, the tracing of the alphabet on the floor, preparation of holy water, mingling of water, salt, ashes and wine, repeated crosses traced with holy water, consecration of the altar, blessing of altar linens, vessels and vestments, deposition of relics and vesting of the altar.

Ordo XLI belongs to Collection B and originated in Gaul. Combining Roman and Frankish elements, it is the result of the Romanizing liturgical reforms of Pepin and Charlemagne.

Its author may have worked as late as the early IX century but, more likely, around 775, before the dissemination of the *Hadrianum*. *Ordo* XLI supposes an older type of sacramentary, such as *Vat. Reg.* 316 or one of the Frankish Gelasians.

Gallican Dedication Rites:

a) The *Sacramentary of Angoulême* (Frankish Gel. family) preserves a Gallican dedication rite uninfluenced by Roman usages: fol. 140^v *Ordo consecrationis basilicae novae* (ed. Cagin, no. 2020). This *ordo* is surrounded by prayers of various origins which also appear in the other Frankish Gelasians but without the *ordo*.[178]

b) The Old Gelasian rite of dedication (*Vat. Reg.* 316) is a Romano-Gallican product of the late VII or early VIII century. *Vat. Reg.* 316 I, LXXXVIII: *Orationes in dedicatione basilicae novae* (Wilson 133-136; Mohlberg 107-110). This rite is composed of both prayers and valuable ceremonial indications in two heterogeneous parts: a) the first two prayers which are of Roman origin (Mohlberg 689 and 690 and b) the rest of the rite, beginning with the blessing of the mingled wine and water (Mohlberg 691-702), which is exactly like the Angoulême rite.[179]

ORDO XLII. ORDO QUOMODO IN SANCTA ROMANA ECCLESIA RELIQUIAE CONDUNTUR.[180]

A rite for the consecration of an altar with the enclosure of relics and three particles of eucharistic bread (no. 11: *tres portiones corporis domini intus in confessione*). It is not, properly speaking, a rite for the dedication of churches but a ceremonial description of the deposition of relics. It reflects the ancient Roman tradition for consecrating a church by the reception of relics. This *sanctificatio* had two moments: the *depositio reliquiarum* and the eucharistic celebration.[181] The rite of *depositio* was much like a Christian funeral: preparation of the *confessio* = the saint's tomb, the translation of the remains, the burial of the *ossa*, the use of perfumed ointments.

Ordo XLII supposes a Gregorian Sacramentary. Belonging to Collection A, this document circulated in Gaul around 750 and may represent something worked out around 720-750. It is clearly Roman in origin and contains no Gallican elements. It seems to have been created for the suburbicarian bishops of Rome.

ORDO XLIII. INCIPIT AD RELIQUIAS LEVANDAS SIVE DEDUCENDAS SEU CONDENDAS.[182]

A brief rite for the transfer of relics (*levare reliquias*)—the place of departure and the origin of the relics is not indicated—and of their deposition in a new church. It was put together by the compiler of the *Collection of St. Amand* around 790; he used *Ordines* XLI and XLII but omitted all the Gallican peculiarities.

ORDO XLIV. ORDO QUALITER DILIGENTIA AGITUR ROMAE, ECCLESIA SANCTI PETRI.[183]

A directory for the so-called *diligentia* rite of ablutions and incensations used in the *confessio* of St. Peter's basilica and for the ritual hanging of the *turribulum* in the shaft of the *confessio* above the apostle's tomb. The same ceremony probably took place on certain days at St. Paul's Outside-the-Walls and in other cemetery churches, both at Rome and outside Rome.[184]

This is clearly a Roman document. The redactor was a Frankish cleric residing in one of the national *scholae* maintained at Rome, around 800.

ORDO XLV. ORDO ROMANUS AD BENEDICENDUM IMPERATOREM QUANDO CORONAM ACCIPIT.[185]

The Roman rite (i.e., originating at Rome) for the coronation of an emperor, contained in the RGP.

Other titles for Ordo XLV: *Römischer Ordo im ottonischen Pontifikale,* (Elze), *Ordo Cencius I, Ordo* B (Schramm, Eichmann), *Ordo* I (Haller).

Ordo XLV is a Roman document composed after the death of Charles the Fat (888), with the assistance of the *ordines* for the coronation of the Frankish kings. It was probably used until the coronation of Berengarius of Friuli (Dec. 915). Although contained from the start in the RGP, it was not used for the coronation of Otto I (962) or those of his immediate successors.[186] It only came into permanent use after it was included in the *Roman Pontifical of the XII Century.*[187] From a literary point of view, this conclusion of Andrieu can be set against Eichmann's; for the latter, *Ordo* XLV would be of German origin and came to Rome through the RGP in company with the prelates of Otto I's entourage. Such a hypothesis would not, however, explain why it was not used for the coronation of Otto I in 962.

The exceptional importance of this document cannot be grasped without comparing it to the whole tradition of *ordines coronationis imperialis.*[188] A list of these will be given later.

ORDO XLVI. ORDO ROMANUS AD BENEDICENDUM IMPERATOREM (*Ordo* of Arras).[189]

A directory for an imperial coronation based, somewhat freely, on older documents (especially *Ordo* XLV) and composing part of a *Liber episcopalis* copied in a monastic scriptorium in the North of France. It cannot be connected with a specific coronation and seems never to have been in Rome.

The MS, Cologne, Dombibl., *codex* 141, completed before 1093, may well be the original. The anonymous French monk who compiled it probably worked at Arras. In any case, the archetype of *Ordo* XLVI is later than 1000, since it employs an Anglo-Saxon *ordo* compiled for a royal coronation around 980.[190]

ORDO XLVII. ITEM BENEDICTIO AD ORDINANDUM IMPERATOREM SECUNDUM OCCIDENTALES.[191]

A Western (i.e., not a Roman or Eastern) rite of imperial coronation, contained in the RGP.

Other titles: *Westlicher Ordo im Ottonischen Pontifikale* (Elze), *Karolingischer Ordo, Ordo* A (Eichmann, Schramm).

This document is certainly of Frankish or Germanic origin; that is clear from the very words used in the title: *secundum occidentales*. The *terra occidentalis* in question is some country in which Saints Hilary, Martin, Germanus and Ambrose labored for Christ or were, at least, venerated (cf. *Ordo* XIX, 39). There is no general agreement as to the nature of this document. It may have been used at Rheims in 816 for the coronation of Louis the Pious by Stephen IV;[192] or it may have been a Frankish *ordo* for a *royal* coronation in the guise of an imperial crowning and meant to serve for the coronation of an emperor outside Rome and any connection with the papacy.[193] In any case, it must have been redacted before 950 since it survives only in copies of the RGP.

ORDO XLVIII. MISSA PRO IMPERATORE.[194]

The Mass of an imperial coronation.

Most scholars (Eichmann, Erdmann, Elze) admit that *Ordo* XLVIII is simply a continuation of *Ordo* XLVII, as all the MSS reveal. Andrieu, however, thinks that, originally, the Mass may have been attached to *Ordo* XLV.

As is clear from the MS tradition, this *ordo* belongs to the same period as the RGP.

Ordines XLV-XLVIII are not the only documents relating to the imperial coronations. Because of their nature and importance, the rites of anointing and crowning had a literary history outside the confines of the major liturgical books. That holds true especially for the coronation rites of the several Christian kingdoms which, for obvious reasons, have left no trace in the Roman books proper.

We must carefully distinguish, first of all, between *imperial* coronation rites and *royal* coronation rites and, then, between those belonging to separate countries.[195]

A.   *Ordines for Imperial Coronations* (according to Elze):

1.   *Ordo romanus ad benedicendum imperatorem quando coronam accipit* (=*Ordo* XLV of Andrieu=*Ordo* Cencius I=*Ordo* B of Eichmann and Schramm=*Ordo* I of Haller=*Ordo* I of Elze); before 962/963.

2.   *Item benedictio ad ordinandum imperatorem secundum occidentales* (=*Ordo* XLVII and XLVIII of Andrieu=*Karolingischer Ordo*=*Ordo* A of Eichmann and Schramm=*Ordo* II of Elze); before 962/963.

3.   The *Ordo* of Florence (950/1000) (=*Appendix* to *Ordo* XLV of Andrieu=*Ordo* IV of Elze). A first attempt at completing *Ordo* XLV.

4.   The *Ordo* of the *Alexandrinus* 173 (*Ordo* V of Elze); around 1000.

5. The *Ordo* of Egilbert of Freising (=*Ordo* VI of Elze), Freising, ca. 1030. A fusion of *Ordines* XLV, XLVII, and XLVIII of Andrieu.

6. The *Ordo* of Verden (=*Ordo* VII of Elze), ca. 1039/1046. A fusion of *Ordines* XLV XLVII, XLVIII of Andrieu, differing from the *Ordo* of Egilbert.

7. *Ordo* VIII of Elze (Mainz, ca. 1000). A recent recension of the RGP resulting from the fusion of *Ordines* XLV, XLVII, XLVIII of Andrieu.

8. The *Ordo* of Arras (=*Ordo* XLVI of Andrieu=*Ordo* IX of Elze =*Ordo* of Cologne), Arras, XI century, before 1093.

9. *Ordo* Cencius I (=*Ordo* X of Elze), Rome, ca. 1100.

10. The expanded *Ordo occidentalis* in a double recension: a) (=*Ordo* XI of Elze=*Karolingischer Ordo*=Ordo A), south of France, ca. 1150/1200 and b) (=Ordo XI A of Elze), Venice?, XII century.

11. The *Ordo* of Apulia (=Ordo XII of Elze), XII century. A compilation between *Ordines* X and II of Elze.

12. The 'Salian' *Ordo* (=*Salischer Kaiserordo* of Schramm=*Ordo* XIII of Elze), Northern Italy, ca. 1050/1100.

13. The *Ordo* Cencius II (=*Ordo* C of Eichmann and Schramm=*Ordo* Ia of Haller=*Ordo* XIV of Elze), the Roman Curia, ca. 1100/1150.

14. The *Ordo* of Apamaea (=*Ordo* XV of Elze=*Ordo* of the Roman Pontifical of the XII Century, XXXV B, ed. Andrieu, 3, 252-254), the Roman Curia, 1150/1200.

15. The *Ordo* of Constantinople (=*Ordo* XVI of Elze), the Roman Curia, 1150/1200.

16. The Hohenstaufen *Ordo* (=*Staufischer Ordo*=*Ordo* of 1209=*Ordo* D=*Ordo* of the third period=*Ordo* II of Haller=*Ordo* XVII of Elze), Roman Curia, end of the XII century. The many titles of *Ordo* XVII of Elze are also applied to the following *ordines*, nos. 17-19.

17. The *Ordo* of the Roman Curia of the XIII century (=*Ordo* XVIII of Elze =*Ordo* of the Pontifical of the Roman Curia of the XIII Century, no. XV B, ed. Andrieu 2, 385-408).

18. The *New Ordo* of the Roman Curia (=*Ordo* XIX of Elze=*Ordo* of the Pontifical of the XIII Century, Andrieu, *ibid.*).

19. The *Ordo* of William Durandus, ca. 1292/1296 (=Ordo XX of Elze=*Pontifical of William Durandus*, liber I, no. XXV, ed. Andrieu 3, 427-435. On the recensions of nos. 14-19, see Elze, *op. cit.*, pp. 124-132.

20. The *Ordo* for the Coronation of Charles IV, May 4, 1355 (=Ordo XXIII of Elze).

21. The *Ordo* of the Roman Curia of the XV Century (=Ordo XXIV of Elze).

22. The *Ordo* of Burchard of Strasbourg and A. Patrizi Piccolomini (=*Caeremoniale Romanum*, ed. 1488, Liber I, tit. V =*Pontificale Romanum*, ed. 1520 by A. Castellani, folios 53-61; ed. M. Dykmans, *L'oeuvre de Patrizi Piccolomini ou le cérémonial de la première renaissance* 1, SeT 293 [Vatican City 1980] 93-117 =*Ordines* XXV and XXVI of Elze). The *editio princeps* of the *Pontificale* edited by Piccolomini-Burchard (Rome 1485) did

not contain an *ordo* for the coronation of an emperor but it did appear in their *Caeremoniale* of 1488 (published by Cristoforo Marcello at Venice in 1516) in an extended dissertation, cited above, Liber I, tit. V: *Titulus de adventu et coronatione electi in imperatorem Romanorum*. A. Castellani's *Pontificale*, (Venice 1520) contained the same *ordo*.

The *ordines* already mentioned were all for the coronation of emperors; the liturgical books also preserve *ordines* for the coronation of empresses:

a) The *Benedicitio reginae* also served for the *benedictio* of an empress (*Francia occidentalis*, ca. 900; it reappeared in the RGP, Mainz, ca. 950, ed. Vogel-Elze, no. LXXVIII, I, 267-269 (=*Ordo* III of Elze).

b) The *Benedictio reginae vel imperatricis* of Gnesen, XIII century (=*Ordo* XVI A of Elze).

c) The *Ordo* of William Durandus cited above at no. 19: *Ordo romanus ad benedicendum regem vel reginam, imperatorem vel imperatricem coronandos* (=*Ordo* XX of Elze).

d) The *Benedictio et coronatio imperatricis* of the XIV century (=*Ordo* XX A of Elze).

e) The *Ordo* of 1488 already cited above at no. 22 in the section *Coronatio imperatricis sine imperatore* (=*Ordo* XXV/XXVI of Elze).

B. *Ordines for Royal Coronations* (according to Schramm):
These *ordines* differ from those proper to imperial coronations. They also differ from one another according to their country of origin.

I. *Ordines for Royal Coronations in France*:

a) *The ordines of Francia occidentalis (843-987)*:
1) The *Ordo* of Judith=the marriage and coronation rite of Judith, daughter of Charles the Bald, with Ethelwulf, at Verberie in 856 (MGH. *Capitularia*, II, 425-427): *Benedictio super reginam quam Ethelulfus rex accepit in uxorem. Coronatio*.
This is the oldest *ordo* for a royal coronation. There were prayers for such occasions in the earlier sacramentaries but no *ordines* (cf. the *Sacramentary of Gellone*, ed. Dumas, nos. 2091-2094, pp. 296-298: *Benedictio regalis* and the *Sacramentary of Angoulême*, ed. Cagin, 130, no. 1857: *Regalis benedictio quando elevatur in regno*). On the two anointings of Pepin the Short (751 and July 28, 754)—the first Frankish king to have been anointed (as against G. Morin in RB 29, 1912)—see the *extra liturgical* documents in J. F. Böhmer—E. Mühlbacher, *Die Regesten des Kaiserreichs* (2nd edition, Hildesheim 1966) 32 and 38; see also E. Caspar, *Pippin und die römische Kirche* (Berlin 1914) 13, no. 2.

2) The *Ordo* for the coronation of Ermintrude, the first wife of Charles the Bald, at Soissons in 866: *Adlocutio duorum episcoporum in ecclesia Sancti Medardi, quando Hermintrudis fuit consecrata in reginam* (MGH. *Capitularia*, II, 453-455).

3) The *Ordo* for the coronation of Charles the Bald as king of Lotharingia, at Metz in 869: *Adnuntiatio Adventii episcopi ... Benedictiones super regem Karolum ante missam et altare sancti Stephani* (MGH. *Capit.*, II, 337-341 and 456-458).

4) *Ordo* for the coronation of Louis the Stammerer at Compiègne in 877: *Ordo qualiter Hludowicus rex ... ab Hincmaro fuit coronatus in Compendio palatio* (MGH. *Capit.*, II, 363-365 and 461-462).

These four *ordines* were most likely composed by or at least inspired by Hincmar of Rheims (ca. 806-882).[196]

5) *Ordo* for the second coronation of Louis II by Pope John VIII at Troyes in 878: *Orationes ad regem benedicendum*, prayers only (ed. Schramm in *Zeitschrift für Rechtsgeschichte* 54, Kan. Abt. 23 (1934) 192-195.

6) *Petitio et Promissio* of Karlomann at Quiercy in 882: *Petitio episcoporum ad domnum Carolomannum regem ... Promissio domni Karlomanni regis ...* prayers only (ed. Schramm, *op. cit.*, 195-196).

7) *Ordo, Petitio, promissio* and festal chants for the coronation of Odo at Compiègne in 888 (ed. Schramm, *op. cit.*, 196-201).

8) Western *Ordo* or *Ordo* of Erdmann or first *Ordo* of Sens, ca. 880/960 (ed. Schramm, *op. cit.*, 201-207.

9) Investiture formulas of Sens, X century (ed. Schramm, *op. cit.* 281-282).

b) *French ordines properly so-called:*

1)The *Memoriale* of Gervase of Rheims on the coronation of Philip I at Rheims in 1059 (Mansi, *Concilia* 19, 923).

2) The *Ordo* of Fulrad (compiled at Saint Vaast of Arras, ca. 980) used since 1108 (ed. Schramm, *op. cit.*, 235-242).

3) The *Ordo* of Rheims, ca. 1270 (ed. U. Chevalier, *Sacramentaire et Martyrologe de l'abbaye de Saint-Rémy; Martyrologe, Calendrier, Ordinaire et Prosaire de la Métropole de Reims*, Bibliothèque liturgique 7 (Paris 1900) 222-226.

4)Compilations of the XIII and XIV centuries (ed. E. Martène, *De antiquis ecclesiae ritibus* 2 [Antwerp 1736] 610-622).

5) The Capetian *Ordo* or the second *Ordo* of Sens, ca. 1300/1320 (ed. Martène, *op. cit.*, 622-624).

6) The *Ordo* of Charles V of 1365 (ed. E.S. Dewick, *The Coronation Book Of Charles V of France*, HBS 15 [London 1899]).[197]

II. *Ordines for the Royal Coronations in Germany:*
The basic documents are the following:

1) Widukind's account (957/958) of the coronation of Otto I at Aachen in 936 (Widukind, *Rerum gest. Saxonicarum* 2, cap. 1-2, see P.E. Schramm in *Zeitschrit für Rechtsgeschichte* 45, Kan. Abt. 24 (1936) 307-308.

2) The *Ordo* of St. Alban's Abbey, Mainz, in its several recensions in the RGP of the X Century.[198]

III. For the *Ordines* of the coronation of the kings of England[199], Navarre, Castile and Aragon, see the bibliography established by P.E. Schramm, *Der König von Frankreich* 2 (2nd edit., Weimar 1960) 6-7 and 33-34.

ORDO XLIX. ORDO QUALITER AGATUR IN OBSEQUIUM DEFUNCTORUM.[200]

A directory for the rites of death (*ut videris cum ad exitum propinquare*) and burial.

This document belongs to Collection A. Its Roman character is proved by the fact that the compiler of the *Roman Pontifical of the XII Century* used *Ordo* XLIX for his purposes. As part of *Collection A*, this *ordo* was in Gaul ca. 750 and had been redacted at Rome ca. 700-750.

Various derivatives of *Ordo* XLIX survive; e.g., an *Ordo infirmorum vel mortuorum* of the XI century (C. Lambot, *Northern Italian Services of the XI Century*, HBS 67 [London 1931] 42-62) and the *Ordo defunctorum* of the Cologne MS, Cathedral Library, *codex* 123 (X century).[201]

A description of an VIII-century Roman funeral rite, having no connection with *Ordo* XLIX, can be found in the Berlin MS, State Library, *codex Phillipps* 1667 (late VIII century)[202], folios 173ʳ-174ʳ: *Incipit de migratione animae.*[203]

ORDO L. ORDO CATHOLICORUM LIBRORUM QUI IN ECCLESIA ROMANA PONUNTUR.[204]

Despite its title, *Ordo L*, also called Hittorp's *Ordo romanus antiquus* (not to be confused with Mabillon's *Ordo romanus primus*=*Ordo* I of Andrieu), is a ceremonial description of the liturgical functions for the entire Church year.

This is the most sizeable of all the *ordines* and constitutes part of the original layer of materials in the *Romano-Germanic Pontifical of the X Century*, edited in the scriptorium of St. Alban's Abbey, Mainz, by the same team of redactors as the rest of the Pontifical.

For the date and origin of *Ordo L*, see the chapter devoted to the RGP (especially pp. 230-237).

The *Ordines romani* are not the only liturgical documents which provide us with information on the ceremonial elements of the rites.

In addition to the literary sources treating of worship matters (see the list given in the first part of this book), the sacramentaries themselves sometimes provide valuable insights. And yet, since the *liber sacramentorum* is, by its very nature, a collection of prayers and not of ceremonial indications, such indicators are usually brief and are often mere titles.

Sometime after the year 1000, collections of *ordines* begin to fall into the background. Actually they were replaced by another category of liturgical book altogether, the pontificals, which gathered together both the ritual directions that are needed and their corresponding prayers. It is from this source that medievalists draw their information as to how the liturgy of the Latin Church was actually conducted.

The following are a few liturgical documents contemporaneous with the *ordines*.

1) The *Prologus Protadii* (early VII century). This is a book of ceremonies of Bishop Protadius of Besançon and the *ordo canonicorum* of St. John of Besançon.[205]

2) The *Ordines de celebrando concilii*. The oldest such *ordo* is of Visigothic origin and is contemporaneous with the Council of Toledo of 633, or a little later, and is preserved in several forms: *Codex Albelden.*, Alvelda, ca. 876 (ed. Mansi, *Concilia* 1, 10), the *Codex Rachionis* for Strasbourg, ca. 785, now lost (ed. P Séjourné, *Isidore de Seville* [Paris 1929] 514-518), *Codex Coloniensis* 138, ca. 800/825 and, later, in the RGP (no. LXXIX: *Ordo romanus qualiter concilium agatur generale*; no. LXXX, *Ordo qualiter agatur concilium provinciale*; ed. Vogel-Elze 1, 269-291).[206]

3) The *ordines* for public penance and for tariff penance.[207]

a) *For Public Penance*:

The oldest surviving rite of public penance is contained in the Old Gelasian Sacramentary (*Vat. Reg.* 316) which was transcribed at the Abbey of Chelles, near Paris, ca. 750. As it stands, it is a complex rite assembled in somewhat disorderly fashion and only a small portion of it seems of early origin (=*Liber* I, XV with the first sentence of the rubric of I, XVI in the second person singular: *Suscipis eum IIII feria mane in capite quadragesimae* ...) As a whole it seems to be a combination of Roman and Frankish elements put together not much earlier than the end of the VII or the beginning of the VIII century. In any case, the Gelasian rite of public penance no longer corresponded with the rite of canonical penance of the early Christian era. The rite may be reconstructed as follows;

Ash Wednesday: Entry into the *Ordo of Penance*:

> Old Gelasian Sacramentary (*Vat. Reg.* 316), Liber I, XV-XVI: *Orations et preces super paenitentes ... Ordo agentibus publicam paententiam* (Wilson, 14-15, Mohlberg, 17-18).

Holy Thursday: Solemn Rite of Reconciliation:

Old Gel. Sac. I, XXXVIII: *Ordo agentibus publicam paenitentiam* (Wilson, 63-65; Mohlberg, 56-57).

The Gelasian Sacramentary also has another rite of public penance (without any ceremonial indications): *Item ad reconciliandum paenitentem*:

Old Gel. Sac. I, XXXVIII: Entry into the Ordo of Penance=4 prayers (Wilson, 65-66; Mohlberg, 57-58); Reconciliation after a period of penance=3 prayers (Wilson, 66; Mohlberg, 58-59).

In addition to these rites of public penance, *Vat. Reg.* 316 contains several other penitential directories for special circumstances:

A rite of *paentitentia in extremis* (at the hour of death): *Old Gel. Sac.* I, XXXVIII: *Reconciliatio paenitentis ad mortem*, (Wilson, 66-67; Mohlberg, 59). A rite *in extremis* for those who cannot speak: *Old Gel Sac.* III, CXVIII (Wilson, 306; Mohlberg, 242) in accordance with the *Statuta Ecclesiae antiqua*, canon 20 (ed. Munier, p. 83) and Leo the Great, *Epistola* 108, 5 (PL 54, 1013 B).

The penitential process described in *Vat. Reg.* 316 reappears in the Frankish Gelasians, in the *Sacramentary of Fulda* and especially in the *Romano-Germanic Pontifical of the X Century* (within the framework of *Ordo* L); (ed. Andrieu, *Ordines romani* 5, 108-124=Ash Wed.; 192-207=Holy Thurs.; ed. Vogel-Elze, RGP 2, 59-67, 224-251).

    b) *For Tariff Penance*:

The very last section of *Vat. Reg.* 316, probably tacked on at the time of its Gallican transcription ca. 750, seems to be a brief rite of tariff or insular penance:

Old Gel. Sac. Liber III, CVII: *Incipit ad paenitentiam dandam* (Wilson, 314; Mohlberg, 248); it bears a marked resemblance to the *ordines* of the *libri paenitentiales*, e.g., the recitation of the psalms.

The oldest *ordines* of tariff penance are preserved in the *libri paenitentiales*.[208] A certain number are included here but it must be remembered that their numbers, chronology and text still await a critical edition.

Poenitentiale Floriacense (early VIII century): *Incipit ordo ad dandam paenitentiam secundum sanctorum patrum traditionem, qualiter confessiones uniuscuiusque sacerdos suscipi debeat* (Wasserschleben, 422).

Poenitentiale Merseburgense (early VIII century): *De capitalibus primum criminibus qui et in legis animadversione plectuntur sciendum est, qualiter suscipi debeant paenitentes* (W, 388).

Poenitentiale Sangallense (Sacramentary of St. Gall, *codex* 150, early VIII century): *Incipit ordo ad dandam paenitentiam secundum sanctorum patrum traditionem . . .* (W, 425).

Poenitentiale Pseudo-Bedae (Wasserschleben: second half of the VIII century): *Qualiter suscipere debeant penitentes espiscopi vel presbyteri* (W, 250-257).

Poenitentiale Pseudo-Egberti (Wasserschleben: VIII century): *Quando aliquis confessorem suum adierit . . . .* (W, 302).

Penitential of Halitgar (Pseudo-Romanum; ca. 817/830): *Quomodo poenitentes sint suscipiendi, iudicandi sive reconciliandi* (W, 360).

Poenitentiale Sangermanense (IX century): *Ordo ad dandam poenitentiam qualiter episcopi vel presbyteri penitentes sucipere debeant* (W, 349-352).

Poenitentiale Vallicellanum II (*codex Vallicell.* E. 62; IX century): *Incipit ordo poenitentiae* (W, 551-557).

And finally, the *Romano-Germanic Pontifical of the X Century* contains a rite of tariff penance: No. CXXXVI: *Qualiter sacerdotes suscipere debeant poenitentes more solito* (ed. Vogel-Elze, 2, pp. 234-245).

4) The Consecration of Virgins.

The *Old Gelasian Sacramentary* (*Vat. Reg.* 316) contains a rite for the consecration of virgins which belongs to a series of pieces added to the sacramentary when it was transcribed outside Rome at the end of the VII or the beginning of the VIII century.

Liber I, CIII: *Consecratio sacrae virginis quae in epiphania vel secunda feria pasche aut in apostolorum natalicio caelebratur* (Wilson, 156-157; Mohlberg, 124-126). This is a Romano-Gallican rite like those of ordination, the dedication of churches, the blessing of holy water, funerals and penance; see Chavasse's commentary in *Le Sacramentaire gélasien,* 28-35. The later evolution of this rite for the consecration of virgins is described by R. Metz, *La consécration des vierges dans l'Église romaine* (Paris 1954) and in several works by the same author listed in Metz, "Les vierges chrétiennes en Gaule au IV siècle," *Studia Anselmiana* 46 (1961) 109-132 and in Metz, "Benedictio sive consecratio virginum," *EL* 80 (1966) 265-293.

5) Weddings.

No *ordo* for weddings appears outside the sacramentaries. The *Old Gelasian* contains an *Actio nuptialis* (III, LII: Wilson, 265-267; Mohlberg, 208-210) which reappears in the Frankish Gelasians (e.g., Gellone, ed. Dumas, CC 159, nos. 2629-2639, pp. 411-414) and in the RGP, no CCLIV (ed. Vogel-Elze 2, 417-419). See B. Binder, *Geschichte der feierlichen Ehesegens,* Abtei Metten, (1938); P.M. Gy, "Le rite sacramental du marriage et la tradition liturgique," *Revue des sciences phil. et théol.* 38 (1954) 258-263; J. Huard, "La liturgie nuptiale dans l'Église romaine," *Questions liturgiques* 38 (1957) 197-205; K. Ritzer, *Eheschlieessung. Formen, Riten u. rel. Brauchtum in d. christliche Kirche des ersten Jahrtausends,* LQF 38 (Münster 1962), Fr. Trans., *Le marriage dans les Églises chrétiennes du I au XI siècle* (Paris 1970); J.B. Molin-P. Moutembe, *Le Rituel de mariage en France du XII au XVI siècle* (Paris 1974); and most especially, K.W. Stevenson, *Nuptial Blessing: A Study of Christian Marriage Rites,* ACC 64 (London 1982 and New York 1983).

C. SYSTEMATIC CLASSIFICATION OF THE ORDINES ACCORDING TO THE RITES THEY CONTAIN.

1. THE EUCHARIST (papal Mass, episcopal Mass, solemn Mass).

Ordo I (Rome, ca. 700; Gaul, 750): the first *ordo* for the papal Mass.

Ordo II (ca. 750): a Roman supplement to the papal Mass.

Ordo III (ca. 750 and 750-780): Frankish supplement.

Ordo IV (ca. 760-770): the second *ordo* for the papal Mass (first Romano-Frankish rite).

Ordo V (ca. 850-900): the third *ordo* for the papal Mass (second Romano-Frankish rite).

Ordo VI (*ordo* of Cassander; later than 850): a poorly abridged version of Ordo I.

Ordo VII (ca. 750-800): signs of the cross during the *canon missae*.

Ordo IX (ca. 880-900): the first Romano-Frankish rite for an episcopal Mass.

Ordo X (ca. 900-950): the second Romano-Frankish rite for an episcopal Mass.

Ordo XVII (ca. 790), nos. 17-63; a simplified and Gallicanized rite of the Mass.

See also the *Ordines* XV, XVI, XVII of the *St. Gall Collection*.

2. BAPTISM.

Ordo XI (Rome, ca. 650; Gaul, ca. 750).

See also the *Ordines* for Lent, Holy Week and Easter Week.

3. ORDINATIONS.

Ordo XXXIV (ca. 700-750)

Ordo XXXV (ca. 925)

Ordo XXXV A (ca. 970)

Ordo XXXV B (ca. 975-1000)

Ordo XXXVI (ca. 850-900)

Ordo XXXIX (late VIII century)

Ordo XL A (VI century; papal ordination)

Ordo XL B (ca. 950; papal ordination)

4. FUNERALS.

Ordo XLIX (ca. 800)

5. IMPERIAL CORONATIONS.

Ordo XLV (888-915; 950)
Ordo XLVI (980-1093)
Ordo XLVII (816, ca. 950)
Ordo XLVIII (ca. 950)
See also the list of imperial *ordines* given above, pp. 183-185

6. THE DEDICATION OF CHURCHES, THE DEPOSITION OF RELICS AND THE CONSECRATION OF ALTARS.

Ordo XLI (ca. 775)
Ordo XLII (ca. 720-750)
Ordo XLIII (ca. 790)

7. THE TEMPORAL CYCLE.

a) The Liturgical year as a whole:
Ordo L (ca. 950) and several sections of the *Capitulare ecclesiastici ordinis* (Ordines XV, XVI).
b) Lent:
Ordo XXII (ca. 790-800)
Ordo XXVIII (ca. 800)
c) Holy Week:
Ordo XXIII (ca. 700-750)
Ordo XXIV (ca. 750-800)
Ordo XXVI (ca. 750-775)
Ordo XXVII (ca. 750-800)
Ordo XXVIII A (ca. 810)
Ordo XXIX (ca. 870-890)
Ordo XXX A (ca. 750-800)
Ordo XXX B (ca. 770-800)
Ordo XXXI (ca. 850-900)
Ordo XXXII (ca. 870-890)
Ordo XXXIII (late X century or late XI century?)
d) Eastertide:
Ordo XXX A (ca. 750-800)
Ordo XXX B (ca. 770-800)

Ordo XXXI (ca. 850-900)
Ordo XXXII (ca. 870-890)
e) The Blessing of the Paschal Candle:
Ordo XXV (ca. 810-820).
f) Ember Days:
Ordo XXXVII A (ca. 813-817)
Ordo XXXVII B (825 and 950)
Ordo XXXVIII (ca. 950).

8. DIRECTORIES FOR FEASTS AND SPECIAL OCCASIONS.

Besides *Ordo* L, see:
a) The Purification:
Ordo XX (ca. 780-790)
b) The Major Litany (April 25):
Ordo XXI (ca. 780).

9. DIRECTORY FOR THE LITURGY OF THE HOURS (READINGS) AT ST. PETER'S AND IN THE ROMAN MONASTERIES.

Ordo XII (ca. 770-795, and 800)
Ordo XIII A (ca. 700-750)
Ordo XIII B (ca. 770-780 and 800)
Ordo XIII C (ca. 1025)
Ordo XIII D (XI century)
Ordo XIV (ca. 650-700)
Ordo XV (ca. 750-787)
Ordo XVI (ca. 750-787)
Ordo XVII (ca. 780-790)
Ordo XVIII (ca. 750-787)

10. DIRECTORY FOR MONASTIC MEALS.

Ordo XIX (ca. 750-787).

11. THE DILIGENTIA RITE.

Ordo XLIV (ca. 800).

12. DIRECTORY FOR LITURGICAL VESTMENTS.

Ordo VIII (ca. 850-900).

To avoid major confusions of text and chronology in regard to the various *ordines*, we supply two concordances for the editions of Mabillon, Duchesne and Andrieu. Until the critical work of the latter scholar, the *ordines* were always cited according ot the editions of Mabillon and Duchesne.

D. MABILLON'S EDITION OF THE ORDINES

Mabillon's Numbering	*Andrieu's Numbering*
1 *Ordo*, nos. 1-21	*Ordo* I
1 *Ordo*, no. 22	*Ordo* II
1 *Ordo*, nos. 23-26	*Ordo* XXII
1 *Ordo*, nos. 27-47	*Ordo* XXVIII
1 *Ordo*, nos. 48-51 (end)	*Ordo* III
1 *Ordo* Appendix, nos. 1-18 (end)	*Ordo* XXVII
2 *Ordo*	*Ordo* V
3 *Ordo*	*Ordo* VI
4 *Ordo* (*Fragmentum* + Mabillon II, pp. 559-560, forming the beginning)	*Ordo* VII
5 *Ordo*, nos. 1-2	*Ordo* VIII
5 *Ordo*, no. 3	*Ordo* IX
6 *Ordo*	*Ordo* X
7 *Ordo*	*Ordo* XI
8 *Ordo*	*Ordo* XXXIV
9 *Ordo*, nos. 1-6	*Ordo* XXXVI
9 *Ordo*, nos. 7-9	*Ordo* XXXVII A
10 *Ordo: Qualiter agendum sit V feria in Coena Domini*	Extracts from the *Pontifical of the Roman Curia of the XIII Century: Qualiter agendum sit V Feria in Cena Domini*, ed. M. Andrieu, *Le Pontifical romain*, 2,
nos. 1-12	pp. 455-464
nos. 13-15	pp. 464-469
nos. 16-23	pp. 470-477 (nos. 1-25)
no. 24	pp. 452-453
nos. 25-29	pp. 479-484
no. 30	pp. 484-486
nos. 31-32	pp. 486-490
no. 33	pp. 491-492
nos. 34-35	pp. 493-495
nos. 36-50 (end)	pp. 505-513
11 *Ordo: Benedicti beati Petri canonici Liber politicus* (the papal liturgy for the whole year).	Part of the *Liber politicus* drawn up by Canon Benedict at the request of Cardinal Guido de Castello, the future Pope Celestine II, between 1140-1143;

ed. P. Fabre-L. Duchesne, *Le Liber Censuum de l'Église romaine* 2 (Paris 1910) 141-177.

12 Ordo: *De consuetudinibus et observantiis . . . in praecipuis solemnitatibus* (papal liturgy from Advent to Sept. 14, papal and imperial coronation.)

Drawn up by Cencius Camerarius (Cencius de Sabellis or Cencio Savelli, the future Pope Honorius III), ca. 1188-1197 for his *Liber Censuum*; cf. E. Eichmann, *Miscellanea F. Ehrle*, 2 (Rome 1924) 322-327 and *Historisches Jahrbuch* 39 (1919)714; 45 (1925)21f; cf. R. Elze, "Der Liber Censuum des Cencius," *Bulletino dell'Archivio paleografico italiano*, N.S., 2-3 (1956/57) 251-270; reprinted in *Päpste-Kaiser-Könige*, edd. B. Schimmelpfennig-L. Schmugge (London 1982) article 3; B. Schimmelpfennig, *Die Zeremonienbücher der römischen Kurie im Mittelalter*, Bibl. des deutschen hist. Inst. in Rom 24 (Tübingen 1973).

13 Ordo: *Caeremoniale Romanum* (election, consecration and functions of the pope)

A Roman *Ceremonial* composed by order of Gregory X (1271-1276), probably before the Council of Lyons (1274), in that city and by a Frenchman (there is no allusion to the constitution *Ubi periculum maius* promulgated by the Council). Partial critical edition by M. Andrieu, *Le Pontifical* 2, 525-541; M. Dykmans, *Le cérémonial papal de la fin du moyen âge à la renaissance*, Bibliothèque de l'Institut historique belge à Rome 24 (Rome-Brussels 1977) 13-66, 155-218.

14 Ordo: *Ordinarium Sanctae Romanae Ecclesiasie* (election, coronation and functions of the pope)

The *Ceremonial* of Cardinal G. Gaetano Stefaneschi († 1341), composed around 1304/1328 at Avignon, in the form reordered after 1341 with the assistance of the *Ceremonial* of Pierre Amiel. Cf. M. Andrieu, in *Miscell. F. Ehrle* (Rome 1924) 348-376, and his "L'Ordinaire de la chapelle papale et le cardinal J.G. Stefaneschi," EL 49 (1935) 230-260, and his *Le Pontifical* 2, 284-288; 3, 36 and 150-157. Critical edition of the *Ceremonial* of Stephaneschi is

15 Ordo: De caeremoniis Sanctae
            Romanae Ecclesiae
            (covering the whole
            liturgical year)

by M. Dykmans, Le cérémonial papal de la fin du moyen âge à la renaissance, 2: De Rome en Avignon ou le cérémonial de Jacques Stefaneschi, Bibl. de l'Institut historique belge à Rome 25 (Rome-Brussels 1981) and 3: Les textes avignonais . . . , ibid. 26 (Rome-Brussels 1983).

The Ceremonial of Pierre Amiel, bishop of Sinigaglia and later patriarch of Grado († 1403), completed by Petrus Oloycensis episcopus (Dulcigno in Dalmatia, 1435-1441); ed. M. Dykmans, Le cérémonial . . . , 4, ibid. 27 (Rome-Brussels 1985) 69-251.

E. CONCORDANCE FOR THE ORDINES ROMANI

(according to the editions of J. Mabillon, L. Duchesne and M. Andrieu)
References to:
J. Mabillon, Museum Italicum, 2 (Paris 1689), reprint PL 78, 861-1408.
L. Duchesne, Christian Worship, Its Origin and Evolution (London 1923) 456-480.

ANDRIEU	MABILLON	DUCHESNE
Ordo I	1 Ordo, nos. 1-21 (pp. 3-16)	
Ordo II	1 Ordo, no. 22 (16-17)	
Ordo III	1 Ordo, nos. 48-51 (29-30)	
Ordo IV		Ordo I (456-465)
Ordo V	2 Ordo (42-51)	
Ordo VI	3 Ordo (53-60)	
Ordo VII	4 Ordo (fragment) (61-62 and 559-560=beginning)	

Ordo VIII	5 Ordo, nos. 1-2 (64-65)	
Ordo IX	5 Ordo, no. 33 (65-69)	
Ordo X	6 Ordo (70-76)	
Ordo XI	7 Ordo (77-84)	
Ordines XII-XIX		
Ordo XX		Ordo IX (479-480)
Ordo XXI		Ordo VI (473-475)
Ordo XXII	1 Ordo, nos. 23-26 (17-18)	
Ordines XXIII-XXVI		
Ordo XXVII	1 Ordo, Append. 1-18 (30-40)	
Ordo XXVIII	1 Ordo, nos. 27-47 (18-29)	
Ordines XXVIII A to XXX A		
Ordo XXX B		Ordines II to V (pp. 465-473)
Ordines XXXI to XXXIII		
Ordo XXXIV	8 Ordo (85-89)	
Ordines XXXV A to XXXV B		
Ordo XXXVI	9 Ordo, nos. 1-6 (83-93)	
Ordo XXXVII A	9 Ordo, nos. 7-9 (93-94)	
Ordines XXXVII B to XXXVIII		
Ordo XXXIX		Ordo VII (475-477)
Ordines XL to XLII		
Ordo XLIII		Ordo VIII (478-479)
Ordo XLIV		
Ordo XLV	12 Ordo, nos. 88-91 (215-217)	
Ordines XLVI to L		

****

NOTES

1. In the proper sense of the term, *ordo* corresponds to what we now call rubrics, i.e., the explanatory notes which accompany the liturgical prayers

and which are printed in red to distinguish them from the euchological formulas. We shall try to avoid using the term 'rubric', however, in order not to confuse the indications provided by the *ordines* with the later, minute and narrow regulations characteristic of what we call rubricism. For *rubrica*, see C. Du Cange, *Glossarium ad scriptores mediae et infimae latinitatis*, 10 vols. (Niort 1883-1887; reprint Paris 1943). —The term 'ritual' designates all the ceremonial gestures of an *actio liturgica*, e.g. the ritual of baptism, the ritual of dedication, etc., and is in this sense synonomous with *ordo*. Ritual can also mean a specific liturgical book containing the rites (prayers and rubrics) used by simple presbyters (as opposed to bishops) for the celebration of the sacraments and sacramentals (except Mass). The term 'rite' is reserved for a particular liturgical function as a whole, e.g. the marriage rite, the rite of consecration, etc., and is synonymous with liturgy. In English, rite is also used for a particular liturgical family, e.g., the Roman, Ambrosian or Gallican rite.

2. The importance Frankish bishops attached to masters of ceremony is well known. We have only to remember Bishop Remedius of Rouen, the brother of Pepin the Short, who in 760 visited Rome with the sole purpose of obtaining from Paul I permission to take back with him Simeon, the *secundus* of the papal *schola cantorum*, to teach the Roman usages to the clerics of his cathedral. Cf. Paul I, *Epistola* 41; MGH, *Epist.* 1, 554; PL 89, 1187. For the historical context of this event, see Vogel, "Les échanges liturgiques," 242-243.

3. For these words, see C. Du Cange, *Glossarium*, under *Ordo, regula, canon.*

4. Innocent I, *Letter to Decentius of Gubbio* (416); PL 56, 513; R. Cabié, *La lettre du pape Innocent I à Decentius de Gubbio*, Bibliothèque de la Revue d'histoire ecclésiastique 58 (Louvain 1973) 18. In this text *ordines* do not stand for *ordo* in the proper sense but for institution, *regula* or *canon*.

5. Tertullian, *De exhortatione castitatis* 7; PL 2, 921-923; CSEL 70, 137-139; CC 2, 1024-1026. Cf. *De oratione* 23; PL 1, 1298-1299; CSEL 20, 196-197; CC 1, 271-272; *De baptismo* 17; PL 1, 1326-1329; CSEL 20, 214-215; CC 1, 291-292; *De monogamia* 7; PL 2, 937-939; CSEL 76, 55-58; CC 2, 1237-1239.

6. There is a larger literature on *ordines* as 'holy orders': J. Morin, *Commentarius historicus ac dogmaticus de sacris Ecclesiae ordinationibus . . .* , 3 vols. (Paris 1655; Antwerp 1695, reprint Farnborough 1970); A. von Harnack, "Zur Geschichte der Anfänge der inneren Organisation der stadtrömischen Kirche," *Sitzungsberichte der preuss. Akademie der Wisssenschaften, Phil.-hist. Kl.* 43 (1918) 954-987; G. Bardy, "Le sacerdoce chrétien du I au V siècle," *Prêtres d'hier et d'aujourd'hui* (Paris 1954) 23-61; W. Plochl, *Geschichte des Kirchenrechts* 1 (Vienna 1935) 165-176; P. M. Gy, "Remarques sur le vocabulaire antique du sacerdoce chrétien," *Études sur le sacrement de l'ordre*, Lex Orandi 22 (paris 1957), ET *The Sacrament of Holy Orders* (Collegeville, MN 1962) 98-115; C. Vogel, "Unité de l'Eglise et Pluralité des formes historiques d'organisation ecclésiastique du III au V siècle," *L'Épiscopat et l'Église universelle*, Unam Sanctam 39 (Paris 1962) 591-636. P. van Beneden, *Aux origines d'une terminologie sacramentelle: Ordo,*

Ordinare, Ordinatio dans la littérature chrétienne avant 313, Spic. sac. lovan. 38 (Louvain 1974). An excellent overview is presented by B. Cooke, *Ministry to Word and Sacrament* (Philadelphia 1976).

7. Braga (573), canon 4; Mansi, *Concilia* 9, 777; J. Vives, *Concilios visigóticos y hispano-romanos,* España cristiana 1 (Barcelona-Madrid 1963) 72. The canon refers to a letter of Pope Vigilius (537-555) to Bishop Profuturus of Braga; PL 69, 18: *ordo precum. Ordo.* here means formulary; F. Probst, *Die ältesten römische Sakramentarien und Ordines* (Münster/Westf. 1982), 400. Unfortunately this *ordo* of the mass and the rite for baptism have not survived.

8. Since the time of Amalarius of Metz, *ordo* has been used in the strict sense. Note its employment in the X century to designate the nascent pontificals; see *infra,* pp. 225-226.

9. Like the *libelli missarum* and the ancient sacramentaries, the *ordines* are anonymous. It is not necessary to know their authors since the authenticity of an *ordo* does not depend on who composed it but on the fact that it served in some manner to regulate the actual worship in any given church. The reader should recall the general principles enunciated *supra,* pp. 62-64, on liturgical texts and their 'originals'.

10. This is as true of the *ordines* as it is of other liturgical documents; cf. Vogel, "Les échanges liturgiques," 227f.

11. Cf., among others, the *Poenitentiale pseudo-Bedae,* as Wasserschleben terms it [Schmitz calls it Beda-Egbert] or *Liber de remediis peccatorum* (Anglo-Saxon; VIII century) *'Non etiam omnes clerici hanc scripturam usurpare debent vel legere qui inveniunt eam, nisi soli illi quibus necesse est, hoc est episcopis et presbyteris. Sicut enim sacrificium offerre non debent nisi episcopi et presbyteri . . . sic nec iudicia ista alii usurpare debent;* H. Wasserschleben, *Die Bussordnungen,* 251. See also C. Vogel, *Les "Libri Paenitentiales",* Typologie des sources du moyen âge occidental 27 (Turnhout 1978)-new edition in preparation; review by A. Frantzen, *Speculum* 55 (1980) 404-405.

12. An *ordo* is 'functional' to the degree that what it describes has an obvious meaning for all present at a given rite. There would be no point in a secret *ordo* for a public rite and consequently, whole *ordines* or parts of them are reproduced in reference books and didactic treatises. The *disciplina arcani* might well apply, however, to the unbaptized (Jews, pagans, catechumens), especially in regard to the Eucharist and the ceremonies of baptism, including the *symbolum fidei* and the Lord's Prayer. According to the testimony of Cyril of Jerusalem, *Procatechesis. Ad Lectorem;* PG 33, 365; FC 61, 84-85, even the preliminary catechetical lectures were reserved to those immediately preparing for baptism: "These catechetical lectures, addressed to candidates for Enlightenment, may be given to those going on forward for Baptism and to the already baptized faithful. They may, on no account, be given to catechumens or to other classes of non-Christians. Anyone making a copy is hereby adjured, as in the sight of the Lord, to preface it with this warning." The *electi* were not even to tell the catechumens what they learned in the catechesis: "If after class a catechumen asks you what the instructors have said, tell outsiders nothing. For it is a divine secret that we deliver to

you, even the hope of the life to come. Keep the secret for the Rewarder."
Protocatechesis 12; FC 61, 79. Another indication that the liturgical texts were
not for transcription comes from the obligation incumbent on celebrants to
know *by heart* several forms of the eucharistic prayer; cf. Augustine, *Contra
litteras Petiliani* 2, 68; CSEL 52, 58: *Si quisquam carmina sacerdotis memoriter
teneat, numquid inde sacerdos est, quod ore sacrilego, carmen publicat sacerdotis;* see
also John Moschus (ca. 550-619), *The Spiritual Meadow* 25; PG 87, 2870.
Clergymen who knew the Scriptures and other sacred texts by heart were
much admired. The best account of the *disciplina arcani* is by O. Perler,
"Arkandisciplin," *Reallexikon für Antike und Christentum* 1 (1950) 667-676.—
For its influence on the liturgy, see G. Rietschel-P. Graff, *Lehrbuch der Liturgik*
1 (Göttingen 1951) 226-231.

13. On the secrecy surrounding the *ordines*, see F. Ehrle, *Archiv für
Literatur und Kirchengeschichte des Mittelalters* 5 (Berlin-Freiburg/Br. 1889) 565.
The mania for secrecy prompted the following papal acts: Alexander VII, *Ad
aures nostras* (Jan 12, 1661) put Joseph Voisin's translation of the Roman
Missal on the Index of Forbidden Books and forbade any translation of the
Roman Missal even for private perusal; Clement XI, *Unigenitus* (Sept 8, 1713)
rejected P. Quesnel's proposition 86: *Eripere simplici populo hoc solatium
iungendi vocem suam voci totius Ecclesiae est usus contrarius praxi apostolicae et
intentioni Dei;* Pius VI (Aug 28, 1794) rejected article 66 of the Synod of
Pistoia: *Propositio asserens fore contra apostolicam praxim et Dei consilia, nisi
populo faciliores viae pararentur vocem suam iungendi cum voce totius Ecclesiae,
intellecta de usu vulgaris linguae in liturgicas preces inducendae: falsa, temeraria,
ordinis pro mysteriorum celebratione praescripti perturbativa.*

14. Although the immediate occasion for his project originated in a
personal betrayal by a colleague, the arguments De Grassis advanced against
publishing the Ceremonial reveal an attitude dead set against the publication
of any liturgical books: Paris de Grassis, *Contra electum Corcyrensem*
(Cristoforo Marcello): *Verum antequam ab eo exordiar quod hae sacrae ceremoniae
in vulgus minime prodendae sunt, respondebo illorum opinioni qui existimat
religionis christianae ceremonias ad publicam mortalium utilitatem esse divulgandas,
moti forsan vel eo argumento quod ipsa divini Numinis deductio et cetera ecclesiae
sacramenta, libris pontificalibus impressa et publicata sunt. Quippe illa ad omnes
ecclesias et singulos quosque sacerdotes pertinent, nec omni recondi poterant. . . . Sed
utinam etiam et illa quae dixi secretiora forent et magis recondita. Non enim ea
quotidie ad profanas manus in sacerdotii contemptum, nec ad alienas sectas in nostrae
religionis irrisionem devenire videremus. . . . Novit iam pridem Sanctitas Tua omnem
Romanorum Pontificum auctoritaem, omnem maiestatem huius sacrosanctae Sedis
pendere ex animis opinionibusque principum, et praelatorum. Dum enim illi summos
Pontifices non tamquam mortales homines, sed tamquam deos in terris existimant et
credunt, illis se sponte sua subiciunt, illis parent, illos suspiciunt ac venerantur et
etiam adorant, incredibili quadam afficiuntur, admiratione, cum aliquando audiunt
aut vident supra humanum opus ab illis per eas, de quibus agimus, ceremonias in
sanctorum numerum quempiam referri, pontifices tanta solmnitate tantaque obser-
vatione eligi atque sanctificari, imperatores coronari, reges inungi, cardinales assumi,*

patriarchas, archipepiscopos, episcopos consecrari ac cetera effici quae tum rerum magnitudine tum varietate divintatem quamdam prae se ferre videntur. Quod si sacrorum arcana pandantur ac sacrae publicentur ceremoniae, illico futurum est ut omnis opinio minatur. . . . Tandem papa mandavit tribus cardinalibus . . . ut petitiones meas ad partes plenius intelligerent et me prout iuris fuerit, ac sibi videretur, expedirent tam super libro [that of Cristoforo Marcello] comburendo, quam auctore castigando et ad Urbem citando personaliter et comparando. Mabillon, *Museum Italicum* 2(Paris 1689) 588-589 and 592=PL 78, 1401-1406; new edition by M. Dykmans, *L'oeuvre de Patrizi Piccolomini,* SeT 293 and 294 (Vatican City 1980-1982) and "Paris de Grassis," EL 96 (1982) 407-486 (to be continued). Despite his previous strictures, in the end Paris De Grassis (†1528) wrote an *ordo* of his own: *De caeremoniis cardinalium et episcoporum in eorum diocesibus libri duo* (Rome 1564)=Martène, *De antiquis Ecclesiae ritibus* 3, 217f. Note the work of J.B. Gattico, *Acta selecta caeremonialia S.R.E. ex variis MSS. codices et diariis saec. XV, XVI, XVII aucta et illustrata* 1 (Rome 1753); publication was stopped "by higher authority" before the second volume was printed in full.

15. See what is said about Collection A, pp. 144-147.

16. The didactic or juridico-liturgical collections which existed for the instruction of the clergy were reference tools, used in the library rather than in church; they remain of great interest for the history of theology and for the general life of the church; see *infra,* pp. 154-155 and notes 35-40.

17. Three essays are of fundamental importance for understanding the liturgical reciprocity which existed between Rome and *Francia*: T. Klauser, "Die liturgischen Austauschbeziehungen zwischen der römischen und der Fränkisch-deutschen Kirche vom 8 bis zum 11 Jhd.," *Historisches Jahrbuch* 53(1933) 169-189; M. Andrieu, "La liturgie romaine en pays franc et les Ordines romani," *Les Ordines romani* 2 (Louvain 1948) xvii-xlix; C. Vogel, "Les échanges liturgiques," 185-295.

18. Survey in Andrieu, *Les Ordines romani* 1, 467-493. The special problems of each *ordo* or group of *ordines* appear before each document.

19. In Collection A *Ordo* XXVII has a certain amount of revision of its basically Roman contents. As a collection, therefore, Collection A could not have been assembled at Rome; its constituent pieces must have crossed the Alps by themselves before being gathered together in a collection. On this point we must correct Andrieu, *Les Ordines* 1, 470 and 3, 342, note 1.

20. The description of the different MSS will be found in Andrieu and in each case we refer the readers to his descriptions. —Liturgical *ordines* are much like conciliar canons and decretals; they normally appear only in collections and not as independent texts. Except for the restricted area of their origin (church, monastery, diocese, the Lateran, etc.), such documents are usually far more important in the later collections than they were when originally promulgated.

21. Ordo XXVII: *De officiis in noctibus a coena Domini usque in Pascha* (Andrieu 3, 347-372), nos. 1-66; compiled in *Francia*.

22. We have already discussed the mid-VIII century as a time of liturgical

renovation. One of its most important manifestations was the creation of the Frankish Gelasian Sacramentary at Flavigny, ca 760-770; see *supra*, pp. 70f.

23. Collection A is not, however, the oldest source for *all* the *ordines*. There are three MSS which help us attain an older recension of certain *ordines* (I, II, XXIII, XXIV, XXVI, VIII, IX): Brussels, Bibliothèque royale, *codex latinus* 10127-10144 (late VIII century; *Francia*, Liège?); Albi, Biblio. municip., *codex* 42 (late IX century; S. France, after 873/885); St. Gall, Stiftsbibliothek, *codex* 614 (2nd half of IX century; St. Gall); this last MS is especially important because it is the source of *Sangallensis* 140 which was used, in turn, for *Sangall.* 446 (a didactic collection of *ordines*) and by the redactors of the Mainz Pontifical of the X Century.

24. The *Veronensis* 92 is described in Andrieu, *Les Ordines* 1, 367-373 and the *Coloniensis* 138, *ibid.*, 101-108.

25. The most important addition in certain MSS is *Ordo* III attached to the end of *Ordo* I. The most interesting divergences—aside from the complex *immixtio* rite in various rencensions of *Ordo* I—relate to the orientation of the celebrant (*Ordo* I, 53); cf. C. Vogel, "Versus ad orientem," *Studi medievali*, 3rd series, 1(1960) 455-459 and in MD 70(1962) 67-99 and "Sol aequinoctialis," *Actes du colloque d'archéologie paléochrétienne et culte chrétien* = RSR 36 (1962) 183-211.

26. For the Frankish rites of ordination, see the information provided after the analysis of *Ordo* XXXVI.—*Veronensis* 92 also contains a series of episcopal *benedictiones* which make this MS a kind of experimental pontifical, as will be explained later.

27. Chronological details in Andrieu, *Les Ordines* 1, 372 and 373.

28. Duchesne, *Christian Worship*, 455-480.

29. Described and analyzed by Andrieu, *Les Ordines* 1, 330-333 and 491-492; 3, 3, 3-21. For the Fragmentary *collectarium* contained in *Sangall.* 349, see O. Heiming, "Das Kollectarfragment des *Sangallensis* 349 (VIII Jhdt.)," "*Mélanges liturgiques offerts à Dom Botte* (Louvain 1972) 175-204.

30. Ordo XIX, 44-45; Andrieu 3, 226-227: *Sex autem* [hereses] *iam surrexerunt in mundo de parte orientali contra sancta romana ecclesia, sed, opitulante gratia Christi, omnes illas hereses fregit sancta sedis beati Petri apostoli atque compotavit* [the first six Ecumenical Councils; number VI in 681]. *Adhuc septima restat* [Nicea II, in 787] *et sic tradunt seniori et sapientes atque doctores sancte sedis romane ecclesie, quia de parte ista occidentali seu et aquilone surgere habet* [an unrealized prophecy!]. S. Bäumer-R. Biron, *Histoire du Bréviare* 1 (Paris 1905) 320, note 3; P. Lejay, "Chronique de littérature chrétienne. La messe," *Revue d'histoire et de littérature religieuse* 2 (1897)180; both these authors drew attention to this chronology.

31. C. Silva-Tarouca, "Giovanni 'archicantor' di S. Pietro a Roma e l'*Ordo Romanus* da lui composto (anno 680)" *Atti della pontificia Accademia Romana di archeologia, Memorie* 1/2 (1923) 159-219; reviewed by L. C. Mohlberg, JfL 4 (1924) 178-182 and A. Baumstark, JfL 5 (1925) 153-158. The definitive refutation of the old view is in Andrieu, *Les Ordines* 3, 3-21. Subsequently the *Capitulare ecclesiastici ordinis* seems to have had very little success as a

collection but, around 780, its redactor must have been a devoted promoter of the Roman liturgy north of the Alps; see *Ordo* XV, nos. 155-156; Andrieu 3, 125; *Hoc iterum atque iterum super omnia admonemus, ut omnis sacerdos qui desiderat racionabiliter sacrificium Deo offerre, ut et complaciat, secundum sanctae institutionis ortodoxorum patrum, beati atque gloriosa sedis sancti Petri apostoli, isto more, cum omni devotione retinire atque celebrare stodit* [= studeat] ... *Qui enim isto modo non offert, postquam cognoverit, non recto ordine offert sed barbarico et suo arbitrio sequitur, vel eorum qui ad voluntatem suam sacras scripturas convetere nituntur.* The mediocre Latinity of this passage shows that it was written before the Carolingian Renaissance.

32. Described by Andrieu, *Les Ordines* 1, 91-96.

33. Cf. Andrieu, *op. cit.*, 1, 343-347.

34. Cf. Andrieu, *op. cit.*, 1, 326-329 and 487-488.

35. The formation and composition of the didactic *ordines* was studied by Andrieu, *op. cit.*, 1, 476-485. The main MSS are the following: Zürich, Zentralbibliothek, *codex* C. 102 (late IX or early X century; Rheinau); St. Gall, Stiftsbibliothek, *codex* 446; Munich, Clm 14581 (early XII century).

36. Carlomann, *Capitulary* (742): *Decrevimus ... ut unusquisque presbyter in parrocchia habitans ... semper in Quadragissima rationem et ordinem ministerii sui, sive de baptismo, sive de fide catholica, sive de precibus et ordine missarum, episcopo reddat et ostendat* (MGH, *Capitularia* 1, 25; *Concilia aevi Carolin.* 1, 3). This text was reissued in the Capitularia of Soissons by Pepin (774) (MGH, *Capitularia* 1, 29) and by St. Boniface as a decree of the pseudo-council of 747 (MGH, *Concilia aevi Carol.* 1, 47). Cf. E. Vykoukal, "Les examens du clergé paroissial à l'époque carolingienne, *Revue d'histoire ecclés.* 14(1913)81-96; R. Amiet, "Une *Admonitio Synodalis* de l'époque carolingienne," *Medieval Studies* 26 (1964)12-82.

37. *Admonitio generalis* (March 23, 789), canon 70: *Ut episcopi diligenter discutiant per suas parrochias presbyteros, eorum fidem, baptisma et missarum celebrationem ut et fidem rectam teneant et baptismum catholicum observent et missarum preces bene intelegent ... et dominicam orationem* (MGH, *Capitularia* 1, 59).

38. Council of Frankfort (794), canon 33: *Ut fides catholica sanctae Trinitatis et oratio dominica atque symbolum omnibus praedicetur et tradatur* (MGH, *Concilia aevi Carol.* 1, 169).

39. *Interrogationes examinationis* (ca. 803), cap. 1, 4, 7, 8 (MGH, *Capit.* 1, 234).

40. Hincmar of Rheims, *Statuta synodalia* (852) 1; PL 125, 773.—Similar texts in Andrieu, *Les Ordines,* 1, 476-479. See P. Riché, *Education and Culture in the Barbarian West, Sixth through Eighth Centuries,* tr. from 3rd French ed. by J.J. Contrani (Columbia, S. Carolina 1975) and *Les écoles et l'enseignement dans l'Occident chrétien de la fin du V siècle au milieu du XI siècle* (Paris 1979).

41. Ed. A. Andrieu, *Les Ordines* 2, 67-108, ET E.G.C.F. Atchley, *Ordo Romanus Primus* (London 1905); the section dealing with the offertory-communion rites has been tranlated by R.C.D. Jasper-G.J. Cuming, *Prayers of*

the Eucharist Early and Reformed (London 1975) 111-115. Commentaries and summaries of Ordo I in P. Battifol, Leçons sur la messe (Paris 1927) 30-64, 65-99 (with reservations); R. Stapper, Ordo romanus primus de missa papali, Opuscula et textus, Series liturgica 1 (Münster/Westf. 1933), using Ms Wolfenbüttel 4175; G. Kunze, Lehre, Gottesdienst, Kirchenbau 1 (Göttingen 1949) 100-107: J.A. Jungmann, The Mass of the Roman Rite 1 (New York 1956) 67-74: T. Klauser, A Short History of the Western Liturgy (New York 1979) 59-72.

42. For the Roman dignitaries who would later be grouped into the Papal Chapel, see R. Elze, "Die päpstliche Kapelle im 12. und 13. Jhd," Zeitschrift der Savigny Stiftung für Rechtsgeschichte, Kan. Abt. 36 (1950) 145-204 including bibliography, and the commentaries in the Introduction to Andrieu's edition of OR I, Les Ordines 2, 38-48. On the stational liturgies, see G. Morin, "Liturgie et basiliques de Rome au milieu du VII siècle," RB 28 (1911) 296-330; G.G. Willis, Further Essays in Early Roman Liturgy, ACC 50 (London 1968) 1-87; J.F. Baldovin, The Urban Character of Christian Worship in Jerusalem, Rome, and Constantinople from the Fourth to the Tenth Centuries, Ph.D. Dissertation (Yale 1982).

43. The use of the term itself, missa privata, is very rare in the early Middle Ages; see note 56.

44. This is the key to A. Häussling's theory as will be explained further on in this section. Vogel, on the other hand, makes bold to say that there is no connection between the small-group masses of antiquity—the "house masses", the shrine masses at martyrs' graves and the refrigeria, etc.—and the later "private" mass. C. Vogel, "Une mutation cultuelle inexpliquée: le passage de l'Eucharistie communitaire à la messe privée," RSR 54 (1980) 231-250, esp. 234-235. Häussling's views on this are summarized in his Mönchskonvent und Eucharistiefeier, LQF 58 (Münster 1972) 238-251.

45. A Häussling, ibid., deals with missa matutinalis on pp. 323-327, missa maior and the other masses, passim and 315-323. C. Vogel, "Une mutation cultuelle," 240, argues that the private mass influenced the appearance of the monk-priest, while noting (note 12) that Nussbaum makes no allusion to this relationship in his "remarquable travail," i.e., O. Nussbaum, Kloster, Priestermönch, und Privatmesse, Theophaneia 14 (Bonn 1961); the latter deals with missae matutinalis et maior on pp. 124-132.

46. On opus bonum see the study of R. Berger, Die Wendung "offere pro" in der römischen Liturgie, LQF 41 (Münster 1965). The rise of the private mass for Nussbaum is explained largely by the change in understanding of the mass as an opus bonum and his entire theory concerning the frequency of mass revolves around the notion of subjective piety; see Nussbaum, Kloster, Priestermönch und Privatmesse, 152-173. This has been challenged by Häussling throughout Mönchskonvent esp. pp. 243-258, 287-288, and 342-344. According to Häussling, the Eucharist was still considered an actio ecclesiae "and not of an isolated individual" even when celebrated by a single representative of the Church. On this see R. Schulte, Die Messe als Opfer der

Kirche. Die Lehre frühmitelalterlichen Autoren über das eucharistische Opfer, LQF 35 (Münster 1959). A. Franz describes the votive masses for various needs in *Die Messe im deutschen Mittelalter,* 268-291; on the so-called Gregorian masses, Franz, *ibid.,* 244 and C.V. Héris, "Théologie des suffrages pour les morts," MD 44 (1955)58-67 R.W. Pfaff, "The English Devotion to St. Gregory's Trental", *Speculum* 49 (1974) 75-90 and A. Angenendt," *Missa specialis.* Zugleich ein Beitrag zur Entstehung der Privatmessen," *Frühmittelalterliche Studien* 17 (1983) 153-221.

47. See C. Vogel, "Une mutation cultuelle," 242-246 and the detailed documentation in his "Composition légale et commutations dans le système de la pénitence tarifée," *Revue de Droit Canonique* 8 (1958) 289-318; 9 (1959) 1-38; 341-359.

48. On the weekly votive masses see H. Barré-J. Deshusses," À la recherche du missel d'Alcuin," EL 82 (1968) 3-44 and J. Deshusses, "Les Messes d'Alcuin," Afl 14 (1972) 7-41. On votive masses in general, A Franz, *Die Messe,* 115-154; Häussling, *Mönchskonvent* 243-246, 255, 283. On the rising cult of the Virgin, see G. Frénaud, "Le Culte de Notre Dame dans l'ancienne liturgie latine," *Maria,* ed. H. Du Manoir, vol. 6 (Paris 1961) 157-211; H. Barré, *Prières anciennes de l'Occident à la mère du Sauveur, des origines à S. Anselme* (Paris 1963). In the X century, Alcuin's *Missa Sanctae Mariae* came to be widely celebrated on free Saturdays but little by little a daily mass known as the *Missa familiaris* or *De Domina* spread everywhere. Accompanied by the ever-more popular *Officium parvum B. M. V.,* it soon required a Lady chapel of its own—usually East of the apse—in every monastery , cathedral and large parish in Western Europe. On the development and spread of the additional Marian Office, see J. Leclercq, "Formes anciennes de l'office marial," EL 74(1960)89-102 and "Fragmenta Mariana," EL 72(1958) 292-305; J. M. Canal, "El oficio parvo de la Virgen," *Ephemerides Mariologicae* 15(1965)463-475; J.B.L. Tolhurst, *The Monastic Breviary of Hyde Abbey, Winchester,* Vol. 6: *Introduction to the English Monastic Breviaries,* HBS 80 (London 1942), 120-129; in addition to the Office of Our Lady, Tolhurst has a full discussion of all the devotional accretions to the medieval office.

49. This was related to the penances as well as the growing concern throughout the Middle Ages with 'intercessory foundations" to pray for the dead, i.e. the founders and their relatives. On masses for the dead see K.J. Merk, *Die messliturgische Totenehrung in der römischen Kirche. Zugleich ein Beitrag zum mittelalterlicher Opferwesen* 1 (Stuttgart 1926); R. Berger, *Die Wendung "offere pro" in der römischen Liturgie,* LQF 41 (Münster 1965) 125-128, 162-167, 212-223. For the enormous proliferation of chantries, chantry priests and chantry chapels, see A.H. Thompson, *The Historical Growth of the Parish Church* (London 1911) 24-50; F. Bond, *An Introduction to English Church Architecture from the Eleventh to the Sixteenth Century* (London 1913) 102-112; J.R.H. Moorman, *Church Life in England in the Thirteenth Century* (Cambridge 1946)15-18; A.H. Thompson, "Chantries and Colleges of Chantry Priests," *The English Clergy and their Organization in the Later Middle Ages* (Oxford 1947;

reprint 1966) chap. 5, 132-160, 247-291; E.E. Williams, *The Chantries of William Canynges in St. Mary Redcliffe, Bristol* (Bristol-Oxford 1950); K.L. Wood-Legh, *Perpetual Chantries in Britain* (Cambridge 1965); G.H. Cook, *The English Mediaeval Parish Church* (London 1956) 47-123; A. Kreider, *English Chantries and the Road to Dissolution* (Cambridge, MA-London 1979), especially chaps. 1-3 on the intercessory institutions, their priests and the chronological contours of the various foundations, 1-92. It must also be remembered that in addition to the cantarists proper, there were large numbers of unbeneficed priests and lesser clerics who constituted a kind of clerical underworld or proletariat, living off occasional stipends for attendance at funerals, the singing of obits, etc.; see Kreider, 19-21. For a perfect description of a chantry college and its intercessory obligations, see A.L. Gabriel, *Student Life in Ave Maria College, Mediaeval Paris* (Notre Dame, IN 1955) especially chap. 11, 199-212. On occasion, whole monasteries were conceived of as chantries, e.g., Sheen and Syon Abbeys, both founded by King Henry V (1413-1422) in reparation for the murder of Richard II. Shakespeare has Henry pray before the battle of Agincourt: "Five hundred poor I have in yearly pay, Who twice a day their withered hands hold up Toward heaven to pardon blood; And I have built Two chantries where the sad and solemn priests Sing still for Richard's soul" (Henry V, lines 317-321).

50. K.J. Merk, *Abriss einer liturgiegeschichtlichen Darstellung des Mess-stipendiums* (Stuttgart 1928), *Das Mess-stipendium. Geschichtlich, dogmatisch, rechtlich und aszetisch erklärt* (Stuttgart 1929), "Das Mess-Stipendium," *Theologische Quartalschrift* 136 (Tübingen 1956) 199-228; K. Mörsdorf, "Mess-Stipendium," *Lexikon für Theologie und Kirche* 7 (1962) 354f; M.F. Mannion, "Stipends and Eucharistic Praxis," *Worship* 57 (1983) 194-214; C.F. Keller, *Mass Stipends* (St. Louis 1926); C.E. Gilpatric, "Mass Stipends and Mass Intentions" *Worship* 38 (1964) 190-201; J.A. Jungmann, "Mass Intentions and Mass Stipends," *Unto the Altar: The Practice of Catholic Worship*, ed. A. Kirchgässner (New York 1963) 23-31; E. Kilmartin, "Money and the Ministry of the Sacraments," *The Finances of the Church*, ed. W. Bassett-P. Huizing, *Concilium 117* (New York 1979) 104-111; K. Rahner-A. Häussling, *The Celebration of the Eucharist* (New York 1968).

51. Nussbaum and Vogel are cited *supra*, note 44.

52. This is the working definition of Vogel based on his own research in the area of evolving penitential discipline and its influence on the frequency of Eucharistic celebrations (see note 47 *supra*). This is also Nussbaum's definition of private mass in his *Kloster, Priestermönch und Privatmesse*, 136. See Vogel, "Une mutation cultuelle," 234-235.

53. Vogel, "Une mutation cultuelle," 241.

54. Vogel, "Une mutation cultuelle," 247: "[the notion of] the Eucharistic celebration as a communal act is reinforced by considering the Eucharist as a 'mystery' in the ancient sense of the term. Thus the notion of *mysterion* is proper to the Christian communities native to the Mediterranean region. One can well imagine that at the beginning of the VII century, the new-

comers to the faith from the North would have found it difficult to conceive of this sort of eucharistic process. . . . This resulted in a kind of degeneration of 'mystery': the cultic society began to consider liturgical activity as an ensemble of practices designed for individual salvation. One could say quite correctly that *mysterium* gradually became *officium quotidianum* or in other words, the progressive divinization of the Christian in and through the Eucharist gave way to a cultic act which is simply an instrument of salvation."

55. *Mönchskonvent und Eucharistiefeier: Eine Studie über die Messe in der abendländischen Klosterliturgie des frühen Mittelalters und zur Geschichte der Messhäufigkeit,* LQF 58 (Münster 1972).

56. Häussling, *ibid.,* 246, n. 336 and 285, note 522 notes that in the Early Middle Ages the actual term *missae privatae* occurs only once: Walafrid Strabo, *De exordiis et incrementis rerum ecclesiasticarum* cap. 26; MGH, *Capitularia* 2, 506 line 26. The context of its occurrence supports Häussling's theory: referring to the Patriarch Paulinus of Aquileia (†802), Strabo says: *saepius et maxime in privatis missis circa immolationem sacramentum ymnos vel ab aliis vel a se compositus celebrasse.* It wouldn't have made much sense to have hymns sung if no one was present save patriarch and server . . . who would have sung the hymns? It is more likely that "even at private masses" signifies the subordinate liturgies celebrated on nonliturgical days in the episcopal chapel attended by the members of his household and at least some who could sing.

57. See the Dissertation of J. Wagner, *Altchristliche Eucharistiefeiern im kleinen Kreis* (Bonn 1949) referred to by Häussling, 229, note 266; Vogel, "Une mutation," 235, note 5; Nussbaum, *Kloster, Priestermönch und Privatmesse,* 134, note 5. Häussling points to the distinction between community-eucharists (Gemeindeeucharistie) and memorial-eucharists (Gedächtnis-eucharistie) 229f. which was apparent already in Jerusalem at the time of Egeria's pilgrimage (late IV century); cf. *Itinerarium Egeriae* c. 43, 2-3; cc. 3:6f; 4:2-4,5,7=CC 175, 84f and 40-43. From Rome, Leo I wrote to the Alexandrian patriarch Dioskorus (ca. 445) concerning the frequency of celebrating the Eucharist on feastdays: *Ut autem in omnibus observantia nostra concordet, illud quoque volumus custodiri, ut cum sollemnior quaeque festivitas conventum populi numerosioris indixerit, et ea fidelium multitudo convenerit quam recipere basilica simul una non possit, sacrificii oblatio indubitanter iteretur; ne his tantum admissis ad hanc devotionem, qui prima advenerint, videantur hi, qui postmodum confluxerint, non recepti, cum plenum pietatis atque rationis sit, ut quoties basilicam, in qua agitur, praesentia novae plebis impleverit, toties sacrificium subsequens offeratur.* Leo, *Epistolae* 9,2; PL 54, 626-627. When the number of pilgrims to the shrines even on 'private days' seemed to demand it, the Eucharist was celebrated for their benefit, as is reported by the anonymous Ambrosiaster (ca 366-384): *Omni enim hebdomada offerendum est, etiam si non quotidie peregrinis, incolis tamen vel bis in hebdomada* (Wednesday and Friday, the most ancient 'liturgical days' after Sunday); *In I Tim 3:12f,* sect. 4=CSEL 81, 3, 269.

58. Häussling, 242-243; J.P. Kirsch, "Die *Memoria Apostolorum* an der

Appischen Strasse und die liturgische Festfeier de 29. Juni," JfL 3 (1923) 33-50, esp 49-50.

59. E.g. the prefaces *post infirmitatem* in the midst of the *libelli* for Peter and Paul in the *Veronense*, ed. Mohlberg, nos. 308, 314, 334 and the reference to the prayers *servi tui Gregorii* in one of the many orations provided in the votive mass *pro sterilitate mulierum* in the *Gelasianum Vetus* (*Vat. Reg.* 316), ed. Mohlberg, no. 1466.

60. See the introduction and notes in J.F. Baldovin, *The Urban Character of Christian Worship in Jerusalem, Rome, and Constantinople from the Fourth to the Tenth Centuries.* PhD Dissertation (Yale 1982) 1-6.

61. Adaptation of the Roman stational system, see Häussling, 201-213; for the relic-cult and multiplication of shrines, see *ibid.*, 214-228.

62. On the change in Eucharistic theology see Häussling, 251-255 and the works cited in his footnotes on those pages. On the new self-conception of the cleric see *ibid.*, 268-271.

63. Vogel, "Une mutation cultuelle," 238.

64. Nussbaum, *op. cit.* provides an overview of references from the IX century and following on pp. 185-202.

65. Häussling, 243-258, 287-288, 342-344.

66. The presence and role of the congregation is still assumed even in the *Ordo servandus per sacerdotem in celebratione Missae sine cantu et sine ministris secundum ritum S. Romanae Ecclesiae* (1508) by J. Burchard. This *ordo* served as a model for the rubrics of the 1570 *Missale Romanum* ,but lost most of its references to congregational presence/participation. See the excellent summary in B. Neunheuser, "The Relation of Priest and Faithful in the Liturgies of Pius V and Paul VI," *Roles in the Liturgical Assembly*, Conférences Saint Serge 23, tr. M. O'Connor (New York 1981) 207-219 esp. 208-209.

67. The editions of the Roman Missal are the following: *Missale Romanum* (Milan 1474); Milan, Bibl. Ambrosiana *Incunabulum* SQN III 14;=*editio princeps.* This was re-issued by R. Lippe, *Missale Romanum Mediolani 1474*, HBS 17 (London 1899) and *Missale Romanum Mediolani 1474. A Collation with other editions printed before 1570. Indices,* HBS 33 (London 1907). See also A.P. Frutaz, "Due edizioni rare del Missale Romanum pubblicate a Milano nel 1482 e nel 1492," *Miscellanea Giulio Belvederi* (Rome 1954/1955) 55-107. The Missal of 1474 was based on the type of mass-book called the *Missale Curiae romanae* or *Ordo missalis secundum consuetudinem romanae Curiae* from the XIII century; cf. M. Andrieu, "Le Missel de la chapelle papale à la fin du XIII siècle," *Miscellanea F. Ehrle* 2, SeT 38 (Rome 1924) 348-376; S.J.P. Van Dijk–J.H. Walker, *The Origins of the Modern Roman Liturgy* (London 1960); S.J.P. Van Dijk, "The Lateran Missal," SE 6 (1954) 125-179, "The Legend of 'the Missal of the Papal Chapel' and the Fact of Cardinal Orsini's Reform," SE 8 (1956) 76-142, and "The Authentic Missal of the Papal Chapel," *Scriptorium* 14 (1960) 257-314. For the formation of the missal, see J.W. Legg, *Tracts on the Mass*, HBS 27 (London 1904-1905) (London 1905); H. Grisar, *Das Missale im Lichte römischer Stadtgeschichte* (Freiburg 1925); J. Ferreres, *Historia del Missal Romano* (Barcelona 1929) and especially, A. Dold, *Vom Sakramentar, Comes und*

Capitulare zum Missale, TuA 34 (Beuron 1943). The extract from the *Missal of Constance,* which was printed before the *editio princeps* (Copinger dates it 1470, Misset argues for ca. 1450 and therefore before the edition of the Psalter of 1457) does not contain the *formulae* for Advent, Sundays after Epiphany, Lent and the Sundays after Easter and Pentecost; it has been edited by O. Hupp, *Ein Missale speciale, Vorlaüfer des Psalteriums von 1457* (Munich 1898); E. Misset, *Un missel spécial de Constance oeuvre de Gutenberg avant 1450* (Paris 1899); H. Stein, *Une production inconnue de l'atelier de Gutenberg* (Paris 1899); A. Stevenson, *The Problem of the Missale Speciale* (London 1967); and G. Widman, (ed.), *Der gegenwärtige Stand der Gutenberg-Forschung,* Bibliothek des Buchwesens 1 (Stuttgart 1972, esp. articles by F. Geldner and S. Corsten). From 1570 up to 1970, the official edition of the Roman Missal was the *Missale romanum ex decreto sacrosancti concilii Tridentini restitutum, Pii V, P.M. iussu editum* (Rome 1570). This *Missale Pianum* was, for all practical purposes, a repeat of the *editio princeps* of 1474, and after it had been aligned with the *editio princeps* of the Breviary (1568), it was promulgated by the Bull *Quo primum tempore* of Pius V on July 14, 1570 [the missal was to be adopted within six months by all churches who had not had their own rite for at least 200 years]. An *Ordo servandus* and *Rubricae generales* based on the work of J. Burchard were joined to this 1570 missal; see note 66 *supra,* and A.P. Frutaz, "Contributo alla Storia della Riforma del Messale Promulgato da San Pio V nel 1570," *Problemi di Vita Religiosa in Italia nel Cinquecento,* Italia Sacra 2 (Padua 1960) 187-214. A bibliography of printed missals by W.H.J. Weale, *Bibliographia liturgica. Catalogus missalium ritus latini ab anno 1475 impressorum* (London 1886) notes the 211 editions/printings of the Missal from 1475 until the official edition of 1570; an enlarged and revised edition is C. Bohatta-W.H.J. Weale, (London 1928).

68. Ed. J. Deshusses, *Le Sacramentaire grégorien: Ses principales formes d'après les plus anciens manuscrits,* Spicilegium Friburgense 16 (Fribourg 1971) no. 1, pp. 85-86. Cf. H. Lietzmann, *Das Sacramentarium Gregorianum nach dem Aachener Urexemplar,* LQF 3 (Münster 1921) 1; and H.A. Wilson, *The Gregorian Sacramentary under Charles the Great,* HBS 49 (London 1915).

69. For a discussion of the evidence regarding the frequency of celebration, see R. Taft, "The Frequency of the Eucharist throughout History." *Can We Always Celebrate the Eucharist?,* edd. M. Collins-D. Power (New York 1982) 13-24; reprint Taft, *Beyond East and West: Problems in Liturgical Understanding* (Washington, D.C. 1984) 61-80.

70. This conclusion runs through the works of M. Andrieu and is to be maintained against the thesis that the longer recension is not Roman in origin as has been proposed by B. Capelle, "Le rite de la fraction dans la messe romaine," *RB* 53 (1942) 5-40; cf. M. Andrieu, *Les Ordines* 2, 56-64.

71. It was when Gregory II instituted masses for the Thursdays of Lent [*Liber pontificalis,* Gregory II; ed. Duchesne 1, 402] that the station for *feria V hebdomadae III* was assigned to the *diaconia*/deaconry of Ss. Cosmas and Damian; cf. *Hadrianum* 56, ed. Deshusses p. 151. For the importance of these Lenten Thursdays for the chronology of the liturgical documents, see M.

Andrieu, "Les messes des jeudis de Carême," RSR 9 (1929) 343-375. As buildings the *diaconiae* are mentioned at the end of the VII century: *Liber pont.*, Benedict II (684-685); ed. Duchesne 1, 354; cf. G. Ferrari, *Early Roman Monasteries... through the X Century*, Studi di antichità cristiana 23 (Rome 1957). The oldest liturgical witness to the Roman stational system is the Lectionary of Würzburg, VII century; cf. G. Morin, "Liturgie et basiliques de Rome au milieu du VII siècle," RB 28 (1911)296-330. The origins of stational liturgies may have been in the East; cf. H.I. Marrou, "L'origine orientale des diaconies romaines," *Mélanges de l'École française de Rome* 57 (1940) 95-142; a different view is given by J. Baldovin, *The Urban Character of Worship in Jerusalem, Rome and Constantinople*, PhD Dissertation (Yale 1982) 182-196, 258-271.

72. *Liber pont.*, ed. Duchesne 1, 371 and 374.

73. In addition to the studies of R. Elze, *supra* note 42, see L. Halphen, *Études sur l'administration de Rome* (Paris 1907).

74. *Liber pont.*, ed. Duchesne 1, 376. See also the works cited *supra*, note 41.

75. Ed. Andrieu, *Les Ordines* 2, 115-116.

76. *Ibid.*, 2, 131-134.

77. *Ibid.*, 2, 157-170; K. Gamber, "Der *Ordo romanus* IV, ein Dokument der ravennatischen Liturgie des 8. Jhdt., "*Römische Quartalschrift* 66 (1971)154-170.

78. Andrieu 2, 209-227.

79. Amalarius is one of the sources of *Ordo* V and not the contrary as A. Franz believed, *Die Messe*, 353.

80. The *Eclogae de ordine romano* were attributed to Amalarius by E. Baluze on the evidence of a note in a later hand contained in *Sangallensis* 614. His text was reprinted in PL 105, 1315-1322. Mabillon, *Museum Italicum* 2, 41, believed that the *Eclogae* were a commentary on *Ordo* V whereas they were one of its sources; they appear in the edition of Amalarius' works edited by J.M. Hanssens, *Amalarii episcopi opera liturgica omnia* 3, SeT 140 (Rome 1950).

81. Edition of the *Expositio missae* by Hanssens, "Le premier traité d'Amalaire sur la messe," EL 44 (1930) 31-42; other *Expositiones* in the *Opera liturgica omnia* 1, SeT 138 (Rome 1948) 255-338.

82. E.g. in Bernhold of Constance (†1100), *Micrologus*; PL 151, 979 and 982-983.

83. Ed. Andrieu, *Les Ordines* 2, 241-250.

84. G. Cassander, *Ordo romanus de officio missae* (Cologne 1561)=M. Hittorp, *De divinis catholicae Ecclesiae officiis* (Cologne 1568) 15-19; reprinted in the *Bibliotheca Magna Patrum* and the *Bibliotheca Maxima Patrum* but not in PL,=Mabillon, *Museum Italicum* 2, 52-60=*Ordo* 3. Cassander's *Ordo* was also used by Onofrio Panvinio (1568) in his MS-collection of liturgical texts; cf. Andrieu, "Note sur quelques MSS et sur une édition de l'*Ordo romanus primus*," RSR 2 (1922)319-330, esp. 328-33.

85. Ed. Andrieu, *Les Ordines* 2, 295-305.

86. *Nam et hoc flagitasti a nobis, sanctissime frater: in sacri canonis predicatione quot in locis cruces facere debeantur, tuae significemus Sanctitati;* MGH, *Tomus Epistolarum* 3, 372; cf. B. Botte, *Le Canon de la messe romaine* (Louvain 1935) 21 and B. Capelle, "Le rite de la fraction," RB 53 (1942) 20-22.

87. For the *Expositiones missae* the best sythesis is still A. Wilmart, *"Expositio missae,"* DACL 5(1922)1014-1027; see also the work of Hanssens, *supra* note 80 and P.M. Gy, *"Expositiones missae,"* *Bulletin du Comité des Études de la Compagnie de St. Sulpice* 22 (1958)223-232; D.F. Wright, *A Medieval Commentary on the Mass: . . . the De missarum mysteriis (ca. 1195) of Cardinal Lothar of Segni.* An unpublished Ph.D. dissertation (Notre Dame, IN 1977) 5-44="Medieval *Expositio missae* literature: Amalarius of Metz to Lothar of Segni"; A. Häussling, "Messe (*Expositiones Missae*)," DS 10(1980)1083-1090.

88. The best documentation of the MS sources of these manuals is Andrieu, *Les Ordines romani* 1, 476-485. Other indispensable studies are A. Franz, *Die Messe im deutschen Mittelalter. Beiträge zur Geschichte der Liturgie* (Freiburg 1902; reprint Darmstadt 1963) and J.A. Jungmann, *The Mass of the Roman Rite,* 2 vols. (New York 1950-1955).

89. As Cabrol believed, DACL 5(1923)1625-1635; see also his "La messe de Flacius Illyricus," RB 22 (1905)151-164.

90. J. Braun, "Alter und Herkunft der sog. *Missa Illyrica,"* *Stimmen aus Maria-Laach* 69(1905)143-155; see also O.K. Olson, *The 'Missa Illyrica' and the Liturgical Thought of Flacius Illyricus.* Ph.D. dissertation, Hamburg University (1966) 95-131.

91. The best synthesis is by F. Cabrol, "Apologies," DACL 1 (1907)2591-2601; N.K. Rasmussen, "An Early *ordo missae* from Hamburg with a *litania abecedaria* addressed to Christ (Rome, Bibl. Vallicelliana, *codex* B 141; XI century)," EL 98(1984)198-211; A. Strittmatter, "An Unknown 'apology' in the Morgan MS 641," *Traditio* 4(1946)179-196.

92. For abuses of the mass, see J.B. Thiers, *Traité des superstitions qui regardent les sacrements,* 4 vols. (Paris 1697-1704). In the absence of an overall synthesis, see A. Franz, *Die Messe im deutschen Mittelalter* (Freiburg 1902); J. Kramp, "Messgebräuche der Gläubigen," *Stimmen der Zeit* (Maria-Laach) 111(1926)206-223; 113(1927)352-367; L. A. Veit, *Volksfrommes Brauchtum und Kirche* (Freiburg 1936)—these last two books are particulary good for bibliography; G. Nickl, *Der Anteil des Volkes an der Messliturgie im Frankenreiche von Chlodwig bis Karl den Grossen* (Innsbruck 1930); L. A. Veit-L. Lenhart, *Kirche und Volksfrömmigkeit im Zeitalter des Barock* (Freiburg 1956); H. Kromler, *Die Eucharistie in Sprache und Volkstum* (Basel 1949): F.X. Weiser, *Handbook of Christian Feasts and Customs* (New York 1958); T.E. Bridgett, *A History of the Holy Eucharist in Great Britain* (London-St. Louis 1908). For a wider perspective, see G. Schreiber, *Die Wochentage im Erlebniss der Ostkirche und des christlichen Abendlands* (Cologne 1959). It is also useful to consult the corresponding articles in H. Bächtold, *Handwörterbuch des deutschen Aber-*

glaubens, 10 vols. (Berlin-Leipzig 1927-1942).—In addition to the books recommended *supra,* pp. 6-9, and the appropriate articles in the encyclopedias, the following books are helpful: A. Fortescue, *The Mass* (London 1912); P. Battifol, *Leçons sur la messe* (8th ed. Paris 1927); A. Baumstark, *Missale Romanum* (Eindhoven 1929) with reservations because of the unusual theories advanced by the author in regard to the evolution of the sacramentaries; S.J.P. van Dijk-J.H. Walker, *The Origins of the Modern Roman Liturgy* (Westminster, MD London 1960).—For the term *missa* and other terms for the Eucharist, see F.J. Dölger, *Antike und Christentum* 6(1950)81-132; A. Pagliaro, *Atti della Accad. Naz. dei Lincei* 19(Rome 1955)104-135; A. Coppo, "Una nuova ipotesi sull'origine di 'missa'," *EL* 71(1957)225-267 and, especially, C. Mohrmann, "Missa," *Vigiliae Christianae* 12(1958)67-92.—For the origins of the eucharistic *rite:* A. Arnold, *Der Ursprung des christlichen Abendmahls* (Freiburg 1939); G. Dix, *The Shape of the Liturgy* (2nd ed. Westminster 1945) 1-267 and especially the following: H. Schurmann, "Die Gestalt der urchristlichen Eucharistiefeier," *Münchener theol. Zeitschrift* 6 (1955) 107-113; H. Lietzmann, *Messe und Herrenmahl* (3rd ed. Berlin 1955) ET *Mass and the Lord's Supper,* by H.G. Reeve-R.D. Richardson (Leiden 1979); J.P. Audet, "Esquisse historique du genre littéraire de la Bénédiction juive et de l'Eucharistie chrétienne," *Revue Biblique* 65 (1958)371-399, ET "Literary Forms and Contents of a Normal *Eucharistia* in the First Century," *Studia Evangelica,* TuU 73 (1959)643-662; T.J. Talley, "From *Berakah* to *Eucharistia:* A Reopening of the Question," *Worship* 50 (1976) 115-137 and "The Literary Structure of the Eucharistic Prayer," *Worship* 58 (1984)404-419; M. Vos, "À la recherche de normes pour les textes liturgiques de la messe (V et VII siècle)," *Revue d'histoire ecclésiastique* 69 (1974) 5-37; K. Gamber, *Sacrificium Laudis. Zur Geschichte des frühchristlichen Eucharistiegebets,* TPL 5 (Regensburg 1973) and "Canonica prex. Eine Studie über den altrömischen Mess-Canon," *Heiliger Dienst* (1963) 1-16.—For the altar and other liturgical furnishings, see J. Braun, *Der christliche Altar,* 2 vols. (Munich 1924) and *Das christliche Altargerät in seinem Sein und in seiner Entwicklung* (Munich 1932); E. Bishop, "On the History of the Christian Altar," *Liturgica Historica* (Oxford 1918; reprint 1962) 20-38; C.E. Pocknee, *The Christian Altar in History and Today* (London 1963); D. R. Dendy, *The Use of Lights in Christian Worship,* ACC 41 (London 1959); E.G.C.F. Atchley, *A History of the Use of Incense in Divine Worship,* ACC 13 (London-New York 1909); J.G. Davies, *The Architectural Setting of Baptism* (London 1962) and *The Origin and Development of Early Christian Church Architecture* (London 1952).—For Holy Communion see P. Browe, *Die häufige Kommunion im Mittelalter* (Munich 1938) and *Die Pflichtkommunion im Mittelalter* (Münster 1940)—For the veneration and reservation of the Eucharist, see E. Dumoutet, *Le désir de voir l'hostie et les origines de la dévotion au Saint-Sacrement* (Paris 1926); P. Browe, *Die Verehrung der Eucharistie im Mittelalters* (Munich 1933), *Die eucharistischen Wunder des Mittelalters,* Breslauer Studien zur historische Theologie, N.F. 4 (Breslau 1938); O. Nussbaum, *Die Aufbewahrung der Eucharistie* (Bonn 1979); G. G. Grant, "The Elevation of the Host: A Reaction to Twelfth Century Heresy,"

Theological Studies 1 (1940) 228-250; V. L. Kennedy, "The Moment of Consecration and the Elevation of the Host," *Medieval Studies* 6 (1944) 121-150; S.J.P. van Dijk-J.H. Walker, *The Myth of the Aumbry: Notes on Medieval Reservation Practice and Eucharistic Devotion* (London 1957)—largely a refutation of G. Dix, *A Detection of Aumbries* (Westminster 1942); A. A. King, *Eucharistic Reservation in the Western Church* (New York 1964); N. Mitchell, *Cult and Controversy: The Worship of the Eucharist outside Mass* (New York 1982) with an excellent bibliography.

93. Ed. Andrieu, *Les Ordines* 2, 321-322.

94. For liturgical vestments, see J. Braun, *Die liturgische Gewandung im Occident und Orient* (Freiburg 1907) and *Die liturgische Paramente* (2nd ed. Freiburg 1924); T. Klauser, *Der Ursprung der bischöflichen Insignien und Ehrenrechte* (Krefeld 1948)—Klauser uses and critiques the works of Delbrueck, Alföldi and others on the imperial vestments; A. Fortescue, *The Vestments of the Roman Rite* (London 1912); P. Salmon, *Étude sur les insignes du pontife dans le rit romain. Histoire et liturgie* (Rome 1955); R. Lesage, *Linges et vêtements liturgiques* (Paris 1954) and *Objects et habits liturgiques* (Paris 1958), ET *Vestments and Church Furniture*, trans. F. Murphy, Twentieth Century Encyclopedia of Catholicism 114 (New York 1960); C. E. Pocknee, *Liturgical Vesture: Its Origins and Development* (London 1960); G. Cope, "Vestments," *A Dictionary of Liturgy and Worship*, ed. J. G. Davies (New York 1972) 365-383; V. Labhart, *Zur Rechtssymbolik des Bischoffsrings*, Rechtshistoriche Arbeitet . . . , ed. K.S. Bader, 2 (Cologne-Graz 1963); O. Nussbaum, *Das Brustkreuz des Bischofs* (Mainz 1964); K. Honselmann, *Das Rationale der Bischöfe* (Paderborn 1975); B. Sirch, *Der Ursprung der bischoflichen Mitra und päpstlichen Tiara*, Kirchengeschichtliche Quellen und Studien 8 (St. Ottilien 1975).

95. Ed. Andrieu, *Les Ordines* 2, 329-336.

96. *Ibid.*, 2, 351-362.

97. *Ibid.*, 2, 417-447.

98. For baptism, see H. Kraft, *Texte zur Geschichte der Taufe, besonders der Kindertaufe in der alten Kirche*, Kleine Texte 174 (Berlin 1953); A. Wilmart "Un florilège carolingien sur le symbolisme des cérémonies du baptême, avec un appendice sur la lettre de Jean diacre," *Analecta Reginensia*, SeT 59 (Rome 1933) 153-179. —A full bibliography on baptism cannot be furnished here but for the rite see A. Chavasse, "Le carême romain et les scrutins prébaptismaux avant le IX siècle," RSR 35 (1948) 325-382; "Les deux rituels romain et gaulois, de l'admission au catéchuménat que renferme le sacramentaire gélasien (*Vat. Reg.* 316)," *Etudes de critique et d'histoire religieuses* (Lyons 1948) 79-78, "La préparation à la Pâque à Rome avant le V siècle," *Memorial J. Chaine* (1950) 61-80, "Temps de préparation à la Pâque d'après quelques livres liturgiques romains," RSR 37 (1950) 125-145, "La structure de câreme et les lectures des messes quadragésimales dans la liturgie romaine," MD 31(1952) 76-119, "Les formulaires du sacramentaire gélasien," *Le Sac. gél.* (Paris 1958) 155-172. An overall synthesis has been attempted by A. Stenzel, *Die römische Taufliturgie. Ein genetische Erklärung*, Forschungen zur Geschichte der Theologie und der innnerkirchlichen Lebens 7-8 (Innsbruck

1958) and "Erwägungen zur Ritus der Erwachsenentaufe," *Liturgisches Jahrbuch* 3(1953) 310-322; see also G. Kretschmar, "Die Geschichte des Taufgottesdienstes in der alten Kirche," *Leiturgia* 5(Kassel 1970) 1-348—a very helpful work. —For the *pompa diaboli*, see J. de Labriolle, *Archivum Lat. Medii Aevi* 2(1926) 170-181; H. Rahner, *Zeitschrift für kath. Theologie* 55(1931) 239-273; J. H. Waszink, *Vigilae Christianae* 1(1947) 13-41. —For the baptismal promises, see F.J. Dölger, *Die Sonne der Gerechtigkeit und der Schwarze*, LQF 14 (Münster/Westf. 1919). —For the blessing of the baptismal water, see E. Stommel, *Studien zur Epiklese der römischen Taufwasserweihe*, Theophaneia 5 (Bonn 1950); S. Benz, "Zur Vorgeschichte des Textes der römischen Taufwasserweihe," RB 66 (1956) 218-285; E. G. C. F. Atchley, *On the Epiclesis of the Eucharistic Liturgy and in the Consecration of the Font*, ACC 31 (London 1935). —For Confirmation as part of the baptismal rite, see F. J. Dölger, *Das Sakrament der Firmung historisch-dogmatisch dargestellt*, Studien der Leo-Gesellschaft 15 (Vienna 1906); J. Brinktrine, "Zur Entstehung der lateinischen. Firmformel," *Theologie und Glaube* 44(1954) 51-53; L. A. Van Buchem, *L'homélie pseudo-eusébienne de Pentecôte. L'origine de la confirmation en Gaule et l'interprétation de ce rite par Fauste de Riez* (Nijmegen 1967); H. Riley, *Christian Initiation*, Catholic University of America Studies in Christian Antiquity 17 (Washington 1974); A. Kavanagh, "Confirmation: A Suggestion from Structure," *Worship* 58 (1984) 386-395; G. Winkler, "Confirmation or Chrismation? A Study in Comparative Liturgy," *Worship* 58(1984) 2-17; L.L. Mitchell, *Baptismal Anointing*, ACC 48 (London 1968); J. D. C. Fisher, *Confirmation. Then and Now*, ACC 60 (London 1978); G. Austin, *Anointing with the Spirit. The Rite of Confirmation: The Use of Oil and Chrism* (New York 1985). —General documentation on the rites of initiation: E. C. Whitaker, *Documents of the Baptismal Liturgy* (London 1960); J. D. C. Fisher, *Christian Initiation: Baptism in the Medieval West*, ACC 47 (London 1965) and *Christian Initiation: The Reformation Period*, ACC 51 (London 1970); E. Yarnold, *The Awe-Inspiring Rites of Initiation: Baptismal Homilies of the Fourth Century* (Slough 1972).

99. See Chavasse, *Le Sac. gél.*, 166-168.

100. For an analysis and the origin of these rites, see Chavasse, *Le Sac gél.* 155-171.

101. *Ibid.*, 172-176.

102. For these problems, see A. Stenzel, *Die Taufe* (Innsbruck 1958).

103. *Romano-Germanic Pontifical of the X Century*, cap. CVII: *Ex authentico libro sacramentorum sancti Gregorii papae urbis Romae. Incipit ordo ad baptizandum infantes*; ed. Vogel-Elze 2, 155-164.

104. The *ordo* is part of a brief *Rituale*; see *infra*, p. 259.

105. Ed. Andrieu, *Les Ordines*, 2, 459-466.

106. *Ordines* XII-XVIII treat, in various ways, of the Roman Liturgy of the Hours although it is difficult to derive an adequate picture of its actual celebration from them. A fully satisfying study of the Office has yet to appear; the following are helpful:

H. Leclercq, "Bréviaire," DACL 2(1925) 1267-1316;

S. Bäumer, *Geschichte des Breviers* (Freiburg 1895) use the revised, French trans. by R. Biron, *Histoire du bréviaire*, 2 vols., (Paris 1905);

P. Battifol, *Histoire du bréviaire romain* (3rd ed. Paris 1911), ET *History of the Roman Breviary*, trans. A. Baylay (New York 1912);

J. Brinktrine, *Das römische Brevier* (Paderborn 1932);

C. Callewaert, *De breviarii romani liturgia*, Liturgicae institutiones 2 (Bruges 1931) and *Sacris erudiri: Fragmenta liturgica collecta a monachis Sancti Petri de Aldenburgo in Steenbrugge* (Steenbrugge 1940);

C. Sanchez Aliseda, *El breviario romano: estudio histórico-litúrgico sobre el oficio divino* (Madrid 1951);

M. Righetti, *Manuale di storia liturgica*, 2: *L'anno liturgico, Il breviario* (3rd ed. Milan 1969);

L. Einsenhofer, *Handbuch der katholischen Liturgik* (Freiburg 1932);

J. A. Jungmann, "Beiträge zur Geschichte der Gebetsliturgie," *Zeitschrift für kath. Theologie* 72 (1950) and following years, (ed.), *Brevierstudien* (Trier 1958), *Der Gottesdienst der Kirche* (Innsbruck 1958), ET *Public Worship*, tr. C. Howell (Collegeville, MN 1957) 149-177; *Liturgisches Erbe und pastorale Gegenwart* (Innsbruck 1960), ET *Pastoral Liturgy* (London 1962), *Christliches Beten* (Munich 1969), ET *Christian Prayer through the Centuries*, trans. J. Coyne but without footnotes! (New York 1978);

J. M. Hanssens, *Aux origines de la prière liturgique: Genèse et nature de l'office des Matines*, Analecta Gregoriana 57 (Rome 1952);

J. Pascher, *Das Studengebet der römischen Kirche* (Munich 1954);

C. Marcora, *La vigilia nella liturgia; ricerche sulle origini e sui primi sviluppi* (sec. I-IV), Archivio Ambrosiano 6 (Milan 1954);

A. Baumstark, *Nocturna laus: Typen frühchristlichen Vigilienfeier und ihr Fortleben vor allem im römischen und monastischen Ritus*, LQF 32 (Münster 1957); *Comparative Liturgy* (London 1958); O. Rousseau *et al.*, *Liturgie monastique et liturgie paroissiale*=MD 51(1957);

P. Salmon, *L'office divin. Histoire de la formation du bréviaire*, Lex orandi 27 (Paris 1959), ET *The Breviary through the Centuries*, trans. Sr. Mary David (Collegeville, MN 1962) and *L'office divin au moyen âge*, Lex orandi 43 (Paris 1967);

V. Raffa, *La liturgia delle ore* (Brescia 1959);

B. Piault. *La prière de l'Eglise: le bréviaire romain* (Paris 1958);

E. Dekkers, "Were the Early Monks Liturgical?" *Collectanea Cisterciensia* 22(1960) 120-137;

O. Heiming, "Zum monastischen Offizium von Kassianus bis Kolumbanus," AfL 7(1961) 89-156;

S. J. P. van Dijk-J. H. Walker, *The Origins of the Modern Roman Liturgy* (Westminster, MD/London 1960);

A. Hamman *et al.*, *Priez sans cesse* = MD 64(1960);

Mgr. Cassien-B. Botte (edd.), *La prière des heures*, Lex orandi 35 (Paris 1963);

A. Schmemann, *Introduction to Liturgical Theology* (London-Bangor, Maine

1966)—largely reflections on the *ordo* of the Byzantine Office but very helpful for all aspects of the liturgy of the hours;

J. Mateos, "The Origins of the Divine Office," *Worship* 41 (1967) 477-484 and "The Morning and Evening Office," *Worship* 42 (1968) 31-47;

W. J. Grisbrooke, "A Contemporary Liturgical Problem: The Divine Office and Public Worship," *Studia Liturgica* 8(1971-1972) 129-168; 9(1973) 3-18, 81-106;

Balth. Fischer, "The Common Prayer of Congregation and Family in the Ancient Church," *Studia Liturgica* 10(1974) 106-124;

C. W. Dugmore, "The Canonical Hours," *A Dictionary of Liturgy and Worship*, ed. J. G. Davies (New York 1972) 113-120;

G. Winkler, "Uber die Kathedralvesper in den verschiedenen Riten des Ostens und Westens," *AfL* 16(1974) 53-102 and "Stundengebet, Offizium," *Kleines Orientalisches Lexikon* (Wiesbaden 1975);

J. D. Crichton, *Christian Celebration: The Prayer of the Church* (London 1976);

W. G. Storey, "The Liturgy of the Hours: Cathedral vs. Monastery," *Worship* 50(1976) 50-70;

A. de Vogüé "Liturgy: The Divine Office," *The Rule of the Master*, trans. L. Eberle (Kalamazoo, MI 1977) 26-42;

C. Jones *et al.*, "The Divine Office," *The Study of Liturgy* (New York 1978) part 5, pp. 350-402;

R.T. Beckwith, "The Daily and Weekly Worship of the Primitive Church in Relation to its Jewish Antecedents," *QL* 62(1981) 5-20, 83-105; P. Bradshaw, *Daily Prayer in the Early Church*, ACC 63 (London 1981);

N. Mitchell, "The Liturgical Code in the Rule of Benedict," *The Rule of St. Benedict*, ed. T. Fry *et al.* (Collegeville, MN 1981) 379-414;

R. Taft, "Thanksgiving for the Light, Towards a Theology of Vespers," *Diakonia* 13 (1978) 27-50 and in *Beyond East and West. Problems in Liturgical Understanding* (Washington, DC 1984) 127-150; "Praise in the Desert: the Coptic Monastic Office Yesterday and Today," *Worship* 56(1982) 513-536; "*Quaestiones disputatae* in the History of the Liturgy of the Hours: the Origins of Nocturns, Matins, Prime," *Worship* 58 (1984) 130-158; *The Liturgy of the Hours in East and West. The Origins of the Divine Office and its Meaning for Today* (Collegeville 1986). Taft presents the best account in English of the crucial distinction—discovered by A. Baumstark and elaborated with full evidence by J. Mateos— between the cathedral and monastic styles of the Daily Office; cf. his excellent bibliography, including all the books and articles of Mateos.

A. G. Martimort, "La prière des heures," *L'Eglise en prière. Introduction à la liturgie*. Ed. nouvelle, 4/3 (Paris 1983) 169-290, ET *The Church at Prayer*, trans. M. O'Connell (Collegeville, MN 1985).

107. Ed. Andrieu, *Les Ordines* 2, 481-488.

108. *Ibid.*, 2, 499-506.

109. *Ibid.*, 2, 513-514.

110. *Ibid.*, 2, 521-526.

111. *Ibid.*, 3, 39-41.

112. The MS was described by G. Silva-Tarouca, *Atti della Pont. Accad. rom. di archeol.*, Series 3, *Memorie* 1/1 (Rome 1923) 173-178.

113. Ed. Andrieu, *Les Ordines* 3, 95-125.

114. *Ibid.*, 3, 147-154.

115. *Ibid.*, 3, 175-193.

116. *Ibid.*, 3, 205-208.

117. *Ibid.*, 3, 217-227.

118. *Ibid.*, 3, 235-236.

119. *Liber pontificalis*, Sergius I (687-701), ed. Duchesne 1, 376.

120. Ed. Andrieu, *Les Ordines* 3, 247-249.

121. Gregory I, *Registrum* 2, 2 (a letter of 592), MGH, *Epist.* 1, 102.

122. Ed. Andrieu, *Les Ordines* 3, 259-262.

123. A. Chavasse, *Le Sac. gél.*, 87-137, 215-272. For the structures of Lent, see, Chavasse, "La préparation de la Pâque à Rome avant le V siècle, *Memorial J. Chaine* (1950) 61-80; "Temps de préparation à la Pâque d'après quelques livres liturgiques romains," RSR 37(1950) 125-145; "La structure du Carême et les lectures des messes quadragésimales," MD 31(1952) 76-119.

124. See J. A. Jungmann, "Flectere pro Carolo rege," *Mélanges Andrieu* (Strasbourg 1956) 219-228.

125. Ed. Andrieu, *Les Ordines* 3, 269-273.

126. *Codex* 326, fol. 86ᵛ-88ᵛ; cf. J. B. de Rossi, *Inscriptiones christianae Urbis Romae* 2, 34-35, reproduced by L. Duchesne, *Christian Worship*, 481-484.

127. For this *Ordo* XXIII, see Chavasse, *Le Sac, gél.*, 88-91.

128. Ed. Andrieu, *Les Ordines* 3, 287-297.

129. For *Ordo* XXIV, see Chavasse, *Le Sac. gél.*, 93-96.

130. Ed. Andrieu, *Les Ordines* 3, 305.

131. *Liber pontificalis*, Zosimus (417-418), ed. Duchesne 1, 225.

132. See E. Stommel, "Die Benedictio fontis in der Osternacht," *Liturgisches Jahrbuch* 7 (1957) 8-24 and Chavasse, *Le Sac. gél.*, 102-103; DACL 13(1938) 1559-1574 under "Pâques;" see also J. Pinell, "La Benedicció del ciri pascual i els seus textos," *Liturgica* 2= *Scripta et Documenta* 10 (Montserrat) 1958 1-119.

133. Ed. Andrieu, *Les Ordines* 3, 325-329.

134. A. Chavasse, "A Rome, le Jeudi-Saint au VII siècle," *Revue d'histoire ecclés.* 50 (1955) 21-25 and *Le Sac. gél.*, 126-139.

135. A. Mundò, *Liturgica* 2= *Scripta et Documenta* 10 (Montserrat 1958) 181-216 (VII-VIII century).

136. Ed. Andrieu, *Les Ordines* 3, 347-372.

137. *Ibid.*, 3, 391-411.

138. *Ibid.*, 3, 421-425.

139. *Ibid.*, 3, 437-446.

140. *Ibid.*, 3, 455-458.

141. *Ibid.*, 3, 467-477.

142. *Ibid.*, 3, 491-509.

143. *Ibid.*, 3, 517-524.

144. *Ibid.*, 3, 531-532. Cf. Chavasse, *Le Sac. gél.* for all the *ordines* relative to Lent and Eastertide; his later works on the same subject are listed in RSR 58(1984) 226-229.

145. Ed. Andrieu, *Les Ordines* 3, 603-613.

146. In addition to the introductory commentaries by Andrieu and the corresponding articles in the encyclopedias and canonical treatises, see A. von Harnack, "Zur Geschichte der Anfänge der inneren Organisation der stadtrömischen Kirche," *Sitzungsberichte der Akad. Wiss. Berlin*, Phil.-Hist. Kl., 43(1918) 954-987; C. Pietri, *Roma Christiana, Recherches sur l'Église de Rome, son organisation, sa politique, son idéologie de Miltiades à Sixte III (311-440)*, 2 vols. Bibliothèque des Écoles françaises d'Athènes et Rome 224 (1976) 684-724 and *passim*; B. Botte, "Holy Orders in the Ordination Prayers," *The Sacrament of Holy Orders* (Collegeville-London 1962) 5-29; H. B. Porter, *The Ordination Prayers of the Ancient Western Churches*, ACC 49 (London 1967); M. Andrieu, "Les ordres mineurs dans l'ancien rit romain," RSR 5(1925) 232-274; and "La carrière ecclés. des papes et les documents liturgiques du moyen áge," RSR 21(1947) 90-120; B. Kleinheyer, *Die Priesterweihe im römischen Ritus*, Trierer theologische Studien 12 (Trier 1962); K. Richter, *Die Ordination des Bischofs von Rom: Eine Untersuchung zur Weiheliturgie*, LQF 60 (Münster 1970); A. Santantoni, *L'ordinazione episcopale: Storia e teologia dei riti dell'ordinazione nelle antiche liturgie dell'Occidente*, Studia Anselmiana 69 (Rome 1976).

147. B. Botte, (ed.), *La Tradition apostolique de saint Hippolyte*, LQF 39 (Münster 1963) 4-17 (bishop), 20-27 (presbyter and deacon). For the widespread dissemination of the *Apostolic Tradition* see B. Botte, "Les plus anciennes collections canoniques," *Orient syrien* 5 (1960) 331-350; J. M. Hanssens, *La liturgie d'Hippolyte: Ses documents, son Titulaire, ses origines et son caractère*, Orientalia Christiana Analecta 155 (Rome 1959) and *La liturgie d'Hippolyte: documents et études* (Rome 1970). Commentary on the orders section of Hippolytus in G. Dix, "The Ministry in the Early Church," *The Apostolic Ministry*, ed. K. E. Kirk, *et al.* (New York 1946); A. G. Hebert, *Apostle and Bishop* (London 1963) 61-66; W. Telfer, *The Office of a Bishop* (London 1962) 200-201; P. M. Gy, "La théologie des prières anciennes pour l'ordination des evêques et des prêtres," *Revue des Sciences phil. et théol.* 58 (1974) 599-617 and "Les anciennes prières d'ordination," MD 138 (1979) 93-122; B. Kleinheyer, "Studien zur nichtrömischen westlichen Ordinations-liturgie," AfL 22(1980) 93-107; 23(1981) 313-366.

148. Verona Sacramentary XXVIII: *Consecratio episcorporum. Benedictio super diaconos. Consecratio prebyteri* (Mohlberg 188-122); *Hadrianum* 2-4: *Benedictio episcoporum. Orationes ad ordinandum praesbiterum. Orationes ad ordinandum diaconum* (Deshusses 92-98). For the anointings of the ordination rites, see G. Ellard, *Ordination Anointings in the Western Church before 1000 A. D.* (Cambridge, MA 1933).

149. *Statua Ecclesiae antiqua*, canons 90-98, ed. C. Munier (Paris 1958) 95-99, 170-206 and *Concilia Galliae A. D. 314-506*, ed. Munier, CC 148, 162-188.

See also B. Botte, "Le Rituel d'ordinations des *Statuta Ecclesiae antiqua*," *Recherches de théol. ancienne et médiévale* 11(1939) 223-241.

150. For this Romano-Gallican rite, see A. Chavasse, *Le Sac. gél.*, 5-27.

151. Chavasse, *op. cit.*, 5-27 has a comparative study of the ordination rites in the *Reg.* 316, the *Index* of Saint Thierry, the *Gellonensis* and the *Missale Francorum*.

152. There is a detailed description of these MSS in Andrieu, *Les Ordines romani* 1 (Louvain 1931); the libraries appear in alphabetical order.

153. *The Romano-Germanic Pontifical of the X Century*, XV: *Ordo qualiter in romana ecclesia sacri ordines fiunt*; XVI: *Ordo qualiter in romana ecclesia presbyteri, diaconi vel subdiaconi eligendi sunt* (ed. Vogel-Elze 1, 13-36). These rites were used at Rome for the first time at the ordinations of Pope Leo VIII (963) and John XIII (965); see *infra*, notes 244-246.

154. Ed. Andrieu, *Les Ordines* 4, 33-57.

155. *Ibid.*,4, 473-75.

156. *Ibid.*,4, 99-110.

157. Hadrian I, Letter to Charlemagne (790/791); MGH, *Epist.* 3, 634.

158. Ed. Andrieu, *Les Ordines* 4, 195-205.

159. There is a comparative study of *Ordines* XXXVI and XXXIX and the corresponding section of *Vat. Reg.* 316 I, XX in Chavasse, *Le Sac. gél.*, 22-27.

160. Ed. Andrieu, *Les Ordines* 4, 235-238.

161. *Liber pontificalis*, Callixtus I (217-222) but which actually belonged to the time of Pope Symmachus (498-514): *Hic constituit ieiunium die sabbati ter in anno fieri, frumenti, vini et olei secundum prophetiam*; ed. Duchesne 1, 141. The prophecy alluded to was that of Zechariah 8:19: *Haec dicit Dominus exercituum: ieiunium quarti et ieiunium quinti et ieiunium septimi et ieiunium decimi erit domui Iuda in gaudium et laetitiam et in solemnitates praeclaras; veritatem et pacem diligite*. Cf. Duchesne, *Christian Worship*, 232-233, 285-286; T. Talley, *The Development of the Emberdays to the time of Gregory VII*. Unpublished Doctoral Dissertation. General Theol. Seminary (New York 1969); G. G. Willis, *Essays in Early Roman Liturgy*, ACC 46 (London 1974) 49-97; A. Chavasse, "L'Avent romain du VI au VIII siècle," EL 67(1953) 297-308). For the relationship between the three early sets of Ember Days and the *feriae conceptivae* or *indictivae* of pagan origin, see G. Morin, "L'origine des Quatre-temps," RB 14(1897) 337-342. In the Old Gelasian Sacramentary (*Vat. Reg.* 316) there still survive two distinct fasts of the first month (March): I, XIX: *Istae orationes quae sequuntur prima sabbato, in mense primo, sunt dicendae. Orationes et preces in XII lectiones, mense primo* (Wilson 21; Mohlberg 23). *Ibid.*, I, XVIII: *Feria septima in Quadragesima*=Sat. of the first week of Lent (Wilson 20; Mohlberg 23). *Hadrianum 44: Sabbatum in XII lectiones ad sanctum Petrum*=Sat. of the first week of Lent (Deshusses 139-141).

162. Council of Mainz (813), canon 34, enjoining observance of the Roman liturgy; Hefele-Leclercq, *Histoire des conciles* 3, (Paris 1910) 1141; Amalarius, *De ecclesiasiticis officiis* (ca. 825) 2, 1, 10-13=Hanssens 2, 200-201; Benedict Levita, *Capitular. collectio* (ca. 850) 1, 151=PL 117, 721; Regino of

Prüm, *De synodalibus causis* 1, 281 = Wasserschleben 132; Burchard of Worms, *Decretum* 20, 13, 2 = PL 140, 885.

163. The Gregorian Sacramentaries (*Paduensis, Hadrianum, Tridentinum*) and especially the paschal decree of 1087, under Gregory VII [Löwenfeld, *Neues Archiv* 14 (1889) 620] as well as the practice of the whole Latin Church until the II Vatican Council.

164. Council of Mainz (813), canon 34; Mansi, *Concilia*, 14, 63. —For the two, three and four Ember periods, see A. Chavasse, "Les Quatre-Temps," in *L'Eglise en prière*, ed. A. G. Martimort (Paris-Tournai 1961) 739-746; G. Morin, "L'origine des Quatre-Temps," RB 14(1897) 337-346; L. Fischer, *Die kirchlichen Quatember* (Munich 1914); M. Andrieu, *Les Ordines romani*, 4, 213-231, 258-263; J. Janini, *S. Siricio y las Quatro Temporas* (Valencia 1958); T. Talley, *The Development of the Ember Days*; G. G. Willis, "Ember Days," in *Essays in Early Roman Liturgy*, ACC 46 (London 1974) 49-97.

165. Ed. Andrieu, *Les Ordines* 4, 249-254.

166. *Ibid.*, 267-269.

167. See *supra, Ordo* XXXVII A.

168. Ed. Andrieu, *Les Ordines* 4, 283-286.

169. See Chavasse, *Le Sac. gél.*, 22-27 for the relationship between *Ordo* XXXIX and the *Ordines* XXXIV, XXXVI and the *ordo* of Vat. Reg. 316 I, XX.

170. See the entry on this collection, *supra*, p. 152.

171. Andrieu, *Les Ordines* 4, 297.

172. As bishop of Rome the pope required the same number of co-consecrators as other bishops; the normal rule was seven but three would suffice. For the bibliography on this subject, see Vogel, "Unité de l'Église et pluralité des formes historiques d'organisation ecclésiastique," *L'Épiscopat et l'Église universelle*, Unam Sanctam 34 (Paris 1962) 591-636 esp. 593; K. Richter, *Die Ordination des Bischofs von Rom: Eine Untersuchung zur Weiheliturgie*, LQF 60 (Münster 1976); A. Sanantoni, *L'ordinazione espiscopale: Storia e Teologia dei riti dell'ordinazione nelle antiche liturgie dell'Occidente*, Studia Anselmiana 69 (Rome 1976) 191-223. Note, however, that when consecrating his own suffragans the pope did not emply co-consecrators but acted alone; cf. Andrieu, *Les Ordines* 3, 583-586

173. *Liber Diurnus*, forumula 57; ed. E. de Rozière (Paris 1869) 99-102; ed. H. Foerster (Bern 1958) 111.

174. Ed. Andrieu, *Les Ordines*, 4, 307-308.

175. *Ibid.*, 4, 339-347.

176. *Vat. Reg.* 316, II, I (Wilson 161: Mohlberg 129): *Denunciacio cum reliquiae ponendae sunt martyrum.*

177. Actually, the Roman Church had two kinds of dedications: a) When relics were not deposited in a church, its consecration was accomplished simply by the first celebration of mass; cf. Vigilius, *Letter to Profuturus of Braga* (538); PL 69, 18-19; b) When relics were deposited in the building for the first time or after a theft, the dedication was accomplished by both the solemn deposition of relics and by the celebration of mass; cf. Vigilius, *ibid.* In

both cases the celebration of the Eucharist remained the essential element. See the reminders in the *Liber diurnus* (ed. Sickel): *Quatenus basilicam debeat sacrosanctis misteriis consecrare* for a public building=formula 10, pp. 9-10; *Predictum oratorium absque missas publicas sollemniter consecratis* for a private oratory in which such an inaugural mass is forbidden=formula 11, p. 10. The celebration of mass is what is fundamental in both cases; the deposition of relics is an accessory rite in the case of a shrine dedicated to a saint. See also S. Benz, "Zur Geschichte der römischen Kirchweihe nach den texten des 7. bis 9. Jahrhunderts," *Enkainia, gesammelte Arbeiten zum Achthundert Weihegedächtnis der Abteirkirche Maria-Laach* (Düsseldorff 1956) 62-109 and K.J. Benz [same as S. Benz], *Untersuchungen zur politischen Bedeutung der Kirchweihe unter teilnahme der Deutschen Herrscher im Mittelalter. Ein Beitrag zum Studium des Verhältnisses zwischen weltlicher Macht und Kirchlicher Wirklichkeit unter Otto III. und Heinrich II.* (Kallmünz 1975) and G. G. Willis, *Further Essays in Early Roman Liturgy,* ACC 50 (London 1968) 133-174.

178. For the *ordo* of Angoulême, see Chavasse, *Le Sac. gél.*, 40-42.

179. For the rite of dedication in the Old Gelasian and its relationship to the *ordines,* see Chavasse, *op cit.*, 36-49. *Vat. Reg.* 316 also has a rite for the making of holy water: III, LXXV-LXXXVI, *Benedictio aquae spargendae in domo* (Wilson 285-288; Mohlberg 224-227), mixed with salt, wine and consecrated oil (not chrism). On this *ordo* which was added to the Old Gelasian after it left Rome in the late VII or early VIII century, see Chavasse, *op cit.*, 50-57. See also M. S. Gros, "El Ordo romano-hispánico de Narbona para la consagracion de iglesias," *Hispania sacra* 19(1966) 321-401.

180. Ed. Andrieu, *Les Ordines*, 4, 397-402.

181. See the remarks in notes 177 and 179.

182. Ed. Andrieu, *ibid.*, 4, 411-413.

183. *Ibid.*, 4, 431-433.

184. In addition to the commentary accompanying the edition of *Ordo* XLIV, see M. Andrieu, "La cérémonie appelée *Diligentia* à Saint-Pierre au début du IX siècle," RSR 1(1921) 62-68.

185. Ed. Andrieu, *Les Ordines*, 4, 459-462 and by Elze, *Ordines coronationis imperialis*, 2-3.

186. Cf. Luitprand of Cremona, *Liber de rebus gestis Ottonis regis*, cap. 3; MGH, *Script.* 3, 340-346 and *Script. rerum germanicarum in usum scholarum* 41 (3rd ed. 1915) 124-136. This *ordo* appears in the RGP under no. LXXV; ed. Vogel-Elze 1, 263-264.

187. *Pontifical romain du XII siècle*, XXXV A; ed. Andrieu, 251-252; this rite is like that in the RGP; cf. *Pont. rom. du XIII siècle*, XV A; ed. Andrieu, 382-385.

188. The *ordines* for imperial coronations have been edited by R. Elze, *Ordines coronationis imperialis*, Fontes iuris germanici antiqui 9 (Hanover 1960). This is now the standard edition = OCI. Bibliography on pp. xliv-l.

189. Ed. Andrieu, *Les Ordines* 4, 483-485 and Elze, OCI, 21-22.

190. This has been established by P. E. Schramm, "Die Krönung bei den

Westfranken." *Zeitschrift für Rechtsgeschichte* 45, Kan. Abt. 23 (1934) 117-242, esp. 226; new edition in *Kaiser, Könige und Päpste* 2 (Stuttgart 1968) 140-248.

191. Ed. Andrieu, *Les Ordines* 4, 503-505 and Elze, OCI, 3-5.

192. E. Eichmann, *Die Kaiserkrönung im Abendland* 1 (Wurzburg 1942) 65.

193. C. Erdmann, *Forschungen zur politischen Ideenwelt des Frühmittelalters* [published by F. Baethgen] (Berlin 1951) 43-46, 77-80.

194. Ed. Andrieu, *Les Ordines* 4, 517-519 and by Elze, OCI, 5-6.

195. In addition to the works cited above in the introductory bibliography (Bouman, Elze, Erdmann, Schramm), see the following: G. Waitz, "Die Formeln der deutschen Königs- und römischen Kaiserkrönung," *Abhandlungen der Gesellschaft der Wissenschaft zu Göttingen* 18 (1972); J. Schwarzer, "Die Formeln der Kaiserkrönung," *Forschungen zur deutschen Geschichte* 22 (1882) 159-212; A. Diemand, "Das Ceremoniell der Kaiserkrönungen von Otto I bis Friedrich II," in T. Heigel-H. Grauert, *Historische Abhandlungen* 4 (Munich 1894); H. W. Klewitz, "Papstum und Kaiserkrönung," *Deutsches Archiv* 4 (1941) 412-443; E. Eichmann *Die Kaiserkrönung im Abendland*, 2 vols. (Wurzburg 1942) and "Um die Kaiserkrönung im Abendland," *Historisches Jahrbuch* 62/69 (1949) 607-618; J. Haller, "Die Formen der deutsch-römische Kaiserkrönung," in his *Abhandlungen zur Geschichte des Mittelatters* (1944) 280-334; E. H. Kantorowicz, *Laudes Regiae*, University of California Publications in History 33 (Los Angeles 1946; reprint *ibid.* 1958); J. Ramackers, "Das Alter des Kaiserkrönungsordo Cencius II," *Quellen und Forschungen aus italienischen Archiven und Bibliotheken* 37 (1957) 16-54; R. Elze, "Der *Liber Censuum* des Cencius (Vat. *lat.* 8486) von 1192-1228. Zur Ueberlieferung des Kaiserkrönungsordo Cencius II," *Archivo paleographico italiano* 213 (1956/1957) 251-270; reprint in *Päpste-Kaiser-Könige und die mittelalterliche Herrschaftssymbolik*, edd. B. Schimmelpfennig - L. Schmugge (London 1982), article three.

196. P. E. Schramm, "Ordines-Studien II. Die Krönung bei den Westfranken und den Franzosen," *Archiv für Urkundenforschung* 15 (1938) 8-16; a better synthesis of this research was given in the author's *Der König von Frankreich*, 2 vols. (Weimar 1939; reprint Darmstadt 1960). The above-mentioned articles have all been reprinted with additions in Schramm's *Kaiser, Könige und Päpste. Gesammelte Aufsätze zur Geschichte des Mittelalters*, 4 vols. (Stuttgart 1971).

197. In addition to the works of Schramm, see M. Bloch, *Les rois thaumaturges, Étude sur le caractère surnaturel attribué à la puissance royale* (Strasbourg 1924), ET *The Royal Touch*, trans. J. E. Anderson (London 1973); and E. H. Kantorowicz, *The King's Two Bodies* (Princeton, NJ 1957) and R.A. Jackson, *Vive le Roi! A History of the French Coronation from Charles V to Charles X* (Chapel Hill, NC 1984).

198. *RGP cap.* LXXII, ed. Vogel-Elze 1, 246-259.

199. In addition to Schramm, *A History of the English Coronation*, trans. L. G. Wickham Legg (Oxford 1937) and Schramm's "Ordines-Studien III: Die

Krönung in England" (cited above), see P. L. Ward, "The Coronation Ceremony in Medieval England," *Speculum* 14 (1939) 160-178.

200. Ed. Andrieu, *Les Ordines* 4, 529-530. Cf. H. Frank, "Der älteste erhaltene *Ordo defunctorum* der römischen Liturgie und sein Fortleben in Totenagenden des frühen Mittelalters," AfL 7 (1962) 360-415; D. Sicard, *La Liturgie de la mort dans l'Eglise latine des origines à la réforme carolingienne* LQF 63 (Münster 1978).

201. G. Haenni, "Un *Ordo defunctorum* du X siècle," EL 73 (1959) 431-434. The *Coloniensis* 123 should be compared with Paris Bibl. Nat. *lat.* 1240, fol. 16^{rv}.

202. The Phillipps MS is a Frankish Gelasian Sacramentary; cf. CLLA no. 853, pp. 390-391.

203. The Old Gelasian Sacramentary contains a funeral *ordo*: III, 91, *Orationes post obitum* (Wilson 295-299; Mohlberg 234-238). This was one of the many items added to this sacramentary after it left Rome in the late VII or early VIII century; see Chavasse, *Le Sac. gél.*, 57-71.

204. Ed. Andrieu, *Les Ordines* 5 and Vogel-Elze, RGP no. XCIX, vol 2, pp. 1-141.

205. Edited by B. de Vregille, "Le rituel de S. Prothade et l'*ordo canonicorum* de Saint-Jean de Besançon," *Revue du moyen âge latin* 5(1949) 97-114. —The so-called *Liturgia sancti Prothadii* in PL 80, 411-422 is of a much later date.

206. For these *ordines*, see M. Andrieu, *Le pontifical romain au XII siècle* (Rome 1938) 26, 53, 67; C. Munier, "L'*Ordo de celebrando concilio* d'après le *Coloniensis* 138," *Recherches de théologie ancienne et médiévale* 29(1962) 288-294 and "L'*Ordo de celebrando concilio* wisigothique. Ses remaniements jusqu'au X siècle," RSR 37 (1963) 250-271; R. Kay, "The Conciliar *Ordo* of Eugenius IV," *Orientalia christiana periodica* 31(1965) 295-304; M. Klöckner, "Eine liturgische Ordnung für Provinzial-Konzilien aus der Karolingerzeit. Der *Ordo romanus qualiter concilium agatur* des *Codex* 138 der Dombibliothek Köln, liturgie-geschichtlich erklärt," *Annuarium Historiae Conciliorum* 12(1980) 109-182; a new critical edition is announced by H. Schneider, *Die Konzilsordines des Früh- und Hochmittelalters* (*Ordines de celebrando concilio*), MGH, *Leges.*

207. For a general introduction to the bibliography on penance, see the works of B. Poschmann in his "Busse und letzte Ölung," in Schmaus-Geiselmann-Rahner, *Handbuch der Dogmengeschichte* 4, 3(Freiburg/Br. 1951), ET *Penance and the Anointing of the Sick*, trans. and revised F. Courtney (New York 1964); C. Vogel, *Le péché et la pénitence. Aperçu sur l'évolution historique de la discipline pénitentielle dans l'Église latine*, Bibliothèque de Théologie 2: Théologie morale 8 (Paris 1961), ET "Sin and Penance: A Survey of the Historical Evolution of the Penitential Discipline in the Latin Church" in *Pastoral Treatment of Sin*, ed. P. Delhaye (New York 1968) 177-282. P. Anciaux, *La théologie du sacrament de pénitence au XII siècle* (Louvain 1949).—On the evolution of the rites of penance, see J. A. Jungmann, *Die lateinischen Bussriten in ihrer geschichtlichen Entwicklung*, Forschungen zur Geschichte der inner-kirchlichen Lebens 3/4 (Innsbruck 1932).—The best commentary on the rite

of penance in *Vat. Reg.* 316 is that of A. Chavasse, *Le Sacramentaire gélasien*, 141-155.—To the rites of public, tariff and private penance, there must be added the many other forms of penance which flourished in the Middle Ages, especially penitential pilgrimages and the observances of the flagellants; for penitential pilgrimages, see C. Vogel, "Le pélerinage pénitentiel," *Atti IV Convegno internazionale Accademia Tudertina* (Todi 1961) 39-94, reprinted in RSR 38(1964) 113-153.

208. G. Le Bras, "Pénitentiels," DTC 12 (1933) 1160-1179; the best synthesis is now C. Vogel, *Les Libri Paenitentiales*, Typologie des sources du Moyen Age Occidental 27 (Turnhout 1978); but see review by A. Frantzen in *Speculum* 55 (1980) 404-405; see also his *La discipline pénitentielle en Gaule dès origines à la fin du VII siècle* (Paris 1952). Aside from certain text editions of *libri paenitentiales*, the best collections of texts are those of F. W. H. Wasserschleben, *Die Bussordnungen der abendländischen Kirche* (Halle 1851, reprint Graz 1958) and H.J. Schmitz, *Die Bussbücher und die Bussdisciplin der Kirche* 1 (Mainz 1883); 2 (Düsseldorf 1898 both vols. reprinted Graz 1958); the latter classifies the penitentials inaccurately. J. Longere (ed.), *Liber Penitentialis de Alanus de Insulis* (Louvain 1965).—Penitentials in English: M. F. Broswell, *The Medieval Sinner: Characterization and Confession in the Literature of the Middle Ages* (London 1983); J. T. McNeill-H. Gamer, trans. *Medieval Handbooks of Penance: A Translation of the Principal libri poenitentiales and Selections from Related Documents* (New York 1938); L. Bieler, ed., *The Irish Penitentials* Scriptores Latini Hiberniae 5 (Dublin 1963). P.J. Payer, *Sex and the Penitentials: The Formation and Transmission of a Sexual Code, 550-1150* (Toronto 1984). New critical editions by R. Kottje announced for the CC.

V. THE ROMANO-FRANKISH/ ROMANO-GERMANIC PERIOD: FROM GREGORY THE GREAT (590-604) TO GREGORY VII (1073—1085). *THE ROMANO-GERMANIC PONTIFICAL OF THE TENTH CENTURY (=RGP)*

Theoretically, the liturgical compilation that we call a Pontifical results from the combining of the non-eucharistic *ordines* with the corresponding prayers from the Sacramentary.[209] In practice, however, the Pontifical did not appear in its fully developed stage all at once. A variety of different attempts and experiments appeared over a considerable range of time before settling into a fairly standard shape. Some collections were more or less complete or more or less disengaged from extraneous elements—didactic, edifying or juridical; some were better arranged than others or were, simply, handier. And this remained true not only during the early stages of experimentation but throughout the entire Middle Ages. As standardized in the late XV century and as corrected and approved by Pope Clement VIII in 1596, the *Roman Pontifical* was the end result of centuries of trial and error.[210]

The new book developed for purely practical reasons: a liturgist found it much handier to have in a *single* volume both the directions he needed to celebrate well and the prayers themselves. This proved a much better arrangement than having to consult two collections, the *ordo* or *ordines*, on the one hand, and the Sacramentary, on the other. Pontificals appeared more for reasons of convenience than because liturgical experts set about constructing them.

For centuries the compilations that we have come to call Pontificals had no proper name of their own. Their text simply began with the first item to appear (prayer, *benedictio*, *ordo*, etc.).

The oldest term used at Rome to designate the Romano-Germanic collection was simply *ordo* or *Ordo romanus*[211]—a term that carries us back to a time when the Germanic origin of the Mainz Pontifical had been completely forgotten. Generic titles like *ordo* were to designate the Pontifical for a long time to come.

The expression *Ordinarium papale* or *Ordinarium domni papae* appeared already in some MSS of the XIII Century Pontifical (e.g., Paris, Biblio. de l'Arsenal, *codex* 333; XIV century).

In the same MSS we can begin to discover such terms as *Liber pontificalis* or *Liber pontificalis secundum ordinationem romanae ecclesiae* (e.g., Paris, Biblio. Nat., *codex lat.* 1219; XV century). Originally, *Liber pontificalis* (=The Book of the Popes) had been used for the papal chronicles but, beginning in the XIV century, it started to replace the older terms, *Ordo, Ordo romanus* and *Ordinarium.*

The use of *Pontificale* as a noun appears already at the end of the XIII or beginning of the XIV century in a Roman Ms (*Vat. lat.* 5791) and in two Lateran MSS: *Pontificale secundum consuetudinem romanae curiae* (*Vat. lat.,* 1155; XIV century and *Parisinus lat.* 960; XIV century).

The famous Philippe de Cabassole, bishop of Cavaillon (1334-1361), patriarch of Jerusalem (1361) and cardinal (1368-1372), bequeathed *Unum Pontificale historiatum ad usum romane curiae* (cf. ed. F. Duchesne, *Histoire des cardinaux francois,* 2 [Paris 1660] 418).

A. FIRST ATTEMPTS AT PONTIFICALS BEFORE THE ROMANO-GERMANIC PONTIFICAL OF THE TENTH CENTURY.

The association of ceremonial indications and the appropriate prayers could have ocurred within the confines of a Sacramentary; in such a case, the prayer formulas would have been supplied with suitable rubrics drawn from the older *ordines,* leaving the *Liber sacramentorum* as it stood. In actual fact, however, such an approach was not used, probably for purely practical reasons, since the already outsized Sacramentaries of the time would have been swollen beyond all proportion.[212]

Rather, insofar as the MSS permit us to ascertain, the combination of *ordines* and Sacramentary took place in two different ways:

1) The non-eucharistic *ordines* were provided with their corresponding prayers from the Sacramentary. This was the older solution and, generally, the poorest, since it tended to get out of balance. There were a few successful attempts along these lines but that was only when the *ordo* or *ordines* in question were in a pure

state, i.e., composed of specifically liturgical elements. Generally speaking, however, the *ordo* was disproportionately large compared to the *formulae*, especially when it was a question of *ordines* crammed with non-liturgical information, e.g., MSS 1-4 of the following list. These are collections of *ordines* in which the prayers are given *in extenso* rather than as *incipits* or as references to a Sacramentary (*ut in sacramentario continetur*).

2) The non-eucharistic *formulae*, detached from the Sacramentary, were provided with rubrics drawn from the corresponding *ordines*. This was the later solution and, generally, gave better results than the former. In this case the prayers are the point of departure and not the *ordines*, e.g., nos. 6-9 of the following list. As a consequence, the Pontifical is, as it were, a limb broken off the trunk of the Sacramentary.

3) N.K. Rasmussen has recently shown that the origins of the pontifical can also be found in the existence of separate *libelli* for particular rites. These *libelli* were subsequently bound together to form a kind of pontifical.[213]

The first attempts at Pontificals appeared in the IX century in Germany, France, Italy and Switzerland. The complete repertory of such attempts cannot be established until a methodical inventory of the libraries of the several countries has been completed. Here are a few major examples:

1. Cologne, Biblio. capit., *codex* 138 (early IX century); described by Andrieu, *Les Ordines* 1, 101-108, 474-475. This MS is a witness to Collection B but it can be considered an attempt at a true Pontifical because of its choice of genuine liturgical items.

2. Verona, Biblio. capit., *codex* 92 (Verona, early IX century); described by Andrieu, *op. cit.*, 367-373 and 473-474. This MS is also a witness to Collection B. Generally speaking, it provides a bishop with what he needs for non-eucharistic services.

3. The *Pontifical* of Wissembourg (Wolfenbüttel, Herzog August Biblio., *codex* 4175; Wissembourg, early IX century). Described by Andrieu, *op. cit.*, 453-458 and 488-490. This work of a monk of Wissembourg prefigures by a century the great Rhenish compilation we call the *Romano-Germanic Pontifical of the X Century*. In its manner of compostion, the *Guelferbytanus* 4175 is even purer than the RGP.

4. The *Pontifical* of St. Emmeram of Ratisbon/Regensburg (Munich, Staatsbiblio., *Clm* 14510; St. Emmeram, early IX century). Described by Andrieu, *op. cit.*, 232-238. A bishop's book like Verona 92.

5. The *Pontifical* of Angers (Angers, Biblio. municip., *codex* 80; St. Aubin of Angers, XI century). Described by V. Leroquais, *Les Pontificaux* 1, 25.

6. The Pontifical called the *Pontifical* of Poitiers (Paris, Biblio. de l'Arsenal, codex 227; St. Pierre de Vierzon, 2nd half of the IX century). A very complex volume described by Leroquais, *op cit.*, 267-270; A. Martini (ed.), *Il Cosidetto Pontificale di Poitiers*, RED, Series Major 14 (Rome 1979).

7. The *Pontifical* of Freiburg (Freiburg/Br., Universitätsbiblio., codex 365; Basel, mid-IX century).

8. The *Pontifical* of Donaueschingen (formerly Donaueschingen, Fürstl. Fürstenberg. Biblio., codex 192; Constance, end of the IX Century).[214] Documents 7 and 8 have been studied and edited by J. Metzger, *Zwei karolingische Pontificalien vom Oberrhein*, Freiburger Theol. Studien 17 (Freiburg/Br. 1914), texts pp. 3* -108*.

9. A fragment of a *Pontifical* of Ratisbon/Regensburg (Vienna, National-biblio. Series nova, codex 2762; Regensburg, mid-IX century). See below after no. 23.

10. The *Pontifical* of Aurillac (Albi, Biblio. municip., codex 14; Aurillac, 2nd half of IX century). Described by Leroquais, *Les Pontificaux* 1, p. 8.

11. The *Pontifical* of Milan (Milan, Biblio. capit. metropol., codex 14; Milan, IX or XI century?). Published by M. Magistretti, *Pontificale in usum Ecclesiae Mediolanensis* (Milan 1897).

12. The *Pontifical* of Cahors (Paris, Biblio. Nat., codex lat. 1217; Cahors, end of the IX century). Described by Leroquais, *Pontificaux* 1, 109.

13. The *Pontifical* of Zürich (Zürich, Zentralbibliothek, codex C. 102; end of the IX century). Described by Andrieu, *Ordines* 1, 458-464.

14. The *Pontifical* of Egbert of York (Paris, B.N. cod. lat. 10575; York, 1000). Ed. by W. Greenwell, *The Pontifical of Archbishop Egbert of York* (Durham 1893).

15. The *Pontifical* of St. Germans of Cornwall (and not of St. Servans d'Alet in Brittany). (Rouen, Biblio. municip., codex 368; IX-X century). Ed. by G.H. Doble, *The St. Germans Pontifical*, HBS 74 (London 1937).

16. The *Benedictional* of Archbishop Robert also known as the Pontifical of Winchester. (Rouen, Biblio. municip., codex 369; X century). Ed. by H.A. Wilson *The Benedictional of Archbishop Robert*, HBS 24 (Cambridge 1902).

17. The *Pontifical* of Sens (Leningrad, Publichnaja Biblioteca im M.E. Saltykova-Schedrina, codex Q.v.I, no. 35; X century). See A. Staerk, *Les Mss latins . . . conservés à l'ancienne Bibliothèque impériale de Saint-Petersbourg* 1 (1910) 156.

18. The *Pontifical* of Sherborne or of St. Dunstan (Paris, B.N. codex lat. 943, end of X century).

19. The *Pontifical* of Central Italy (Vat. lat. 7701, IX-XI century). Short description in P. Salmon, *Les MSS liturgiques latins de la Bibliothèque Vaticane* 3, SeT 260 (Rome 1970) 47.

20. The *Claudius Pontificals* (London, British Library MS, Cotton Claudius A iii). D.H. Turner, (ed)., HBS 97 (Chichester 1971).

21. The *Anderson Pontifical* (London, Bodleian Library MS Audit. 57.337). Found in a stable at Brodie Castle, Moreyshire in 1971. See J. Brückmann,

"Latin Manuscript Pontificals in England and Wales," *Traditio* 29 (1973) 431-432.

22. Lerida, (Lleida) (Archives of the Cathedral, *Cod.* 16). A Pontifical from ca. 1000, ed. J.R. Barriga-Planas, *El Sacramentari, Ritual i Pontifical de Roda,* Publicacion del Fundació Salvador Vives Casajuana 37 (Barcelona 1975).

23. Cracow (Jagellonian Library, MS 2057, XI century), ed. Z. Obertynski, *The Cracow Pontifical,* HBS 100 (Manchester 1977).

A special place belongs to the *Pontifical* of Bishop Baturich of Ratisbon/ Regensburg (817-848) (Vienna, Nationalbiblio., *Series nova, codex* 2762. Ed. by F. Unterkircher, *Das Kollektar-Pontifikale des Bischofs Baturich von Regensburg,* Spicilegium Friburgense 8 (Freiburg. 1962) 53-131 (the *Collectarium,* a collection of the prayers for the Liturgy of the Hours, nos. 1-449; the *Pontifical,* nos. 450-563). This document is a unique combination of a Collectar and a Pontifical which can be explained by the fact that the bishop of Regensburg was also the abbot of St. Emmeran. The Collectar is made up of excerpts from the *Hadrianum authenticum* (without its Supplement). The Pontifical is different from the Rhenish Pontificals published by Metzger and from the RGP; it numbers among the oldest attempts at creating a Pontifical.

As the Pontifical was elaborated along the lines already indicated, the non-eucharistic *formulae* gradually disappeared from the *Liber sacramentorum.* As this occurred, the Sacramentary tended to become a Missal. Examples: the Sacramentary of Amiens (Paris, Biblio. Nat., *codex lat.* 9432; 2nd half of the IX century), the Sacramentary of Tours (Paris, Biblio. Nat., *codex lat., nouvel acquis.* 1589; 2nd half of IX century), the Sacramentary of St. Amand (Paris, Biblio. Nat., *codex lat.* 2291; 2nd half of IX century),[215] the Sacramentary of Arles (Paris, Biblio. Nat., *codex lat.* 2812; 2nd half of IX century). In the X century, as the Pontifical matured and spread, the Sacramentary became more and more a book for the Eucharist alone. Examples of exceptions for this period are the Sacramentary of Rotradus or of Corbie (*Parisinus* 12050), the Sacramentary of Beauvais (*Parisinus* 9429) and the Sacramentary of St. Vaast or of Ratoldus (*Parisinus* 12052). One should not confuse the Sacramentary of Beauvais with the MS of Leyden, University Library *codex* 111-112; cf. N.K. Rasmussen, "Le 'Pontifical' de Beauvais (IX/X s.)," *Studia Patristica* 10=TuU 107 (Berlin 1970) 413-418.

In the XI century, Pontificals multiplied at an accelerated rate. We cannot examine them here in detail since we are engaged in discerning only the main lines of the evolution of the liturgical books.[216] Medievalists will have no difficulty using these Pontificals whose dates and origins are becoming clearer and clearer.

Among the Pontificals of the X century we shall stress the one that was destined to become the point of departure for all later episcopal books. Its extraordinary career was as much the result of favorable political circumstances as it was of its own intrinsic merits.

B. THE ROMANO-GERMANIC PONTIFICAL OF THE TENTH CENTURY (ca. 950-962) = RGP.

The compilation which Michel Andrieu identified and called the *Romano-Germanic Pontifical of the Tenth Century* is also called the Pontifical of Otto the Great (*Ottonisches Pontifikale*) or the Mainz Pontifical; Andrieu's title is preferable, however, because it expresses best the hybrid or mixed nature of this famous document, now in a critical edition by C. Vogel–R. Elze, *Le Pontifical romano-germanique du X siècle*, 1-2: *Texte*; 3: *Introduction générale et Tables*, SeT 226, 227, 269 (Vatican City 1963, 1972).[217]

1. The Manuscripts.

In the IX century, the collections of *ordines* (the very Roman Collection A and the several Gallicanized Collections) stopped appearing as separate booklets and completed their literary career in two sorts of ways:

a) Combined with juridico- or theologico-liturgical texts, the *ordines* become didactic treatises for the instruction of the clergy; at this stage they are no longer liturgical books properly speaking but reference volumes.[218]

b) Combined with excerpts from the Sacramentaries, as we have described above, they become experimental Pontificals of greater or lesser worth depending on their organization and completeness.[219]

In the X century, these two traditions merge in the RGP. Some fifty MSS of the RGP survive and permit no doubt as to their common origin.[220] As a whole, the MSS are German or Germanic in origin and even the Italian, French, English and Polish examples clearly depend upon German models.[221]

The most important MSS are the following; they are divided into four groups or families:

a) Monte Cassino, Abbey Library, *codex* 451 (copied in Beneventan script, a little before 1050, from a Rhenish MS which had been interpolated at Rome, between 996 and 1002);

Rome, Biblio. Vallicelliana, *codex* D.5 (Beneventan script; a little after the *Cassinensis* 451);

b) Bamberg, Oeffentl. Biblio., *codex lit.* 53 (Bamberg, XI century). Eichstätt, Episcopal Archives, *Pontifical of Gondekar II* (1057-1075);

Lucca, Biblio. capit., *codex* 607 (copied at Lucca from a Mainz model, second half of X century);

Pistoia, Biblio. capit., *codex* 141 (from a Mainz model; XI century). It has the same contents as *Lucensis* 607;

c) Rome, Biblio. Alessandrina, *codex* 173 (copied in Italy, perhaps at Rome itself, from a Salzburg model; early XI century).

Vendôme, Biblio. municip., *codex* 14 (copied from a Salzburg model, first half of XI century). This MS is the source of the following two:

Paris, Biblio. Nat., *codex lat.* 820 (2nd half of XI Century); Vitry-le-François, Biblio. municip., *codex* 36 (late XI or early XII century);

d) Vienna, Nationalbiblio., *codex lat.* 701 (St. Alban's Abbey, Mainz, XI century);

London, British Library, *codex addit.* 17004 (a German scriptorium, XI century).[222]

2. Contents of the RGP.

Only an overview of this vast compilation can be given here; it includes some 258 titles of varying dimension, running from a simple *benedictio* or Mass formula to veritable treatises and collections of documents.[223] This work is a genuine Pontifical and not a collection of *ordines* because the relevant prayers figure *in extenso* at the required places. Nevertheless, it is not yet a 'pure' Pontifical.

It still remains attached to the earlier didactic tradition: in it we find sermons for special occasions (the dedication of churches, synods, etc.), *Expositiones missae*, explanations of the Lord's Prayer, the Creed and the Office of the Dead. Actually the RGP is less 'pure' than some earlier attempts which had fewer didactic materials, e.g., the *Veronensis* 92, *Coloniensis* 138 or the *Pontifical of Wissembourg*, the *Guelferbytanus* 4175. There are also a considerable number of Mass propers that would be more logically located in the Sacramentaries or the Missal[224]—as they came to be, little by little, in subsequent books.

Aside from these two categories, the RGP contains a good many archaic *ordines* (destined to disappear as it continued to be copied), some contemporary *ordines* of the mid-IX century and various Roman, Frankish and German rites worked out in Neustria, Austrasia or the Rhineland since the Carolingian era, series of *benedictiones* for various circumstances, and an important series of *Iudicia Dei* for ordeals.

For medievalists interested in divine worship, the RGP is a veritable mine of information regarding the actual liturgical usages of those Western churches which adopted this book after the X century.

Not only was the RGP the meeting place of ancient traditions and the repository of the ritual practices worked out in the IX and X centuries, it was also the point of departure for a later evolution of liturgy that we shall discuss; it survived in the Roman Pontificals of the High Middle Ages, in the Pontifical of Trent (1596), and, to some extent, even in the Pontifical of the II Vatican Council (1978).

Just as the eucharistic liturgy reached a kind of apogee in the *Hadrianum* revised and supplemented by St. Benedict of Aniane, so *non*-eucharistic worship (aside from the Divine Office) reached a kind of peak in the contents and arrangement of the RGP.

3. *Provenance of the RGP.*

The paleography of the MSS indicates Germany and, to be more exact, the city of Mainz. Examination of the text reveals that the different witnesses all derive from a single prototype compiled in the Benedictine monastery of St. Alban of Mainz.

The following evidence all points in this direction:

Ordo L (*Ordo romanus antiquus*=RGP, no. XCIX of the Vogel-Elze edition) is an authentic and primitive part of the RGP. *Ordo* L has no MS tradition apart from the RGP and seems never to have existed independently before being incorporated into it.[225] Now, in the Rogation Days of this *ordo*, we find a well-known hymn from St. Gall composed ca. 925: *Humili prece et sincera devotione*[226] which contains some important and characteristic variants on the original:

a) a new stanza is added in honor of St. Disibodius, the patron saint of Disibodenberg, near Mainz, and of St. Boniface, the patron saint of the city itself.[227]

b) the St. Gallus of the original is replaced by a celebrated holy monk, Theodolus, whose body Charlemagne brought from Rome and deposited in the abbey of Clingenmünster, near Landau, in the diocese of Spire, where it became the object of special devotion for the monks of St. Alban's abbey.[228]

c) *Albanus pater* is substituted for the original *Ottmarus pater*, i.e., Ottmar, the founder-protector of the abbey of St. Gall gives way before St. Alban, the protector of the abbey bearing his name.

These additions and substitutions were obviously made after the hymn left St. Gall. The names *Albanus, Theodolus* and *Disibodius* were only significant in the scriptorium of St. Alban's, Mainz.[229]

d) The Vienna MS, Nationalbibliothek, *codex latinus* 1888, is a copy made in the late X century of a compilation assembled at St. Alban's between 936 and 962.[230] This *codex* is used both in *Ordo* L (RGP, no. XCIX) and in other places in the RGP, and in the same way. That seems to mean that the compiler(s) of *Ordo* L and of the RGP must have worked in the same scriptorium.[231]

Still, we cannot say without qualification that *Ordo* L and the RGP had the same authors; several awkward textual blunders even seem to indicate the opposite.[232] Nevertheless, we must affirm that both works came from the same workshop and form a single whole which, if it is not a logical one, is at least, a *de facto* one.

It must be added that an important work like the RGP, which had such an exceptional and widespread influence, supposes both an official sponsor and a well-equipped scriptorium: Mainz fills the bill exactly. The archbishop of Mainz occupied a preeminent position in the religious and feudal life of X-century Germany and the popes of that century confirmed again and again his ancient title: *vicarius et missus in cunctis regionibus totius Germaniae.*[233] In addition to being primate of all Germany, he was the archchancellor of the Empire; between 954 and 968, this great personage was William of Mainz, the son of Otto the Great, whose connections with St. Alban's are so well documented.[234] Moreover, given the reforming tendencies of Otto I and of the *episcopi* and *archiepiscopi* who surrounded him, we can appreciate the climate that favored an undertaking like that of the RGP. It was one of *two* major liturgical monuments of the Ottonian Renaissance, the other being the Sacramentary of Fulda (Göttingen, Universitätsbibliothek, *codex theol.* 231).

4. Date of the RGP.

It was compiled around 950-962;[235] every indication points to these years.

a) *The terminus ante quem non.*

Ordo L (Vogel-Elze, no XCIX) uses Pseudo-Alcuin's *Liber de divinis officiis* (ca. 910),[236] Remigius of Auxerre's (†ca. 908) *Expositio de celebratione missae* and Regino of Prüm's (†915) *De synodalibus causis.*[237] In addition, through the intermediary of another St. Alban's *codex* (*Vindobonensis* 1888) it also contains the hymn *Humili prece,* probably composed by Hartmann of St. Gall (†925): the progress accomplished by this metrical item—it left St. Gall after 925, was retouched at St. Alban's, transcribed for the model of *Vindobonensis* 1888 and used again in *Ordo* L—brings us up to the year 950 or thereabouts—and more likely after it rather than before it. The dating for the model of *Vindobonensis* 1888 (936/962) supports such a *terminus ante quem non*.

   b) *The terminus post quem non.*

   The age of the oldest MS witnesses or of their immediate models assist us in discovering the latest date the RGP could have been compiled.

   Thus, the Lucca MS, Biblio. capit., *codex* 607, probably the work of a Luccan copyist (since the German saints are eliminated from the litanies and St. Martin, the patron of Lucca's cathedral, closes the list of confessors) working from a model originating at Mainz (fol. 76ʳ: *Vis sanctae Mogontiensi Ecclesiae, mihi et successoribus meis*, etc.) was transcribed between the years 960-1000.[238]

   Rome, Biblio. Alessandr., *codex* 173, copied in Italy (Rome?) from a Mainz Pontifical originating at Salzburg (fol. 18ᵛ: *Vis sanctae Iuvavensi Ecclesiae, mihi et successoribus meis*, etc.) dates from around the years 1005-1010.[239]

   Monte Cassino, Abbey Library, *codex* 451 and the *Vallicellanus* D. 5, are direct copies of an RGP, and were interpolated around 996-1002 before being copied, as follows: *Gaudeat omnis homo quia regnat tertius Otto Illius imperio* (May 21, 996-Jan 3, 1002).[240] The interpolation must have occurred on the occasion of Otto III's 999 visit to Rome, on Aug. 15, a feast to which the acclamation of the *Carmen in Assumptione sanctae Mariae* refers.[241]

   Vienna, Nationalbibliothek, *codex latinus* 1817 is a copy of the RGP executed ca. 1002-1024, because in the *laudes imperiales* we find the names of Pope Sylvester II (999-1003) and King Henry II (1002-1024): *Silvestro summo pontifici et universali papae, vita! Heinrico a Deo coronato magno et pacifico regi, vita!*[242]

   All these chronological indications, plus the fact that none of these MSS are either the archetype or the original, when added to the astonishing dissemination of the *codices* in question, demand a date closer to 950 than to 1000.

   A certain amount of additional cross checking even allows us to get a little closer to the exact date.

   The Caroline handwriting of *Lucensis* 607 points to the second half of the X century; the codex was copied from a model originating at Mainz. It may well have been transcribed at Lucca during one of the visits of Otto I, March, 962 or July-Aug., 964.[243]

   In the description of the ordinations received by Pope Leo VIII

(Dec. 6, 963), we see that he was ordained over a period of two days, to the orders of *ostiarius, lector, acolytus, subdicaconus, diaconus et presbyter.*[244] In the description of the ordinations of John XIII, drawn up between Oct. 1, 965 and Dec. 965, the same *cursus honorum* reappears: *ostiarius, psalmista, lector, acolitus, subdicaconus, diaconus.*[245] But such a *cursus* is a Frankish or Gallican one, absolutely foreign to the Roman documents.[246] Consequently, we may suppose that these ordinations were conferred with the help of a copy of the RGP, especially since Leo VIII was a creation of Otto I and was ordained in his presence and that of his episcopal entourage who surely possessed a book like that of Mainz.[247]

The German *ordo* for royal coronations (*Ordo ad regem benedicendum quando novus a clero et populo sublimatur in regnum*) appears in the RGP in three different versions.[248] This *Ordo* cannot be found outside the MSS of the RGP and seems to have had no older literary model.[249] Thanks to Widukind's account, we know the ceremonies used at the royal coronation of Otto I at Aachen, Aug. 7, 936.[250] But the *Ordo ad regem benedicendum* does not correspond with the information provided by Widukind[251] although it does agree perfectly with what we know about the royal coronation of Otto II at Aachen, May 26, 961.[252] At this latter ceremony, the officiant was the archchancellor of the Empire, Archbishop William of Mainz, the protector of St. Alban's abbey.[253] It is not too far fetched to suppose that this prelate asked the scriptorium of that monastery to supply him with an *ordo* for the coronation.[254]

If these bits of additional information are valid, the *terminus post quem non* of the RGP must lie between the years 961-963; that means it must have been assembled between 950 and 961-963.

5. The Earliest Arrangement of the RGP.

All the copies of the RGP that survive derive from a common archetype, but none of them can be considered the archetype or even a faithful copy of it, much less the original itself.

We must not think of this 'original' too simplistically. Given its sheer volume and its importance for worship, several redactors must have worked on it, i.e., it was assembled by a team of editors rather than by a single person. We can be equally sure that a work that concerned the very foundation of the Church's worship was not a mere private project; some great ecclesiastic must have either supervised or, at least, stood guarantor of its execution. This would have been Archbishop William of Mainz (954-968), brother of the emperor, protector of St. Alban's and primate of Germany, probably with the direct encouragement of Otto I who took such an interest in matters liturgical. As copies succeeded one another, revisions of various sections must have appeared at St. Alban's itself without necessarily rearranging the general framework of the Pontifical; on the other hand, the instant success of the RGP must have obliged the team of redactors to increase their pace of production. As a consequence, several recensions of the same basic work could have issued from the same scriptorium, each one being as original as the next.

On the other hand, it is conceivable that as later copies appeared— at Mainz or elsewhere—a revised selection or section might appear in a more archaic setting or a more archaic piece might appear in a more modern setting. When dealing with a compilation as voluminous as the RGP, the literary history of each section or item is quite different than the overall arrangement of the collection itself.

The surviving MSS represent the Mainz Pontifical in several stages of its evolution or, if we prefer, they bear witness to the transformation undergone by the primitive redaction as it was copied. Despite the often important differences among the MSS, each witness is authentic because each of these books was meant for the day-to-day worship of a given church. As we said earlier on, a liturgical text is not in the same category as classic literary texts.

The overall plan of the Pontifical in its earliest surviving form appears in the MSS *Cassinensis* 451 and *Vallicellanus* D. 5; in these MSS, the older *ordines* are more numerous than in the other MSS, no *ordo* appears elsewhere which does not figure already in these two *codices*. The large number of didactic and juridical pieces reveal a strong connection with earlier collections, and eucharistic formularies appear more frequently than in other witnesses.[255] All this proclaims the archaic character of *Cass.* 451-*Vallicell.* D.5.

The fact that some rites appear in these two witnesses in a more modern form does not stand in opposition to above conclusion; neither does the fact that other MS witnesses present the same rites in an older recension.[256] E.g., the consecration of bishops and the coronation of *German* kings appear in an archaic recension in the MSS Bamberg 53, Lucca 607, Pistoia 141 and Eichstätt, the *Pontifical of Gondekar*, while Monte Cassino 451 and *Vallicell* D. 5 have revised recensions of the same *ordines*.[257] As was mentioned above, the recension of parts is quite different from the recension of the whole.

The text and arrangement of *Cass.* 451-*Vallicell.* D.5 must be completed by two additional sets of liturgical items: a series of *Benedictiones* and a series of *Iudicia Dei* which are missing from group A, because of a faulty and incomplete transcription, while they appear in all the witnesses of group B.[258] We know that both series were known at St. Alban's because they figure in *Vindobonensis* 1888 (*Benedictiones*) and 701 (*Iudicia Dei*).[259]

C. DIFFUSION OF THE RGP AND ITS INTRODUCTION AT ROME.

The intrinsic value alone of the RGP is not enough to explain its rapid dissemination and its immediate popularity in other medieval churches.[260] The real reason for its success is that it appeared at Mainz as part and parcel of the *Renovatio imperii*. The whole central portion of the Empire belonged to the ecclesiastical province of Mainz (18 dioceses) and the neighboring provinces (Besançon, Cologne, Trier, Salzburg, Hamburg-Bremen, and Magdeburg) were much under its influence.[261] It is no surprise, therefore, that the new book found a warm welcome in these very territories. From 954-968 the primate-successor of St. Boniface, Archbishop William, was an outstanding personage with an eminent political role in the Empire. There can be little doubt that the political and religious position of this great prelate contributed to the success of a book that must have been under his protection if it were not produced at his command. Moreover, the restoration of the Empire and the politico-religious initiatives of the Ottonian emperors would seem to have spread the new book far and wide.

Very soon the RGP passed outside the boundaries of the Empire: at least one copy survives in Poland (Cracow, Jagellonian Library, *codex* 2057;XII century; cf. Andrieu, *Ordines* 1, 116). Probably as early as 956, thanks to Bishop Beranger, it was at Cambrai (Cologne Biblio. capit., *codex* 141; XI century; cf. Andrieu, 1, 108-114). It is also found at Amiens, ca. 1104-1105 (London, British Library, *codex addit*. 17004; XII century; cf. Andrieu, 1, 144-154), at Besançon in the XI century (Wolfenbüttel, Herzog-August Biblio., *codex lit*. 4099 B; XI century; cf. Andrieu, 1, 441-451) and, at the same period, at Vendôme (Loir-et-Cher) (Vendôme, Biblio. munic., *codex* 14; XI century; cf. Andrieu, 1, 351-366) at Sées (*Salariensis eccles.*) (Paris, Biblio. Nat., *codex lat*. 820; XI century; cf. Andrieu, 1, 352) and at Châlons-sur-Marne (Vitry-le-François, Biblio. munic., *codex* 36; XI century; cf. Andrieu 1, 352).

In England, there were copies of the RGP in circulation from the time of Edward the Confessor (1042-1066) at Winchester (Cambridge, Corpus Christi College, *codex* 163; cf. Andrieu 1, 96-99) and at Worcester (Cambridge, Corpus Christi College, *codex* 265; cf. Andrieu 1, 99-101).

The establishment of the RGP at Rome is a major event in the history of Christian worship. The migration of the Mainz Pontifical from the valley of the Rhine to the banks of the Tiber inaugurated the second great stage in the liturgical development of the Latin Church. The freshly minted book arrived in Rome on the occasion of one of the many sojourns of Otto I in Italy (951, 952, 961-965, 966-972). The great emperor's concern for liturgy is a well-attested fact.[262] The numerous bishops and abbots of his entourage carried with them the books and liturgical utensils they needed for worship. There can be no doubt that the new Mainz Pontifical was the book they used.[263]

Tenth-century Rome was suffering from profound liturgical decadence and had lost any grip it once had on its own best traditions; consequently, the City was vulnerable to any outside liturgical influences and we can note that happening even before the new German books were introduced in the time of the Ottos.[264] Nevertheless, the main reason the RGP was established at Rome was the determination of Otto I to remedy the scandalous decadence of the Roman Church.[265]

We have abundant evidence for the arrival and establishment of the RGP at Rome: the papal ordinations of 963 and 965 suppose a Romano-Germanic rite that would be difficult to find except in the RGP;[266] a copy of the RGP brought from Mainz (*Cass.* 451 and *Vallicell.* D.5 being Beneventan copies of it) was in use in Rome between the years 996 and 1002;[267] the *Vindocinensis* 14 (first half of the XI century) was a copy of a model of the RGP which left Salzburg for Rome and then Rome for Vendôme without significant changes;[268] the *codex Alexandrinus* 173 (early XI century) is a copy of an RGP modified at Rome or in some suburbicarian diocese in the section on episcopal consecrations but otherwise very faithful to its Rhenish model;[269] in 1020, Benedict VIII very probably had in hand the *Bambergensis* 53, which he considered a Roman book.[270] When Gregory V (996-999) granted the privilege of immunity to the abbey of Reichenau, he demanded in exchange a regular supply of liturgical books from its scriptorium;[271] without doubt these MSS would have been Romano-Germanic in character. During the reign of Henry II (1004-1024), the same close ties existed between him and the popes as under the Ottonian emperors. Then, beginning in Dec. 1046, the Roman See was occupied by a series of German popes: Clement II

(Suidger of Bamberg) in 1046, Damasus II (Poppo of Brixen) in 1047, Leo IX (Bruno of Toul) in 1048, Victor II (Gebhard of Eichstätt) in 1054, Stephen IX (Frederick of Lorraine) in 1057. Once established in Rome, these prelates continued to use the same liturgical books to which they were accustomed in Germany. We also have other serious, non-liturgical evidence of the presence of the RGP at Rome down to the time of Gregory VII (1073-1085).[272]

Even as late as 1150, when the *Ordo officiorum Ecclesiae Lateranensis* cited the RGP, it called it an *Ordo romanus*.[273] We could hardly have a stronger testimony to how well acclimated to the banks of the Tiber the Rhenish book had become: the RGP had become simply 'Roman'.

Outside Rome, the RGP was no less prestigious; for centuries to come, Western *scriptoria* reproduced this book for Latin churches across the whole face of medieval Europe. Suitable inventories, however, remain to be produced for the period after the XI century.

XI-century copies: the *Vindobonensis* 701 (St. Alban's, before 1070), the *Londoniensis Addit.* 17004 (XI century), the *Guelferbytanus* 4099 A and B (Besançon, XI century), the *Bambergensis lit.* 59 (Verden, 1025-1050).

XII-century copies: the RGP preserved in the *Guelferbytanus* 503 (Franconia, early XII century), the *Guelferbytanus* 164 (Verden, early XII century); (for these MSS, see Andrieu, *Les Ordines*, 1, 542-545). All these copies reproduce the old RGP more or less completely but they all re-arrange the materials to some degree; such re-orderings seem to be of purely local interest but could help the historian to understand how a certain historic rite might have been conducted in a given church at a given period.

At Rome itself, the RGP was destined to become the immediate source for the Roman Pontificals of the XII and XIII centuries, and it was through the latter that the Romano-Germanic book ultimately provided the core of the *official* Pontifical of the entire Latin Church.

NOTES

209. In the same way, in theory, the *missale plenarium* results from combining the lectionary with the eucharistic *ordines* and the sacramentary; in the case of the *Missale Romanum*, the sacramentary in question is the *Hadrianum* as it was revised and supplemented by Benedict of Aniane.

210. As in so many other instances, our great authority here is M. Andrieu (†1956). —Important studies on the evolution of the liturgical books: T. Klauser, "Die liturg. Austauschbeziehungen zwischen. der römischen und der fränkischdeutschen Kirche vom 8. bis zum 11. Jahrhundert," *Historisches Jahrbuch* 53(1933) 169-189 and *Abendländische Liturgiegeschichte* (Bonn 1949), and *Kleine abendländische Liturgiegeschichte* (Bonn 1965), ET *A Short History of the Western Liturgy*, trans. from the 5th German edition (New York 1979); M. Andrieu, *Les Ordines romani du haut moyen âge*, 5 vols. (Louvain 1931-1956), especially the comprehensive views in vol. 1, pp. 465-548 and in vol. 2, pp. xvii-xlix (the Roman liturgy in *Francia* and the *Ordines romani*); M. Andrieu, *Le Pontifical romain au moyen âge*, SeT 76-79, 99 (Rome 1938-1941); C. Vogel, "Les échanges liturgiques entre Rome et les pays francs jusqu' à l'époque de Charlemagne," *Settimane di studio del Centro italiano di studi sull'alto medio evo* 7(Spoleto 1960) 185-295.—There is still no complete *repertorium* of the MS-Pontificals in the libraries of different countries, outside of France: V. Leroquais, *Les pontificaux manuscrits des bibliothèques publiques de France*, 3 vols. and 1 vol. of plates (Paris 1937) and England and Wales: J. Brückmann, "Latin Manuscript Pontificals and Benedictionals in England and Wales," *Traditio* 29(1973) 391-458; see the orientation to other collections provided by T. Klauser, "*Repertorium liturgicum* und liturgischer Spezialkatalog," *Zentralblatt für Bibliothekwesen* 53(1936) 2-16 and, of course, the MSS described by Andrieu in his edition of the medieval Pontifical. —Within the limits of this introduction to the sources, we cannot indicate the commentaries on the pontifical rites, but see *supra*, pp. 6-21. The following books are listed because of their extensive documentation and full bibliographies: P. de Puniet, *Le Pontifical romain. Histoire et commentaire*, 2 vols. (Louvain 1930-1931), ET *The Roman Pontifical: A History and Commentary*, trans. M. V. Harcourt (London 1932); J. Catalani, *Pontificale romanum . . . nunc primum prologomenis et commentariis illustratum* (Rome 1738) based on the Pontifical of Clement VIII and Urban VIII (Rome 1645) and a new edition with fresh notes in brackets by Dom Guéranger *et al.*, 3 vols, (Paris 1850-1852); N. K. Rasmussen, *Les Pontificaux du haut moyen âge: Genèse du livre de l'évêque* which will soon appear in *Spicilegium sacrum Lovaniense*.

211. Cf. Anselm of Lucca, VI, 166: *Ex ordine romano* (=Ordo III); ed. F. Thaner, *Anselmi episcopi Lucensis collectio canonum*, 2 fascicles (1905-1915) 345-346; *Ordo* was used for the Mainz Pontifical as a whole rather than for any part of it (cf. Andrieu, *Les Ordines*, 1, p. 522, note 2); Bernard, prior of the Lateran (1145): *Unde in ordine romano dicitur*, etc. (=Ordo L=RGP, no. XCIX); ed. L. Fischer, *Bernardi cardinalis et Lateranensis ecclesiae prioris ordo officiorum ecclesiae Lateranensis*, Historische Forschungen und Quellen 2-3 (Munich-Freising 1916) 60.

212. Actually all sacramentaries have some ceremonial indications but they are never copious enough to assist the celebrant in performing a full liturgy. The *Missale Francorum*, which is sometimes referred to as a kind of incipient Pontifical, is no different, in this regard, than other sacramentaries,

e.g., *Vat. Reg.* 316. See V. Leroquais, *Les Pontificaux Manuscripts* 1 (1937) i-cxxix.

213. Rasmussen, "Le 'Pontifcal' de Beauvais," *Studia Patristica* 10=TuU 107 (Berlin 1970) 413-418; "Unité et diversité des Pontificaux latins aux VIII, IX et X siècles," *Liturgie et l'Église particulière et liturgie de l'Église universelle* =Conférences Saint-Serge 1975 (Rome 1976) 393-410; *Les Pontificaux du haut moyen âge: Genèse du livre de l'évêque,* to appear in *Spic. sac. Lov.*

214. This pontifical has been sold to an undisclosed buyer and is no longer at Donaueschingen; see the catalogue of Sotheby Parke Bernet & Company, Auction date June 21, 1982, lot 5 (with erroneus attribution).

215. See S. Rehle-K. Gamber, *Sacramentarium Gelasianum mixtum von Saint Amand: Mit einer sakramentargeschichtlichen Einfuhrung . . . .,* TPL 10 (Regensburg 1973); on the remarkable series of Sacramentaries produced at Saint-Amand, see J. Deshusses, "Chronologie des grands sacramentaires de Saint-Amand," RB 87(1977) 230-237 and "Encore les sacramentaires de Saint-Amand," RB 89 (1979) 310-312.

216. Leroquais estimates that in the X century the non-eucharistic elements predominated by 2/3 over the eucharistic ones and that, therefore, the Pontifical was already becoming a specifically episcopal book like those of later centuries; cf. *Les Pontificaux manuscrits* (Paris 1937).

217. One of the great accomplishments of the French liturgist Michel Andrieu was the identification of a family of MSS witnessing to a common archetype which had issued from the *scriptorium* of Mainz, around the middle of the X century. The title he conferred upon this collection—the Romano-Germanic Pontifical—accurately described the mixed character of this remarkable compilation. His first studies appeared in 1924—*Immixtio et consecratio* (Paris 1924) 63, note 5, 126, 138 and *passim*—with a faulty chronology which he later rectified. The basic story of the RGP is contained in his *Les Ordines romani* 1 (Louvain 1931)494-548 and 5(Louvain 1961)72-79. Andrieu himself was unable to publish the text of the RGP which was subsequently produced by Vogel-Elze from his notes.

218. For these collections, which are of the greatest interest for the history of the education of both clergy and people in the Middle Ages, see Andrieu, *Les Ordines romani* 1, 476-485 and E. Vykoukal, "Les examens du clergé paroissial à l'époque carolingienne," *Revue d'histoire* ecclés. 14(1913)81-96.

219. Refer to what was said *supra* on the early attempts at producing Pontificals before the RGP.

220. The list of MSS is contained in Andrieu, *Les Ordines romani* 1, 497-498 and their description, in the alphabetical order of their libraries, in the first part of the same volume.

221. According to Andrieu, 21 MSS come from Mainz, 11 from Salzburg, and 1 from Cologne. MSS from other countries are clearly connected to the German ones. Their relationship with a given metropolitan see can be established both by the ordinary comparative method and from common faults perpetrated by the copyists. For example, in the rite for the

consecration of bishops, when the consecrating prelate (the metropolitan) asks the bishop-elect: *Vis sanctae N. Ecclesiae, mihi et successoribus meis fidem et subiectionem exhibere?*, the copyist often leaves the name of the original see: *Moguntinae Ecclesiae* or *Mogotiensis Eccl.*, i.e., Mainz; this can be seen in Italian, French and English MSS. All the non-German MSS are connected to Mainz, either directly or through some other German intermediary. Even the 11 MSS of Salzburg, as unlike as they are in many ways, all depend in one way or another on Mainz; cf. Andrieu, *Les Ordines romani* 1, pp. 498-500.

222. A fragmentary Pontifical with a text like that of the RGP is described by Bogdan Bolz, *Nieznane Fragmenty pontyfikalu XI s. wieku* (Gniezno, Poland, Cathedral Library, codex Fr. 10), in *Naszej Przeszlosci* 35(1971)47-67.

223. Vogel provided the first inventory of its contents: "Le PRG du X siècle. Eléments constitutifs avec l'indication des sections imprimées," RSR 32 (1958) 113-167. See the critical edition of Vogel-Elze, *supra*.

224. The list was established by Bourque, *Étude sur les sacramentaires romains* 2/2 (Rome 1958) 362-376.

225. Andrieu's critical edition of *Ordo* L effectively replaces that of Melchior Hittorp, *De divinis catholicae ecclesiae officiis et mysteriis varii . . . libri* (Colgone 1568, reprint Farnborough 1968) 1-160 under the general title of *Ordo romanus de divinis cath. Ecclesiae officiis et ministeriis per totius anni circulum*, a text corresponding to a type of RGP not presently found in any of the surviving MS witnesses. Our *Ordo* L appears as *Ordo romanus antiquus de reliquis anni totius officiis ac ministeriis* in the *editio princeps* of 1568, pp. 19-85 [= *Magna Bibliotheca Patrum* 10 (Paris 1610) 21-93 = *Maxima Bibliotheca Patrum* 13 (Lyons 1677) 666-702]. Migne did not reproduce the text of Hittorp in his *Patrologia latina*. -*Ordo* L is an integral and authentic part of the earliest layers of the RGP and not an older *ordo* reproduced by the compilers; this can be proved by the fact that a) this *ordo* figures in the witnesses to the RGP and only in these MSS and b) MSS containing *Ordo* L can be found in all the groupings of the RGP.

226. This hymn can be found *in extenso* in *Cassinensis* 451, *Vallicellanus* D.5, *Vindobonensis* 701 and 1817, *Guelferbytani* 530 and 4099. It was composed by Abbot Hartmann of St. Gall (†925), according to Ekkehard, the abbey's historian. Editions in G.M. Dreves-C. Blume, *Hymnographici latini: Analecta hymn. medii aevi* 50(Leipzig 1907)253-256; MGH, *Poetae latini aevi carolini* 4(1899)319-321; PL 138, 1082-1084.

227. Strophe 9: *Disibodo pius atque Bonifatius;* cf. Andrieu, *Les Ordines romani* 1, 500-505.

228. In addition to St. Alban's, Theodolus is venerated in two other abbeys of the diocese of Mainz, Fulda and Saint Wigbert of Hersfeld [Rabanus Maurus, *Carmina* 43 and 78; MGH, *Poetae latini aevi carolini* 2(1884)210 and 229]. For the *cultus* of Theodolus, see Mabillon, *Annales O.S.B.* 3(1739)9; cf. N. Falk, *Forschungen zur deutschen Geschichte* 22(1882)436.

229. These modifications could, of course, have occurred at Clingen-münster, Disibodenberg or even at Mainz itself.

230. *Vindobonensis* 1888 is not one of the RGPs but a compilation used for

the RGP by the editors of St. Alban's. In the litany (fol. 109^r and 115^r) Otto I is called *rex* and not *imperator* and this puts it in the years 936-962. For a description of this MS, see Andrieu, *Les Ordines* 1, 404-419.

231. If such is not the case we would have to conceive of two different teams of redactors, working in different *scriptoria*, around the same period, who would have produced the same kind of work; cf. Andrieu, *Les Ordines*, 5, 72-79.

232. E.g. a certain amount of duplication: *Ordo de IV temporibus ieiuniorum I. V. VII. et X mensis* (=*Ordo* XXXVII B) appears both in Ordo L and in another section of the RGP (no. VII; ed. Vogel-Elze 1, 8-9). This is one of the reasons why it seems better to think of a *team* of redactors who worked on the RGP rather than of a single editor. If several different monks worked on different sections, it is easy to understand why there survive differences of detail.

233. See, among others, the letters of Pope Leo VII to Archbishop Frederick in (937/939) (P. Jaffé, *Regesta pontificum romanorum* ... [Leipzig 1885] 363); of Marinus II to the same archbishop in 946 (Jaffé, 3631); of Agapitus II, Letter of 955 (Jaffé, 3668) and of Benedict VIII to Willigis in 975 (Jaffé, 3784).

234. See E. Dümmler, *Kaiser Otto der Grosse*, Jahrbücher der deutsch. Geschichte (Leipzig 1876) *passim*; K. Wenck, "Die Stellung des Erzstiftes Mainz in Gange der deutsche Geschichte," *Zeitschrift der Vereins für hessische Geschichte und Landeskunde* 43(1909)278-318.

235. Andrieu, *Les Ordines*, 1, 505-506 (a little after 950; this corrects his earlier dating to the XI century in his first studies of the Roman *ordines* in 1931); T. Klauser, "Die liturgischen Austauschbeziehungen," *Historisches Jahrbuch* 53(1933)187 (before 962/964); P.E. Schramm, "Die Krönung in Deutschland," *Zeitschrift fur Rechtsgeschichte*, Kan Abt. 24(1935)227 (ca. 961/ 962); C. Erdmann, *Forschungen zur polit. Ideenwelt des Mittelalters* (Berlin 1951) 52 (the same dating as that proposed by Andrieu; earlier on Erdmann had proposed a date around 1000); Vogel, "Précisions sur la date et l'ordonnance primitive du PRG," EL 74 (1960)145-162 (between 950 and 961/963).

236. For the dating of this work, see Andrieu, "L'*Ordo romanus antiquus* et le *Liber de divinis officiis* du ps.-Alcuin," RSR 5(1925)642-650.

237. All the sources used in *Ordo* L were carefully noted by Andrieu, *Les Ordines* 5, 83-365.

238. Andrieu, *Les Ordines* 1, 156-165.

239. Andrieu, *ibid.* 282-287.

240. *Carmen: Sancta Maria quid est?*, ed. Andrieu, *Les Ordines* 5, 359-362; Vogel-Elze, *PRG du X siècle* 2(1963)138-140 (procession with the famous ikon of Christ from the Lateran to St. Mary Major on the feast of the Assumption, in *Ordo* L).

241. For the residence of Otto III in Rome on Aug 15, 999, see W. von Giesebrecht, *Geschichte der deutschen Kaiserzeit* 1 (5th ed., Leipzig 1881) 886. This poem with its allusion to Otto III could have been inserted either at Rome itself—in the MS of which the *codices Cassinensis* 451 and *Vallicell.* D.5 are copies, or at Mainz—in the model which turned up in S. Italy and was

transcribed by the Beneventan scribes to whom we owe the two *codices* in question. Chronologically, our conclusions would be the same.

242. Andrieu, *Les Ordines* 1, 388-397.

243. The connection between the redaction of *Lucensis* 607 and Otto I's visit to Lucca was discovered by Andrieu, *Les Ordines* 1, 157, note 1 and reproduced by T. Klauser, "Die liturg. Austauschbeziehungen," *Hist. Jarhbuch* 53(1933)186. *Lucen.* 607 must have been copied from a Mainz MS since a careless scribe copied *Mogontiensis Ecclesia* in the vow of obedience. The presence of saints native to Lucca and the absence of the redaction in their original German couterparts makes the redaction of this MS at Lucca practically certain. On Otto at Lucca, see W. Dümmler, *Kaiser Otto,* 336-337.

244. Synod of the Lateran (Feb 964); Mansi, *Concilia* 18(1902)472.

245. *Liber pontificalis,* ed. Duchesne 2(1892)247=a notice between Oct 1, and Dec 965. This is a part of a rather flat continuation of the L.P. proper which had been discontinued after 891 with Stephen V.

246. For the old *cursus honorum* of the Roman clergy, see the bibliography in notes 146-173, *supra.*—On the evolution, disappearance and restoration of the minor orders at Rome, see Andrieu, "Les ordres mineurs dans l'ancien rit romain," RSR 5 (1925)232-274 and "La carrière ecclésiastique des papes et les documents liturgiques du moyen âge," RSR 21(1947)90-120.—For the Frankish *cursus* see the *Statuta Ecclesiae antiqua,* 90-98, ed. C. Munier, (Paris 1960) 95-99.—During the Laurentian Schism (498-505), there appeared at Rome the so-called Symmachan Forgeries, such as the *Synodus Sinuessana* or *Gesta Marcellini,* the *Constitutum Silvestri* (not to be confused with the *Donatio*) and the Council of 275 Bishops (*Liber pontificalis,* ed. Duchesne 1(1886) CXXVIII-CXLI) which contain a complete enumeration of the stages of the ecclesiastical *cursus*; they are, however, *pia desiderata* rather than descriptions of the real situation.

247. Theoretically, an independent *ordo* like *Ordo* XXXV (ed. Andrieu, *Les Ordines* 4, 3-46), a Frankish edition of *Ordo* XXXIV, could have been used for these new-style ordinations, but it is much more likely that, for the ordinations of 963 and 965, the consecrating bishops employed a full-scale episcopal book like the RGP.—The section on ordination in the RGP is nos. XV-XVI, ed. Vogel-Elze 1, 13-36.

248. RGP, no LXXII: *Incipit ordo ad regem benedicendum quando novus a clero et populo sublimatur in regnum* (ed. Vogel-Elze 1, 246-259).—This *ordo* for the coronation of a German king must not be confused either with the *ordines* for imperial coronations or with those for the coronations of French, English or Spanish kings, which have no literary connection with the RGP.

249. This view relies on the work of Eichmann, Schramm and Erdmann (*supra,* nos. 185-198) and the MS tradition set forth in Andrieu, *Les Ordines* 1, 194; all the MSS containing the *Ordo ad regem benedicendum* are copies of the RGP. The stylistic likenesses were pointed out by P.E. Schramm, "Die Krönung in Deutschland bis zum Beginn des Salischen Hauses (1028)," *Zeitschrift für Rechtsgesichchte,* Kan. Abt. 24(1935)223 and 310-322.—When we say that the *Ordo ad regem benedicendum* had no older literary model, we do

not mean to say that the redactor had no similar materials at hand (he could have used the *Ordo* of the Sacramentary of Warmund [Ivrea, Bibl. capit., *codex* 86, fol. 2ᵛ-7ᵛ] and the *Ordo* of the Seven Formulae" [Brussels, *codex* 2067-2073 from Stavelot]). Nevertheless, the *Ordo ad regem benedicendum* is a *new* composition produced at St. Alban's, Mainz, and had no direct ancestor. Cf. especially P.E. Schramm, "Die Krönung", 223, 310-322 and C. Erdmann, *Forschungen zur politischen Ideenwelt des Frühmittelalters* (Berlin 1951) 54-70, 83-89.

250. Widukind, *Res Gestae Saxonicae*, 2, 1-2: MGH, *Scriptorum* 3(1839) 437-438.

251. On this point see Schramm, "Die Krönung," 235, 244-251.

252. For the fragmentary information on the coronation of Otto II in 961, see Schramm, *op. cit.*, 244-251.

253. Ruotger, *Vita Brunonis*, cap. 41: *Caesar ipse futurus* (Otto I crowned emperor at Rome on Feb 2, 962) *electum* (=his son, Otto II) *summo consensu ab omni populo regem esse constituit, unxeruntque Ottonem aequivocum patris, Bruno archiepiscopus* (archbishop of Cologne) *Wilhelmus* (William, archbishop of Mainz) *et Heinricus caeterique sacerdotes Domini regem in Aquisgrani palatio* (MGH, *Scriptorum* 4(1841)270=Schramm, *op. cit.*, 246, note 1).—On the connections of Archbishop William of Mainz with St. Alban's Abbey, see Dümmler, *Kaiser Otto der Grosse*, 228, 290-291, 438; Andrieu, *Les Ordines* 1, 508 and Schramm, *op. cit.*, 224.

254. It is possible that the *Ordo ad regem benedicendum* is the written redaction of what occurred a little earlier at Aachen in 961; what is important is the connection with 961 and not the exact redactional date.—In the mind of its redactors, the *Ordo ad regem benedicendum* was created for general use and not for a particular occasion and, in fact, it was used so long as the German kings were crowned at Aachen (until 1531). The changes introduced in the first half of the XII century and in 1307, did not affect the structure of this *ordo*. If the *Ordo ad regem benedicendum* can be dated to around 961, this helps provide a more accurate date for the Sacramentary of Fulda (Göttingen *codex theol.* 231; ed. G. Richter-A. Schönfelder, Fulda 1912 reprint HBS 101 [London 1977] which was used by the redactor of this *ordo*. Cf. Schramm, *op. cit.*, 315-316.

255. See the comparative tables published by Vogel-Elze in their edition of the RGP 1, xxxii f.

256. This fact spoils a certain hypothesis: that *Cass.* 451 and *Valli.* D.5 represent either the archetype or the original or are direct copies of them. Such an hypothesis is simply untenable. Several transcriptions intervene between the archetype and the MS witnesses which have preserved it for us; the *Cassinensis*, in particular, is a faulty and incomplete transcription and does not represent well the RGP as it issued from St. Alban's *scriptorium*. It is only by comparing it to the other witnesses that we discover that its overall arrangement is probably more archaic.

257. RGP, no. LXIII (*Ordinatio episcopi*), ed. Vogel-Elze 1, 200-226 and no. LXXII. *Incipit ordo ad regem benedicendum*, ed. Vogel-Elze 1, 246-259.—This fact

has been brought out by C. Erdmann, *Forschungen zur politischen Ideenwelt*, 52, note 3 and, with a certain amount of reserve, by P.E. Schramm, "Die Krönung," 229, note 2; and updated by C. Vogel, "Précision sur la date et l'ordonnance primitive du PRG," EL 74(1960)158-162.

258. As a result of its faulty transcription, *Cassinensis* 451 stops at section CLXX. The *Benedictiones* and the *Iudicia Dei* are in sections CLXXI-CCLVIII of the RGP.

259. Both these MSS come from St. Alban's; see Andrieu, *Les Ordines*, 1, 404-419, 373-388.

260. Such popularity is obvious because of the extraordinarily rapid dissemination of the RGP both in Germany and elsewhere.—The RGP was not yet a real Pontifical because it still contained too many didactic and eucharistic elements. From this point of view many earlier attempts were actually more specifically bishops' books (*libri pontificales*), e.g., *Coloniensis* 138 *Veronensis* 92 and, especially, *Guelferbytanus* 4175, which was at least a century earlier than the Pontifical of Mainz.

261. For the ecclesiastical geography of the Empire, see A. Werminghoff, *Verfassungsgeschichte der deutschen Kirche im Mittelalter* (Leipzig-Berlin 1913) 118-124.

262. *Continuator Reginonis, anno* 967; PL 132, 174: *"Inde progrediens per Spoletum, Ravennam adiit ibique Pasca celębrans cum domno Iohanne papa* (John XIII), *plurimos ibi ex Italia et Romania episcopos coadunavit et, habita synodo, multa ad utilitatem sanctae Ecclesiae adinvenit."* A similar text appears in the *Translatio Epiphanii* cap., 1 (ca. 962/964), MGH, *Scriptorum* 4 (1841) 249.

263. In 951/952, the archbishops of Mainz and Trier, the bishops of Metz, Verdun and Toul accompanied Otto I; in 961, the same Otto was surrounded by a *compta grex episcoporum* (cf. Dümmler, *Kaiser Otto*, 194 and 326, n.1); in 936 he had gone to Rome *cum suis archiepiscopis atque episcopis* (Duchesne, *Liber pontificalis*, 2, 246). The archbishop of Mainz made several trips to Rome by himself; cf. J.F. Böhmer, *Regesta archiepiscoporum Maguntinensium* 1 (Innsbruck 1877; reprint Darmstadt 1966) 104-105.

264. For example the attempt at restoration made by the patrician Alberic (932-954), *senator et dux Romanorum*, during the five pontificates from John XI (931-935) to Agapitus II (946-955) with the support of Odo of Cluny, "archimandrite" of monasteries located in papal territory [cf. F.A. Gregorovius, *The History of the City of Rome* 1, tr. A. Hamilton (London 1894; reprint New York 1967) 15-19 and L. Duchesne, *Les premiers temps de l'état pontifical* (Paris 1911) 334-335] simply resulted in the contamination from Frankish sources of the already badly decayed liturgy of the City. This comes from an analysis of *Ordo* XXXIV as it is found in London, British Library *Addit. codex* 15222, whose primitive redaction places it ca. 900/925, and which is a "gallican" edition of the ancient Roman rite of ordinations contained in *Ordo* XXXIV (ca. 700): cf. M. Andrieu, "Les ordres mineurs ... " RSR 5 (1925) 252.

265. We are fully informed concerning the cultural and cultic decadence by Luitprand of Cremona, *"Liber de rebus gestis Ottonis Magni imperatoris,"* cap.

4 and 10: MGH, *Scriptores rerum germanicorum in usum scholarum* 43 (2nd ed. Hanover 1877) 125, 130: PL 136, 900, 903-904.

266. See *supra*, notes 244-254.

267. See *supra*, notes 240-241.

268. For other details on this important MS, see M. Andrieu, *Les Ordines romani*, 1, 352f.

269. Description of the MS in Andrieu, *Les Ordines* 1, 282-287.

270. Description, *ibid*, 41-63.—On folio 2^r there is a miniature representing, most probably, the emperor Henry II (1002-1024) between two prelates, one of whom could be Benedict VIII who visited Bamberg on the 14 of April.

271. Gregory V, to the Abbey of Reichenau (April 22, 998): *statuens ut monasterium debeat pensionis nomine in sui* (i.e. abbatis) *consecratione codice sacramentorum* I, *epistolarum* I, *evangeliorum* I, *equos albos* II; A. Brackmann, *Germania Pontificia* 2/1 (Berlin 1923) 152. At this time, Rome no longer had *scriptoria* capable of transcribing a liturgical *codex*. Cf. Arnulf of Orleans to the council of Sainte-Basle de Versy (near Rheims) in 991: *Sed cum hoc tempore Romae nullus pene sit, ut fama est, qui litteras didicerit, sine quibus, ut scriptum est, vix ostiarius efficitur*; MGH, *Scriptorum* 3, 673. The situaiton thus had not changed much since the days of Martin I (649-655); cf. C. Vogel, "Les échanges liturgiques," 228.

272. Thus the extracts from the RGP which appear in the common source to which Anselm of Lucca and Deusdedit both had access; cf. P. Fournier, "Les collections canoniques romaines de l'époque de Grégoire VII," *Mémoires de l'Académie des Inscr. et Belles-Lettres* 41 (Paris 1918) 271-397; material gathered by M. Andrieu, *Les Ordines*, I, 519-522.

273. *Ordo officiorum Ecclesiae Lateranensis*: ed. L. Fischer (Munich-Freising 1916) 60,=*Ordo L*; Andrieu, *Les Ordines* 5, 297=RGP; Vogel-Elze 2, 112; 1, 15-17.

VI. THE PERIOD OF GRADUAL UNIFICATION: FROM GREGORY VII (1073-1085) TO THE EDITIO PRINCEPS OF THE PONTIFICAL (1485) BY A.P. PICCOLOMINI AND J. BURCHARD OF STRASBOURG.

Under Gregory VII (1073-1085) and during the confrontation between the Papacy and the Empire, the influx of liturgical books from beyond the Alps dried up little by little. Within its own defined geographical and ecclesiastical territories (the City and the suburbicarian dioceses), Rome seized the initiative in matters liturgical. German control of ecclesiastical affairs came to an end, as Gregory VII informs us:

Illi autem [those whom Gregory is attacking] *qui in diebus cotidianis tres psalmos et tres lectiones videntur agere, non ex regula sanctorum patrum, sed ex fastidio et neglegentia comprobantur facere. Romani autem diverso modo agere ceperunt, maxime a tempore quo Teutonicis concessum est regimen nostrae Ecclesiae. Nos autem et ordinem romanum et antiquum morem investigantes, statuimus fieri nostrae Ecclesiae sicut superius praenotavimus, antiquos imitantes patres.*[274]

In large part, such a declaration was still a mere statement of intent since neither he nor anyone else could escape the impress of the Romano-Germanic books. The so-called *Roman* Pontificals which began to be compiled by the second half of the XI century are striking proof of their abiding influence.

A. THE ROMAN PONTIFICALS OF THE XII CENTURY.

The Pontificals compiled at Rome from the reign of Gregory VII until around the end of the XII century call for two observations:

a) All the surviving copies diverge to such a degree that there could not have been a common Roman archetype; the various

Roman churches (the Lateran and the suburbicarian cathedrals) and the Roman *scriptoria* each worked up its own Pontifical. That means that in the XII century there was no single, official version of the RGP that established itself in the City of the Popes. Nevertheless, the surviving witnesses form a family of MSS which may be called by the generic title: *Roman Pontificals of the XII Century*. As a result, these *Roman Pontificals of the XII Century* can be easily distinquished from others of the same era which were descendants of the RGP and copied north of the Alps.

b) As regards both prayers and rites, the RGP remained the source *common* to all the Roman episcopal books of the XII century.[275] Consequently, we may classify the surviving MSS according to their greater or lesser proximity to the RGP.

For his edition, Andrieu used nine MSS according to the principle just enunciated:

MS witnesses still very close to the RGP:

Troyes, Biblio. municp., *codex* 2272 (late XI century; Pavia?)

Rome, Biblio. Vat., *codex lat.* 7114 (2nd half of the XIII century; Auch)

Rome, Biblio. Vat., *codex lat.* 7818 (XII century; Chieti)

Rome, Biblio. Vat., *codex Borghes. lat.* 49 (XIII century; Naples area, then Sora)

Grenoble, Biblio. municip., *codex* 140 (2nd half or end of the XII century; perhaps from the time of Bishop John I, 1163-1220; Grenoble)

Aoste, R. Amiet (ed.), *Pontificale Augustanum, Le Pontifical du XI siècle de la Bibl. Capit. d'Aoste,* Monumenta Liturgica Ecclesiae Augustanae 3 (Aoste 1975)

MS witnesses that are more specifically Roman:

Rome, Biblio. Vat., *codex Barber.* 631 (end of the XI century; Monte Cassino)

Rome, Biblio. Vat., *codex Ottobon. lat.* 270 (XII century; Rome)

London, British Library, *codex addit.* 17005 (2nd half of the XII century; German copy of a Roman Pontifical; south of Mainz)

An original witness by a Roman liturgist:

Lyons, Biblio. municip., *codex* 570. This is the famous MS containing the *Pontifical of Apamea* (cf. M. Andrieu, "Le Pontifical d'Apamée," RB 48 (1936)321-348) The *codex* includes copies of five Pontificals executed around 1676 by Jean Deslions for Martène's *De antiquis Ecclesiae ritibus:* 1) the *Pontifical of Troyes* (or pseudo-Pontifical of Prudence; a copy of Paris, Biblio. Nat., *codex lat.* 818), 2) a *Pontifical of Amiens*, 3) a *Pontifical of Cambrai*, 4) the *Pontifical of Apamea* (in the Latin Patriarchate of Antioch) copied from a Roman model at the end of the XII century. Once considered lost, this pontifical was found again by F. Wormald who bequeathed it to the British Library. It is now MS Addit. 57.528. Cf. A.G. Martimort, *La documentation liturgique de Dom Edmond Martène, Étude codicologique*, SeT 279 (Vatican City 1978) no. 25; and 5) the *Pseudo-Pontifical of Poitiers* (a copy of Paris, Biblio. Arsenal, *codex* 227; now edited by A. Martini).

The MSS of groups two and three constitute the two authentic forms of the *Roman Pontifical of the XII Century*.

The labor of adapting the RGP to the new Roman situation (topographically, ecclesiastically and politically) took place in the several Roman *scriptoria*—quite independently of one another—and proved to be a work of substantial reduction. The Roman liturgists aimed at eliminating a good deal of archaic and unnecessary material from the Mainz Pontifical: archaic *ordines*, the *ordo* for royal coronations, which neither Rome nor its suffragans needed, didactic sections, rites of exorcism and excommunication, and the *Benedictiones* and *Iudicia Dei* deemed unsuitable to the Roman religious temperament.

The rites that were retained were either simplified by the elimination of exuberant or interchangeable *formulae* (series of *aliae*) or adapted to the peculiar conditions of the Church of Rome (episcopal ordination, celebrations linked to particular sites in the City, e.g., the Purification, Lent, etc.).[276]

The various offshoots of the RGP came to be disseminated rather widely: first of all, in the dioceses directly subject to or in close relation with the pope and, then, throughout the whole Latin Church.[277] After the I Lateran Council (1123), Rome had every intention of extending its supervisory role in Latin Christendom: papal legates traveled all over Europe to enforce the disciplinary decrees of 1123 and the popes themselves, from the death of Gregory VII (1085) through the reign of Innocent III (1198-1216), were often obliged to take the road of exile, finding asylum in different parts of Italy and France (Papal authority was growing in the Christian world as a whole but at Rome itself it was precarious at best).[278] In their far-flung travels, the popes carried with them their new Roman books and thus contributed to their diffusion; of the nine MSS used by the editor of the *Roman Pontifical of the XII Century*, only one was executed at Rome (Rome, *Vaticanus Ottobon. lat.* 270).[279]

The success of the XII-century experiments was, therefore, sure but limited: the freshly adapted book soon gave way before the Roman Pontifical associated with the liturgical reforms of Innocent III, *The Pontifical of the Roman Curia of the XIII Century*.

B. THE PONTIFICAL OF THE ROMAN CURIA OF THE XIII CENTURY.

The thirty-three complete MSS used by Andrieu for his edition of this Pontifical form a more coherent family of witnesses than those for the *Pontifical of the XII Century* and suppose a common archetype; it must have been the result of initiatives taken by the masters of ceremonies of the Lateran at the time of Innocent III.[280]

The text survives in three recensions, but only the first and last can be dated exactly. Nevertheless, the essence of the *Roman Pontifical of the XII Century* can be found in all three (the prayer *formulae* in particular) through the intermediary of the Roman *Pontifical of Apamea* (ca. 1200).[281]

The first recension (=*alpha* of Andrieu) is later than the *Pontifical of Apamea* (very end of the XII century) and very likely belongs to the pontificate of Innocent III. Evidence comes from the oath included in the section for imperial coronations (Andrieu, p. 387) which sounds like the promises Otto IV made to Pope Innocent between 1201 and 1209.[282] This recension was created at the Lateran by the masters of ceremonies of the Roman curia and enjoyed a kind of official status. The first recension would suffice for any bishop celebrating in churches directly dependent on the papacy.

The third recension (=*gamma* of Andrieu) must be located before the pontificate of Innocent V (1276) and probably in the time of Innocent IV (1243-1254). To this latter reign belongs best the acclamation contained in the papal coronation rite: *Domino nostro I. a Deo decreto summo pontifici et universali papae, vita!* (Andrieu, p. 375).[283] This third and last form of the Pontifical came from the same enviroment as the *alpha* recension; it is simply an enlarged edition for the use of the Roman curia.

The three editions existed side by side (along with copies of the *XII Century Pontifical*) but in the XIV century the third recension came to predominate, and it was that edition which accompanied the popes to Avignon (1305/1309) and came to compete with the Pontifical of William Durandus, Bishop of Mende.

The Curial Pontifical of the XIII Century was used at the Lateran and in the Italian churches immediately subject to the Holy See of Rome. After the popes established themselves in France, the new Pontifical became the official book of the papal court and spread throughout the south of France.

C. THE PONTIFICAL OF WILLIAM DURANDUS (ca. 1293-1295).[284]

In the South of France, towards the end of the XIII century, the *Pontifical of the Roman Curia* encountered the Pontifical in three books compiled and arranged by the celebrated William Durandus, Bishop of Mende. After a period of reciprocal exchanges,[285] Durandus' book won the day because of its instrinsic qualities and its clarity of arrangement. Durandus had never intended producing either a scholarly study of the liturgy or a Pontifical destined only *ad usum ecclesiae Mimatensis*. Rather, without every saying so explicitly, the Bishop of Mende prescribed all the episcopal functions for every bishop in Latin Christendom.

The papal schism of the late XIV century contributed to the success of this book, especially during the pontificates of Robert of Geneva (Clement VII, 1378-1394) and Pedro da Luna (Benedict XIII, 1394-1417, † 1423). It is a well-known fact that Durandus' Pontifical served as a model for A. P. Piccolomini and the famous Burchard of Strasbourg and their printed edition of the *Pontificale* in 1485. And so it was that the rites and ceremonies worked out, in the first instance for the diocese of Mende, survived in all the dioceses of the Latin patriarchate until the II Vatican Council.

Of the twenty-one MSS he described, Andrieu used fourteen for his edition.[286] The Pontifical bears no name: *Pontificalis ordinis liber incipit*, but there is no doubt that the author was William Durandus (born ca. 1230 at Puimisson, N. of Béziers; bishop of Mende in 1285, died at Rome, Feb 1, 1296), the famous composer of the *Speculum iudiciale* (ca. 1276) and the *Rationale divinorum officiorum*, a veritable *summa* of medieval liturgical information (ca. 1286).

Signs of authorship:

a) In the oath of obedience to the ordinary, the bishop is designated by the letter G, Liber I, cap. XX, no. 9: *Ego . . . talis monasterii ordinandus abbas vel abbatissa, promitto . . . tibique G. domino meo, eiusdem ecclesiae episcopo . . .* (Andrieu, p. 402);

b) there are many explicit references to the other works of Durandus, proving that the *Pontifical* and the rest belong to the same author: e.g., Liber III, cap. XVIII, no. 50 (Andrieu, p. 642): *De premissis singulis et aliis in Rationali nostri posuimus rationes*; Liber III, cap. VII, no. 27 (Andrieu, p. 609): *Haec autem in Speculo iudiciali, in tertia parte, sub titulo: De accusatione, in secundo loco, plenius duximus explicanda.*

c) the author claims to be the bishop of Mende: Liber III, cap. XXII, no. 2: *In ecclesia tamen Mimatensi cui, auctore Deo, presidemus* (Andrieu, p. 650).

William began his *Pontifical* around 1292 and finished it between 1293 and the autumn of 1295.[287]

His *Pontifical* was a liturgical book in the strict sense, i.e., a book designed for actual liturgical use. Its subject matter was clearly arranged in three books; although this was the first time such a tripartite division had been used, it was to become standard for the future:

1. *In prima (parte) de personarum benedictionibus, ordinationibus et consecrationibus agitur . . . .*

II. *In secunda parte de consecrationibus et benedictionibus aliarum tam sacrarum quam prophanarum rerum agitur . . . .*

III. *In tertia parte de quibusdam ecclesiasticis officiis agitur . . . .* (*Prologus* 1, 2, and 3; Andrieu, pp. 327, 328, and 331).

The rock foundation of William's work was, beyond all question, Roman, but he also knew how to take into account local usages. Among the immediate sources of his edition were the *Roman Pontifical of the XII Century*, and *Pontifical of the Roman Curia of the XIII Century* in its several recensions (when he cites an *Ordo romanus*, he means the *usus romanae curiae*) and even the RGP, independently of the materials which had passed into the several *Roman Pontificals*.[288]

In addition, Durandus made some important modifications and some new contributions.

a) Modifications:

He eliminated everything that related to the functions of simple priests/presbyters and that makes his book the first Pontifical strictly speaking (*Prologus*; Andrieu, p. 327). Purely priestly functions are set forth elsewhere, in his *Instructiones*.[289] Every section of the *Pontifical of the Roman Curia* appears in Durandus, every prayer is reproduced in its entirety and he limits his elaboration of the rubrics of his sources to a more methodical arrangement.

b) Fresh Contributions:

By this we mean the arrangements proper to the Bishop of Mende, even if the prayer itself or other indications are themselves old. In the *Pontifical* of William Durandus, the following elements are peculiarly his:

Liber I, cap. XIX, XXII, XXVI-XXVIII.

Liber II, cap. XIII, XIV, XVII, XX, XXX, XXXII, XXXIV, XXXV, XXXVII.

Liber III, cap. V, VII-XVI.

The final sections, Liber III, cap. XVII-XXX, can be easily distinguished from the body of the *Pontifical* since they are didactic in nature and not designed for liturgical use.

D. THE *EDITIO PRINCEPS* OF THE *PONTIFICALE* BY A.P. PICCOLOMINI AND J. BURCHARD OF STRASBOURG (ROME, 1485).

The first printed edition of the *Pontificale* was the joint work of Agostino Patrizzi Piccolomini (Augustinus Patricius de Piccolominibus), the adopted son and secretary of Pius II, bishop of Pienza and Montalcino (*episcopus Pientini et Ilcinensis*) who died in 1496 and of John Burchard (or Burckhard), provost of the church of St. Florentius of Haslach (near Molsheim) in the diocese of Strasbourg, master of ceremonies to Popes Sixtus IV, Innocent VIII and Alexander VI, and author of the famous *Diarium* and of many liturgical directories; it was clearly John who did most of the work on the *Pontificale*,[290] whose title was:

Pontificalis ordinis liber incipit in quo ea tantum ordinata sunt que ad officium pontificis pertinent, qui tres in se partes continet. In quarum prima, de benedictionibus, ordinationibus et consecrationibus personarum. In secunda, de consecrationibus et benedictionibus. In tertia vero, de quibusdam sacramentis et ecclesiaticis officiis agitur. Romae, apud Steph. Planck, 1485.

Then there follows a dedicatory letter to Innocent VIII.

Explicit. Explicit pontificalis liber, magna diligentia Rev. in Christo patris D. Augustini Patricii de Piccolomnibus, ep. Pientini et Ilcinensis, ac Ven. viri D. Ioannis Burckhardi, prepositi et can. eccles. S. Florentii Haselacensis, Argent. Dioc., capelle SS. D.N. Papae caeremoniarum magistri, correctus et emendatus.[291]

In the letter dedicated to his "all-seeing Holiness" (*Oculatissima Sanctitas*), the authors explicitly acknowledge that they have faithfully reproduced the *Pontifical* of William Durandus and have confined themselves to correcting the text from several different MSS:

Tum maxime Guillelmi Durantis, episcopi Mimatensis auctoritas, qui pontificalem librum, quo maxime hoc tempore utuntur antistites, edidit. . . . Cuius editioni manus apponere piaculum ducerem, nisi post ea tempora multa addita, pleraque intermissa, plurima vero vitiata reperirentur. . . . Nos vero illum, quantum potuimus, secuti, adhibitis pluribus ac diversis exemplaribus. . . . [292]

Obviously, the *editio princeps* of the *Pontificale* procedes directly and of set purpose from that of William Durandus.[293] The distribution of subject matter corresponds to the threefold division the Bishop of Mende had introduced; to announce such a division the 1485 editors even borrowed the very words of Durandus cited above.

Piccolimini-Burchard were content with suppressing the sections of the *Pontifical* which had become obsolete (e.g., the expulsion of penitents on Ash Wed. and their reconciliation on Holy Thurs.),[294] with completing the rubrics from the *Ceremonial of Bishops*,[295] and with setting aside, once and for all, any purely presbyteral functions which, they thought, should appear in a special collection, which they proposed to edit: *collecturi, si vita supererit, in alio volumine omnia quae ad simplices sacerdotes spectant.*[296]

The new Pontifical was reissued at Rome in 1497 by Jacobus de Luciis (or Lutiis), bishop of Caiazzo (*episcopus Caiacensis*) and the same John Burchard;[297] at Lyons and Venice in 1511,[298] and again at Venice by the Dominican F. Alberti Castellani in 1520.[299] It was the Castellani edition that was reproduced almost word for word in the first *official* edition of the *Pontifical* at Rome in 1595 under Pope Clement VIII (1595 on the title page, 1596 in the introductory papal constitution, *Ex quo in Ecclesia Dei*).[300] Any supressions in this official edition affect almost exclusively the third book. Everything was eliminated that was better located in the *Ceremonial of Bishops*, e.g., the rubrics for pontifical Vespers, for masses *coram episcopo*, precise directions for the *mitra* and the *baculus* and minor ministers and anything relating to the pope alone. All such information was to be relegated to the *Caeremoniale Romanum*.

There is no room in an introduction like this for the period extending from the Council of Trent (1545-1563) to the II Vatican Council (1962-1965). Suffice it to say that it was an era of rigid unification and of rubricism in matters liturgical.[301] But we must take note of the fact that the official Roman books which became obligatory in the whole Latin Church issued directly from their Romano-Frankish and Romano-Germanic ancestors and remained normative throughout the entire era of Tridentine Catholicism.[302]

E. RITUALS

Until the accomplishment of William Durandus (1293-1295) and the Pontificals that issued directly from it, the Pontifical—which, in principle, includes the rites for all the sacraments and sacramentals reserved to a bishop—contained, *de facto*, rites and formulae for any celebrant, whether bishop or simple presbyter.

As a specific liturgical book, the Ritual contains forms for the administration of all those sacraments and sacramentals which are not reserved exclusively to bishops; it is a book for priests having between its covers everything he needs for non-eucharistic, non-office worship. For the latter, he possesses the *Missale* and the *Breviarium*. Theoretically, the Ritual derives directly from the Pontifical but, as a matter of fact, it had a much more complicated origin and history.

The Ritual is a liturgical book in the strict sense and must be distinguished from the *Pastorale* (or *Sacramentale* or *Manipulus*) and from the *Manuale curatorum* which contained pastoral advice and directions in addition to the sacramental rites and ceremonies.[303]

Medievalists investigating the normal and regular worship of the parish churches will find the Ritual more valuable than the Pontifical since it approximates actual liturgical practice more closely.[304] Remarkable differences often show up in the various diocesan Rituals in regard to baptism, marriage rites, the *cura circa morientes* and *pro mortuis gerenda*, the blessing of bells, pilgrimages, the numerous medieval rites for warding off evil, etc. Scholarly research into the Rituals is, and would be, of the greatest service to medievalists.[305]

1. SOURCES AND STUDIES

In the present case, it is not easy to separate sources and studies except when dealing with liturgical books strictly speaking. Most editions of texts contain valuable introductions, commentaries and repertories. It is impossible to provide a complete bibliography in the area of Rituals; important works in progress may well modify our presently accepted ideas.

a) *General Studies:*

J. Catalani, *Rituale Romanum Benedicti papae XIV perpetuis commentariis exornatum*, 2 vols. (Padua 1760). Like all Catalani's works this is a mine of valuable information.

A. Franz, *Die kirchlichen Benediktionen im Mittelalter*, 2 vols. (Freiburg/Br. 1909; reprint Graz 1961). Rituals, pp. xxx-xxxiv.

_____, *Das Rituale von S. Florian aus dem XII Jahrhundert*. (Freiburg/Br. 1904);

_____, *Das Rituale des Bischofs Heinrich von Breslau* (XIV century) (Freiburg/Br. 1912).

B. Löwenfeld, *Das Rituale des card. Julius Antonius Sanctorius. Ein Beitrag zur Enstehungsgeschichte des Rituale Romanum* (Munich 1937).

_____, "Die Erst-Ausgabe des Rituale Romanum (1614)," *Zeitschift für kathol. Theologie* 66(1942) 141-147.

A. Dold, *Die Konstanzer Ritualientexte in ihrer Entwicklung von 1482 bis 1721*, LQF 5-6 (Münster/Westf. 1923); texts and history.

H. Johansson, *Hemsjömanualet* (Stockholm 1950). A catalogue of Rituals up to 1530.

J. B. Molin, "Introduction à l'étude des Rituels anciens," *Bulletin du Comité des Études* (Saint-Sulpice) 3(1959)675-692.

_____, "Un type d'ouvrage mal connu, le Rituel. Son intérêt et ses caractéristiques bibliographiques," *Bulletin d'information de l'Association des Bibliothécaires français* 31(1960) 9-18; reprinted in *EL* 63(1959) 218-224.

P.M. Gy, "Collectaire, Rituel, Processional," *Revue des Sciences phil. et théol.* 44(1960)441-469.

W. von Arx, "Zur Entstehungesgeschichte des Rituale," *Zeitschrift für schweizerische Kirchengeschichte* 63 (1969) 39-57.

H.J. Spital, *Der Taufritus in den deutschen Ritualien, von den ersten Drucken bis zur Einführung des Rituale Romanum*, LQF 47 (Münster/W 1968).

b) *Studies relating to various Countries:*

FRANCE:

Ritual of Autun (1545): J.B. Molin, "Monitions sacramentelles au XVI siècle," LMD 61 (1960) 56-57.

Ritual of Coutances: J.L. Adam, "Le Manuel de Coutances imprimé à Rouen en 1494," *Revue Catholique de Normandie* 18 (1908) 185-199.

Ritual of Chartres (1580): Philippeau, *Paroisse et Liturgie* 34 (1952) 360-364.

Ritual of Alet (1667): P. Guéranger, *Institutions liturgiques* 2 (Paris 1841) 60-66; P. Broutin, *La réforme pastorale en France au XVII siècle* 2 (Paris 1956) 399-411; J. Dubu, "Racine et le Rituel d'Alet," *Studi in onore di V. Lugli e D. Valeri* (Venice 1960) 350-352.

Ritual of Aix en Provence (1577): L. Marrot, *La liturgie aixoise* (Aix 1899) 83-88.

Rituals of Toul and Verdun: M. Beaupré, *Notice bibl. sur les livres liturgiques des diocèses de Toul et Verdun* (Nancy 1843) 35.

Ritual of Strasbourg: F. Fues in *Katholisches Kirchen-und Schulblatt* (1857) 97.

J.B. Molin-A. Aussedat-Minivelle, *Répertoire des rituels et processionaux imprimés conservés en France* (Paris 1984).

ITALY:

Refer to what will be said on the studies of Castello, Samarino, Santori (Sanctorio) and Catalani. For Northern Italy, C. Lambot, *North Italian Services of the Eleventh Century* (Milan, Biblio. Ambros. *codex* T. 27, Sup.) HBS 67 (London 1931). A collection of XI-century *Ordines*.

GERMANY, AUSTRIA AND GERMAN SWITZERLAND:

In addition to the studies of Franz, Löwenfeld and Dold, consult for the Ritual of Magdeburg: C.E. Luthardt, "Agenda Magdeburgensis," *Zeitschrift für kirchl. Wissenschaft und kirchl. Leben* 10(1889)32f.

Ritual of Augsburg: J.A. Hoeynck, *Geschichte der kirchl. Liturgie des Bistums Augsburg* (Augsburg 1889).

Ritual of Freising: *Die Spendung der Sakramente nach den Freisinger Ritualien*, Münchener theologische Studien 2 (Munich 1967).

Ritual of Salzburg: H. Mayer, "Geschichte der Spendung der Sakramente in der alten Kirchenprovinz Salzburg," *Zeitschrift für kath. Theologie* 37 (1913)760-804; 38(1914)1-36 and 267-296.

Ritual of Rheinau (Zürich, *codex Rh.* 114; early XII century): ed. G. Hürlimann, *Das Rheinauer Rituale*, Spicilegium Friburgense 5 (Fribourg 1959).

Ritual of Chur: H. Bissig, *Das Churer Rituale (1503-1927)*, Studia Friburgensia N.F. 56 (Fribourg 1979).

See also H. Reifenberg, "Gottesdienst . . . ," *infra*, p. 285.

ENGLAND:

Ritual of York: W.G. Henderson (ed.), *Manuale et Processionale ad usum insignis Ecclesiae Eboracensis*, Surtees Soc. 53 (Durham 1875). Comparisons with other English Rituals.

Ritual of Durham: H. Thompson-Lindelöf (ed.), *Collectar-Ritual of Durham*, Surtees Soc. 140 (Durham 1927).

Ritual of Salisbury: A.J. Collins (ed.) *Manuale ad usum percelebris Ecclesiae Sarisburiensis*, HBS 91 (London 1960).

SPAIN AND PORTUGAL:

Ritual of Toledo: I. García Alonso in *Salmanticenses* 5(1958)3-79, 351-450; 6(1959) 187-198, 323-399.

Ritual of Tarragona: A.M. Franquesa, "El Ritual Tarraconense," *Liturgica* 2 (Montserrat 1958) 249-298; and *Liturgia* 13 (Burgos 1958) 193-204.

Ritual of Coimbra: J.O. Bragança, *Ritual de Santa Cruz de Coimbra* (Lisbon 1976).

BELGIUM:

G. Malherbe, "Les Rituels liègeois," *Bulletin de la Société d'Art et d'Histoire du diocèse de Liège* 37(1951) 27-81.

SCANDINAVIA:

H. Johansson, *Hemsjömanualet* (Stockholm 1950).

_____, *Bidrag till den svenska Manualettraditionen* (Lund 1951).

E. Segelberg, *Manuale Stregnense* (Strengnäss, Sweden). (Uppsala 1950).

K. Ottosen, *The Manual of Notmark*, Bibli. lit. danica 1 (Copenhagen 1970).

B. Strömberg, *The Manual from Bystorp*, Bibl. lit. danica 2 (Egtved 1982).

M. Parvio, *Manuale seu exequiale aboense 1522. Editio stereotypa* (Helsinki 1980).

Further information for the ecclesiastical province of Nidaros (Trondheim), Norway in A.A. King, *Liturgies of the Past*, (Milwaukee 1959) 375-466.

POLAND:

W. Wrona in *Polania Sacra* (1951) 368-372.

2. FORMATION OF THE RITUAL.

Theoretically, as was said earlier, the Ritual is made up of liturgical items excerpted from the Pontifical; we have already related the proposals of William Durandus and of A.P. Piccolomini and J. Burchard on this matter. As a matter of fact, however, the Ritual has a long and complicated history (and even a pre-history), especially down to the XII century.

a) The Libellus.

When any *ordo* is provided with the appropriate prayers from the Sacramentary, we already have a Ritual-booklet serving *one* particular liturgical function (baptism, funerals, etc.). Normally, however, such a collection serves several possible liturgical events for which a *sacerdos/presbyter* (as opposed to an *episcopus*) is the ordinary minister; such a booklet always unites the description of the ritual process (*ordo*) with the corresponding prayer-*formulae* drawn from the Sacramentary. The practical advantages of such booklets are clear: the convenience of the celebrant, savings on parchment and copying time.

We know that such booklets existed already at the beginning of the X century[306] and a few of them still survive:

Paris, Biblio. Nat., *codex latinus* 13764, fol. 90ʳ-116ᵛ (St. Amand, 900/950). The rite of penance and the *cura circa morientes*.

Paris, B.N., *codex lat.* 2984 A (ca. 975), fol. 87-90ʳ. The rite of the *commendatio animae* and of burial.

Paris, B.N., *codex lat.* 1240 (St. Martial of Limoges; early X century), fol. 12-16ᵛ. The rite for the anointing of the sick and for funerals.

b) The Ritual-Collectar and the Ritual-Sacramentary.

In the X century there also appeared Rituals that were bound up with Collectars containing the *capitula* and collects (*orationes*) needed by the officiant at the Liturgy of the Hours; sometimes the Collectar was termed *Orationale*, especially in Italy, or *Portiforium*, especially in England.

According to the discoveries of P.M. Gy, some five X-century and a dozen XI-century MSS still survive in various libraries:

X Century:

Collectar-Ritual of St. Thierry (Rheims, Biblio. municip., *codex* 304). It includes monastic profession and the *cura circa morientes* and *pro defunctis*.

Collectar-Ritual of Durham (Durham, Chapter Library, *codex* A. IV. 19), ed. H. Thompson-Lindelöf, Surtees Soc. 140 (Durham 1927).

Collectar-Ritual of Vercelli (Vercelli, Biblio. capit., *codex* 178; late X or early XI century). It includes baptism, penance, the *cura circa morientes* and *pro defunctis*.

Ritual of Asti (Paris, Biblio. Mazarine, *codex* 525). Baptism, penance, marriage, *cura circa morientes* and *pro defunctis*.

Collectar-Ritual of Rheims (Rheims, Biblio. munic., *codex* 305). Baptism, monastic profession, *cura circa morientes* and *pro defunctis*, and various blessings.

For the XI-century MSS of this type, see the list established by P.M. Gy, "Collectaire, Rituel, Processional," *Revue des Sciences phil. et théol.* 44 (1960) 455-456.

On occasion, a partial Ritual is associated with certain types of Sacramentaries or Missals containing selected *formulae* for special feasts or circumstances. To this category belong:

Paris, Biblio. Mazarine, *codex* 525. A Ritual + a votive Sacramentary, ed. A. Gastoué, "Un rituel noté de la province de Milan du X siècle," *Rassegna Gregoriana* 2 (1903)137f.

Paris, Biblio. Nat., *codex latinus* 5251 (end of the X century). A Ritual + a festive Missal of St. Martial of Limoges.

Paris, B.N., *Nouv. acquis. codex* 557. A Ritual + festive Missal + festive Breviary.

Several such texts have been gathered together by A. Mundó, "Librorum liturgicorum Cathaloniae s. IX ad XVI" in *Biblio. abbatiae Montisserrati catalogus* (Montserrat 1958) 9.

3. THE PURE RITUAL.

The pure Ritual, i.e., one that is completely independent of other liturgical books (Collectar, Sacramentary, Breviary, Missal), began to appear in the XI century; e.g., the monastic Ritual of Jumièges (Rouen, Biblio. munic., *codex* 395; XI century) and the collection of *ordines* from Northern Italy published by C. Lambot (Milan, Biblio. Ambros., *codex* T. 27. Sup.).[307]

With the XII century, the Ritual began to exist as an automomous liturgical book and, as such, became more and more common in the following centuries.[308] No longer were they *ordines* with references to a Sacramentary or with the mere *incipits* of prayers but contained the prayers themselves *in extenso*. They did not yet bear the title *Rituale*; the more usual names were the following: *baptisterium* (Wissembourg, A.D. 1043: *baptisteria* VI; Becker, *Catalogi* [Bonn 1885] 73 and 171) or *orationale* (inventory of S. Angelo in Formis, near Capua; 2nd half of the XII century: *orationalia, orationalia defunctorum, orationale de benedicenda aqua*; ed. M. Inguanez, *Miscell. Cassinense* 21 [Monte Cassino 1941] 53.

Catalogues or inventories contemporary with the Rituals sometimes provide definitions for the ones they list:

Reginbert of Reichenau (835-842): *In XXVIII libello continentur orationes*
sufficientes ad sepulturam fratrum et orationes per singula monasteria et lectiones vel
tractatus ad vigilias defunctorum (Lehmann, *Mittelalterliche Biblio. Kataloge* 1
[Munich 1918] 261).

Catalogue of Pfafers (1151): *Exorcismus maior* (and not *maioris*) *aquae.*
Baptisteria in quibbus benedictio ferri et aquae et alia continentur et in uno obsequium
mortuorum (Becker, p. 208).

Like its predecessors the Ritual-Collectar and the Ritual-Missal,
until the XII century inclusively, the pure Rituals always show some
sign of monastic influences, even though the rites they contain are
never exclusively monastic in character. There seems to be a double
explanation of this fact: first of all, it was only monasteries that
possessed *scriptoria* and they apparently inserted in the Rituals they
assembled the elements they themselves needed; secondly, throughout the Middle Ages, monks almost always had some connection
with pastoral work.

The most famous XII-century Rituals are the following:

The Ritual of St. Florian ed. A. Franz, *Das Rituale von S. Florian aus dem XII Jhd.*
(Freiburg/Br. 1904);

The Ritual of Rheinau (Zürich, *codex Rh.* 114), ed. G. Hürlimann, *Das*
Rheinauer Rituale, Spicilegium Friburgense 5 (Fribourg 1959).

In the XIII century, the Rituals grow more frequent and more
parish oriented and lose their monastic connections. This fact seems
to be related to the new synodical legislation which ordered pastors
of parishes to own a *Manuale*.

For example: the Statutes of Odo of Sully, bishop of Paris (1200-1208) VII,
4: *Librum qui dicitur Manualis habeant singuli sacerdotes parochiales ubi continetur*
ordo servitii extremae unctionis, catechismi, baptismatis et huiusmodi (PL 27, 63
A);

the Synodical Statues of Fulk Basset, Bishop of London (1245/1259), cap.
54: *Precipimus in virtute obedientie ut quilibet rector ecclesie parochialis et vicarius*
habeat in ecclesia sua librum qui dicitur Manuale in quo contineatur totius ordo officii
sacramentorum que per sacerdotem possunt conferri, scilicet exorcismus salis et aque,
servitium cathecismi et baptismi, sponsaliorum, extreme unctionis, commendationis,
Placebo, Dirige, et servitium selpulture ad usum ecclesie sancti Pauli London' . . .
(edd. F.M. Powicke and C.R. Cheney, *Councils and Synods . . . relating to the*
English Church 2, part 1 [Oxford 1964] 645).

As Rituals multiplied, the Pontifical tended to become a book reserved for bishops exclusively. The *Pontifical* of William Durandus is the most famous example of this work of elimination and specification.[309] Even before his effort, a Pontifical of Meaux had put into an appendix any rites that belonged to presbyters alone.

In the XIV century, diocesan bishops took the place of monasteries in the production of Rituals. In this category stands the Ritual of Bishop Henry I of Breslau (1301-1319), ed. by A. Franz (Freiburg/Br. 1912).

None of the Rituals mentioned above were compiled in any particular order; they were simply a series of *ordines* with the necessary prayers in place. It was not until after the Reformation that the Ritual would be divided into books and chapters.

4. PRINTED RITUALS.

By and large the Rituals that were printed *before the Reformation* kept the same aspect as those that had appeared before the printing press; they also retained a variety of titles: *Agenda* or *Obsequiale* (Germany, before the XVII century), *Manuale* (England, France, Spain until the XVI century), *Rituale* (only in Italy before 1614), *Ordinarium* (Catalonia, S. France).

After the Reformation, under the titles *Liber sacerdotalis*, *Sacerdotale* or *Rituale*, these books came to be arranged more methodically, were divided into books and chapters and were enlarged by pastoral directives in many places. Three Italian editions prepared the way for the official edition of the *Rituale*, in 1614.

1. Albert Castellano (or de Castello or Castellani), *Liber sacerdotalis* (Venice 1523); it became the *Sacerdotale iuxta Sanctae Romanae Ecclesiae ritum* after 1537. It had three sections: sacraments, blessings, processions. This book spread far and wide (Italy, S. and W. of France, Lyons, Basle, Rheims) and after 1545, many diocesan Rituals began to shape themselves along the lines of Castellano's *Rituale*. After the Reformation, certain dubious elements disappeared from the Ritual, vernacular sections began to appear and catechetical concerns manifested themselves.[310]

2. F. Samarino, *Sacerdotale* (Venice 1579). Redone by Angelo Rocca, *Sacerdotale sive sacerdotum thesaurus* (Venice 1593). Based on the Ritual of Castellano.

3. J. A. Santori (Sanctorio), *Rituale sacramentorum Romanum Gregorii XIII* (Rome 1584-1612) 708 pages in 4°. This work was begun by Cardinal Santori in 1578 at the orders of Pope Gregory XIII; it was not completed

until after the death of Santori in 1602. It was a liturgical-didactic production which became the immediate source of the official *Rituale* of 1614.[311]

4. *Rituale Romanum Pauli V P. M. iussu editum* (Rome 1614) This official Ritual was recommended but not imposed on other churches; essentially, it was a somewhat abbreviated version of Santori's voluminous collection. Introduced by the Bull *Apostolicae Sedi* of June 17, 1614, the Roman Ritual did not eliminate the diocesan Rituals all at once. In Italy, its adoption was more rapid, but in France it was not accepted unanimously until 1853[312]; in Spain, it came into general use only at the beginning of the XIX century; in Germany, it established itself through the intermediary of the *Ritual of Constance* (XVII century) which was, for all practical purposes, the *Rituale Romanum*.[313]

NOTES

274. Gregory VII, *Regula canonica (canonicorum)*, codex Vat. lat. 629; 1095-1099): ed. G. Morin, *Études, textes découvertes*, Anecdota Maredsolana, series 2, vol. 1 (Maredsous-Paris 1913) 459-460. This passage deals with a rather futile controversy regarding the number of psalms and readings to be recited during the Office. [According to J. Mabillon, *Annales O.S.B.* 4, Appendix n. 77, the passage is actually taken from words spoken by Hildebrand, the future Gregory VII, at the Lateran council held under Nicholas II May 1, 1059.] In addition to the efforts which produced the Roman Pontifical of the XII century, one can cite as proof of a Roman liturgical renewal after the middle of the XI century, the insertion of feasts of the popes in the sanctoral, unknown in the Frankish books [cf. L. Guérard, "Un fragment de Calendrier romain au moyen-âge." *Mélanges d'archéologie et d'histoire* 13 (1893)169] which according to Bernhold of Constance, were to be celebrated *solemniter ubique cum pleno officio* (*Micrologus*, cap. 43; PL 151, 1010). A complete list of Pontifical MSS, subdivided into families, still needs to be made. See R. Kay, "The twelfth-Century Tournai Pontifical," *Scriptorium* 16 (1962) 239-245; and "A Chalons Pontifical of the Thirteenth Century," *Scriptorium* 19 (1965) 201-213.

275. The XII-Century Roman Pontifical has been edited by M. Andrieu, *Le pontifical romain au moyen-âge*, 1=SeT 86 (Vatican City 1938). The editor indicates the passages borrowed from the RGP by printing them in smaller characters; a simple glance at this edition informs the reader that the RGP provided most of the material contained in the new episcopal book.

276 The MS, Rome, Bibl. Alessandrina, *codex* 173 is an excellent example of what happened to an RGP during the XI century at Rome before the Gregorian liturgists attempted to compile a new book (description in Andrieu, *Les Ordines* 1, 282-287). This allows us to distinguish between the earlier, modest and rather limited adaptation and the later Roman Pontifical of the XII century.

277. This limited geographical area should not be considered insignificant; it includes the hundred bishops who were suffragans of the Pope and would need the new book. The number of bishops under the special jurisdiction of the Roman See would remain the same during the XII and XIII centuries; cf. Albinus and Cencius in Fabre-Duchesne-Mollat, *Le Liber Censuum* 1 (Paris 1905) 243 and 2 (Paris 1915) 104-106.

278. Various unexpected circumstances—exiles and journeys of the popes, who were always in a precarious position at Rome—helped to increase the authority of the Roman customs in the places and countries wherever they happened to find asylum. See the classical histories of the Popes, J. Haller, *Das Papsttum, Idee und Wirklichkeit*, 5 vols. (Stuttgart 1934-53); F.X. Seppelt-C. Löffler, *A Short History of the Popes*, adapted by H.A. Frommelt (St. Louis-London 1932) as well as A. Werminghoff, *Verfassungsgeschichte der deutschen Kirche im Mittelalter* (Leipzig-Berlin 1913) 194-215 for the splendor and influence of the papacy during the XII century. See also F. Kempf, *et al.*, (edd.), *The Church in the Age of Feudalism*, Handbook of Church History 3 (New York 1969) 351-403 and H.G. Beck, *et al.*, (edd.) *From the High Middle Ages to the Eve of the Reformation*, Handbook of Church History 4 (New York 1970) 3-81; D. Knowles–D. Obolensky, *The Middle Ages*, The Christian Centuries 2 (London-New York 1969) 198-234.

279. All of the MSS are described by M. Andrieu, *Le Pontifical romain*, 1, 21-88. F. Combaluzier, "Un pontifical du Mont Saint-Michel (Paris, Bibl. Nat. cod. 14832)," *Millénaire monastique du Mont Saint-Michel* 1 (Paris 1967) 383-398, identifies another from the XIII century.

280. Critical edition, M. Andrieu, *Le Pontifical de la Curie romaine du XIII siècle=Le pontifical romain au moyen âge* 2, SeT 87 (Vatican City 1940).

281. In the edition of the XIII-century book, Andrieu printed the texts taken from the XII-century Pontifical in small characters; all of the formularies were taken from the earlier book, which in turn had borrowed from the RGP.

282. See P.E. Schramm, "Die *Ordines* der mittelalterlichen Kaiserkrönung," *Archiv für Urkundenforschung* 11 (1930) 338-340.

283 See Andrieu, *Le Pontifical* 2=SeT 87, 310f. for the different recensions.

284. Critical edition, M. Andrieu, *Le Pontifical de Guillaume Durand,= Le Pontifical romain au moyen âge* 3, SeT 88 (Vatican City 1940). Tables and indices for the three types of Roman Pontificals, M. Andrieu, *Le pontifical romain au moyen âge* 4, SeT 91 (Vatican City 1941).

285. Andrieu describes mixed or 'contaminated' examples in *Le pontifical* 3, 88-95.

286. Cf. *Le pontifical* 3, 23-283.

287. Cf. *Le pontifical* 3, 4-10.

288. The editor of Durandus' pontifical has carefully indicated all of the sources used by the author.

289. J. Berthelé, "Les instructions et constitutions de G. Durand le spéculateur, d'après le MS de Cessenon," *Mémoires de la section des lettres de*

l'Académie des Sciences et Lettres de Montpellier, ser. 2, vol. 3 (Montpellier 1900-1907) 13-48.

290. In the 1497 edition of the Roman Pontifical, the name of the bishop of Pienza and Montalcino († 1496) was replaced by that of Jacobus de Luciis (Lutiis) but the name of J. Burchard remained. Cf. P. Battifol, "Le Pontifical romain. La tradition du texte du P.R. Les éditions imprimées," *Bulletin d'ancienne littérature et d'archéologie chrétiennes* 2 (1912) 134-140. On J. Burchard, see L. Oliger, "Der päpstliche Zeremonienmeister J. Burchard," *Archiv für elsässischen Kirchengeschichte* 9 (1934) 199-232 and J. Lesellier, "Les méfaits du cérémoniare J. Burchard," *Mélanges de l'École française de Rome* 44 (1927) 11-34

291. The 1485 *Pontifical* is not the only liturgical production of the famous J. Burchard. We owe to him an *Ordo missae secundum consuetudines S.R.E.* or *Ordo servandus per sacerdotem in celebratione missae sine cantu et sine ministris secundum ritum S.R.E.* (Rome 1495, 1498, 1502, 1505). Noted for its detailed rubrics, Burchard's *Ordo* was adapted for inclusion in the *Missale Romanum* (Pius V) of 1570. [This *Ordo* was not for a "private" mass; see article of B. Neunheuser mentioned in note 66 on p. 208]. Along with A.P. Piccolomini, Burchard finished a *Liber caeremonialis S.R.E.* (Papal ceremonial) in 1488 and dedicated it to Innocent VIII; this was only published in 1516 thanks to Cristoforo Marcello; see *infra*, note 295.

292. *Ponificalis ordinis liber* (Rome 1485), letter of dedication to Innocent VII.

293. This fact was recognized by J. Catalani, *Pontificale Romanum Commentariis illustratum*, 3 vols. (Rome 1738; Augsburg 1878; Paris 1850) t. 2, p. 45, while he was commenting on the *Pontifical*. After the discovery of Vat. lat. *codex* 4744 [H. Ehrensberger, *Libri liturgici Bibliothecae apostolicae Vaticanae MSS* (Freiburg/Br. 1897) 530-532] this was forgotten, [thus Dom Baudot, *Le Pontifical* (Paris 1910)]. P. Batiffol has fortunately reminded liturgists of this fundamental equivalence which is so important for our knowledge of the development of the liturgical books.

294. The liturgy of public penance [Ash Wednesday and Holy Thursday] was reintroduced into the *Pontifical* by Clement VIII in the official 1596 edition for historical, not pastoral, reasons.

295. We must distinguish carefully between the *two* types of *Caeremoniale*: 1) the *Caeremoniale episcoporum* or Ceremonial of bishops (the pope excepted), which is a rubrical complement to the *Pontifical* (pontifical vespers, mass in the presence of a bishop, etc., *de mitra, de baculo, de officio ministrorum* at a pontifical mass). The edition of the *Caeremoniale episcoporum* (Rome 1600) promulgated by the Bull *Cum novissime* July 14, 1600 of Clement VIII, relied on the work of the *ceremoniarius* Paris de Grassis, *De caeremoniis cardinalium et episcoporum in eorum diocesibus libri duo* (Rome 1564) = E. Martène, *De ant. Ecclesiae ritibus* 3 (Venice-Bassano 1788) 217f., and was prepared by a commission set up by Gregory XIII in 1582. The *editio typica* of the Ceremonial in use until Vatican II was that of Leo XIII (Regensburg 1886). See the commentaries by J. Catalani, *Caeremoniale*

episcoporum commentariis illustratum, 2 vols. (Rome 1747; Paris 1860); J. Nabuco, "La liturgie papale et l'origine de Cérémonial des évêques," *Miscellanea Mohlberg* 1 (Rome 1948) 283-300, and *Jus Pontificalium. Introductio in Caerem. episcoporum* (Tournai 1956) for bibliography and list of editions; P. Martinucci, *Manuale sacr. caeremon. Pars altera pro episcopis aliisque pontificalium privilegio insignitis* (2nd ed. Regensburg, 2 vols., 1914-1915). 2) the papal *Caeremoniale*, which has no official title, was referred to by Pius XI as the *Liber sacrorum rituum S.R.E.* [*Acta Apostolicae Sedis* 26 (Aug. 15, 1934) 501] and as the *Caeremoniale Romanum* by Pius XII [AAS 38 (Dec. 12, 1945) 97]. It contains the liturgical functions reserved to the pope: *ordines* of papal election and coronation, *ordines* for imperial and royal coronations, the election of cardinals, etc. The papal *Caeremoniale* was derived from the *Liber caeremoniarum Romanae Curiae* (MSS date from the XV century) which stems from the *Caeremoniale* of Cardinal G. Gaetano Stefaneschi composed ca. 1311 at Avignon and revised after 1341 (=Ordo 14 of Mabillon, *Mus. Italicum* 2, 243-443; cf. M. Andrieu, "L'Ordinaire de la Chapelle papale et le card. J.G. Stefaneschi," EL 49 (1935) 230-260). The *Liber caeremoniarum Romanae Curiae* was revised and improved by A.P. Piccolomini and J. Burchard, *Liber Caeremonialis S.R.E.* (1488) and dedicated to Innocent VIII but only published by Cristoforo Marcello, bishop of Corfu, as *Rituum ecclesiasticorum sive sacrarum caeremoniarum S.E.R. libri tres* (Venice 1516), dedicated to Leo X. The latter is the edition which excited the wrath of Paris de Grassis who demanded (letters of April 11 and 25, 1517) that the work be burnt and the pseudo-author (Marcello) chastised; cf. Mabillon, *Iter Italicum*, 2, 587-592=PL 78, 1401-1406. There have been frequent re-editions and a critical edition with copious annotations by M. Dykmans, *L'Oeuvre de Patrizi Piccolomini*, 2 vols., SeT 293-294 (Vatican City 1980-82). On the papal ceremonial see J. Catalani, *Sacrum Caeremoniale sive rituum S.R.E. libri tres*, 2 (Rome 1750-51) which is a reprint of the Marcello edition; F. Ehrle, "Zur Geschichte des päpstlichen Hofzeremoniells im 14 Jhd.," *Archiv für Literatur- und Kirchengeschichte des Mittelalters* 5 (1889) 565-602; F. Wasner, "Fifteenth-Century texts on the Ceremonial of the Papal *legatus a latere*," *Traditio* 14 (1958) 295-358; 16 (1960) 405-416, and "Tor der Geschichte. Beiträge zum päpstlichen Zeremonienwesen im 15. Jahrhundert," *Archivum Historiae Pontificiae* 6(1968) 113-162. Medieval papal ceremonial texts are edited by S.J.P. van Dijk–J.H. Walker, *The Ordinary of Innocent III*, Spicilegium Friburgense 22 (Fribourg 1975); and by B. Schimmelpfennig, *Die Zeremonienbücher der römischen Kurie im Mittelalter*, Bibliothek des deutschen historischen Instituts im Rom 40 (Tübingen 1973). M. Dykmans has edited *Le Cérémonial papal de la fin du moyen âge à la Renaissance*. Bibliothèque de l'Institut historique belge de Rome 24-27. (Brussels–Rome 1977–1985);

296. From the dedication to Innocent VIII of the Piccolomini-Burchard *Pontificalis Ordinis Liber* (Rome 1485)—the two authors did not have time to complete their proposed *Ritual* (*ad simplices sacerdotes*), see *supra*, p. 256.

297. On this edition see P. Batiffol, "Le Pontifical Romain," *Bulletin d'anc. litt. et d'archéol. chrétiennes* 2 (1912) 138.

298. *Pontificale noviter impressum perpulchrisque characteribus diligentissime ornatum* (Lyons-Venice 1511) = Pontifical of Julius II.

299. *Pontificale secundum ritum romanae Ecclesiae emendatum primum a Jacobo de Lutiis, ep. Caiacensi et Joanne Burchardo Romae, typis Steph. Plannck, 1497, cum multis additionibus ex recognitione Fr. Alberti Castellani* (Venice 1520).

300. *Pontificale Romanum Clementis VIII P.M. iussu restitutum atque editum* (Rome 1595) on the title page; 1596 on the introductory Constitution, *Ex quo in Ecclesia Dei.* Clement VIII wanted to do for the Pontifical what Pius V had done for the Missal (*Missale Romanum ex decreto sacrosancti concilii Tridentini restitutum, Pii V P.M. iussu editum,* Romae 1570), and the Breviary (*Breviarium Romanum ex decreto sacros. concilii Trident. restitutum. Pii V P.M. iussu editum,* Romae 1568). The latter came after two unsuccessful attempts at Breviary reform: a) Z. Ferreri, *Hymni novi ecclesiastici iuxta veram metri et latinitatis normam ab patre Clemente VII P.M. ut in divinis quisque eis uti possit approbati,* (Rome 1525)—the breviary properly speaking, announced by the author, never appeared; and b) F. Quignonez, *Breviarium Romanum ex sacra potissimum scriptura et probatis sanctorum historiis collectum et concinnatum* (Rome 1535)—more than 100 editions appeared between 1535 and 1568. A reprint and study of the Quignones Breviary is by W. Legg, HBS 35 and 42 (London 1908-1912); a commentary on the Pontifical in use before Vatican II is J. Nabuco, *Pontificalis Romani expositio iuridico-practica* (Tournai 1963). See W.H. Frere-F.C. Eeles-A. Riley, *Pontifical Services, Descriptive Notes and a Liturgical Introduction,* ACC 3, 4, 8, 12, (London 1920-25). The history of the first printed Pontificals is now available in M. Dykmans, *Le pontifical romain révisé au XV siècle,* SeT 311 (Vatican City 1985).

301. A general introduction to the liturgy of this period can be found in T. Klauser, *A Short History of the Western Liturgy* (Oxford 1979) 117-152; the essays of J.A. Jungmann in his *Pastoral Liturgy* (London-New York 1961) 80-101 *et passim*; T. Klauser, *The Western Liturgy Today* (London 1963); G. Ellard, *The Mass in Transition* (Milwaukee 1956) and N.K. Rasmussen, "Liturgy, Liturgical Arts" chapter in J.W. O'Malley (ed.), *Catholicism in Early Modern History (ca. 1540-1700): A Guide to Research* (St. Louis 1986).

302. See the outline which sketches the development of *Ordines* and pontificals in Table E.

303. The *Rituale* used until the reforms of Vatican II was a liturgical book of mixed or hybrid origin. It contained simultaneously a *Ritual* and a *Pastoral* (liturgically related guidelines for the *cura animarum*). Sometimes the name *Missale* was given to the Ritual from the XIV to XVI centuries since one could often find therein, not only the usual items found in a Ritual, but also a *Canon missae,* certain votive masses and the masses for the Dead. The *Manuale Carnotense* (1490) is called a *Missale* in the preface. Certain *Libri paenitentiales,* supplied with *ordines* for tariff penance, are also *Rituals* designed for the administration of penance.

304. cf. M. Andrieu, "La liturgie et les travaux d'histoire locale," *Revue d'histoire de l'Église de France* (1928) 289-303.—The Ritual is one of the most authentic sources of medieval popular piety. It is beyond the scope of this introduction to list the works which deal with this subject. See the extensive bibliography in H. Bächtold-Stäubli, *Handwörterbuch d. deutschen Aberglaubens*, 10 vols. (Berlin-Leipzig 1927-1942); M. Rumpf, *Religiöse Volkskunde* (Stuttgart 1933); O.A. Erich–R. Beitl, *Wörterbuch der deutschen Volkskunde* (2nd ed. Stuttgart 1955); L.A.Veit–L. Lenhart, *Kirche und Volksfrömmigkeit im Zeitalter des Barock* (Freiburg/Br. 1956); L.A. Veit, *Volksfrommes Brauchtum und Kirche im deutschen Mittelalter* (Freiburg/Br 1936); G. Schreiber, *Forschungen zur Volkskunde* (Münster/Westf. 1933-); A. Franz, *Die Messe im deutschen Mittelalter, Beiträge zur Geschichte der Liturgie und des religiösen Volkslebens* (Freiburg 1902; reprint Darmstadt 1963), and *Die kirchlichen Benediktionen im Mittelalter*, 2 vols. (Freiburg 1909; reprint Graz 1960); H. Dausend, *Germanische Frömmigkeit in der kirchlichen Liturgie* (Berlin 1936).—For France documentation and bibliography are provided in the remarkable work of A. van Gennep, *Manuel de folklore français contemporain*, 8 vols. (Paris 1938-1953). See also A. Bruford, *Gaelic Folktales and Medieval Romances* (Dublin 1969); W.C. Hazlitt, *Faiths and Folklore of the British Isles* (New York 1965); M. Baker, *Folklore and Customs of Rural England* (Totowa, NJ 1974); *Archivio per la raccolta e lo studio delle tradizioni popolari italiane* (Naples 1925–) a quarterly publication.

305. In addition to the works of A. Franz, we are especially indebted to the research of P.M. Gy, J.B. Molin, and G. Hürlimann for the information in this section. A more recent introduction of the history of the *Rituale* is included in J. B. Molin–A. Aussedat-Minivelle, *Répertoire des rituels et processionaux imprimés conservés en France* (Paris 1984).

306. Riculf, bishop of Elna, *Testamentum* (915): "*Orationarios libros II . . . ad aecclesiam consecrandum quaterniones duos, ad visitandum infirmum quaterniones duos, ad ordinationes ecclesiasticas quaternionem unum*" (PL 132, 467 D); Alcuin, *Epistola 65* (PL 100, 234 C).—It is possible that these texts are simple *ordines* provided with the *formulae* of the corresponding rites; the expression *orationarius* indicates a euchological formulary. Perhaps these were extracts from a sacramentary, but more probably from a formulary which included ceremonial indications, thus, a ritual-booklet.

307. C. Lambot, *North-Italian Services of the XI Century*, HBS 67 (London 1931).

308. This point has been elucidated by A. Franz and P.M. Gy in the works cited above.

309. See above, pp. 253-255, on the Pontifical of William Durandus (1293-1295).

310. For diocesan or national *Rituals*, see above pp. 258-260. Note also E. Cattaneo, "Il Rituale Romano de Alberto Castellani," *Miscellanea liturgica in onore di sua Eminenza il Cardinale G. Lercaro* 2 (Rome–New York 1967) 629-647.

311. On Sanctorio's Ritual, see B. Löwenfeld, *Das Rituale des Kardinal Julius*

Antonius Sanctorius. Ein Beitrag zur Entstehungsgeschichte des Rituale Romanum (Munich 1937) and "Die Erstausgabe des Rituale Romanum von 1614" *Zeitschrift für katholische Theologie* 66 (1942) 141-147 The original MS was discovered by Balt. Fischer, "Das Originalmanuskript des Rituale Romanum," *Trierer theologische Zeitschrift* 70 (1961) 244-246; cf. G.J. Sigler, "The Influence of Charles Borromeo on the Laws of The Roman Ritual," *The Jurist* 24 (1964) 119-168; 319-334.

312. Cf. H. Leclercq, "Liturgies, néo-gallicanes, DACL 9 (1930) 1694-1729 and C. Johnson, *Prosper Guéranger (1805-1875): A Liturgical Theologian*, Studia Anselmiana 89 (Rome 1984).

313. See A. Dold, *Die Konstanzer Ritualientexte in ihrer Entwicklung von 1382-1721*, LQF 5-6 (Münster 1923). This is a bibliography of various editions of the Rituals by Kolberg, Freisen, Schönfelder, Stapper and Collin.

APPENDIX II

THE NON-ROMAN WESTERN RITES

Before the Roman liturgy, i.e., the liturgy of the City and of *Italia suburbicaria*, succeeded in implanting itself almost everywhere in Western Europe, several different families of Latin rites existed in the West. Unfortunately, most of them are not well known in their original form since their liturgical books are either lost, heavily Romanized or too late to be of much assistance.

The basic bibliography given below emphasizes source materials and a few foundational studies. The sacramentaries proper to these liturgies are given above, pp. 107-110.

GENERAL DOCUMENTATION

J. A. Assemani, *Codex liturgicus Ecclesiae universalis in XV libros distributus* (incomplete), 13 vols. (Rome 1749-1766; reprint Paris-Leipzig 1902 and Farnborough 1968-1969. This work is still indispensable.

H. A. Daniel, *Codex liturgicus Ecclesiae universae in epitomen redactus*, 4 vols. (Leipzig 1853; reprint of vols 3-4, Hildesheim 1966).

C. E. Hammond, *Liturgies Eastern and Western: Being a Reprint of the Texts either Original or Translated of the most Representative Liturgies of the Church* (Oxford 1878).

R. C. West, *Western Liturgies* (London 1938). ET of the Roman, Ambrosian, Gallican, Mozarabic, Celtic, and Sarum Eucharists.

A. Hänggi-I. Pahl, *Prex Eucharistica: Textus e variis liturgiis antiquioribus selecti*, Spicilegium Friburgense 12 (Fribourg 1968).

E. Lodi, *Enchiridion euchologicum fontium liturgicorum*, Bibliotheca Ephemerides Liturgicae Subsidia 15 (Rome 1979).

In addition to the articles contained in the great encyclopedias: *Dictionaire d'Archéologie chrétienne et de Liturgie* (=DACL), 15 tomes in 30 vols. (Paris 1907-1953) under the editorship of F. Cabrol-H. Leclercq-H. Marrou; *Lexikon für Theologie und Kirche* (=LTK), 2nd ed., 1957- (cf. Balt. Fischer, "Liturgie," LTK 6 (1961) 1092-1095), the catalogues of MSS published by E. Dekkers and K. Gamber and the general histories of the liturgy provided in our introductory bibliography (*supra*,pp. 5-9), we must always have recourse to

the following studies for an overall view of the non-Roman, Western
liturgies:

L. Duchesne, *Origines du culte chrétien. Etude sur la liturgie latine avant
Charlemagne*, (5th ed. Paris 1925), ET *Christian Worship: Its Origin and
Evolution*, trans. M.L. McClure (London 1925);

A. Baumstark, *Comparative Liturgy*, trans. F.L. Cross from B. Botte's 3rd rev.
French ed. (1953) of the original German ed. of 1939 (Westminster, MD–
London 1958);

A.A. King, *Liturgies of the Religious Orders* (London 1955);

_____, *Liturgies of the Past* (London 1959);

_____, *Liturgies of the Primatial Sees* (London 1957);

F. Heiler, *Altkirchliche Autonomie und päpstlicher Zentralismus*, Die katholische
Kirche des Ostens und Westens 2, 1 (Munich 1941).

A. *The Liturgy of North Africa.*

Aside from a few Arian fragments (Rome, *Vat. lat. codex* 5760, fol. 73-74;
early VI century) ed. L. C. Mohlberg, *Sacramentarium Veronense* (Rome 1956)
201, there are no surviving texts of the African liturgy. The non-liturgical
texts relating to African worship have been compiled by F. Cabrol–H.
Leclercq, *Reliquiae liturgicae vetustissima*, Monumenta Ecclesiae Liturgica 1
(Paris 1900-1902) pp. LXXXVIIf. See also G. Morin, "Formules liturgiques
orientales et occidentales aux IV-V siècle," RB 40 (1928) 134-138.

Studies:

E. Schelestrate, *De fide et ritibus Ecclesiae africanae* in *Antiquitates Ecclesiae*
(Rome 1692). Like the studies of Grancolas (Paris 1704), Morcelli (Brixen
1816), and Bunsen (London 1854), this work is inadequate.

F. G. Mone, *Lateinische und griechische Messen aus dem 2 bis 6 Jhd.* (Frankfurt/
Main 1850). French trans. in *Revue catholique de Louvain* 8 (1850-1851) 149f.
In spite of its title, this contains excellent insights on the African liturgy.

F. Probst, "Die afrikanische Liturgie, hauptsächlich nach den Schriften des hl.
Augustinus," *Liturgie des 4 Jhds. und deren Reform* (Münster/Westf. 1893)
272-307.

W. C. Bishop, "The African Rite," JTS 13 (1912) 250-279.

B. Capelle, "Un homéliaire de l'évêque arien Maximen," RB 34 (1922) 81-
108; 40 (1928) 49-86.

F. Cabrol, "Africaine, liturgie," DACL 1 (1924) 591-657.

W. Roetzer, *Des hl. Augustinus Schriften als liturgiegeschichtliche Quelle* (Munich
1930).

A. Schwarze, *Untersuchungen über die aüssere Entwicklung der afrikanische Kirche*
(Leipzig 1892).

F. Heiler, *Altkirchliche Autonomie und päpstlicher Zentralismus* (Munich 1941).

G.G. Willis, *St. Augustine's Lectionary*, ACC 44 (London 1962).

F. van der Meer, *Augustinus de Zielzorger* (Utrecht 1949); ET *Augustine the Bishop*, trans. B. Battershaw–G.R. Lamb (New York–London 1961) chaps. 10-13, 17-19.

V. Saxer, *Vie liturgique et quotidienne à Carthage vers le milieu du III siècle*, Studi di antichità cristiana 29 (Rome 1969).

K. Gamber, "*Ordo Missae Africanae*: der nordafrikanische Messritus zur Zeit des hl. Augustinus," *Römische Quartalschrift* 64 (1969) 139-153.

C. Casati, "La liturgia della Messa al tempo di S. Agostino," *Augustianum* 9 (1969) 484-514.

A. Coppo, "Vita cristiana e terminologia liturgica a Carthagine verso la metà del III secolo," EL 85 (1971) 70-86.

B. *The Liturgy of Gaul.*

This is usually called the Gallican liturgy and refers to the style of worship prevalent in Gaul before the Carolingian reforms.

The surviving sacramentaries (see *supra*, pp. 108) of this rite need to be supplemented by the Merovingian authorities such as Gregory of Tours and the *Statuta Ecclesiae antiqua* (ed. C. Munier, Paris 1958).

1) *Liturgical Documents* (other than Sacramentaries).

a) *Inquisitio de lege ad missam celebrare* (Bobbio Missal, Paris Bibl. Nat. *lat* 13246, fols 292^v-293^v; VIII century) ed. E. A. Lowe, HBS 58 (London 1920) 177-178; A. Wilmart, "Une curieuse instruction liturgique du Missel de Bobbio," *Revue Charlemagne* 2 (1912) 1-16.

b) *Pro quale virtute cantantur omnes cursus*, The Bobbio Missal, HBS 58, 180-181; cf. A. Wilmart, RB 33 (1921) 4, note 1.

c) Germanus of Paris, *Expositio antiquae liturgiae gallicanae*, ed. E.C. Ratcliff, HBS 98 (London 1971). Other editions by E. Martène, *Thesaurus novus anecdotorum* 5 (Paris 1717) 91-100 (=PL 72, 89-98) and J. Quasten, *Expositio antiqua liturgiae gallicanae Germano Parisiensi ascripta*, Opuscula et textus. Series liturgica 3 (Münster/West. 1931). Despite the high authority of A. Wilmart, (DACL 6 (1924) 1049-1102), the *Expositio* may be an authentic work of St. Germanus, bishop of Paris (555-576): cf. A. van der Mensbrugghe, "L'*Expositio missae gallicanae* est-elle de Saint Germain de Paris († 576)?" *Messager de l'Exarchat du Patriarchat russe en Europe occidentale* 8 (1959) 217-249 and "Pseudo-Germanus Reconsidered," *Studia Patristica* 5, TuU 80 (Berlin 1962) 172-184.

d) *Gallican Benedictionals* (collections of episcopal blessings conferred after the *Pater Noster* and before communion):
Benedictionale of Freiburg (Freiburg/Br., Universitätsbibl. *codex* 363; IX

century); ed. M. J. Metzger, *Zwei karolingische Pontifikalien vom Oberrhein* (Freiburg/Br. 1914) 87-92, 18*-25*.

Benedictionale of Freising (Munich, Clm 6430; VIII-IX century); partial ed. W. Dürig, AfL 4 (1956) 223-244; critical edition by R. Amiet, *The Benedictionals of Freising (Munich Bayerische Staatsbibliothek codex lat. 6430)*, HBS 88 (Maidstone, Kent 1974).

Benedictiones gallicanae (Munich, Clm 29163 [6211]; IX–X century); cf. W. Dürig, RB 64 (1954) 168-175.

e) The *Gallican Lectionaries* are listed below (*infra*, pp. 320-326); see also E. Dekkers, *Clavis Patrum latinorum* (2nd ed. Steenbrugge 1961) nos. 1947-1975.

2) Studies

The best overall bibliography is by A. G. Martimort, EL 72 (1958) 446f. See also A. Baumstark, *Comparative Liturgy* (London 1958) 31-51 and H. Leclercq, "Liturgies gallicanes," DACL 6 (1924) 473-596.

Reconstructions of the Gallican Mass:
L. Duchesne, *Christian Worship* (London 1925) 189-227.
H. Lietzmann, *Ordo missae gallicanus*, Kleine Texte 19 (Bonn 1923) 21-29.
W. S. Porter, *The Gallican Rite* (London 1958) 24-53.
K. Gamber, *Ordo antiquus gallicanus*, TPL 3 (Regensburg 1965).
   Origins of the Gallican Liturgy:
E. Griffe, "Aux origines de la liturgie gallicane," *Bulletin de littérature ecclésiastique* 52 (1951) 17-43. A basic article on the Mass in Gaul in the V century.
L. Duchesne, "Sur l'origine de la liturgie gallicane," *Revue d'histoire et de littérature religieuse* 5 (1900) 31-47.
G. Mercati, "Sull'origine della liturgia gallicana," *Antiche reliquie liturgiche*, SeT 7 (Rome 1902) 72-75.
J. Thibaut, *L'ancienne liturgie gallicane: Son origine et sa formation en Provence aux V et VI siècles* (Paris 1929).
F. Cabrol, "Les origines de la liturgie gallicane," *Revue d'histoire ecclésiastique* 26 (1930) 951-962.
R. Cabié, "Les lettres attribuées à saint Germain de Paris et les origines de la liturgie gallicane," *Bulletin de littérature ecclésiastique* 73 (1972) 183-192.
   On the Rite as a whole:
J. Mabillon, *De liturgia gallicana libri tres* (Rome 1685) = PL 72, 99-448.
J. M. Neale–G. H. Forbes, *The Ancient Liturgies of the Gallican Church* (Burntisland 1855-1857).
E. Marchesi, *La liturgie gallicane dans les huit premiers siècles de l'Eglise* (Lyons 1869).
R. Buchwald, *De liturgia gallicana* (Breslau 1898).

P. de Puniet, "La liturgie baptismale en Gaul avant Charlemagne," *Revue des questions historiques* 72 (1902) 382-423.

L. Duchesne, *Christian Worship* (London 1925) 86-105, 151-160; Mass 189-227, baptism 316-327, ordinations 363-375, dedications of churches 407-418.

K. Berg, *Caesarius von Arles als liturgiegeschichtliche Quelle* (Gregorian University 1946), unpublished dissertation.

H. G. J. Beck, *The Pastoral Cure of Souls in South-East France during the 5th Century*, Analecta Gregoriana 51 (Rome 1950).

J. Quasten, "Oriental Influence in the Gallican Liturgy," *Traditio* 1 (1943) 55-78.

C. G. Austin, *The Trinitarian Doctrine in the Gallican Liturgy according to the Missale Gothicum*, (Paris, Institut Catholique 1968), unpublished dissertation.

For the *Neo*-Gallican liturgies of the XVII, XVIII, and XIX centuries see:

H. Leclercq, "Liturgies néo-gallicanes," DACL 9 (1930) 1636-1729.

A. A. King, *Liturgies of the Primatial Sees* (London 1957) 139-153.

G. Fontaine, "Presentation des missels diocésains français du 17 au 19 siècle," LMD 144 (1980) 97-166.

P. Jounel, "Les missels français du 18 siècle," LMD 144 (1980) 91-96.

A. Ward–C. Johnson, "Où en sont les études sur les liturgies de France aux 17, 18, et 19 siècles," EL 96 (1982) 265-270.

F. Brovelli, "Per uno studio dei missali francesi del secolo XVIII: Saggi di analisi," EL 96 (1982) 279-406; 97 (1983) 482-549.

C. Johnson, *Prosper Guéranger (1805-1875): A Liturgical Theologian. An Introduction to his Liturgical Writings and Work*, Studia Anselmiana 89 (Rome 1984), espec. ch. 3.

C. *The Old Spanish Liturgy.*

This liturgy is also called Visigothic or Mozarabic because it was developed and maintained for so long under Visigothic and then Arabic rulers; cf. review by L. Brou, "Liturgie 'Mozarabe' ou liturgie 'hispanique'?" EL 63 (1949) 66-70. This liturgy was abolished by Pope Gregory VII; cf. the Council of Burgos (1080) in C. J. Hefele– H. Leclercq, *Histoire des Conciles* 5 (Paris 1912) 284-285, n. 4, as well as the summaries of studies on the suppresssion of the Mozarabic rite with complete bibliographies in the various "Bulletin(s) de liturgie mozárabe," which appeared in *Hispania Sacra* (=HS) by L. Brou, HS 2

(1949) 466-469; J. M. Pinell, HS 9 (1956) 415; and J. M. de Mora Ontalva, HS 26 (1973) 211.

1) *Liturgical Documents* (other than sacramentaries).

a) *Liber commicus sive lectionarius missae quo Toletana Ecclesia ante annos MCC utebatur*, Anecdota Maredsolana 1 (Maredsous 1893); new and more complete edition by J. Perez de Urbel–A. Gonzales, 2 vols., Monumenta Hispaniae Sacra. Series liturgica 2-3 (Madrid 1940-1955).

b) *Liber Commicus* of the province of Narbonne (VIII-IX century); ed. A. Mundó, "El Commicus palimsest Paris *lat.* 2269: Amb notes sobre litúrgia i manuscrits visigótics a Septimània i Catalunya," Liturgica I, Scripta et documenta 7 (Montserrat 1956) 151-275.

c) *Liber ordinum en usage dans l'église wisigothique et mozarabe d'Espagne du V au XI siècle*; ed. M. Férotin, Monumenta Ecclesiae Liturgica 5 (Paris 1904).

d) *Missale mixtum secundum regulam beati Isidori dictum mozarabes*; ed. A. Ortiz (Toledo 1500) revised by A. Lesley, *Missale mixtum* (Rome 1755) = PL 85.

e) *Oracional visigótico*; ed. J. Vives, Monumenta Hispaniae Sacra 1 (Barcelona 1946). Prayers for the Liturgy of the Hours. Also on the psalm-prayers, *Liber orationum psalmographus: Colectas de Salmos del antiguo Rito Hispanico: Recomposición y edicion critica*; ed. J. M. Pinell, Monumenta Hispaniae Sacra 9 (Barcelona-Madrid 1972). cf. A. Triacca, "Liber orationum psalmographus. A proposito della sua re-composizione e recente edizione critica," EL 87 (1973) 284-300.

f) *Breviarium secundum regulam beati Isidori*; ed. A. Ortiz (Toledo 1502) revised A. Lorenzana, *Breviarium gothicum* (Madrid 1775; reprint Rome 1804) = PL 86. cf. J. M. Pinell, *Hispania Sacra* 10 (1957) 385-427.

g) *Antifonario visigótico mozárabe de la Catedral de León* (X century); edd. J. Vives–A. Fabrega–L. Brou, Monumenta Hispaniae Sacra 5/1 and 5/2 (Madrid-Barcelona 1953-1959). The second of these is a facsimile; cf. *Archivos Leoneses* 8 (1954).

h) *Hymnodia gothica*; ed. C. Blume, *Analecta hymnica medii aevi* 27 (Leipzig 1897).

Himnario sacro liturgico de España; ed. J. Zahonero–L. Casanoves (Alcoy 1957).

The Mozarabic Psalter; ed. J. P. Gilson, HBS 30 (London 1905).

i) *Pasionario hispánico* (VII-XI century), 2 vols; ed. A. Fábrega Grau, Monumenta Hispaniae Sacra 6 (Madrid-Barcelona 1953-55).

j) *Liber misticus de Cuaresima* (*Codex Toledo* 35.2; now Madrid

Bibliotheca Nacional 10110); ed. J. Janini–A. Mundò, Series Liturgica 1 (Toledo 1979).

k) *Liber Ordinum sacerdotal* (*Codex* Silos, Arch. Monastico 3); ed. J. Janini, Studia Silensia 7 (Silos 1981).

2. Studies.

Bibliographies by H. Engberding, "Die spanische-westgotische Liturgie," *Liturgische Zeitschrift* 4 (Regensburg 1931-1932) 155-166, 241-249; L. Brou, "Bulletin de liturgie mozarabe, 1936-1948," HS 2 (1949) 459-484; J. M. Pinell, "Boletín de liturgia hispano-visigótica," HS 9 (1956) 405-427; J. M. de Mora Ontalva, "Nuevo boletín de liturgia hispánica antigua," HS 26 (1973) 209-237; along with the lists provided in the works of J. M. Pinell and A. Triacca mentioned above under e) *Oracional visigótico*, contain an almost complete listing of studies devoted to the Old Spanish Liturgy. See also H. Ashworth, "Dom Louis Brou, OSB (1898-1961). Obituary and Bibliography," EL 75 (1961) 356-361.

F. Cabrol, "Liturgie mozarabe," DACL 12 (1935) 390-491.

Moraleda y Estaban, *El rito mozárabe* (Toledo 1904).

W. C. Bishop, *The Mozarabic and Ambrosian Rites* (London 1924), this was re-edited by C. L. Feltoe and appeared under the same title in Alcuin Club Tracts 15 (London 1940).

A. A. King, *Notes on the Catholic Liturgies* (London 1930) 249-321.

G. Prado, *Manual de liturgia hispano-visigótica o mozárabes* (Madrid 1927).

_____, *Historia del rito mozárabe y Toledano* (Silos 1928).

_____, *Textos ineditos de la liturgia mozárabes* (Madrid 1926).

W. S. Porter, "Early Spanish Monasticism," *Laudate* 10 (1932) 2-14, 66-79, 156-167; 11 (1933) 199-207; 12 (1934) 31-52; the last two articles are specifically devoted to monastic liturgy.

_____, "Studies in the Mozarabic Office, 1: The Verona Orationale and the León Antiphoner," JTS 35 (1934) 266-286.

_____ "Cantica Mozarabici Officii," EL 49 (1935) 126-145.

A. Baumstark, "Orientalisches in altspanischer Liturgie," *Oriens Christianus* 3rd series 10 (1935) 3-37.

L. Brou, "Liturgie 'Mozarabe' ou liturgie 'Hispanique'?" EL 63 (1949) 66-70.

J. M. Pinell, "Las *Missae*, grupos de cantos y oraciones en el officio de la antigua liturgia hispanica," *Archivos Leoneses* 8 (1954) 145-185.

_____, "El oficio hispano-visigótico," *Hispania Sacra* 10 (1957) 385-427.

———, "Los textos de la antigua liturgia hispanica," *Estudios sobre la Liturgia Mozárabe*, ed. J. F. Rivera Recio (Toledo 1965) 109-164; the whole volume is a valuable contribution to the topic.

J. A. Jungmann, "The pre-monastic Morning Hour in the Gallo-Spanish Region in the 6th century," *Pastoral Liturgy* (London 1962) 122-157.

D. M. Randel, *The Responsorial Psalm Tones for the Mozarabic Office*, Princeton Studies in Music 3 (Princeton 1969); *An Index to the Chant of the Mozarabic Rite*, Princeton Studies in Music 6 (Princeton 1973).

T. C. Akeley, *Christian Initiation in Spain c. 300-1100* (London 1967). Review by B. de Gaiffier, *Analecta Bollandiana* 87 (1969) 473-474.

D. *The Celtic Liturgy.*

This is the ancient liturgy of the British Isles, Galicia, and Brittany before these churches gradually adopted the calendar and liturgy of Rome: Galicia accepted Roman dating at the Council of Toledo in 633; S. Ireland adhered to the Roman order in 636; Northumbria in 664 at the Synod of Whitby; N. Ireland in 696 at the Synod of Birr; N. Wales ca. 750 and S. Wales some time later; Devon and Cornwall preferred their own ways until the X century; Brittany was ordered to conform to Roman usages by Louis the Pious in 818; Scotland held out until the X century and it was only in the time of the saintly Margaret of Scotland that it fully conformed to the Roman liturgy late in the XI century. Cf. N.K. Chadwick, *The Age of the Saints in the Early Celtic Church* (London 1961) 126-140.

1) *Liturgical Documents.*

a) The Stowe Missal (Dublin, Library of the Royal Irish Academy, *codex* D. II. 3: late VIII century and later interpolations; originated at Tallaght in Leinster, near Dublin); ed. with facsimiles, G. F. Warner, HBS 31-32 (London 1906-1915); cf. B. MacCarthy, "On the Stowe Missal," *Royal Irish Academy Transactions* 27 (1886) 135-268, and T. F. O'Rahilly, "The History of the Stowe Missal," *Eriu* 10 (1926) 95-109.

b) The St. Gall Fragments (Stiftsbibliothek, *codices* 1394 and 1395; VIII-IX century); ed. F. E. Warren, *The Liturgy and Ritual of the Celtic Church* (Oxford 1881).

c) H. M. Bannister, ed., "Liturgical Fragments. A) Anglo-Saxon

Sacramentaries," JTS 9 (1907-08) 398-411; and "Fragments of an Anglo-Saxon Sacramentary," JTS 12 (1910-11) 451-454.

d) The *Murbach Fragments* (Colmar, Bibl. mum, *codex* 144; VIII century); ed. L. Brou, *Bulletin de Littérature ecclésiastique* 56 (1955) 65-71. These are fragments of an Irish Pontifical.

e) The *Antiphonary of Bangor* (Ulster; 680/691), 2 vols; ed. F. E. Warren, HBS 4, 10 (London 1893, 1895); M. Curran, *The Antiphonary of Bangor and the Early Irish Office* (Dublin 1984).

f) The *Computation* of Sillan Moccu Min, the abbot of Bangor, (†610); cf. P. Grosjean, *Analecta Bollandiana* 64 (1946) 215f.

g) *The Irish Liber Hymnorum*, edd. J. H. Bernard–R. Atkinson, HBS 13-14 (London 1898).

h) *The Irish Penitentials*; ed. L. Bieler, Scriptores Latini Hiberniae 5 (Dublin 1963).

i) *The Martyrology of Oengus the Culdee*; ed. W. Stokes, HBS 29 (London 1905, reprint Dublin 1985).

j) *The Psalter and Martyrology of Ricemarch*, 2 vols; ed. H. J. Lawlor, HBS 47-48 (London 1914).

k) For the *Loricae* or breastplates recited to ward-off danger see DACL 9 (1930) 2515 and L. Bieler, *The Works of St. Patrick*, ACW 17 (London 1953) 67-72.

2) Studies.

W. Delius, *Geschichte der irischen Kirche* (Münster/Westf. 1954).

F. E. Warren, *The Liturgy and Ritual of the Celtic Church* (Oxford 1881).

L. Gougaud, *Christianity in Celtic Lands* (London 1932).

———, "Celtiques, liturgies," DACL 2 (1925) 2969-3032.

H. Zimmer, "Ueber die Bedeutung des irischen Elements für die mittel-alterliche Kultur," *Historisches Jahrbuch* 59 (1939) 31f.

G. Manz, "Wisigotische Orationen in irischen Messbücher," *Ausdrucksformen* (Beuron 1941) 23-25.

J. F. Kenney, *The Sources for the Early History of Ireland. 1: Ecclesiastical* (New York 1929; reprint New York–Dublin 1966).

J. Hennig, "The Feast of All Saints in Europe," *Speculum* 21 (1946) 49-66.

———, "Studies in the Liturgy of the Early Irish Church," *Irish Ecclesiastical Record* 75 (1951) 318-333.

———, "Studies in the Literary Tradition of the *Martyrologium Poeticum*," *Proceedings of the Royal Irish Academy* 56 (1954) 197-226. *Opera* of Hennig in E. V. Severus, "Rückwärts schauen und vorwärts blicken. Zur Bibliographie Dr. phil. h. c. John Hennig. Nachträge und Erganzung," AfL 19 (1977) 98-105.

B. Capelle, "Alcuin et l'histoire du symbole de la messe," *Recherches de théologie ancienne et médiévale* 6 (1934) 249-260.
A. A. King, "The Celtic Rite," *Liturgies of the Past* (London 1959) 186-275.
J. Ryan, "The Mass in the Early Irish Church," *Studies, an Irish Quarterly Review* 50 (1961) 371-384.
H. B. Swete, *Church Services and Service Books before the Reformation*, rev. ed. A. J. Maclean (London-New York 1930).

E. The Ambrosian or Milanese Liturgy.

1) Documents (other than the sacramentaries).

A. M. Ceriani, *Notitia liturgiae Ambrosianae ante saeculum XI medium* (Milan 1895).
M. Magistretti, *Beroldus sive Ecclesiae Ambrosianae Kalendarium et ordines saec. XII* (Milan 1894, reprint Farnborough 1968).
————, *Pontificale in usum Ecclesiae Mediolanensis necnon ordines ambrosiani ex codicibus saec. IX-XV*, Monumenta veteris liturgiae ambrosianae 1 (Milan 1897).
————, *Manuale Ambrosianum ex codici saec. XI olim in usu Canonicae Vallis Travaliae*, Monumenta veteris liturg. ambros. 2-3 (Milan 1904-1905).
G. Mercati, *Antiche reliquie liturgiche ambrosiane e romane*, SeT 7 (Rome 1902).
Antiphonale Ambrosianum = *Paléographie musicale* 5 (Solesmes 1896).
A. Paredi, "L'Evangeliario di Busto Arsizio," *Miscellanea liturgica in onore di Sua Em. il cardinale G. Lercaro* 2 (Rome 1967) 207-249.
For other Ambrosian MSS see *Archivio Ambrosiano* 2 (1950) 79-88. For the calendars see O. Heiming, "Die ältesten ungedruckten Kalender der Mailändischen Kirche," *Colligere Fragmenta* = *Festschrift Alban Dold . . .* , ed. B. Fischer–V. Fiala, TuA I, Abteilung, Beiheft 2 (Beuron 1952) 214-235. For the *Praefationale* see O. Heiming, AfL 1 (1950) 128-132.

2) Studies.

E. G. C. F. Atchley, *The Ambrosian Liturgy* (London 1909).
W. C. Bishop–F. C. Feltoe, *The Mozarabic and Ambrosian Rites*, Alcuin Club Tracts 15 (London 1924).
P. Borella, "Influssi carolingi e monastici sul Messale Ambrosiano," *Miscellanea Mohlberg* 1 (Rome 1949) 73-115.
————, "Rito Ambrosiano antico e sue variazioni locali," EL 61 (1948) 369-374.
————, in M. Righetti, *Storia liturgica* 3 (Milan 1966) 508-516.
————, in *Archivio Ambrosiano* 2 (1950) 79-203.
————, "Materia e forma dell'Estrema Unzione nell'antico rito ambrosiano," *Ambrosius* 20 (1944) 13-18.

———, "Gli esorcismi nel battesimo e nell'Estrema Unzione," *Ambrosius* 20 (1944) 40-45.

———, "L'orazione e l'imposizione delle mani nell'Estrema Unzione," *Ambrosius* 20 (1944) 49-57.

These last three articles were reprinted in M. Righetti, *Manuale di storia liturgica* 4: *Sacramenti* (2nd ed. Milan 1959) 597f and in *Ambrosius* 38 (1962) 89-95; 153-161.

———, "L'evoluzione dei riti sacramentali nell'antica liturgia ambrosiana," *Liturgie, Gestalt und Vollzug* (Munich 1963) 48-59.

———, *Il rito ambrosiano*, Brescia, Biblioteca di scienze religiose, sez. 3 (Brescia 1964); this book contains the best available bibliography.

A. Paredi, *I prefazi ambrosiani* (Milan 1937).

———, La liturgia di San Ambrogio," *Sant'Ambrogio nel XVI centenario* (Milan 1940) 71-157.

———, "Influssi orientali sulla liturgia milanese antica," *Scuola cattolica* 68 (1940) 574-579.

———, "Messali ambosiani antichi," *Ambrosius* 4 (1959) 1-25.

C. Coebergh, "Tre antiche anafore della liturgia di Milano," *Ambrosius* 29 (1953) 219-232.

H. Frank, "Das Mailandische Kirchenjahr in den Werken des hl. Ambrosius," *Pastor Bonus* 51 (1940) 40f.

F. Heiler, *Altkirchliche Autonomie und päpstlicher Zentralismus* (Munich 1941) 91f.

J. Schmitz, *Gottesdienst im altchristlichen Mailand*, Theophaneia 25 (Cologne 1975).

A. M. Triacca, *I prefazi ambrosiani del ciclo 'De tempore' secondo il Sacramentarium Bergomense* (Rome 1970).

———, "Per una migliore ambientazione delle fonti liturgiche ambrosiane. Note metodologiche," *Fons Vivus: Miscellanea liturgica in memoria di E. M. Vismara* (Zürich-Rome 1971) 163-220.

———, "L'Unzione degli ammalati presso l'antica liturgia ambrosiana," *Eulogia: Miscellanea liturgica in onore di B. Neunheuser*, Studia Anselmiana 68 (Rome 1979) 509-590.

———, "In margine al Sacramentario Gregoriano recentemente edito," EL 87 (1973) 415-433.

A. A. King, *Liturgies of the Primatial Sees* (London 1957) 286-456.

F. *The Rite of Aquileia* (suppressed in 1594/1595).

This rite was connected with the Milanese Liturgy.

Missale Aquileyensis Ecclesie (Venice 1519, reprint Brussels 1963).

A. De Rubeis, *De antiquis Foroiuliensium ritibus* (Venice 1754).

R. Althan, *Iter liturgicum Foroiuliense* (Rome 1749).

———, *De calendariis* (Venice 1753).

E. Dichlich, *Rito veneto antico detto Patriarchino* (Venice 1823).

A. Baumstark, *Liturgia Romana e Liturgia dell'Esarcato: Il rito detto in seguito Patriarchino* (Rome 1904).

H. B. Porter, "Maxentius of Aquileia and the North Italian Baptismal Rites," EL 69 (1955) 5f.

P. Paschini, *Sulle origini della chiesa di Aquileia* (Udine 1909).

F. Spessot, "I codici liturgici aquileiesi di Gorizia," *Studi Goriziani* 7 (1930).

_____, "I codici liturgici della Basilica aquileiese," *Aquileia nostra* 3 (1932).

For more bibliography, see G. Vale, EL 65 (1951) 113f; CLLA 287-291, 397-407.

G. *The Rite of Ravenna.*

F. Cabrol, "Autour de la liturgie de Ravenne," RB 23 (1906) 489-500.

E. Caronti, "Liturgia Ravennate del IV-V sec.," *Revista diocesana di Ravenna e Cervia* 13 (1922) 27-32.

A. Baumstark, *Liturgia Romana e Liturgia dell'Esarcato* (Rome 1904).

K. Gamber, "Der *Ordo Romanus IV*, ein Dokument der ravennatischen Liturgie des 8. Jhds.," *Römische Quartalschrift* 66 (1971) 154-170.

_____, *Sakramentartypen*, 43-46; CLLA 295-330.

S. Benz, *Der Rotulus von Ravenna nach seiner Herkunft und seiner Bedeutung für die Liturgiegeschichte kritisch untersucht*, LQF 45 (Münster/Westf. 1967).

H. *The Beneventan Rite.*

K. Gamber, "Die mittelitalienisch-beneventanischen Plenarmissalien," SE 9 (1957) 265-285.

_____, *Sakramentartypen*, 64-73; CLLA 238-258, 465-467.

R. J. Hesbert, "L'*Antiphonale missarum* de l'ancien rit bénéventain," EL 52 (1938) 28-66, 141-158; 53 (1939) 168-190; 59 (1945) 69-95; 60 (1946) 103-141; 61 (1947) 153-210.

_____, ed., *Graduel bénéventain: Le Codex 10673 de la Bibliothèque Vaticane, fonds latin. XI siècle*, Paléographie Musicale 14 (Tournai 1931-36; reprint Berne 1971).

S. Rehle, "*Missale Beneventanum (Codex VI. 33 des erzbischöflichen Archivs von Benevent)*," SE 21 (1972-73) 323-405.

_____, ed. *Missale Beneventanum von Canosa*, TPL 9 (Regensburg 1972).

A. Odermatt, *Ein Rituale im beneventanischer Schrift. Roma, Biblioteca Vallicelliana, Codex C. 32, Ende des XI Jhdts.*, Spicilegium Friburgense 26 (Fribourg 1980).

I. *Medieval English Rites/Uses.*

A. A. King, "English Medieval Rites," *Liturgies of the Past* (London-Milwaukee 1959) 276-374.

R.W. Pfaff, *New Liturgical Feasts in Later Medieval England* (Oxford 1970); *Medieval Latin Liturgy. A Select Bibliography* (Toronto-Buffalo-London 1982), "English Liturgy," pp. 103-109.

J. *The Rite of Nidaros* (Trondheim).

A. A. King, "Rite of Nidaros," *Liturgies of the Past* (1959) 375-466.
H. Faehn, *Manuale norvegicum*, Libri liturgici provinciae nidrosiensis medii aevi 1 (Oslo 1962).
L. Gjerlöw, *Ordo nidrosiensis ecclesiae*, Libri liturgici prov. nidros. med. aevi 2 (Oslo 1968).
_____, *Antiphonarium nidrosiensis ecclesiae*, Libri liturg. prov. nidros. med. aevi 3 (Oslo 1979).
_____, *Liturgica islandica*, 2 vols. Bibliotheca Arnamagnaeana 35-36 (Copenhagen 1980).

K. *Medieval German Rites.*

H. Reifenberg, "Gottesdienst in den Kirchen des deutschen Sprachgebietes. Bestand und Wünsche wissenschaftlicher Bemühungen um die teilkirchliche Liturgie im Laufe eines Jahrhunderts," AfL 22 (1981) 30-92. A very important repertory for the study of local diocesan liturgies in German-speaking and neighboring countries.

L. *Monastic Rites.*

For the specialized liturgies of the monastic orders, see:
E. Martène, *De antiquis monachorum ritibus libri quinque* (Paris 1690) = *De antiquis ecclesiae ritibus* 4.
A. A. King, *Liturgies of the Religious Orders* (London-New York-Toronto 1955).
K. Hallinger, ed. *Corpus Consuetudinum Monasticarum* (Siegburg 1963-). 10 vols. have appeared as of 1983.
J. B. Tolhurst, *Introduction to the English Monastic Breviaries* = *The Monastic Breviary of Hyde Abbey, Winchester* 6, HBS 80 (London 1942).
P. Tirot, "Un '*Ordo Missae*' monastique: Cluny, Cîteaux, La Chartreuse," EL 95 (1981) 44-120 and 220-251; reprinted as *Bibliotheca Ephemerides Litugicae Subsidia* 24 (Rome 1981).

1) *Carthusians*:

A. Degand, "Chartreux, Litugies des," DACL 3 (1924) 1045-1071; A. A. King, *Liturgies of the Religious Orders* (London 1955) 1-61; and A. Gruys, *Cartusiana. Un instrument heuristique. A Heuristic Instrument. Ein heuristischer Apparat.* Vol 1: *Bibliographie générale* (Paris 1976) provide a useful introduction.

a) *Documents*.

Guigonis Carthusiae Maioris, prioris quinti (†1137), Consuetudines (ca. 1127), called the *Consuetudines Guigonis* = PL 153, 631-760.

Statuta Jancelini (ca. 1222) by Jancelinus, prior of the Chartreuse. Unpublished.

Consuetudines Carthusiae or *Statuta Antiqua* (1259). A combination the *Consuetudines Guigonis* and the *Statuta Jancelini* (Basel 1510).

Libellus declarationis tam confirmationum quam caeremoniarum Ordinis Cartusiensis, Boniface Ferrer (Prior General of the Carthusians, 1402-1410) Unpublished.

b) *Studies*.

E. M. Thompson, *The Carthusian Order in England*, Church Historical Publications, New Series 3 (London 1930).

J. Hourlier–B. Du Moustier, "Le Calendrier cartusien," *Études grégoriennes* 2 (1957) 151-161.

R. Etaix, "L'Homiliaire cartusien," SE 13 (1962) 67-112.

J. Hogg, ed. *Mittelalterliche Caerimonialia der Kartäuser*, Analecta Cartusiana 2 (Salzburg 1971).

————, *Late Fifteenth-Century Rubrics for the Deacon and the Sacristan from the MS Valsainte 42/T.I.8*, Analecta Cartusiana 4 (Salzburg 1971).

H. Becker, *Die Responsorien der Kartäuserbreviers: Untersuchungen zu Urform und Herkunft des Antiphonars der Kartäuse*, Münchener theologische Studien, II. Systematische Abteilung 39 (Munich 1971).

2) *Cluniacs*:

The following contain much information that is useful for the study of the liturgy at Cluny and its several priories: A. Wilmart, "Cluny," DACL 3 (1925) 2074-2092; G. de Valous, *Le monachisme clunisien*, 3 vols. (Ligugé-Paris 1935-38); L. H. Champly, *Histoire de l'abbaye de Cluny* (3rd ed. Paris 1939): "Cluny," *Dictionnaire d'Histoire et de Géographie ecclésiastique* 13 (1956) 35-174.

a) *Documents*.

Consuetudines Cluniacenses antiquiores; ed. B. Albers, Consuetudines Monasticae 2 (Monte Cassino 1905).

Ordo Cluniacenses per Bernardum saeculi XI scriptorem; ed. M. Herrgott, *Vetus Disciplina Monastica* (Paris 1726) 133-364.

Liber tramitis aevi Odilonis abbatis; ed. K. Hallinger, Corpus Consuetudinum Monasticarum 10 (Siegburg 1983).

Udalric, *Consuetudines Cluniacenses*, PL 149, 643-778.

Several monasteries reformed by the Cluniacs adopted the Customary of Cluny: the following are especially important for the liturgical information they contain:
Consuetudines Farfenses (XI century; Farfa, Italy); ed. B. Albers, Consuetudines Monasticae 1 (Stuttgart 1899).
Consuetudines Hirsaugenses (drawn up under the orders of Abbot William the Blessed of Hirschau [1065-1091] ca. 1080); ed. M. Herrgott, *Vetus Disciplina Monastica* (Paris 1726) 36-132 = PL 150.

b) Studies.

B. Albers, "Le plus ancien coutumier de Cluny," RB 20 (1903) 174-184.
C.J. Bishko, "Liturgical Intercession at Cluny for the King Emperors of León," *Studia Monastica* 3 (1961) 53-76.
K. J. Conant, *Cluny: les églises et la maison du chef d'ordre* (Macôn 1968).
J. Evans, *Monastic Life at Cluny, 950-1157* (Oxford 1931).
N. Hunt, *Cluny under St. Hugh, 1049-1109.* (Notre Dame, IN 1967).
R. Etaix, "Le Lectionnaire de l'office à Cluny," *Recherches augustiennes* 11 (1976) 91-159.
K. Hallinger, "Liturgisch-monastische Gegensätze zwischen Gorze und Kluny," *Gorze-Kluny* 2, Studia Anselmiana 24-25 (Rome 1951) 869-983.
_____, "Klunys Bräuche zur Zeit Hugos des Grossen (1049-1109)," *Zeitschrift für Savigny-Stiftung*, Kanonistische Abteilung 45 (1955) 99-140.
_____, "Überlieferung und Steigerung in Mönchtum des 8. bis 12. Jahrhunderts," *Studia Anselmiana* 68 (1979) 125-187.
J. Hourlier, "Le Bréviaire de Saint-Taurin: Un livre liturgique clunisien à l'usage de l'Echelle-Saint-Aurin," *Études grégoriennes* 3 (1959) 163-173.
D. Knowles, "The Monastic Horarium, 970-1120," *Downside Review* 51 (1933) 706-725.
V. Leroquais, *Le Bréviaire-Missel du prieuré clunisien de Lewes* (Paris 1935).
R. Monterosa, "Canto gregoriano e riforma tra Cluniacensi e Cistercensi," *Chiesa e riforma nella spiritualità del sec. XI*, Convegni del centro di studi sulla spiritualità medievale 6 (Todi 1968) 191-219.
P. Schmitz, "La Liturgie de Cluny," *Spiritualità cluniacense*, Convegni del centro di studi sulla spiritualità medievale 2 (Todi 1960) 83-99, a popular survey.

3) Cistercians:

a) Documents.

The MS of Dijon, Bibliothèque municipale, *codex* 114 (82) (ca. 1173-1191) contains all the liturgical books used by the Cistercians:
Breviarium, Epistolare, Textus evangeliorum, Missale, Collectaneum,

Kalendarium, Regula, Consuetudines or *Liber usuum* (which includes the *Liber usuum* or *Ecclesiastica officia, Institutio generalis capituli, and the Usus conversorum)*, *Psalterium, Cantica, Hymnarium, Antiphonarium, Gradale.*

This MS is available on microfiche from CIPOL, 4 Avenue Vavin, F-75006 Paris.

The *Annalia* (or *Statuta) capituli generalis* (1157-1786) contained in the two MSS of Lucerne (Staatsarchiv, *codex*. H. 544) and Paris (Bibliothèque de l'Arsenal, *codex* 926) were partially edited by E. Martène, *Thesaurus novus anecdotorum* 4, 1244f.

b) Studies.

J. Agricola, *Caeremoniale divini offici sacris Ordinis Cisterciensis usibus et definitionibus accomodatum,* (1648) = *Cistercienser-Chronik* 15 (1903) 23f.

R. Trilhe, "Cîteaux, liturgie de l'ordre de," DACL 3 (1925) 1779-1811.

_____, *Mémoire pour le cérémonial cistercien* (Toulouse 1900).

G. Müller, "Zur Geschichte unseres Rituals," *Cistercienser-Chronik* 4 (1892) 342 f.

J. M. Canivez, "Le rite cistercien," EL 63 (1949) 276-311.

A. A. King, *Citeaux and her Elder Daughters* (London 1954).

_____, "The Cistercian Rite," *Liturgies of the Religious Orders* (London 1955) 62-156.

B. Schneider, "Cîteaux und die benediktinische Tradition," *Analecta S. O. Cisterciensium* 16 (1960) fasc. 3-4; 17 (1961) fasc. 1-2 = sources of the *Liber Usuum.*

B. Backaert, "L'Évolution du calendrier cistercien," *Collectanea ordinis Cisterciensium reformatorum* 12 (1950) 81-94, 302-316; 13 (1951) 108-27.

B. Lackner, "The Liturgy of Early Citeaux," *Studies in Medieval Cistercian History* 1, ed. J. F. O'Callaghan, Cistercian Studies 13 (Spencer, MA 1971) 1-34.

C. Waddell, "The Early Cistercian Experience of Liturgy," *Rule and Life: An Interdisciplinary Symposium,* ed. M. B. Pennington, Cistercian Studies 12 (Spencer, MA 1971) 77-116.

4) Premonstratensians, Carmelites, Franciscans and Dominicans:

A. A. King, *Liturgies of the Religious Orders* (London 1955) 157-234.

See also the list in R. C. Pfaff, *Medieval Latin Liturgy: A Select Bibliography* (Toronto 1982) 96, 99-101.

M. *The Uses of Lyons and Braga.*

A. A. King, *Liturgies of the Primatial Sees* (London-New York-Toronto 1957).

R. Amiet, *Inventaire général des livres liturgiques du diocèse de Lyon* (Paris 1979).

D. Buenner, *L'ancienne liturgie romaine: Le rite lyonnais* (Lyons 1934; reprint Farnborough 1969).

M. Bernard, "Un Missel manuscrit de Saint-Nizier de Lyon (Ecole des Beaux-Arts, coll. Masson 121; fin XV siècle)," *Études grégoriennes* 10 (1969) 117-124.

J. O. Bragança "A Liturgia de Braga," *Miscellànea en Memoria de D. M. Férotin* (Madrid-Barcelona 1965) 259-281.

_____, "O Santoral do 'Missal de Mateus'," *O Distritto de Braga* 4 (1967) 1-52.

_____, "Preces galicanas no Missal de Braga," *Lusitania sacra* 7 (1964/66) 217-236.

_____, "O '*Ordo Missae*' de Braga," *O Distritto de Braga* 5 (1968) 1-34.

_____, "Die '*Benedictiones episcopales*' des Pontifikale von Coimbra (Porto, Municipal Library, *codex* 353," *Aufsätze zur portugiesischen Kulturgeschichte* 6 (1966) 7-27.

_____, *Missal de Mateus*. Manuscrito 1000 de la biblioteca pública e arquivo distrital de Braga (Lisbon 1975).

VII. THE LITURGICAL READINGS

A. PRELIMINARIES.

In addition to its ceremonial and ritual aspects, Christian worship includes another essential element: the reading of the Holy Scriptures and preaching. For Christian believers, God is present in the act of worship (especially in the eucharistic *actio*) and in the Word that is announced and proclaimed. In the Christian liturgy Word and Sacrament are inseparable and probably from the very beginning the Liturgy of the Word and the Liturgy of the Table were brought together in a single *actio liturgica*.[1]

In this chapter we shall consider the reading of Scripture as it appears in the context of the eucharistic liturgy.[2] The lessons included in the Liturgy of the Hours demand special treatment elsewhere while the act of preaching raises peculiar problems of its own.[3]

1. STUDIES.

Since the XVI century, historians have been attracted to the study of the origin, purpose and organization of the liturgical readings.[4] In spite of this early interest, however, it has only been since the mid-XIX century that such investigations have been pursued scientifically. Besides the articles appearing in the major encyclopedias, the following studies will prove helpful:

E. Ranke, *Das kirchliche Pericopensystem aus den ältesten Urkunden der römischen Liturgie* (Berlin 1847).
S. Beissel, *Entstehung der Perikopen des römischen Messbuches*, Ergänzungshefte z. d. Stimmen aus Maria-Laach 96 (Freiburg/Br. 1907; reprint Rome 1967).
_____, *Geschichte der Evangelienbücher* (same series, 92 and 93) (Freiburg/Br. 1906).
G. Godu, "Épîtres," DACL 5 (1922-1923) 245-344.
_____, "Évangiles," DACL 5, 852-923. Excellent articles based on a plan worked out by A. Wilmart, EL 51 (1937) 136, 2.
R. J. Hesbert, "La liturgie bénéventaine dans la tradition manuscrite," *Paléographie musicale* 14 (1931) 60-465.

W. H. Frere, *Studies in Early Roman Liturgy*. 1. *The Kalendar*. 2. *The Roman Gospel Lectionary*. 3. *The Roman Epistle Lectionary*, ACC 28, 30, 32 (Oxford-London 1930, 1934, 1935).

T. Klauser, *Das römische Capitulare Evangeliorum*. 1. *Typen* (the only vol. to appear), LQF 28 (Münster/Westf. 1935). This basic work sets out the state of the question and provides a bibliography. It analyzes more than 1300 MSS.

G. Kunze, *Die Gottesdienstliche Schriftlesung*. 1. *Stand u. Aufgabe der Perikopenforschung* [the only vol. to appear] (Göttingen 1947).

A. Chavasse, "Les plus anciens types du lectionnaire et de l'antiphonaire romain de la messe," RB 62 (1952) 1-91.

————, "Le calendrier dominical romain au VI siècle. L'épistolier et l'homéliaire prégrégoriens," *Recherches de science religieuse* 38 (1951/1952) 234-246; 41 (1953) 96-122. Basic articles to orient one's research.

S. J. P. van Dijk, "The Bible in Liturgical Use," in G. W. H. Lampe (ed.), *The Cambridge History of the Bible* 2 (Cambridge 1969) 220-252; 520-521.

A. Dold, "Das Donaueschinger Comes-Fragment B. II. 7, ein neuer Text-Zeuge f. d. Alt-überlieferte Feier der Stations-festage Mittwoch und Freitag. Zugleich ein Beitrag z. Geschichte der Sonn-u. Stations-Festags-perikopen in der Zeit von Pfingsten bis zum Advent," JfL 6(1926) 16-53.[5]

————, *Vom Sakramentar, Comes und Capitulare zum Voll-Missale* [on *Cassinensis* 271]. *Mit Beitragen von A. Baumstark*, TuA 34 (Beuron 1943).

In addition to the works just cited, one should consult the numerous articles published by G. Morin (1861-1946), A. Wilmart (1876-1941), A. Dold (1882-1960) and K. Gamber.[6]

Briefer studies of the Liturgy of the Word may be found in:

A. Baumstark, *Comparative Liturgy* (London-Westminster, MD 1958) 111-129.

H. Chirat, *L'assemblée chrétienne à l'âge apostolique*, Lex orandi 10 (Paris 1949) 74-90.

J. A. Jungmann, *The Mass of the Roman Rite* 1 (New York 1951) 391-461.

————, *The Liturgy of the Word* (Collegeville 1966).

————, *The Mass* (Collegeville, MN 1975) 174-184.

B. Botte *et al.*, *La parole dans la liturgie* (Paris 1970).

C. Jones *et al.*, *The Study of the Liturgy* (New York 1978) 179-188.

A. Chavasse, "L'Épistolier romain du *codex* de Wurtzbourg, son organisation," RB 91 (1981) 280-331.

————, "L'Évangéliaire romain de 645: un recueil. Sa composition, façons et matériaux," RB 92(1982) 33-75.

————, "L'organisation stationale du Carême romain avant le VIII siècle. Une organisation pastorale," RSR 56(1982) 17-32.

A. G. Martimort, "A propos du nombre des lectures à la messe," RSR (1984) 42-51.

2. THE LANGUAGE OF WORSHIP.

Outside Palestine itself, the early Christian message was expressed in *koine* Greek, which was not only the popular language of the Eastern half of the Roman Empire but of large sections of the population in the West as well. Only Syriac—in the East—was of any comparable importance.

Although in the beginning and for many centuries thereafter, Rome was more an international capital than simply the leading city of the West and more Greek than Latin, recent research helps us observe the transition from Greek to Latin on the part of the Church of Rome.[7]

When the Roman community of Christians was first founded (ca. 40?; certainly by 64), the population of the City was largely composed of those who spoke Greek; as the satirist Juvenal expressed it: *Non possum ferre, Quirites, graecam urbem (Satyricon* III, 58-60).[8] The composition and personnel of the Roman Church also reflected this situation: in the first two centuries, ten of its fourteen known bishops were Greek; its oldest burial inscriptions were in Greek and its most ancient liturgical treatise, the *Apostolic Tradition* of Hippolytus of Rome (ca. 215), was originally composed in Greek.[9] For some two hundred years this situation remained unchanged.

It was the African rather than the Roman Church that first expressed itself in Latin and it was the North Africans Tertullian, Cyprian, Arnobius, Lactantius and Augustine who created the juridical and liturgical vocabulary of the Latin Church of the West: *ius, cathedra, institutio, disciplina, regula, successio, sacramentum, ordo, plebs, primatus,* etc.[10] The Latinization of the Roman Church was a gradual process which did not exclude the coexistence of Greek and Latin over a rather lengthy period of time. Before adopting Latin completely, the Christian community of the imperial capital was undoubtedly bilingual for a fairly long period.

a. *The Early Latin of the Roman Church.*

The earliest Latin texts originating in Rome (ca. 150) were translations from the Greek: a Latin version of Clement's *Letter to the Corinthians* (the Greek original was composed ca. 96; the Latin translation appeared in the second half of the II century), the vulgate version of the *Shepherd* of Hermas (mid-II century), and a Latin version of the *Teaching of the Apostles (Didascalia Apostolorum*—Syriac, III century).

These translations were made at Rome (Bardy, Harnack, Mohrmann) rather than in Africa (Haussleiter) and reveal the need to use both Latin and Greek in order to reach the whole Christian population. The first influx of Latin may well have come during the pontificate of the African, Victor I (193-203).

It was only around 250 that texts began to appear which were originally composed in Latin: Novatian's great treatise *De Trinitate* (ca. 256)[11], the *Letter of the Roman Clergy* to the clergy of Carthage after Bishop Fabian's death (250-251)[12], the seven *Letters of Cornelius of Rome* to Cyprian of Carthage (252)[13] and the *Letter of Stephen of Rome* to Cyprian (256).[14] These are sure indications that Latin had already come into current usage.

Since the reading of Holy Scripture is an essential part of the liturgy, translations of the Bible are of the greatest importance to worship. After an initial period of oral translation during the liturgy itself, written translations began to appear in the II century. Often they were versions sponsored or approved by the bishops but sometimes they were the product of private individuals of somewhat doubtful character (the *Diatesseron* of Tatian, the *Corpus Paulinum* of Marcion, the Latin version of the Bible so much criticized by Tertullian). The first sign of an authorized Latin version appeared in North Africa (ca. 250) and it was this version that Cyprian of Carthage cited so often throughout his works. The Latin authors of Africa did not have recourse to the original Greek but merely used the current Latin versions that lay at hand. At Rome, the first indications of a Latin Bible appear in Novatian, but from the IV century on, a variety of biblical translations was evident.[15] Several coexisting translations were not, however, a sign of linguistic or liturgical chaos. It simply meant that earlier versions were reviewed and revised in the light of fresh linguistic and critical evidence and were designed to be very straightforward, literal versions of the original.[16] Learned versions of the Scriptures were normally not employed in the liturgy (e.g., Origen's *Hexapla* or Jerome's psalter *Iuxta Hebraeos*) and even revisions sometimes created an uproar; witness the excitement Augustine alluded to when a bishop, who had adopted Jerome's new translation of the Book of Jonah, substituted 'ivy' for the 'gourd' of the Old Latin version.[17]

b. Latin as the Official Language of the Roman Church.

As the bilingual character of the City gradually disappeared, Latin came to predominate at Rome. After 250, the correspondence of the

Roman bishops and clergy reveals that they were now willing to employ the language of the persons and communities they addressed in their letters rather than Greek. Bishop Cornelius of Rome died and was buried at Centumcellae in 253; towards the end of the century, his body was translated to the catacomb of St. Callixtus on the *Via Appia* where his funeral inscription appeared in Latin—an official first; nevertheless, the names of his successors continued to appear for a while in Greek: Loukis or Lucius (†254), Eutychianos (†283), Gaios (†296). This seems to indicate that Latin did not come to predominate until the late III century.

We also know that, from around 250, the sociological composition of the Roman community underwent modification; as the *pars orientalis imperii* became more stable, the flood of easterners dried up, and although Greek colonies still existed in Rome for a long time to come, they seem to have been of little importance.[18]

It was also around 250, as Latin began to become the offical tongue of the Roman Church, that the Christian community began to lose any knowledge it once had of the Greek sources of its own history and it was only to rediscover them much later in the Latin translations of Eusebius' *History of the Church* and his *Chronicle*.[19] It also lost all trace of its ancient martyrs and retained only confused memories of its earlier bishops; accurate dates for the bishops of Rome begin only after 235.[20]

c. Latin as the Liturgical Language of the Roman Church

The Roman liturgy did not make an immediate transition from Greek to Latin during the crucial years described above. On the other hand, it is practically certain that the readings were put into Latin more quickly than the rest of the liturgy. Several literary landmarks testify to this Latinizing process.

In 360, C. Marius Victorinus, *Adversus Arium* II, 8, although writing in Latin, cited a section of the eucharistic anaphora in Greek: *Hinc oratio oblationis intellectu eodem precatur eum:* σῶσον περιούσιον λαὸν ζηλωτὴν καλῶν ἔργων.[21]

Between 374-382, an anonymous Roman writer, 'Ambrosiaster,' the author of the *Quaestiones Veteris et Novi Testamenti* CIX, 20, also cited the canon of the mass but he did so in Latin: *Spiritus sanctus missus, quasi antistes sacerdos appelatus est Excelsi Dei, non summus sicut nostri* (i.e. romani) *in oblatione praesumunt*[22].

It is apparent, then, that between 360-382 Latin became the language of the liturgy—at least for the anaphora. This does not, however, imply that earlier on there had not been other attempts at Latinizing various aspects of the liturgy or that a Latin and Greek eucharistic prayer may not have existed side by side according to the respective needs of two distinct linguistic groups in the Roman Church. The likelihood of such coexistence is, indeed, very strong (Baumstark, Eizenhofer, Leclercq, Klauser). In any case, the transition to Latin must have taken place before the pontificate of Damasus I (366-384); he probably composed several of the liturgical *formulae* appearing in the so-called Leonine Sacramentary and certainly composed his celebrated *epigrammata* in Latin.[23] Moreover, St. Ambrose's *De sacramentis* (before 387/391), which contains a fragment of a Latin eucharistic prayer very much like the same passage in the medieval *canon missae*, obliges us to push the date for the Latinizing of the Roman liturgy further back into the IV century— unless we want to admit the Milanese origin of the Roman canon.[24]

The Latin liturgy which came into use at Rome in the IV century was not a simple translation of a Greek original but a fresh creation— despite the attractive arguments of A. Baumstark to the contrary.[25] Whichever hypothesis we support, one fact is clear; the language of the liturgy was about a century behind the language current in the City and among the faithful.

At a later date, in the VII century, when many Eastern Christians again poured into Rome, the Roman liturgy became bilingual once more—at least for the readings and for some ceremonies of the catechumenate. Between 638-772, i.e., from the reign of Honorius I (625-638) to that of Hadrian I (772-795), nine of the twenty-five popes were easterners (3 Greek, 3 Syrian, 2 Antiochene, 1 Thracian)—a sure sign of the renewed cosmopolitan character of the Roman Church. In the face of such a foreign influx, perhaps only the Frankish intervention in matters of worship saved the Latin and Roman liturgy.[26]

No bilingual lectionaries survive but traces of their existence are to be found in several biblical MSS: the *Codex Cantabrigiensis/Codex Bezae*[27] (V/VI century) and the *Codex Claromontanus* (VI century) give the same texts in both Greek (*verso*) and Latin (*recto*); the same is true of the *Mengeringhausen Fragment*, while the *Wolfenbüttel Fragment* (*Carolinus Fragment*) provides a text in parallel columns of Latin and Gothic.[28]

Greco-Latin readings continued to be used at Rome for special occasions:

a) at Christmas and Easter (Sun. and Mon.): cf. *Ordines* 11, nos. 20 and 34 (*Liber politicus*) and 12, nos. 4 and 47 (Cencius) of Mabillon (PL 78, 1033 B/C and 1044B/C, 1066B/C and 1079 B);

b) for the Vigils of Easter and Pentecost: cf. *Ordo* XXVIII, Appendix 2-11: *In primis greca legitur, dein statim ab alio latina* (Andrieu 3, 412-413);

c) on the four Ember Saturdays: *Sabbato in XII lectionibus*, when the six lessons of the Vigil were each read twice, once in Greek and once in Latin (Bede and Amalarius);

d) and at the mass for the ordination of a pope (Mabillon's *Ordo* 12).

Unfortunately, the IV-century linguistic revolution was the only language change to take place in the Latin Church throughout the Middle Ages. As national tongues emerged, the Latin liturgy was stubbornly maintained even in the face of liturgical necessity.[29] Throughout the entire medieval period, the only sensible liturgical adaptation was promoted—in the face of inveterate hostility—by Sts. Cyril and Methodius (IX century), the apostles of the Slavs.[30]

3. ROMAN SPHERES OF INFLUENCE.

Until the II Vatican Council (1962-1965), Latin liturgy was almost synonymous with Roman liturgy, i.e., the liturgy proper to the city of Rome. But such was not always the case and Roman hegemony in matters liturgical resulted from a variety of circumstances and intiatives rather than simply from the persistent intervention of popes.

a. *The Patristic Period* (II-VI centuries).

In the city of Rome proper, its bishop exercised all the normal prerogatives of a bishop in his community. Outside Rome, but in certain regions only, the bishop of Rome came to enjoy several extended forms of jurisdiction. Already the Council of Nicea (325), canon 6, compared his prerogatives to the *exousia* exercised by the bishop of Alexandria in Egypt, Libya and the Pentapolis, but without specifying it any further. According to a Latin gloss of Rufinus, this canon designated the rights the bishop of Rome enjoyed in regard to the suburbicarian churches. By such a term we must understand not only the seven suburban bishoprics of the City (Porto and San Rufino, Ostia, Albano, Sabina, Velletri, Frascati or Tusculum and Praeneste or Palestrina) but all the churches of the ten provinces of the civil diocese of *Italia suburbicaria*: Tuscia-Umbria, Campania, Lucania-Bruttium, Apulia-Calabria, Samnium, Picenum, Valeria, and the three islands of Sicily, Sardinia and Corsica. *Italia suburbicaria* was under the authority of the *Vicarius urbis* just as in the North *Italia annonaria* was governed by the *Vicarius Italiae*. Similarly, the bishop of Milan was the primate of *Italia annonaria* and the bishop of Rome the primate of *Italia suburbicaria*; as such he was, in theory at least, able to impose the Roman rite on the churches of his 'diocese'. Naturally he had no such authority in *Italia annonaria*, anymore than he had in North Africa where the bishop of Carthage was primate. As a matter of course, the bishop of Rome carried on a direct correspondence with the bishops of his 'diocese' whereas he did not do so directly with the bishops of other regions, but only contacted them indirectly through their own primate or metropolitan bishop.[31]

In matters of worship, the Roman bishops confined themselves to their own 'diocese' and to this section of the Western Church alone; they exercised no jurisdiction whatsoever in N. Italy, Africa, Gaul, Spain, the British Isles or Germany.

Towards the end of the early Christian era (ca. 570-650), Roman influence became even more circumscribed in Italy because of the Lombard occupation of all but the coastal region between Rome and Naples. The *ducatus Romae* of the Exarchate of Ravenna was gradually isolated from the rest of the peninsula. Moreover, if we draw a line to the south of Rome passing through Monte Cassino, Naples, Capua and Benevento, we can observe a frequent time-lag between these sections and Rome itself; changes and developments observable at Rome were not immediately reflected in the above-mentioned regions which continued to follow older Roman usages.[32]

In suburbicarian Italy as a whole, one can detect liturgical influences stemming from both N. Italy and even from beyond the Alps. Nevertheless, such influences do not normally explain the liturgical peculiarities of the suburbicarian churches as compared to Rome. Most of the time they are manifestly dependent upon Rome rather than upon other churches.

b. *From the Late Patristic Period to the Liturgical Renewal of Gregory VII (1073-1085).*

During this long period, Roman liturgical decadence was so pronounced that there was no question of Rome influencing other churches. It was the period in which, as Gregory VII remarked: *Teutonicis concessum est regimen Ecclesiae nostrae.*[33] We have only to recall the significant role played by the Carolingian rulers in things liturgical. The Romanizing process they set on foot for both political and religious reasons resulted in a freshly evolved liturgy bearing the marks of its Roman, Frankish and Visigothic background. By the mid-X century, this Romano-Frankish/Romano-Germanic liturgy was being transported back to Rome by the Ottonian emperors and there it took root so firmly that it was shortly considered authentically Roman even by the Romans themselves. Subsequently, this 'Roman' liturgy became the liturgy of the whole medieval Latin Church since, whatever the influence of the Gregorian reformers, they did no more than prune the somewhat luxuriant overgrowth of the German books they had inherited; they did not touch, much less transform, their substance.

Throughout the West, the Romanizing process was never uniform and depended a great deal on the country in question. It was a gradual, step-by-step process that imposed itself through the reformed books characteristic of the Gregorian renewal.[34]

In Italy of the XI and XII century, Roman liturgical influence was confined below a line passing through Umbria and Nursia (between Spoleto and Ascoli). Arezzo and Tuscany were already more under N. Italian influence. In the South of the peninsula, the old patristic boundaries remained unchanged, except where the Beneventan rite became influential.

Strangely enough, while from the XIII century on, the ecclesiastical province of Rome shrank and came to include only some seventy dioceses situated between Pisa and Capua, its liturgical influence never ceased expanding. The development and dissemination of the Roman Pontifical from its earliest stages in the XII century through its *editio princeps* of 1485 is a perfect example of this expansiveness.

4. CONTINUOUS OR CONSECUTIVE READING, DISCREET OR SELECTED READINGS.

Many scholars used to assert that until the era of fixed lessons (V-VI centuries), the Bible was used in the liturgy in a series of continuous or consecutive readings (*lectio continua, Scriptura currens*). In such an approach, the reader would have simply continued the sacred text where he had left off at the previous celebration. To support such a view these authors referred to series of readings appearing in the lectionaries which seemed to be relics of this ancient usage.[35]

Such a view is, however, very problematic, especially if we understand *lectio continua* as a systematic reading of the whole Bible in the course of the Eucharist. Such a way of reading the Bible for purposes of instruction and edification certainly existed in the early Church but not at the Eucharist.[36]

Probably from the earliest times and certainly from the II century on, the annual recurrence of special feasts and seasons suggested the use of proper readings in harmony with the meaning of the feast or season in question. This was especially true of Easter and Pentecost and, a little later, of Christmas and Ascension, but it was also true of the weeks preparing for Easter and for the great Fifty Days which followed. Churches also maintained the festivals of their own special martyrs, e.g., Peter and Paul at Rome, Polycarp at Smyrna, Cyprian at Carthage, etc. and would select their readings accordingly.[37] This choice of scriptual passages separated from their biblical context (pericopes) is a kind of discontinuous reading of the Bible which became more and more common as seasons found their special definition and more and more feasts made their appearance. The progressive organization of the liturgical year rendered any *lectio continua* at the Eucharist less and less probable; the books of the Bible are organized along lines quite different than those of the liturgical commmmemorations.[38]

Moreoever, while improvisation was still the rule, i.e., precisely during the time when *lectio continua* was supposed to have prevailed, it was the bishop who determined both the choice and the length of what was read at mass.[39] There is no evidence that bishops were obliged to adhere to the order of the Bible in any systematic or wholesale manner. A *lectio continua* of the Old Testament would be even more difficult to maintain; there isn't even a smattering of evidence for such a use of the Old Testament in the Eucharist.

As a matter of principle, any book of the scriptual canon could furnish lessons for the liturgy of the Word although it took some time for a general canon of scripture to establish itself.[40] Churches had somewhat variable lists of authorized books; some communities used the *Apocalypse of Peter*, the *Shepherd* of Hermas and Clement of Rome's *Letter to the Corinthians*, while others omitted one or more of the books that most Christians recognized as canonical.[41] In the IV century, the councils of Laodicea (372) and of Hippo (393) felt obliged to forbid sharply the use of non-canonical materials.[42] The eventual establishment of a clear-cut canon of Scripture did not, however, mean that certain kinds of non-biblical readings could not be used in the liturgy, e.g., the Acts of the Martyrs in some churches.[43]

Normally, the reading of the Sacred Scriptures at mass was surrounded by ceremonies to highlight the importance of the *lectio* and the *virtus* that resided in it.[44] On the other hand, readings were also used in less solemn ways at Vigils or in order to fill in gaps or to occupy people as they waited for the beginning of a liturgy.[45]

At least in theory, readers faithfully followed the text they had before their eyes, often using not a special book of selected readings but a whole Bible specially marked for liturgical use. Centonization, on the other hand, was not unheard of, especially in the Gallican liturgy.[46] A cento is a text composed of a variety of scriptural passages drawn from different parts of the Bible and assembled like a quilt or a mosaic.[47] It is not the same as harmonization which means weaving together several parallel passages of the Gospels into one continuous reading.[48]

5. EVIDENCE FOR THE LITURGICAL READINGS.

No liturgical document survives from before the VI century with information on the nature and arrangement of the readings in the liturgy[49] but there can be no doubt about the existence of such readings.[50] It also appears to be indisputable that the Christian custom of reading the Holy Scriptures derives from the Jewish custom of reading the Law and the Prophets in the liturgy of the synagogue.[51] For both Jews and Christians, the reading of the Sacred Page was seen to confer strength and life and the Holy Book itself could only be handled with covered hands.[52]

We cannot be sure that all the apostolic communities continued reading the Law in their assemblies. We can be quite sure the Judeo-Christian churches persisted in doing so, but we are less sure about the practice of the Hellenistic churches.[53] On the other hand, it is clear that everyone read the Pauline letters.[54] As the canon of Scripture was gradually agreed upon, other New Testament writings were added to Paul's letters, as were certain apocryphal documents and other non-biblical texts, as we have said.

Justin Martyr (ca. 150/155) testified that, on Sundays at Rome, the regular reading of "the memoirs of the apostles or the writings of the prophets" was already a traditional practice.[55] Toward the end of the II century, Tertullian witnessed to the same custom: [the Roman Church] *legem et prophetas cum evangelicis et apostolicis litteris miscet unde potat fidem . . . apud quas [ecclesias apostolicas] ipsae authenticae litterae eorum recitantur.*[56] The existence of a special category of clerics to do the readings is also a clear proof of the existence and regularity of the liturgical *lectiones*. Such lectors were not, however, ordained but merely appointed by being handed the book of readings by the bishop.[57]

The fact that the readings for the annual festivals were specially selected and followed no particular biblical order does not exclude the possibility that at the same period there existed something like and overall arrangement of readings for the entire year. As in the case of the prayer *formulae*, the bishop was perfectly free to choose the passages that were to be read. Such episcopal freedom seems to have endured until at least the end of the IV century.

The first trace we have of a fixed set of readings is in Ambrose of Milan and is good at least for his church: [During Holy Week] *audistis Librum Iob qui solemni munere est decursus et tempore . . . sequenti die lectus est de more liber Ionae.*[58]

In North Africa, ca. 400, certain liturgical times had fixed readings in an overall arrangement that could only be interrupted on special occasions. In a sermon preached at Hippo on Easter Monday, 416, Augustine remarked: *Meminit sanctitas vestra, evangelium secundum Iohannem ex ordine lectionum nos solere tractare: sed quia nunc interposita est solemnitas sanctorum dierum quibus certas ex evangelio lectiones oportet in ecclesia recitari, quae ita sunt annuae ut aliae esse non possint, ordo ille quem susceperamus, necessitate paululum intermissus est, non amissus.*[59]

Sidonius Apollinaris, the bishop of Clermont (470-480/90), reports that Claudianus, the brother of bishop Mamertus and a presbyter of Vienne, prepared a set of texts for the liturgical festivals: *Vicarius in ecclesiis [Claudianus], procurator in negotiis, villicus in praediis, tabularius in tributis, in lectionibus comes, in expositionibus interpres, in itineribus contubernalis,*

> Psalmorum hic modulator et phonascus
> Ante altaria, fratre gratulante,
> Instructas docuit sonare classes.
> Hic solemnibus annuis paravit
> Quae quo tempore lecta convenirent.[60]

According to Gennadius (†492/505), the presbyter Museus of Marseilles (†458/9), composed a lectionary for the entire liturgical year at the request of his bishop Venerius (†452): *Musaeus Massiliensis Ecclesiae presbyter . . . hortatu sancti Venerii episcopi, excerpsit de sanctis scripturis lectiones totius anni festivis diebus aptas; responsoria etiam psalmorum capitula temporibus et lectionibus congruentia.*[61] This is the oldest reference we have to a complete lectionary. Unfortunately, the lectionary itself no longer survives and attempts to confuse it with the palimpsest lectionary of Wolfenbüttel (*codex Weissenburgensis* 76) are dubious at best.[62]

The lectionary of the Church of Arles can be restored in part from the sermons of St. Caesarius (502-543).[63] The information provided by Bishop Caesarius is so detailed and precise that is supposes the existence of a well-arranged and fixed lectionary.[64]

Bishop Germanus of Paris (ca. 496-576) set out the Gallican system of readings for us: *De Prophetia et Apostolo. Lectio vero prophetica suum tenet ordinem Veteris videlicet Testamenti . . . De Apostolo. Quod enim propheta clamat futurum, apostolus docet factum. Actus autem Apostolorum vel Apocalypsis Iohannis pro novitate gaudii paschalis leguntur, servantes ordinem temporum, sicut historia testamenti veteris in Quinquagesima vel Gesta sanctorum confessorum ac martyrum in solempnitatibus eorum . . . Egreditur processio Evangelii.*[65]

Eucharistic lectionaries began to appear in the VI century: the Wolfenbüttel Lectionary (*codex Weissenb.* 76) and the Lectionary of Capua, (ca. 546) are, therefore, among the oldest surviving books of the Latin liturgy.

6. THE NUMBER OF LITURGICAL READINGS.

To understand the number of readings, it is helpful to distinguish between the Roman rite, i.e., the liturgy of the City and of suburbicarian Italy, and the non-Roman, Latin rites of the West, often called Gallican. In this case the non-Roman evidence is the oldest.[66]

a. *The Non-Roman System.*

The arrangement of readings in these Latin rites (Gallican, Milanese, Visigothic, etc.) is far from uniform. Actually the greatest diversity characterized the lectionary systems of these several churches. On the other hand, all the non-Roman documents reveal certain common features which permit us to speak of a 'Gallican' system of readings as contrasted to a Roman one.[67] The general rule was three readings at mass: the first lesson from the Old Testament (usually a prophetic lesson), the second from the New Testament and the third from the Gospels. The *Acts of the Apostles* and the *Apocalypse* were reserved for Eastertide. Some days had a (optional?) reading from the *Acts of the Martyrs*.[68] In the texts themselves, *Dominus Iesus* appears more frequently than *Dominus* or *Iesus* alone. All these characteristics can be found in *Weissenburgensis 76*, the *Lectionary of Luxeuil*, the *Bobbio Missal*, the *Liber commicus* of Silos and in the Milanese books.

In North Africa, Augustine is our witness to the use of three readings at the Eucharist.[69]

b. *The Roman System.*

Normally the Roman lectionaries have only two lessons, an epistle[70] and a gospel. A number of indications survive, nevertheless, which suggest that early on Rome too had a system of three lessons. The Epistolary of Würzburg (ca. 600), our earliest exemplar, provides a series of readings which includes sometimes an epistle, sometimes an epistle followed by an Old Testament reading (or conversely) and then a gospel. Apparently at Rome in the VII century—when this lectionary was in use—a three-lesson system was still employed but was perhaps beginning to disappear or was in use only at the discretion of the celebrant. A fragmentary S. Italian missal also contains three lessons.[71] Another indication of the primitive use is the survival of two chant pieces, the Gradual and the Alleluia, which seem originally to have separated the three readings.[72] One of the non-gospel readings seems to have fallen out of use in the last half of the VI century. In any case, when the Roman books entered Gaul in the VII and VIII centuries, the two-lesson system was fully operative.[73]

B. THE CHRONOLOGICAL FRAMEWORK: THE LITURGICAL YEAR.

The arrangement of liturgical readings raises the problem of how the liturgical year was organized. Research on the origin and selection of the *pericopes* allows a fuller grasp of the *circulus anni* in which Christian worship takes place. Here we shall consider only the *Temporale*, with its movable feasts and seasons, and only to the degree such an analysis helps us understand the liturgical documents.[74] The

Sanctorale, with its fixed feasts, poses far less complicated problems.[75]

Early Christians sanctified the week before they did the year and kept the Lord's Day long before they observed Easter. The weekly cycle existed before the yearly cycle; it included Sunday and the weekly celebration of the Lord's Supper, and Wednesday and Friday, which were days of fast and non-eucharistic gatherings (synaxes).

As the annual cycle developed, it had only one focal point, the feast of Easter.

1. EASTER

The feast of Easter has been celebrated everywhere since the II century. The early paschal controversies were never about the celebration itself but about certain aspects of its observance, such as the date, the method of computing it, fasting and feasting, meaning. Since the *Didache*, the Apostolic Fathers and Justin Martyr do not mention the observance of Easter, no evidence for its existence can be ascertained before the late II century.

We do not have to discuss the meaning of this festival, but we must take note of the fact that *Passa/Pascha* was not reserved simply to the celebration of Easter Sunday; it was also an annual commemoration of the passion and death of Jesus Christ which culminated in his resurrection.[76] In the IV century, Easter became the celebratory conclusion to a rigorous period of fasting which came to an end after the all-night Vigil (Sat.-Sun.) with the celebration of the Eucharistic Sacrifice *in galli cantu*.[77]

In spite of its completely new meaning, the Chrisian *Passa* remained attached to the old Jewish chronology; that is why the Jewish Passover, observed during the night of 14-15 Nisan at the full moon of the first lunar month, remained the point of departure for calculating the Christian festival. The result is that the date of Easter is different every year and the further result of its movable character is that the entire liturgical year is also essentially movable.[78]

a. ASSIGNING EASTER A FIXED DATE.

Many attempts have been made to assign Easter a fixed date. In the East, according to Clement of Alexandria (†before 215), *Stromata* 1, 21, some people proposed March 21, April 14 or 20. According to Epiphanius of Salamis, *Panarion* (ca. 374/377) 51, 24-26, Christ was born on Jan 6, baptized on Nov 8 in his 29th year and died on March 20 (*XIII Kalendas Aprilis*) when he was 34 years old; but he also says that others think he died on March 23 (*X Kal. Aprilis*).

At Rome and in the West generally, a tradition which assigned March 25 as the date of the Passion (*VIII Kal. Aprilis*=the Spring equinox of the Julian calendar) appeared rather early and lasted for a long time. One of its most precious legacies is the expressive Roman collect introduced in the mid-VII century for the *Adnuntiatio Sanctae Dei Genetricis et Passio eiusdem Domini: Gratiam tuam, quaesumus, Domine, mentibus nostris infunde, ut qui angelo nuntiante Christi filii tui incarnationem cognovimus, per passionem eius et crucem ad resurrectionis gloriam perducamur* (*Paduense* 385, ed. Deshusses, p. 635). This prayer continued to be used in the papal sacramentary (*Hadrianum* 143) and in the Frankish Gelasian Sacramentares of the late VIII century (*Gellone* 850; *Angoulême* 879) and in the Tridentine Missal. It still remains the prayer concluding the *Angelus* three times a day.

The year of Christ's death came to be fixed in 29 A.D., in the consulate of the Gemini, the consuls C. Fufius Geminus and L. Rubellius Geminus: Tertullian, *Adversus Iudaeos* (ca. 207), cap. 8: *Passio perfecta est sub Tiberio Caesare, consulibus Rubellio Gemino et Fufio Gemino, mense Martio, temporibus Paschae, die VIII Kalendas Aprilis, die primo Azymorum* (March 25 of 29 A.D., the XV regnal year of Tiberius). Lactantius, *Divin. Instit.* 4, 10, 18 gives a different date (March 23 of 29) from that of the dominant tradition. The *Chronography* of Philocalus of the year 354, in the *Liberian Catalogue* of the Popes (L. Duchesne, *Liber pontificalis* 1, 3; T. Mommsen, MGH, *Auctores Antiquissini* 9, 73) maintains the classic tradition: *Imperante Tiberio Caesare, passus est Dominus noster Iesus Christus, duobus Geminis consulibus, VIII Kalendas Aprilis* (March 25 of 29). The same is true of the *Prologus Paschae ad Vitalem* of 395 (Mommsen, MGH, *Auct. Antiq.* 9, 737) and Q. Julius Hilarianus, *De ratione Paschae et mensis* of 397 (PL 13, 1114 A/B): *eo quippe anno ut Supputationis* [the *Supputatio Romana*] *fides ostendit, et ratio ipsa persuadet, passus est idem Dominus Christus, luna XIV, VIII Kalendas Aprilis, feria sexta*. Supporting the same tradition is Sulpicius Severus, *Chronicon* 2, 27 (CSEL 1, 82): *Fufio Gemino et Rubellio Gemino consulibus* and Augustine, *De civitate Dei* 18, 54 (CSEL 40, 2, p. 360): *Mortuus est ergo Christus duobus Geminis consulibus, octavo Kalendas Aprilis* (March 25 of 29). Prosper of Aquitaine, *Chronica* of 433 (Mommsen, MGH, *Chronica minora* 1, 409) indicates the consular year but not the date. The *Computatio anni* 452 (MGH, *Chronica minora* 1, 153) puts the passion in Jesus' 31st year in the same consulate of the Gemini. The *Liber pascalis codicis Cizensis* of 447 (MGH, *Chronica minora* 1, 507) gives the date March 25 under the Gemini. Victor of Aquitaine, *Cursus pascalis* of 457, in spite of the difficulties attached to his canon, maintains the consulate of the Gemini as the year of the passion but puts the Last Supper, rather than Christ's death, on March 25. For the testimony contained in the *Acta Pilati* (325/376), see M. Richard, "Comput et chronographie chez S. Hippolyte," *Mélanges de science religieuse* 7(1950) 237-268; 8(1951) 19-50.

Another ancient tradition portrayed Jesus as having lived a perfect number of years and that, consequently, the date of his conception and of his death must have been the same. He was conceived on March 25, the spring equinox (the feast of the Annunciation), and died on the same date; he was born, of course, on Dec 25, the winter solstice. If the feast of John the Baptist, his forerunner and herald, is added to these, the cycle of feasts then includes all the solstices and equinoxes of the year. Patristic testimony on these points is abundant: Augustine, *De Trinitate 4, 5* (PL 42, 894): *VIII Kalendas Aprilis conceptus* [Christus] *creditur quo et passus; De diversis quaestionibus* 83, qu. 56 (PL 40, 39): [VIII Kal. Apr.] *quo die conceptus Dominus creditur, quia eodem die etiam passus est, usque ad VIII Kalendas Ianuarii quo die natus est.* For this symbolism of the number of years, the dates of his conception and birth and the origins of Christmas, see B. Botte, *Les origines de la Noël et de l'Épiphanie*, Textes et études liturgiques 1 (Louvain 1932); H. Frank, "Frühgeschichte und Ursprung des römischen Weihnachtsfestes im Lichte neuer Forschung," AfL 2(1952) 1-24 and H. Engberding, "Der 25. Dezember als Tag der Feier der Geburt des Herrn," *ibid.*, pp. 25-43; these last two articles draw different conclusions from the evidence they present but they are excellent summaries of the different theories and contain a full bibliography.[79] The basis for the parallelism between the feasts of John the Baptist and Jesus is furnished by the words of the angel at the annunciation (Luke 1:36): *Et ecce Elisabeth cognata tua et ipsa concepit filium in senectute sua et hic mensis sextus est illi quae vocatur sterilis.* See table K.

The quartodeciman controversies which occurred from 165-325 and the arguments over how to compute the proper date of Easter (V-VI century) need not detain us here. Only the chronological decisions provided by the Council of Nicea (325) are of interest:

a) the Spring equinox is fixed on March 21;

b) the first lunar month of Spring is the one whose 14th day (full moon) falls on March 21 or whose full moon occurs immediately after March 21;

c) Easter must not be celebrated on the Jewish Passover. If the 14th falls on a Sunday, Easter is observed a week later. This means that the *termini pascales* (=Sundays) are March 22 (the earliest possible date) and April 25 (the latest);

d) Easter must always be celebrated on a Sunday.

To be more explicit, since the Council of Nicea until the present, Easter has been celebrated on the Sunday following the first full moon of the Spring equinox. In spite of the efforts of Nicea to make the Alexandrian method of computation prevail everywhere, Rome itself continued to use the *Supputatio romana* until the VI century (ca. 525/530).[80]

b. THE ROMAN WAY OF COMPUTING EASTER.

a) *From 222 to the end of the III century.*

The equinox is fixed on March 25 (the Julian calendar). The 16-year cycle is that of Hippolytus of Rome (222).[81] The *termini pascales: luna XVI-XXII*, i.e. March 20 to April 19 (?); March 18 is the earliest possible date for the first full moon of Spring (14 Nisan). If the 14th falls on a Friday, Easter Sunday is on the 20th, or five days before the Spring equinox, the Roman rule being that Easter must not fall before two days after the 14th of Nisan, namely the day of the resurrection.

b) *From the end of the III century until 313/343.*

The cycle of 84 years or the Augustalis cycle.[82] *Termini pascales: luna XIV-XX*, i.e. March 25 and April 21.

c) *From 313/343 until Dionysius Exiguus (ca 525/530).*

The use of the *Supputatio romana* continued under varying conditions and with many attempts at adaptation, a system usually called the Old Roman Computation—important for understanding the liturgical year. It had an 84-year cycle beginning in 298 (*Supputatio romana* proper) or in the year 29 *Termini pascales: luna XVI-XXII*, i.e. March 22 to April 21.

d) *The cycle of 19 years (the Alexandrian or Anatolian cycle).*[83]

In spite of Nicea's decision in favor of the Alexandrian way of computing Easter, Rome continued for centuries to follow its own method until Dionysius Exiguus (Denis the Short) worked out a fresh Easter cycle in conformity with the decisions of 325. To do so, he continued the *Paschal Tables* of Cyril of Alexandria, which ran from 340-512, extending them from 532-626 in a way that could be easily continued. *Termini pascales: luna XIV-XXI*, i.e. March 22 to April 25 (See the Tables G and H.)

It was also Dionysius who first established the Christian Era, taking 753 *ab Urbe condita*—his best calculation for the Incarnation—as his point of departure; he was at least 4 years too late.

Ultimately Dionysius' method of computing Easter won out in the West over both the 84-year cycle and the Cycle of Victorius which was used in the Frankish kingdom until the VIII century. Comparative tables can be found in Cappelli and Grotefend, see note 78 on p. 383.

The *Tabula pascalis* of Dionysius included the following items in 8 columns: 1) *Anni Domini Nostri Iesu Christi;* 2) the *Indictiones;* 3) the *Epactae lunares;* 4) the *Concurrentes;* 5) the *Lunaris cyclus;* 6) the *Luna quarta decima Paschae;* 7) the *Dies dominicus Paschae;* 8) the *Luna ipsius diei (paschae).*

The feast of Easter is preceded by a period of preparation and followed by fifty days of festivity or Pentecost. Pentecost was originally the term for the whole fifty-day period before it became restricted to its final day. The two periods—one before and one after the central feast of Easter—are the two primitive constants of the annual liturgical cycle.

2. THE FIRST PERIOD: THE PREPARATION FOR EASTER.

The period preparing for Easter was gradually established by working back from the feast itself. The step-by-step formation of a full Lent can only be understood by working back from Easter through the *Triduum*, Holy Week and, ultimately, all the weeks of Lent and even pre-Lent.[84]

a. *The Paschal Triduum.*

The *Triduum* was composed of Good Friday, Holy Saturday and Easter Sunday and not of Holy Thursday, Good Friday and Holy Saturday as it was later. This *triduum* had a special liturgical organization of its own; Friday and Saturday were days of strict fast since at least the beginning of the III century and this fast was broken only by the celebration of the festal Eucharist at dawn on Easter Sunday.[85] Each day of the *triduum* began on the preceding evening.

The paschal *triduum* of Friday through Sunday still existed in the V century and was considered *outside* Lent which ended on Holy Thursday.[86]

b. *The Week before Easter: Holy Week or de Passione.*

This week existed as a liturgical entity already in the V century and was a kind of extension of the *triduum* (moving backward from Easter itself) and encroached somewhat upon it.[87] It was a complete liturgical unit in itself and was called *hebdomada maior* or *authentica*.[88] The Sunday before Easter was known as the *Dominica de Passione* and later as *Dominica in Palmis*.[89] We do not know if at Rome, so long as this was the only preparation for Easter, the liturgical observances involved an all-week fast, as was the case at Alexandria after 250.[90]

c. *The Fast of Three Weeks before Easter.*

According to Socrates the historian (ca. 439): "At Rome they fast for three weeks in succession before Easter, except on Saturday and Sunday."[91] These three weeks existed before Lent proper was established in Rome, i.e., before 384/7, and were not a simple subdivision of it.[92] They are to be seen as one continuous period and not as separate weeks of fasting.[93] In addition to what we have from Socrates, two major indicators in favor of a three week fast can be ascertained:

1) In the oldest liturgical texts, the V Sunday of Lent was called *Dominica mediana* and the week preceding it *septimana* or *hebdomada mediana*.[94] The adjective *mediana* only makes sense in the context of a three-week fast before Easter where *Dominica mediana* would stand

between the IV Sunday of Lent and Palm Sunday; 2) From the IV Sunday of Lent (=the I Sunday of the old fast of three weeks), the gospel readings were all taken from John (except on Thursdays which had no Mass until 715/731), the Gospel proper to Paschaltide. The three weeks preceding Easter seem, then, in continuity with Eastertide itself.

We can deduce the reason for the three-week preparatory fast. Since the Roman year began on March 1, there were exactly three weeks available before March 22, the earliest possible date of Easter. In such a case one would have a beginning of the year fast that would coincide with a fast before Easter (see Table F). In any case, the three week period could not begin before New Year's (March 1) since Easter could not fall earlier than March 22.[95]

d. *The Roman Fast of Six Weeks: Quadragesima or Lent.*

Except for Sundays, the six-week fast was also continuous and began with the I Sunday of Lent and ended on Holy Thursday, the paschal *triduum* always standing outside Lent proper. Taken as a whole, the six weeks counted as a forty-day fast.

Lent is attested in this form in 384 but probably did not exist before 350.[96] Before the end of the V century, the Wednesday and Friday before the I Sunday of Lent were added to it, Wednesday being called *feria IV in capite Quadragesimae.*[97]

In the VII century, the paschal *triduum* as a distinct entity faded from view and the fast days were henceforth calculated backwards from Easter Sunday, rather than from Holy Thursday as before. Lent now contained forty-three days and thirty-six fast days (43 minus 7 Sundays). Forty days of fasting were obtained by adding Ash Wednesday and the Thursday, Friday and Saturday before I Lent.[98] Under this new system Lent usually began before the old New Year (March 1), sometimes even in February.

e. *Quinquagesima.*

Quinquagesima first appears in the notice devoted to Pope Telesphorus in the *Liber pontificalis,* a notice drawn up under Pope Hormisdas (514-523)[99] and again under Pope Vigilius in 538.[100] The fifty days were counted backwards from Easter to the Sunday which was still called *Dominica in Quinquagesima* in the Tridentine Missal. Outside Rome, this new liturgical unit was vigorously resisted as an unwelcome innovation.[101]

f. *Sexagesima.*

The new period of sixty days, which was unknown in the time of Pope Vigilius, appears in the Old Gelasian Sacramentary (*Vat. Reg.* 316) and in the Epistolary of Victor of Capua (546).[102] The number sixty was obtained by adding a week before the *Dominica in Quinquagesima* and the three days after Easter (Mon. through Wed.).[103]

g. *Septuagesima.*

This new and final addition to the pre-Easter period appears in the Roman lectionaries of the VII century but after the Roman model (643) used by the *Comes* of Alcuin and therefore after Gregory the Great († 604).[104] To get seventy days, a new week was added before *Dominica in Sexagesima* and all the days of Easter Week as well (Sunday-Saturday).

Lent and Eastertide form two fixed liturgical seasons revolving around Easter Sunday. They include fourteen Sundays in all: the six Sundays of Lent + Easter Sunday = seven Sundays and the seven Sundays after Easter, including Pentecost.

3. THE SECOND FIXED PERIOD: THE GREAT FIFTY DAYS (PENTEKOSTE).

In the beginning Pentecost meant the whole fifty days of Eastertide and not just the day of Pentecost itself. It was only in the IV century, when the event character of the feasts was worked out, that the fiftieth day was singled out and became the feast of Pentecost proper.[105] The Fifty Days always include the six weeks between Easter and Pentecost and, with the paschal *triduum*, form the *tempus pascale*.[106]

4. ORDINARY TIME.

The early liturgical year at Rome began in March and concluded in February.[107] There are no surviving liturgical documents which permit us to study that period directly but traces of the ancient system still surface in the later liturgical books, e.g., the designations *ieiunium primi, quarti, septimi et decimi mensis* to indicate the quarterly fasts of March (the first month), June (the fourth month), September (the seventh month) and December (the tenth month).[108] Despite this venerable method of dating, however, in the Old Gelasian Sacramentary (*Vat. Reg.* 316) the first day of the Christian year has become Dec. 25 and the last day Dec. 24. Until the VI century, the Nativity of Christ had belonged to the *Sanctorale*, where Christ was counted as the first of the martyrs,[109] but then it passed into the

Temporale and became the opening day of the liturgical year, as we see in the Old Gelasian. In the VIII-IX century, the beginning of the liturgical year shifted again and became the I Sunday of Advent. All in all, the liturgical year never did come to have an absolutely fixed beginning.[110]

In the liturgical year that began according to the old Roman system (March 1), the off-season or ordinary time included the Sundays extending from Pentecost to Lent (which was three weeks long at first and then forty days). Its only high-points were three sets of fastdays: Pentecost (one of the Ember Day sets since the VII century) or the fast of the fourth month (June) in existence since Gelasius I (492-496), and the fasts of the seventh (Sept.) and the tenth month (Dec.); these latter two were the earliest and were observed even before Leo I (440-461). See Tables H and I.

a. *The Ember Days; Quattuor tempora.*

At first only the Wednesday, Friday and Saturday at the beginning of the seventh and tenth months (Sept. and Dec.) were special fast days; they probably existed as early as the IV century. The fast days of Pentecost week, marking the resumption of fasting after the Easter festivities, came to be observed as the fast of the fourth month (June, approximately, depending on the date of Easter) since the time of Gelasius I (†496). That produced three seasonal fasts (*ieiunium quarti, septimi et decimi mensis*). It was in the V century, too, that the fast of the first month (March) was instituted, although it did not necessarily coincide with the first week of Lent—as it did in the Middle Ages. Early on, the primary day for ordinations at Rome had been the Ember Saturday of December, but in the V century the first Saturday of Lent became an ordination day and, consequently, a special day for fasting and keeping vigil. That meant that there could be two fasts of the first month, as we can see in the Old Gelasian (*Vat. Reg.* 316).[111] The Gregorian Sacramentaries combine both of these observances into a single fast of the first month. It was only in the XIII century that the dates of all four sets of Ember Days became fixed once and for all:

Ieiunium primi mensis (March): the first week of Lent;

Ieiunium quarti mensis (June): the week after Pentecost;

Ieiunium septimi mensis (Sept.): the week after Sept. 14 (Holy Cross):

Ieiumium decimi mensis (Dec.): the week after the III Sunday of Advent.

The institution of the seasonal Ember Days was of Roman origin, but their observance spread throughout the entire Latin Church. The fasting on Wednesday and Friday derived from the primitive Christian practice of fasting every Wednesday and Friday; the Saturday fast was simply a prolongation of that of Friday and was connected to the great Vigil of Twelve Lessons characteristic of Ember Saturday night.[112] As Leo the Great put it: "On Wednesday and Friday, then, we shall fast, and on Saturday we shall keep vigil at the church of the holy Apostle Peter."[113]

b. *The Ides of September* (Sept 13).

Traces of a reorganization of the liturgical year before the time of Gregory the Great († 604)—probably in the V or VI century—are still apparent. The maximum number of Sundays between the first Sunday after Pentecost (termed *Dominica vacat* but later known as Trinity Sunday) and January 1 is thirty-two (see Table I).

When Easter falls between March 22 and 24 (=Pentecost between May 10 and 12), sixteen of these thirty-two Sundays come before the Ides of September, whose chronological importance is revealed in the Rule of St. Benedict and its derivatives: [*Ieiunium monasticum*] *ab Idus autem Septembres usque caput quadragesimae* (cap. 41).[114] Thus there are two equal groups of Sundays during the great off-season extending from the Sunday after Pentecost until January 1 and they are divided by Sept. 13.[115]

The number of Sundays between Jan. 1 and the beginning of Lent obviously depends on the date of the latter, i.e., five, nine or ten Sundays.[116] The importance of this series of Sundays was bound to decrease with the institution of *Quinquagesima* (ca. 530), *Sexagesima* (ca. 590-604) and *Septuagesima* (ca. 650).

When the beginning of the liturgical year was pushed back from March 1 to December 25, the period between Christmas and Lent or, later, between Christmas and the season of Septuagesima was severely modified, while the Sundays between Pentecost and Christmas were only slightly affected. New groups of Sundays appeared: *Dominicae post Natale* and *post Epiphaniam*, although the actual number of Sundays varied from one liturgical text to another. The minimal system was calculated on Easter falling on March 25 which had the I Sunday after Epiphany fall on January 7, the very day after the feast.[117]

A final rearrangement of the Sundays took place after the new beginning of the liturgical year was fixed on December 25; it was the adoption of the season of Advent, sometime before the pontificate of Gregory I (590-604).[118] The number of Sundays assigned to Advent fluctuated somewhat but became fixed at four in the Gregorian books and for the rest of the Middle Ages.

In the course of the VII century, although the papal, stational sacramentary never developed a full set of Sunday propers after Pentecost, other derivative usages, such as that of St. Peter's basilica, divided this long series of common Sundays into five groups, each depending on a fixed major festival of the *Sanctorale*: e.g., the *Paduense* had:

5 *dominicae post Pentecosten*;

5 *dominicae post octavas Apostolorum* (Peter and Paul);

5 *dominicae post natale S. Laurentii* (Aug. 10);

9 *dominicae post sancti Angeli* (Sept. 29);

4 *dominicae de Adventu* (see Table J).[119]

The influential Frankish Gelasians of the late VIII century, on the other hand, had twenty-six to twenty-seven Sundays after Pentecost and five *ante Natale Domini*.[120] Employing largely the same texts to supplement the supposed deficiencies of the *Hadrianum*, Benedict of Aniane supplied twenty-four Sundays after Pentecost[121] and this arrangement became standard until the II Vatican Council.

C. TYPES OF LITURGICAL READINGS AND THEIR TERMINOLOGY.

Several different systems were worked out to help lectors find the proper readings for the recurring festivals. The remarkable inventories of T. Klauser (1935) make it possible to ascertain both the origin and nature of these several systems. Of thirty-eight *codices* (Roman and non-Roman) before 800, nineteen indicate the pericopes (liturgical readings of set length) by marginal notes to the text of a New Testament; eight *codices* by marginal notes and lists of *incipits* and *explicits* for each reading—often of different periods and origins—; three *codices* provide the readings *in extenso*, i.e., they are lectionaries properly speaking; and two *codices* give the pericopes in full in the context of a sacramentary.[122] We can at least learn from such statistics that, in the oldest documents we have, the use of marginal notes was more frequent than the use of lists of pericopes, lectionaries or sacramentaries with the readings included. It would be a mistake, however, to conclude that these four ways of providing readings were simply four consecutive stages of a gradual evolution: marginal notes, lists, lectionaries, sacramentaries with readings. The fact is that these four systems coexisted side by side for hundreds of years until, finally, the lectionary with full readings won the day.

There is evidence for all four methods already in the V/VI

centuries and all four continued to exist until the XIV century.[123] The use of marginal notes lasted so long as readings were relatiely few and the Bible itself remained a liturgical book. The lists of *incipits* and *explicits* became necessary as the number of readings increased while the Bible still remained the sole book of readings. The lectionary with the lessons *in extenso* appears to have been, at first, rather a luxury item; it came into more general use as the biblical *codices* stopped being employed as liturgical books and as the rites became settled. The combining of the lectionary and the sacramentary in a single book coincided with the development of the plenary missal; the latter was unknown before the X century, a relatively late date.[124]

The book of pericopes that was joined to the sacramentary and the *Antiphonale missae* to make the missal was not a complete lectionary with epistles and gospels selected for each day according to some coherent principle. Originally the choice of epistles and gospels had been made separately and they maintained their distinct character very largely even when combined into a single mass lectionary; rarely were they adapted or adjusted to one another. They were united far more by chance than by design. Moreover, none of the ancient sacramentaries coincide with any surviving system of readings (marginal notes, lists or lectionaries). Only the Comes of Murbach has some connection with a particular type of sacramentary, the Frankish Gelasians. From our evidence it is clear that not only did the different systems for indicating the pericopes evolve separately, but the arrangement of epistle and gospel readings also developed in isolation from one another and were only combined much later in a purely haphazard manner.

We shall survey the three basic systems of providing readings that were prevalent in the Middle Ages.

1. MARGINAL NOTES.

Marginal notes are indications provided in the margins of Bibles— either complete Bibles or ones divided into Old Testament and New Testament.[125] These notes consisted of crosses or other reference signs placed in the margin of a *codex* at the beginning of each pericope; its conclusion was not always similarly indicated. This rudimentary system seems awkward at first glance but was actually the only one possible in ancient Bibles without either chapter or verse; the best references available were the Eusebian sections or canons,[126] but only for the Gospels. The older Bibles, then, could hardly be used with lists of *incipits* and *explicits* since it would have been difficult or impossible to find the pericopes in the text without the marginal indications. Although infrequent, marginal notes continued to be used in Bibles until the XIV century. Klauser lists eleven for the period from the VII to the XIV century: two for each century from the VII to the XII; one for the XIII and one for the XIV century.[127] Sometimes, too, marginal notes coexisted in the same *codex* with lists of pericopes at the beginning or end of the volume, although they were usually not the same!

2. CAPITULARIA OR LISTS OF PERICOPES.

Most are arranged in the same way:

a) the day and the month, as in present-day usage (dating by Kalends, Ides and Nones is rare in these lists);

b) the indication of the liturgical day and the stational church;

c) the indication of the biblical book (chapter or Eusebian section for the gospels);

d) the *incipit* and the *explicit* of the pericope connected by *usque*; e.g. *Die X mensis Maii. Natale sancti Gordiani. Scd* [=secundum] *Matth. cap XCV* [=Mt 10:34-42]. *Nolite arbitrari quia veni pacem* usque *Amen dico vobis non perdet mercedem suam.*

Ebdomada III [of Lent] *die dominica ad scum Laurentium. Scd. Luc. cap. CXXVI* [=Lk 11:14-28]. *Erat Iesus eiciens daemonium* usque *Beati qui audiunt verbum Dei et custodiunt illud.*

In the oldest surviving MSS, the lists begin with the midnight mass of Christmas and arrange all the masses of both the Sanctoral and the Temporal cycle in a single series of *formulae*.[128] Even before the VIII century, however, some MSS begin their lists with the Vigil of Christmas, as in the sacramentaries. In the IX century, there appeared the first list with the I Sunday of Advent as its point of departure (Rome, *Vat. lat.* 5465), an arrangement that was to become predominant in the X century.

The generic term *Capitulare* for a list of pericopes appeared in the VIII century:

Ordo XXIV, 7 (ca. 750/787; *Roma suburbicaria*): *Legitur lectio una sicut in capitulare commemorat* (Andrieu, *Ordines* 3, 289);

Ordo XV, 104 (ca. 750/787; Frankish): *Et inde leguntur lectiones duae quas in capitulare commemorat* (Andrieu, *Ordines*, 3, 118):

the *Comes* (=Capitulare) of *Würzburg* (*codex* M.p. Th. f. 62, ca. 700):

Incipiunt capitula lectionum anni circuli. Incipiunt capitula sancti evangelii lectionum.

Rome, *Vat. Pal. lat.* 46, ca. 800: *Incipit capitulare lectionum evangeliorum de circulo anni.*

In these quotations *capitulare* is a collective term designating the *capitula*, i.e., the pericopes that were to be read.[129] *Capitulare* should not be confused with *comes*; *capitulare* means a list of pericopes; *comes* means a collection of pericopes copied out in full.[130]

As regards their content; there are three kinds of lists:

1. *Capitulare lectionum or Lists of non-Gospel Readings:*

The term *capitulare lectionum* is not explicitly used either in the literary texts or in liturgical MSS. The *Comes (sic)* of Würzburg carries the title *capitula lectionum*. Compared to the two other kinds of lists, the *cap. lect.* are few in number. According to Klauser (p. xxxvi), between the VIII and the XV century there are only seven *cap. lect.*, the oldest being from around 700 (Würzburg) and the six others scattered from the XIII to the XV century. None survive from the IX, X, XI, or XII centuries. Perhaps the small number of *capitularia* can be explained by the absence of chapters in the non-gospel parts of the New Testament. In any case, such lists or readings can be found both in complete Bibles and in MSS of the New Testament.

2. *Capitulare evangeliorum or Lists of Gospel Pericopes.*

The term *capitulare* was used around 800 (Trier, Stadtbibliothek, *codex* XXII). It also appears in the masculine form, *capitularis* (Liège, Biblio. univer., *codex* 4; X century; Vienna, Nationalbiblio., *codex* 1190, IX century). For such lists of gospel readings other names are even more common: *Breviarius/breviarium lectionum evangelii, breviarium quattuor evangeliorum, breviarium* alone, *tituli evangeliorum, ordo evangeliorum per annum, index evangeliorum, capitulatio, tabula, quotationes evangeliorum, registrum.* According to Klauser (pp. xxxvii-lxx), the 429 MSS of the *cap. evang.* are catalogued by century as follows:

VIII:	2 MSS	XII:	63 MSS
IX:	140 MSS	XIII:	13 MSS
X:	96 MSS	XIV:	6 MSS
XI:	101 MSS	XV:	8 MSS

The *capitularia evangeliorum* are found in *codices* of the four Gospels (usually in an appendix at the end but sometimes at the beginning) but also in full Bibles and in New Testaments.

3. *Captularia lectionum et evangeliorum.*

Although never actually used in any of the MSS, this would be the most appropriate title for such lists of readings. For this third type of list, the MSS use the following titles: *cotationes/quotationes epistolarum et evangeliorum, tabula evangeliorum et epistolarum, inventarium evangeliorum et epistolarum, breviarium, intitulationes, registrum, pronunciatio, ordo legendi, terminationes, opusculum evangeliorum et epistolarum.* According to Klauser (pp. lxxi-lxxxi), the Roman *capitularia evang. et epist.* can be arranged as follows: VIII-XII: 1 MS per century; XIII: 83 MSS; XIV: 53 MSS; XV: 40 MSS; XVI: 1 MS.

3. BOOKS OF PERICOPES WITH THE TEXT IN EXTENSO.

Books containing the pericopes are arranged in the same way as the lists of pericopes but give the full passage to be read rather than just its opening and closing words. Such a book dispenses a reader from using a Bible any longer and greatly facilitates his task. It was, however, a luxury which many churches could not afford.[131] There survive:

1. Books of gospel readings: *Evangelary;*[132]
2. Books of non-gospel readings: *Epistolary;*[133]
3. Books of both gospel and non-gospel readings together: *Mass Lectionary.*[134]

Klauser (pp. lxxxi-cxx) helps us establish a lexicon for these three kinds of Roman documents:

a) *Epistolary: Apostolus,*[135] *Comes, Liber comitis, Epistolare (-ium, -ius),*[136] *Epistolium, Collectarium, Liber* or *Ordo epistolarum, Lectionarius,*[137] *Lectionarius plenarius.*

b) *Evangelary: Evangelium excerptum* (X century), *Evangeliare, Evangelistale, Evangelistarium, Liber* or *Libellus* or *Ordo evangelii (-iorum), Plenarium.*

c) *Mass Lectionary: Comes* (ca. 800), *Epistolae cum evangeliis, Lectionarius epistolarum et evangeliorum* or *de epist. et evangel., Liber comitis, Liber lectionum, Liber commicus.*[138]

In the MSS, the book of pericopes is designated by a great variety of confusing terms. Rather than trying to ferret out *termini technici*, it is better to employ the nomenclature commonly used by liturgical scholars:

1. The term *Epistolary* means a complete series of non-gospel readings, either in the form of simple lists or *in extenso;*

2. The term *Evangelary* means a complete series of gospel readings, either in the form of simple lists or *in extenso;*

3. The term *Mass Lectionary* means documents containing both the Epistolary and the Evangelary. The Mass Lectionary must be distinguished from the *Office Lectionary* which contains all the readings from the Bible, the legends of the saints and the homilies of the Fathers for the use at Vigils of the daily Office.

The analysis of any given series of readings is equally well served by a *list* of pericopes or by a *book* of pericopes.[139]

Practically speaking, we use the term *lectionary* in a general sense to designate any document which indicates liturgical readings.

COLLECTIONS OF MSS.

There is no full inventory of the *codices* of lessons for the Eucharist, both because of the immense number of MSS involved and because of the difficulty in classifying them. The works cited below usually contain both catalogues of MSS and studies. The bibliographical notices they include—especially the more recent ones—will help us to get our bearings in the midst of such a vast amount of material. The innumerable articles which have appeared on some of these MSS cannot be listed here; most will be found in the works given below.

E. Ranke, *Das kirchliche Pericopensystem* (Berlin 1847), with appendices.

S. Beissel, *Entstehung der Perikopen des römischen Messbuches*, Ergänzungsband 93 zu den *Stimmen aus Maria Laach* (Freiburg/Br. 1907; reprint Rome 1967).

E. Baudot, *Les Lectionnaires* (Paris 1908).

G. Godu, "Épîtres-Évangiles," DACL 5 (1922/23) 245-344; 852-923.

R.J. Hesbert, *Paléographie musicale* 14 (Tournai 1931)

T. Klauser, *Das römische Capitulare Evangeliorum*, LQF 28 (Münster/Westf. 1935), a basic text for both its methodology and its inventory of MSS. Cited from now on as "Klauser" with no other indications, except the page numbers.

W.H. Frere, *Studies in Early Roman Liturgy. 1: Calendar; 2: The Roman Gospel-Lectionary; 3: The Roman Epistle-Lectionary*, ACC 28, 30, 32 (Oxford-London 1930, 1934, 1935).

P. Salmon, *Le Lectionnaire de Luxeuil* (Paris, codex *lat.* 9427), 2 vols., Collectanea biblica latina 7, 9 (Rome 1944, 1953).

G. Kunze, *Die gottesdienstliche Schriftlesung* (Göttingen 1947);

_____, "Die Lesungen," *Leiturgia* 2 (Kassel 1955) 87-180.

A. Chavasse, "Les plus anciens types du lectionnaire et de l'antiphonaire romain de la messe," RB 62 (1952) 1-91.

S.J.P. Van Dijk, *Latin Liturgical Manuscripts* (Oxford 1952).

E. Dekkers, *Clavis Patrum Latinorum* (2nd ed. Steenbrugge 1961) 442-450—excellent repertory for the pre-carolingian period.

K. Gamber, *Codices liturgici latini antiquiores—second, enlarged, ed.*–2 vols., Spicilegii Friburgensis Subsidia 1 (Fribourg 1968)—excellent inventory with bibliography; classifications made following the principles set out in his *Sakramentartypen* (Beuron 1958); the first edition of *Codices liturgici latini antiquiores* appeared in one volume in 1963.

A. Chavasse, "L'Épistolier romain du *codex* de Wurtzbourg. Son organisation," RB 91 (1981) 280-331.

_____, "L'Évangeliaire romain de 645: un recueil. Sa compositions, façons et materiaux," RB 92(1982)32-75.

D. THE LECTIONARIES OF MEROVINGIAN GAUL.

Before enumerating the principal documents relating to the Gallican readings, it is well to cite the celebrated letter of Pseudo-Jerome which figures as a prologue to so many of these MSS: *Ad Constantium Constantinopolitanum. Quamquam licenter adsumatur . . venerabilis mihi et amantissime frater.* Since Alan of Farfa (†770), the Middle Ages believed that this was an authentic letter of St. Jerome. As a matter of fact it is a text drawn up a shortly before the end of the VIII century and had little or no connection with Rome.[140] It is probably a Gallican type *consuetudo* and was not originally meant to introduce a eucharistic lectionary. The anonymous author may have wanted, however, to compose something didactic and edifying along the lines of a book of liturgical readings: . . . *lectiones utriusque Testamenti . . . Sed et nonnulla alia aedificationis causa multa illic aggregata sunt atque suis apellationibus inserta, id est in Capite Quadragesimae de abstinentia sanctorum et sobrietate. Item, in Quadragesima de penitentia, de pudicitia, de remissione inimicitiarum vel alia multa. Haec enim omnia ad multorum equidem utilitatem . . . scribere curavi.*[141]

1. *The Wolfenbüttel Palimpsest.*

Library: Herzog-August Bibliothek, *codex* 4160 (*Weissenburgensis* 76).

Date: ca. 500.

Origin: S. Gaul=Septimania, between Perpignan and Marseilles (Dold) or S.E. Gaul (Klauser, JfL 15 [1935] p. 467), and finally at Wissembourg, France.

Author: The author is unknown but may have been Musaeus of Marseilles (†461?), according to Morin and Gamber, or Claudius Mamertus (†ca. 474), according to G. Berti.

Edition: A. Dold, *Das älteste Liturgiebuch der lateinischen Kirche,* TuA 26-28 (Beuron 1936).[142]

Bibliography: G. Morin, "Le plus ancien monument qui existe de la liturgie gallicane," EL 51(1937)3-12; K. Gamber, "Das Lectionar und Sakramentar des Musäus von Massilia," RB 69(1959) 118-215; G. Berti, "Il più antico lezionario della Chiesa," EL 68(1954) 147-154. CLLA, no. 250, pp. 174-176.

This lectionary is a true *comes* with all its lessons copied out in full and a palimpsest preserving more than half of the original content, although the original order of its pages cannot be ascertained for sure. In accordance with Gallican usage, it gives three lessons (Old Testament, Pauline letters, Gospel) for each celebration. The liturgical year begins with the Easter Vigil and closes with Holy Saturday, following an arrangement already attested by Zeno of Verona (✝ 380). Many of its lessons are centos, i.e., isolated passages of Scripture assembled as a literary whole, but they have no connection with the *Diatesseron* or *Gospel Harmony* of Tatian (late II century).

2. *Fragment of a Palimpsest Lectionary of Paris* (sometimes called the second lectionary of Luxeuil).

Library: Paris, Biblio. Nat. *codex latinus* 10863.

Date: late VI/early VII century and therefore before the Lectionary of Luxeuil.

Origin: Merovingian Gaul.

Edition: E. Chatelain, "Fragments palimpsestes d'un lectionnaire mérovingien," *Revue d'histoire et de littérature religieuse.* 5(1900) 193-199; DACL 6, 513-514. CLLA, no. 258, p. 277.

The 69 palimpsest leaves have not yet been studied scientifically. This lectionary has the usual three readings of the Gallican system but they rarely if ever agree with those of the Lectionary of Luxeuil.

3. *The Lectionary of Luxeuil.*

Library: Paris, Biblio. Nat., *codex latinus* 9427.

Date: late VII or very early VIII century.

Origin: Merovingian Gaul, probably Paris (St. Denis or Langres?); at Luxeuil until the French Revolution.[143]

Author: unknown; possibly Claudius Mamertus? (✝ 474).[144]

Edition: J. Mabillon, *De liturgia gallicana* (1685), pp. 106-173; this is an abidged edition, the lessons being reduced to lists; PL 72,99-448; P.

Salmon, *Le lectionnaire de Luxeuil,* Collectanea biblica latina 7 and 9 (Rome 1944 and 1953), critical edition with facsimiles.
Bibliography: DACL 5, 274-277 and 863-869; 9, 2748-2769; P. Radó, "Das älteste Schriftlesungssystem der altgallischen Liturgie," EL 45(1931) 9-25; 100-115; C. Charlier, "Note sur les origines de l'écriture dite de Luxeuil," RB 58(1948)149-157; E. A. Lowe, "The 'Script of Luxeuil': a Title Vindicated," RB 63(1953) 132-146; F. Masai, "Pour quelle Église fut exécutée le lectionnaire de Luxeuil," *Scriptorium* 2(1948)37-46; 3(1949)172. See also the remarks of M. Bogaert, "Un témoin liturgique de la vieille version latine du Livre de Judith," RB 77 (1967) 7-28. CLLA, no 255, p. 176.

This *codex* is not complete; it begins with the Vigil of Christmas (not preserved) and breaks off in the middle of the *lectiones cotidianae.* It is a pure Gallican book untouched by Roman influences. It contains the three lessons *in extenso* (prophetic, pauline, evangelical) as well as readings drawn from non-biblical sources.[145] A few masses have two or four lessons. Its readings differ completely from those of the Lectionary of Wolfenbüttel.

4. *The Lectionary of Sélestat.*

Library: Sélestat (Schlettstadt), France, Bibliothèque de la Ville, *codex* 1 (*olim* 1093).
Date: ca. 700.
Origin: N. Italy, not Merovingian Gaul (Lowe).
Edition and Bibliography: G. Morin, "Le lectionnaire mérovingien de Sélestat," RB 25(1908)161-166 and in *Études, textes, découvertes* 1 (Maredsous 1913) 440-456; DACL 5, 277-279; 6, 514-516; K. Gamber, "I più antichi libri liturgici dell 'alta Italia," *Rivista di storia della Chiesa in Italia* 15(1961)74-75. Klauser, p. xxxiv, no. 31., CLLA no. 265, p. 179.

This lectionary contains 59 pericopes and is complete for the first OT lesson of the Gallican system, but it does not have the second or third reading, except for the period extending from the Vigil of Easter to Pentecost *(Acts of the Apostles).* The set of readings goes from the I Sunday of Advent to Good Friday. The partially edited text is that of some pre-Jerome recension of the Bible. Because of its Gallican and Milanese characteristics, this lectionary may be a transitional form between the two rites.

5. *The Fragmentary Epistolary of Sélestat.*

Library: Sélestat, France, Biblio. de la Ville, *codex* 1 (B).
Date: ca. 700.
Origin: N. Italy.
Edition and Bibliography: G. Morin, "Le lectionnaire mérovingien de Schlettstadt," RB 25(1908)166. CLLA no. 266, p. 179.

This fragment has 7 leaves containing the epistles from Advent to the *Dominica de Samaritana* (II Sun. of Lent).

6. *A List of Pauline Readings; the List or Epistolary of Bobbio.*

Library: Rome, *Vat. lat., codex* 5755.
Date and Origin: VI/VII century; N. Italy (Bobbio).
Edition: A. Dold, *Geschabte Paulustexte der I. Hälfte des VII. Jhs. mit einer gleichzeitigen unbekannten Liste paulinischer Leseabschnitte,* TuA 19-20 (Beuron 1931) 64-83. Klauser, p. xxxiv, no. 29; CLLA no. 240, pp. 170-171.

This is a Pauline text with marginal notes and a somewhat more recent list of readings, in two columns, containing 57 pericopes (VIII century); the list which has been added to the original MS does not always correspond with the marginal notes. The period covered extends from Advent to the Saturday before Easter. The basic arrangement is that of Bobbio, but this fundamentally Gallican system also contains Mozarabic, Milanese and even Roman characteristics. It belongs to the same type as the marginal notes of Freising (*Clm* 6229, *infra*). *Vat. lat.* 5755 must not be confused with the pericopes of the Bobbio Missal (*Parisinus lat.* 13246).

7. *The Bobbio Missal.*

Library: Paris, Biblio. Nat., *codex lat.* 13246 (*olim* St. Germain des Prés, 1488).
Date: VIII century; the *Parisinus* 13246 is a distant copy of what was probably a VI-century original contemporaneous with the Lectionary of Luxeuil.
Origin: N. Italy (Pavia?, Gamber), later at Bobbio, rather than in S. Gaul (Morin).

Editions: J. Mabillon, *Museum Italicum* 1(1687) 278-397 (*Sacramentarium gallicanum*), reproduced by L. Muratori, *Liturgia Romana vetus* (1748) 2, col. 775-968 and in PL 72, 451-574 (*Sacramentarium gallicanum a Muratorio* (sic!) *in lucem editum*); critical edition by E.A. Lowe and J. W. Legg, *The Bobbio Missal: A Gallican Mass-Book*, HBS 53 and 58, 1: Facsimile (London 1917), 2: Text (London 1920); Lowe-Wilmart-Wilson, *The Bobbio Missal*, HBS 61, 3: Notes and Studies (London 1924); K. Gamber, *Sakramentartypen*, p. 39; and "Die Ostermessen im Missale Gallicanum Vetus," *SE* 12(1961)89-96. The pericopes of the Bobbio Missal must not be confused with those of the Bobbio Epistolary (*Vat. lat.* 5755, *supra*). Klauser, p. xxxiii, no. 24; CLLA, no. 220, pp. 167-168.

In conformity with Gallican usage, three readings usually appear before each mass formulary and the texts are provided in full. Although the Bobbio Missal is a rather poor witness to the Gallican rite because of its mixed character (Romano-Gelasian *formulae*), the arrangement of its pericopes is remarkably helpful for an understanding of the Gallican system of readings.

8. The Marginal Notes of the Gospel Book of St. Kilian.

Library: Würzburg, Universitätsbibliothek, *codex* M.p.th.q.1a.

Date and Origin: VI/VII century; from an area which used the Gallican rite.

Edition and Bibliography: G. Morin, "Liturgie et basiliques de Rome au VII siècle," RB 28(1911) 328-330; P. Salmon, "Le système des lectures liturgiques contenues dans les notes marginales du MS M.p. th. Q. I a de Wurzbourg," RB 61(1951) 38-53; 62(1952) 294-296; P. Radó, "Die Perikopennotierungen im Evangeliar des Hl. Kilian," EL 45(1931) 113-114; B. Bischoff and J. Hoffman, *Libri Sancti Kyliani*, Quellen und Forschungen zur Geschichte des Bistums und Hochstifts Würzburg 6 (Würzburg 1952) 92. Klauser, p. xxxv, no. 38. CLLA no. 250, pp. 175-176.

These are marginal notes extending from the VII-IX century attached to a text of the Four Gospels. They are of the same type as those in the lectionary of Wolfenbüttel (*Weissenburgensis* 76) but they are not of the same type as those of the Lectionary of Luxeuil (*Parisinus* 9427); e.g. the *cento* Jn 6: 1, 2, 5a, 14 and Lk 24:13-14, 30-31, *In epyfania* is only to be found in the lectionary of Wolfenbüttel.

9. *The Marginal Notes of the Pauline Letters of Freising.*

Library: Munich, Bayerische Staatsbibliothek, *Clm* 6229.
Date and Origin: from the time of Bishop Arbeo of Freising (764-784).
Edition and Bibliography: B. Bischoff, "Gallikanische Epistelperikopen," *Studien und Mitteilungen O.S.B.* 50(1932) 516-519. Klauser, p. xxxiii, no. 20; CLLA no. 240, p. 171.
The marginal notes are affixed to each chapter and are of the same type as those of the Bobbio Epistolary (*Vat. lat.* 5755).

10. *The Lectionary of Tegernsee.*

Library: Munich, Bayerische Staatsbibliothek, *Clm* 19126 (two leaves at the beginning and the end of the MS).
Origin and Date: end of the VIII century; probably for the monastery of Tegernsee.
Edition: A. Dold, *Ein rätselhaftes Lektionar aus Tegernsee,* TuA 35 (Beuron 1944) 39-52.
Bibliography: G. Kunze, *Die Gottesdienstliche Schriftlesung* (Göttingen 1947) 42. CLLA no. 1625, pp. 588-589.
This lectionary contains only short readings which may be *lectiones breves* for Prime rather than readings for the Eucharist. It appears to be a Gallican document.

11. *Marginal Notes of the Pentateuch of Lyons.*

Library: Lyons, Bibliothèque municipale, *codex* 403 (*olim* 329) and 1964 (*olim* 1840).
Date: VII century.
Edition: U. Robert, *Pentateuchi versio latina antiquissima e cod. Lugdunensi,* 1 (Paris 1881), pp. xix-xli; 2 (Lyons 1900), p. xiii. Klauser, p. xxxii, no. 14; CLLA no. 260ᵃ, p. 177.

12. *The Marginal Notes of the Gospel Book of Trier.*

Library: Trier, Dombibliotek, *codex* 420 (*olim* 134).
Date and Origin: VIII century; Trier? Echternach?
Edition and Bibliography: D. De Bruyne, "Les notes liturgiques du MS 134 de la cathédrale de Trèves," RB 33(1921) 45-52; P. Radó, "Die Heimat des Pericopenssytems im Thomas-Evangeliar," EL

45(1931) 208-210. There are 125 marginal notes indicating gospels to be read and they are of the Gallican type. Klauser, p. xxxiv, no. 33; CLLA no. 260^d, p. 177.

13. *The Marginal Notes of the Gospel Book of St. Denis.*

Library: Paris, Biblio. Nat., *codex latinus* 256.
Date: VII century, but the notes belong to the beginning of the VIII century.
Edition and Bibliography: G. Morin, "Le lectionnaire de l'Eglise de Paris au VII siècle," RB 10(1893) 438-441; P. Salmon, "Le texte biblique de l'Évangeliaire de Saint-Denis," *Miscellanea Mercati* 1 (Rome 1946) 103-106. There are 30 marginal notes of the Gallican type. G. Morin used them, somewhat imprudently, to complete the Lectionary of Luxeuil. Klauser, xxxiii, no. 22; CLLA no. 260c, p. 177.

14. *The Marginal Notes of the Gospel Book of Durham.*

Library: Durham, Chapter Library, MS A.II.16+MS A.II.17.
Date: beginning of the VIII century, but the marginal notes extend from the VIII to the IX century.
Edition: C.H. Turner, *The Oldest MS of the Vulgate Gospels* (Oxford 1931) 217. There are 17 marginal notes in the first MS and 27 in the second. Klauser, p. xxxi, no. 6 and 7; CLLA no. 260^d, p. 178.

The marginal notes contained in the books described above (nos. 11-14) were compared by P. Salmon, *Le lectionnaire de Luxeuil* (Rome 1944) lxxxi-cxxiii. See also the inventories of Klauser and Gamber cited under each description.[146]

Several of the Gallican MSS described above can also appear among the lectionaries of N. Italy given below.

E. THE LECTIONARIES OF NORTHERN ITALY.

1. *The Marginal Notes of the Gospel Book of Vercelli.*

Library: Vercelli, Tesoro della Cattedrale, no number.
Date: The Four Gospels are of the IV century; the marginal notes extend from the VII to the VIII century.
Bibliography: A. Gasquet, *Codex Vercellensis* 1 (Rome 1914) pp. xvi-xix.

The arrangement of the readings is proper to Vercelli. Klauser, p. xxxv, no. 34; CLLA no. 062, p. 89.

2. *The Marginal Notes of the Gospel Book of St. Marcellinus.*

Library: Ancona, Biblio. capit., *codex Evangel. S. Marcellini.*
Date: the marginal notes extend from the VII to the IX century.
Bibliography: T. Klauser, "Der *Codex* S. Marcellini in Ancona," RB 50(1938) 309-323; reprinted in *Gesammelte Arbeiten,* Jahrbuch für Antike und Christentum Ergänzungsband 3 (Münster 1974) 71-81.
The 35 marginal notes provide the arrangement of pericopes called that of Ancona.[147]

3. *The Marginal Notes of the Gospel Book of St. Gall.*

Library: St. Gall, Stiftsbibliothek, *codex* 1395.
Date: the Book belongs to the end of the V century but the notes are of the VII (?).
Edition and Bibliogaphy: C.H. Turner, *The Oldest MS of the Vulgate Gospels* (Oxford 1931) 71; D. De Bruyne, *Bulletin d'ancienne littérature chrétienne latine* 2(1922) no. 281. Klauser, p. xxxi, no. 10; CLLA no. 073, p. 99.
The notes belong to the liturgy of N. Italy.

4. *The Marginal Notes of the Codex Valerianus or the Gospel Book of St. Corbinianus.*

Library: Munich, Bayerische Staatsbibliothek, *Clm* 6224.
Date and Origin: The Gospel Book belongs to the beginning of the VI century; the marginal notes extend from the VII to the IX century; N. Italy (Milan? Verona?).
Edition and Bibliography: G. Morin, "Un systeme inédit de lectures liturgiques en usage au VII/VIII siècle dans une église de la Haute Italie," RB 20(1903) 375-388; D. De Bruyne, "Notes sur le *Clm* 6224," RB 28 (1911) 75-79 and *Bulletin d'ancienne littérature chrétienne* 1 (Maredsous 1921) no. 432; G. Leidinger, *Wissenschaftliche Festgabe zur 1200. Jubiläum des hl. Korbinian* (Munich 1924) 79-102. Klauser, p. xxxiii, no. 19; CLLA no. 247, pp. 173-174.
The notes provide an arrangement of readings proper to N. Italy; Gamber prefers the region around Aquileia.

5. *Marginal Notes to the Gospel Book of Milan.*

Library: Milan, Biblioteca Ambrosiana, *codex* C. 39 inf.

Date and Origin: The Gospel Book belongs to the beginning of the VI century; the marginal notes extend from the VII to the IX century; N. Italy (Milan? Verona?).

Edition and Bibliography: G. Morin, "Un systeme inédit de lectures liturgiques en usage au VII/VIII siècle dans une èglise de la Haute Italie," RB 20(1903)375-388; D. De Bruyne, "L'origine des processions de la chandeleur et des rogations à propos d'un sermon inédit," RB 34(1922) 26, no. 1. Klauser, p. xxxii, no. 16. CLLA no. 247[b], p. 174.

The arrangement of readings is related to that of the Gospel Book of St. Corbinianus (*Clm* 6224) and is a mixture of N. Italian and Roman characteristics.

6. *Capitulare Evangeliorum of the Codex Foroiuliensis.*

Library: Cividale, Museo civico (archeologico), *Codex Foroiuliensis* (CXXXVIII).

Date: The Gospel Book belongs to the beginning of the VI century; the fragmentary list of gospel pericopes (IV Sunday of October to the II Sunday of November) belongs to the VII century; the marginal notes extend from the VI to the VIII century; the two lists do not agree with one another.

Edition: D. De Bruyne, "Les notes liturgiques du *codex Foroiuliensis,*" RB 30(1913) 208-218. Klauser, p. xxx, no. 4; CLLA no. 246, pp. 172-173.

The marginal notes seem to be of the same type as those of the Capitulary of the *codex Rehdigeranus (infra)*. The arrangement is probably that of Aquileia.

7. *The Capitulare Evangeliorum of the Codex Rehdigeranus.*

Library: Wroclaw (Breslau), *olim* Stadtbibliothek, *codex Rehdigeranus* 169 (fol. 92ᵛ); destroyed during World War II.

Date: This codex belongs to the first half of the VIII century; the fragmentary list of gospel readings *(In nomine Domini incipit Capitulare Evangelii)* from December to the vigil of St. John the Baptist (June 23) and the marginal notes belong to the same era.

Edition and Bibliography: H. J. Vogels, *Codex Rehdigeranus*, Collectanea biblica latina 2 (Rome 1913) 95-97 and xxii-xxv; DACL 1, 2685-2688; G. Morin, "L'année liturgique à Aquilée antérieurement à l'époque carolingienne d'après le *Codex Evangelorium Rehdigeranus*," RB 19(1902) 1-12; K. Gamber, "Die älteste abendländische Evangelien-Perikopen-Liste, vermutlich von Bischof Fortunatianus von Aquileja," *Münchener Theol. Zeitschrift* 13(1962) 181-201. Klauser, p. xxx, no. 3; CLLA no. 245, p. 172.

The *Capitulare* represents the Aquileian arrangement of lessons; it probably does not go back as far as Bishop Fortunatianus (†after 360).

8. *The Gospel Book of Constance.*

Library: Darmstadt, Landes- und Hochschulbibliothek, Hs. 895 (a single leaf)+Donaueschingen, Hofbibliothek, *codex* 925 +Stuttgart, Würtemberg. Landesbibliothek, HB VI 114, VII 29, VII 64, XIV 15 (a single leaf in each instance).
Date and Origin: VII century; N. Italy, rather than S.E. Gaul.
Edition and Bibliography: A. Dold, *Konstanzer altlateinische Propheten- und Evangelienbruchstücke mit Glossen*, TuA 7/9 (Beuron 1923) 194-224; K. Gamber, "Die älteste abendländische Perikopen-liste," *Münchener Theol. Zeitschrift* 13(1962) 181-201. Klauser, p. xxxii, no. 11; CLLA no. 261, p. 178.

This fragmentary Gospel Book supposes a *Capitulare* like that of the *Codex Rehdigeranus* (Aquileia). It also has some relationship with the Gospel Book of Verona, Biblioteca capitulare, *codex* VII, of the VIII century; see H. Vogels, *Colligere Fragmenta*, TuA 2 (Beuron 1952) 1-12.

9. *The Libellus Missae of Benediktbeuern* (Diocese of Augsburg)

Library: Munich, Bayerische Staatsbibliothek, *Clm* 6333: a *libellus missae* with epistles and gospels.
Date and Origin: VIII/IX century; Benediktbeuern, then Freising.
Edition and Bibliography: A. Dold, *Die Liturgischen Texte des Clm 6333*, TuA 15/18 (Beuron 1930) pp. 24-75; and *Palimpsest-Studien* 2, TuA 48 (Beuron 1957) passim. CLLA no. 704, p. 331.

The lesson arrangement has the same characteristics as that of the Epistolary of Bobbio (*Vat. lat. 5755*), *supra.*

10. *The Pauline Readings and Marginal Notes of Vat. Reg. 9.*

Library: Rome, *Vat. Reg. lat.* 9 (initial pages).
Date and Origin: Mid-VIII century; N. Italy (Ravenna).
Edition and Bibliography: G. Morin, "Les notes liturgiques du MS
   Vat. Reg. lat. 9 Les épîtres de S. Paul," RB 15(1898) 104-106; A.
   Dold, *Die im codex Vat. lat. 9 vorgeheftete Liste paulinischer Lesungen für
   die Messfeier,* TuA 35 (Beuron 1944); K. Gamber, "Eine altraven-
   natische Epistel-Liste aus der Zeit des hl. Petrus Chrysologus,"
   Liturgisches Jahrbuch 8(1958) 73-96; A. Olivar, "Sobre el *Capitulare
   Lectionum* del *Codex Vat. Reg.* 9," EL 74(1960) 393-408; and in *Scripta
   et Documenta* 13(Montserrat 1962) 429-435. Klauser, p. xxxiv, no.
   27; CCLA no. 242, p. 171.
   The lost Pauline readings which once stood at the beginning of the
MS were found by G. Morin at St. Paul's Abbey in Lavanttal,
Carinthia; see H. Quentin, "Manuscrits démembrés. MS 9 du Fonds
de la Reine à la Bibliothèque Vaticane et Fragment de l'abbaye de
Saint-Paul en Carinthie," RB 28(1911) 257-269. They had been
published previously by Tommasi, *Antiqui libri missarum Romanae
Ecclesiae,* Opera omnia 5, 424-427 (ed. Vezzosi) and by Georgi, *De lit.
Rom. pontif.* 3, 72. The text of the Pauline epistles belongs to the end of
the Merovingian era; see S. Berger, *Histoire de la Vulgate pendant les
premiers siècles du moyen âge* (Paris 1893) 85. This list was probably
used at Ravenna but it is highly doubtful that Peter Chrysologus,
archbishop of Ravenna († 450), had any knowledge of it. The 30
marginal notes from the VII/VIII century in Merovingian script do
not agree with the list of epistles. This list is of the same type as that
of Bobbio (*Vat. lat.* 5755), although it is about a century later.

11. *The Lectionary of Beuron.*

Library: Beuron, Klosterbibliothek, *Fragment* 47.
Date and Origin: X century; N. Italy (Ravenna?).
Edition and Bibliography: A. Dold, "Das Beuroner Fragment-Dop-
   pelblatt no. 47 mit vollständig ausgeschriebenen Texten eines Lec-
   tions-Sakramentars," EL 73(1959) 31-37. CLLA no. 1290, p. 489.
   This MS has the epistle and gospel pericopes *in extenso* after the
oratio, from the I Sunday of Advent to the *feria IV* after the II Sunday
of Advent. The church that used this arrangement cannot be
identified but it was probably N. Italian.

F. MILANESE LECTIONARIES

The Milanese books of readings are peculiar in two ways: From the IX century, they are joined to the sacramentary; only the *lectiones*, (i.e., the first lesson before the epistle in the Gallican system), are assembled into separate books. The other readings are attached to another liturgical book.

1. *The Milanese Lectionary of Orleans.*

Library: Orléans, Bibliothèque municipale, *codex* 184 (161).
Date and Origin: VI/VII century; N. Italy (Ambrosian).
Edition and Bibliography: K. Gamber, "Leimabdrücke eines mailändischen Lektionars aus dem 6/7 Jh.," *Scriptorium* 15(1961) 117-121; and, *Ambrosius* 37(1961) 16-19. CLLA no. 540, pp. 271-272.

Two gospel readings, probably from the *missae cotidianae*, and an epistle for the vigil of St. Lawrence; these fragments are characteristic of an Ambrosian missal. They possess both Gallican and Ambrosian peculiarities: *Dominus Iesus* for *Iesus* and *Lectio sancti evangelii* instead of *Sequentia*.

2. *Capitulare Evangeliorum and the Gospel Book of Busto Arsizio.*

Library: Busto-Arsizio, San Giovanni Battista, *codex* M.I. 14.
Date and Origin: IX century (Borella); X/XI century (Heiming); Busto Arsizio, for the church of St. John the Baptist.
Edition and Bibliography: P. Borella, "Il Capitolare ed Evangeliare ambrosiano di San Giovanni Battista in Busto Arsizio," *Ambrosius* 10(1934) 210-232; A. Paredi, "L 'evangeliario di Busto Arsizio," *Miscellanea liturgica in onore di sua Em. il card. G. Lercaro* 2 (Rome 1967) 207-249. O. Heiming, "Die Episteln der Montage, Dienstage, Mittwoche und Donnerstage der Mailänder Quadragesima," JfL 7(1928) 141-144; and, "Altliturgische Fastenferien in Mailand," AfL 2(1952) 44-60. CLLA no. 541, p. 272.

This is the oldest Milanese *Capitulare evangeliorum* we have and its original seems to have been pre-Carolingian. There are gospel readings only for the Fridays, Saturdays and Sundays of Lent; the other Lenten weekdays were aliturgical until the Romanization of the Milanese rite in Carolingian times. The Gospel Book to which the

Capitulare is attached provides gospel readings for every day but Friday. It is an example of a partial *lectio continua:* the Gospel according to St. Matthew is used until the Saturday before the IV Sunday of Lent.

3. *The Sacramentary of Biasca.*

Library: Milan, Biblioteca Ambrosiana, *codex* A. 24 bis inf.
Date and Origin: X century; Biasca.
Edition and Bibliography: O. Heiming (ed.), *Corpus Ambrosiano-Liturgicum,* 2: *Das Ambrosianische Sakramentar von Biasca,* LQF 51 (Münster 1969); M. Ceriani, *Missale Ambrosianum vetus,* Monum. sacra et profana 8 (Milan 1912); O. Heiming, "Die Episteln der Mailänder Quadragesima," JfL 7 (1927) 141-144. CLLA no. 515, pp. 266-267. This is the Milanese arrangement of readings.

4. *The Sacramentary of Bergamo.*

Library: Bergamo, Biblioteca di S. Allessandro-in-Colonna, no number, fol. 12^r-19^v.
Date and Origin: This fragmentary lectionary belongs to the IX/X century and is in a much later hand than the body of the sacramentary itself: Bergamo.
Edition and Bibliography: P. Cagin, *Codex Sacramentorum Bergomensis,* Auctuarium Solesmense 1 (Solesmes 1900) 187-192; A. Paredi, *Sacramentarium Bergomense,* Monumenta Bergomensia 6 (Bergamo 1962) 28-37. The fragment begins with the *lectio* which precedes the epistle of the II Sunday of Lent.

5. *The Gospel Book of Milan.*

Library: Milan, Biblioteca Ambrosiana, *codex* A 28 inf.
Date and Origin: IX century; Milan.
Edition and Bibliography: P. Borella, *Ambrosius* 10(1934) 210-232.

This Gospel Book begins with the I Sunday of Advent. At the end of the *codex* there are 20 epistles and 4 hagiographical lessons according to the Milanese arrangement.[148]

G. SPANISH LECTIONARIES (Visigothic/Mozarabic).

The Spanish lectionary or *Liber commicus* (and not *comicus*) is characterized by a kind of uniformity and stability unknown to the lectionaries of other countries.[149]

1. *The Liber Commicus of Silos.*

Library: Paris, Biblio. Nat., MS *nouvelles acquisitions lat.* 2171.

Date and Origin: Before 1041/1067; Silos Abbey.

Edition: G. Morin, *Liber commicus sive lectionarius missae quo Toletana Ecclesia ante Mille et ducentos utebatur,* Anecdota Maredsolana 1 (Maredsous 1893) based on the *Parisinus nouv. acq. lat. 2171* alone; F.J. Perez de Urbel and A. Gonzales y Ruiz-Zorilla, *Liber commicus. Edición critica,* Mounumenta Hispaniae sacra. Series liturgica 2-3 (Madrid 1950-1955) = a reconstruction of the *Liber commicus* from the *Parisinus nouv. acq. lat.* 2171, Toledo, Bibl. capit. (Catedral) *codex* 35.4 and 35.8, Madrid, Acad. de la Historia, *codex* 22 (Aemilianus 4), and León, Bibl. capitular (Catedral) *codex* 2.

Bibliography: M. Férotin, *Liber mozarabicus sacramentorum* (Paris 1912) 885-888; DACL 5, 261-271, 857-863; 9, 220-243. CLLA no. 360, p. 215. The surviving witness is a distant copy of the VII-century original from the time of Bishop Ildefonse (657-667) and represents the usages of Toledo. The three series of readings (Old Testament or prophetic *lectio,* epistle and gospel) are given *in extenso* and the year begins with Advent.

2. *The Liber Commicus of Paris.*

Library: Paris, Bibl. Nat., MS *lat.* 2269.

Date and Origin: Late VIII or early IX century; church of St. Nazarius of Carcassonne (France).

Edition: A. Mundó, "El *commicus* Palimsest Paris *lat.* 2269. Amb notes sobre litúrgia i MSS visigòtics a Septimània y Catalunya," *Liturgica* 1, *Scripta et Documenta* 7 (Montserrat 1956) 151-276; and "Frammenti palinsesti del *liber commicus* visigotico," *Analecta Gregoriana* 70(1954) 101-106. CLLA no. 361, p. 215.

The 16 surviving folios of this lectionary begin with January 6 and run to the IV Sunday of Lent. The arrangement does not agree with the later MSS.

3. *The Liber Commicus of Toledo.*

Library: Toledo, Bibl. capitular (Catedral), *codex* 35.8.
Date and Origin: IX/X century; Toledo.
Edition: See the Lectionary of Silos, *supra*.
Bibliography: J.F. Rivera, *Estudios biblicos* 7(1948) 335-359, CLLA
   no. 362, pp. 215-216.
This mutilated lectionary contains prophetic lessons, even for
the weekdays of Lent.

4. *The Liber Commicus of Toledo.*

Library: Toledo, Bibl. capitular (Catedral) *codex* 35.4 (folios 173-
   174).
Date and Origin: End of the IX century; Toledo.
Edition: See the Lectionary of Silos.
These two leaves have the title: *Incipiunt lectiones de cotidiano* and
are followed by readings for a sick person, for a dead lay person
and for dead priests.

5. *The Liber Commicus of León.*

Library: León, Bibl. capitular (Catedral), *codex* 2.
Date and Origin: 1065/1071; León.
Edition: See the Lectionary of Silos. CLLA no. 354, pp. 216-217.
This *codex* has fragments of Advent, Eastertide and some votive
masses.

6. *The Liber Commicus of San Millàn de la Cogolla.*

Library: Madrid, Academia de la Historia, *codex* 22 (*Aemilianus* 4).
Date and Origin: 1073; for the church of San Millàn.
Edition: See the Lectionary of Silos. CLLA no. 363, p. 216.
This is a complete Mozarabic lectionary of a later period: *In
nomine Domini Nostri Iesu Christi incipit liber comicus de toto anni
circulo.*

7. *The Marginal Notes of Aniane* (near Montpellier).

Library: Montpellier, Bibliothèque municipale, *codex* 6.
Date and Origin: VIII/IX century; for the Abbey of Aniane.
Edition: A. Wilmart, "Un lectionnaire d'Aniane," *Revue Mabillon*

13(1923) 40-53; P. Salmon, "Le texte des épîtres de S. Pierre, S. Jean et S. Jude dans le MS 6 de Montpellier," JTS n.s. 2(1951) 170-177; A. Mundó, *Liturgica* 1 (Montserrat 1956) 155; H. Engberding, "Die spanisch-westgothische Liturgie. Eine Einführung in ihr Wesen," *Liturgische Zeitschrift* 4(1931/1932) 155-166; 241-249. CLLA no. 369ᵇ, p. 217.

This codex of Pauline letters has 32 marginal notes. It is a Mozarabic book with many Gallican peculiarities.

8. *The Marginal Notes of the Alcala Bible.*

Library: Madrid, Bibl. univers. *codex* 31 (*Biblia Complutensis*).
Date and Origin: IX/X century; the notes are a little later than the text of the *Complutensis*.
Edition: D. De Bruyne, "Un système de lectures de la liturgie mozarabe," RB 34(1922) 147-155; DACL 12, 402-404. CLLA no. 369ᶜ, p. 217.

This codex has 216 marginal notes, but none for the Gospels. They represent an arrangement that has to be situated sometime between the *Liber commicus* of Silos and the *Liber sacramentorum mozarabicus* (Toledo usages).[150]

H. NON-ROMAN LECTIONARIES OF CENTRAL ITALY (CAMPANIA, BENEVENTO).

A few liturgical documents of VI and VII-century Campania still survive and are available either directly or through Anglo-Saxon copies.[151] They are all free of any Roman influence. On the other hand, none of the Beneventan documents are earlier than the X century and all are Romanized to some extent.[152]

1. *The Epistolary of Capua.*

Library: Fulda, Landesbibliothek, *codex Bonifatianus* 1.
Date and Origin: ca. 545; it was written for Victor of Capua (signature of April 19, 546) and was taken to England, probably by Abbot Hadrian of Nisida (an island near Naples), the companion of Archbishop Theodore of Canterbury, around 668; it was later used by St. Boniface († 754).
Edition and Bibliography: E. Ranke, *Codex Fuldensis NT latine, interprete Hieronymo* (Marburg-Leipzig 1868) 165-168; G. Morin,

"Lectiones ex epistolis paulinis excerptae quae in ecclesia Capuana saec. VI legebantur," *Anecdota Maredsolana* 1, Appendix 5 (Maredsous 1893) 436-444; M. Gerbert, *Monumenta veteris liturgiae alemannicae* 1(1777), 409-416; J. Chapman, *Notes on the Early History of the Vulgate Gospels* (Oxford 1908) 130-133; DACL 5, 297-300; 8, 2276-2283; E. von Dobschütz, "Wann las Victor von Capua sein NT," *Zeitschrift für NT Wissenschaft* 10(1909) 90-96; G. Kunze, *Die gottesdienstliche Schriftlesung* (Göttingen 1947) 47-52; K. Gamber, "Vergleich zwischen den kampanischen Perikopenlisten und dem *Codex V*," *SE* 12(1961) 56-67; 13(1962) 326-334. Klauser, p. xxxi, no. 9; CLLA no. 401, pp. 227-228.

The *Codex Fuldensis* or *Bonifatianus* contains the purest surviving version of Jerome's translation of the Gospels and the Pauline Letters and is closely related to the *Codex Amiatinus* and the *Codex Ambrosianus* C. 39. The Gospels are given in Tatian's arrangement although what we have is a *Diapente* rather than a *Diatesseron*. The liturgical readings drawn from the Pauline Epistles are mentioned twice: in a list appearing before the collection of epistles and in marginal notes to the text. The list and the notes are contemporaneous but they do not correspond exactly. The list begins with Advent; in Lent there are lessons only for Wednesday, Friday and Sunday. The only feasts that are mentioned are those of Saints Peter and Paul, Lawrence and Andrew, although there are pericopes provided for feasts of martyrs in general. The *Fuldensis* documents for us the use of epistles at Capua in an unique and remarkable fashion. It also furnishes solid information on the formation of the pre- and post-paschal periods of the liturgical year.

2. *The Lindisfarne Gospels,* sometimes called the Gospel of St. Cuthbert, the Book of Durham or the *Comes* of Naples.

Library: London, The British Library, *codex Cottoniensis Nero D. IV.*

Date and Origin: ca. 700; Lindisfarne (England), but from a Neapolitan original containing the feast of San Gennaro (!).

Edition and Bibliography: W.W. Skeat, *The Book of Lindisfarne* (Cambridge 1871-1887); Facsimile edition=*Evangeliorum Quattuor Codex Lindisfarnensis,* 2 vols. (Olten-Lausanne 1956-1960); G. Morin, "La liturgie de Naples au temps de S. Grégoire," RB 8(1891); 481-493; 529-537 and *Anecdota Maredsolana* 1, Appendix 4 (Maredsous 1892) 426-435; DACL 9, 2373-2377; 12, 758-761; K. Gamber, "Die Kampanische Lektionsordnung," SE 13(1962) 326-352; Klauser, p. xxxii, nos. 12 and 13; CLLA no. 405, p. 229.

A list of pericopes appears before each of the Gospels but these four lists are not arranged according to the liturgical year but according to their appearance in each of the Gospels. Moreover, although each list indicates the day the selection is to be used, the pericope itself is not clearly indicated, making for difficult use. G. Morin attempted a definition of each pericope. The model for the Lindisfarne Gospels came from Naples (or from Lucullanum near Naples?) and appeared in England in 668 (Morin) or 678 (Chapman).

Two copies of the Lindisfarne Gospels survive: a) the *Codex Regius* (London, The British Library, Royal, *codex* I. B VII; VIII century; Northumbria; see CLLA no. 406, p. 229) and b) a Rheims MS (Bibliothèque municipale, *codex* 41; X century).

3. *The Marginal Notes to the Gospel Book of Burchard of Würzburg.*

Library: Würzburg, Universitätsbibliothek, *codex M. p. th. f. 68.*

Date and Origin: Burchard, the bishop of Würzburg (741-753) carried this *codex* from England to the Continent; the marginal notes and the text are contemporaneous, ca. 700, but the Roman model was of the VI/VII century.

Edition and Bibliography: G. Schepss, *Die ältesten Evangelien-Hss. der Würzburger Universitätsbibl.* (Würzburg 1887); G. Morin, "Les notes liturgiques de l'Evangéliaire de Burchard," RB 10 (1893) 113-126; DACL 12, 762-768; B. Bischoff and J. Hoffmann, *Libri S. Kyliani* (Würzburg 1952) 93; J. Hoffman, "Angelsächsischen Hss. in der Würzburger Dombibliothek," *Heiliges Franken:* Festchronik zur Jahr der Frankenapostel (Würzburg 1952) 172-176; K. Gamber, "Die Kampanische Lektionsordnung," SE 13(1962) 326-352, Klauser, p. xxxv, no. 37; CLLA no. 407, p. 230.

At the top of the page appears the day for which a pericope is provided on that page; crosses in the text indicate the exact selection; the notes and the text are in the same hand; and the arrangement has both Neapolitan and Roman characteristics.

4. *Pericope Notes in the Codex Amiatinus.*

Library: Florence, Biblioteca Laurenziana, *codex* 1 *(Amiatinus).*

Date and Origin: Copied at Wearmouth-Jarrow (England) under Abbot Ceolfrith (678-715) from the Gospel Book of Eugippius as revised by Cassiodorus.

Edition and Bibliography: C. Tischendorf, *Codex Amiatinus* (Leipzig 1850). Klauser, p. xxxi, no. 8.

Four pericope indications survive in the text of Luke and John; they are probably the remains of a system of marginal notes which had figured in the Gospel Book of Eugippius and were omitted by the English copyist of the *Amiatinus*. The arrangement is Neapolitan.

5. The Missale Plenum of Benevento.

Library: Benevento, Archivio arcivescovile, *codex* VI. 33.
Date and Origin: X/XI century; Benevento.
Edition and Bibliography: K. Gamber, "Väterlesungen innerhalb der Messe in beneventanischen Messbüchern," EL 74(1960) 163-165 and "Die Sonntagsmessen nach Pfingsten im *codex* VI. 33 von Benevent," *ibid.*, pp. 428-431 and, SE 12(1961) 71; K. Gamber, *Missale Beneventanum*, TPL 9 (Regensburg 1972). CLLA no. 430, pp. 239-240.

The epistles appear in the Roman arrangement but the gospels still bear traces of an old Beneventan system.

6. Missal Fragments of Zürich, Peterlingen and Lucerne.

Library: Zürich, Staatsarchiv, W.3.A.G.19, fol. 6-15; Zürich, Zentralbibliothek, Z.XIV. 4; Peterlingen (Payerne), Communalarchiv, no number; Lucerne, Stiftsarchiv, no. 1912.
Date and Origin: End of the X century; S. Italy (Bari).
Edition and Bibliography: A. Dold, *Die Zürcher und Peterlinger Messbuchfragmente*, TuA 25 (Beuron 1934); G. Morin, "Le missel de Payerne," *Zeitschrift für schweizerische Kirchengeschichte* 25 (1931) 102-111; E. Omlin, "Ein Messbuch Fragment im Stiftsarchiv Luzern," *Innerschweitzerisches Jahrbuch für Heimatkunde* 8/10 (1944/1946) 39-60; K. Gamber, SE 12(1961) 21-28; 52-56; 77-82.

The 23 mass *formulae* normally have three readings (OT, epistle, gospel). In spite of its fragmentary character, this is the oldest and most important document of the ancient Beneventan liturgy.

MSS are plentiful after the X century[153] but they have all been Romanized to some degree; nevertheless they contain vestiges of a non-Roman system of readings, e.g., for the Sundays of Lent.[154]

I. ROMAN LECTIONARIES

Only a few major documents of the *consuetudo* of the City will be indicated here. The further development of the different kinds of lectionaries for the Eucharist will be spelled out in the following section.[155]

1. *The Capitulary of Würzburg.*

Library: Würzburg, Universitätsbibliothek, codex M. p. th. f. 62.
Date and Origin: ca. 700 (ca. 750, Lowe, Gamber); England.
Edition and Bibliography: Facsimile: *Comes Romanus Wirziburgensis*: Facsimilie edition of Codex M. p. th. f. 62 of the University Library at Würzburg, Codices selecti phototypice impressi 17 (Graz 1968); G. Morin, "Les plus ancien *Comes* ou lectionnaire de l'Église romaine," RB 27(1910) 41-74 (epistle list); and "Liturgie et basiliques de Rome au milieu du VII siècle d'après les listes d'évangiles de Wurzbourg," RB 28(1911) 296-330 (gospel list); DACL 5, 312-316; G. Kunze, "Das Rätsel der Würzburger Epistelliste," *Colligere Fragmenta*, TuA 2 (Beuron 1952) 191-204; W.C. Rush, "A Possible Explanation of the Calendar in the Würzburg Lectionary," JTS 21 (1970) 105-111. CLLA no. 1001, pp. 431-432.

Codex 62 contains three divisions: a) folios 1ʳ-2ᵛ have a calendar of the Roman Church with 211 entries and indications of the stational churches which are closely related to the lessons which follow; b) folios 2ᵛ-10ᵛ have a list of epistles with *incipit* and *explicit: Incipiunt capitula lectionum de circulo anni* with 255 entries; c) folios 10ᵛ-16ᵛ have a list of gospels with *incipit* and *explicit: Incipiunt Kapituli Sancti Evangelii Lec.* with 237 entries (see pp. 342-343). Both lists are Roman and done by the same scribe but they come from different eras and do not correspond to one another. The lists of epistles is abridged from a book which contained the full text for each pericope and seems to have been from the early VII century; see no. XCI: *Feria VI. Ad sca. Maria Martyra,* which means the station was held at the Pantheon, dedicated to St. Mary and all the Martyrs in 609 by Pope Boniface IV (608-615). G. Kunze, *op. cit.,* pp. 191-204, puts it before Gregory the Great (590-604), in the mid-VI century. He regards it as a collection of materials to be used as readings rather than a list of epistles properly speaking. This collection would be like the *Veronensis* as compared with later sacramentaries. In any case, this is the oldest surviving lectionary of the Roman Church with many archaic features, e.g., no masses for the Thursdays in Lent, *dominica vacans* in Lent with no readings, and survivals of an older system of three readings. The final pericopes (nos. 214-255) are rather mysterious but are perhaps a *lectio continua* for the lesser Sundays.

2. *The Epistolary of Corbie/Comes of Leningrad.*

Library: Leningrad, Publichnaja Biblioteka, *codex*, Q. V. I, no. 16 (*olim Sangerman.* 842).

Date and Origin: ca. 772/780, under Abbot Maurdramnus of Corbie; cf. A. Wilmart, "Le lectionaire d'Alcuin," EL 51(1937) 140; Frere is wrong in dating it to the X century! CLLA no. 1005, p. 432.

Edition and Bibliography: W. H. Frere, *Studies in Early Roman Liturgy*, 3: *The Roman Epistle-Lectionary*, ACC 32 (Oxford 1935) 1-24; R. Dubois (in process); DACL 14, 649; A. Staerk, *Les MSS latins conservés à la Bibliothèque impériale de Saint-Petersbourg* 1 (Leningrad 1910) 135-171.

This epistolary is basically a Romano-Frankish document adapted to a IX-century sacramentary. It has the same lessons as the *Comes* of Murbach and belongs among the Type III lectionaries.

3. *The Comes ab Albino Ordinatus/Comes or Epistolary of Alcuin.*

The *Comes* of Alcuin comes down to us in two forms, one with and one without a Supplement. CLLA nos. 1040-1041, pp. 438-439

a) *The Epistolary without a Supplement.*
Library: Cambrai, Bibliothèque municipale, *codex* 553.
Date and Origin: Beginning of the IX century for the Church of Cambrai; 2nd quarter of the IX century (Bischoff).
Edition and Bibliography: A. Wilmart, "Le lectionnaire d'Alcuin," EL 51(1937) 136-197; also printed separately in *Bibliotheca Eph. lit.* 2 (Rome 1937).

b) *The Epistolary with a Supplement.*
Library: Paris, Bibl. Nat. *codex latinus* 9452.
Date and Origin: First quarter or first half of the IX century;

Abbey of St. Amand (Bischoff) and, later, the cathedral of Chartres.

Edition and Bibliography: A. Wilmart, Le lectionnaire d'Alcuin," EL 51 (1937) 151-168; J. M. Tommasi, *Opera omnia* 5 (ed. Vezzosi, Rome 1750) 297-318 (with only the *incipits* and *explicits* of the pericopes); E. Ranke, *Das kirchliche Pericopensystem* (Berlin 1847); DACL 5, 300-311, 335-342; Frere, 3 (1935) 40-48; A. Wilmart, "Le lectionnaire de Saint-Père," *Speculum* 1(1926) 269-278. For his edition Tommasi used a copy made by Arnoul (not Arnaldus) de Loo from a MS belonging to the chapter library of Notre Dame de Chartres, the present *Parisinus* 9452.[156]

The title *Comes ab Albino ex Caroli imperatoris praecepto emendatus* or *Comes ab Albino ordinatus* is not in the MSS but was provided by Tommasi from the preface to the Supplement. The *Comes* of Alcuin is an Epistolary properly speaking, i.e., a book containing the prophetic readings and epistles, but not the gospels, for the *Temporale* and *Sanctorale* of 216 liturgical celebrations, some with more than one reading.

The Supplement is preceded by a *praefatio: Hunc codicem qui ab ecclesiasticis viris Comes appelatur, tua, lector, noverit perspicacitas ab eo codice sumptum quem constat ab Albino eruditissimo viro (Carolo sapientissimo imperatore praecipiente), lima rectitudinis esse politus atque emendatus . . . imitando ac sequendo libellum pp. Gregorii sacramentorum.*[157] The author of the preface was probably Helisachar, the chancellor of Louis the Pious; cf G. Morin, "Une rédaction inédite de la préface au Supplément du *Comes* d'Alcuin," RB 29(1912)341-348. The Supplement includes 65 OT and NT readings, but no gospel pericopes. They are drawn from a book like the *Comes* of Murbach rather than from the family of the Epistolary of Würzburg. The *Comes* proper draws upon the Epistolary of Würzburg and not conversely. Alcuin's role in the *Comes* is certain; Helisachar says in his preface: *hunc codicem . . . ab eo codice sumptum quem constat ab Albino . . . esse politum atque emendatum.* In addition, the inventory of St. Riquier (831) mentions a *lectionarius plenarius a supradicto Albino ordinatus.* In spite of what Helisachar says, however, Alcuin made only the most minor changes in a Roman epistolary put together in Rome in 626 under Honorius I on the basis of an earlier text by Theodore (642-649); it had the structure of a type II Evangelary and was retouched in 627 (Chavasse). It must have left Rome before Gregory II (715-731), since the readings for the Thursdays of Lent are not those used in Rome, and was known in N.

Italy around the beginning of the VIII century [A. Wilmart, "Un missel grégorien," RB 26 (1909) 281-300; A. Dold, *Vom Sakramentar, Comes und Capitulare zum Missale,* TuA 34 (Beuron 1943)]. From N. Italy it migrated to Gaul and came into the possession of Alcuin. What Alcuin did to it is hard to discern in any detail. In any case, whatever he accomplished was minor and did not drastically reorganize the Roman model. Certainly the *Comes* that circulated under Alcuin's name was a purely Roman document aside, naturally, from a few minor items like the vigil and feast of All Saints and the vigil of St. Martin; it had acquired its fixed arrangements in 626/627 and was, therefore, of a more recent vintage than the Epistolary of Würzburg.

Did Alcuin compose or revise a Gospel Book? Probably not, given our lack of documentation. The Roman Gospel Book (type Δ, ca. 750) was already a set item in the time of Alcuin and needed no further work.[158]

4. The Capitularia evangeliorum (Lists of Gospel Pericopes).

T. Klauser reduces these lists of pericopes to four basic types: Π, Λ, Σ, Δ.[159] More recent research, which will be reported below under the development of the mass lectionary, enables us to improve upon Klauser's remarkable analyses and to locate his findings in a wider framework of MSS and classifications. Klauser's first three types, Π, Λ, Σ[160], are in fact variations on Chavasse's second type of evangelary. Klauser's fourth type[161], Δ, is a variant of family B of Chavasse's third type of evangelary.[162] Here we shall use the nomenclature adopted by Frere along with the types defined by Klauser.[163]

a) Klauser Type Π=Frere Earlier Type=a variation of Chavasse's Type 2=pure Roman Gospel Book, ca. 645.

The following are the main witnesses to this type.

Library: Würzburg, Universitätsbibliothek, *codex* M. p. th. f. 62.

Date and Origin: See the Capitulary of Würzburg (*supra.*)

We are now looking at the third section of this MS, folios 10ᵛ-16ᵛ, containing 237 gospel listings; they come from a different period than the epistles and have no relation to them. This *capitulare evangeliorum* was probably put together under Vitalian (657-672) and reflects the Roman *consuetudo* around 650. It does not contain the Lenten Thursdays, but it does mention Sts. Primus and Felicianus who were translated from the *Via Nomentana* to Rome under

Theodore (642/649). On the other hand, it does not refer to the translation of Leo I in 688.

It bears the title: *Incipiunt Kapituli Sancti Evangelii Lec.* and opens with the Midnight Mass of Christmas: *In natale Domini ad scam Mariam Maiorem*, and not with the vigil of Christmas as the Epistolary of the MS does. Intermediate title: *Incipiunt lectiones* (=gospels) *a Septuagesima usque in Pascha*. Explicit: *Expliciunt capitula anni circuli de sollemnitatibus vel nataliciis sanctorum*. Finally, for a fresh series of readings of special circumstances: *Incipiunt capitula necessaria*.

Besides the Würzburg MS, Klauser gives as the oldest witnesses of Type Π the *codices* of Rome, *Vat. Pal. lat.* 46 (ca. 800); Paris, Bibl. Nat. *codices lat.* 260 (early IX century), 274 (*idem*), 266 (mid-IX century), 9385 (*idem*), 269 (IX century); 11959 (X century)[164]

b) Klauser Type Λ=Frere Martina Type=a variation on Chavasse's Type 2 Evangelary=pure Roman, ca. 740.
Library: Trier, Stadtbibliothek, *codex* 22 (*Codex aureus*), fol. 161ʳ-171ʳ.
Date and Origin: ca. 800; Abbey of St. Maximinus, Trier.

The *incipits* of the pericopes are introduced by *In illo tempore*. The secular name for each month appears before the first feast of the month, as in the *libelli missarum* of Verona. Rome, *Vat. Pal. lat.* 50 (early IX century); Zürich, Zentralbibliothek, *codex* Rh. 20 (X century); Paris, Bibliothèque Ste. Geneviève, *codex* 1190 (mid-IX century); Rome, *Vat. lat.* 7016 (ca. 800); Aachen, Cathedral Treasury, Carolingian Evangelary (early IX century).[165]

c) Klauser Type Σ=Frere Standard Type=a variation on Chavasse's Type 2=pure Roman Evangelary; ca. 755.
Library: Paris, Bibl. Nat., *Nouvelles acquisitions latines* 1588 (ca. 800; Autun), *lat.* 17227 (ca. 800), 11958 (IX century); 9386 (late IX century); 11956 (X century); Rome, *Ottobon. lat* 79 (X century).[166]

d) Klauser Type Δ=Frere Vitus-Type=a variant of Chavasse's Type 3 of the B family of Evangelaries=a Romano-Frankish book based on a pure Roman *capitulare* of ca. 650; it was completed in ca. 750, emigrated to Gaul and had Gallican elements added to it.

Douai, Bibliothèque municipale, *codex* 12 (late VIII century); Paris, Biblio. Nat. *lat.* 11957 (IX/X century); Rome, Vat. lat. 8523 (*idem*); Paris, Biblio. Nat. *lat.* 11963 (X/XI century).[167]

The *Capitularia evangeliorum* are mere lists of pericopes, providing only the *incipit* and *explicit* of each lesson. The MS tradition preserves many other books in which the lessons are given *in extenso*. See

Klauser[168], and the works of R. J. Hesbert, A. Chavasse and K. Gamber cited above.[169]

5. *Lectionaries with Full Readings* (Epistles and Gospels *in extenso*).

As was said above, the various ways of indicating readings for the Eucharist coexisted for centuries, and we must not conceive of a rectilinear evolution from marginal notes through lists of readings to the complete Mass lectionary; actually, some of the full lectionaries are very old.[170]

We must also remember that epistles and gospels were not logically coordinated but were assembled in a purely haphazard fashion.

a) The Fragmentary Lectionary of Munich.

Library: Munich, Bayerische Staatsbibliothek, *Clm* 29155.
Date and Origin: Late VI century; N. Italy, although it is a pure Roman type.
Edition and Bibliography: K. Gamber, "Das Münchener Fragment eines Lectionarium Plenarium," EL 72 (1958) 268-280.

This fragment preserves only the gospel of the Monday of Holy Week (Jn 12:1-36) and the epistle of the Tuesday of the same week (Jer. 11:18-20).

b) The Verona Lectionary (or the Lectionary of Monza).

Library: Paris, Biblio. Nat. *codex lat.* 9451.
Date and Origin: VIII/IX century; N. Italy (Monza? Verona?)
Edition and Bibliography: R. Amiet, "Un *Comes* carolingien inédit de la Haute Italie," EL 73 (1959) 335-367; DACL 5, 335-342; 13, 2107; K. Gamber, "Die Lesungen und Cantica an der Ostervigil im *Comes Parisinus*," RB 71 (1961) 125-134; A. Wilmart, EL 71 (1937) p. 140, n. 16 (Verona).

This is a *lectionarium plenarium* which is probably of the same type as that of *Clm* 29155. After Pseudo-Jerome's preface, *Ad Constantium*, the lectionary begins with the vigil of Christmas. It is certainly a Roman lectionary but was copied outside the City since it contains a few N. Italian peculiarities, such as *Dominica in Trigesima, in Viginsima,* etc. for the Sundays of Lent.

c) The Fragmentary Lectionary of the Vatican.

Library: Rome, *Vat. Reg. lat.* 74.
Date and Origin: Late VIII century; N. Italy (Bobbio?) or even Gaul, although it is a pure Roman lectionary.
Edition and Bibliography: A. Dold, "Ein Ausgeschriebenes Perikopenbuch des 8. Jhs.," EL 54 (1940) 12-37.
Closely connected to the *Comes* of Murbach.

d) The Fragmentary Lectionary of Stuttgart.

Library: Stuttgart, Würtemb. Landesbibliothek, *codex frag.* 47 from Incunab. 6769 and H. 5385.
Date and Origin: Late VIII century; German (Constance?).
Edition and Bibliography: A. Dold, "Zwei wichtige Fragmente eines Doppel-*Comes* aus dem 8. Jh.," EL 65 (1951) 77-86 and "Ein Vorläufer des *Comes* von Murbach," EL 65 (1951) 237-249, 251.

According to the editor, the Roman model for the Stuttgart lectionary must have been earlier than Gregory II (715-731) since the Thursdays of Lent are still missing.

e) The Abridged Lectionary of Regensburg.

Library: Prague, Metropolitni Kapitoly, *codex* O.83 (Sacramentary of Prague), fol. 121-130.
Date and Origin: Second half of the VIII century; Regensburg.
Edition and Bibliography: A. Dold, *Das Prager Sakramentar*, TuA 38/42 (Beuron 1949) 188*-195*. The epistles and gospels for four Sundays, for four masses *de Communi* and for four votive masses are in the same hand as the Sacramentary (CLLA no. 1220, pp. 475-476). Roman arrangement.

f) The Lectionary of the Sacramentary of Monte Cassino.

Library: Monte Cassino, Abbey Library, *codex* 271 (*olim* 348).
Date and Origin: ca. 700, perhaps a bit earlier (Lowe, Bischoff); N. Italy but reflecting Roman usages.
Edition: A. Dold, *Vom Sakramentar, Comes und Capitulare zum Missale*, TuA 34 (Beuron 1943); full bibliography in CLLA no. 701, pp. 330-331 but one must now add the crucial article of A. Chavasse, "Les

fragments palimpsestes du *Casinensis* 271 (Sigle Z 6)," AfL 25 (1983) 9-33. This unusual sacramentary-lectionary inserts the epistles and gospels of the temporal cycle after the *oratio* of each mass. It is a Roman type lectionary of ca. 660-680.

g) The Fragmentary Lectionary of Donaueschingen.

Library: Donaueschingen, Hofbibliothek, *codex* B. II. 2 and Heidelberg, Gerhard Eis-Sammlung, *codex* 82.
Date and Origin: VIII/IX century; S. Germany.
Edition and Bibliography: A. Dold, JfL 3 (1923) 52-54; and EL 65 (1951) 250-252. CLLA no. 1233, p. 479.
These are the remains of a Mass lectionary in a Roman arrangement.

h) The Munich Lectionary Fragments.

There is a full listing of the MSS in Gamber, CLLA no. 1240, pp. 480-481.
Edition and Bibliography: *ibid.*
These fragments are of the same type as the lectionary of Murbach and the *Comes* of Würzburg but they are more recent.

i) The Lectionary of Chartres.

Library: Chartres, Bibl. municip., *codex* 24 (*olim* 32) (destroyed in an air-raid May 26, 1944).
Date and Origin: First half of the IX century; by Andradus, Saint Père near Tours.
Edition and Bibliography: A. Wilmart, "Remarques sur un lectionnaire de Chartres copié à Tours," *Comptes rendus de l'Académie des Inscriptions et Belles Lettres de Paris* 13 (1925) 290-298; Frere, *Studies* 3 (1935) 71. CLLA no. 1229, pp. 477-478.
This Chartres MS has often been confused with *Parisinus* 9452 (a *Comes* of Alcuin without the Supplement) because of a misunderstood remark of Mabillon, *Annales O. S. B.* 2 (1704) 328. After the prologue of Pseudo-Jerome, *Ad Constantium*, there is the title: *Incipiunt lectiones* (epistles and gospels) *libri comitis anni circuli*. The arrangement is the same as the *Comes* of Alcuin.[171]

j) The Lectionary of Murbach (Comes Murbacensis).

Library: Besançon, Bibl. municip., *codex* 184, fol. 58-74.
Date and Origin: Late VIII century; Abbey of Murbach (Alsace).
Edition and Bibliography: A. Wilmart, "Le Comes de Murbach," RB 30
   (1913) 25-69; DACL 5, 316-321; 908-914. CLLA no. 1226, p. 477.
   This is a list of epistles and gospels, in the form of a *capitulare*,
giving the *incipit* and *explicit* for each lesson. The list has been
compiled from a book which contained the pericopes *in extenso*. After
Pseudo-Jerome's prologue, *Ad Constantium*, the list begins: *In vigilia
natalis Domini ad nonam ad sanctam Mariam* and continues for the rest
of the year. Chronologically, the *Comes* of Murbach is later than the
Comes of Alcuin and represents a Romano-Frankish arrangement of
the readings connected with the Frankish Gelasian Sacramentary.
Genetically, this MS belongs to Chavasse's family B or the third type
of Mass lectionary. The systems of readings appearing in the *Comes* of
Murbach is essentially the one that became mandatory in the whole
Latin Church with the *Missale Romanum* of 1570. It has a fully
developed Sunday cycle: 5 *dominicae post Theophaniam*, 4 *dominicae*
after the octave of Easter, 1 *dominica* after the Ascension, 25 after
Pentecost, 5 before Christmas. In addition to Sundays, each Wed-
nesday and Friday has readings provided: Wed. = epistle and gospel;
Fri. = gospel only. Lent and Paschaltide are complete; Lent has the
Thursday masses, although they do not correspond with those of the
Comes of Alcuin. The calendar is that of the Frankish Gelasian
Sacramentary (Flavigny, ca. 760-770), which means that this lec-
tionary is an adaptation of the Roman lectionary to the newly
elaborated sacramentary based on both a Gregorian and a Gelasian
Sacramentary. Once again, we discern the basic law of our liturgical
history: the Roman liturgy we have inherited is, in fact, Romano-
Frankish (or Romano-Germanic), and that includes the system of
readings at Mass.

k) The Lectionary of Theotinchus (Comes Theotinchi).

Library: Beauvais, *codex* 23 (lost).
Date and Origin: IX century; from the Abbey of St. Riquier (Centula),
   for Amiens.
Edition and Bibliography: É. Baluze, *Capitularia regum Francorum* 2

(Paris 1677) 1309-1351= a copy of the lost MS of Beauvais, reproduced in PL 30, 487-532; E. Ranke, *Das kirchliche Pericopensystem* (Berlin 1847) Append. lxxxiv-xcii; V. Fiala, "Neue Beobachtungen zum Sanctorale des *Comes Theotinchi*," *Colligere Fragmenta*=Festschrift A. Dold, TuA 2 (Beuron 1952) 205-213; A. Baumstark, *Missale Romanum* (Eindhoven-Nijmegen 1929) 100 and 188, note 43; Frere, *Studies in the Early Roman Liturgy* 3(1935) 84-91. CLLA no. 1050, p. 439.

This work has a rather enigmatic title: *In Christi nomine anni circuli liber comitis incipit, auctus a Theotincho indigno presbytero, rogatu viri venerabilis Hechiardi, comitis Ambianensis.* Neither the presbyter Theotinchus nor Hechiardus, the count of Amiens, can be identified. The lectionary includes a list of pericopes (epistles and gospels) for the entire liturgical year with the *incipit* and *explict* for each reading. Both readings appear side by side for each day—as in the *Comes* of Murbach—and not in separate lists as in so many MSS. An analysis of the contents points to the IX century. The author seems to have completed an older document in which the lessons are given *in extenso*: *Liber comitis auctus a Theotincho ... ita ... ut sancta evangeliorum dicta necnon et apostolorum ac prophetarum immota atque inconcussa servarentur et diebus quibus deerant propriae sanctae lectiones adhiberentur.* As a matter of fact, however, he combined two different documents; the first was one like the *Comes* of Murbach with the epistle and gospel located on the same day; the second was an older and purely Roman document like the *Comes* of Alcuin (with Supplement) and the *Comes* of Würzburg; see A. Wilmart, RB 30 (1913) 159. The *Comes Theotinchi* does not get us back to an older source (ca. 401-417), as Baumstark claimed.

1) The Comes of Pamelius.

Edition: J. Pamelius, *Liturgicon Ecclesiae latinae* 2(Cologne 1571; reprint Farnborough 1970) 1-61; reedited by E. Ranke, *Das kirchliche Pericopensystem* (Berlin 1847), Append. IV, pp. lii-lxxxiii. Pamelius compiled this edition from several MSS but without indicating either their date or exact nature. One of the MSS belonged to the church of St. Donatianus of Bruges and several others were at Cologne where they were examined by Hittorp. Analysis of the contents indicates that Pamelius used Frere's Standard Type of the same family as the *Comes* of Murbach. Pamelius printed his compilation as a complete *capitulare* (epistles and gospels but with only their *incipits* and *explicits*). This text is hard to use because we cannot be sure of the sources that were actually employed.[172]

J. THE DEVELOPMENT OF THE ROMAN LECTIONARY.

We cannot study the growth of the lectionary as if it happened all at once. Rather, certain groups of readings appeared early on and some at a much later date.

1) The period between Septuagesima and Easter, which had been organized before Gregory the Great, formed a fixed and autonomous liturgical unit throughout the Middle Ages. Naturally, there was no fixed arrangement of pericopes before the VI century, since the choice of readings, like the formulation of the eucharistic prayer, was left to the euchological skills of the celebrant.

2) All Roman lectionaries agree on Easter Week, Pentecost Week and the intervening six Sundays. After Lent itself, this period contained the oldest section of lessons and remained stable for the future.

3) Lectionaries diverge for the period between Christmas and the last Sunday after Epiphany (=the Sunday before Septuagesima) and the period after Pentecost (=the Sunday after Pentecost to the last Sunday before Christmas), including Advent.

It is much easier to study the lessons of the *Sanctorale* than those of the *Temporale* since chronological data is far more exact for the former than the latter.[173]

No lectionary was simply and absolutely fixed once it appeared, either for every subsequent year or for a wide collection of churches. In the Early Church and in the Medieval Church, liturgical uniformity was unheard of. Not only were there different liturgical families of rites, each with its own distinct lectionary, but even within a given family, lectionaries did not always agree at all times and in all places. Churches used books of readings that came from different periods and belonged to different types. The fact that a Roman lectionary or, rather a Romano-Frankish lectionary like the *Comes* of Murbach, finally prevailed in the West is an accidental result of the Romanization of worship brought about by the Carolingian reformers.

Nowhere is there to be found a systematic attempt at organizing or reforming a system of readings; neither Rome nor any other primatial see tried to impose its choices on others. As head of his church and its liturgist par excellence, each bishop was perfectly free to both create his prayer *formulae* and choose appropriate readings. Once certain series of readings appeared in a MS tradition, they tended to spread far and wide according to the vagaries of a more or less accidental dissemination. That means that, generally speaking, they came to have the influence they did more for extrinsic than for intrinsic reasons. We have to recall that the process that assured the success of the Roman books was the result of religious and political moves on the part of Pepin III and Charlemagne and had no connection with the intrinsic qualities of the documents in question. Moreover, their efforts never aimed at simple uniformity either in the case of the lectionary or the other liturgical books; the *Comes* of Murbach (late VIII century), the ancestor of the medieval system, was also a Romano-Frankish, i.e., a hybrid document.

All liturgical historians acknowledge the existence of different types of authentic epistolaries and evangelaries.[174] They also agree on the following points:

a) The existence of three types of epistolary: *Comes* of Würzburg, *Comes* of Alcuin, later witnesses.[175]

b) The evangelary had an older form represented by types Π, Λ, Σ of Klauser or the Earlier-, Martina- and Standard-Type of Frere, but this older form is still not the primitive form, which is no longer accessible paleographically.[176]

c) It is possible to establish some kind of correspondence between the three types of evangelaries and the epistolary.[177]

We have to distinguish carefully between the Gospel Book in its three appearances (Four Gospels + marginal notes, lists, books of pericopes *in extenso*) and the Book of Epistles (*Apostolus* + marginal notes, lists, books of pericopes *in extenso*). For a very long time, these two kinds of books existed simply in their own right and had no direct connection with one another. The *Comes* of Murbach (late VIII century) is the first surviving document in which epistles and gospels appear side by side for each day of the full cycle of Sundays and feasts. Before this date, the development of the epistolary was quite different than that of the evangelary. If Rome had a kind of primacy in regard to the gospel lists, thanks to the *Comes* of Würzburg and the *codex Vat. Pal.* 46, it never had the same in regard to the epistle lists. The arrangement that finally came to prevail in the Latin Church was a Romano-Frankish one rather than a purely Roman one. Neither the Epistolary of Würzburg nor *Comes* of Alcuin ever succeeded in imposing themselves as completely or as 'purely' as the Gospel Book of Würzburg and *Vat. Pal.* 46.

The following schematic arrangement represents the gradual formation of the Roman lectionary for the Eucharist (according to Chavasse):

EPISTOLARY	EVANGELARY
Type 1 Comes of Würzburg; late VI century.	No surviving MSS: it must be reconstructed from Klauser's Π family of MSS.
Type 2 Comes of Alcuin = a Roman comes, ca. 626/627, slightly corrected by Alcuin.	Represented by Klauser's Π, Λ, Σ or by Frere's Earlier-, Martina-, Standard types, ca. 595-657.
Type 3 Chavasse's Family A = Roman witnesses, ca. 700.	Chavasse's Family A = Roman MSS, ca. 700.
Chavasse's Family B = other witnesses, ca. 700/740.	Chavasse's Family B = other witnesses, ca. 700/740; a variant = Klauser Δ = Frere Vitus type.

1) The Comes of Würzburg (Würzburg, Universitätsbibl., codex M. p. th. f. 62; ca. 700; ca. 750, Gamber, Lowe) contains the first type of Roman epistolary. For intrinsic reasons (the absence of VII century feasts, the Thursdays of Lent, etc.), its Roman model can be located in the late VI century, in the time of Gregory the Great (✝604). Certain portions of this epistolary existed, however, before this pope, namely, the readings for those periods which had been already organized: Easter Week and the six Sundays post Pascha. The Comes of Würzburg is the oldest Roman epistolary for which we have direct MS evidence. It represents Roman usage around the years 600/625.[178]

To this first type of Roman epistolary corresponds a gospel book of the first type. Although we have no MSS for it, traces of it can be found in Klauser's Π family of MSS. This evangelary, which was earlier than Gregory I, had Johannine readings for the six Sundays post Pascha, ten formulae post Theophaniam and sixteen pericopes for the time after Pentecost.

2) The Comes of Alcuin has the second type of Roman epistolary; its Roman model can be located around the years 626/627.

A second type of evangelary corresponds to this second type of epistolary, namely, the evangelary which is the common source of Klauser's families: Π (ca. 645), Λ (ca. 740), Σ (ca. 755). These three families are simply variations of the same basic type of Gospel Book. Given that Λ and Σ are directly attached to Π, the basic system can be discerned by examining Π alone. Klauser used the *Sanctorale* to get his chronology; it was completed under popes Theodore (642-649), Martin (649-654) and Eugenius (654-657) but organized under Honorius I (625-638).[179] The *Temporale* was revised towards the beginning of Honorius I's pontificate and under Sabinianus (604-606). In its earliest state, evangelary Π seems to have been contemporaneous with Gregory the Great (590-604).[180]

The chief MS witnesses for type Π (Roman, ca. 645) are: Würzburg, Universitätsbibl. codex M. p. th. 62, fol., 10ᵛ-16ᵛ which is a *Capitulare evangeliorum* of insular origin, ca. 700; Rome, Vat. *Pal. lat.* 46 (Carolingian, ca. 800); Paris, Bibl. Nat. *codices* 260 (ca. early IX century; Tours), 274 (ca. 807/834; Tours), 266 (mid-IX century; Tours), 9385 (ca. 860; Tours), 269 (second half of the IX century; Limoges), and 11959 (X century; St. Germain des Prés?).[181] The principal MS witnesses for type Λ (Roman, ca. 740) are: Trier, Stadbibl. *codex* 22=*Codex aureus* (ca. 800; Mainz); Rome, Vat. *Pal. lat.* 50 (early IX century; Lorsch?); Rome, Vat. *lat.* 7016 (ca. 800; Lucca?); Aachen, Cathedral Treasury, Carolingian Evangelary (early IX century; Aachen). The main MS witnesses for type Σ (Roman; ca. 755) are: Autun, Bibl. municip., *codex* 4 + Paris, Bibl. Nat. *nouv. acq. lat.* 1588 (VIII/IX century); Paris, 17227 (first half of the IX century).[182]

3) The greatest confusion has reigned for years in regard to the third type of mass lectionary. In his inventory of MSS, Klauser does not refer to it at all. Type Δ (Romano-Frankish of 750, based on a Roman text of 650) is only a variation on family B of type three. Frere did not distinguish clearly enough between the witnesses to this third group.[183] More systematic investigations were, however, conducted by A. Wilmart, R. J. Hesbert and especially by A. Chavasse.[184] The latter succeeded in separating out two families of MSS in type three (A and B). For the gospel pericopes the A and B witnesses are revisions of the second type of evangelary which is the foundation of Klauser's groups Π, Λ, Σ; for the epistle pericopes the compilers of families A and B drew upon the *Comes* of Alcuin (epistolary of the second type) and directly upon the Epistolary of Würzburg (first type). When we compare the two families, there can be no doubt that family A best preserves the primitive form of the third type of lectionary. Family B is a revision of A and its epistolary is less well organized and later than its evangelary. Where it was revised cannot be ascertained; we could hardly be mistaken, however, in situating it

in one of those countries where the liturgy of the Latin Church was continually in process during the early Middle Ages: N. Italy, Switzerland or Frankish Gaul.

The witnesses to family A are Roman, i.e., they originated in the City or suburbicarian Italy. The witnesses to family B come from countries that were not immediately influenced by Rome.

From the evidence of the MSS, both families belong to the VIII century, but family A is certainly later than Gregory II (715-731) because of its Lenten Thursdays, the addition of the untitled feasts of the Nativity of Mary (Sept. 8) and the Exaltation of the Cross (Sept. 14), established by Sergius I (687-701), and because of the most recent feast added to the lectionary under Gregory III (731-741), that of St. Urban (May 25). Family A seems to be the result of a recasting of the second type of lectionary made about 700. Family B is a little later than 700 but probably before 740. Both families are, therefore, somewhat contemporaneous.

THE PRINCIPAL WITNESSES TO FAMILY A.

Rome, Bibl. Vallicelliana, *codex* B. 8.
Date and Origin: Early X century; Abbey of San Eutizio di Norcia, Umbria.
Edition and Bibliography: J. M. Tommasi, *Opera omnia* 5 (ed. Vezzosi; Rome 1750) 320; K. Gamber, *Sakramentartypen*, p. 68 and in SE 12 (1961) 84; as well as *Heiliger Dienst* 15 (1961) 114-118; R. Amiet, EL 71 (1957) 92, note 2. This is a *missale plenum*.

Rome, Bibl. Vallicell., *codex* C. 10, fol. 139-280.
Date and Origin: Late X century; Valcassoriana monastery, near Nursia.
Edition and Bibliography: Frere, *Studies* 3, p. 68; A. Wilmart, EL 51 (1937) 136-197; This so-called Epistolary of Nursia has the same arrangement as that of *Vallicellianus* B. 8.

Rome, Vatican Library, Archivio di San Pietro, *codex* F. 7 (6). This is a XII-century evangelary with the epistles indicated in the margins. Ed. J.M. Tommasi, *Opera omnia* 5, 468-473.

Geneva, Bodmer Collection, former Private Library of Sir Sydney Cockerell (XII century). This is a complete lectionary drawn up for the church of St. Cecilia, Rome. Edition and Bibliography: Frere, *Studies* 3, p. 70.

Rome, Vatican Library, Archivio di San Pietro, *codex* F. 1. This is a
XIII-century epistolary for St. Peter's.

Several Beneventan witnesses to family A have been collected by
R. J. Hesbert and A. Chavasse.[185]

THE PRINCIPAL WINTESSES TO FAMILY B.

Paris, Bibl. Nat., *codex lat.* 9451 (late VIII century; Verona).
This is the Verona Lectionary (see *supra*).

Chartres, Bibl. municip., *codex* 32 (*olim* 24) (ca. 820; by Andradus, a
monk of St. Martin of Tours, for Saint Père, near Vézelay) (see
supra).

Leningrad, Publichnaja Bibliotheka, *codex* Q.V.I. 16 (772-780;
Corbie), the Epistolary of Corbie (see *supra*).

Besançon, Bibl. municip. *codex* 184 (late VIII century; Murbach);
the Lectionary of Murbach (see *supra*).

Rome, *Vat. Reg. lat.* 74 (VIII century; Gaul), (see *supra*).

Rome, *Vat. lat.* 7018 (IX century; Reggio Emilia? Bologna?) a *Missale
plenum* (see *supra*).

Rome, Bibl. Vallicell. *codex* E. 16 (1100; Farfa? Subiaco?) a *Capitulare
evangeliorum*; see Klauser, *Das römische Capit. evangel.*, p. lxiv, no.
337.

To this same family belong some fifty plenary missals (X-XV
century) listed by Hesbert.[186]

The witnesses of Klauser's type Δ constitute a variant of family B;
they are of Romano-Frankish character and were compiled about 750
but stem from a pure Roman capitulary of 650.[187]

K. THE TRIDENTINE SYSTEM OF READINGS.

The Roman system of readings fixed in the *Missale Romanum* of
Pius V (July 14, 1570) was a Romano-Frankish system worked out
during the Carolingian era and had the same arrangement as the
Comes of Murbach. It was, therefore, essentially an VIII-century
Roman system. The *Comes* of Murbach was a lectionary of the third
type and therefore a Frankish revision—for the gospels—of type 2
which was basically Klauser's Π, Δ, Σ groups and—for the epistles—
a Frankish revision of the *Comes* of Alcuin.

Since no complete inventory of MSS for the lectionary exists, the
full development of this lectionary cannot be traced from the X-XVI
century.[188]

A variety of medieval liturgists can assist us in classifying the surviving witnesses; Amalarius of Metz (†ca. 850), Berno of Reichenau (†1048), Bernhold of Constance (†1100), Honorius of Autun (†ca. 1145), Rupert of Deutz (†1135), and William Durandus (†1296).[189]

From the time of Charlemagne until the II Vatican Council, the same readings were used in Lent, Holy Week, Easter Week and for the Ember Days. Throughout Paschaltide and until the feast of the Apostles (June 29), the lessons were drawn from the Epistle to the Romans, and the Epistles to the Corinthians, the Galatians, the Ephesians, the Phillippians and the Colossians. After Pentecost, the readings were from the Acts of the Apostles.

Although the juxtaposition of epistle and gospel readings had come about more by chance than by design, it was destined to endure from more than a thousand years.[190]

APPENDIX III

THE ROMAN ANTIPHONARY FOR MASS
(Antiphonale missarum).

In principle, the Mass Antiphonary (*antiphonarius, antiphonale, liber antiphonarius missarum*)   contains all the texts meant to be sung at Mass: the Introit and its corresponding psalm, the Gradual and its Response, the Tract, the Alleluia and its verse, and the Offertory and Communion verses. As in the case of all medieval liturgical books, however, rarely was the content of the antiphonary so carefully defined. Any given *codex* might be missing one or more of the items just mentioned or they could be gathered together in a special book, a kind of subdivision of the antiphonary.[191]

Amalarius of Metz (†ca. 850) had already noted that Roman nomenclature did not always coincide with that used in Frankish Gaul.

Notandum est volumen quod nos vocamus Antiphonarium, tria habere nomina apud Romanos: quod dicimus Gradale, illi vocant Cantatorium qui adhuc iuxta morem antiquum apud illos in aliquibus ecclesiis uno volumine continetur. Sequentem partem dividunt in nominibus; pars quae continet responsoria vocatur Responsoriale et pars quae continet antiphonas vocatur Antiphonarius. Ego secutus sum nostrum usum et posui mixtim responsoria et antiphonas secundum ordinem temporum in quibus solemnitates nostrae celebrantur.[192]

According to Amalarius, therefore, the Romans had several distinct chant books while the Frankish churches used a single collection. The Frankish *Gradale* corresponded to the Roman *Cantatorium*, i.e., the book containing the Gradual, the Tract and the alleluia verses. The term *Gradale (Graduale)* derives from the word *gradus*, the steps of the ambo where the cantor stood to sing what came between the epistle and gospel. The responses were contained in the *Responsoriale* while the antiphons for the introit and communion were in the *Antiphonarius*. In Frankish usage all these chant pieces were contained in a single book bearing the title of Antiphonary. Medieval terminology for designating liturgical books never became fixed.[193] It should also be recalled that the books of chant, whether antiphonaries or more specialized collections of Tropes, Sequences or

Hymns, were meant for those who   directed the choirs *(magister, primus, secundus scolae)* rather than for the singers who normally sang from memory.

According to a medieval tradition originating in a biography by John the Deacon (825-880), it was Pope Gregory I (†604) who composed a *liber antiphonarius* for the Roman *scola cantorum:*

In domo Domini, more sapientissimi Salomonis, propter musicae compunctionem dulcedinis Antiphonarium centonem cantorum studiosissimus [Gregorius I] nimis utiliter compilavit.[194] Clearly such a tradition is without foundation; John the Deacon's testimony is far too tardy to be of value.[195] We have to be just as careful about attributing parts of the Antiphonary to Celestine I (422-432) or to Damasus I (366-384).[196]

On the other hand, the Roman Antiphonary and Responsorial were certainly introduced into the Frankish Kingdom in the time of Pepin the Short:

Direximus itaque excellentissimae praecellentiae vestrae et libros quantos reperire potuimus, i.e., antiphonale et responsale, insimul autem et grammaticam Aristotelis, Dionisii Ariopagitae geometriam, orthographiam, grammaticam, omnes greco eloquio scriptas.[197]

As in the case of the Roman sacramentaries and *ordines,* the chant books must have penetrated north of the Alps before that period, but in an unofficial manner. As is clear from Egbert of York (732), the chant books were known in England in the VIII century.[198]

From the period it is first accessible in the MSS (VIII/IX century), the Roman Antiphonary remained exceptionally stable. All the surviving antiphonaries begin with Advent whereas all the sacramentaries and lectionaries begin the liturgical year with the vigil of Christmas or with Christmas. During Advent the antiphonaries combine the *Temporale* and the *Sanctorale* into a single series of masses, like the Frankish Gelasians and the lectionary of Murbach. They do the same for the time after Epiphany, like the Frankish Gelasians, the Paduan type Gregorian, the *Comes* of Murbach and the Evangelary of Würzburg, whereas the *Hadrianum* relegates these Sundays to an appendix. For the time after Easter and after Pentecost, they separate the Temporal and the Sanctoral, like the Old Gelasian. In all the liturgical books, Lent and the three Sundays which precede it (Septuagesima, Sexagesima, Quinquagesima) and the octave of Easter form a single block of material which excludes all elements from the *Sanctorale.*

The following are the oldest and best witnesses to the Roman Antiphonary:

1. *The Cantatorium of Monza.*

Library: Monza, Tesoro della basilica S. Giovanni, *codex* CIX.
Date and Origin: ca. 800; Monza.
Edition and Bibliography: R.J. Hesbert, *Antiphonale Missarum sextuplex* (Brussels 1935) 1-196; *Le Graduel romain: Édition critique par les moines de Solesmes.* 2: *Les sources* (Solesmes 1957) 77.
    This is the oldest surviving witness to the Roman Gradual.
Title: *In nomine Dei summi. Dominica prima de adventu.* Secondary title before the 22 Sundays after Pentecost: *Incipiunt responsoria gradualia in dominicis diebus a pentecosten usque ad adventum Domini. Ebdomata prima.*[199]

2. *The Antiphonary of Rheinau.*

Library: Zürich, Zentralbibl., *codex Rh.* 30, fol. 1ᵛ-13ᵛ.
Date and Origin: VIII/IX century; abbey of Nivelles or Chur ?; later at the abbey of Rheinau.
Edition and Bibliography: M. Gerbert, *Monumenta veteris liturgiae Alemannicae* 1 (Saint Blaise 1777) 362-399; R.J. Hesbert, *Antiphonale*, p. xii. The *Rhenaugiense* 30 is a complex MS. The antiphonary is followed by the *Poenitentiale Cummeani* (fol. 14ʳ-24ᵛ), edited by J. Schmitz, *Die Bussbücher und die Bussdisciplin der Kirche*, 1(1883) 611-645, and by a Frankish Gelasian Sacramentary (but not the *Triplex* published by Gerbert). These books are all independent of one another and have no essential connection. Title of the Antiphonary: *Incipiunt dominicales anni circuli. Dominica quinta ante natale Domini.*

3. *The Antiphonary of Mont Blandin/Antiphonary of Pamelius.*

Library: Brussels, Bibl. royale, *codex* 10127-10144, fol. 90-115.
Date and Origin: VIII/IX century; abbey of Mont Blandin, near Ghent.
Edition and Bibliography: Pamelius, *Liturgicon Ecclesiae latinae* (1571); R. J. Hesbert, *Antiphonale Missarum sextuplex* (Brussels 1935); and, "L'antiphonaire de Pamelius," EL 49 (1935) 348-359; *Le Graduel romain* 2: *Les sources*, p. 37; M. Huglo, "Le chant 'vieux-romain'," SE 6 (1954) 111, no. 13.
    This antiphonary is part of a MS containing a collection of *ordines;* cf. M. Andrieu, *Les Ordines* 1 (1931) 81-100. Title: *Incipit antephonarius ordinatus a sancto Gregorio per circulum anni.*

4. *The Antiphonary of Compiègne/Antiphonary of Charles the Bald.*

Library: Paris, Bibl. Nat. *lat.* 17436.
Date and Origin: ca. 860/880; Abbey of St. Cornelius of Compiègne for a church dedicated to St. Médard or St. Vaast.

Edition and Bibliography: Maurist edition in PL 78, 641-724; R.J. Hesbert, *Antiphonale missarum sextuplex* (Brussels 1935); P. Cagin, *Un mot sur l'antiphonale missarum* (Solesmes 1890).

The *Parisinus* 17436 contains an antiphonary for Mass on fol. 1^v-30^v and an antiphonary for the Office *(Liber responsorialis sive antiphonarius)* on fol. 31^v-107^v; PL 78, 725-850. The Antiphonary for Mass has the title: *Incipit dominica prima de adventu Domini. Statio ad S. Andream ad praesepe.*

5. *The Antiphonary of Corbie.*

Library: Paris, Bibl. Nat., *lat.* 12050, fol. 3-17.

Date and Origin: After 853; written by the priest Hrodratus at Corbie; at St. Germain-des-Prés from 1638 to 1795.

Edition and Bibliography: R.J. Hesbert, *Antiphonale missarum sextuplex* (Brussels 1935); M. Huglo, *Revue grégorienne* 21 (1952) 230-296.

This MS contains the antiphonary for Mass on leaves 3-10, 11-17 (one leaf is missing) and the famous Sacramentary of Rodradus, a fine witness to the supplemented *Hadrianum* by Benedict of Aniane (see *supra*, p. 90).

6. *The Antiphonary of Senlis.*

Library: Paris, Bibl. Ste. Geneviève, *codex lat.* 111(*olim* BB I fol. 20).

Date and Origin: Between 877 and 882; St. Denis for Senlis.

Edition and Bibliography: R.J. Hesbert, *Ant. miss. sext.* (Brussels 1935); *Le Graduel romain* 2: *Les sources,* 113.

The antiphonary is followed by a sacramentary and begins without a title with *Dominica prima de adventu Domini.*

More recent antiphonaries for the Mass have been catalogued by K. Gamber and in the comprehensive list in *Le Graduel romain 2: Les sources.*[200]

APPENDIX IV

THE NON-ROMAN ANTIPHONARIES FOR MASS.

1. *Mozarabic Antiphonaries.*

In the Visigothic (Old Spanish) liturgy, the antiphonary for the Mass and the antiphonary for the Office appear in the same volume.[201] Only a single, somewhat late example survives.

Library: León, Bibl. catedral, *codex* I.

Date and Origin: Under Abbot Akilia (917-970); León.

Edition and Bibliography: *Antiphonarium mozarabicum de la Catedral de León* (León 1928); L. Brou-J. Vives, *Antifonario visigótico mozárabe de la catedral de León*, Monumenta Hispaniae sacra, Series liturgica 5, 1 and 2 (Barcelona-Madrid 1953/1959); M. Ravanal Alvarez, "Sobre algunas piezas del Antifonario visigótico-mozárabe de la Catedral le León," *Archivos Leoneses* 13 (1959) 67-85; J.M. Martin Patino, "El antifonario hispánico de Adviento: Contribución al estudio de las fuentes," *Miscelánea Commillas* 45 (Santander 1966) 189-243.

Title: *Incipit liber antiphonarium de toto anni circulo a festivitate sancti Acicli usque in finem* (Nov 17).

Fragments of antiphonaries:

M.S. Gros, "Les fragments parisiens de l'antiphonaire de Silos," RB 74 (1964) 324-333; J. Janini, "Los fragmentos visigóticos de San Zoilo de Carrión," *Liturgica* 3=Scripta et Documenta 17 (1966) 73-83.[202]

2. *Beneventan Antiphonaries.*

Basically, these antiphonaries agree with the corresponding Roman books, although they contain some characteristics which connect them with the Milanese antiphonaries.[203] Although most of them are fragments and rather recent, the most important witnesses to this tradition are: Rome, *Vat. lat. codices* 10673 (X/XI century) and 10657 (XI century), Benevento, Archiv. arcivescovile, *codices* VI. 40 (XI century), VI. 38 (XI century), VI. 34 (XI/XII century), VI. 39 (late XI century), VI. 35 (XII century), Farfa, Palmieri I and II (XI century).[204]

3. *Ambrosian Antiphonaries.*

Aside from a late MS, the Antiphonary of London, the surviving Ambrosian antiphonaries are mere fragments.[205]

Library: London, British Library, *Add.* 34.209.

Date and Origin: Early XII century; Milan or its environs.

Edition and Bibliography: *Paléographie musicale* 1, 5, 6, (Tournai 1889, 1896, 1900); M. Huglo, *Fonti e paleografia del canto ambrosiano* (Milan 1956) 39-44.

This is the oldest Ambrosian antiphonary with musical notation; used for the *Antiphonale Missarum iuxta ritum S.E. Mediolanensis* (Rome 1935).

APPENDIX V

BOOKS OF HOMILIES AND ANTIPHONARIES FOR THE DIVINE OFFICE

At present, given the complexity of the situation, it would be almost impossible to provide a description of the *status quaestionis* on the history of the Liturgy of the Hours and its various components in the Middle Ages. The following items merely permit a certain orientation to the sources.

R. Grégoire, *Les Homéliaires du moyen âge. Inventaire et analyse des manuscrits*, RED, Series maior, Fontes 4 (Rome 1966) is fundamental along with his *Homéliaires liturgiques médiévaux*, Biblioteca degli 'Studi medievali' 12 (Spoleto 1980) with very useful tables and bibliographies; "La collection homilétique du MS Wolfenbüttel 4096," *Studi medievali* 14 (1973) 259-286; "L'Homéliaire de Saint-Pierre au Vatican (*codex lat.* C 105)," *Studi medievali* 13 (1972) 233-255. See also H. Barré, *Les Homéliaires carolingiens de l'école d'Auxerre*, SeT 225 (Vatican City 1962).

A careful description of the MSS will be found in CLLA and in E. Dekkers, *Clavis patrum latinorum* (2nd ed. Steenbrugge 1961).

A. Chavasse has new approaches in his edition of the *Tractatus* of Leo the Great, CC 138, xix-lxxxiii; see also his "Le sermonnaire d'Agimond," *Kyriakon, Festschrift J. Quasten* (Münster/Westf. 1973) 800-810 and "Le sermonnaire du Vatican du VII siècle," SE 23 (1978/79) 225-289.

1. *The Homiliary of Charlemagne or of Paul the Deacon.*

Several books were needed for a proper celebration of the Canonical Office: an Antiphonary, a Homiliary containing extracts from the Fathers and other ecclesiastical writers, a Hymnary, a Psalter and a Bible. Here we shall only address the first two.

We know that Charlemagne asked Paul the Deacon to compose a Book of Homilies for the Office that would be both grammatically and liturgically correct. Paul Warnefrid did as he was asked and composed a two-volume Book of Homilies which King Charles subsequently imposed on the churches and monasteries of his dominions. Charlemagne's *Epistola generalis* of 768/800 confirms this:

Accensi praeterea venerandae memoriae Pippini genitoris nostri exemplis, qui totas Galliarum ecclesias romanae traditionis suo studio cantibus decoravit, nos nihilominus solerti easdem curamus intuitu praecipuarum insignire serie lectionum. Denique quia ad nocturnale officium compilatas quorumdam casso labore, licet recto intuitu, minus tamen idonee repperimus lectiones, quippe quae et sine auctorum suorum vocabulis essent positae et infinitis vitiorum anfractibus scaterent, non sumus passi nostris in diebus in divinis lectionibus inter sacra officia inconsonantes perstrepere soloecismos, atque earumdem lectionum in melius reformare tramitem mentem intendimus. Idque opus Paulo diacono, familiari clientulo nostro, elimandum iniunximus, scilicet ut, studiose catholicorum patrum dicta percurrens, veluti e latissimis eorum pratis certos flosculos legeret, et in unum quaeque essent utilia quasi sertum aptaret. Qui nostrae celsitudini devote parere desiderans, tractatus atque sermones diversorum catholicorum patrum perlegens et optima quaeque decerpens, in duobus voluminibus per totius anni circulum congruentes cuique festivitati distincte et absque vitiis nobis obtulit lectiones. Quarum omnium textum nostra sagacitate perpendentes, nostra eadem volumina auctoritate constabilimus vestraeque religioni in Christi ecclesiis tradimus ad legendum. MGH, *Capitularia regum Francorum* 1, 80-81.

Only a few studies have appeared on this Homiliary: see F. Wieland, *Das Homiliarium Karls des Grossen auf seine ursprüngliche Gestalt hin untersucht* (Leipzig 1897; repr. Aalen 1972) and "Ein Vorläufer des Paulus-Homiliars," *Theologische Studien und Kritiken* 75 (1902) 188-205; G. Morin, "Les sources non identifiées de l'Homéliaire de Paul Diacre," RB 15 (1898) 400-403. In this instance Charlemagne proceeded differently than usual. Instead of procuring an authentic Roman homiliary or having one copied—as he had done for other liturgical books—this time Charles asked his Lombard monk to compose a new book by selecting his own passages from the writings of the Fathers. The result was a two-volume work *per totius anni circulum* that Charlemagne imposed on his churches. It was a particularly curious way of proceeding since Charles claimed only to be continuing the work of his father in favor of the Roman rite. What was apparently at work was a desire to have pure and authentic texts of the Fathers. In this instance he seemed less interested in a Roman book and more interested in a *correct* book. As far as the free choice of patristic texts was concerned, the *Ordines romani* were agreed in authorizing it. While for the Biblical readings there were precise indications and often even set *incipits* and *explicits*—as in *Ordo* XIII A (700-750), XIII B (late VIII century), XIII C (in the lifetime of Burchard of Worms), XIII D (XI century) and in *Ordo* XIV (Gaul, 750-787)—these same *ordines* are more relaxed in regard to the patristic readings. They seem quite content to indicate what they have in mind in very general terms: *Tractatus patrum, sermones atque homeliae ad ipsum diem pertinentes* and refer in a general way to the four great Latin Fathers without further specification. *Ordo* XIII A, no. 13: *sermones vel omeliae catholicorum patrum* seems echoed in Charlemagne's *Epistola generalis: Catholici patres, tractatus atque sermones Catholicorum patrum.*

In addition to Paul the Deacon's work, we learn from the *Vita Alcuini* that Alcuin also composed an analogous work in two books: *Collegit multis de patrum operibus omeliarum duo volumina*: MGH. *Script.* 15, 1, 195. Possibly the author of the *Vita* confused his evidence and thought that the *duo volumina* of the *Epistola generalis* were to be attributed to Alcuin. In any case such a work by Alcuin has never been found although it was mentioned in the old catalogue of Fulda; cf. G. Becker, *Catalogi bibliothecarum antiqui* nos. 13 and 17, pp. 30 and 37. G. Morin thought he had discovered this homiliary of Alcuin in the *Parisinus lat.* 14302, Morin, "L'Homéliaire d'Alcuin retrouvé," RB 9 (1892) 491-497, but his so-called discovery was disputed from the start; cf. the exchange of letters between Morin and C.J.B. Gaskoin in E.S. Duckett, *Alcuin, Friend of Charlemagne* (New York 1951) 199, note.

2. *Other Homiliaries.*

In addition to the titles above, the studies of R. Etaix are essential: "L'Homéliaire d'Ebardus retrouvé (Paris, Bibl. Nat. *latin* 19604)," *Revue d'histoire des textes* 8 (1978) 309-317; "Homiliaires wisigothiques provenant de Silos à la Bibliothèque Nationale de Paris," *Hispania Scara* 12 (1959) 213-224; "L'Homiliaire conservé au Museo Diocesano de Gerona," *Analecta sacra Taraconensia* 34 (1961) 1-9; "L'Homiliaire cartusien," SE 13 (1962) 67-112; "Un homiliaire ancien à Vérone (Bibl. capit., *codex* LII)," RB 73 (1963) 289-306; "Le prologue du sermonnaire d'Alain de Farfa," *Scriptorium 18 (1964)* 3-10; "Les homiliaires patristiques du Mont-Saint-Michel," *Millénaire monastique du Mont-Saint-Michel* 1 (Paris 1967) 339-415; "Le lectionnaire de l'Office à Cluny," *Recherches augustiniennes* 11 (1976) 91-159; "Nouvelle collection des sermons rassemblés par. S. Césaire, RB 87 (1977) 7-33; "Le sermonnaire carolingien de Beaune," *Revue des études augustiniennes* 25 (1979) 106-149; "Les homiliaires liturgiques de Saint-Thierry," *Saint Thierry, une abbaye du VI au XX siècle. Actes du colloque international d'histoire monastique* (Saint-Thierry 1979) 147-158.

3. *The Antiphonary of Amalarius of Metz.*

The Antiphonary of the Divine Office was only amended and corrected under Louis the Pious (814-840) through the intermediary of the learned Amalarius of Metz. In contrast to what Charlemagne had done in the case of the Homiliary, Amalarius went to Rome for his information.

He had discovered great discrepancies among the various antiphonaries used in the Frankish churches and made no attempt to hide his dismay:

Cum longo tempore taedio affectus essem propter antiphonarios discordantes inter se in nostra provincia [Lotharingia], moderni enim alio ordine currebant quam vetusti, et quid plus retinendum esset nesciebam [De ordine antiphonarii, Prologus; PL 105, 1243; ed. J.M. Hanssens, *Amalarii episcopi opera liturgica omnia*, SeT 138 (Vatican City 1948) 361.]

At Rome a cruel surprise awaited him; Pope Gregory IV (827-844) informed him that he no longer had an antiphonary! All the copies he had once possessed he had bestowed upon Abbot Wala of Corbie at an earlier date:

Antiphonarium non habeo quem possim mittere filio meo domino imperatori, *quoniam hos quos habuimus, Wala, quando functus est huc legatione aliqua, abduxit eos hinc secum in Franciam (Ibid.).*

At Corbie Amalarius was to find an abundant supply of antiphonaries but they were all different from those used at Metz:

Inventa copiam antiphonarium . . . volumnina contuli cum nostris antiphonariis, invenique ea discrepare a nostris non solum in ordine, verum etiam in verbis et multitudine responsorium et antiphonarum, quas nos non cantamus (ibid.).

His solution for at least some of the new book was to combine a Metz antiphonary with the Roman copies and thus produce a new antiphonary—a clear case of hybridization:

Ex utrisque [romanis et mettensibus] collegi ea quae recta mihi videbantur, et rationabili cursui congruere, atque ea redacta in unum corpus posui sub uno textu in fine antiphonarii nostri. [Liber de ordine antiphonarii, cap. 79; PL 105, 1314; ed. Hanssens, vol. 3, SeT 140, p. 108].

Cf. R.J. Hesbert, "L'Antiphonaire d'Amalaire," EL 94 (1980) 176-194.

The oldest antiphonaries for the Office are available in R.J. Hesbert, *Corpus Antiphonalium Officii,* 5 vols., RED, series major 7-12 (Rome 1963-79).

Additional Notes:

1. The *libri ordinarii.*

An inventory of all those published until 1957 in A. Hänggi, *Der Rheinauer Liber ordinarius* (Zürich, *RH.* 80, XII century), Spicilegium Friburgense 1 (1957) xxv-xxxvi, to be completed by A. Jacob, "A propos de l'édition de l'Ordinaire de Tongres," *Revue d'histoire ecclés.* 65 (1970) 789-797.

2. *The liturgical readings from the Martyrologies.*

An analysis of the Martyrologies and the *Passionaria* cannot be provided here but see B. de Gaiffier, "De l'usage et de la lecture du martyrologe," *Analecta Bollandiana* 79 (1961) 40-59 and *Recherches d'hagiographie latine,* Subsidia hagiographica 52 (Brussels 1971).

3. *The Episcopal Benedictionals.*

F. Combaluzier, "Un Bénédictionaire épiscopal du X siècle," SE 14 (1963) 286-342 with bibliography; E. Moeller, *Corpus Benedictionum Pontificalium,* 4 vols., CC 162, 162 A, 162 B, 162 C (Turnhout 1971-1979).

4. *Hymns and Hymnaries.*

For the Latin hymns and collections of hymns current in the Middle Ages, see:
F.J. Mone, *Lateinische Hymnen des Mittelalters,* 3 vols. (Freiburg 1853-1855); G.M. Dreves-C. Blume, *Analecta Hymnica Medii Aevi,* 55 vols. (Leipzig 1886-1922, reprint New York 1961); M. Lütolf (ed.), *Register* (Indices), 2 vols. in 3 (Berne 1978);

U. Chevalier, *Repertorium Hymnologicum. Catalogue des chants, hymnes, proses, sequences, tropes en usage dans l'Église latine* ..., 6 vols. (Louvain 1892-1912, Brussels 1920-1921);

J. Julian, *Dictionary of Hymnology*, 2nd ed. (London 1908, reprint New York 1977);

J. Mearns, *Early Latin Hymnaries: An Index of Hymns in Hymnaries before 1100* (Cambridge 1913, reprint Hildesheim 1970);

The best overview of the present state of research in hymnology is J. Szövérffy, *Die Annalen der lateinischen Hymnendichtung*, 2 vols. (Berlin 1964-1965).

Hymns, of course, must be seen within the whole context of medieval poetry:

F.J.E. Raby, *A History of Christian Latin-Poetry from the Beginnings to the Close of the Middle Ages* (Oxford 1927, reprint 1953);

A. Michel, *In Hymnis et Canticis. Culture et beauté dans l'hymnique chrétienne latine*, Philosophes médiévaux 20 (Louvain 1976).

For the hymns of the Divine Office/Liturgy of the Hours, consult:

A.S. Walpole-A.J. Mason, *Early Latin Hymns*, Cambridge Patristic Texts (Cambridge 1922). Walpole presents the medieval texts of the hymns and not those revised under Urban VIII, the last of the humanist popes. The authentic, unrevised texts have recently reappeared:

Liturgia Horarum iuxta Ritum Romanum, 4 vols. (Vatican City 1971);

A. Lentini, *Te Decet Hymnus, L'innario della Liturgia Horarum* (Vatican City 1984).

English translations of the revised Latin text with helpful notes:

M. Britt, *The Hymns of the Roman Breviary and Missal* (New York 1936);

J. Connolly, *Hymns of the Roman Liturgy* (Westminster, MD 1957).

5. *Tropes and Sequences.*

A great deal of research has been done recently on the medieval poetical compositions used in the celebration of the Eucharist. Sequences have been listed and studied by R.J. Crocker, *The Early Medieval Sequence* (Berkeley 1977). For the tropes—poetical compositions which were interpolated into the sung parts of the mass—a major editorial work has been undertaken by scholars of the University of Stockholm under the auspices of the European Science Foundation: *Corpus Troporum*, Studia Latina Stockholmiensis, Stockholm: R. Jonsson (ed.), *Tropes du propre de la messe* 1, Cycle de Noel, CT 1, SLS 21 (Stockholm 1975); O. Marcusson (ed.), *Prosules de la messe* 1, Tropes de l'alleluia, CT 2, SLS 22 (Stockholm 1976); G. Björkvall, G. Iversen, R. Jonsson (edd.), *Tropes du propre de la messe* 2, Cycle de Pâques, CT 3, SLS 25 (Stockholm 1982): G. Iverson, *Tropes de l'Agnus Dei*, CT 4, SLS 26 (Stockholm 1980). See also G. Iversen (ed.), *Research on Tropes. Proceedings of a Symposium Organized by the Royal Academy of Letters, History and Antiquities and the Corpus Troporum*, Konferenser 8 (Stockholm 1983).

Notes: Chapter Seven and Appendices III, IV and V.

1. O. Cullman, *Early Christian Worship*, trans. A.S. Todd-J.B. Torrance (London 1953) 26-32.

2. We are not concerned here with the private reading of Scripture; for this see A. Harnack, *Über den privaten Gebrauch der heiligen Schriften in der alten Kirche* (Leipzig 1912), ET *Bible Reading in the Early Church*, trans. J.R. Wilkinson, Crown Theological Library 36 (New York-London 1912). For a more general view see L. Koep, "Buch," *Reallexikon für Antike und Christentum* 2 (1954) 720-724.

3. The history of preaching still leaves much to be desired. See the summary and bibliography in Y.T. Brilioth, *A Brief History of Preaching* (Philadlephia 1958); C.E. Fant-W.M. Pinson (edd.), *Twenty Centuries of Great Christian Preaching* (Waco, TX 1972); R.G. Turnbull, *A History of Preaching*, 3 vols. (Grand Rapids, MI 1974); B.J. Cooke, *Ministry to Word and Sacraments* (Philadelphia 1976); D.T. Holland, *The Preaching Tradition: A Brief History* (Nashville, 1980).

4. For a bibliography of studies before those of E. Ranke (1847), see T. Klauser, *Das römische Capitulare Evangeliorum*, LQF 28 (Münster 1935) xxiii-xxv.

5. A. Dold's bibliography can be found in *Colligere Fragmenta*, TuA 2 (Beuron 1952) ix-xx (by A. Fiala)=122 titles; and in K. Gamber, *Sakramentartypen*, TuA 49-50 (Beuron 1958) viii-x,=34 titles from 1952-1958.

6. For exhaustive bibliographies of G. Morin, A. Wilmart, K. Gamber and others, see Gamber, *Codices liturgici latini antiquiores* (CLLA), Spicilegii Friburgensis Subsidia 1, 2 vols. (2nd ed. Fribourg 1968) 170-180, 214-219, 226-230, 430-491 *et passim*.

7. Basic bibliography: C.P. Caspari, "Griechen und Grieschisches in der römischen Gemeinde in den ersten 3 Jh. ihres Bestehens," *Ungedruckte, unbeachtete und wenig beachtete Quellen zur Geschichte des Taufsymbol und der Glaubensregel* 3 (Oslo 1875) 267-466 and "Über den gottesdienstlichen Gebrauch des Griechischen im Abendlande während des frühen Mittelalters," *ibid.*, 466-510; G. Morin, "Formules liturgiques orientales en Occident aux IV et V siècles," RB 40 (1928)134-137, on Marius Victorinus; A. Baumstark, "Ein Übersetzungsfehler im Messkanon," *Studia Catholica* 5 (1929) 378-382: *summus sacerdos tuus Melchisedech*; M. Müller, *Der Übergang von der griechischen zur lateinischen Sprache in der abendländischen Kirche von Hermas bis Novatian* (Rome 1943); F. Cumont, "Pourquoi le latin fut la seule langue liturgique de l'Occident," *Mélanges Paul Frédéricq* (Brussels 1904); T. Klauser, "Der Übergang der römischen Kirche von griechischen zur lateinischen Liturgiesprache," *Miscellanea Giovanni Mercati* 1 (SeT 121 (Rome 1946) 467-482; reprinted in *Gesammelte Arbeiten*, Jahrbuch für Antike und Christentum Ergänzungsband 3 (Münster 1974) 184-194. A. G. Martimort, "La discipline de l'Église en matiére de langue liturgique. Essai historique," MD 11 (1947) 39-54 and "Le problème des langues liturgiques," MD 53 (1958) 23-56; G. Bardy, *La question des langues dans l'Église ancienne* (Paris 1918), which does not treat of the change of language at Rome; C.

Mohrmann, "Les origines de la latinité chrétienne à Rome," *Vigiliae Christianae* 3 (1949) 162-182.—On the nature of liturgical Latin see a synthesis and bibliography in C. Mohrmann, "Die Rolle des Lateins in der Kirche des Westens," *Theologische Revue* 52 (1956) 1-18; C. Mohrmann-B. Botte, "Le latin liturgique, "*L'Ordinaire de la messe. Études litugiques* 2 (Paris-Louvain 1953) 29-48.—On the cosmopolitan and eastern character of the Christian community at Rome, see A.M. Schneider, "Die ältesten Denkmäler der römischen Kirche," *Festschrift zur Feier des 200 Jhr Bestehens der Akad. Wiss. in Göttingen* 2 Phil.-hist. Kl. (Berlin-Göttingen-Heidelberg 1951) 166-198; C. Pietri, *Roma Christiana: Recherches sur l'Église de Rome, son organisation, sa politique, son idéologie de Miltiade à Sixte III (311-440)*, 2 vols, Bibliothèque des Écoles françaises d'Athènes et de Rome 224 (Rome 1976).

8. G. La Piana, "The Roman Church at the End of the Second Century," *Harvard Theological Review* 18 (1925) 201-277 and "L'immigrazione a Roma nei primi secoli dell'Impero," *Ricerche religiose* 2 (1926) 485-547; 3 (1927) 36-75 and *Foreign Groups in Rome during the First Centuries of the Empire* (Cambridge 1927).

9. B. Botte, (ed.), *La Tradition Apostolique de Saint Hippolyte,* LQF 39 (Münster 1963). For the oldest documents on the Christian community at Rome see A.M. Schneider, *op. cit.* above in note 7.

10. The disappearance of the Latin language used for worship in North Africa, which was not assimilated by either the native Berbers or the conquering Vandals, meant the disappearance of the Church as well; see C. Courtois, *Les Vandales et l'Afrique* (Paris 1955) 126-130.—On the role and significance of the North African Church in the ancient period, see F. Heiler, *Altkirchliche Autonomie und päpstlicher Zentralismus* (Munich 1941) 3-51, 187-203; W.H.C. Frend, *The Donatist Church* (Oxford 1952) and *Martyrdom and Persecution in the Early Church* (New York 1967).

11. W.Y. Fausset, (ed.), *Novatiani Romae Urbis presbyteri De Trinitate liber* (Cambridge 1909).

12. *Epistola* 8 in the *corpus* of Cyprian's Letters; CSEL 3, 485-488; FC 51, 20-23.

13. *Epistolae* 49 and 50 in the Cyprian *corpus;* CSEL 3, 608-614; FC 51, 121-125.

14. Cyprian to Stephen; *Epistolae* 68 and 72; CSEL 3, 744-749 and 775-778; FC 51, 239-43 and 265-68.

15. See P. Sabatier, *Bibliorum sacrorum latinae versiones antiquae* (Rheims 1745); Bon. Fischer *et al., Vetus Latina. Die Reste der altlateinischen Bibel nach Petrus Sabatier neu gesammelt und hrsg. von der Erzabtei Beuron,* vols. 1, 2, 11, 24, 25, 26 (Beuron-Freiburg, 1949-1984); J. Gribomont, "L'Église et les versions bibliques," MD 62 (1960) 41-68; P. Salmon, "Le texte biblique des lectionnaires mérovingiens," *La Bibbia nell'alto medioevo,* Settimane di studi 10 (Spoleto 1963) 491-519; J. Quasten, "The First Latin Versions of the Bible," in *Patrology* 2 (Westminster, MD 1953; reprint 1983) 244-245, with bibliography.

16. Jerome, *Epistola,* 57, 7; CSEL 54, 512-516, PL 22, 371 : *Ego enim non solum fateor, sed libera voce profiteor me, in interpretatione Graecorum absque*

Scripturis sanctis, ubi et verborum mysterium est, non verbum e verbo, sed sensum exprimere de sensu.—It is not at all sure that Jerome's work was meant to remedy a kind of linguistic chaos.

17. Augustine, *Epistolae* 71, 3, 5; 75, 6, 21; 77, 22; and 82, 5, 35; CSEL 34, 250-253, 289, 320-321; 355-356, 386. See F. van der Meer, *Augustine the Bishop*, (London-New York 1961) 341 and note 95.

18. C. Wessel, *Inscriptiones graece christianae veteres Occidentis*, Dissertation (Halle 1936).

19. The *Liberian Catalogue* (352-354) of the Chronographer of 354 (MGH, *Auctores Antiquissimi* 9, 73; L. Duchesne, *Liber pontificalis* 1, 1-9) contains a few historical references to the bishops of Rome (after 235) such as anniversaries of their ordinations and their burials; the Chronographer's other information comes from the letters of Cyprian and not from contemporaries; A.M. Schneider, *Die ältesten Denkmäler*, 166-168.

20. On this point see H. Delehaye, *Origines du culte des martyres* (2nd ed. Brussels 1933) 262. No authentic *Passio* of a martyr survives in Latin and the Church of Rome always viewed with considerable suspicion the later hagiographical writings: . . . *gesta sanctorum martyrum . . . secundum antiquam consuetudinem, singulari cautela in sancta Romana ecclesia non leguntur; Decretum Gelasianum* 4, 4; ed. Dobschütz, TuU 38, 4 (1912) 9. In composing his famous marble inscriptions for the tombs of the Roman martyrs, Pope Damasus (366-384) had very little historical material to work with. The poet Prudentius summarized the situation very nicely: *Sunt et muta tamen tacitas claudentia tumbas marmora; Peristephanon* 9, 9; ed. M.P. Cunningham, CC 126 (1966) 370. As for the tombs of Peter and Paul, it seems that the two apostles did not enjoy a *cultus* at Rome until the time of Constantine; even the date of their *depositio* is unknown; see T. Klauser, *Die römische Petrus-Tradition im Lichte der neuen Ausgrabungen unter der Peterskirche* (Cologne-Opladen 1956) 21-28; on the other hand, J. Toynbee-J.W. Perkins devote a full chapter to "The Pre-Constantinian Shrine," *The Shrine of St. Peter and the Vatican Excavations* (London-New York-Toronto 1956) 134-194. For the list of Roman bishops, see E. Caspar, "Die älteste römische Bischofsliste," *Schriften der Königsbergergesellschaft* 2/2 (Berlin 1926).

21. PL 8, 1094; SC 68, 416.

22. CSEL 50, 268.

23. The interpretation of the expression *loqui lingua/linguis* of Ambrosiaster in the time of Damasus (366-384) in his *Commentarius in 1 Cor.* 14; PL 17, 253-260, given by T. Klauser as meaning a foreign language, unintelligible to the community ["Der Übergang," 475-477; see *supra* note 7] has been contested by C. Mohrmann, "Le latin liturgique," *L'Ordinaire de la messe* (Paris-Louvain 1953) 34-35.—Cf. A. Stuiber, *Libelli sacramentorum romani*, Theophaneia 6 (Bonn 1950); A. Ferrua, *Epigrammata Damasiana*, Sussidi 2 (Vatican City 1942).

24. Such is Klauser's theory (*op. cit.*, 481) as opposed to that of B. Botte, *L'Ordinaire de la messe*, 17,—Ambrose of Milan, *De sacramentis, De mysteriis,*

(ed.), B. Botte, SC 25bis (Paris 1961); T. Thompson, *St. Ambrose: On the Sacraments and On the Mysteries* (London 1950), with introduction and notes by J.H. Srawley; R. Deferrari, *St. Ambrose: Theological and Dogmatic Works,* FC 44 (Washington, DC 1963).

25. A. Baumstark, "Ein Übersetzungsfehler im Messkanon," *Studia catholica* 5 (1929) 378-382 and in his *Missale Romanum* (Eindhoven-Nijmegen 1929) 13, thought he had discovered in the Latin *Canon missae* an erroneous translation of a Greek text. The passage in Genesis 14:18 had been translated by *summus sacerdos tuus Melchisedech* instead of by the more exact translation [*Melchisedech*] *sacerdos Dei Altissimi* or *Summi* or, in the canon itself, *quod tibi obtulit Melchisedech sacerdos tuus, Altissime.* His whole argument rested on the supposedly strange translation *summus sacerdos tuus Melchisedech* which he thought to be a mistranslation of the original Greek; but such is not the case. Cf. B. Botte, *Le canon de la messe romaine* (Louvain 1935) 42 and his references to the *Apostolic Constitutions* 8, 12, 23; ed. Funk 1, 502; G. Bardy, "Melchisédech dans la littérature patristique," *Revue Biblique* 35 (1926) 496-509; 36(1927)25-45.

26. See *supra,* pp. 61-62, 147-150, 237-239 on the Romanization process undertaken in the Carolingian period and the role of the Ottos of Germany in regard to the liturgy of the City in the last half of the X century.

27. J. Mizzi, "The Vulgate Text of the Supplemental Pages of *Codex Bezae Cantabrigiensis,*" SE 19 (1969) 149-163.

28. On these bilingual documents, see P. Glaue, *Die Vorlesung der hl. Schriften im Gottesdienst* 1: *Bis zum Entstehung der altkatholischen Kirche* (Leipzig 1907); A. Hermann, "Dolmetscher," *Reallexikon für Antike und Christentum* 4 (1959) 41-44.

29. See P. Frédéricq, "Les conséquences de l'évangelisation par Rome et par Byzance sur le développement de la langue maternelle des peuples convertis," *Académie royale de Belgique. Bulletin Classe des Lettres* (1903) 738-751; F. Cumont, "Pourquoi le latin fut la seule langue liturgique de l'Occident," *Mélanges Paul Frédéricq* (Brussels 1904) 63-66; F. Lot, "À quelle époque a-t-on cessé de parler le latin?" *Bulletin du Cange* (1931) 97-159; D. Norberg, "À quelle époque a-t-on cessé de parler latin en Gaule?" *Annales, Écomomies, Sociétés, Civilisations* 21 (1966) 346-356 reprinted in his *Au seuil du Moyen Age. Études linguistiques, métriques et littéraires,* Medioevo e Umanesimo 19 (Padua 1974) 3-16; J. Gülden, "Deutsche liturgische Texte. Versuch eines geschichtlichen Überblicks," *Werkblätter* 11 (1938-1939) 183-187; Balt. Fischer, "La grand-messe allemande," *Questions liturgiques et paroissiales* 35 (1954)22-33; C. Korolevsky, *Living Languages in Catholic Worship,* trans. D. Attwater (London 1957).

30. Pope Hadrian II (867-872) originally defended the brothers against their enemies and had them celebrate the Slavonic liturgy in Roman churches, but a later pope, Stephen V (885-891), succumbed to German episcopal pressure and closed the door permanently to the Roman liturgy in a vernacular tongue. Only among the Orthodox Slavs was a Slavonic liturgy

to continue as a phenomenon of Church life; cf. F. Kempf, *et al.*, *The Church in the Age of Feudalism*, Church History 3 (New York 1969) 147-151 and 512 (bibliography). Although Latin was maintained as *the* liturgical language, no universal way of pronouncing came to prevail in either the medieval or the modern Church. Latin was commonly pronounced in the same manner as the current vernacular tongue. The so-called Roman or Italian pronunciation promoted for the past few decades is an artificial, ultramodernist innovation; cf. F. Brittain, *Latin in Church. The History of its Pronunciation*, Alcuin Club Tract 28 (London 1955).

31. Regarding the liturgy, the bishops of Rome had quite different approaches to their own primatial region (*Italia Suburbicaria*) and to the more distant provinces. On the one hand, there is the liberalism of Vigilius (538-555) who sent Profuturus of Braga, the metropolitan of Galicia, an *ordinarium missae* and a baptismal formulary (now lost) by way of liturgical example without demanding that he use them; Vigilius, *Letter to Profuturus* (538); PL 69, 18. Canons 4 and 5 of the Synod of Braga (563) certainly went beyond the intentions of Vigilius by declaring the Roman *consuetudines* to be obligatory; Mansi, *Concilia* 9, 777. In North Africa, Augustine of Hippo († 430) proved to be equally tolerant: *Faciat ergo quisque quod in ea ecclesia in quam venit invenit . . . Propter fidem aut propter mores vel emendari oportet quod perperam fiebat vel instituti quod non fiebat. Ipsa quippe mutatio consuetudinis* [liturgical usages] *etiam quae utilitate adiuvat, novitate perturbat; Epistola* 54, 5, 6; CSEL 34/2, 165. The same broadmindedness is apparent in Gregory the Great († 604); when Augustine of Canterbury asked him why the churches of Gaul and Rome had different liturgical usages and which he should adopt for England, he responded: *Novit fraternitas tua romanae Ecclesiae consuetudinem, in qua se meminit nutritam; valde amabilem te habeat. Sed mihi placet, sive in Romana sive in Galliarum sive in qualibet ecclesia aliquid invenisti, quod plus omnipotenti Deo possit placere, sollicite eligas et in Anglorum ecclesia quae adhuc ad fidem nova est, institutione praecipua, quam de multis ecclesiis colligere potuisti, infundas. Non enim pro locis res, sed pro bonis rebus loca amanda sunt. Ex singulis ergo quibusque ecclesiis quae pia, quae religiosa, quae recta sunt elige et haec quasi in fasciculo collecta apud Anglorum mentes in consuetudinem depone;* MGH, *Epistolarum* 2, (1899) 334. To an objection that the pope himself had borrowed certain usages from Constantinople [*in ordinandis missae ritibus quibusdam Constantinopolitanae Ecclesiae consuetudines fuisse imitatum*], Gregory I replied to John of Syracuse that he found such an approach to be perfectly normal: *Veniens quidam de Sicilia dixit mihi quod aliqui amici eius vel Graeci vel Latini, nescio, quasi sub zelo sanctae romanae Ecclesiae de meis dispositionibus murmurarent dicentes: Quomodo ecclesiam Constantinopolitanam disponit comprimere, qui eius consuetudines per omnia sequitur? . . . cui ego respondi, quia in nullo eorum aliam ecclesiam secuti sumus . . . Si quid boni vel ipsa vel altera ecclesia habet, ego et minores meos quos ab inlicito prohibeo, in bono imitari paratus sum. Stultus est enim quo in eo se primum existimat, ut bona quae viderit, discere contemnat;* MGH, *Epistolarum* 2, 59. Cf. G. Gassner, "Das Selbstzeugniss Gregors des Grossen über seinen liturgischen Reformen," JfL 6 (1926) 218-223; T. Michels, "Prex quam scholasticus composuerat,"*ibid.*, 223-225. —On the other hand, this

eclecticism and tolerance of the popes in regard to those outside their immediate jurisdiction has to be contrasted with their intransigence in regard to their own suffragans; cf. Innocent I, *Letter to Decentius of Gubbio* (416): *Si instituta ecclesiastica ut sunt a beatis apostolis tradita integra vellent servare Domini sacerdotes, nulla diversitas, nulla varietas in ipsis ordinibus, et consecrationibus haberetur. Sed dum unusquisque non quod traditum est sed quod visum sibi fuerit hoc aestimat esse tenendum, inde diversa in diversis locis vel ecclesiis aut teneri aut celebrari videntur, ac fit scandalum populis, qui dum nesciunt traditiones antiquae humana praesumptione corruptas, putent sibi aut ecclesias non convenire aut ab apostolis vel apostolicis viris contrarietatem inducta;* PL 20, 551; R. Cabié *La Lettre du Pape Innocent I à Decentius de Gubbio* (Louvain 1973) 18. Such a letter not only betrays a different temperament from that of Gregory I but a difference of tone and attitude that depends on the addressee.

32. The liturgy of these frontier districts was often of a somewhat mixed character. Monte Cassino was obviously not completely under Roman influence, as can be seen in a remark of Leo of Ostia on Stephen IX's intervention of 1058: *Ambrosianum cantum in Ecclesia ista* [Montecassino] *cantari penitus interdixit; Chronica monasterii Cassinensis* 2, 94; MGH, *Scriptorum* 7 (1866) 693. Naples, on the other hand, showed by one of its calendars that it wanted to be in accord with Rome: *Kalendarium marmoreum Neapolitanum* (800/850); DACL 2 (1925) 1591-1592. Cf. A. Ehrhardt, "Der Marmor-Kalender von Neapel," *Rivista di archeologia cristiana* 9 (1934) 119-150.

33. Gregory VII, *Regula canonicorum: Romani autem diverso modo agere coeperunt maxime a tempore quo Teutonicis concessum est regimen Ecclesiae nostrae. Nos autem et ordinem Romanum et antiquum morem investigantes, statuimus fieri nostrae Ecclesiae sicut superius praenotavimus, antiquos imitantes patres;* G. Morin (ed.), *Études, textes, découvertes,* Anecdota Maredsolana, series 2, vol. 1 (Maredsous-Paris 1913) 459-460.

34. There is a considerable contrast, however, between what happened in France and Germany under the Carolingians and Ottonian emperors and what occured in Spain and N. Italy. In Spain, the Synod of Gerona (571), canon 1 (Mansi 8, 549) and the Synod of Braga (563) canons 4 and 5 (Mansi 9, 777) ordered liturgical uniformity on the basis of the Roman *consuetudo* although such had not been the intent of Pope Vigilius in his famous letter to Profuturus of Braga (538). Whatever was actually accomplished must have vanished during the reign of Leovigild (586) and was not restored under the new Catholic monarchy of Reccared and his successors. Instead, Toledo became the political and ecclesiastical capital of Spain and the great national councils which met there under the presidency of king and primate worked toward the liturgical unification of the entire peninsula; cf., e.g., Synod of Toledo (633) canon 2 (Mansi 10, 617) which sanctioned liturgical uniformity for all of Spain and its Gallic appendage across the Pyrenees in Septimania. In fact, however, there were always two Spanish uses, that of Toledo and that of Seville. As the Carolingians encroached on Spain in the VIII century, Synods like that of Frankfurt (794) tried to eliminate the Visigothic liturgy but its brutal suppression was not to be accomplished until the XI century

under popes Nicholas II, Alexander II, Gregory VII, and Urban II; bibliography in the various "Boletíns" by Brou, Pinell, and Mora Ontalva in *Hispania Sacra* 2 (1949) 459-484; 9 (1956) 418-421; 26 (1973) 211. —The Milanese/Ambrosian liturgy of N. Italy was much more influenced by Rome; cf. K. Gamber, CLLA pp. 259-286 = *Libri liturgici ambrosiani*. It cannot be determined whether or not Charlemagne attempted a systematic Romanization of the Milanese liturgy. The testimony of Landulph (ca. 1085), *Historia Mediolanensis*, is too late to be considered: *Ut quicquid in cantu et ministerio divino inveniret* [Charlemagne] *a romano diversum, totum deleret et ad unitatem ministerii uniret*; according to Landulph, Charlemagne carried off and systematically destroyed all the Ambrosian liturgical books: *ultra montes* [deportavit] *quasi in exilium omnes libros ambrosianos titulo sigillatos quos vel dono vel pretio vel vi habere potuit*; PL 147, 853.

35. The Gospel readings for the three weeks before Easter and for Paschaltide (Tridentine Missal) were drawn from St. John, although the pericopes did not appear in their biblical order. The Epistolary of Würzburg indicates 42 pericopes after the liturgical cycle proper, without assigning them to particular days, and does so in the New Testament order from Romans 5: 6-11 to Hebrews 13: 7-21. The same is true of the *Comes* of Donaueschingen (Frag. B. II. 7). Although such readings appear in their biblical order, they do not constitute a *lectio continua* in the proper sense since so much of each book is omitted; they are rather *morceaux choisis* or purple patches. Sometimes a continuous reading of the Bible at the liturgy seems proved by the fact that patristic commentaries on whole books of the Old and New Testaments still survive; even when they appear in the form of homilies, however, we cannot be sure they were actually delivered. In fact, there are simply no proofs of a *lectio continua*. Despite the fact we can discover a certain amount of continuity in the pericopes (especially for the Gospel at certain times of the year) a true *lectio continua* cannot be proved. A quotation from Caesarius of Arles, *Regula monachorum*, cap. 69 (G. Morin, (ed.), *S. Caesarii episcopi arlatensis Opera omnia* 2 [Maredsous 1942] 122): *Privatis vero diebus in vigiliis ordine suo libri Novi vel Veteris Testamenti legantur*, proves nothing in regard to a *lectio continua*. Not only does it refer to lessons for the office and not for mass, but the expression *ordine suo* may simply mean that the readings are done in some traditional sequence; of itself this proves nothing about how the Bible was read or how much of it was read.

36. For the reading of Holy Scripture outside the liturgy, see A. von Harnack, *Bible Reading in the Early Church* (New York-London 1912). The original reading of an apostolic letter in its entirety to a given community was certainly an example of a continuous reading but cannot be called a liturgical reading in any proper sense; cf. Col. 4:16; 1 Thess. 5:27. —Early on the private reading of the sacred books was recommended to believers; cf. Hippolytus of Rome, *The Apostolic Tradition*, cap. 41: *Si dies est in qua non est instructio* [catechesis or liturgy of the Word], *cum unusquisque in domo sua erit, accipiat librum sanctum et legat in eo sufficienter quod videtur ei ferre utilitatem* (ed. Botte, LQF 39, 88). At the time of Augustine, Scripture was read (and

commented upon ?) in the churches of N. Africa even outside the Eucharist; cf. Augustine, *Confessiones* 5, 9, 17: *viduae* [Monica] . . . *bis die, mane et vespere, ad ecclesiam tuam . . . venientis . . . ut te audiret in tuis sermonibus.* Apparently Augustine himself preached nearly every day at mass and at vespers; cf. F. van der Meer, *Augustine the Bishop* (London-New York 1961) 172. Although psalms and hymns followed by intercessory prayer were to remain the core of the morning and evening cathedral offices, several other churches— notably those of Egypt—used Bible readings in these services; cf. R. Taft, *The Liturgy of the Hours in the Christian East* (Rome 1984) 37-38, 41, 44. A very curious example of organized readings of the Scriptures can be found in the writings of pseudo-Euthalius, a deacon of Alexandria and later the bishop of Sulci (S. W. Sardinia), ca. 460; PG 85, 627f. The 57 readings it contains probably date from 396 and were certainly in existence in 508; they appear to be arranged for the Sundays and feasts of an entire year and are drawn from the Acts of the Apostles and the NT letters; they are of varying length: the longest, Acts 11:27-14:28; the shortest, Acts 1:15-26, and are a series of discontinuous readings. This collection could have served for either personal or liturgical use and an attempt has been made to divide the 57 readings into 365/366 capitula; cf. E. von der Goltz, *Eine textkritische Arbeit des zehnten bezw. sechsten Jahrhunderts, herausgegeben nach einen Kodex des Athosklosters Lawra,* TuU 14/4, N. F. 2/4 (Leipzig 1889) 4.

37. Evidence collected by S. Beissel, *Entstehung der Perikopen*, 41-51, 59-65; Godu, DACL 5 (1922) 246-249; W. Roetzer, *Des hl. Augustinus Schriften als liturgiegeschichtliche Quelle* (Munich 1930); A. Baumstark, *Missale Romanum*, 16. —Both Tertullian and Augustine tell us that certain liturgical occasions called for appropriate lessons. Tertullian, *Apologeticum* 39; PL 1, 532; CSEL 69, 91-95; CC 1, 150-153: *Coimus ad litterarum divinarum commemorationem, si quid praesentiam temporum qualitas aut praemonere cogit aut recognoscere;* Augustine, *Tractatus in epist. Iohannis prol.*; PL 35, 1977: *Lectiones oportet in ecclesia recitari quae ita sunt annuae ut aliae esse non possunt.* That meant that during the *triduum sacrum* one read the accounts of the Passion and during Easter Week the accounts of the Resurrection; Augustine, *Sermo* 247 *in diebus Paschae*; PL 38, 1156; ET *St. Augustine: Sermons on the Liturgical Seasons*, FC 38 (New York 1959) 297-300. For a general understanding see G.G. Willis, *St. Augustine's Lectionary*, ACC 44 (London 1962). Acts 1 and 2 and Joel 2:28-3:8 were read on Pentecost Sunday. The accounts of the Nativity and of the Baptism of Jesus were naturally used at Christmas and Epiphany. Once the Ascension was separated from Pentecost proper and was commemorated on the 40th day after Easter, it too acquired proper lessons. During Holy Week Job was read, according to Ambrose, *Epistola* 20, 14; PL 16, 998; and on Holy Thursday extracts from the book of Jonah; *ibid.*, and ET *St. Ambrose: Letters*, FC 26 (New York 1954) 365f, especially 369-371 and 374. Palm Sunday had Mt 21:1-9 as its Gospel reading; Ambrose, *De Elia et ieiunio* 21; PL 14, 697-731. On the feast of Peter and Paul (June 29) extracts from Lk 5:1-11 were used.

38. Definitive objections to a *lectio continua* have been formulated by G.

Kunze, "Die Lesungen," *Leiturgia* 2 (1955) 87-180 and *Die gottesdienstliche Schriftlesung* (Göttingen 1947) 12, 20, 75, 98 and *passim*. One of the oldest examples of a series of select readings detached from their context is preserved in the London *codices*, British Library, *Syr. Add.* 14528 and *Add.* 14457, 12140, 17113, 17116, 17717 and *Vat.* 12 which were published and studied by F. C. Burkitt, "The Early Syriac Lectionary System," *Proceedings of the British Academy* 10 (1921/1923) 301-338; cf. Kunze, *Leiturgia* 2, 130-132. Examples of a discontinuous reading are provided in the Epistolary of Würzburg, nos. 214-255 = Pauline pericopes which were to be reproduced as they stood in the Lectionary of Alcuin, and in the fragmentary *Comes* of Donaueschingen (*Fragmentum* B. II. 7); A. Dold, "Das Donaueschinger Comesfragment B. II. 7," Jfl 6 (1926) 16-53.

39. Justin Martyr, *First Apology* 67 (PG 6, 430): "On the day which is called Sunday, all who live in the cities or in the country gather together in one place and the memoirs of the apostles and/or the writings of the prophets are read as long as time permits" [trans. J. Quasten, *Patrology* 1 (Westminster, MD 1962) 216].

40. As soon as they had acquired sufficient authority, the New Testament writings were combined with those of the Old Testament (Septuagint); cf. Tertullian, *De praescriptione haereticorum* 36: [*Ecclesia*] *legem et prophetas cum evangelicis et apostolicis litteris miscet* (CSEL 70, 46). Justin Martyr, *First Apology* 67: "The memoirs of the apostoles and (or?) the writings of the prophets are read" shows that the Gospels came to occupy the place that Torah had in the synagogue liturgy.

41. The *Muratorian Fragment*: *Apocalypsis etiam Iohannis et Petri tantum recipimus, quam quidam ex nostris legi in ecclesia nolunt. Pastorem vero nuperrime temporibus nostris in urbe Roma Hermas conscripsit ... et ideo legi eum quidem oportet, si publicare vero in ecclesia populo neque inter prophetas completo numero neque inter apostolos in fine temporum potest;* (H. Lietzmann (ed.), *Das Muratorische Fragment und die monarchianischen Prologe zu den Evangelien,* Kleine Texte 1 [4th ed. Bonn 1933] 9), ET "We also receive the Apocalypse of John and that of Peter, although some of us do not want them read in church. But Hermas wrote the *Shepherd* very recently, in our own time, in the city of Rome ... and therefore it too should be read but it must not be read publicly to the people in church either among the prophets since their number is complete or among the apostles who came at the end of time." —Eusebius, *The History of the Church from Christ to Constantine* 3, 16: "Clement has left us one recognized epistle, long and wonderful, which he composed in the name of the church at Rome and sent to the church at Corinth, where dissension had recently occurred. I have evidence that in many churches this epistle was read aloud to the assembled worshippers in early days, as it is in our own"; trans. G. A. Williamson (New York 1966) 124-125. —Sozomen also tells us that in the V century they were still reading the Apocalype of Peter on Good Friday in some Palestinian churches; *Historia eccles.* 7, 19; PG 67, 1478.

42. Council of Laodicea (372), canon 60; Mansi 2, 573; includes a list of canonical books, Old and New Testaments. Council of Hippo (393) canon 47

= Carthage (397) canon 47: *ut praeter scripturas canonicas, nihil in ecclesia legatur sub nomine divinarum scripturam;* Mansi 3, 879.

43. III Council of Carthage (397), canon 36; Mansi 3, 924: *Liceat etiam legi passiones martyrum, cum annniversarii dies eorum celebrantur.* Augustine, *Sermo* 309; PL 38, 1410: *Sermonem a nobis debitum auribus et cordibus vestris exigit tam grata et religiosa solemnitas qua passionem beati Martyris celebramus . . . . Placet itaque universam illam fidelissimi et fortissimi et gloriosissimi Martyris passionem cum exultatione recordari praeteritam, quam tunc fratres cum sollicitudine sustinere futuram.* Cf. W. Roetzer, *Des hl. Augustinus Schriften als liturgiegeschichtliche Quelle* (Munich 1930) 62-107; F. van der Meer, *Augustine the Bishop* (London-New York 1961) 472-497; L. Koep, "Antikes Kaisertum und Christus-bekenntnis im Widerspruch," *Jahrbuch für Antike und Christentum* 4 (1961) 58, note 3.—In Gaul: Germanus of Paris, *Expositio antiquae liturgiae gallicanae* (ed.), E. C. Ratcliff, HBS 98 (London 1971) 6: *Leguntur . . . gesta sanctorum confessorum ac martyrum in solempnitatibus eorum;* Lectionary of Luxeuil; P. Salmon (ed.), (Rome 1944-1953) 27, 181: *XVIII. Legenda in vigiliis Epiphaniae. Vita et Passio Sancti ac beatissimi Juliani Martyris. LXIII. Legenda in festivitate sanctorum Petri et Pauli. Passio Sanctorum Apostolorum Petri et Pauli.* See also Gregory of Tours, *De gloria martyrum* 1, 86: PL 71, 781; and *De miraculis sancti Martini* 2, 29 and 49; PL 71, 954 and 967. —For the Church of Milan, see Mabillon, *Museum Italicum* 1 (Paris 1724) 97. —The liturgical use of the Acts of the Martyrs explains the conclusion of some of their texts: *Regnante vero Dominus noster Iesus Christus cui est honor et gloria in saecula saeculorum. Amen: Acta proconsularis Cypriani* of 257/258, cap. 6; CSEL 3, 3, cxiv. —For the liturgical reading of the Acts of the Martyrs, see B. de Gaiffier, "La lecture des Actes de Martyrs dans la prière liturgique en Occident," *Analecta Bollandiana* 72 (1954) 134-166.

44. For the ceremonies surrounding the readings at mass, see J. A. Jungmann, *The Mass of the Roman Rite* 1 (New York 1951) 403-419.

45. In addition to the text of Justin, *First Apology* 67 quoted in note 39 *supra*—whose meaning is somewhat ambiguous—see the *Canons of Hippolytus* (ca 500), canon 47: "The readers succeed one another until the community has assembled;" W. Riedel, *Das Kirchenrechtsquellen des Patriar-chats Alexandrien* (Leipzig 1900) 224; and the *Canons of Basil,* canon 97: "The mysteries must not be celebrated in a disorderly fashion but await the arrival of the whole community. While the faithful are still arriving, the Psalms are to be read. After the community has assembled, extracts from the sacred books are to be read;" Riedel, *op. cit.,* 273. Similar customs still survive among the Russian Orthodox.

46. Among others, see the Lectionary of the *Codex Weissenburgensis* 76; A. Dold, *Das ältesteLiturgiebuch der lateinischen Kirche,* TuA 26/28 (Beuron 1936) where the Gospel for the mass of a dedication of a church is composed of 13 extracts from the four Gospels. In the Lectionary of Luxeuil the Gospel for the *Cathedra Petri* (Jan. 18) is made up of extracts from Mt 16: 13-19 and Jn 21: 15-19; ed. P. Salmon (Rome 1944) 67-68.

47. Some pericopes are made up of excerpts drawn from a single book of

the Bible and are not *centos* properly speaking, e.g., the OT reading for the Wed. of the V week of Lent (Tridentine Missal) is composed of Lev 19: 1-2, 11-19, and 25; the OT readings *Ecce sacerdos* of the *commune* of bishops is composed of extracts from two different chapters of the same book, Ecclesiasticus 44: 17-27 and 45: 3-20.

48. The Lectionary of the *Codex Weissenburgensis* 76 contains an attempt at harmonization of the readings for Holy Thurs. and Good Friday. Apparently Augustine already knew of harmonization; cf. *Sermo* 232; PL 38, 1108.

49. The palimpsest lectionary of Wolfenbüttel, i.e. *codex Weissenburgensis* 76, is the oldest collection of pericopes in the Latin language, dating from the beginning of the VI century. It is not, however, the oldest liturgical book of a Western church. That honor belongs to the *Apostolic Tradition* (in Greek) of Hippolytus of Rome (ca. 215); its Latin translation dates from the last quarter of the IV century; the *Verona Fragments*, E. Hauler (ed.), *Didascaliae Apostolorum fragmenta Veronensia latina* (Leipzig 1900); E. Tidner (ed.), *Didascaliae apostolorum, canonum ecclesiasticorum, traditionis apostolicae versiones Latinae*, TuU 75 (Berlin 1963). The Verona MS itself, *codex LV* (53), dates from the VIII century but the palimpsest pages had been borrowed from a *codex* of ca. 494 and that MS is a copy of the original Latin translation from ca. 375/ 400. At Rome the Latin and Greek versions may well have served side by side in the bilingual situation that prevailed there in the IV century; see C. Pietri, *Roma Christiana*, 2 vols., Bibliothèque des Écoles françaises d'Athènes et Rome 224 (Rome 1976).

50. The evidence cited in the following notes all contributes to prove this point. From the very beginning, Christians gathered together to listen to readings, even though such readings could not be called liturgical in a strict sense; cf. Col 4:16 "After you read this letter, make sure that it is also read in the Church at Laodicea. At the same time, you are to read the letter that the brothers in Laodicea will send you."—I Thess 5:27, "I urge you by the authority of the Lord to read this letter to all the believers."

51. The liturgical reading of the *Torah* (=Pentateuch) is very old and was already mentioned in Biblical times; cf. Dt 31: 10-13; Neh 8: 1-8. Early on in the history of the synagogue, *Torah* came to be read on Sabbaths and festivals, fast days, Mondays and Thursdays, New Moons, Chanukah, Purim and the intermediate days of Pesach (Passover) and Sukkot (Tabernacles). A fixed lectionary gradually emerged in the Rabbinic period and took two forms. In Palestine the Torah was divided into 175 pericopes and was read in its entirety over 3 or 3 1/2 years. In Babylonia the Torah was divided into 54 pericopes and read once a year. It was this annual cycle of much longer readings that came to prevail in the medieval period. It also became customary to conclude the liturgy of the Word on Sabbaths and festivals by reading an appropriate selection from the Prophets (*Haftarah* = conclusion or dismissal because read last in the service). Such a practice is well attested in the Mishnah (ca 200 C. E.), although a complete lectionary was a long time in coming. Early in the Rabbinic period it also became customary to read the

pericopes first in Hebrew and then in a vernacular translation or paraphrase (Aramaic) and then to expound them in a sermon; cf. L. A. Hoffman, *Gates of Understanding: Notes to Shaarei Tefillah* (New York 1977) 18-19, 230-232; the table of the 54 Torah readings and their corresponding *Haftarot* are on pp. 271-284. See also L. Zunz, *Die Ritus der synagogalen Gottesdienstes* (Berlin 1859) and his *Die gottesdienstliche Vorträge der Juden* (Frankfurt 1892; reprint Hildesheim 1966) 6 and 188; A. Z. Idelsohn, *Jewish Liturgy and its Development* (New York 1932; 1967) 3-33; A. I. Schechter, *Studies in Jewish Liturgy* (Philadelphia 1930); J. Mann, *The Bible as Read and Preached in the Old Synagogue*, 2 vols. (Cincinnati 1940) esp. the prologue; R. Posner, *et al.*, *Jewish Liturgy* (Jerusalem 1975) 91, 248 *et passim*; L. Hoffman, *The Canonization of the Synagogue Service* (Notre Dame 1979); A. Büchler, "Reading of the Law and Prophets in a Triennial Cycle," *Contributions to the Scientific Study of Jewish Liturgy*, ed. J. J. Petuchowski (New York 1970) 181-302; K. Hruby, "Die jüdische Liturgie zur Zeit Jesu," *Judaîca* 18 (1962) 104-126 and "Geschichtlicher Überblick über die Anfänge der synagogalen Liturgie und ihre Entwicklung," *Judaîca* 18 (1962) 193-214; 19 (1963) 1-25; C. W. Dugmore, *The Influence of the Synagogue upon the Divine Office* (Oxford 1944) 10-25; P. F. Bradshaw, *Daily Prayer in the Early Church*, ACC 63 (London 1981) 19-21; H. H. Rowley, *Worship in Ancient Israel* (London 1967) 213-245; J. Heinemann, *Prayer in the Talmud: Forms and Patterns*, Studia Judaica 9 (Berlin-New York 1977) 123-138; I. Elbogen, *Der jüdische Gottesdienst in seiner geschichtlichen Entwicklung* (Hildesheim 1962) 155-174 (Torah); 174-184 (Haftarah). The New Testament also indicates the use of both readings in the synagogue: Acts 15:21, 13:27; Lk 4:16, followed by a commentary: Lk 4:20-21.

52. On the sacred character and power inherent in the reading, see L. Koep, "Buch," *Reallexikon für Antike und Christentum* 2, 719; G. Kunze, "Was bedeutet das Heilige-Schriftlesen?" *Leiturgia* 2 (1955) 91-102.

53. On Judaeo-Christian usages in regard to the readings, see P. Glaue, *Die Vorlesung der hl. Schrift im Gottesdienst* (Göttingen 1907). Early Gentile communities of Christians probably also used OT readings in their worship. St. Paul referred to OT passages in his letters (Rom 7: 1; 2 Cor 6: 16, 9: 13) and that means that his converts must have had some acquaintance with them.

54. The Pauline letters were not yet read as Holy Scripture but as works of edification and catechesis (1 Thess 5: 27; 2 Cor 1: 13; Col 4: 16). See G. Kunze, "Die Lesungen," *Leiturgia* 2 (1955) 115-126.

55. See supra, note 39.

56. *De Praescriptione haereticorum* 36; PL 2, 58; CC 1, 216-217; and *Apologeticum* 39; PL 1, 532; CC 1, 150-153; *De anima* 9; PL 2, 701, CC 2, 791-794.

57. Lectors are already mentioned in a letter of Cornelius of Rome (253-255) to Fabius of Antioch (Eusebius, *History of the Church*, 6, 43); in Cyprian of Carthage, *Epistola 29: Optatum inter lectores doctorum audientium constituimus*

(CSEL 3, 547-548); and Hippolytus of Rome, *Apostolic Tradition* 11: A reader is appointed by the bishop giving him the book, for he does not have hands laid on him (trans. G. J. Cuming, p. 15).

58. Ambrose (340-397), *Epistola 20 ad Marcellinam* 14 and 25; PL 16, 1040 and 1044. —The role Bishop Ambrose may have played in the formation of the Milanese liturgy cannot be ascertained. When he became bishop of Milan in 373, the city already had a well-developed liturgy; cf. the text for the consecration of baptismal water which he quoted; *In Lucam* 10, 48; F. Probst, *Die ältesten römischen Sakramentarien und Ordines*, 223-224; J. Schmitz, *Gottesdienst im altchristlichen Mailand*, Theophaneia 25 (Cologne-Bonn 1975). From Augustine we learn that Ambrose introduced the singing of hymns to Milan; cf. *Confessiones* 9, 7: *Tunc* [during the persecutions of 386] *hymni et psalmi ut canerentur secundum morem orientalium partium, ne populus maeroris taedio contabesceret, institutum est.* For Ambrose and the fragments of the *Canon missae* he cites in the *De sacramentis*, see Klauser and Botte on the *Canon* and K. Gamber, *Ostkirchliche Studien* 7 (1958) 153-172; 9 (1960) 123-173. The *Liber notitiae sanctorum Mediolani*, edd. M. Magistretti-U. Monneret (Milan 1917) 369, 370, attributes a certain amount of liturgical activity to Bishops Simplicianus (†401) and Eusebius (†462). —For these problems, see Borella-Cattaneo-Villa, *Questioni e bibliografia ambrosiane*, Archivio Ambrosiano 2 (Milan 1950) 79-101 which contains a complete bibliography up to 1950 and additional material can be found in AfL 2 (1952) 195-197; O. Heiming, AfL 2 (1952) 44-60 and in *Colligere Fragmenta*, TuA 2 (Beuron 1950) 214-235; E. Cattaneo, *Rito Ambrosiano e liturgia orientale*, Archivio Ambrosiano 2 (Milan 1950) 19-42; A. A. King, *Liturgies of the Primatial Sees* (London 1957) 286-457; R. Amiet, *Scriptorium* 14 (1960) 16-60. For the liturgical books of the Ambrosian rite, see CLLA 501-596, pp. 259-291, and *supra* pp. 282-283.

59. Augustine, *Tractatus in epistola Iohannis ad Parthos*; PL 35, 1977. — Augustine, *Tractatus VI in Iohannem* 18; PL 35, 1433: *Actus Apostolorum, ille liber canonicus omni anno in ecclesia recitandus. Anniversaria solemnitate post passionem Domini a nostris illum librum recitari; Sermo* 315, 1; PL 38, 1426: *Ipse liber* [Actus Apostolorum] *incipit a dominico Paschae sicut se consuetudo habet ecclesiae.* —Cf. W. Roetzer, *Des hl. Augustinus Schriften als liturgiegeschichtliche Quelle* (Munich 1930) 104-108. —For the African liturgy (the African Church was the cradle of Latin Christianity and forged its liturgical and theological vocabulary), see E. Dekkers, *Tertullianus en de geschiedenis van de liturgie* (Brussels 1947) and "Afrikaanse liturgie," *Liturgisch Woordenboek* 1 (1958) 64-74; G. G. Willis, *St. Augustine's Lectionary*, ACC 44 (London 1962); K. Gamber, *Sakramentartypen*, 8-14 and CLLA 001-029, pp. 29-55. See also S. Poque, "Les lectures liturgiques de l'octave pascale à Hippone d'àprès les traités de S. Augustin," RB 74 (1964) 217-242.

60. Sidonius Apollinaris, *Epistulae* 4, 11, 6; MGH, *Auctores antiquissimi* 8, 63; PL 58, 616. —According to his own testimony, (*Epist.* 7, 3) Sidonius composed *contestatiunculae* (prefaces) which were later collected by Gregory of Tours (†594) into a *libellus missarum*; cf. *Historia Francorum* 2, 22; MGH, *Scriptores rerum merovingicarum* 1, 1; PL 71, 218.

61. Gennadius of Marseilles, *De scriptoribus eccles.* 79; PL 58, 1103-1104.

62. K. Gamber, "Das Lektionar und Sakramentar des Musaeus von Massilia," RB 69 (1959) 198-215, resuming an hypothesis first presented by G. Morin, "Le plus ancien monument qui existe de la liturgie gallicane," EL 51 (1937) 3-12, thinks that the lectionary of Musaeus is preserved in the palimpsest MS of Wolfenbüttel, Herz. August-Bibl., *codex Weissenburgensis* 76 (S. Gaul, early VI century). —According to Gamber, Gennadius of Marseilles, *De script. eccles.: sacramentorum egregium et non parvum volumen*, attributes to Musaeus the composition of a sacramentary preserved in the present palimpsest of Milan, Biblioteca Ambrosiana, *codex* M. 12 *Sup.* (S. Gaul, ca. 700).

63. G. Morin (ed.), *S. Caesarii episcopi Arelatensis Opera omnia*, 3 vols. (Maredsous 1937-1942, reedited CC 103-104. —K. Berg, *Die Werke des hl. Caesarius von Arles als liturgiegeschichtliche Quelle*, Doctoral Dissertation, Gregorian University (Rome 1946).

64. Caesarius of Arles, *Sermo* 84, 1; ed. Morin 1, 330; CC 103, 245: *Lectio illa qua beatus Abraham, Isaac filium suum in holocaustum legitur obtulisse, ideo in ordine suo diebus quadragesimae non recitatur quia, sicut ipsi nostis, in vigiliis Paschae propter sacramentum dominicae passionis reservatur.*

65. E. C. Ratcliff (ed.), *Expositio Antiquae Liturgiae Gallicanae*, HBS 98 (London 1971) 5-6., cf. R. Cabié, "Les lettres attribuées à Saint Germain de Paris et les origines de la liturgie gallicane," *Bulletin de Littérature ecclésiastique* 73 (1972) 183-192. —Jerome, *De viris illustribus, cap.* 79 notes that Hilary of Poiters (✝367) composed a *Liber mysteriorum* but it is impossible for us to know what kind of book this might have been; cf. K. Gamber, "Der *Liber mysteriorum* des Hilarius von Poitiers," *Studia Patristica* 5, TuU 80 (Berlin 1962) 40-49.

66. See pages 273-289 for the various Latin rites of the West.—We have to remember that all the books of the Gallican rite relating to the liturgical readings are either mutilated, fragmentary or palimpsest; all the other Gallican liturgical books are Romanized. It is possible that during the Carolingian period all the liturgical books of the Gallican rite were systematically destroyed and that the only survivors are the mixed or hybrid examples. —A. G. Martimort, "À propos du nombre des lectures à la messe," RSR 58 (1984) 42-51.

67. See *infra* for the main examples of this liturgical family.

68. Gregory of Tours, *Historia Francorum* 4, 16; MGH, *Script. rerum merovingicarum* 1, 154-155, *Liber in gloria martyrum* 86; MGH, *ibid.*, 546, and *De virtutibus S. Martini* 1, 5 and 2, 29 and 40; MGH, *ibid.*, pp. 591, 620 and 623. Germanus of Paris, *Expositio: Gesta sanctorum confessorum ac martyrum*; ed. Ratcliff, 6. —Medieval Breviaries often had sanctoral readings in all three nocturns of Matins and the scriptural and patristic readings were cancelled or deferred to the refectory. "The reasons for these exceptions were many. Yet they can be reduced to one, namely that the stories available were too long for a single nocturn;" S. J. P. van Dijk-J. H. Walker, *The Origins of the Modern Roman Liturgy* (London 1960) 131.

69. Augustine, *Sermo* 45, 1: *Animadvertit, caritas vestra, primam lectionem Isaiae prophetae...Deinde ascendit apostolica lectio* and then the gospel, of course (PL 38, 262; cf. also *Sermo* 48, 1; PL 38, 216-317). Augustine's terminology is not always the same; In *sermo* 176 he speaks of three lessons but they are the *Apostolus*, the *Psalmus* and the Gospel (PL 38, 950). Cf. W. Roetzer, *Des hl. Augustinus Schriften als liturgiegeschichtliche Quelle* (Munich 1930).

70. The term epistle does not always mean a reading drawn from the Pauline letters; it can designate an OT reading or one from the Acts of the Apostles or the Revelations of St. John.

71. A. Dold, *Die Zürcher und Peterlinger Messbuchfragmente aus der Zeit des 1. Jahrtausends im Bari-Schrifttyp*, TuA 25 (Beuron 1934); cf. CLLA no. 431, pp. 240-241.

72. For all the evidence available on the old Roman system of three readings at mass, see A. Chavasse, "Le calendrier dominical romain au sixième siècle," *Recherches de science religieuse* 41 (1953) 96-122, espec. 101-106; and *Le Sac. gél.* 186-195; G. Kunze, *Die gottesdienstliche Schriftlesung* 1 (Göttingen 1947) 140-143; W. Roetzer, *Des hl. Augustinus*, 110-102.—Ralph de Rivo († 1403), *De canonum observantia liber, propositio* 23; L. C. Mohlberg (ed.), *Radulph de Rivo der letzte Vertreter der altrömischen Liturgie* 2: *Texte* (Louvain 1915) 139, says that even in his time there were still three readings on Christmas and on Christmas Eve.—Despite the evidence given above, more recent research suggests that originally only two readings existed in the Roman mass; cf. Martimort, *supra*, note 66.

73. The best witness to this fact is the Lectionary of Alcuin (*Comes ab Albino ordinatus*) which contains only one lesson before the gospel reading. Its pericopes correspond better with a Frankish Gelasian Sacramentary than with the *Hadrianum* which is a good indication that the lectionary was Romanized long before the arrival of the *Hadrianum* in Gaul.—Charlemagne, *Epistola generalis* (ca. 786-800): *Accensi praeterea venerandae memoriae Pippini genitoris nostris exemplis, qui totas Galliarum ecclesias romanae traditionis suo studio cantibus decoravit, nos nihilominus solerti easdem curamus intuitu praecipuarum insignire serie lectionum* (MGH, *Capit. regum Francorum* 1, 80).

74. The connections which exist between research on the liturgical readings and on the organization of the liturgical year are very evident in the writings of Klauser, Chavasse and Hesbert.

75. Consult K. A. H. Kellner, *Heortologie oder das Kirchenjahr und die Heiligenfeste in ihrer geschichtlichen Entwicklung* (Freiburg 1901), ET *Heortology; A History of the Christian Festivals from their Origin to the Present Day* (London 1908); T. Klauser, *Das römische Capitulare*, 184-185; H. Quentin-H. Delehaye, *Commentarius perpetuus in Martyrologium Hieronymianum*, Acta Sanctorum Nov. 2, 2 (Brussels 1931) and H. Delehaye, *Martyrologium Romanum scholiis historicis instructum*, Acta Sanctorum, Propylaeum Dec. (Brussels 1940) with the classic reference works of the Bollandists: *Bibliotheca Hagiographica latina*, 2 vols. (Brussels 1891-1901, reprint 1939) with the *Supplementum* by A.

Poncelet (2nd ed. Brussels 1911) and the *Bibliotheca Hagigraphica graeca* by F. Halkin (3rd ed., Brussels 1957); G. Schreiber, *Die Wochentage im Erlebniss der Ostkirche und des christlichen Abendlandes* (Cologne 1959); J. Hennig, "Kalender und Martyrologium als Literaturformen," AfL 7 (1961) 1-44; 423-427; A. Vogel, "Der Einfluss der Heiligenfeste auf die Perikopenwahl an den Sonntagen nach Pfingsten," *Zeitschrift für katholische Theologie* 69 (1947) 100-118; A. A. MacArthur, *The Evolution of the Christian Year* (New York 1955); N. Denis-Boulet, *The Christian Calendar* (New York 1960); P. Jounel, *Le culte des saints dans les basiliques du Latran et du Vatican au douzième siècle*, Collection de l'École française de Rome 26 (Rome 1977); A. Adam, *The Liturgical Year* (New York 1981); T. J. Talley, *Origins of the Liturgical Year* (N.Y. 1986).

76. For the meaning of Easter, see O. Casel, "Art und Sinn der ältesten christlichen Osterfeier," JfL 14(1938) 1-78; cf. O. D. Santagada, AfL 10 (1967) 7-77 for a bibliography of O. Casel; H. Rahner, *Griechische Mythen in christlicher Deutung* (Zürich 1945) 149-171, ET *Greek Myths and Christian Mystery* (New York 1963) 109-129; B. Botte, "La question pascale. Pâque du Vendredi ou Pâque du Dimanche?" LMD 41(1955)84-95; Balt. Fischer-J.Wagner, *Paschatis Sollemnia* (Freiburg-Basel-Vienna 1960). A Baumstark tried to make a case for a primitive distinction between *Pascha anastasimon* and *Pascha staurosimon (Comparative Liturgy* [Westminster, MD 1958] 141, 144, 168) but, against this opinion, see C. Mohrmann, "Pascha, Passio, Transitus," *Études sur le latin des chrétiens*, 1 (Rome 1958) 205-222; B. Botte, "Pascha," *L'Orient syrien* 8(1963) 213-226 (the best synthesis); R. Cantalamessa, *La pascua nella Chiesa antica* (Turin 1978; Berne 1980; German trans., Berne 1981).

77. The Easter Eucharist which brought the fast to an end was celebrated shortly before dawn and not at midnight—as in current practice. Friday's and Saturday's fast was simply the normal Friday fast observed every week of the year and extended by way of *superpositio* throughout Saturday and the entire Easter Vigil.

78. The movable nature of Easter and the difficulty of calculating it each year have occasioned enormous chronological difficulties. See the following studies: H. Grotefend, *Zeitrechnung des deutschen Mittelalters und der Neuzeit*, 3 vols. (Hanover 1891-1898) and *Handbuch der historischen Chronologie* (Hanover 1872); H. Grotefend-T. Ulrich, *Taschenbuch der Zeitrechnung des deutschen Mittelalters und der Neuzeit* (Hanover 1960); H. Lietzmann-K. Aland, *Zeitrechnung der römischen Kaiserzeit, des Mittelalters und der Neuzeit für die Jahre 1-2000 nach Christus* (Berlin 1956); A. Capelli, *Chronologia, cronografia e calendario perpetuo* (Milan 1930, reprint 1969). One may also consult B. M. Lersch, *Einleitung in die Chronologie, 2: Der christliche Kalender, seine Einrichtung, Geschichte und chronologische Verwertung* (Freiburg 1899); L. Ideler, *Handbuch der mathematischen und technischen Chronologie*, 2 vols. (Berlin 1825); V. Grumel, *La chronologie*, Traité d'études byzantines 1 (Paris 1958).

79. For additional articles, see O. Cullmann, *Der Ursprung des Weihnachtfestes* (2nd ed. Zürich 1960); a first edition of this article was translated as

"The Origin of Christmas," *The Early Church* (London 1956) 17-36; J. Lemarié, *La manifestation du Seigneur: La liturgie de Noël et de l'Epiphanie*, Lex orandi 23 (Paris 1957).

80. For the decree of the Council of Nicea on how to calculate Easter (which is lost but known from other sources), see J. B. Pitra, *Iuris ecclesiastici Graecorum historia et momumenta* 1(Rome 1864; reprint Farnborough 1966) 453 and *Spicilegium Solesmense* 4(Paris 1858) 540-55; L. Duchesne, "La question de la Pâque au concile de Nicée," *Revue des questiones historiques* 28(1880) 5-42. —For the problems of how to compute Easter, see—in addition to the works given in note 78, H. Leclercq, "Pâques," DACL 13.2 (1938) 1521-1574; M. Richard, "Comput et chronographie chez S. Hippolyte," *Mélanges de science religieuse* 7 (1950) 237-268; 8(1951) 19-50 on the work of P. Nautin, *Hippolyte et Josippe. Contribution à l'histoire de la littérature chrétienne du III siècle* (Paris 1947); A. Jaubert, *La date de la Cène. Calendrier biblique et liturgie chrétienne* (Paris 1957), ET *The Date of the Last Supper*, trans. I. Rafferty (Staten Island, NY 1965) on the differences between the chronology of the Synoptic Gospels and that of John regarding the day of Christ's death and on the patristic tradition which held that Jesus celebrated the Passover on Tuesday evening and died on Friday. —In conformity with standard liturgical usage, we use the terms *termini paschales* to indicate the earliest and latest dates for Easter Sunday. More strictly speaking, *terminus paschalis* means the first full moon after the Spring equinox = *Luna XIV Paschae* or *luna quartodecima*. Since Easter can fall at the earliest a day after this *luna quartodecima*, the Paschal full moon is called the *terminus paschalis*. The preceding new moon is called *incensio lunae paschalis*. March 21, the earliest possible date of the Paschal full moon, is called *luna XIV prima*; April 18, the latest possible date of the Paschal full moon, is called *luna XIV ultima*. Consequently, the earliest date for Easter Sunday is March 22 and the latest April 25. —See also A. Strobel, *Ursprung und Geschichte des frühchristlichen Osternkalenders*, TuU 121 (Berlin 1971) and *Texte zur Geschichte des frühchristlichen Osternkalenders*, LQF 64 (Münster 1984); P. Harnoncourt, "Oster-komputation-Geschichtstheologie-Theologiegeschichte. Kalendarische Fragen und ihre Theologische Bedeutung nach den Studien von A. Strobel," AfL 27(1985) 263-272.

81. Hippolytus' paschal cycle appears on the base of his statue that used to be in the Lateran Museum but which now stands at the entrance to the Vatican Library; J. Ficker, *Die altchristlichen Bildwercke im christlichen Museum des Laterans* (Leipzig 1890) 166-175 and H. Leclercq, "Hippolyte (Statue et cimetière de saint)", DACL 6(1925) 2419-2483; Grumel, *La chronologie*, 6-17.

82. The best study of the Cycle of 84 Years is B. Krusch, *Studien zur christlichmittelalterlichen Chronologie. Der 84 jahrige Ostercyclus und seine Quellen* (Leipzig 1880) and *Neues Archiv* 9(1883) 99-169; Grumel, *op cit.*, 18-22.

83. For the Cycle of 19 Years, see M. da Leonessa, *La tavola pasquale di Anatolio* (Tivoli 1934).

84. Studies that have contributed a great deal to an understanding of the period before Easter are: A. Chavasse, "La préparation à la Pâque à Rome avant le VI siècle. Jeûne et organisation liturgique," *Mémorial J. Chaine*, Bibliothèque de la Faculté catholique de Lyon 5 (Lyons 1950) 61-80; "Le Carême romain et les scrutins prébaptismaux avante le IX siècle," *Recherches de science religieuse* 35(1948) 325-381; "Temps de préparation à la Pâque d'après quelques livres liturgiques romains," *ibid.* 37(1950) 125-145; "Le calendrier dominical romain au VI siècle," *ibid.* 38(1951) 234-246; 41(1953) 96-122; "À propos d'une anticipation du jeûne quadragésimal. Deux sermons d'un même auteur du VI siècle," RSR 52(1978) 3-12; "L'organisa-stationale due Carême romain avant le VIII siècle, une organisation pastorale," RSR 56(1982) 17-32; *Le Sac, gél.* 185-266; 403-422; J. Baldovin, *The Urban Character of Christian Worship in Jerusalem, Rome and Constantinople from the Fourth to the Tenth Centuries: A Study in Stational Liturgy*. Ph.D. Dissertation, (Yale University 1982).

85. Ambrose, *Epistula* 23 (A. D. 386) *Triduum sacrum ... intra quod ... et passus est et quievit et resurrexit* (PL 16, 1030); Augustine, *Epistula* 55 *ad inquisit. Ianuarii* 1, 14, 24: *sacratissimum triduum crucifixi, sepulti et resuscitati* (PL 33, 215); Hippolytus of Rome, *Traditio apostolica*, cap. 33: "At the Pascha no one may eat before the offering is made. If anyone does so, it does not count for him as fasting." (trans. Cuming, 26; ed. Botte, *cap.* 33, p. 78). Early on the time of fasting before Easter may have varied from one to two days or even more; cf. Irenaeus, Letter to Bishop Victor in Eusebius, *Historia eccles.* 5, 24, 12, trans. G. A. Williamson, 232: "The dispute is not only about the day, but also about the actual character of the fast. Some think they ought to fast for one day, some for two, others for still more; some make their 'day' last forty hours on end. Such variation in the observance did not originate in our own day, but very much earlier, in the time of our forefathers ... In spite of that, they all lived in peace with one another, ... the divergency in the fast emphasizes the unanimity of our faith."

86. Leo I (440-461), *Sermo* 44: *Cum ad istos recurrimus dies ... qui vicino ordine atque contiguo festum pascale precedunt* (PL 54, 285; CC 138 A, 258); *Sermo* 47: *Praesentes dies ... quos illi sublimissimo ... sacramento scimus esse contiguos* (PL 54, 295; CC 138 A, 274).

87. We can deduce this from the fact that the readings of the Passion on Palm Sunday, Tuesday, Wednesday and Good Friday constitute a kind of early liturgical unit. Such originality is reinforced by certain ceremonial peculiarities belonging only to Holy Week.

88. Cf. *Praedestinatus*, (ca. 432/440); PL 53, 615.

89. In the Old Gelasian Sacramentary (*Vat. Reg.* 316) of the mid-VIII century it is still called: *Dominica in Palmas de Passione Domini* (ed. L. C. Mohlberg XXXVII, 329, p. 53).

90. Dionysius of Alexandria (248-265), *Epistula ad Basilidem*, cf. M. J. Routh, *Reliquiae sacrae* 3 (1846) 229; Athanasius of Alexandria, *The Festal Epistles* (329-336); PG 26, 1366, 1422, 1379; Coptic version ed. L. T. Lefort, *Lettres Festales et Pastorales de S. Athanase en copte*, Corpus Scriptorum Christianorum

Orientalium 150 (Louvain 1955) 1-72, ET *The Festal Epistles of S. Athanasius,* trans. H. Burgess, Library of the Fathers 39 (Oxford 1854).

91. Socrates (ca. 493), *Historia ecclesiastica* 5, 22; PG 77, 632.

92. Jerome, *Epistula* 24, 4 *ad Marcellam* (A. D. 384); CSEL 54, 216; speaks of a Lent of six weeks duration. Given the circumstances of the letter, such a Lent may even have existed before 350. —The *Depositio martyrum* of the Chronographer of 354 (ed. T. Mommsen, *Chronica minora* 1, MGH, *Auctores antiquissimi* 9, 71) contains an empty space from March 7 to May 19: *Nonas Martias: Perpetuae et Felicitatis, Africae* (=March 7) . . . *XIV Kalendas Iunias: Partheni et Caloceri in Callisti, Diocletiano IX et Maximiano VIII* (=May 19) [A. D. 304] This space in the *Sanctorale* allows for the three-week fast before Easter and the fifty days of Eastertide. That may mean that the three-week fast was already observed in Rome in 354; cf. A. Chavasse, "Temps de préparation à la Pâque d'après quelques livres liturgiques romains," *Recherches de science religieuse* 37 (1950) 125-145.

93. L. Duchesne, *Christian Worship* (London 1925) 243, note 1 gives a wrong interpretation of the quotation of Socrates cited above; he viewed it as a discontinuous fast of the first, fourth and sixth weeks before Easter; C. Callewaert, "La semaine *Mediana* dans l'ancien carême romain et les quatre-temps," RB 36 (1927) 200-228 and *Sacris Erudiri: Fragmenta Liturgica* (Steenbrugge 1940) 561-588 thought that the three weeks noted by Socrates were three weeks of more rigorous fasting than usual. However, Socrates' testimony on three continous weeks is clear; he is wrong only about Saturday not being a fast day in the West. Since 416 at least, and probably as early as 384/387, the Saturdays of Lent were all fast days at Rome; cf. Augustine, *Epistula 36 ad Casulanum* (ca. 396/397) 14, 32; PL 33, 151 on the years 384/387. See also Jerome, *Epistula 71* (A. D. 398) *ad Lucinum* 6; CSEL 55, 6; John the Deacon, *Epistula ad Senarium* 13, PL 59, 406 and ed. A. Wilmart, *Analecta Reginensia,* SeT 59 (Vatican City 1933) 178; Innocent I, *Epist. ad Decentium Egubinum* (A. D. 416) 4; PL 20, 554 and ed. R. Cabié, 24-27. Gelasius I (492-496), *Epist. ad episcopos Lucaniae, cap.* 2; ed. A. Thiel, *Epistulae romanorum pontificum* (Braunsberg 1868) 368.

94. Cf. *Ordines* XXVI-XXIX, XXXI, XXXVI-XXXIX; Andrieu, *Les Ordines romani* 3 and 4 (1951 and 1956). See also the *Comes* of Würzburg, nos. 65 and 68 [RB 27 (1910) 52-53] and the *Comes* of Murbach nos. 51 and 53 [RB 30 (1913) 40] and the *Comes* of Alcuin, nos. 58 and 65 [A. Wilmart, "Le lectionnaire d'Alcuin," EL 51 (1937) 154.]; G.G. Willis. "What is Mediana Week?" *Essays in Early Roman Liturgy,* ACC 46 (London 1964) 101-104.

95. See tables F-H.

96. The Council of Nicea (325), canon 5 alluded to a "tessarakosti," but did not describe it more fully. The passage in Origen, *In Lucam homilia* 10 (PG 13, 1823-1826) is of dubious authenticity and can only be found in Rufinus. Beginning with Athanasius, however, we have direct testimony to a forty-day fast in Egypt as early as 330; it began on the Monday of the sixth week before Easter; *Festal Letters,* AD. 329-348; PG 26, 1431-1444; cf. J. Quasten, *Patrology* 3

(Westminster, MD 1963) 53. The first Latin evidence appears in Jerome, *Letter to Marcella* (A.D. 384): *tum vere in Quadragesima* (PL 30, 50-55). After that there were more and more testimonies: *Praedestinatus* (under Sixtus III, 432-440): *in ipso initio Quadragesimae* (PL 53, 615); Leo I (440-461), *Sermo 41*, 2 (PL 54, 273; CC 138 A, 234) and *Sermo 45*, 1 (PL 54, 288; CC 138 A, 263): *Quadraginta dierum continentia* or *ieiunium.* See the texts given *supra*, note 86, on Lent or *Quadragesima* as preceding the ancient *triduum pascale.*

97. The Old Gelasian Sacramentary (*Vat. Reg.* 316) I, 16: *Suscipis eum* [=paenitentem publicum] *IV feria mane in capite Quadragesimae* (Wilson 15; Mohlberg 18).

98. For the progressive extension of Lent see the studies of Chavasse given in note 84 and P. Jounel, "Le cycle pascal," *L'Église en prière* 4 (Paris 1983) 45-90, ET "The Easter Cycle," The Church at Prayer 4 (Collegeville 1986), 33-76.

99. *Liber pontificalis* (ed. Duchesne 1, 129): *Hic constituit ut septem hebdomadae ante Pascha ieiunium celebretur.*

100. Cf. J. Froger, "Les anticipations du jêune quadragésimal," *Mélanges de science religieuse* 3 (1946) 207-234, espec. 215-216 and A. Chavasse, "Messes du pape Vigile (537-555) dans le sacramentaire léonien," EL 64 (1950) 161-213, espec. 162, and 66 (1952) 145-219.

101. The Councils of Orleans (511), canon 24 and (541), canon 2: *Concilia Galliae*, ed. C. de Clercq, CC 148A (Turnhout 1963) 11 and 132.

102. The Epistolary of Capua, nos. 56-58; cf. DACL 5 (1922) 298: *In Sexagesima*—The Old Gelasian (*Vat. Reg.* 316) I, 14: *In Sexagesima* (Wilson 13; Mohlberg 16).

103. The Epistolary of Capua, nos. 56-58: *In II, III, IV feria Paschae*, followed immediately by no. 59 = *In Pascha annotina*, i.e., the date of Easter of the preceding year; DACL 5(1922) 299.

104 In the time of Gregory I, the gospel of Septuagesima (used in Tridentine Missal) was employed on the feast of St. Lawrence (Aug 10); cf. Gregory I, *Homelia* 19 (PL 76, 1153-1159). At the end of the VII century, this gospel pericope passed to Septuagesima Sunday along with its station of St. Lawrence-outside-the-walls. Septuagesima appears in the Old Gelasian Sacramentary (Vat. Reg. 316) I, 13: *In Septuagesima* (Wilson 12; Mohlberg 16).

105. Tertullian, *De idolatria* 14, CC 2, 1113-1115; *De corona* 3, CC 2, 1042-1043; *De baptismo* 19. CC 1, 293-294. —Origen, *Adversus Celsum* 8, 22; PG 11, 1549-1552; SC 150, 222-225. —Later development of the Fifty Days: the feast of the Ascension appeared about 350; cf. Socrates, *Historia eccles.* 7, 26 and Augustine, *Epistula 54 ad Ianuarium*; PL 33, 200; on the fortieth day after Easter in accordance with a somewhat dubious interpretation of Acts 1: 6-9 which stands in opposition to Mark 16:19 which fixes the Ascension on the day of the Resurrection. —See the Council of Elvira (314), canon 43: *Pravam institutionem emendari placuit iuxta auctoritatem scripturarum, ut cuncti diem Pentecostes celebremus, ne si quis non fecerit novam haeresim induxisse notetur;* Mansi, *Concilia* 2, 13. This text simply means that they are fifty days after

Easter and not merely forty: *post Pascha quinquagesima teneatur, non quadragesima*. Cf. Hefele-Lerclercq, *Histoire des conciles* 1 (1907) 245-246 which contains all the evidence.

106. Eusebius, *Vita Constantini* 4, 64; PG 20, 1219-1220. For the development of the fifty days after Easter, see R. Cabié, *La Pentecôte. L'évolution de la Cinquantaine pascale au cours des cinq premiers siècles*, Bibliothèque de liturgie 1 (Tournai 1965). On the Easter Octave see H. A. J. Wegman, *Pâques, du premier Jour au huitième: Étude sur l'histoire de la semaine de Pâques en Occident*. Doctoral Dissertation Gregorian University (Rome 1959), Dutch edition: *Het Paasoktaaf in het Missale Romanum en zijn geschiedenis* (Assen 1968).

107. February, the last month of the year, had been traditionally dedicated to the commemoration of the dead. The festival of the dead, called *Feralia* or *Parentalia*, began on Feb. 13 and ended on Feb. 22 with a funeral feast in honor of one's dead relatives; Feb. 22 was called *Charistia or Cara cognatio*; cf. Valerius Maximus, *Facta et dicta memorabilia* 2, 1, 8: *convivium etiam solemne maiores instituerunt idque Caristia appelaverunt*; the calendar of Polemius Silvius, compiled in Gaul ca. 448, has, under Feb. 22; *VIII Kalendas Martias. Depositio SS. Petri et Pauli. Cara cognatio ideo dicta quia tunc etsi fuerint vivorum parentum odia, tempore obitus deponantur* (*Corpus inscriptionum latinorum* 2, 2 259). This latter quotation seems to suggest that a festival of Peter and Paul had been introduced on Feb. 22 to replace the pagan feast and to commemorate the two chief apostles, martyrs and 'founders' of the Roman Church. In the *Philocalian Calendar* of 354, Feb. 22 is entered as: *VIII Kalendas Martias. Natale Petri de cathedra* and should probably be understood as the anniversary of the establishment of Peter's chair, i.e., his teaching authority, at Rome. Here *cathedra* also has a funereal meaning; see H. Lietzman, *Petrus und Paulus in Rome* (2nd ed., Berlin 1927) 19-21; T. Klauser, *Die Cathedra im Totenkult*, LQF 21 (Münster/ West. 1927) 152-183 and 2nd revised edition (1971) 205-206; and Klauser, *Die römische Petrus-Tradition im Lichte der neuen Ausgrabungen unter der Peterskirche*, Arbeitsgemeinschaft für Forschung des Landes Nordrhein-Westfalen 24 (Cologne 1956) 27-28.

108. The collection of *libelli missarum* now called the Verona Sacramentary (VI century) is organized according to the months of the civil calendar, beginning in January and ending in December. —Old Gel. Sac. (*Vat. Reg.* 316): I, 82: *Denuntiatio ieiuniorum quarti, septimi et decimi mensis*; I, 20: *Mensis I, IV, VIII et X sabbatorum die in XII lectiones* (Wilson 124 and 22; Mohlberg 101 and 24).

109. Old Gel. Sac. (*Vat. Reg.* 316) I, 1: *Incipit liber sacramentorum romanae aeclesiae ordinis anni circuli. Orationes et preces in vigiliis Natalis Domini.* (Wilson 1; Mohlberg 1). —The same is true of the various Gregorian Sacramentaries, the *Capitularia evangeliorum* (Klauser, type II and the Epistolary of Würzburg. —The *Depositio martyrum* of the Chronographer of 354 places the Nativity at the head of its festal calendar: *VIII Kalendas Ianuarii* = Dec 25 *natus Christus in Betleem Iudeae* (Mommsen 71), Jesus being the protomartyr.

110. The year began in six different ways in the Middle Ages: a) on Jan. 1, the feast of the Circumcision, b) on March 1, the old Roman manner, c) on

March 25, the feast of the Annunciation, d) on Easter day (*a cereo pascali*), e) on Sept. 1, Byzantine style, and f) on Dec. 25, Christmas. March 1 and Dec. 25 were the most popular. For the calendar situation in different countries, see B. M. Lersch, *Einleitung in die Chronologie* 1 (1899) 235-241; and especially, H. Grotefend, *Taschenbuch der Zeitrechnung* (Hanover 1960) 11-14.

111. Old Gel. Sac. I, 18: *Orationes et preces Dominica in Quadragesima inchoantis ieiunium*; I, 19: *Istae orationes quae sequuntur prima sabbato in mense primo* [= March] *sunt dicendae* (Wilson, 17 and 21; Mohlberg, 20 and 23).

112. For the four Ember periods, their origin (early on there were only three such periods corresponding to the Roman *feriae sementivae, messis et vindemiales*) and their development, see G. Morin, "L'origine des Quatres-Temps." RB 14 (1897) 337-346; L. Fischer, *Die kirchlichen Quatember. Ihre Entstehung, Entwicklung und Bedeutung* (Munich 1914); M. Andrieu, *Les Ordines romani* 4 (1956) 213-231, 258-263; J. Janini, *S. Siricio y las cuatro Témporas* (Valencia 1958); G. G. Willis, "Ember Days," *Essays in Early Roman Liturgy*, ACC 46 (London 1964) 49-97; T. J. Talley, *The Development of the Ember Days to the Time of Gregory VII*, Ph. D. dissertation (New York: The General Theological Seminary, 1969). Talley destroys Morin's thesis *re* connection with the pagan feasts of sowing, harvest and wine and connects them with intentional duplications of the Paschal fast, for '*revival*' purposes.

113. Leo I, *Epistula* 12, 4; PL 54, 171.

114. T. Fry *et al.* (edd.), *The Rule of St. Benedict. In Latin and English with Notes* (Collegeville, MN 1981) 240-241.

115. See Table I,1.

116. See Table I,2.

117. This is perhaps a survival of the ancient tradition that Jesus was both born and died on the same day, March 25, the Spring equinox. See *supra* for the attempt to assign Easter a fixed date.

118. Advent appears for the first time in the Old. Gel. Sac. (*Vat. Reg.* 316) II, 80-84 (5 *formulae*) (Wilson 214-219; Mohlberg 169-173) and in the Epistolary of Würzburg nos. 170-174; G. Morin (ed.), RB 27 (1910) 64-65. See M. Grégoire, "La dernière phase du cycle," *Questions liturgiques et paroissiales* 9 (1924) 174-180 (before Advent proper there was a kind of pre-Advent beginning with the XVIII Sunday after Pentecost). See espec. A. Chavsse, *Le Sac. gél.* 412-433.

119. Cf. *Sacramentarium Paduense*, ed. J. Deshusses, *Le Sac. grég.* 1 (Fribourg 1971) 609-684. For the Sundays after Pentecost, see L. Brou, "Étude historique sur les oraisons des dimanches de la Pentecôte," SE 2 (1949) 123-224; and "Les oraisons des dimanches après la Pentecôte," *Paroisse et liturgie* 38 (Bruges 1959); A. Chavasse, *Le Sac. gél.*, 496-497; R. J. Hesbert, *Antiphonale missarum sextuplex* (Brussels 1935) lxxii-lxxix; "Les dimanches verts," (= dimanches après la Pentecôte) LMD 46 (1956) 35-59; and most especially A. Chavasse, "Les oraisons pour les dimanches ordinaires," RB 93 (1983) 31-70, 177-244 for an explanation of the *orationes cottidianae* of the *Hadrianum* 202 and their use for the ordinary Sundays throughout the year in the Lateran Sacramentary.

120. E.g., A. Dumas (ed.), *Liber Sacramentorum Gellonensis*, CC 149 and P. Cagin (ed.), *Le Sacramentaire gélasien d'Angoulême* (Angoulême 1918); the late VIII-century sacramentaries present the Sundays and the Saints in a single series of masses.

121. *Supplementum Anianense* XVIII-XLI, ed. Deshusses, 390-407.

122. T. Klauser, *Das römische Capitulare Evangeliorum*, xxx and *passim*.

123. There survive, however, only eleven examples of the use of marginal notes between the VII and the XIV centuries; cf. Klauser, *op. cit.*, xxxv-xxxvi. —The coexistence of different types is well attested by the following two witnesses: one could still find a Bible with marginal notes produced in the XIV century (Amsterdam, Universiteits Bibliothek, *codex* 84) while the famous *Weissenburgensis* 76 is an example of a lectionary with three series of pericopes given *in extenso* which belonged to the end of the V or the beginning of the VI century; cf. A. Dold, *Das älteste Liturgiebuch der lateinischen Kirche. Ein altgallikanisches Lektionar des 5/6. Jhrs.*, TuA 26/28 (Beuron 1930). —We must remember that although the *Weissenburgensis* 76 is the oldest liturgical document preserved in Latin, it is considerably younger than the *Apostolic Tradition* of Hippolytus of Rome composed ca. 215; the Latin version of the latter may also have been used for worship; cf. note 49 *supra*.

124. The famous Sacramentary-Lectionary of Monte Cassino (*Casinensis* 271) is not a missal in any proper sense of that term. It is a fragmentary Gregorian Sacramentary closely related to the *Paduense* and the *Hadrianum* and is remarkable for the fact that it experiments with inserting the scriptural readings (epistle and gospel) in the masses of the *temporale* (but not in the *sanctorale*). The text of this palimpsest was written ca. 700 or a bit earlier (Lowe, Bischoff); cf. A. Chavasse, "Les fragments palimpsestes du *Casinensis* 271," AfL 25 (1983) 9-33; K. Gamber, CLLA 701, pp. 330-331; ed. A. Dold, *Vom Sakramentar, Comes und Capitulare zum Missale*, TuA 34 (Beuron 1943) with facsimiles. According to Dold, progress towards the plenary missal came about as follows: marginal notes, lists, lectionaries, sacramentaries and antiphonaries; *libelli missarum*, sacramentaries with readings but without chants and, finally, sacramentaries with readings and chants in a single volume=a plenary missal.

125. As a liturgical book, the Bible was called *bibliotheca* and was contained in one or two volumes; cf. the catalogue of Saint Wandrille of Fontenelle (823/833): *Bibliothecam optimam continentem Vetus et Novum Testamentum* [ed. G. H. Becker, *Catalogi Bibliothecarum Antiqui* (Bonn 1855; reprint Hildesheim 1973) 13, note 7]; Catalogue of St. Riquier (831): *bibliotheca integra ubi continentur libri LXXII in uno volumine, bibliotheca dispersa in voluminibus quatuordecim* (Becker, 24, note 11); Catalogue of St. Amand (XII century): *Duo magna volumina, in quibus separatim Vetus et Novum Testamentum continetur, preter evangelium et psalterium* [L. V. Delisle, *Le cabinet des manuscrits de la Bibliothèque impériale* 2 (Paris 1870) 449, note 2]. This last notice proves that on occasion the two Testaments were copied into two separate volumes.

126. The Eusebian canons can be found in *Novum Testamentum graece et*

latine, new ed. by E. Nestle-K. Aland (Stuttgart 1964) 32*-37* and in A. Merk, *Novum Testamentum Graece et Latine* (Rome 1964) 853-854.

127. T. Klauser, *Das römische Capitulare Evangeliorum*, xxxv-xxxvi.

128. Such an arrangement is maintained for the rest of the Middle Ages although after 850/900 sometimes the Temporal and Sanctoral lists appear separately.

129. According to Klauser, *capitulare* had been used in this sense since the V century; as meaning a section of a book it had appeared in Tertullian, *De exhortatione castitatis* 3, 10; CC 2, 1020 and *De idolatria* 19, 1; CC 2, 1120; as meaning a liturgical reading *capitulum* appeared in Augustine *Sermo* 164, 2; PL 38, 896: *in ipso quippe capitulo lectionis habes positum*, ="In the same chapter from which our reading is taken . . . ."

130. See Klauser, *op. cit.*, xv-xvi.

131. Books of pericopes were rare before around 1000. —The papal mass of the VII century supposed two distinct books of readings and not a complete lectionary; cf. *Ordo* I, 20 (Andrieu, *Les Ordines*, 2, 73): *Apostolum* [=epistolary] *autem subdiaconus qui lecturus est sub cura sua habebit, evangelium* [evangelary] *archidiaconus*.

132. The oldest example is from the VIII century: Paris, Bibliothèque Nationale, *nouvelles acquisitions latines* 1203 = *Evangelia anni circuli secundum ordinem romanam* (Evangelary of Godescalc), ca. 781/783; cf. Frere, *Studies* 2 (1934) 214-216 and S. Beissel, *Entstehung der Perikopen des römischen Messbuches; zur Geschichte der Evangelienbücher in der ersten Hälfte des Mittelalters* (Rome 1902; reprint Rome 1967) 157-170, espec. 164-167; CLLA 1120, p. 454. In English an *evangelary* means a books of selected gospel readings; the full text of the Gospels is called the *Four Gospels*, e.g., the Book of Kells. In German *Evangeliar* means the Four Gospels and *Evangelistar* a book of gospel pericopes.

133. The oldest examples are from the VIII/IX century: the Epistolary of Corbie (*Liber comitis*); Leningrad, *Publichnaja Biblioteka im. M.E. Saltykova-Shchedrina, codex*, Q. v. I, no. 16 of the VIII/IX century and the *Comes ab Albino ordinatus*, ca. 800; see *infra* for a full description of these MSS. —The term *epistle* came to mean the first reading at mass, even when it was drawn from the OT. John Beleth (†1182) already used *epistle* in this way: *Summa de ecclesiastic officiis, cap.* 38, ed. H. Douteil, CC, *Cont. med.* 41; PL 202, 46.

134. The oldest examples are from the IX century: the *Liber comitis* of Saint-Père, Chartres, Bibliothèque municipale, *codex* 24 (32), ca. 800, destroyed in air-raid, May 26, 1944; the Donaueschingen *Fragment* B. II. 2 of the IX century; the Milanese Lectionary, Biblioteca Ambrosiana, *codex* C *inf.* 228 of the IX century; the Zürich Lectionary, Zentralbibliothek, *codex* 77 of the IX century; see *infra* for full description of these MSS.

135. *Apostolus* means St. Paul the Apostle and by extension the collection of Pauline letters; cf. Augustine, *Sermo* 172: *Apostolum cum legeretur, audistis,* . . . (PL 38, 909); the Council of Toledo (400), canon 2: *Item placuit, ut de poenitente non admittatur ad clerum, nisi tantum si necessitas aut usus exegerit,*

inter ostiarios deputetur, vel inter lectores: ita ut evangelia et apostolum non legat (Mansi, *Concilia* 3, 998-999). *Apostolus* often meant the Book of Epistles = Epistolary, composed largely but not exclusively of the Pauline epistles; cf. *Ordo* I, 20: *Apostolum autem subdiaconus qui lecturus est sub cura habebit, evangelium archidiaconus* (Andrieu, *Les Ordines* 2, 73); the *Hadrianum* 1: *deinde sequitur apostolum. Item gradalem seu alleluia* (ed. J. Deshusses, 86).

136. *Epistolarium (-are, aris)* has a more precise meaning than *lectionarius*; it is the book of non-gospel readings.

137 The term *lectionarius* stands for two different books: the mass-lectionary (as here) and the lectionary of reading for the Liturgy of the Hours. In principle, the *lectionarius* contains both sets of pericopes (epistle and gospel), although sometimes the term is used simply for an epistolary and sometimes for an evangelary. Medieval catalogues set *lectionarius* besides *evangelia, libri sacramentorum* and *missalia* (Becker, pp. 4, 9, 35, 36, 73) and *epistolaria (-ares)*. —Catalogue of Saint Riquier (831): *lectionarii epistolarum et evangeliorum mixtim et ordinate compositi, quinque* (Becker p. 28): Testament of Eberhard of Friuli (837): *lectionarium de epistolis et evangeliis* (Becker p. 29).

138. *Comes* or *Liber comitis* stands for a book which contains the readings *in extenso*; whenever it is used for mere list of the readings it means that the list is taken from an originally complete lectionary; see the proof of this in Klauser, *Das römische Capitulare*, xv-xvi. *Comes* can also mean an epistolary with the readings intact or an entire lectionary containing both readings: thus the *Comes ab Albino emendatus* or *Comes* of Alcuin is an epistolary although it often appears in the catalogues as a *Lectionarius plenarius a supradicto Albino ordinatus* (Catalogue of Saint Riquier of 831: Becker p. 28). Under the title *Divi Hieronymi comes*, Pamelius published a list of two series of readings deriving from several MS witnesses; see *infra* for a description of this document. Two series also appear in the *Comes auctus a Theotincho presbitero*. Some catalogues classify lectionaries and *comites* separately: Catalogue of Fulda (XII century): *Missales III, Evangelium I, Lectionarium I . . . Liber comes, Psalterium* (Becker, 266). Catalogue of Marchiennes (XII/ XIII century): *lectionarii duo . . . liber comitis* (Delisle, *Cabinet des MSS* 2, 513). Bernhold of Constance, *Mircologus* 25, seems to confuse *lectionarius* and *comes: Liber etiam comitis sive lectionarius* (PL 151, 999). Obviously a standard terminology did not prevail in regard to the books of liturgical readings. —As early as 471, the *Charta Cornutiana*, a foundation charter for a church near Tivoli, mentions a *comes: Item codices Evangelia IV apostolorum* (Mabillon: *Apostolum*), *Psalterium et Comitem* (L. Duchesne, *Liber pontificalis* 1, cxlvii). Given the date of the *Charta Cornutiana*, *comes* here may mean a didactic or edifying collection of readings rather than a book of liturgical readings. —In the Old Spanish rite, the term for the *liber comitis* or *comes* was *liber commicus*. *Commicus* probably derives from *comma* = section or pericope (A. Mundó, "Frammenti palinsesti del 'Liber Comicus' visigotico" *Analecta Gregoriana* 70 [1954] 101). The term *Comes* does not derive from the word *comes* = companion.

139. On the other hand, for historians of the Latin versions of the New Testament, full readings are of capital importance since they reveal variant

readings to those of the Vulgate. In this regard, however, we have to remember that copyists often cited from memory and that, consequently, variants are often mere *lapsus memoriae*.

140. Pseudo-Jerome, *Epistola ad Constantium*, ed. L. d'Achery, *Spicilegium* (Paris 1723) 3, 301 = PL 30, 487-488 and 501-503; E. Ranke, *Das kirchliche Perikopensystem* (Berlin 1847), Appendix 1; W. H. Frere, *Studies in Early Roman Liturgy* 3, 75-76. —For the inauthentic character of this letter and for the difficulty in discovering its real author, see the various opinions of G. Morin, "L'auteur de la lettre à Constantius," RB 7 (1890) 416-423 (the author would have been Victor of Capua [541-554] and the addressee, Constance of Aquino [525-573]; *idem,* "Constantius, évêque de Constantinople, et les origines du *Comes* romain," RB 15 (1898) 241-246 (in some MSS the words *ad Constantium Constantinopolitanum* became *Constantiae episcopum*, who would have been the bishop of Constantia, = Cosenza, Bruttium); *idem,* "Le plus ancien *Comes* ou Lectionnaire de l'Église romaine," RB 27 (1910) 41-74; *idem,* "La lettre-préface du *Comes, Ad Constantium,* se rapporterait au lectionnaire de Claudien Mamert?" RB 30 (1913) 228-231 (the addressee would have been the presbyter Constantius of Lyons who had been considered a bishop since Isidore of Seville). —W. H. Frere, *Studies* 3, 74-77; Klauser, xx, no. 17; K. Gamber, "Das älteste Fragment des *Comes* des hl. Hieronymus," EL 75 (1961) 214-222 (Gamber says the letter's inauthenticity has not been fully decided). —In the main the letter descends through a series of Gallican witnesses: Lectionary of Corbie, the *Comes* of Paris (*Parisinus* 9451), the Lectionary of Chartres (*Carnotensis* 24), the *Comes* of Murbach (Bensançon 184).

141. Ed. W. H. Frere, *Studies*, 3, 76.

142. Dold's text had been corrected in a few places by P. Salmon, *Le lectionnaire de Luxeuil* (Rome 1944); cf. also P. McGurk, *Latin Gospel Books from 400-800* (Antwerp 1961).

143. The exact origin of this MS has not been determined. Several localities have been suggested: Around Paris (Duchesne, Morin), Morigny, near Étampes, Seine-et-Oise (Masai), S. E. of France or around Autun (Charlier), Luxeuil, for a parish church (H. Philippeau, *Revue du moyen âge latin* 2 [1946] 183), a Colombanian abbey, for the church of Langres (P. Salmon, *Mélanges colombaniens* [Paris 1951] 254).

144. See Sidonius Apollinaris on Claudius Mamertus: *Hic sollemnibus annuis paravit quae quo tempore lecta convenirent* (MGH, *Auctorum Antiquissimorum* 8, 63; PL 58, 516); see also G. Morin, "La lettre-préface du Comes . . . ," RB 30 (1913) 228-233.

145. See A. Wilmart, "La lettre LXIII de Cyprien parmi les lectures non bibliques," RB 28 (1911) 228-233.

146. The following documents can be added to those listed above: the Marginal Notes of the Pentateuch of Tours, Paris, Biblio. Nat. *nouv. acq. lat.*. 2334; first half of the VI century, which is a mixed Gallican-Visigothic book (P. Salmon, *Le lectionnaire de Luxeuil,* lxxxiii) and the Notes to the Evangelary of the *Codex Palatinus,* Vienna, Nationalbibliothek, *codex* 1185 + Dublin,

Trinity College, no. 4, 18; V century. The notes are of the VII/VIII century and appear to be older than those of the Lectionary of Luxeuil; cf. Klauser, xxxv, 35 and D. de Bruyne, "Notes liturgiques inédites du *Codex Palatinus* des évangiles," RB 45 (1933) 255.

147. Similar notes appear in the marginal notes of an evangelary of Split (Spalato) discovered by C. Kniewald, "De Evangeliario Spalatensi," EL 71 (1957) 408-427.

148. For other examples of the Milanese lectionaries, see CLLA 540-549, pp. 270-275.

149. For the spelling *commicus* (and not *comicus*) derived from *comma*= section (and not from *comes*), see J. F. Rivera, *Estudios biblicos* 7(1948) 339 and T. Ayuso, *ibid.* 10 (1951) 299-300. —For bibliographies and MSS, see D. De Bruyne, "Manuscrits wisigothiques," RB 35 (1924) 7-20; M. Dietz, *Gebetsklänge aus Altspanien* (Bonn 1947); L. Brou, "Bulletin de liturgie mozarabe," HS 2 (1949) 459-484; J. M. Pinell, "Boletín de Liturgia hispano-visigóthica," HS 9 (1956) 418-421; J. M. Mora-Ontalva, "Nuevo boletín de Liturgia hispano-visigótica," HS 26 (1973) 209-237; A. Millares Carlo, "MSS visigóticos. Notas biliograficas," HS 14 (1961) 337-444; F. M. Rodriguez, "La antigua biblioteca de la Catedral de Salamanca," HS 14 (1961) 281-323; J. Janini, "Hacia el inventorio de MSS litúrgicos de las bibliotecas de España, Primeras etapas de un *Iter Hispanicum*," HS 14 (1961) 465-471.

150. Other examples of Visigothic lectionaries in CLLA nos. 360-377, pp. 214-219.

151. Introductory bibliography for the ancient liturgy of Campania: J. Chapman, "The Capuan Mass-Books of Northumbria" in *Notes on the Early History of the Vulgate Gospels* (Oxford 1908) 144-161; A. Baumstark, *Die northumbrischen alten und neuen Messbücher*, in L.C. Mohlberg, *Die älteste erreichbare Gestalt* LQF 11-12 (Münster 1927; repr. 1967) 62*-70*; K. Gamber, "Die kampanische Lektionsordnung," SE 13 (1962) 326-352.—The Epistolary of Capua or *Codex Fuldensis* is, however, the first direct document of the Campanian liturgy.

152. Introductory bibliography for the ancient liturgy of Benevento: R. Andoyer, "L'ancienne liturgie de Bénévent," *Revue du chant grégorien* 20 (1912) 176-183; 21 (1913) 14-20; 22 (1914) 8-11; 24 (1920) 48-50; R. J. Hesbert, "Le *codex* 10.673 de la Bibliothèque Vaticane fonds latin (XI siècle). Graduel bénéventain," *Paléographie musicale* 14 (Tournai 1931) (Hesbert reveals a basic fact about this liturgy: the only vestiges that survive are available only through Roman usages); *idem*, "Les dimanches de Carême dans les MSS romano-bénéventains," EL 38 (1934) 198-222; *idem*, "L'*Antiphonale missarum* de l'ancien rit bénéventain," EL 52 (1938) 22-26; 141-158; 53 (1939) 168-190; 59 (1945) 69-95; 60 (1946) 103-141; 61 (1947) 153-210; J. Gajard, "Le *codex* VI, 34 de la Bibliothèque capitulaire de Bénévent. Graduel avec prosaire et tropaire," *Paléographie musicale* 15 (Tournai 1937); G. Morin, "Le missel de Payerne," *Zeitschrift für Schweitzerische Kirchengeschichte* 25 (1931) 102-111; A. Dold, *Zürcher und Peterlinger Messbuch-Fragmente aus der Zeit der Jahrtausendwende*, TuA 25 (Beuron 1934);

idem, "Im Escorial gefundene Bruchstücke eines Plenarmissals in beneventanischer Schrift des 11 Jhrs.," *Spanische Forschungen der Görresgesellschaft* 5 (1935) 89-96; *idem,* "Umfangreiche Reste zweier Plenarmissalien des 11. und 12. Jhs.," EL 53 (1938) 11-167; *idem,* "Fragmente eines um die Jahrtausendwende in beneventanischer Schrift geschrieben Vollmissales aus *codex Vaticanus latinus* 10645," JfL 10 (1931) 40-55; *idem,* "Eine alte Bussliturgie aus *codex Vaticanus latinus* 1339," JfL 11 (1932) 126; *idem,* "Untersuchungsergebnisse einer doppelt reskribierten Wolfenbütler Hs.," *Zentralblatt für Bibl.wesen* 34 (1917) 233-244; M. Avery, "The Beneventan Lections for the Vigil of Easter and the Ambrosian Chant Banned by Pope Stephen IX at Montecassino," *Studi Gregoriani* 1 (1947) 433-458; K. Gamber, "Die mittelitalienisch-beneventanischen Plenarmissalien," SE 9 (1957) 265-285; *idem,* "La liturgia delle diocesi dell' Italia centro-meridionale dal IX all'XI secolo," Atti del Convengo di storia della Chiesa in Italia (Rome 1963); A. A. King, *Liturgies of the Past* (London 1959) 52-77; K. Gamber, *Missale Beneventanum von Canossa* (Baltimore, Walters Art Gallery, MS W 6), TPL 9 (Regensburg 1972).

153. See CLLA nos. 1170-1179, pp. 465-467.

154. See *infra* for the Families A and B of A. Chavasse, belonging to the third type of lectionary.

155. See *infra,* pp. 349-352.

156. The *Parisinus* 9452 or *Comes* of Alcuin must not be confused with the complete lectionary (epistles and gospels) of Chartres, Bibliothèque municipale, *codex* 24 (32) of the early IX century; cf. A. Wilmart, "Le lectionnaire de Saint-Père," *Speculum* 1 (1926) 269-278. Such confusion was occasioned by a misunderstood remark of Mabillon, *Annales O. S. B.* 2 (1704) 328, a confusion continued by Berger, *Histoire de la Vulgate pendant les premiers siècles du moyen âge* (Paris 1893) 180. —The Chartres MS was destroyed in May, 1944; CLLA no. 1229, pp. 477-478.

157. Edition of the preface by A. Wilmart, "Le lectionnaire d'Alcuin," EL 51 (1937) 164-165; E. Ranke, *Das kirchliche Pericopensystem,* Appendix, p. xii.

158. See also the numerous epistolaries enumerated in CLLA nos. 1001-1037, pp. 429-438.

159. T. Klauser, *Das römische Capitulare Evangeliorum.*

160. The first three types Π, Λ, Σ appear in Klauser, 1-130.

161. The fourth type Δ in Klauser, 131-172.

162. A. Chavasse, "Les plus anciens types du lectionaire et de l'antiphonaire romains de la messe," RB 62 (1952) 1-94.

163. W. H. Frere, *Studies in Early Roman Liturgy* 2, ACC 30 (London 1934).

164. One must not confuse the epistolary and evangelary contained in the Würzburg MS M. p. th. f. 62. The two lists of readings are of utterly different age and provenance. —See other examples in Klauser, 13-46.

165. Examples and text in Klauser, 47-92.

166. Examples and text in Klauser, 93-130.

167. Examples and text in Klauser, 131-172.

168. *Ibid.*, cxiv-cxx.

169. R. J. Hesbert, "La liturgie bénéventaine dans la tradition manuscrite," *Paléographie musicale* 14 (Brussels 1931) 60-465; A. Chavasse, "Les plus anciens types du lectionnaire . . . ," RB 62 (1952) 1-51; *idem*, "L' évangeliaire romain de 645, un recueil, sa composition," RB 92 (1982) 33-75; CLLA, nos. 1101-1114, pp. 446-452.

170. See *supra* in the chapter on the literary types of books of readings.

171. Other examples in CLLA nos. 1201-1229, pp. 470-478; Klauser, cxiv-cxx.

172. The surviving books of homilies serve as an invaluable complementary source for understanding the system of readings. Research in this field has barely begun; see A. Chavasse, "Le calendrier dominical romain au VI siècle. L'Épistolier et l'Homéliaire prégrégoriens, *Recherches de science religieuse* 38 (1951) 234-240; 41 (1953) 96-122, the article cited *supra* note 169 and "Le sermonnaire vatican du VII siècle," SE 23 (1978-1979) 225-289.

173. A table of the feasts that were added to the *Sanctorale* from the VII-IX century appears in Klauser, 184-185 and in Frere, *Studies* 1. See also note 75, *supra*.

174. We have to remember that the authenticity of a liturgical text depends on the simple fact that it was actually used in the liturgy.

175. Both Frere and Wilmart agree on this point. Wilmart was the first to point to the existence of two families of MSS within the large collection of lectionaries of the third group. Hesbert and Chavasse continued and expanded in this area.

176. Klauser and Frere worked independently on the lectionaries but their work agreed upon the existence of three variants or types. Chavasse succeeded in establishing that the three types of Klauser and Frere were in fact three variants of the same type of evangelary.

177. Chavasse was the first to show this.

178. We must remember that by Roman usage we mean that of the City and of the suburbicarian dioceses. —For the date of the Würzburg epistolary, see A. Chavasse, "Le lectionnaire et l'antiphonaire romains: Semaines de Pâques, Pentecôte et les dimanches après Pâques," RB 62 (1952) 72-94 and "Les lectures; la formation de l'Épistolier romain (Comes de Wurzbourg)," *Recherches de science religieuse* 41 (1953) 101-111. In any case, the Würzburg epistolary is earlier than Pope Gregory II (†731) since it has no masses for the Thursdays of Lent; it is probably later than 608 since it does contain the dedication of the Pantheon (*S. Maria ad martyres*) which was accomplished in the reign of Boniface IV (608-615).

179. Klauser, 1-3.

180. Chavasse, "Le lectionnaire et l'antiphonaire romains antérieures à 650," RB 62 (1952) 28-49.

181. MSS and text in Klauser, 1-46.

182. MSS and text in Klauser, 93-130.

183. Frere, *Studies* 2 and 3.

184. See the works indicated *supra*, pp. 291-292.

185. Chavasse, "Le lectionnaire . . . ," RB 62 (1952) 8-9: Hesbert, *Paléographie musicale* 14, 136-137.

186. Hesbert, *Paléog. musicale* 14, 134.

187. MSS and text in Klauser, 131-172.

188. The only repertories we presently possess are those of Klauser, Chavasse, Hesbert and Gamber—which we have cited so often.

189. Amalarius, *De ecclesiasticis officiis libri IV* (ed. Hanssens, *Opera liturgica omnia*, 2, 401-543). —Berno of Reichenau, *De officiis eccles.* (PL 97, 1055-1088), *De celebratione Adventus* (PL 47, 1079-1087), *De ieiunio IV Temporum* (PL 97, 1087-1098). —Bernhold of Constance, *Micrologus* (PL 151, 973-1022). —Honorius of Autun, *Gemma animae* (PL 172, 541-738). —Rupert of Deutz, *De divinis officiis* (ed. H. Haacke, CC, *Cont. med.* 7; PL 170, 9-332). —William Durandus of Mende, *Rationale divinorum officiorum* (many MSS and *incunabula* but no modern edition; French trans. by C. Barthélemy, *Rational ou manuel des divins offices*, 5 vols. (Paris 1854); ET of Book 1, J. M. Neale-B. Webb, *The Symbolism of Churches and Church Ornaments* (London 1843) and of Book 3, T. H. Passmore, *The Sacred Vestments* (London 1899).

190. With the II Vatican Council, the medieval system of pericopes disappeared from the Roman Catholic Church; it survives in part in some Lutheran Churches. The new Roman system (3-year Sunday cycle, 2-year ferial cycle) is contained in the *Ordo Lectionum Missae* (Vatican City 1969).

191. See the MSS listed in CLLA nos. 380-384, pp. 220-223; nos. 470-484, pp. 250-254; nos. 550-557, pp. 275-278; nos. 1301-1398, pp. 492-526. and in the classic work of R. J. Hesbert, *Antiphonale missarum sextuplex* (Brussels 1935); descriptions of the MSS ix-xxx; introduction xxxi-cxxvi; J. R. Bryden-D. G. Hughes, *An Index of Gregorian Chant*, 2 vols. (Cambridge, MA 1969).

192. Amalarius, *Liber de ordine antiphonarii*, Prologus 17 (ed. Hanssens 1, 363), cf. R. J. Hesbert, "L'Antiphonaire d'Amalaire," EL 94 (1980) 176-194; M. Huglo, "Les remaniements de l'Antiphonaire grégorien au IX siècle: Hélisachar, Agobard, Amalaire," *Culto cristiano-Politica imperiale carolinga* (Todi 1979) 87-120. For MSS of the *Antiphonarii officii*, see CLLA nos. 1301-1308, pp. 492-500. For the *lectionaria, passionaria* and *homiliaria* of the divine office, see CLLA nos. 1625-1665, pp. 588-602.

193. One of the major results of the research done by A. Chavasse is to have proven that the *antiphonale missarum* and the mass lectionary evolved in tandem; cf. Chavasse," "Le Lectionnaire . . . ," RB 62 (1952) 1-94 and "Cantatorium et Antiphonale missarum. Quelques procédés de confection. L'Antiphonaire des dimanches après la Pentecôte. Les graduels du Sanctoral," *Ecclesia orans* 1 (1984) 15-55.

194. John the Deacon, *Vita Gregorii* 2, 6; PL 75, 90.

195. For the role of Gregory I in the composition of an antiphonary, see C. Callewaert, "L'oeuvre liturgique de S. Grégoire. La Septuagésime et l'Alleluia," SE 1 (1940) 635-653; G. Verbrecke, "S. Grégoire et la messe de sainte Agathe," EL 52 (1938) 67-76; W. Lipphardt, "Gregor der Grosse und sein Anteil am römischen Antiphonar," *Atti del Congresso internazionale di Musica sacra*, 1950 (Tournai 1952) 248-254; B. Stäblein, "Zur Frühgeschichte des römischen Chorals," *ibid.* 271-275 and "Zur Entstehung der gregorianischen Melodien," *Kirchenmusikalisches Jahrbuch* 35 (1951) 5-9; H. Hucke, "Die Entstehung der Überlieferung von einer musikalischen Tätigkeit Gregors des Grossen," *Die Musikforschung* 8 (1955) 259-265; S. Corbin, *L'Église à la conquête de sa musique* (Paris 1960) 172-189. S.J.P. van Dijk, "Gregory the Great, Founder of the Urban *Schola Cantorum*," EL 77 (1963) 335-356.

196. *Liber pontificalis*, Celestine I (Duchesne 1, 230); P. Jeffery, "The Introduction of Psalmody into the Roman Mass by Pope Celestine I (422-432)," AfL 26 (1984) 147-165.

197. Paul I, *Epistula* 24 to King Pepin III, ca. 757/767; MGH, *Epist.* 3, 529.

198. Egbert, *De institutione catholica quaest.* 16: *Quod non solum nostra testantur antiphonaria, sed et ipsa quae cum missalibus suis conspeximus apud Apostolorum Petri et Pauli limina* (PL 89, 441).

199. Other *cantatoria* in CLLA nos. 1310-1319, pp. 500-503.

200. CLLA nos. 1320-1372, pp. 503-517.

201. G. Suñol, *Introduction à la paléographie musicale grégorienne* (Paris 1935) 311-352; L. Brou, "Le *Psallendum* de la messe et les chants connexes d'après les sources manuscrites," EL 62 (1947) 13-54 and "L'Antiphonaire wisigothique et l'antiphonaire grégorien au début du VIII siècle," *Annuario musical* 5 (1950) 3-10; T. Marín, "Bibliografía del Antifonario," *Archivos Leoneses* 7 (1954) 318-326; G. Prado, "Estado actual de los estudios sobre la musica mozarabe," *Estudios sobre la liturgia mozarabe* (Toledo 1965) 89-106; C.W. Brockett, *Antiphons, Responsories and Other Chants of the Mozarabic Rite*, Musicological Studies 15 (New York 1968).

202. For other fragmentary antiphonaries, see CLLA nos. 382-384, pp. 222-223.

203. R. J. Hesbert, "L'*antiphonale missarum*. L'ancien rit bénéventain," EL 52 (1938) 28; M. Huglo in *Ecclesia Orans* 2 (1985) 265-293.

204. CLLA nos. 470-484, pp. 250-254.

205. CLLA nos. 550-557, pp. 275-278.

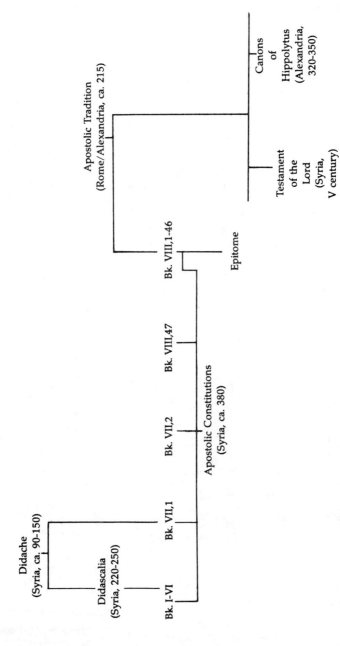

A. The Early Church Orders

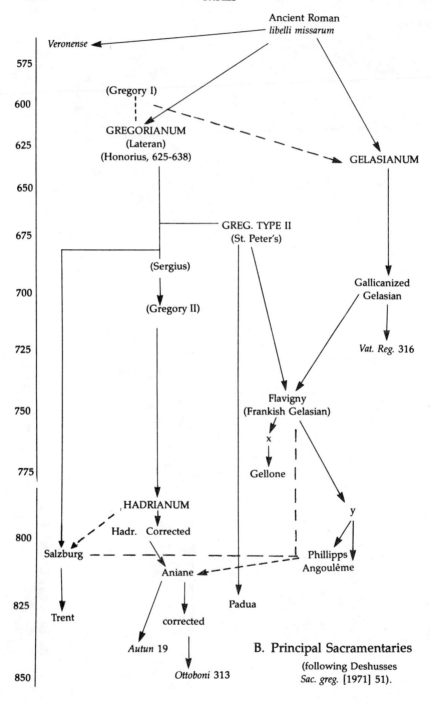

Ancient Roman
libelli missarum

Veronense

575

(Gregory I)

600

GREGORIANUM
(Lateran)
(Honorius, 625-638)

625

GELASIANUM

650

GREG. TYPE II
(St. Peter's)

675

(Sergius)

700

(Gregory II)

Gallicanized
Gelasian

725

Vat. Reg. 316

Flavigny
(Frankish Gelasian)

750

x

775

Gellone

HADRIANUM

Hadr. Corrected

y

800

Salzburg

Phillipps
Angoulême

Aniane

825

Trent

Padua

corrected

Autun 19

B. Principal Sacramentaries

850

Ottoboni 313

(following Deshusses
Sac. greg. [1971] 51).

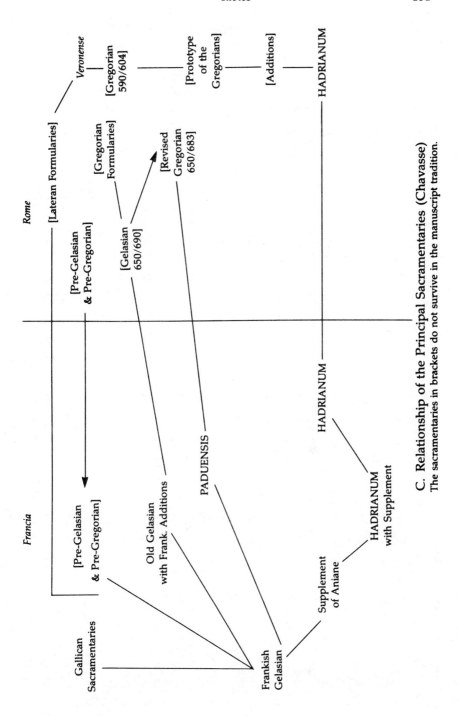

C. Relationship of the Principal Sacramentaries (Chavasse)
The sacramentaries in brackets do not survive in the manuscript tradition.

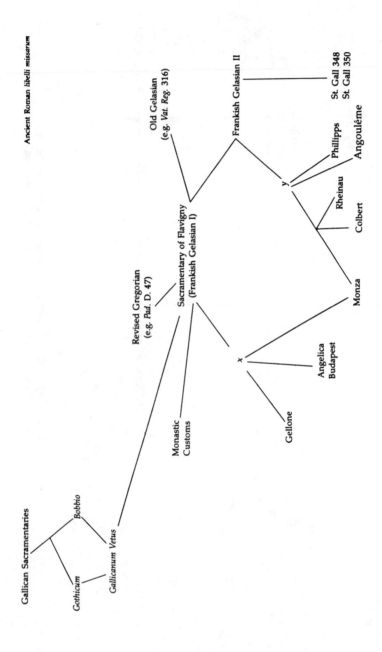

D. Origin and Evolution of the Frankish Gelasian
(present state of the question, following J. Deshusses, *Liber Sac. Gellonensis:* Intr., xxv)

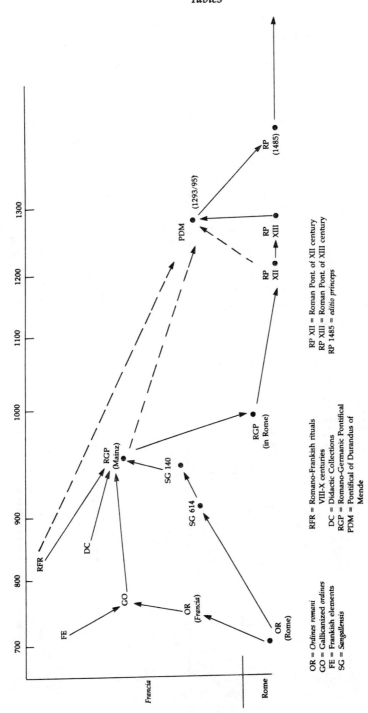

E. General Overview of the 'Migration' of *Ordines* and Pontificals

OR = *Ordines romani*
GO = *Gallicanized ordines*
FE = *Frankish elements*
SG = *Sangellensis*

RFR = Romano-Frankish rituals
        VIII-X centuries
DC = Didactic Collections
RGP = Romano-Germanic Pontifical
PDM = Pontifical of Durandus of
        Mende

RP XII = Roman Pont. of XII century
RP XIII = Roman Pont. of XIII century
RP 1485 = *editio princeps*

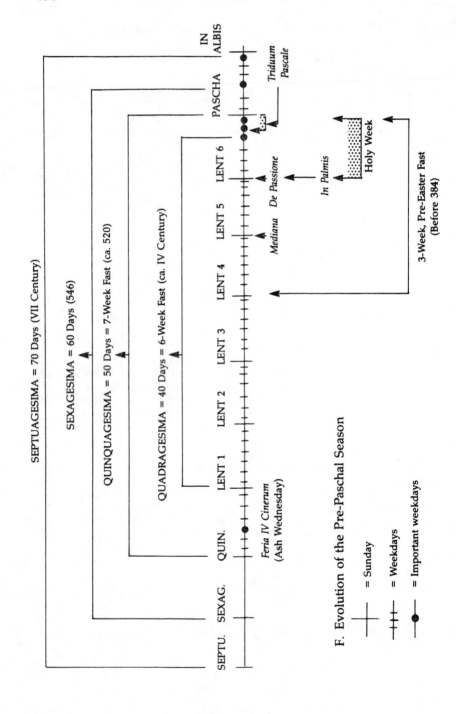

F. Evolution of the Pre-Paschal Season

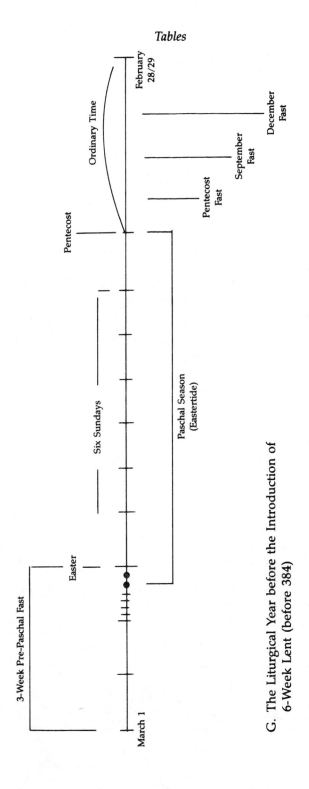

G. The Liturgical Year before the Introduction of 6-Week Lent (before 384)

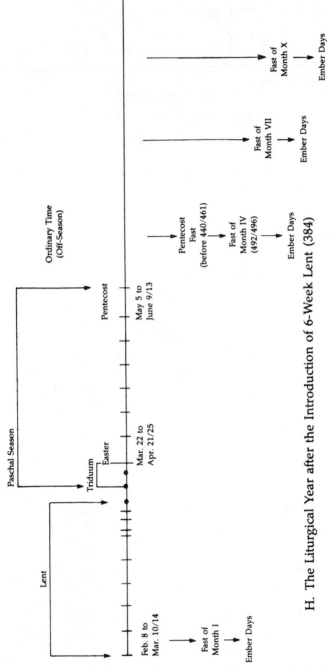

H. The Liturgical Year after the Introduction of 6-Week Lent (384)

Indication of extremes for the date of Easter, Pentecost and beginning of Lent—Roman computations before/after the year 530.

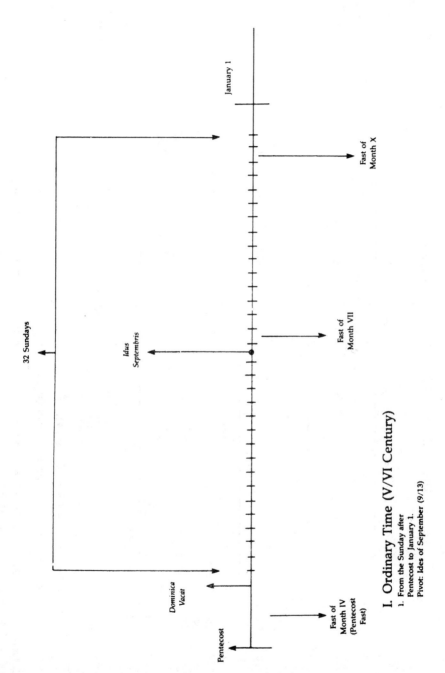

I. Ordinary Time (V/VI Century)

1. From the Sunday after
   Pentecost to January 1.
   Pivot: Ides of September (9/13)

January 1

Fast of
Month X

Fast of
Month VII

*Idus
Septembris*

32 Sundays

*Dominica
Vacat*

Pentecost

Fast of
Month IV
(Pentecost
Fast)

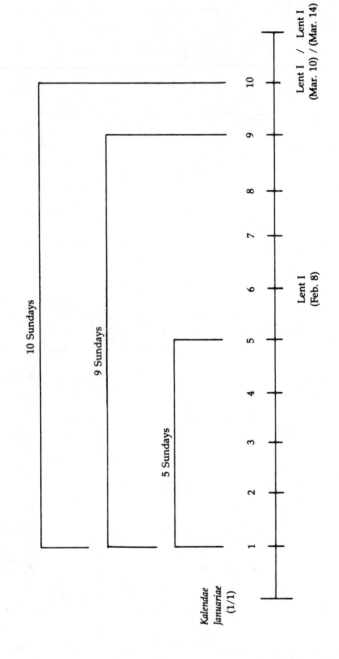

TABLE I. ORDINARY TIME (V/VI Century)

1. Ordinary Time (V/VI Century).

2. From January 1 to the First Sunday of Lent . . .

2. From January 1 to the First Sunday of Lent. Indications of extremes for the date of Lent I—before and after the revised Roman computation for Easter.

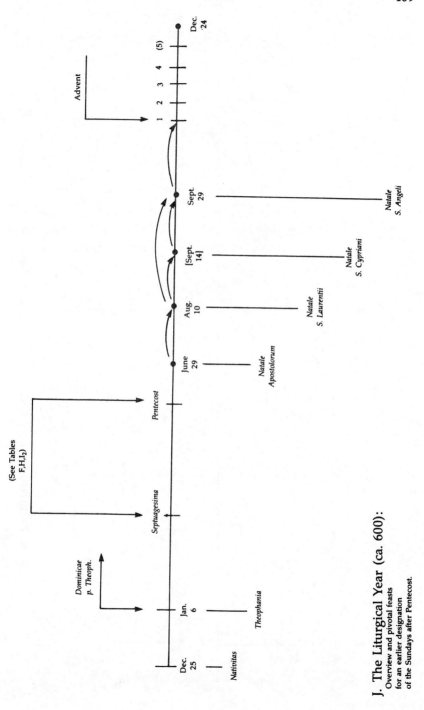

J. The Liturgical Year (ca. 600):
Overview and pivotal feasts
for an earlier designation
of the Sundays after Pentecost.

K. Relationship of the Festal Cycles of the Lord and of John the Baptist.

BIBLIOGRAPHY OF CYRILLE VOGEL

A. *BOOKS*

La discipline pénitentielle en Gaule des origines à la fin du VII siècle (Paris 1952) 206 pages. This study was 'crowned' by the Académie des Inscriptions et Belles-Lettres.

A new edition of L. Duchesne, *Le Liber Pontificalis* [original edition: 2 vols., Paris 1886 and 1892] (Paris 1955) with an new volume 3: *Additions et Corrections* containing the *Histoire du Liber Pontificalis depuis l'édition de L. Duchesne, Bibliographie et Tables générales* (Paris 1957) 400 pages; reprinted in 1971 and 1981.

Le Pontifical romano-germanique. Text: vols. 1 and 2, SeT 226 and 227 (Vatican City 1963) 370 and 446 pages; vol. 3: *Introduction générale et Tables,* SeT 269 (Vatican City 1972) 228 pages.

Césaire d'Arles. Introduction et choix de textes (Paris 1964) 150 pages.

Introduction aux sources de l'histoire du culte chrétien au moyen âge. First edition, 1966, 385 pages; second edition, Biblioteca degli Studi Medievali 1 (Spoleto-Turin 1975) 407 pages. This edition was 'crowned' by the Académie des Inscriptions et Belles-Lettres; third edition (Spoleto 1981) 407 pages.

Le pécheur et la péniténce dans l'Église ancienne (Paris 1966) 214 pages with Italian and Spanish translations; new French edition, Paris: Editions du Cerf, 1982.

Le pécheur et la pénitence au moyen âge (Paris 1969) 245 pages with an Italian translation; new French edition, Paris: Éditions du Cerf, 1982.

Ordinations inconsistantes et caractère inamissible, Études d'Histoire du culte et des Institutions chrétiennes 1 (Turin 1978) 212 pages.

Les "Libri paenitentiales," Typologie des sources du moyen âge occidental 27 (Turnhout 1978) 116 pages.

Institutions cultuelles aux II et III siècles. This will eventually appear in the collection Histoire du Droit et des Institutions de l'Église, ed. by J. Gaudemet.

B. *ARTICLES*

"Les sanctions infligées aux laïcs et aux clercs par les conciles gallo-romains et mérovingiens," *Revue de Droit Canonique* 2 (1952) 5–29; 171–94; 311–328.

"La discipline pénitentielle dans l'Église orthodoxe de Grèce," *Revue des Sciences Religieuses* 27 (1953) 374–399.

411

"Fiançailles, mariage et divorce dans les pays de religion orthodoxe grecque," *Revue de Droit Canonique* 4 (1954) 298–328.

"La discipline pénitentielle en Gaule des origines au IX siècle. Le dossier hagiographique," *Revue des Sciences Religieuses* 30 (1956) 1–26; 157–186.

"La *Descriptio Ecclesiae Lateranensis* du diacre Jean. Histoire du texte manuscrit," *Mélanges M. Andrieu, Revue des Sciences Religieuses* (1956) 457–476.

"Mgr. Michel Andrieu (1886–1956)," *Ephemerides liturgicae* 71 (1957) 34–36.

"L'oeuvre liturgique de Mgr. M. Andrieu. Un bilan provisoire," *Revue des Sciences Religieuses* 31 (1957) 7–19 and *Revue de Droit Canonique* 7 (1957) 1–14.

"Le Pontifical romano-germanique du X siècle. Éléments constitutifs avec indication des sections imprimées," *Revue des Sciences Religieuses* 32 (1958) 113–167.

"L'hymnaire de Murbach contenu dans le manuscrit *Junius* 25 (Oxford, Bodleian 5137). Un témoin du *cursus* bénédictin ou *cursus* occidental," *Archives de l'Église d'Alsace* 9 (1958) 1–42 (with a bibliography of earlier studies).

"Composition légale et commutations dans le système de la pénitence tarifée," *Revue de Droit Canonique* 8 (1958) 289–318; 9 (1959) 1–38; 341–359.

"Précisions sur la date et l'ordonnance primitive du Pontifical romano-germanique," *Ephemerides liturgicae* 74 (1960) 145–162.

"*Versus ad Orientem*. L'orientation dans les *Ordines romani* du haut moyen âge," *Studi medievali* 3rd series 1/2 (1960) 447–469.

"Note sur la théologie du péché dans les Églises protestantes," *Théologie du péché*, Bibliothèque de théologie, series 2. Théologie morale 7 (Tournai 1960) 519–528.

"Le péché et la pénitence. Aperçu sur l'évolution historique de la discipline pénitentielle dans l'Église latine," *Pastorale du péché*, Bibliothéque de Théologie, series 2. Théologie morale 8 (Tournai 1961) 147–235.

"La législation actuelle sur les fiançailles, le mariage et le divorce dans le Royaume de Grèce" *Istina* (1961/62) 151–182.

"L'organisation de la paroisse orthodoxe en Grèce." *Istina* (1961/62) 295–320.

"Un problème pastoral au VI siècle. La *paenitentia in extremis* au temps de Césaire, évêque d'Arles (503–542)," *Parole de Dieu et sacerdoce* (Tournai 1962) 125–137.

"La *paenitentia in extremis* chez saint Césaire, évêque d'Arles (503–542)," *Studia Patristica* 5, Texte und Untersuchungen 80 (Berlin 1962) 416–423.

"*Sol aequinoctialis*. Problèmes et technique de l'orientation dans le culte chrétien," *Revue des Sciences Religieuses* 36 (1962) 175–211 (Colloqium "Archéologie paléochrétienne et culte chrétien," Dec. 7–9, 1961).

"Contributions des Abbayes de Murbach et de Wissembourg à l'élaboration de la liturgie chrétienne durant le haut moyen âge," *Les lettres en Alsace,*

Publication de la Société savante d'Alsace et des régions de l'Est 8 (Strasbourg 1962) 35–45.

"*Versus ad Orientem.* L'orientation dans les *Ordines Romani* du haut moyen âge," *La Maison-Dieu* 70 (1962) 67–99.

"Contenu et ordonnance primitive du Pontifical romano-germanique,"*Atti del VI Congresso Internazionale di Archeologia Cristiana* (Ravenna, Sept. 23–29, 1962) 243–265.

"La signation dans l'Église des premiers siècles," *La Maison-Dieu* 75 (1963) 37–51.

"Le Pontifical romano-germanique du X siècle. Nature, date et importance du document," *Cahiers de civilisation médiévale* 6 (1963) 27–48.

"L'orientation vers l'Est du célébrant et des fidèles pendant la célébration eucharistique," *L'Orient syrien* 9 (1964) 3–37.

"Le pèlerinage pénitentiel," *Revue des Sciences Religieuses* 38 (1964) 113–153; reproduced from *Convegno Studi Todi* 4 (1963) 39–94.

"Unité de l'Église et pluralité des formes historique d'organisation ecclésiastique du III au V siècle," *L'épiscopat et l'Église universelle*, Unam Sanctam 39 (Paris 1964) 591–636.

"La réforme liturgique sous Charlemagne," *Karl der Grosse* 2(Düsseldorf 1965) 217–232.

"La discipline pénitentielle dans les inscriptions paléochrétiennes," *Rivista di Archeologia Cristiana* 42 (1966) 317–325 (Miscellanea in onore di Enrico Josi 1).

"Le repas sacré au poisson chez les chrétiens," *Revue des Sciences Religieuses* 40 (1966) 1–26.

"Les rites de la pénitence publique aux X et XI siècles," *Mélanges R. Crozet* 1 (Poitiers 1966) 137–144.

"*Facere cum virginia (—o) sua (—o) annos* . . . L'âge des époux chrétiens au moment de contracter mariage, d'après les inscriptions paléochrétiennes," *Revue de Droit Canonique* 16 (1966) 355–366.

"Nomination et installation du Primat d'une Église autocéphale. Sa Béatitude Mgr. Ieronimos Kotsonis, Archevêque d'Athènes et de toute la Grèce," *Revue de Droit Canonique* 17 (1967) 177–201.

"La croix eschatologique," *Noël-Épiphanie-Retour du Christ*, Lex orandi 40 (Paris 1967) 85–108.

"Saint Chrodegang et les débuts de la romanisation du culte en pays franc," *Saint Chrodegang*, Communication présentée au Colloque tenu à Metz à l'occasion du douzième centenaire de sa mort (Metz 1967) 91–109.

"La Faculté de Théologie Catholique de 1902 à 1918," *Revue des Sciences Religieuses* 43 (1969) 37–75 (Mémorial du Cinquantenaire de la Faculté de Théologie Catholique, 1919–1969).

"Simples réflexions sur l'institution pénitentielle dans l'Église latine," *Catéchèse* 37 (1969) 489–496.

"Réflexions de l'historien sur la discipline pénitentielle dans l'Église latine," *Vérité et vie* 620, Formation doctrinale (Strasbourg 1969/1970).

"Le repas sacré au poisson chez les chrétiens," *Eucharisties d'Orient et d'Occident* 1, Lex orandi 46 (Paris 1970) 83–116.

"L'imposition des mains dans les rites d'ordination en Orient et en Occident," *La Maison-Dieu* 102 (1970) 57–72.

"Chirotonie et Chirothésie. Importance et relativité du geste de l'imposition des mains dans la collation des ordres," *Irénikon* 45 (1972) 7–71; 207–238.

"*Vacua manus impositio*. L'inconsistance de la chirotonie absolue en Occident," *Mélanges liturgiques offerts au R.P. Bernard Botte* (Louvain 1972) 511–524.

"Le ministère liturgique dans la vie de l'Église. Aliénation du culte par rapport à la communauté chrétienne," *Concilium* 72 (1972) 11–22 (English, German, Italian, Spanish and Dutch translations).

"*Laica communione contentus*. Le retour du presbytre au range des laïcs," *Revue des Sciences Religieuses* 47 (1973) 56–122.

"Titre d'ordination et lien du presbytre à la communauté locale dans l'Église ancienne," *La Maison-Dieu* 115 (1973) 70–85.

"Le développement historique du culte chrétien en Occident. Résultats et problèmes," *Problemi di Storia della Chiesa. L'alto medioevo*. Il corso di aggiornamento per professori di storia ecclesiastica (Milan 1973).

"*Vulneratum caput*. Position d'Innocent I (402–417) sur la validité de la chirotonie presbytérale conférée par un évêque hérétique," *Rivista di archeologia cristiana* 49 (1973) 375–384 (Miscellanea in onore di L. de Bruyne e A. Ferrua 2).

"Le ministre charismatique de l'Eucharistie. Approche rituelle," *Ministère et célébration de l'Eucharistie. Sacramentum* 1, Studia Anselmiana 61 (Rome 1974) 181–209.

"Pratiques superstitieuses au début du XI siècle d'après le *Corrector sive medicus* de Burchard, évêque de Worms (965–1025)," *Mélanges E.-R. Labande* (Poitiers 1974) 751–761.

"L'environnement cultuel du défunt durant la période paléochrétienne," *La maladie et la mort du chrétien dans la liturgie*, Biblioteca Ephemerides liturgicae. Subsidia 1 (Rome 1975) 381–413.

"Le *Liber Pontificalis* dans l'édition de Louis Duchesne. État de la question," *Monseigneur Duchesne et son temps*, Collection de l'École Française de Rome 23 (Rome 1975) 99–127.

"Pénitence et excommunication dans l'Église ancienne et durant le haut moyen âge," *Concilium* 107 (1975) 11–22. This has been translated into several languages.

"*Rata sacerdotia*. Position de Léon I (440–461) sur les ordinations conférées irrégulièrement," *Revue de Droit Canonique* 25 (1975) 19–27.

"Le caractère inamissible de l'ordre d'après de Décret de Gratien," *Studia Gratiana* 20 (1976) 437–452 (Mélanges G. Fransen 2).

"Le banquet funéraire paléochrétien. Une fête du défunt et des survivants," *Le christianisme populaire. Les dossiers de l'histoire*, edd. B. Plongeron and R. Panet (Paris 1976) 61–78.

"Symboles cultuels chrétiens. Les aliments sacrés: poisson et *refrigeria*,"

Settimane di Studia del Centro italiano di Studi sull' Alto Medioevo 23 (Spoleto 1976) 197–266.

"Le 2 Congrès international des Facultés de Théologie orthodoxe (Athens, Aug. 19–28, 1976)," *Revue de Droit Canonique* 27 (1977) 179–183.

"La chirotonie presbytérale du liturge comme condition de la célébration eucharistique?" *L'assemblée liturgique et les différents rôles dans l'assemblée,* Conférences Saint Serge. XXIII Semaine d'Études liturgiques, Paris, June 28–July 1, 1976; Bibliotheca *Ephemerides liturgicae.* Subsidia 9 (Rome 1977) 307–320.

"Les pénitentiels depuis l'époque de Colomban jusqu'à Burchard de Worms (2 moitié du VI siècle à 1008/1012)," *Pauvreté et pénitence.* X Cahier (1974/1976). Centre de Recherches d'histoire du moyen âge (Paris-Sorbonne 1977) 70–81.

"Les rites da la célébration du mariage: leur signification dans la formation du lien durant le haut moyen âge," *Il matrimonio nella società altomedievale,* Settimane di studio del Centro italiano di studi sull' alto medioevo 24, 1 (Spoleto 1977) 397–472.

"Le poisson, aliment du repas funéraire chrétien?" *Paganisme, Judaisme, Christianisme. Influences et affrontement dans le monde antique,* (Mélanges offerts à Marcel Simon (Paris 1978) 233–243.

"La fin d'une Église autocéphale. Le dernière Loi organique de l'Église orthodoxe d'Albanie du 04.05.1950," Recueil d'Études et d'information en hommage à Mgr. Charles Lefèbvre, L'Année canonique 22 (Paris 1978) 149–164.

"Autonomie de la communauté paléochrétienne et organes de coordination supra-locaux (III-V siècles)," *Communion et Communication,* 3 cycle romand en theologie pratique—1976/1977 (Geneva 1978) 13–30.

"*Peregrina communio,*" Études offertes à J. Gaudemet 2, *Revue de Droit Canonique* 29 (1979) 178–182.

"Les motifs de la romanisation du culte sous Pépin le Bref (751–768) et Charlemagne (774–814)," *Atti del XVIII Convegno di Studi sulla spiritualità medievale.* Università di Perugia, Sept. 9–12, 1977 (Todi 1979) 15–41.

"Symboles cultuels chrétiens: Aliments et boissons," *Concilium* 152 (1980) 83–89.

"Anaphores eucharistiques préconstantiennes. Formes non traditionelles," *Ecclesia orans,* Mélanges offerts à A.G. Hamman, *Augustinianum* 20 (1980) 401–410.

"Le rôle du liturge dans la formation du lien conjugal," *Revue de Droit Canonique* 30 (1980) 1–27.

"Une mutation cultuelle inexpliquée: le passage de l'eucharistie communautaire à la messe privée," *Revue des Sciences Religieuses* 54 (1980) 231–250.

"Primatialité et synodalité dans l'Église locale durant la période anténicéenne," *Aspects de l'Orthodoxie,* Travaux du Centre d'Études supérieures d'Histoire des Religions de Strasbourg. Colloque de novembre 1978 (Paris 1981) 53–66.

"La multiplication des messes solitaires au moyen âge. Essai de statistique," *Revue des Sciences Religieuses* 55 (1981) 206–213.

"Circonscriptions ecclésiastiques et ressorts administratifs civils durant la première moitié du IV siècle. Du concile de Nicée (325) au concile d'Antioche (341)," *La géographie administrative et politique d'Alexandre à Mahomet*, USHS. Centre de Recherches sur le Proche-Orient et la Grèce antique (Leyden 1981) 273–291.

"Communion et Église locale aux premiers siècles. Primatialité et synodalité durant la période anténicéenne," *l'Année Canonique* 25 (1981) 169–177.

"Prière ou intercession? Une ambiguïté dans le culte paléochrétien des martyrs," *Communio Sanctorum*, Mélanges offerts à J.J. von Allmen (Geneva 1982) 284–289.

"La Règle de s. Benoît et le culte chrétien. Prêtre-moine et moine-prêtre," *Atti del 7 Congresso internazionale di Studi sull' Alto Medioevo (Nurcia-Subiaco-Montecassino, Sept. 29–Oct. 5, 1980)* 2 (Spoleto 1982) 409–427.

"La compilation veronaise des *libelli missarum*," *Verona in età gotica e longobarda (Dec. 6–7, 1980)*, Atti (1982) 77–95.

"Application du principe de l'économie en matière de divorce dans le Droit canonique oriental," *Revue de Droit Canonique* 32 (1982) 81–100.

"Les rituels de la pénitence tarifée," *Liturgia opera divina e umana*, Studi offerti a S.E. Mons. Annibale Bugnini in occasione del suo 70 compleanno, a cura di P. Jounel, R. Kaczynski, G. Pasqualetti (Rome 1982) 419–427=Biblioteca *Ephemerides liturgicae* Subsidia 26.

"Le culte des morts au moyen âge et les livres liturgiques," *Le Codex Guta-Sintram* (1154) 2 (1983) 66–78.

"Histoire du culte chrétien: histoire d'un cérémonial ou d'une institution?" *La liturgie; son sens, son esprit, sa méthode*, Conférences Saint-Serge 28 and Semaine d'études liturgiques, Paris, June 30–July 3, 1981 (Rome 1982) 339–348=Biblioteca *Ephemerides liturgicae* Subsidia 27.

"La femme du prêtre," *Revue des Sciences Religieuses* 57 (1983) 57–63.

"Busse," (Entwicklung bis zum Bussakrament, Bussgebet) *Lexikon des Mittelalters* 2 (1983) 1131–1137.

"Ordo," *Catholicisme* 10 (1983) 208–209.

"Handauflegung," *Reallexikon für Antike und Christentum*.

N.B. This bibliography contains all the books and articles written by C. Vogel up to the time of his death on Nov. 24, 1982. It does not, however, include his book reviews.

We are much indebted to Madame Michelle Seyler, the librarian of the Catholic Faculty of Theology of the University of Strasbourg, for permission to use the literary remains of Professor Vogel, our colleague and friend.

Alexandre Faivre
189b Route du Polygone
67100 Strasbourg

This Bibliography originally appeared in the *Revue des Sciences Religieuses* 57 (1983) 4–9 and is reproduced with the permission of Monsieur le professeur Faivre and the directors of the *Revue*.

INDEX OF PERSONS, PLACES, AND THINGS

INDEX OF MANUSCRIPTS